A Psychological Examination

of Political Leaders

A Psychological Examination
of Political Leaders

Edited by

Margaret G. Hermann

with Thomas W. Milburn

THE FREE PRESS
A Division of Macmillan Publishing Co., Inc.
NEW YORK

Collier Macmillan Publishers
LONDON

The Free Press
A Division of Macmillan Publishing Co., Inc.
866 Third Avenue, New York, N.Y. 10022

Collier Macmillan Canada, Ltd.

Library of Congress Catalog Card Number: 75-32366

Printed in the United States of America

printing number

1 2 3 4 5 6 7 8 9 10

Library of Congress Cataloging in Publication Data
Main entry under title:

A Psychological examination of political leaders.

    Includes index.
    1. Political psychology.   2.   Leadership.
I. Hermann, Margaret G.
JA74.5.P75   320'.01'9   75-32366
ISBN 0-02-914590-2

To Harold Guetzkow
and Richard C. Snyder

Contents

Contents ix

Preface

With his book on political leadership in 1972, Glenn Paige sought to establish a new field of inquiry in the social sciences. He visualized that the study of political leadership would incorporate a disparate body of research now falling under such rubrics as political elites, political biography, community power studies, and political roles. The study of political leadership would build on the theoretical and empirical foundations already present in research on leadership in psychology, sociology, public administration, and anthropology. Paige (1972, p. 69) defined political leadership as "the interaction of personality, role, organization, task, values, and setting as expressed in the [political] behavior of salient individuals . . ." who can have an effect on public policy. The present volume follows in the Paige tradition. It, too, focuses on political leadership, seeking to ascertain who becomes a political leader and how a political leader's personal characteristics affect political behavior. The chapters that follow are intended to further the creation of political leadership as a separate field of inquiry.

Empirical research on the personal characteristics of political leaders is recent. As the varied disciplines of the contributors to this volume indicate (psychology, political science, sociology), the research is scattered throughout the social sciences. To date much of this research has been circulated as unpublished material. The present book attempts to bring such research together, to suggest the kinds of issues it addresses, to describe in more detail the kinds of techniques used to generate it, and to present some ways of integrating it for future study.

As editor, I am indebted to several groups of people who made this book possible. First, and foremost, are the contributors who were most patient with deadlines and demands. I feel fortunate that these talented researchers were able to find time to write chapters for this book, detailing their research.

A second group of individuals are responsible for my own continuing interest in the study of the personal characteristics of political leaders. The dedication of the book to Harold Guetzkow and Richard C. Snyder is only a small token of my appreciation for the intellectual stimulation and encouragement which these gentlemen have afforded me. Similar debts of gratitude are owed Maurice East, Charles Hermann, James Robinson, Barbara Salmore, and Stephen Salmore. Without their challenges, criticisms, and willingness to talk, my own research probably would not have been done nor this book undertaken.

A special acknowledgement is due Thomas Milburn who started out as a co-editor of this book but because of time conflicts was able to participate only peripherally in its preparation. His continued interest in considering and discussing the issues in the study of political leadership was most helpful and gratifying.

The preparation of this book was aided immensely by the skills of Susan Trice and Sally Levine. I thank them for their calmness under fire and promise "things will get better."

Margaret Hermann
Columbus, Ohio

CHAPTER 1

Introduction: A Statement of Issues

Margaret G. Hermann

"Goldwater is a die-hard conservative!"
"I am sure Daley rarely delegates authority."
"Rodino has risen to meet the challenge of the committee chairman-
   ship."
"DeGaulle got crowds because he was charismatic."
"I think Dulles truly believed in the Communist menace."

HOW OFTEN OBSERVATIONS such as these are made as conversation turns to politics and politicians. There is a certain fascination in analyzing political leaders. As a result, biographies on current political figures become best sellers and the triumphs as well as the tragedies of political leaders become newspaper headlines. The authors in this book are not unlike the above speakers in their interest in the political leader as a person. Going deeper than the pieces of conversation above, however, the authors have tried systematically to explore the impact of a political leader's personal characteristics on his choice of job and on the political environment in which he finds himself. In the course of their explorations, they have renovated old techniques for use in a new setting and devised new techniques in order to ascertain the personal characteristics of the political leaders under study. The purpose of this chapter is to set the stage for the research reports to follow by discussing some of the issues faced in studying the personal characteristics of political leaders.

1

Relevant Definitions

Before raising the issues, our first task is to state what we mean by *political leader* and *personal characteristics.* With regard to the definition of political leader we are, in effect, asking who are the subjects in the research described in subsequent chapters? By political leader we mean an individual who has the authority to commit the resources and select the goals of a political unit and, in turn, to affect its policies (cf. Katz, 1973). Such individuals can be at all levels of government (i.e., local, state, regional, national) and can achieve office by election, appointment, revolution, or assassination. We have tried in this book to examine political leaders at these various levels of government and with these different entrance routes. Moreover, we present cross-national data on political leaders to avoid limiting our study to American politicians.

As noted in the preface, an objective of this book is to build on Paige's (1972) conceptualization of political leadership. According to Paige (1972, p. 69), political leadership is "the interaction of personality, role, organization, task, values, and setting as expressed in the [political] behavior of salient individuals . . ." who can affect public policy. In urging that political leadership become a field of study, Paige indicated the importance of describing and explaining the concepts included in his definition and of working out the linkages among the concepts. The chapters that follow focus on the concept of personality as it relates to political leadership. The authors consider the import for political leadership of the variables this concept denotes.

Having stated what we mean by political leader and political leadership, we need to indicate our conceptualization of what Paige refers to as "personality" and what we call *personal characteristics.* (In order to avoid misunderstandings because of the many and varied definitions of personality—Allport (1937) noted some 50 different definitions of personality—we will use the term personal characteristics instead of personality.) Personal characteristics are all aspects of an individual *qua* individual—his biographical statistics (e.g., age, place of birth), his capabilities and skills, his training, his work experiences, his motives, his cognitions, his affect, his attitudes and beliefs, his role perceptions, and his values. Such a definition permits us to examine, as the psychobiographer often does (see, e.g., George and George, 1964; Mazlish, 1972; Rogow, 1963; Wolfenstein, 1967), the relationship between early childhood experiences and political behavior as well as to explore the relationship between a contemporary belief—say in the importance of international involvement—and political behavior. We can examine "deep" personal characteristics such as basic needs; we can study "manifest" personal characteristics such as a general belief in the ability to control one's environment where there is an *evident* relationship to the behavior being studied; and we can explore "situationally-oriented" personal characteristics such as preference for national health care where the characteristic is specific to a situation, role, or issue. Thus, we can describe a political leader's personal characteristics at both a general (across situations, issues, and roles) and a specific (applicable to particular situations, issues, or roles) level.

Although we recognize that an individual's behavior is determined not by a single personal characteristic but by a mix of characteristics, most of the studies in this book examine one characteristic at a time instead of the interrelationship among characteristics. As a first step, it appeared to the authors to make sense to determine how personal characteristics singly relate to being a political leader and to political behavior before examining combinations of characteristics. Knowledge about relationships with single characteristics can aid in suggesting propositions concerning their interrelationships. An important next step in research on the personal characteristics of political leaders is to explore how various personal characteristics interact to affect becoming a political leader and political behavior.

As the definition of personal characteristics implies, we are interested in both *traits* and *states* of political leaders. Traits are personal characteristics which are consistent across different kinds of situations whereas states are personal characteristics specific to a particular kind of situation. We are using situation here to refer to differences in role and policy issues as well as setting. Trait and state may be viewed as lying at opposite ends of a continuum emphasizing consistency in behavior. Probably most personal characteristics fall somewhere near the middle of the continuum, consistent for certain kinds of situations and either not relevant or inconsistent for others. For example, a political leader may be nationalistic across all foreign policy issues, but nationalism is less germane to discussions of domestic policy. Or, as a second example, Congressmen may cast most issues with which they deal into simplistic black-white, either-or terms but become more cognitively complex for those issues studied by the committees of which they are members. Committee assignments help the Congressmen to develop areas of expertise so that they begin to perceive the many ramifications of the problems. To provide the reader some examples of research on both traits and states, the chapters that follow discuss personal characteristics at many points along this consistency continuum.

Issues Explored

ASSESSMENT

How do we go about assessing or measuring a political leader's personal characteristics? What techniques does one use? Political leaders pose an assessment problem. They often have very limited time to participate in research and, at the higher governmental levels (e.g., foreign minister, head of state), may be virtually inaccessible to the researcher. Such is particularly the case for national political leaders outside one's own country. Moreover, political leaders are wary of research whose results might prove politically damaging to them. Note, for example, how the psychiatric data released on Thomas Eagleton during his bid for the 1972 U.S. Vice-Presidency forced him to drop out as a candidate. Furthermore, political leaders spend their lives creating and maintaining an image. They are generally quite adept at detecting what behavior is seen as desirable.

On the other hand, political leaders present at least one advantage to the researcher. Only movie stars and hit music groups probably have more traces of their behavior in the public arena than politicians. Speeches of political leaders are regularly transcribed, their votes—if any—are recorded, their biographical statistics are maintained and printed, their autobiographies and biographies are fairly commonplace, and television and radio news programs feature interviews with them. Many political forums such as city councils and legislatures are open to the public and can be observed. These potential data sources have just begun to be tapped by social scientists.

Most techniques available to the student of personality can be used with political leaders. Among these are questionnaires, interviews, observation, content analysis, biographical statistics, and simulation. Each has advantages and disadvantages that must be kept in mind when used with political leaders. At least one example of the application of each technique to the study of political leaders is found in the chapters which follow.

Questionnaires. The technique which generally has carried the burden to date in most personality research, the questionnaire (or personality inventory), is perhaps the most difficult to employ in research on political leaders for the reasons mentioned at the outset of this discussion, i.e., accessibility, willingness to cooperate, and image maintenance. When used, questionnaires are probably more easily administered to political leaders at the local or state levels of government, becoming progressively more difficult to administer as one moves to the national government where time and energy are at a premium. Two of the chapters which follow employ the questionnaire to ascertain the personal characteristics of political leaders. Using one ten-item scale (dogmatism), DiRenzo (Chapter 7) combined the questionnaire and interview, embedding the scale toward the end of the interview when some rapport was already established with the political leader. By limiting his sample and spending much time in and around their offices, DiRenzo was able to employ this technique with Italian Deputies at the national level. Ziller, Stone, Jackson, and Terbovic (Chapter 8) used a questionnaire to examine self-other orientations of candidates for state legislative positions and of freshman legislators. They were successful in gaining cooperation through the use of a letter explaining the research, a visit by a member of the research team to each candidate or legislator, and the fact that the questionnaire took only 15 minutes to complete.

As these examples suggest, there is much scheduling time involved in pursuing the political leader to elicit his help. The patience of the researcher must be high. Moreover, only a limited amount of questionnaire information can be gained at a time. Generally there is some antagonism among politicians, as other busy people, to formatted items (e.g., multiple choice, true-false questions). The greater the rapport with the person administering the questionnaire, the more open-ended the questionnaire is, or the more discussion the researcher allows in the process of answering items, probably the less antagonism incurred on the part of the political leader.

We have spoken about the problems of accessibility and gaining cooperation. The researcher using questionnaires with political leaders also needs to guard against the effects of image maintenance on the part of the political leader in his questionnaire responses. Items may elicit socially desirable responses rather than describe the personal characteristics of the political leader. If there is not enough time for a questionnaire or some items which measure the tendency of the political leader to respond in a socially desirable manner, provision for discussion of the items, notes on rapport between tester and testee, and observations on the amount of time spent reflecting on the items may provide some clues on the nature of the individual's responses.

One distinct advantage that the questionnaire has over other techniques because of its frequent usage in psychological research is that it permits a comparison between the personal characteristics of political leaders and the personal characteristics of other groups. The instruments used with each group can be the same. As a result, hypotheses from previous research can be tested with political leaders or can be suggestive of possible relationships between the characteristic and political behavior.

Interviews. The interview also ranks near the top in popularity as a technique for assessing personality. As we have already noted, questionnaires are often administered within an interview setting. There are several types of interviews that are relevant to the study of political leaders. First is the *research interview*. Here the researcher conducts the interview with the political leader. Such interviews can take a variety of forms, for example, building rapport, in-depth discussion, clarification of missing information. The DiRenzo (Chapter 7) chapter mentioned previously is an example of a study with political leaders that employed the research interview. Johnson (Chapter 4) also uses the research interview as one way to gain information in formulating Senator Frank Church's operational code.

The second type of interview is the *acquired interview* or recorded interview conducted by one or more interviewers not connected with the research. For example, transcripts are made of Face the Nation interviews and presidential press conferences. Sources like the *Foreign Broadcast Information Service Daily Report* contain interviews with foreign leaders. The Frank (Chapter 3) and Hermann (Chapter 14) chapters use this second type of interview. Frank examines the first 1972 California primary debate between Hubert Humphrey and George McGovern; Hermann uses CBS news interviews with major participants in the New York City transit strike of 1965.

What are the relative advantages and disadvantages of these two types of interviews? Quickly apparent is the fact that in the research interview the researcher has more control over the material covered. In the acquired interview, there is little control over topics unless the interviews are chosen because they focus on a specific issue. On the other hand, the acquired interview permits the researcher to delve into the past and to have access in most instances to the verbatim content of the interview. Verbatim transcripts of research interviews are only feasible if tape recordings are made at the time of the interview—often a sensitive issue with political leaders. Moreover, with the research interview one delves into the past by questioning the political leader about his participation in an event and using his recollections. Another advantage of the acquired interview is that it generally does not require the cooperation of the political leader whereas the research interview does.

Probably the chief problem with the use of the research interview with political leaders is their tendency toward image maintenance. As Paige (1972, pp. 195-196) notes:

> Most political leaders are highly skilled at answering questions and have had enormous interview experience. The more competitive the political system, the more competitive and diversified the communications media, and the more open to foreign journalism the society, the greater the expected question-answering experience of political leaders in the direction of public policy defense or offense. For a political leader, every question offers the possibility of strengthening or weakening his public position.

Paige (1972, p. 196) suggests several ways to cope with this habit of the political leader. "The researcher should plan to take a nonjudgmental position, to respect confidences, to translate sensitive particulars into general statements . . ., and to report back to the cooperating leaders insights gained that may be useful to them."

The acquired interview is also subject to image maintenance. Recall De Gaulle's carefully orchestrated press conferences where questions were submitted in advance. One method of coping with this problem in the acquired interview is to observe who the questioners are and to analyze their questions as well as the political leader's responses. Does the political figure change the content or style of his communication in response to certain interviewers? What can one learn about the relationship between such interviewers and the politician? Note the oft cited hostile relationship between Dan Rather of CBS News and President Nixon during the Watergate affair or the close rapport Roger Mudd of CBS News is reputed to have with Congressmen. A second way of dealing with image maintenance is to examine interviews at several points in time.

Observation.   A third technique that can be used with political leaders is observation. Because political leaders are often observed by the news media or participate in forums which are open to the public, much observable data is accessible to the researcher. Several types of observation can be done with political leaders. There is *self-observation* or notes by the political leader about himself. Letters, diaries, and autobiographies provide insights into individual political figures and indicate rationales for their political behavior. For example, we have Dag Hammarskjold's (1964) *Markings* which, though not about his political life, bares his character. Druckman (Chapter 16) uses anecdotes from Harold Nicolson's reports of his experiences as a diplomat to suggest how propositions tested in a laboratory setting illustrate occurrences in international negotiations.

A second type of observation uses *informants.* One can gain information about political leaders by asking their colleagues, staff members, journalists assigned to them, political interns, or area scholars to describe the leaders' personal characteristics and the effects of these characteristics on their political behavior. Examples in this book of the use of informant observation are found in the Johnson (Chapter 4), Stogdill et al. (Chapter 5), and Milburn (Chapter 6) chapters. Johnson used informants to learn about Senator Church in his youth; Stogdill, Goode, and Day asked staff associates of U.S. senators to describe their senators' leadership behaviors; Milburn requested area specialists to indicate characteristics that were descriptive of certain world political leaders. In the use of informants with political leaders, the researcher must guard against the halo effect (the informant has strong feelings either for or against the individual and gives stereotyped observations to match his feelings). By gaining information from individuals who support the political leader, from individuals who do *not* support the political leader, and from individuals without strong convictions either way, some perspective is possible in the reports. The characteristics which appear common to all informants are probably those with most relevance to the political leader.

A third type of observation is *participant observation.* Here the observer is also a participant in the process he is observing. Johnson's chapter (Chapter 4) on Senator Church was conceived as a result of such observation. Part of the information Johnson uses in constructing Church's operational code comes from his experiences as an intern in Church's office on the Congressional Fellowship Program. J. Robinson's (1969) recent article on participant observation as a way of learning about political processes suggests the wide-ranging uses and problems with this kind of observation.

A last type of observation possible with political leaders, i.e., *field observation,* is only indirectly illustrated in this book. In field observation the researcher observes the political leader in his natural setting (city council, legislature, press conference, party caucus), not as a participant but as a recorder of what transpires. Frank's (Chapter 3) analysis of the first Humphrey-McGovern California primary debate involves field observation. He noted nonverbal behaviors of the two politicians in the context of the debate. Frank's chapter suggests the impact of the electronic media on field observation. By using a videotape of the debate, Frank was able to observe the actions of these two political leaders without being physically present at the debate. Television coverage of news events and political leaders provides a vast arena for field observation. Because such materials do not require the cooperation of the political leader yet catch him in his natural setting, field observation eliminates the accessibility problem often encountered in studying political leaders. Some check, however, should still be made on the political leader's tendency toward image maintenance. Among the questions that need asking are: What does the political leader hope to convey to the audience, reporters, or colleagues in this setting? Does his behavior differ from that characteristic of him previously in the same setting? Are there changes in the people present or the issues under examination which can explain any differences that are found? The answers to these questions suggest how image maintenance is affecting what one is observing.

Content Analysis.   A fourth technique that can be used with political leaders is content analysis, which involves taking what someone has spoken or written and coding it into a set of meaningful categories. Winter and A. Stewart (Chapter 2) present an excellent list of criteria for use in content analysis. To some extent content analysis is a more basic tool than the others mentioned thus far since it is often involved in their successful implementation. For example, content analysis is used in categorizing responses to open-ended personality question-naires (e.g., projective tests); content analysis is frequently employed to ascer-tain what one has gotten from an interview; and content analysis often aids in selecting the appropriate category in observation.

In doing content analysis with political leaders, there are a series of options or choice-points for the researcher. The first choice-point is whether to employ *quantitative* or *qualitative* content analysis. Quantitative content analysis in-volves (1) counting the amount of material assigned to a set of categories and (2) the assumption that someone else using your rules and your material could arrive at a count similar to yours. Qualitative content analysis, on the other hand, involves a thorough examination of some body of material but no exact counting process. In fact, as George (1959b) maintains, one mention of a topic or characteristic may be as important as 25; it all depends on its salience to the political leader. Moreover, some characteristics can only be inferred from what is spoken or written; there is no explicit mention of them to count. The chapters by Winter and A. Stewart (Chapter 2), Frank (Chapter 3), P. Stewart (Chapter 10), and Hermann (Chapters 12 and 14) in the present book use quantitative content analysis. The Johnson chapter (Chapter 4) employs qualitative content analysis. Political biographies are another example of qualitative content analysis.

A second choice-point for the researcher is the *focus* of the content analysis. One interest a researcher may have is the amount of attention a political leader pays to the content included in a particular category. In other words, how many times can a leader's statements be classified into that specific category? Here the emphasis is on the frequency of occurrence of the category. An assumption of this type of content analysis *(frequency analysis)* is that the more relevant the personal characteristic to a political leader, the greater the number of references he will make that can be classified as indicating the characteristic. So, for example, if the personal characteristic we are studying is belief in one's own ability to control events, one way to determine its presence for a political leader using frequency analysis would be simply to count the number of times the political leader indicated he had or would have what was needed to control events. Or, the researcher using content analysis with political leaders can be interested not merely in the frequency with which a personal characteristic appears, but in the political leader's evaluation of the characteristic. How important is the personal characteristic to the individual? Do the indicators of the characteristic appear in a favorable or unfavorable context? Thus, using our example of belief in ability to control events, this type of content analysis *(evaluation assertion analysis)* allows the researcher to develop a scale ranging from a low score for very unfavorable words or statements surrounding indicators of belief in one's ability to control events to a high score for very favorable words or statements in the context of indicators of belief in internal control over events. A third focus for content analysis involves several personal characteristics instead of just one. Here the researcher is interested in the association among the personal characteristics in the political leader's statements. This type of content analysis is called *contingency analysis.* Which characteristics appear to be associated in the political leader's communication? For example, do indicators of belief in internal control over events and cognitive complexity generally appear together in the political leader's responses to reporters? This focus on association among personal characteristics is important to the study of types of political leaders where the relationship among several personal characteristics defines a specific kind of leader. For the most part, the chapters in this volume which use content analysis involve frequency analysis. Discussions and illustrations of evaluation assertion analysis and contingency analysis can be found in Holsti (1969) and Pool (1959).

A third choice-point in using content analysis centers on the *material* which is analyzed. The researcher can examine the *content* of the communication or the *structure* of the communication. In other words, one can study what is said or how it is said. Generally an examination of content has been associated with studying traits or personal characteristics which are more consistent across time; an examination of the structure of a communication generally has been related to an interest in states of the political leader or personal characteristics which are fairly situation-specific. Some examples of structural categories are number of "ah's" the individual uses, number of repetitions in a speech, number of different words used, and rate of speaking. These particular structural categories seem to indicate the levels of anxiety and uncertainty of the communicator. While the Winter and A. Stewart (Chapter 2), P. Stewart (Chapter 10), and Hermann (Chapter 12) chapters in this book examine content of the communication, the Frank (Chapter 3) and Hermann (Chapter 14) chapters look at structure. The Frank and Hermann chapters focus on indicators of stress in the political leader.

Because of the public visibility of political leaders, there is often an accumulation of material which can be subjected to content analysis. Generally, use of the material does not involve the cooperation of the political figure and, therefore, accessibility to the individual—two problems we have noted in assessing the personal characteristics of political leaders. As with each technique discussed thus far, however, there needs to be some check on the effect of a leader's tendencies toward image maintenance on the results of a content analysis. One may want to examine material on various topics, material presented to varying audiences, and material at different points in time so as to gain some information on the possible effects of image maintenance.

Biographical Statistics.   Biographical statistics, a fifth way of looking at the personal characteristics of political leaders, are indicators of an individual's social and career background. For example, what is the political leader's present age; what was his occupation before entering politics; how much education did he have; what was his prior political experience; what is the extent of his foreign travel? Biographical statistics are available in directories such as the *Congressional Directory* and *Statesman's Yearbook* as well as from biographical and autobiographical statements. Three chapters in the present volume use biographical statistics to examine political leaders. L. Stewart (Chapter 9) is interested in the effects of birth order on becoming president or prime minister and, more particularly, in holding such positions during periods of crisis. P. Stewart (Chapter 10) examines how social and career information relates to specific attitudes for regional Party first secretaries in the Soviet Union. Welsh (Chapter 11) uses social and career data to predict participation in *coups* and general revolutionary behavior in Latin America.

Biographical statistics are commonly used in the study of elites (see, e.g., Edinger and Searing, 1967; Quandt, 1970; Rustow, 1966). However, to date such studies have remained fairly descriptive. Chinese Communist leaders are "this" age and have achieved "that" level of education; American state legislators did "X" before being elected, coming generally from "Y" profession. Little attempt has been made to relate these indicators to political behavior or to explore whether they differentiate political leaders from their constituents or from other types of political leaders. The L. Stewart, P. Stewart, and Welsh chapters tackle these problems head-on.

Biographical statistics provide the "hardest" data on personal characteristics of the techniques mentioned thus far. It is difficult to see how scholars can disagree over variables such as age. Searching for the data and cross-checking sources for agreement are the major tasks involved in the use of biographical statistics with political leaders. Lest we become too cavalier, however, Quandt (1970) notes that comparative cross-national studies using biographical statistics can have problems when it comes to categorizing variables like occupation and education so that they are comparable across nations.

Biographical statistics help the researcher to avoid the three assessment problems mentioned at the beginning of this section. They do not necessarily require access to the political leader nor his cooperation. Moreover, there should be little effect of image maintenance, presuming one can find similar data in several reliable sources. Perhaps these reasons explain the wide use of biographical statistics in the study of elites.

Simulation. The last technique that we will discuss is simulation. Simulation refers here to "a flexible imitation of processes and outcomes for the purpose of clarifying or explaining the underlying mechanisms involved" (Abelson, 1968b, p. 275). In this discussion we are interested in both computerized working models of behavior and research in an enriched experimental setting. Other terms for these types of simulations are *computer simulation* and *all-person* or *person-machine simulation.*

Recently several computer simulations of the cognitive processes of political leaders have been attempted. Abelson and Carroll (1965) have developed a computer simulation called the "ideology machine" and have experimented with it using the beliefs of Senator Barry Goldwater as gleaned from his public statements (see also Abelson, 1968a, 1971, 1973). The ideology machine, or model of a closed belief system, suggests how an individual reacts to questions or statements about international relations based on his beliefs. Of particular interest to Abelson and Carroll were simulating denial and rationalization as ways of cognitively dealing with statements inconsistent with one's beliefs. A second computer simulation focusing on political leaders is that constructed by Pool and Kessler (1965). Programming well-documented psychological propositions regarding the effects of information selection and retention, these investigators used the communications of Kaiser Wilhelm and Czar Nicholas in the summer of 1914 to replicate the kind of information processing which characterizes decision making in crisis situations. A third computer simulation is in the development stages. Shapiro and Bonham (1973) are simulating foreign policy decision making. These researchers are interested in the decisions foreign policy makers reach in reaction to events as a result of their beliefs and their information search behaviors.

These computer simulations are fascinating, but narrow in scope. Their narrow focus results from the precision of statement which is necessary in programming the computer. However, as Abelson (1968b, p. 292) observes: "One virtue for the investigator in struggling with flow-charting problems is that he may be forced into closer scrutiny of his theory. . . ."

The simulations which are illustrated in the present book are of the second type—all-person and person-machine simulations. These simulations focus on complex phenomena such as national policy making, about which we know enough to structure some but not all of the variables. The researcher relies on the simulation participants to supply the complexity which is as yet not completely understood. The Driver chapter (Chapter 13) uses the Inter-Nation Simulation (INS) to explore the relationship between several cognitive characteristics of decision makers and aggression (i.e., war, arms increases). The INS is a person-machine simulation in which participants play the roles of top-level national decision makers who interact with one another in allocating the resources of their nation. The effects of the resource allocations are determined by the programmed aspects of the model. Crow and Noel (Chapter 15), on the other hand, use an all-person simulation (Algonian Exercise) to investigate the relative effect of personal characteristics, organization, and situation on national policy making. Participants were presented with a scenario indicating that there was an insurrection in one of the provinces of their country. After receiving other information about the insurrection, the participants were asked to decide among a series of military alternatives of increasing severity.

The use of this second type of simulation in studying political leaders avoids all the assessment problems posed at the beginning of this section. Such simulations do, however, pose a problem of their own—that of validity. Can one use high-school students and navy recruits, as Driver and Crow and Noel do, as a lens to study the behavior of political leaders? How well do the INS and Algonian Exercise replicate the reference systems they were designed to reflect? Lengthy discussion of simulation validity is beyond the scope of this chapter. The interested reader is directed to several discussions of the validity issue, in addition to that in the Crow and Noel chapter, which suggest ways of dealing with questions of this nature; for example, see Abelson (1968b), Dutton and Starbuck (1971), Guetzkow (1968), C. Hermann (1967), C. Hermann and M. Hermann (1967), and Smoker (1972).

PART ONE

Part One of this book focuses on techniques for assessing the personal characteristics of political leaders. Although we have examples of each of the six techniques just described somewhere in the book, the chapters in Part One focus on two of the techniques, content analysis and observation. By taking advantage of materials in the public record, these two techniques can enable a researcher lacking a large research grant, travel money, sufficient equipment, and political contacts to do research on the personal characteristics of political leaders. In effect, these two techniques can involve the study of political leaders at a distance, as the title of this section suggests. Moreover, more young scholars are taking advantage of the availability of public material on political leaders, resulting in a growing number of studies on leaders' personal characteristics using these two techniques.

Chapters 2, 3, and 4 deal with content analysis. In Chapter 2, Winter and A. Stewart use quantitative content analysis to explore motive imagery in the inaugural addresses of twentieth-century American presidents. Moreover, they review studies of the personal characteristics of political leaders that have been done using quantitative content analysis. Frank in Chapter 3 also employs quantitative content analysis but he looks at the structure of the political leaders' verbal statements rather than their content (the focus of Winter and A. Stewart). Frank examines verbal indicators of stress in the responses of Humphrey and McGovern during their first 1972 California presidential primary debate. In delimiting Senator Frank Church's operational code, Johnson in Chapter 4 provides an example of qualitative content analysis.

The Frank and Johnson chapters (Chapters 3 and 4) are also illustrations of observation along with Chapters 5 and 6. Frank observed the movements that Humphrey and McGovern made during their first 1972 California primary debate. In effect, Frank uses field observation, observing the political leader in action. Johnson employs participant observation in doing Church's operational code—being on Church's staff gave him insights into Church's beliefs, accessibility to Church for interviews, and knowledge of where information on or by Church was available. Chapter 5 by Stogdill, Goode, and Day, and Chapter 6 by Milburn use informant observation. Stogdill and his associates learn about the personal characteristics of senators by questioning members of their staffs; Milburn ascertains data on the personal characteristics of Soviet political leaders by querying academic political specialists.

For further discussion of the four techniques that are not focused on in Part One and excellent examples of their use with political leaders, see:

Questionnaire
Cantril (1965)
DiRenzo (Chapter 7)
McClosky (1967)
Oppenheim (1966)
Robinson and Shaver (1969)
Sniderman and Citrin (1971)
Ziller, Stone, Jackson, and Terbovic (Chapter 8)

Interview
Barber (1965)
Clapp (1964)
Dexter (1970)
Hermann (Chapter 14)
Hunt, Crane, and Wahlke (1964)
Johnson (Chapter 4)
Manley (1969)
Wahlke, Eulau, Buchanan, and Ferguson (1962)

Biographical Statistics
Edinger and Searing (1967)
Frey (1965)
Matthews (1954, 1960)
Nagle (1973)

Quandt (1970)
Rustow (1966)
Scalapino (1972)
Schlesinger (1966)
Searing (1969)
L. Stewart (Chapter 9)
P. Stewart (Chapter 10)
Welsh (Chapter 11)

Simulation

Abelson and Carroll (1965)
Barber (1966)
Browning (1968)
Cherryholmes and Shapiro (1969)
Crow and Noel (Chapter 15)
Driver (Chapter 13)
C. Hermann and M. Hermann (1967)
Pool and Kessler (1965)
Shapiro and Bonham (1973)

WHO BECOMES A POLITICAL LEADER?

Given some way of measuring the personal characteristics of political leaders, what are we interested in learning? Why assess leaders' personal characteristics anyway? One research question of interest to the student of political leadership centers around the leader's reasons for seeking office. Are there personal characteristics which enable an individual to become a political leader? This question has led to several types of research. The personal characteristics of political leaders have been compared to those of their constituents; the personal characteristics of certain groups of political leaders have been described; and the relationships between political role, recruitment process, and personal characteristics have been explored.

In some of the earliest systematic studies of the personal characteristics of political leaders, researchers (e.g., Hennessy, 1959; McConaughy, 1950; Milbrath and Klein, 1962) were interested in comparing the characteristics of such figures to their constituents. Are there personal characteristics that differentiate political leaders from the public-at-large, that is, the nonpoliticians? This type of research compares the scores on a specific personal characteristic of a sample of political leaders with a sample from the nonpolitician population. For example, McConaughy (1950) compared the scores of 18 South Carolina legislators on the Bernreuter Personality Inventory to the adult male norms for the general population; Hennessy (1959) compared 72 politically active (including local office-holders) Tucson, Arizona residents with 66 apolitical residents matched for education and socio-economic status; Browning and Jacob (1964) compared 23 businessmen who had held elective or appointed community offices with 18 businessmen who were politically inactive—the two groups were matched on type and size of business, occupational status, religion, age, education, ethnic background, and place of residence; Hedlund (1973) compared 119 of 124 members of the 1965 Iowa House of Representatives to 597 Iowa adults interviewed as part of a household probability sample by the Iowa Poll— education, occupation, income, age, and residence were controlled during the analysis. Some commonsense notions about political leaders were examined in these studies. Such observations include: "Political leaders are extroverts." "Political leaders seem to be more power-hungry than the ordinary citizen." "Political leaders almost have to like and enjoy being with people." "Political leaders are more dogmatic or authoritarian than most people." Moreover, the writings of such scholars as Lane (1959), Lasswell (1948), Matthews (1954), and Milbrath (1965) contain propositions suggesting personal characteristics peculiar to political leaders.

The results of this type of research are essentially contradictory. For instance, where in one study (Hennessy, 1959) the political leaders show a greater need for power than their constituents, in another (Browning and Jacob, 1964) there is a nonsignificant difference in need for power between political leaders and their constituents. The two propositions that receive support in at least two studies suggest that, at least in the United States, political leaders tend to be white males of upper- or middle-class backgrounds (see Prewitt and Stone, 1973) and are highly sociable (see McConaughy, 1950; Milbrath and Klein, 1962). In effect, however, for most other personal characteristics examined to date there is little homogeneity among political leaders.

Should we expect homogeneity in the personal characteristics of political leaders? If we stop to think about these leaders, there are many possible distinctions to be made. For example, some political leaders are elected, some are appointed, while others achieve office by revolution, assassination, or *coup d'etat.* Moreover, there are political leaders with roles at various levels of government—local, state, national, and international. Particularly at the local governmental level, leaders are often part-time politicians. In other words, we have avocational versus professional political leaders. Furthermore, in the re- cruitment process some political leaders are coopted while others seek the job. It seems unlikely that the same personal characteristics would depict such diverse people.

Taking such diversity into account, researchers have sought to describe the personal characteristics of a particular set of political leaders. Much of the work on social and career background variables is of this nature. Thus, for example, we have Matthews' (1960) description of U.S. senators, Frey's (1965) examina- tion of the deputies to the Grand National Assembly in Turkey, and Lasswell and Lerner's (1965) look at revolutionary political leaders. Let us examine one study of this genre in more detail—Barber's (1965) research on Connecticut legislators.

Barber (1965) was interested in why people become and remain lawmakers. To explore this question, he studied freshman state legislators in the 1959 Connecticut House of Representatives, interviewing in depth some 27 of these legislators and analyzing questionnaire responses of 96. Dividing these freshmen legislators according to the intensity of their legislative behavior (i.e., their activity in the legislative session as noted in bills introduced, committee comments, and speeches on the House floor) and their interest in the job (i.e., response to a question concerning their willingness to return to the legislature in future sessions), Barber arrived at a four-fold typology: lawmaker (high activity, high interest), advertiser (high activity, low interest), spectator (low activity, high interest), and reluctant (low activity, low interest). He found distinct personal characteristics associated with each type of freshman legislator; each type had different motivations in becoming a state legislator, different backgrounds, and different decision styles. Thus, the lawmaker was a young, mobile person with a need to achieve who stressed rationality and was task-oriented. The advertiser was a young lawyer with a need for power who was competitive and used the legislature as a forum for self-advancement. The spectator was a middle-aged, lower status housewife with a need for approval who was submissive and essentially an observer in the legislative process. The reluctant was an elderly, retired person with a need to be useful who had a moral sense of social responsibility that he exhibited in the legislative arena.

In addition to differences in personal characteristics, Barber's four types of legislators differed in the processes by which they were recruited and their perceptions of the legislative role. One way to begin to study systematically who becomes a political leader, taking into account the diverse kinds of political leaders already noted, is to explore how personal characteristics, political role, and recruitment process interrelate. Do different political roles demand different personal characteristics in their execution? Do different recruitment processes necessitate different personal characteristics?

Seligman (1971) in his theoretical discussion of elite political recruitment suggests how personal characteristics, political role, and recruitment may affect one another in the choice of a political leader. Given a particular political role which we are interested in studying, the first thing we need to know is the opportunity it affords. Who can hold the position? In other words, what are the formal requirements for the role (e.g., age, training needed, party affiliation, time involved) and what are the informal expectations about the position (e.g., power of role, flexibility of role, usefulness of role as stepping stone to higher office)? Knowing the answers to these questions, we can begin to propose what personal characteristics might be associated with holding that role. In effect, we can begin to define who might be interested in such a position.

But what about the risks that are involved in trying for the role? What is the probability of winning; what are the costs for losing; what must one give up in order to assume the position; what does one gain by taking it? These queries concern the uncertainties which are part of deciding on a political position. Say the answers to these questions indicated high risk, then, for example, a person who was interested in the position and who was fairly confident, who enjoyed situations involving high stakes, and who believed he had some control over events might be more likely than his opposite to try for the role. Thus, opportunity defines who can and might be interested in a political role; risk suggests who will try for it.

There is also the selection process itself. Who does the selecting (e.g., political party, a political leader, electorate)? How is selection generally made (e.g., cooptation, conscription, self-selection)? How complex is the selection process—how many steps or stages are there? What happens in the selection process suggests the control that others have over the position. If control is tight, the personal characteristics demanded of the role occupant will be those desirable to the selectors, or sponsors. They will set the criteria for selection. Under such circumstances personal characteristics like loyalty, conformity, and agreement in political beliefs and motivations with the sponsor may be important. In looking at the opportunity and risk afforded by the role, we learn who the possible candidates are and can infer what they may be like. The selection process indicates who among the possible candidates will be chosen.

A study by Browning and Jacob (1964) illustrates the process we have been discussing. These researchers were interested in when individuals high in need for achievement and power would seek political office. Their subjects were local political leaders in a "middle-sized Eastern city" and two Louisiana parishes. One question Browning and Jacob asked concerned whether the personal characteristics demanded by the role matched the personal characteristics of the incumbents. Were the political positions with a higher potential for achievement and power activities occupied by political leaders with higher needs for achievement and power? Such was indeed the case. The opportunity the position afforded was perceived.

Browning and Jacob also noted that the political positions in the Eastern city and the Louisiana parishes differed in selection process and risk. In the Eastern city, there was intense party competition, with each party tightly controlled so that mobility within the party hierarchy was small. Movement from local to state and national politics was likely, however, and politics performed an important function in the community. The Louisiana parishes, on the other hand, had fragmented and factional parties; many important decisions were made outside the political process. Furthermore, there was little mobility from local to higher level office. This observation led to the proposition—which was confirmed—that the local political leaders in the Eastern city would be higher in need for achievement and power than those in the Louisiana parishes. The positions in the Eastern city would appear to have more appeal (be of more potential benefit) to persons high in need for achievement and power than the positions in the Louisiana parishes. And, given the emphasis on these motives in the political process of the Eastern city, it is not surprising that political leaders high in need for achievement and power were chosen.

PART TWO

The chapters in Part Two of this book deal with the question of who becomes a political leader. They examine in more detail some of the issues which we have just raised. In Chapter 7, DiRenzo studies how political leaders in two cultures (U.S. and Italy) differ on dogmatism from their constituents. We have already noted some of the problems with this type of study. DiRenzo, however, does not stop here. He also explores within the political leader samples differences in dogmatism by party, by career orientation, by social background, by pattern of recruitment, and by culture. We learn more about how and why dogmatic individuals become politicians as DiRenzo defines political leader more specifically (in Party A, recruited by Method B, in Culture C, for example).

Are there personal characteristics which increase the probability of a political candidate winning an election? Ziller and his associates in Chapter 8 propose two characteristics—self-esteem and complexity of the self concept—which in combination seem important to increasing a candidate's chances of being selected by the electorate. Moreover, they examine how successful elected freshman state legislators with the various combinations of these two characteristics are in the legislature. They conclude by reporting two experiments which study the mechanisms enabling one type of candidate to be elected where another type fails.

In Chapter 9, L. Stewart investigates what kinds of individuals become presidents of the U.S. and prime ministers of England during crisis periods. Are there certain characteristics relevant to selection for these positions under such conditions which are not relevant in periods of calm? Stewart focuses on a variable which has generated much interest among social psychologists, but for which research results are often ambiguous—birth order. Unlike most researchers using birth order, however, Stewart is concerned with sibling relationships rather than parent-child relationships as an explanatory mechanism. The individual with many siblings experiences early, for example, the importance of coalitions, how interest groups function, and the role of elites, while the individual with few or no siblings must wait for such experiences.

Writers on Soviet elites have proposed three types of political leaders, having certain backgrounds and certain attitudes, to account for who becomes a political leader in the Soviet Union. In Chapter 10, P. Stewart systematically explores the backgrounds and attitudes of regional party secretaries in the Soviet Union to see which, if any, of these types of political leaders appear. He examines the secretaries' writings to see what their political attitudes are, and then relates these attitudes to social and career background information to see which attitudes arise out of which backgrounds.

The ultimate in self-selection in the political process is the *coup d'etat*. Here the individual leader becomes his own sponsor in selecting a political position. In Chapter 11, Welsh examines the social and career backgrounds of Latin American participants in *coups d'etat*. He also explores the relationship between certain biographical statistics and revolutionary behavior.

PERSONAL CHARACTERISTICS AND POLITICAL BEHAVIOR

In addition to learning about the personal characteristics of individuals who become political leaders, can we examine what impact a political leader's personal characteristics have on political behavior? Let us turn to this topic now. In effect, do a political leader's personal characteristics affect political behavior? This question has been debated across the ages, for example, in Plato's *Statesman,* in Kautilya's *Arthashastra,* in Machiavelli's *Prince.* Several issues lie at the heart of the debate, not the least of which is the centuries old "great man" versus "zeitgeist" controversy. Must the times be right for the man, or will the man be a great leader regardless of the times? Greenstein (1969), M. Hermann (1976b), Holsti (1973), and Searing (1972) discuss this issue as well as others generally raised when research on the effects of a political leader's personal characteristics on political behavior is contemplated. Three questions appear germane to research on the impact of personal characteristics on political behavior: (1) Whose political behavior are we interested in predicting? (2) What personal characteristics are most likely to affect such political behavior? (3) Are there role, situational, and/or organizational factors which might enhance the particular effect of personal characteristics on political behavior we are seeking to demonstrate?

In examining political behavior, we can look at the individual leader's behavior. How do his personal characteristics affect what he does politically—e.g., how he votes, the meetings he attends, how active he is, the content of his speeches, the people he chooses for his staff. Or, we can examine the political behavior of the group he is leading. How do his personal characteristics affect the policy of the group—e.g., how active it is, its commitments, the problems it tackles. It is easier to postulate a relationship between what a political leader is like and what he does politically than between what a political leader is like and what the political body of which he is part will do. The individual leader's political philosophy, his cognitive map of the political environment, his motives, his decision style, his political training help him to interpret in-coming stimuli, to develop strategies, and to choose tactics. As Holsti (1962, p. 244) observes, a political leader "acts upon his 'image' of the situation rather than upon 'objective' reality." The relationship between what a political leader is like and what the political body he leads does is more complex. Several conditions seem necessary before a political leader's personal characteristics will relate to collective political behavior.

First, how well-defined is the political leader's role? Are the tasks which he is to perform delineated or is there room for the leader to interpret what his functions are to be? Here we are interested in the degree to which the formal requirements of the role circumscribe what the political leader can do. The more opportunity the political leader has to specify what his job does and does not entail—the things he can and cannot do—the more impact he can have on the position. If such a role involves policy making for a group, personal characteristics of the political leader will affect group policy. For example, the city engineer role is probably more circumscribed than that of mayor; the position of state superintendent for education probably has more delineated formal requirements than governor; a desk officer in the foreign ministry probably has his functions fairly delimited in comparison to a foreign minister. Thus, we are suggesting that the personal characteristics of the mayor, governor, and foreign minister will affect policy for their respective political groups more than the personal characteristics of city engineers, state superintendents for education, and desk officers.

These examples indicate a second role characteristic which increases the likelihood that a political leader's personal characteristics will affect public policy. How responsible is the political leader for the decisions of the political body? Is he ultimately accountable for the policies or behavior of the group or organization or is he merely a part of a chain of command? The political leader who has the authority to make policy for a political group or organization has the power to shape that policy. He can negate or approve policies which come through the ranks. He can bypass the chain of command if the situation warrants it. He often can appoint people to political positions subordinate to his own. He can affect the objectives of the political body. As the sign on Truman's desk stated: "The buck stops here." It is likely that the beliefs, attitudes, motives, decision style, and training of the political leader who has ultimate responsibility for the policies of a political body will influence those policies. The opportunity exists for the personal characteristics of the political leader to have an impact on what the group or organization does.

These two role conditions suggest the following proposition: The higher the level of the role in a political group or organization which a political leader holds, the more likely his personal characteristics are to influence that group's or organization's decisions. As Snyder and Robinson (1961, p. 158) have observed: "When asked if personality plays as great (or greater) a part in behavior as organizational factors such as communication, officials who are at lower echelons tend to say no, while those at high echelons tend to say yes." Such high level roles tend to be less well-defined. Moreover, there are few people with more authority who can change or modify a decision. Furthermore, if high-level political leaders can appoint the lower-level officials, chances are their attitudes, beliefs, and values will permeate the group or organization. The high-level leaders are likely to select individuals whose basic political views match their own. The discussion to this point suggests that if the researcher is interested in the effect of political leaders' personal characteristics on political unit behavior, he will be more likely to find such an effect if he studies high-level political leaders.

Even with a focus on high-level political leaders, however, the researcher is urged to also consider situational conditions in predicting when such political leaders' personal characteristics are likely to have an impact on the decisions of a political body. In another place, this author (Hermann, 1976a) has proposed eight circumstances which enhance the relationship of high-level political leaders' personal characteristics to public policy. These situations appear to be of three broad types. The first type involves situations which force the high-level political leader to define or interpret them. Ambiguous situations are of this sort. Either because of too few cues, too many cues, or contradictory cues, the political leader must give some definition to the event. The personal characteristics which generally affect how he processes information will come into play. The second type of situation includes circumstances when the high-level political leader is likely to participate in the decision-making process. Some instances when high-level policy makers are likely to participate are in discussions where issues of major concern to them or their administration are being decided, in crises, and in high-level bargaining or "personal diplomacy." As Janis (1972) argues in *Victims of Groupthink,* when high-level policy makers participate in the decision-making process, their positions, options, and beliefs are often accepted without question by the group. The third type of situation centers on conditions when the political leader assumes office through dramatic means, such as a landslide election, revolution, assassination, or *coup d'etat.* For a period of time (the "honeymoon") following such occurrences, the new high-level political leader can institute his policies with almost a free hand. Constituency criticism is held in abeyance during this time. Moreover, the political leader will probably have some policies to implement.

We have addressed two of the three questions posed at the beginning of this section. There are two kinds of political behavior with which to relate a political leader's personal characteristics—his own and that of the political unit of which he is a part. We have argued that for a political leader's personal characteristics to affect the behavior of his political unit, he must hold a high-level position in that unit. Moreover, the most direct relationships with public policy even for high-level political leaders are expected when certain situational conditions hold. Now, what about the personal characteristics we think are most likely to influence political behavior. We have already mentioned several candidates in the course of our discussion. A search of writings on political leaders—both journalistic and scholarly—suggests four broad types of personal characteristics which seem relevant to the content and means of making and implementing political decisions. These four types are a political leader's beliefs, motives, decision style, and modes of interpersonal interaction.

By *beliefs* we mean the political leader's fundamental assumptions about the the world and, in particular, political reality. Are events predictable, is conflict basic to human interaction, can one have some control over events, is the maintenance of national sovereignty and superiority an important objective of most nations? Answers to questions such as these suggest some of a political leader's beliefs. A political leader's beliefs are proposed by many (e.g., DeRivera, 1968; Frank, 1968; Holsti, 1967; Jervis, 1969; Osgood, 1962; Verba, 1969) to affect his interpretation of his environment and, in turn, the strategies which he employs. Recently under the rubric "operational code," researchers have examined the belief systems of political leaders like Dean Acheson (McLellan, 1971), Willy Brandt (Ashby, 1969), Mao Tse-Tung (White, 1969), and Pierre

Trudeau (Thordarson, 1972). Johnson's operational code for Senator Frank Church in Chapter 4 is one such study.

It is hard to find journalistic political analysis which does not at some point consider the reasons why a political leader is doing what he is doing—in effect, the political leader's *motives*. Probably the most mentioned motive is the need for power. But others, such as the need for achievement and the need for approval, also appear regularly in such writings. Motives seem to affect the strategies which the leader employs. Recall the distinctive legislative strategies of the four types of state legislators which Barber found and their corresponding motives.

Decision style is the third type of personal characteristic which has been proposed to relate to political behavior (see, e.g., M. Hermann, 1974; Snyder and Robinson, 1961). How does the political leader go about making decisions? Are there certain ways of approaching a policy-making task which characterize him? Possible components of style are openness to new information, preference for certain levels of risk, ability to tolerate ambiguity, preference for compromise as a tactic, and willingness to use a satisficing as opposed to an optimizing mode of decision making. Differences in decision style are probably the first differences noted when political leaders change. Decision style is expected to affect the means by which policy decisions are made and implemented. The reader should be alerted to several interesting discussions of high-level political leaders' decision style and its effect on policy. First is T. Robinson's (1972) comparison of the decision styles of Chou En-Lai and Lin Piao. Second is Manley's (1969) description of how Wilbur Mills' decision style influenced committee behavior of the House Ways and Means Committee.

Another type of personal characteristic which will affect the means by which policy is reached and implemented we will call the political leader's *modes of interpersonal interaction*. These are the usual ways in which the political leader deals with others. Two modes of interpersonal interaction—paranoia (excessive suspiciousness) and Machiavellianism (unscrupulous, manipulative behavior)—are often noted as peculiarly pronounced in political leaders and are suggested to account for the "behind-the-scenes" behavior of such leaders (see, e.g., Christie and Geis, 1970; Guterman, 1970; Hofstadter, 1965; Rutherford, 1966). Tucker (1965) has proposed that these two modes of interpersonal interaction are related in a type of political leader having a "warfare personality," for example, Stalin and Hitler. The political behavior of such a leader is combative in nature. Other modes of interpersonal interaction which might prove relevant to political behavior are the political leader's means of persuading others (does he use threats or promises?) (cf. Osgood, 1962), his sensitivity to others, and his leadership style (is he task-oriented or person-oriented?) (cf. Byars, 1973; Verba, 1961).

These four types of personal characteristics focus on what we have called traits or characteristics consistent across situations and issues. Are there any situation-specific characteristics or states of a political leader which might affect political behavior? Several come to mind which are indicators of how stressful the situation is to the political leader. How anxious is he, how defensive is he, how much uncertainty is he experiencing? Once stress is suspected, the ways the political leader copes with it will affect his political behavior—and, if he is a high-level policy maker, public policy. Issue-specific attitudes are also expected to help determine positions on those issues.

One last personal characteristic is important in any discussion of the impact of personal characteristics on political behavior. This characteristic is the political leader's *training* for the position he holds. In other words, what expertise does he have relevant to his political role? With little experience or expertise on which to draw, the political leader may, particularly in the beginning of his tenure, proceed very cautiously. He will rely heavily on his natural problem-solving predispositions. The political leader, however, with some experience or expertise already has some sense of efficacy concerning the role. He has some idea of what will and will not work. As a result, he may move ahead more boldly with the strategies he considers workable. In another place, this author (Hermann, 1974) has shown how training acts as an intervening variable in the personal characteristic-political behavior relationship.

PART THREE

The chapters in Part Three of the book explore in more detail how political leaders' personal characteristics affect their own and their group's political behavior. In Chapter 12, Hermann explores the straight bivariate hypothesis that a political leader's personal characteristics will influence what he does politically. She studies the relationship between certain characteristics of members of the U.S. House of Representatives and their votes on foreign aid. The specific personal characteristics examined were chosen because of their relationship in previous psychological research to an attitude on international involvement.

Driver in Chapter 13 uses simulation to investigate how certain personal characteristics affect when high-level political leaders in a nation will go to war. Here the focus is on the political behavior of the unit, the nation. Simulation participants are given high-level policy maker roles in the nation (e.g., head of state, foreign minister) to increase the likelihood that their personal characteristics will affect national policy. Participants differed in four characteristics which have been found in other research to relate to aggressiveness.

Chapters 14, 15, and 16 examine more specifically how role and situation affect the relationship between personal characteristics and political behavior. Hermann in Chapter 14 studies the behavior of high-level negotiators in a stress situation. She seeks to explore if, as pressures mount in a negotiation, negotiators exhibit more anxiety, uncertainty, and stereotyping behavior in their verbal statements and what the implications of their reactions are for the negotiations.

In Chapter 15, Crow and Noel tackle the question of the relative importance of situational, organizational, and personal characteristics in political unit behavior. Using simulation and a masked historical situation, Crow and Noel study the impact of each of these types of variables by itself and in combination with the others. The simulation participants assume the roles of high-level national decision makers.

Druckman in Chapter 16 focuses on one type of national political behavior, international negotiations, and asks how the personal characteristics of the chief negotiators, their roles vis à vis their nations and opponents, and the characteristics of the negotiation situation itself affect what takes place. He reviews the vast negotiation literature bearing on these components of bargaining and suggests the implications of this research for international negotiations. Moreover, Druckman attempts to indicate how these types of variables interact in determining negotiation outcomes.

Overview of Book

In sum, like ancient Gaul, the chapters that follow are divided into three parts, each part dealing with an issue highly germane to the exploration of the personal characteristics of political leaders. These three issues are: problems of assessment, who becomes a political leader, and the effect of a leader's personal characteristics on political behavior. The chapters examine the issues in some detail, providing illustrations of systematic research on each issue. Moreover, the chapters cover the various alternative ways of assessing the personal characteristics of political leaders and focus on political leaders at the local, state, and national levels, as well as on political leaders from various countries. Preceding each chapter is an editor's introduction which places the chapter in perspective. Where material in one chapter is relevant to an issue other than the one on which it is focused, the relevance will be made explicit in the editor's introduction.

Whereas the present introductory chapter sets the stage for the book by explicating the issues which the chapters are intended to address, the final chapter of the book (Chapter 17) presents some directions for future research on the personal characteristics of political leaders based on an integrative summary of the studies reported in the chapters. The final chapter asks the following questions: Where are we now? What problems arose in using the six techniques which we have just described with political leaders? What personal characteristics were found to relate to becoming a political leader or to political behavior? How can these relationships be linked or integrated? Does what we learned about becoming a political leader have implications for political behavior? From the answers to these questions come the recommendations for future research.

PART 1

POLITICAL LEADERS AT A DISTANCE— PROBLEMS OF ASSESSMENT

CHAPTER 2

Content Analysis as a Technique for Assessing Political Leaders

David G. Winter and
Abigail J. Stewart

Editor's Introduction

Chapters 2, 3, and 4 illustrate the use of content analysis as a means of assessing
the personal characteristics of political leaders. Each deals in a different way
with the choice-points that we proposed in the introductory chapter are involved
in using content analysis. The present chapter focuses on quantitative as opposed
to qualitative content analysis. As the authors note, they are interested in
". . . the systematic, objective study of written and transcribed oral
material . . ." (p. 29). They are interested in counting references to specific
categories which appear in the text of a communication. Moreover, they propose
nine criteria for the researcher to use in deciding whether quantitative content
analysis is applicable to the study under consideration. In their emphasis on
quantitative content analysis, Winter and Stewart differ from Johnson (Chapter
4) who uses qualitative content analysis.

   With regard to the material examined, the content analyses which Winter and
Stewart describe and perform are concerned with the content of a
communication. This type of content analysis contrasts with that of Frank in
the next chapter (Chapter 3) who uses quantitative content analysis to study the
structure of the communication. How is it said? What kinds of words were used?
Several other differences are noteworthy between the content analysis of Winter

27

and Stewart and that of Frank. Winter and Stewart use the theme as the coding unit, whereas in most instances Frank counts single words. Moreover, Winter and Stewart are interested in studying traits or personal characteristics which are generally consistent across issues and situations while Frank is interested in states or personal characteristics that are usually situation or issue specific.

In addition to illustrating the use of quantitative content analysis in the study of traits, the Winter and Stewart chapter is also relevant to research on the effect of personal characteristics on political behavior. In their own study, Winter and Stewart are interested in characterizing twentieth-century presidents on three motives and ascertaining the effect of these motives on both presidential and national political behavior. The authors have a distinct advantage in focusing on these particular personal characteristics (i.e., need for achievement, need for power, and need for affiliation) for there is a rich empirical research history on these motives which suggests the kinds of behavioral correlates to expect. Moreover, the previous studies used content analysis in determining motive scores.

Winter and Stewart not only investigate how the three motives relate to political behavior; they also examine how the motive scores relate to a typology of twentieth-century presidents proposed by Hargrove (1966) and Barber (1972). One criticism often made of this typology concerns its lack of explicitness in suggesting personal characteristics which determine the defining criteria. Winter and Stewart indicate some motive correlates for the various types of presidents, thus beginning the process of identifying personal characteristics which might account for why a president is of a certain type.

This chapter builds on other research by Winter, particularly his research on the power motive (Winter, 1973b) and his original study of presidential motives (Donley and Winter, 1970). Currently Winter is associate professor of psychology at Wesleyan University. Stewart is an assistant professor of psychology at Boston University.

THE STUDY AND ANALYSIS of the words of statesmen and political men of importance has long been a valued technique of historians, commentators, and journalists. The primitive notion is that what people say or write about their actions is useful in interpreting the actions themselves, in assessing the meaning or intention which gave rise to the actions, and in predicting the course of future actions. Because most of the really significant political actors are not available for more direct study through questioning and interviews (by reason of death or sheer unavailability), the student often finds that written products and written transcriptions of oral products are the only available source or, at least, the most convenient source for assessing political leaders. The recent increased interest of political scientists in psychological techniques and modes of explanation and the growing interest of psychologists in studying politics and politicians will surely accelerate the reliance on some form of content analysis. Although lower-level political actors have been studied directly through psychological interviews (e.g., Lasswell, 1930) and systematic testing (e.g., Kaltenbach and McClelland, 1958; Browning and Jacob, 1964), one simply cannot imagine that students will ever be able to administer a Thematic Apperception Test, an F-Scale, or a behavioral observation inventory to the President of the United States, a foreign minister, or a key political advisor. It is, therefore, important to take stock of the ways in which content analysis of written material can be used to make psychological inferences about political leaders.

This chapter will discuss content analysis as a technique for *making psychological inferences about politically relevant aspects of the personality of political actors from the systematic, objective study of written and transcribed oral material.* Such a definition of content analysis is much more circumscribed than usual. Our intention is not to cover the entire field of content analysis (for which an excellent review can be found in Holsti, 1969), but rather to focus on the ways in which it can be used as a psychological technique for the study of political leaders. We will first discuss some early clinical attempts to analyze the written content of political figures to illustrate both the kinds of explanations and interpretations that might be expected from use of the technique and the major problems with the method. Then we will review some of the early and more recent attempts at systematic, comparative content analysis concluding with a discussion of a relatively new technique, first used by Donley and Winter (1970), in which speeches or other content can be scored for motives. Because we believe that this technique holds great promise for the psychological study of political leaders, we will present some further data using the technique and discuss specific procedures and problems that the technique involves.

Issues in Content Analysis

A CLINICAL EXAMPLE

Some might quarrel with our definition of content analysis as being "systematic" and "objective" on the grounds that the introduction of such canons, presumably drawn from the use of the scientific method, is in fact only a pseudo-scientific attempt to obscure the obvious with the mystification of numbers and arcane techniques. The informal and intuitive analysis of speech content and document content has a long and honorable history, from Prince Hamlet's inferences about the complicity and guilt of his own mother down to the esoteric inferences that the "Kremlinologist" draws from single occurrences of single words or the substitution of one subtly shaded term for another in Soviet pronouncements. During the summer of 1973, the American people spent hours before their television sets trying to make inferences from the lengthy testimony of witnesses concerned with the Watergate scandal about "who really intended or knew what, and when they intended or knew it." George (1959a,

1959b) argues that *qualitative* content analysis (a concept to be discussed in more detail below), drawing on an analyst's extensive experience and intuitive inferences, has often proven accurate in the sense of leading to important predictions of action that could not have been made by systematic, objective, and quantitative techniques. George concludes that against the base line of the performance of the best intuitive commentators, or the best clinicians, systematic and objective content analysis has not always performed at a superior level, in the sense of producing interesting, useful, and nonobvious interpretations and predictions about politically relevant behavior.

Based on George's comments, an appropriate point of departure for our survey of content analysis studies of political actors is probably the psychoanalytic study of Woodrow Wilson by Freud and Bullitt (1967—the manuscript was substantially completed by 1932).[1] Psychoanalysis can be understood as a procedure for inferring meaning from the use of special, and unusual, techniques of analysis of written and oral communication *content* (see Rycroft, 1966); thus, for an example of the clinical, nonquantitative, intuitive technique of psychological content analysis, one could scarcely do better than to turn to the works of Freud. The book on Wilson was Freud's only attempt to analyze a prominent political person. And while the authors recognized that they could not "hope to comprehend the decisive events in his [Wilson's] psychic life either in all their details or in all their connections" because Wilson was not accessible in the same way that a patient undergoing psychoanalysis is, they nevertheless argued that the techniques and principles of psychoanalysis, applied "at a distance," could be the basis of a valid and useful psychological study (Freud and Bullitt, 1967, pp. 59-60). The analysis of the content of particular speeches and recorded remarks assumed a major role in their investigation. It is useful to examine the kinds of content analytic evidence that they cite implicitly to justify their analytic conclusions. We will discuss two specific conclusions and some of the corroborative evidence below.

According to Freud and Bullitt (1967, Chapter 3), one of the major themes of Wilson's personality was a *submissive passivity to his father,* identification with his mother, and, consequently, an accentuation of the *feminine* aspect of the human being's essentially bisexual nature. Whether such an interpretative conclusion is justified is not at issue; for present purposes, we wish to cite a typical quotation from Wilson which Freud and Bullitt offer in support of their conclusion in order to give the flavor of this subtle clinical analysis of content.

> My election to the presidency of Princeton has done a very helpful thing
> for me. It has settled the future for me and given me a sense of *position*

[1] There is some dispute about how much Freud himself actually participated in the writing and analysis "at a distance" of Wilson. Although aspects of the style and the use of concepts differ from Freud's other writings, Bullitt states that both authors were agreed on the outline and text of the final result (Foreword to Freud and Bullitt, 1967, by W. C. Bullitt). Judgments about the validity of the product should not, in any case, affect the usefulness of the book as an illustration of the clinical method.

and of definite, tangible tasks which takes the *flutter* and restlessness from my spirits. (Letter to his wife in 1902; "flutter" taken as feminine in connotation; Freud and Bullitt, 1967, p. 141.)

Related to this is a second theme in which Wilson's father and the image of God were fused in an extraordinarily strong superego, with the result that while Wilson was, on occasion, supremely confident, at times of greatest triumph he was driven, as if by a scourge, to the realization that what was done was never enough.

Whether you did little or much, remember that God ordained that I should be the next President of the United States. Neither you nor any other mortal or mortals could have prevented it. . . . I do not feel exuberant or cheerful. I feel exceedingly solemn. . . . A weight of seriousness and responsibility seems to be pressing down upon me. (Statements to his campaign chairman and to Princeton students, respectively, after his election in 1912; Freud and Bullitt, 1967, p. 180.)

The moral obligation that rests upon us not to go back on those boys [American casualties], but to see the thing through, to see it through to the end and make good their redemption of the world. For nothing less depends upon this decision, nothing less than the liberation and salvation of the world. (Speech at Pueblo, Colorado, in September 1919, hours before his collapse and paralysis; Freud and Bullitt, 1967, p. 333.)

We have quoted these brief examples, not to discuss whether Freud and Bullitt's analysis was correct or complete, but rather to illustrate certain problems and issues that are inherent in any use of psychological content analysis. These issues are framed in the form of nine questions or tests which we propose as a guide to evaluating the usefulness and explanatory power of any procedure for psychological content analysis of the communications of political actors. The issues derive directly from the three principal parts of our definition of content analysis: (a) systematic, objective study, (b) making psychological inferences, (c) about politically relevant aspects of personality.[2]

ISSUES RESULTING FROM SYSTEMATIC, OBJECTIVE STUDY

1. *Is the sample of documents (speech transcripts) representative of the verbal output of the persons studied?* Is any further sampling within documents also representative? The temptation is natural to interpret prominent public figures on the basis of remembered phrases or a particular, influential speech with the result that the analyst may be working from primary data that are misleading because they are not representative. The representativeness of sampled

[2] These issues are related to Holsti's (1969, pp. 653-663) survey of general problems of content analysis, but are phrased more specifically to fit the needs of studies relevant to this chapter.

content can be of three different sorts: (1) Representative of the entire corpus of written and verbal output—everything spoken or written by the political leader; (2) representative of a certain class of output for the leader—e.g., a type of speech such as State of the Union or Inaugural speeches; or (3) representative of output on a certain topic—such as foreign policy or morality in government. The kind of representativeness to be sought depends upon the purpose of the investigation or, more precisely, upon the range of the domain of personality which is being studied.

Representativeness in any sense of the word actually involves several different concerns. The first is whether the content analyst acquired a complete, or representative set, of the relevant "universe" of communications by the political leader so that he is acquainted with the entire corpus of output. Failure to do so simply means that data contradictory to an interpretation are not considered. With regard to the Freud-Bullitt analysis of Wilson, Bullitt's remarks in his preface suggest reasonable thoroughness with respect to Wilson's published written documents and speeches, but perhaps (and necessarily) incomplete, nonrepresentative, and possibly faulty sampling of conversational remarks as recalled by Wilson's associates.

> We read all Wilson's published books and speeches, and all the volumes concerning Wilson published by Ray Stannard Baker who had been chosen by the President as his biographer and had access to all Wilson's private papers. . . . I read scores of volumes that dealt with aspects of Wilson's career. . . . I set out to try to collect [private unpublished] information. I was helped by many of my friends among Wilson's associates; some of whom put at our disposal their diaries, letters, records and memoranda, while others talked frankly about him. Thanks to their assistance we felt confident that, although subsequent publication of private papers would amplify and deepen our knowledge of Wilson's character, no new facts would come to light which would conflict vitally with the facts upon which we had based our study (Freud and Bullitt, 1967, pp. vi-vii).

A second concern of representativeness centers on the question of analysis—more loosely, the question of whether to count frequencies or to look for the single, striking metaphor, slip of the tongue or pen, or suggestive image. There seems to be no single best strategy. While counting permits more precise comparison to other political actors, many highly significant psychological characteristics may manifest themselves only in a fleeting sentence or single reference. For example, Wilson only had to write that "I read detective stories to forget, as a man would get drunk" one time for Freud and Bullitt to formulate a hypothesis about his sexual identity. The genius of Freud lay in his ability to attend to such single statements, connect them with a wide variety of seemingly unrelated other evidence, and draw a striking conclusion. As we noted earlier, George (1959a, 1959b) argues plausibly that this kind of inference, made without regard to counting frequencies, often reveals an impressive record of accuracy. Moreover, M. Stewart (1943) demonstrated with newspaper content analysis that mere frequency does not always relate to other forms of "channel prominence devices" such as space, emphasis, sequential order, and intonation. We have no final preference for quantitative methods over nonquantitative "clinical" analysis, beyond noting that frequency counting makes possible the use of statistical techniques to establish validity and to make confident inferences (see below). The key issue may be to determine what it is important to count—e.g., words, phrases, symbols, themes.

2. *Are the categories for the analysis of content described or defined in such a way that different people, working independently, will make the same judgments when using the same material?* In plainer language, this question refers to the reliability of the coding system, an obvious requirement for scientific objectivity. In general, the simpler the code and the more quantitative the analysis, the easier it will be to obtain reliability with only a minimum of training or orientation for the coders. Reliability does not mean that the codes have to be so obvious that an untrained person off the street could apply them with perfect agreement; the amount of training or skill required to code reliably reflects the efficiency or usability of the research rather than reliability as such. Thus, the Freud and Bullitt "coding" of Wilson probably could be duplicated only by another student of psychoanalysis with considerable training. Usually this sort of checking is not done with qualitative or "clinical" coding, so that we do not know the "coding reliability" of the Freud-Bullitt analysis. While reliability is important, we must add the caution that the ease of training coders to be reliable should not completely override considerations of interest and relevance of the categories. Probably any person could obtain a high reliability by counting the number of occurrences of the word "the," but such a variable does not have great interest or explanatory power.

ISSUES RESULTING FROM MAKING PSYCHOLOGICAL
    INFERENCES

3. *Are the variables assessed through content analysis explicitly linked to psychological theory?* Answers to this question differentiate general content analysis, which may be carried out for a variety of purposes (see Holsti, 1969, pp. 601-602), from psychological content analysis. Two separate matters may be considered under this heading. It seems obvious that for the results to be meaningful at the psychological level of explanation, the categories or variables used in content analysis must be anchored in some psychological theory—they must "mean something" in terms of prior clinical experience or research. Nevertheless, this is not always the case in content analysis (see Stone et al., 1966). Freud and Bullitt's concepts are in this respect exemplary, in that they draw up the entire systematic collection of observations and interpretations of psychoanalysis. "Feminine identification" and "extraordinarily strong superego" are major psychoanalytic concepts, central to Freud's entire conception of the organization, functioning, and pathology of human personality. From them, we

are able to make all sorts of further inferences, predictions, and explanations of Wilson's behavior, accomplishments, and final breakdown. Whether all psychologists find these interpretations acceptable is not at issue; only through using theoretically rich constructs is it possible to make any further interpretations and predictions.

While a particular content category may be "linked" to a broader theoretical construct, it is also necessary that there be evidence of the category's validity. Put in terms of the examples given, it must be shown that the use of phrases such as "the moral obligation that rests upon me . . ." or "we desired to offer ourselves as a sacrifice for humanity" are reliable and valid indicators of superego strength. The categories used must be part of the range of operational definitions associated with the theoretical construct, and they must be valid predictors of other manifestations of that construct. The status of Freud and Bullitt's technique on this count is not fully clear. Freud (1949, p. 26) cautioned against establishing fixed ranges of interpretative "meaning" for verbal content (especially of dreams) on the grounds that the unique meaning of the content could only be established through study of the unique associations of the author. Hence, there can never be any exact series of operational definitions for the manifestation of psychoanalytic entities or processes in verbal content.[3] Nevertheless, psychoanalytic practice usually assumes that one can specify manifestations of processes in such a way that examples will be readily recognized, at least when studying personality at a distance (as in the case of Freud's studies of Leonardo, Dostoevsky, and so forth).

4. *Are the psychological variables related to normal functioning as well as (perhaps) to psychopathology?* While Lasswell (1930) has argued that most prominent political figures show signs of abnormality, the fact is that they are not usually thought of as being definitely abnormal or pathological, nor have they usually been treated in any of the ways that so-called "abnormal" persons are treated. In any case, it is well to remember that some substantial proportion of their political action is not "abnormal." Erikson (1964, p. 203) puts the point succinctly in distinguishing the political innovator from the crank: "Such men and women also display an unusual energy of body, a rare concentration of mind, and a total devotion of soul, which carries them through trials and errors and near catastrophes, and, above all, helps them to bide their time. . . ." Choosing variables exclusively associated with abnormal functioning is likely to diminish the interest, relevance, and empirical usefulness of the inferences that can be made to political behavior. With respect to Freud and Bullitt, one observes that psychoanalysis is often accused of an exclusive preoccupation with the abnormal to the neglect of mature, healthy functioning. In fact, however, this is a slight misconception. Whatever the general public may think, Freud considered his concepts adequate for dealing with the entire range of normal

---

[3]Many other theorists who at one time were related to the psychoanalytic movement, notably Jung and Stekel, appear to have accepted more precise and fixed definitions than Freud did.

behavior, and he often demonstrated the "normal" functioning of psycho-analytic mechanisms in his interpretations of errors, dreams, artistic content, and the like. Freud viewed no sharp demarcation between normal and abnormal behavior. Whether one accepts this claim is not relevant to the question stated here: the variables must be related to "normal" behavior as that behavior is conceptualized within the theory in which one works.

5. *Are the psychological variables to be coded in the analysis drawn from a number of different, independent dimensions?* The greater the number of different and independent variables that are being assessed, the broader and fuller will be the resulting set of inferences to political behavior and the richer the overall interpretation. Obviously this issue involves matters of preference. Single-dimensional explanations are not in themselves wrong or undesirable, if they are not exaggerated or extended beyond their reasonable validity. Assessing several different dimensions usually permits a fuller explanation. Even if some of the dimensions are not relevant to a particular political actor, their careful assessment will permit more precise comparison with other political actors (see below). We have emphasized two of the major variables postulated by Freud and Bullitt to account for Wilson's behavior. While they do mention others (such as principal kinds of defense mechanisms, characteristic sources of anxiety, object choices), their analysis taken as a whole is more in the nature of a clinical portrait organized around a few major themes rather than a careful specification of the strength or level of several different variables.

ISSUES CONCERNING POLITICALLY RELEVANT ASPECTS
OF PERSONALITY

6. *Is the content analysis carried out and reported in such a way that comparison with other, similar political actors is facilitated?* This issue entails the use of content categories which are clearly and operationally defined (issue 2) and which include several independent variables (issue 5). Moreover, it usually entails reduction of the data to frequency counts and quantitative values, although "present/absent" or "high/low" dichotomies would permit comparison. Here the Freud and Bullitt study shows several major deficiencies. A researcher who wanted to compare Wilson to other presidents with respect to feminine identification, reaction formation to feminine identification, or super-ego strength would be somewhat at a loss as to how to proceed. He could doubtless find imagery in the speeches and documents of the other president that is quite similar to what Freud and Bullitt found in Wilson's, but how could he decide whether to code the other president as "high" or "low"? The issue is certainly not trivial. One might suppose that the kind of rhetoric Freud and Bullitt consider as reflecting superego strength is quite common in American political speeches on great issues—at least speeches of the early twentieth century. Perhaps all American presidents are high in superego strength because they are elected by a superego-driven population and, thus, reflect population characteristics (see Gorer, 1948). If this is so, then the variable of superego

strength by itself cannot explain the decisive differences in political action between Wilson and other American presidents.

Research by McDiarmid (1937) illustrates the necessity of making comparisons and suggests another problem with the analysis of Freud and Bullitt. McDiarmid coded first inaugural speeches for American presidents from 1881-1933 for the frequency of several different categories, including references to "God," "the Almighty," "Divine Providence." His study indicates that if frequency of occurrence of references to God can be taken as a measure of superego strength, Wilson was not substantially higher than other presidents of his era in either total or relative frequency and was actually lower than the president who succeeded him. Of course, it may be argued that frequency of references to "God" in a single speech is not a sensitive indicator of superego strength; but in that case the burden of definition, and the burden of proof that Wilson was high in superego strength, fall squarely on the clinical analyst who makes the assertion.

7. *Are the content samples of the actor (and of comparison actors) drawn from standardized or otherwise comparable documents or speeches?* To the extent that certain content categories vary with the occasion, purpose, or type of speech or document, comparisons across different political actors may be contaminated if the selections from the types of occasions are not made in the same way for each. Thus, Freud and Bullitt quote extensively from Wilson's speeches in defense of the Versailles Treaty, even though these were speeches made in response to an extraordinary situation. We simply do not know the extent to which any other president might use similar imagery in a similar situation. The Freud and Bullitt interpretation of Wilson may be biased by the uniqueness of the kinds of speeches sampled. At the very least, it will be necessary to specify the exact circumstances in which the content was elicited or occurred to facilitate precise comparison with content drawn from similar circumstances (types, purposes) by comparable political actors. McDiarmid's findings illustrate the importance of using a standardized speech—e.g., the first inaugural speech of the president. Inaugural speeches are the first official statement of a President; they record his fundamental hopes, fears, aspirations, and goals. They establish a distinctive tone and atmosphere for his incoming administration. While they are, of course, influenced by the issues of the day, they are usually more abstract and generalized. Therefore, for the purposes of comparing presidents, the inaugural speeches constitute one source of standardized verbal behavior which occurred in a reasonably standardized situation. To a lesser extent, State of the Union speeches, nomination acceptance speeches, and, under some circumstances, press conference transcripts represent standardized sources of content.

8. *Are the psychological variables presumed to be related directly to significant political actions or is provision made for the operation of moderator variables?* This issue does not concern the categories used in content analysis, but rather the theory from which they are derived and the ways in which the

results are further linked to political inferences. One has the impression that Freud and Bullitt sometimes considered that most of Wilson's behavior was the inevitable product only of the hypothesized personality characteristics rather than the product of these characteristics in combination with important contingent events of the times (World War I, the personalities of Lloyd George, Clemenceau, and Senator Lodge, and so forth). To the extent that research makes explicit provision for the operation of moderator variables, mediating the relationship between personality and behavior, the breadth and convincingness of the final explanation is likely to improve.

9. *Is the behavior that can be predicted by the psychological variables of sufficient political interest and relevance?* This issue concerns the theory from which the variables are derived. There are many psychological variables useful for the analysis of content which relate to behaviors that are rather unlikely to be of clear political relevance—e.g., the adjective-verb ratio which differentiates normals from schizophrenics, the type-token ratio which increases with successful psychotherapy, and the discomfort-relief quotient which has shown some relationship to physiological measures of arousal or anxiety (see Holsti, 1969, pp. 627-634; Garraty, 1959). It is, of course, possible that any measure might predict important political behavior; but one gets the impression that many categories have been used in the psychological content analysis of political actors merely because the categories were there—because they were in the literature. The use of categories solely for this reason, in the absence of a special theory (e.g., differences in stress responses in negotiation or crisis situations predicted by a measure that is related to stress in clinical research), is likely to give disappointing results. Clearly the variables inferred from Freud and Bullitt's analysis—for example, superego strength—may be thought of as potentially related to behaviors which are of very great political significance.

Having discussed at length one clinical example using content analysis to study a political leader and having raised what we feel are nine important issues or considerations in the design of such research, we shall discuss briefly some of the other major content analytic studies of political leaders that have been carried out to date. We shall refer to the issues raised above in commenting on these studies.

Types of Content-Analytic Studies of Political Leaders

Many of the more recent psychological or "psychohistorical" studies of significant political actors make at least some informal use of content analysis of the actors' speeches or writings. Because these studies, insofar as their use of content analysis is concerned, are substantially similar to the Freud and Bullitt work with respect to the nine issues that we have suggested, we shall only mention them briefly here. From the orthodox psychoanalytical perspective, there is Langer's (1972) work on Hitler; more eclectic in its approach is the Georges'

(George and George, 1956) work on Wilson. Erikson's "psychohistory" approach, foreshadowed in his essay on Hitler (Erikson, 1950) and brought to its richest demonstration in his study of Gandhi (Erikson, 1969), has been used by Mazlish (1973) to study Richard Nixon. Finally, using what might be termed an informal "learning theory" approach, Barber (1968) has studied Calvin Coolidge and Herbert Hoover.

EARLY NONPSYCHOLOGICAL, QUANTITATIVE STUDIES

One of the earliest applications of quantitative content analysis to political actors is McDiarmid's (1937) study of first inaugural speeches. He defined four broad categories of symbols such as *national/identity* (form of government, America, our/my country), *historical reference* (glorious past, forefathers, etc.), *fundamental concepts* (God or the Almighty, Constitution, freedom, etc.) and *fact and expectation* (present prosperity, confidence in the future). While these categories may be somewhat naive from a psychological point of view, they are an attempt to analyze content in such a way that the study can be used, in principle at least, to test one of Freud and Bullitt's hypotheses. By restricting himself to the first inaugural speech of each president, McDiarmid provides a way to compare different actors' behavior in a relatively standardized situation. However, his own conclusion that there is fundamental continuity in the symbolic usage of American presidents probably would not stand up to closer scrutiny. Furthermore, the fact that he does not adjust raw frequency of symbol usage for length of speech makes correction necessary before any comparison can be made.

Prothro (1956) attempted to test a relatively precise hypothesis about levels of acceptance and rejection of the New Deal in the first nomination acceptance, inaugural, and State of the Union speeches of Eisenhower as compared with those of Hoover, Franklin Roosevelt, and Truman. Prothro used broad categories of *political appeal* (e.g., community cooperation, government regulation) and *demand symbols* (e.g., national unity, social security). Prothro's conclusions are reached by a rather complex process of reasoning and have been challenged (H. White, 1956). What is of interest here is the design of the study, intended as a direct comparison of several different political actors, and the clear definition of categories. Nevertheless, the variables as such appear to be taken from political science and are not intrinsically of psychological interest.

Knepprath (1962) compared the 1956 campaign speeches of Eisenhower and Stevenson in terms of subjects talked about, motives appealed to, and verbal forms of presentation. He noted that Eisenhower appealed to economic motives and capitalized on public opinion; whereas, Stevenson increasingly came to stress safety motives and did not take advantage of relevant public opinion. Knepprath does not appear to have used any psychological theory in the design or analysis of the categories, but concepts such as "motives appealed to" are perhaps a step toward the psychological use of content analysis.

VALUE-ANALYSIS

Perhaps the first specifically psychological theory and categories used in the content-analytic study of political leaders was the method of *value-analysis* developed by R. White (1951). White (1951, p. 13) defines a "value" as "any goal or standard of judgment which in a given culture is ordinarily referred to as if it were self-evidently desirable (or undesirable)." He compiled a list of 50 such values, each defined with examples and taken from traditional lists of human needs, instincts, and propensities (e.g., those of Murray and McDougall), from his own experience in reading content, and from the use of thesauruses and analytic dictionaries. While White claims that the list is fairly exhaustive with respect to Western culture, he allows the possibility of both additions or refinements as well as combinations or simplifications. The complete system also includes person-symbols and scales of frustration-disapproval, satisfaction, other-referents, and means-ends connections. White (1951, pp. 4-9) suggests that all these categories, taken together, enable inferences to be made about psychological dimensions such as hostility, self-approval, stereotypes, ego ideal, frustration areas, and empathy. For purposes of analysis of content of political actors, however, the basic categories are those 27 of the 50 values which are particularly relevant to propaganda and politics and for which White (1951, pp. 44-55) provides additional, expanded definitions. Results are expressed in terms of the percentage of overall emphasis units devoted to each value, where emphasis units are simply the total of all value judgments which have been recorded. (Sometimes a specially emphasized value may be weighted as three emphasis units.)

The first application of this technique to political research was R. White's (1949) study of systematic samples of the speeches of Hitler and Roosevelt during the years 1935-1939. One outgrowth of this study was the war propaganda index. In designing this index White assumed that Hitler could be considered a criterion case of war propaganda and, as a result, that the actual characteristics of such propaganda could be inferred from those categories which differentiated between Hitler and Roosevelt such as strength values, aggression values, and welfare-of-others values. Eckhardt (1965) added value-analysis studies of books by Churchill, Mussolini, Hoover, Stalin, Goldwater, Marx, and Engels, as well as speeches by Kennedy and Khrushchev, to White's original data on Hitler and Roosevelt. Further reference points were provided by the New Testament, social work case reports, *The God That Failed,* and Alcoholics Anonymous case histories—the intention being to validate specific scales (religious, welfare, intellectual, and alcoholic values, respectively), to compare political with nonpolitical writings, and to validate the war propaganda index derived from White's earlier study. Eckhardt's results validated four of the seven categories in the war propaganda index. War propaganda (and hence "warlike" intentions) consists of increased statements of persecution, increased references to strength, increased concern with aggression in the service of self-defense, and decreased consideration for the welfare of others.

A further study by Eckhardt and White (1967) directly compared Kennedy and Khrushchev in a test of the "mirror-image" hypothesis, that is, that American perceptions of the Soviet Union and Soviet perceptions of America are both distorted in similar ways. They found that Kennedy and Khrushchev did not differ significantly from each other in any of the various indices previously validated by Eckhardt as reflecting war propaganda. Moreover, while they did significantly differ in relative frequency on 21 of the 31 values, the correlation between the profiles of relative values for the two was +.56 ($p < .01$).

The technique of value-analysis as it has been used in these studies certainly deserves a high rating with respect to many of the nine issues we raised previously. The concept of value, and the lists of values, are drawn directly from psychological theory and are clearly defined (issues 2 and 3); they represent several different dimensions of normal behavior and functioning (issues 4 and 5); and they have been validated (albeit in a rather impressionistic way) as predicting significant political behavior (issue 9). The nature of the category definition and coding permits comparison among actors (issue 6). Both White and Eckhardt stress the interaction of situation with the expression of values (e.g., both Roosevelt and Hitler were high in percentage of statements of persecution after World War II started, but only Hitler was high before the war), so that there is some provision for interaction of inferred psychological characteristics and external political reality (issue 8). There are some problems with respect to the issues of obtaining representative and standardized samples of content (issues 1 and 7). Eckhardt (1965) compared books from some actors and speeches from others, and Eckhardt and White (1967) used speeches of Kennedy and Khrushchev that had already been selected by other compilers. Nevertheless, there is nothing in the method of value-analysis as such that makes it impossible to improve the representativeness and the standardization of the sources of content.

One major problem with value-analysis, however, is the nature of the concept of value itself (issue 3). While White borrowed *labels* from a wide variety of psychological sources, it is not clear that the values as operationally defined in value-analysis have any linkage to other psychological theory and research. White's (1947) own study of the autobiography of Richard Wright suggests that value-analysis reveals variables that are important in the sense that they help to explain behavior and supplement intuitive impressions; but beyond this single study we have almost no evidence of the nature, origins, and relationship to behavior of "values" as defined in this way. To be sure, Eckhardt's work suggests that the measures may have important predictive capacity when applied to political speeches and writings. However, in order to achieve a psychological level of explanation for political actors, one would expect that variables with a history of research and validation at the level of individual and small group studies would be necessary. Eckhardt and White (1967, p. 326) recognize this problem in their conclusion when they state: "Whether these 'values' reflect sincere beliefs, or how they will be expressed in action, cannot be determined by value-analysis as such, but is a matter of inference and interpretation." Value-analysis, then, is a way of summarizing manifest content of verbal productions; but it is unclear whether it has yet become an instrument for *psychological* investigation.

EVALUATION ASSERTION ANALYSIS

The technique of *evaluation assertion analysis* grew out of research by Osgood (1959) on the dimensions of meaning and on the tendency toward congruity among the objects of cognition (see Brown, 1965, Chapter 11). First, the researcher selects an *attitude object,* the *value* of which along some dimension is calculated from the written or verbal content of some actor. Then all statements containing that attitude object are reduced to two different kinds of assertions. One type of assertion links the attitude object by a verbal connector to an adjective or "common meaning evaluator" as, e.g., the Soviet Union (attitude object) is (verbal connector) hostile (adjective). The other type of assertion links the attitude object by a verbal connector to a second attitude object as, e.g., the Soviet Union (attitude object) usually opposes (verbal connector) American interests (attitude object). For each verbal connector and for each predicate, values from +3 to −3 are supplied on a theoretical basis. For example, "is" and "supports" indicate strong connection and would be valued at +3, while "sometimes is" might be +1 and "never is" would be −3. Moreover, suppose that "goodness" was the dimension under study, the predicate adjective "hostile" might be taken as −3. Other attitude objects appearing as predicate objects would be assigned arbitrary values—for example, "American interests" might be given a +3. The numbers for each verbal connector and predicate are multiplied in order to determine the value of the particular attitude object along the dimension under consideration. When this is done for every relevant assertion in the text, an average value for each attitude object along the relevant dimension can be calculated.

Holsti (1962) and Finlay, Holsti, and Fagen (1967) used evaluation assertion analysis in a study of Dulles' belief system and images of the Soviet Union during his tenure as Secretary of State. On the basis of every publicly available statement of Dulles, Holsti and his colleagues calculated values for each of the following dimensions by three-month time periods: Soviet policy (friendship vs. hostility), Soviet capabilities (strength vs. weakness), Soviet success (satisfaction vs. frustration), and general evaluation of the Soviet Union (good vs. bad). The major result is that Dulles' perception of Soviet friendship varied inversely with his perception of Soviet strength and satisfaction (or, in other words, Soviet hostility varied directly with strength and satisfaction). The dimension of hostility-friendship was unrelated to that of general evaluation. Holsti and his colleagues conclude that Dulles was able to view Soviet friendship as *only* the result of weakness or failure and, thus, was not inclined to perceive and take at face value any change of policy by the Soviet Union. That is, Dulles perceived the Soviet Union through the lens of the so-called model of "inherent bad faith."

Evaluation assertion analysis derives from a good deal of psychological theory and research on meaning and cognition (Osgood, Suci, and Tannenbaum, 1957; Osgood, 1959) and provides the possibility for comparing political actors along a wide variety of different dimensions that are of political relevance. There are no barriers to the systematic sampling of representative speeches of the political actor(s) in question. Overall, the technique may be thought of as measuring *beliefs, attitudes,* and, possibly, *expectancies* about objects (other actors, nations, etc.) of political relevance in contrast to White's technique of measuring *values* or conceptions of the self-evident good. Alternatively, White's technique for the measurement of *values* might be thought of as providing the basis for supplying the appropriate numbers to be inserted in place of predicates in evaluation assertion analysis. Since many psychological theories postulate behavior as some combination of, or interaction between, values and beliefs it appears that a combination of value-analysis and evaluation assertion analysis would be quite fruitful in the content analysis of political actors.

PSYCHO-LOGIC

Shneidman (1961, 1963) devised another psychological content analysis procedure which is useful for political analysis. The text is coded for the presence of 32 different *idiosyncrasies of reasoning* and 65 *cognitive maneuvers.* Then the researcher articulates the premises which would make each idiosyncrasy of reason, or fallacy, correct. These premises (or "contralogic") are the basis for inference about the psychological state (or "psycho-logic") of the actor. Shneidman (1961, 1963) applied the method to the 1961 Kennedy and Nixon debates and to Khrushchev's speeches in 1960. The results are of interest even though the method itself lacks validation in the sense that there has been little research on the behavior characteristics associated with different "logical styles." Comparisons among different actors are possible in terms of frequency of different idiosyncrasies of reasoning or cognitive maneuvers; but Shneidman's overall characterizations of actors, taking into account somewhat intuitive weightings of the "psycho-logic" statements, is essentially a clinical procedure for making inferences from text.

GENERAL INQUIRER

With the advent of computers has come at least one computer-based technique for the psychological content analysis of political writings and speeches, the General Inquirer system developed by Stone and his colleagues (Stone, Dunphy, Smith, and Ogilvie, 1966). In essence, the General Inquirer is a procedure for counting the frequency of concepts given a "dictionary" or series of text words that are to be taken as equivalent manifestations of the concept. Additional options permit counting of certain patterns of concepts (e.g., co-occurrences within the sentence of concept A and concept B; sentences with concept A as subject, concept B as verb, and concept C as object). When the system is viewed in this way, we see that despite the sophistication and complexity of its computer-oriented nature it is essentially a way of operationalizing some prior psychological theory or set of variables within the constraint of the sentence as a unit of analysis. In other words, the dictionary set of concept definitions or equivalencies must be supplied by the user on the basis of some psychological theory, although Stone et al. make available a series of dictionaries that have been used in prior research.

The major application of the General Inquirer to the psychological analysis of political content is a study of Smith, Stone, and Glenn (1966) which analyzes the frequency of certain concepts in nomination-acceptance speeches of presidential candidates of the two major parties from 1928 through 1964. Examples of the concepts used include the following: ideal-value, urge, artistic, economic. By factor analyzing the frequency of different concepts these authors identified such overall factors as universalistic leadership and normative community structure. Smith et al. confined their analysis to comparison of the two major parties' candidates and trends over time for these factors.

Our view of the General Inquirer is that it is essentially a technological device for performing content analysis and not a separate psychological theory. There is always the danger that premature concentration upon computer techniques will obscure the often quite incomplete, or imperfect, ways in which available computer techniques are an accurate operationalization of the psychological theory that is intended. One awaits with interest further use of systems such as the General Inquirer, while remaining cautious about the capacity of present-day computer systems to reflect fully and accurately the subtlety inherent in the operational definitions of many important psychological categories of content.

MOTIVE IMAGERY

We conclude with an extensive discussion of a new method of psychological content analysis of speeches of political actors which was originally developed by Donley and Winter (1970), further discussed by Winter (1973b), and is supplemented in the present chapter with additional data. This method involves scoring for *motive* imagery, using procedures for assessing motives in individuals which have been empirically developed and validated in the psychological laboratory (see Atkinson, 1958; Winter, 1973b, Chapters 2-3). The motive scoring systems were designed for coding content from brief imaginative stories written to the stimulus of a picture (the Thematic Apperception Test or TAT); yet they have also been used to code children's readers, folktales, diaries, writings of classical authors and dramatists, and even reports of dreams (see Donley and Winter, 1970, p. 229). In fact, the systems appear to be applicable to any kind of verbal or written material that is at least partly imaginative—in the sense that it describes some kind of action (real, imagined, or planned)— rather than being purely factual. In the present case, the first inaugural speeches of American presidents from 1905 through 1974 were scored for three important human motives: the achievement motive (*n* Achievement), the affiliation motive (*n* Affiliation), and the power motive (*n* Power).[4]

In terms of the nine issues we raised earlier, this general procedure has several positive features. First, the first inaugural speeches are a representative and reasonably standardized sample of the verbal production of the presidents (issues 1 and 7). As the initial speech of a president, it is better suited to the expression of his motives than are later speeches or statements, which are usually called forth or strongly influenced by specific issues or external events. Second, the motive measures are both explicitly defined and strongly linked to psychological theory and research on normal human persons (issues 2, 3, and 4), as illustrated in Table 2.1. Achievement, affiliation, and power are surely three important dimensions of human behavior (issue 5) which are likely to have important political consequences and relevance (issue 9). The measurement systems yield comparable scores that permit comparison of the different presidents (issue 6). Finally, the theory of motivation from which these measures are drawn makes provision for the interaction of the motives with external events and pressures (issue 8) which are conceptualized as the moderator effects of expectancies and incentives (see Atkinson and Feather, 1966). The present discussion is devoted mainly to summarizing the existing psychological theory and research on these motives, to giving an account of the procedures used to score the speeches, and to presenting evidence that the motives, thus scored, have important action correlates among the presidents.

Examining Inaugural Speeches for Motive Imagery

HYPOTHESES

Table 2.1 presents brief definitions of the motive imagery which is coded for each of the three motives, lists the behaviors that have been found to be associated with each motive in previous research, and gives the major references for this research. Of special interest is a study by Terhune (1968a, 1968b) in which subjects who were relatively pure types on each of the three motive measures were examined in interpersonal bargaining situations (using the familiar "Prisoner's Dilemma" paradigm) and in an inter-nation simulation. One might expect that these results would be most directly useful for predicting the effects of motives on political behavior in real life.

We shall discuss each of these three motives briefly in order to establish some general hypotheses about the kinds of behavior that they should predict among

[4]Scores for *n* Achievement and *n* Power are taken directly from Donley and Winter (1970). *N* Affiliation was scored by the second author of the present chapter, with reliability checks by the first author.

presidents. *N Achievement,* defined as a concern for excellence, is actually associated with "achievement behavior" of a rather specific and narrowly-defined type, namely *entrepreneurial* or business achievement. The preference for moderate risks (or moderate aspirations) plus modification of behavior on the basis of feedback and the use of "expert" advice—all three behaviors associated with *n* Achievement—are instrumental to success in the business world; but it is not clear how relevant they would be to success in a position such as the presidency which is probably more political than entrepreneurial. For example, reliance on advice that is technically "expert" may erode and jeopardize political alliances. The best person politically for the job may not be necessarily the person with the most relevant technical knowledge. Moreover, creating and maintaining a successful political image may require a president or other political leader to control or "manage" expert opinion rather than to use it, even though this may reduce the achievement of the political system in the narrow sense of the word. Modifying performance on the basis of results is an obvious strategy in the business world; but in politics such behavior may be seen as inconsistency of principle or disinterest in the lives and destinies of political associates. As a result, characteristics associated with *n* Achievement may not be necessarily adaptive in politics. We expect that the high *n* Achievement president will be active—although he may not necessarily like the job, that he will choose advisors on the basis of their expert knowledge rather than upon personal or political considerations, and that he may not necessarily achieve very much or be rated as a "good" or "excellent" president.

The affiliation motive is associated with seeking the security of friendship, although not necessarily with finding it. Perhaps because people high in *n* Affiliation are defensive or oversensitive under conditions of risk or competition, they are often rated as relatively *less* popular than those not so high in the motive. In any case, they are usually passive and are easily influenced by other people in general or people who are perceived as attractive (rather than expert, as in the case of *n* Achievement). In contrast to *n* Achievement, the affiliation and power motives are social motives. Thus, we expect that they will be related more often to aspects of the presidents' behavior. Presidents high in *n* Affiliation will seek to surround themselves with advisors who are similar to them, they will be readily influenced by these advisors, and they will be loyal to them. Because such presidents select advisors on the basis of perceived similarity or attractiveness rather than on the basis of expert knowledge or political sensitivity, the quality and effectiveness of the advice that they receive will be relatively low; hence, their rated accomplishments as president will be low. In fact, their style of selecting and being influenced by advisors may very well make their administrations likely settings for political scandal. They will be relatively loyal "party men" and their motive to seek friendship, if not threatened, will be associated with attempts to achieve peace and friendship among nations.

On the basis of its behavioral correlates, *n* Power should fit a president for successful performance in office for it is associated with a wide variety of

Table 2.1. Characteristics of the Achievement, Affiliation, and Power Motives in Verbal Content, General Behavior, and Interpersonal Bargaining Studies

	n Achievement	n Affiliation	n Power
Manifestation in Content Imagery	Concern with standards of excellence, unique accomplishments, long-term involvement; success in competition.	Concern with establishing, maintaining, or restoring warm and friendly relationships; concern for friendly, convivial activity.	Concern with impact on others; through inherently powerful actions, arousal of strong emotions in others; concern with reputation.
Associated Characteristics in Behavior	Succeed in entrepreneurial occupations. Take moderate risks. Modify performance on the basis of results. Choose experts over friends to help on a task. Exhibit restless expressive movement. Dishonest when it is necessary to achieve a goal. Delinquent.	Engage in warm, friendly behavior when secure. Spend time talking with others. Choose friends over experts to help on a task. Influenceable by others who are perceived as attractive; conforming. React to disagreement with dislike. Sometimes rated as relatively *less* popular.	Attain positions of formal social power. Concerned with prestige and prestige possessions. Consume liquor. Take relatively great risks in gambling situations. Are hostile toward higher status persons. Surround self with low prestige friends. Active and influential in small groups. Are sexually precocious.
Behavior in Interpersonal Bargaining			

Short Term	Cooperative	Cooperative under low risk; under high risk apprehensive and defensive, vacillating between defensiveness and exploitation.	Exploitative, especially if cooperation expected from partner.
Long Term	Very cooperative, especially if they encounter cooperation early. Send many messages to coordinate joint action. Articulate strategy reasons for behavior. Perceive partner as cooperator.	Passive communicators. Least able to articulate clear reasons for behavior. Perceive partner as "fellow worker" *or* as opportunist.	Exploitative, especially if they encounter cooperation early. Engage in mutual deadlocks. Send ambiguous messages. Articulate selfish reasons for behavior. Perceive partner as yielder, gambler, competitor, resister.
Inter-Nation Simulation	More cooperative than conflictful; least military effort.	More passive; least manipulative action.	More conflictful than cooperative; greatest military effort and manipulative actions.
Source of Scoring System	Atkinson (1958)	Atkinson (1958)	Winter (1973b)
References	Cortés and Gatti (1972); McClelland (1961); McClelland and Winter (1969); Mischel and Gilligan (1964); Terhune (1968a, 1968b)	Boyatzis (1973); Terhune (1968a, 1968b)	McClelland (1975); McClelland and Watson (1973); Terhune (1968a, 1968b)*; Winter (1973a, 1973b); Winter and A. Stewart (1976)

*Terhune's interpersonal bargaining research is based on an earlier version of the *n* Power scoring system.

behaviors and characteristics that, taken together, are likely to lead to formal social power. Presidents high in *n* Power will be active, vigorous, and happy in the world of intense political bargaining and conflict. If necessary, they will be able to remain "on top" by exploiting associates and attacking enemies. Because they do not have the *n* Achievement tendency to consult experts and to modify their own performance, they may find themselves trapped with the consequences of actions which were undertaken to secure their prestige, but which failed or had other bad consequences. Such a situation of stress may constitute a perceived threat to their power and under such circumstances they may retreat into an unreal subjective world of risk, prestige, and concern with their inner sense of potency. In an extreme case, they may react to defeat by trying to take much of their world (friends, enemies, possessions, civilization itself) with them—the *Götterdämmerung* gesture of Hitler in World War II (see Winter, 1973b, p. 140). Thus, high *n* Power presidents will be more prone to involve the country in wars. More generally, *n* Power in political leaders will be associated with combat against political, personal, and system foes.

SCORING PROCEDURES

Donley and Winter (1970) adopted certain rules for the application of the achievement and power motive scoring systems to presidential inaugural addresses. These rules were followed by the present authors in scoring *n* Affiliation. Because they may prove helpful to readers interested in scoring for the motive imagery of other political actors, we present these rules below.[5]

1. Score only imagery; ignore the motive subcategories.
2. In general, the sentence is the unit of scoring for motive imagery. This means that:
   a. A single sentence can be scored only once for any particular motive imagery (although it can be scored for two or more different motives).
   b. If the same motive appears in two (or more) separate but consecutive sentences, it can be scored only once.
   c. However, if the same motive appears more than once in consecutive sentences, but the two occurrences are separated by imagery of another motive, then both occurrences can be scored.

   Points (b) and (c) are intended to distinguish between imagery which is repeated merely to clarify the speaker's stand and imagery which is repeated because the speaker is especially concerned with a certain motive theme.

   [5]The reader may find it useful to consult the actual motive scoring systems (references given in Table 2.1) when considering these rules. In any case, the rules listed here are not detailed enough to use in scoring material for these motives. These rules were adapted from scoring criteria in Donley (1968).

3. References to "this nation" or "the American people" along with first person pronouns can be taken as the equivalent of a "character" or "the concern of a character" in the motive scoring systems.

4. Specific modifications of imagery criteria were made as follows:

   a. *Achievement Imagery:* Comparisons of nations are the most frequent examples of competition with others. The scorer should be conservative in scoring "unique accomplishment," since things that are unique for the ordinary person may be routine for the president. In general, do not score as "unique accomplishment" anything that is merely a maintainance of the status quo. Long-term involvement can be scored on the basis of maintaining or enlarging some aspect of the nation's greatness.

   b. *Affiliation Imagery:* Bonds between peoples or nations are the most frequent images. Use of terms such as "friends" or "friendship" are almost always scored, but mere reference to "happiness" or well-being are not sufficient. References to conferences among nations, as such, are not scored unless they contain strong overtones of affiliation (cooperation among nations, among allies, etc.). Help of peoples and nations is scored unless the helping image clearly does not involve affiliative feeling or is merely one unemphasized element of a long list of nonaffiliative goals.

   c. *Power Imagery:* Descriptions of past events, unless elaborated with instrumental activity, are not scored under the "inherently powerful actions" criterion; the list of such actions can be considered as including: stemming a crisis; achieving or seeking economic success, freedom, democracy. "Improving the standard of living" or "securing justice" are considered routine goals in this context and are not scored.

These motive scoring systems have shown high inter-scorer reliability in research with individual human subjects. Moreover, this reliability does not appear to diminish appreciably when two trained and experienced scorers code short passages removed from the context and other identifying cues. Donlcy and Winter (1970) report inter-rater agreement of .85 (percentage category agreement; see Atkinson, 1958, p. 688) for *n* Achievement and *n* Power. The present authors had inter-rater agreement of .93 for *n* Affiliation.

Before presenting the motive scores for the presidents we need to discuss several problems which arise as a result of using inaugural speeches as our content for analysis (see H. White, 1956). Since inaugural speeches are often written in large part by other persons (advisors, speechwriters), can they be taken as a measure of the *president's* motives? Galbraith (1969), for example, recounts the complex process of proposal, revision, deletion, and editorial shaping—each step involving several persons—that can go into the construction of an inaugural speech. Actually several considerations are relevant to this point. First, the president is likely to assign the task of speech construction to speechwriters whom he trusts, in the sense that he relies upon them to produce the specific content, phrasing, and imagery which he finds congenial. Second, experienced speechwriters surely develop the ability to phrase content in ways congruent with the president's style. Third, the president himself is likely to make (or at least decide on) final changes in phrasing and imagery which are precisely the sorts of things that determine whether motive imagery will be scored (see Table 2.2 below). All of these considerations are particularly relevant to the first inaugural speech. There is evidence that many presidents wrote these speeches themselves (see Donley and Winter, 1970, p. 229). After discussing this issue with us, Aram Bakshian, a White House speechwriter, agreed that the presidents' scores are likely to reflect their motives rather closely, especially in the case of major speeches. Even if it is granted that the measures used here reflect not only the motives of the president, but also those of his inner circle of advisors—that is, the "atmosphere" of the administration—this should not rule out their predictive value, since many presidential decisions and behaviors are also likely to be the products of this same circle.

Another problem, first raised by H. White (1956) when using speeches for making psychological inference, is that the content of a speech may be affected by pressures of public opinion or elite group opinion, burning issues of the day, external events not under presidential control, and so forth. Of course, what the president says is affected by a wide variety of factors apart from his personality; but the way in which he says it is more likely to manifest his personality. And it is these subtle shades of image or emphasis that form the coding criteria for the motive scoring systems. Table 2.2 illustrates pairs of passages from different inaugural speeches, each dealing with the same general issue. It should be clear from this table that the topic under consideration does not in and of itself determine whether any particular type of motive is scored. Nevertheless, more research is needed to determine the general influence of topic or issue on motive imagery. One might naturally expect that all political leaders will show more power imagery when they are talking about war, more achievement imagery when discussing economic growth (or perhaps problems such as resource scarcity), and so forth.

A final problem is the fact that the inaugural speech, and most other formal presidential speeches, are calculated, crafted, and controlled communications designed to produce a particular effect in a particular audience. As Downs (1963) suggests, the content may vary with the audience. Speeches are thus quite different from the spontaneous communication characteristic of, for example, a press conference. In a comparison of more and less "controlled" communication, LeVine (1966) found that the more spontaneous communication (report of a dream) gave more valid motive scores than did the more controlled communication (essays). So far as American presidents go, we do not know whether "controlled" speeches will give valid scores until we look at the results.

Table 2.2. Samples from Various Inaugural Speeches Scored and Not Scored for Motive-Related Imagery

	Passages Not Scored	Passages Scored
1.	*On Man's Condition* "We dedicated ourselves to the fulfillment of a vision—to speed the time when there would be for all the people that security and peace essential to the pursuit of happiness." F. Roosevelt (2nd); not scored.	"We are beginning to wipe out the line that divides the practical from the ideal; and in so doing we are fashioning an instrument of unimagined power for the establishment of a morally better world." F. Roosevelt (2nd); scored for *n* Achievement.
2.	*On Defense* "The strong man must at all times be alert to the attack of insidious disease." Hoover; not scored.	"[We must be prepared] in order to prevent other nations from taking advantage of us and of our inability to defend our interests—and assert our rights with a strong hand." Taft; scored for *n* Power.
3.	*On Assisting Other Nations* "We have emerged from the losses of the Great War and the reconstruction following it with increased virility and strength. From this strength we have contributed to the recovery and progress of the world." Hoover; not scored.	"If we fail, the cause of free self-government throughout the world will rock to its foundation, and therefore our responsibility is heavy, to ourselves, to the world as it is today, and to the generations yet unborn." T. Roosevelt; scored for *n* Achievement and *n* Power.
4.	*On Securing Peace* "Seeking to secure peace in the world, we have had to fight through the forests of the Argonne, to the shores of Iwo Jima, and to the cold mountains of Korea." Eisenhower; not scored.	"The physical configuration of the earth has separated us from all of the Old World, but the common brotherhood of man, the highest law of all our being, has united us by inseparable bonds with all humanity...." Coolidge; scored for *n* Affiliation.

Note: Passages one through three of this table are taken from Donley and Winter (1970, p. 232), and are reprinted from *Behavioral Science* by permission of James G. Miller, editor.

RESULTS

Table 2.3 presents the scores on the three motives for the 13 presidents from 1905-1974. Since there was a considerable range in the length of the inaugural speeches, and therefore correlations of length times score, we have used a simple correction procedure of dividing raw scores by length to yield corrected scores of motive images per 1,000 words.[6]

While n Achievement and n Affiliation are only slightly correlated (r=.07) for these presidents as are n Affiliation and n Power (r=.13), n Achievement and n Power are highly correlated (r=.70). Although such a high correlation is unusual in prior research with these motive measures (see Bowen, 1972), Winter (1973b, pp. 213-214) argues that the correlation is probably an artifact of the American political system. Presidents are probably either active (high in achievement and power) or passive (low in both). The high-achievement, low-power man is unlikely to be drawn to seek office, while the high-power, low-achievement man is probably perceived as too "ruthless" or self-seeking to be acceptable to the electorate as its Chief Executive. In any case, such a high correlation suggests the importance of using partial correlations when relating the motive scores to other variables; that is, the effects of the two other motives are controlled (partialled out) in the relationship between each motive and another variable.

As a result of their examination of the n Achievement and n Power data in Table 2.3, Donley and Winter (1970) argued that the motive scores of the presidents seemed valid in the sense that they fit with the consensus of historians and observers about the behavior of the presidents and with specific predictions derived from the study of biographies of these presidents. The reader also may wish to consider the scores reported in Table 2.3 as well as the behavioral correlates associated with the motives which are reported in Table 2.1 and decide whether the score of any particular president "fits" his own sense of that president's administration. We can cite several positive relationships which we perceived in such a comparison of these two tables. As predicted, the more significant scandals that have reached into the White House or the Cabinet in this century are associated with high n Affiliation presidents (Teapot Dome, various scandals of the Truman administration, Sherman Adams in the Eisenhower administration, and Watergate). The peculiar "Kennedy mystique" involved a combination of all three motives, while Franklin Roosevelt's more "Olympian" style was associated with high n Achievement and n Power but low n Affiliation.

So far these standardized motive scores confirm the obvious and the already-known. These confirmations certainly increase our confidence in the validity of the procedures that we have used. Nevertheless, the more interesting question is whether the scores suggest interpretations of presidential behavior that are new,

[6]Ideally, a more sophisticated correction involving calculation of regression scores on length and computation of discrepancies between predicted and actual scores is the best way to correct for length effects (see Winter, 1973b, pp. 104, 147), but the small number of cases made this procedure unwise in the present research.

Table 2.3. Motive Scores from Presidential Inaugural Speeches, 1905-1974

President	Approximate Number of Words	n Achievement		n Affiliation		n Power	
		Raw Frequency	Frequency/1,000 Words	Raw Frequency	Frequency/1,000 Words	Raw Frequency	Frequency/1,000 Words
T. Roosevelt (1905)	970	6	6.19 (H)*	2	2.06 (L)	8	8.25 (H)
Taft (1909)	5,570	5	.90 (L)	4	.72 (L)	11	1.97 (L)
Wilson (1st–1913)	1,670	5	3.00 (L)	2	1.20 (L)	9	5.39 (H)
Harding (1921)	3,540	8	2.26 (L)	10	2.82 (L)	13	3.67 (L)
Coolidge (1925)	4,200	7	1.67 (L)	6	1.43 (L)	13	3.10 (L)
Hoover (1929)	3,960	16	4.04 (L)	8	2.02 (L)	12	3.03 (L)
F. D. Roosevelt (1st–1933)	1,900	10	5.26 (H)	2	1.05 (L)	12	6.32 (H)
Truman (1949)	2,460	10	4.07 (L)	9	3.66 (H)	18	7.32 (H)
Eisenhower (1st–1953)	2,460	7	2.85 (L)	11	4.47 (H)	10	4.07 (L)
Kennedy (1961)	1,320	9	6.82 (H)	7	5.30 (L)	11	8.33 (H)
Johnson (1965)	1,460	11	7.53 (H)	3	2.05 (L)	10	6.85 (H)
Nixon (1st–1969)	2,130	18	8.45 (H)	11	5.16 (L)	11	5.16 (L)
Ford (1974)	848	2	2.36 (L)	9	10.61 (H)	4	4.72 (L)
Mean			4.26		3.27		5.24
Standard Deviation			2.39		2.69		2.06

Note: Data for n Achievement and n Power in this table are taken from Donley and Winter (1970), and are reprinted from *Behavioral Science* by permission of James G. Miller, editor.

*Letter in parentheses indicates whether frequency per 1,000 words is above or below motive mean; H indicates high or above mean while L indicates low or below mean.

or not obvious, and whether the use of motive scores can resolve points of persisting confusion or uncertainty in the study of the presidents. For example, Wilson's inaugural speech showed a relatively high *n* Power score and a relatively low *n* Achievement score. This pattern tends to support the "revisionist" historian's view of Wilson's life and administration. Such historians argue that Wilson's idealistic aspirations (achievement) were more in the nature of rationalizations or covers for his strong power strivings (cf. George and George, 1956; also, to an extent, Freud and Bullitt, 1967).

The curious motive pattern of Nixon (high achievement and affiliation but low power) deserves further comment, although at the date of this writing (October 1974) it is too early to try to integrate these scores with the biographical and psychohistorical accounts of Nixon's political and presidential career (cf. Mazlish, 1973). We can, however, discuss the ways in which Nixon's pattern of motive scores fits with some aspects of the Watergate scandal even though Nixon's full and precise role in the many aspects of Watergate may never be known. (1) With regard to Nixon's high *n* Achievement score (his is the highest among twentieth-century presidents), the research of Cortés and Gatti (1972) and Mischel and Gilligan (1964) suggests that *n* Achievement may lead to cheating and other illegal behaviors, *at least if cheating is perceived as the only way to reach the valued achievement goal.* Since public opinion polls suggested that Nixon trailed his major potential rivals during 1971-72, the "Watergate strategy" may have been viewed as the only way to win the election—although, as Nixon is alleged to have revealed on the tapes, "Why did they do it then?" just before the McGovern nomination. (2) Nixon is also quite high in *n* Affiliation, a motive associated with taking advice from admired and similar friends. Thus, he, like other high *n* Affiliation presidents, was vulnerable to the self-serving behavior of others and to scandal. (3) Nixon is relatively low in *n* Power. Before Watergate, Winter (1973a, p. 285) discussed Nixon's power motive and his power behavior in the following words: "Someone with a low need for power is confronted with power situations, events, and demands [i.e., the office of the presidency]. He responds . . . with widely fluctuating, exaggerated and ambivalent power-actions" essentially because there is a lack of congruence between motive and role demands. Applied to Watergate, such an explanation indicates that the Watergate strategy and the cover-up were more or less what one would expect of someone under pressure in a power situation *who lacked the appropriate motive for dealing with that situation.* It was a clumsy, badly managed attempt to grab power without reckoning with the possible consequences, followed by a series of similarly clumsy, badly managed cover-up actions that lacked political foresight. Alternatively, one could argue that in the case of Nixon the power motive was "split off" on to certain of his advisors who planned Watergate and secured Nixon's cooperation and trust on the basis of his high *n* Affiliation. None of these explanations of Watergate excludes any of the others; they are presented in order to demonstrate the usefulness of the motive scores taken by themselves and applied to the interpretation of events in a single president's administration.

While it is interesting to use the motive scores in this way, the more profound issue is the objective validity of the scores—that is, the extent to which they are related to objectively measurable aspects of presidential (or presidential administration) performance. While the small sample size makes drawing any firm conclusions difficult, it is true that the 13 presidents in this list are a total sample of a group—twentieth-century American presidents—which has had an enormous impact on the history of the world and the lives of millions of people. Thus, the behavioral correlates of the three motives among these presidents are interesting both insofar as they confirm the results of laboratory studies of individuals and insofar as they demonstrate the capacity of motive-related content analysis to relate to significant political behavior.

Table 2.4 gives the relationships between motives and behavior for the 13 presidents. We shall discuss each dependent variable in turn, commenting on details of its measurement. Perhaps the first question that occurs to the reader is which motives tend to be associated with good performance in office. We hypothesized earlier in this chapter that *n* Power would be positively associated with and *n* Affiliation negatively associated with performance, assuming that active and vigorous presidents are positively evaluated by history and, thus, historians. Scholars of American history have been polled twice in recent years regarding their assessment of American presidents (Schlesinger, 1962; Maranell, 1970). Rankings on overall performance solicited by Schlesinger from 75 historians are positively associated with *n* Achievement and negatively associated with *n* Affiliation, although neither partial correlation is significant. Maranell asked 571 historians for ratings along seven different dimensions which, from the pattern of intercorrelations among them, amount to two clusters. Cluster A (high prestige, strong, active, accomplished much, well-known to the historian) is positively associated with *n* Power and negatively associated with *n* Affiliation. In other words, high *n* Power and low *n* Affiliation appear to be characteristics of the "better" presidents, at least in terms of historians' rankings. This same motive pattern (high *n* Power, low *n* Affiliation) at the national level has sometimes been found to be associated with totalitarian governments (McClelland, 1961, pp. 167-170; Winter, 1973b). Moreover, McClelland (1975) has found at the individual level that managers with this pattern appear to generate the highest morale among their subordinates. Overall, it appears that the power motive is associated among these presidents as among individuals with acting powerfully and effectively, and that *n* Affiliation is associated with less effective action *in a political role.* In fact, *n* Affiliation is associated with the flexibility scale in cluster B, supporting the findings among individuals that link the affiliative motive to conformity and changing opinion to that of the majority or that of specifically liked other persons. As shown below, the "flexible," high *n* Affiliation president is also more vulnerable to scandal.

How do the motive scores relate to the more sophisticated typologies of presidential performance proposed by Hargrove (1966) or Barber (1972)? Barber proposes two basic dimensions along which presidents can be classified:

Table 2.4. Presidential Motives and Associated Behaviors

Behavior Measure	Partial Correlations[a]		
	n Achievement	n Affiliation	n Power
Historians' Ratings			
Schlesinger (1962) ratings on "Overall Contribution as President"[b]	.41	-.49	.02
Maranell (1970) dimensions[c]			
Cluster A			
1. General prestige	-.17	-.52[+]	.63*
2. Strength of action	.05	-.72*	.74**
3. Presidential activeness vs. passivity	.19	-.65*	.68*
6. Accomplishments of administration	-.13	-.63*	.66*
7. Amount of information about the president possessed by respondent	.05	-.13	.59*
Cluster B			
4. Idealism vs. practicality	-.20	-.04	.19
5. Flexibility vs. inflexibility	.03	.53[+]	-.01
Barber (1972) Analysis[d]			
Activity (vs. passivity)	.57[‡]	-.44[‡]	.44[‡]
Positive affect (vs. negative affect)	-.44[‡]	.03	.46[‡]
Assassination Attempts[e]	-.41[‡]	-.02	.81**
Executive Turnover[f]	.59*	-.11	.00
First Cabinet Appointees[g]			
Discrepancy from president in age	.42[+]	-.42[+]	.66*

Behavior Measure	Partial Correlations[a]		
	n Achievement	n Affiliation	n Power
Discrepancy from president in number of children	-.19	-.29	.46‡
Proportion who were lawyers	-.26	-.54‡	.60*
Proportion with previous experience in the department of their appointment	.35	-.15	-.20
Proportion with previous experience in Congress and/or state legislature	-.85**	.20	.69**
Prior Legal Training	.10	-.33	-.39
Scandal			
Pages on misconduct per year in office in Woodward (1974) report	-.51	.55*	.10
Forced resignation or indictment of cabinet or staff member	-.40	.68**	.15
Entry of United States into War[h]	-.14	-.27	.62*
Agreement on Arms Limitation[i]	.44+	.80**	-.63*

+ p<.13, 1-tailed; ‡ p<.10, 1-tailed; *p<.05, 1-tailed; **p<.01, 1-tailed.

[a] Correlations for each motive with each behavior are with the effects of the other two motives partialled out, using the appropriate n in each case.

[b] Nine presidents (T. Roosevelt through Eisenhower); Kendall's partial tau used. Schlesinger asked 75 historians to rate the presidents on a generalized dimension of "contribution as president" which included having a creative approach to events, being the master and not the servant of events, using the prestige of office to improve public welfare, etc.

[c] Eleven presidents (T. Roosevelt through Johnson); the numbers refer to Maranell's (1970) dimensions; the letters refer to clusters of these dimensions based on the intercorrelation matrix reported by Maranell, who also gives the full definitions of each dimension.

[d] Eleven presidents (Taft through Nixon).

[e] Twelve presidents (T. Roosevelt through Nixon).

[f] Twelve presidents (T. Roosevelt through Nixon). Executive turnover is the number of changes in Cabinet posts per department per year; vice-presidents taking office on the death of a president are counted (for changes and for years in office) only from their inauguration in their own right (see Winter, 1973b, pp. 218-219 for details).

[g] Twelve presidents (T. Roosevelt through Nixon). First Cabinet appointees include first Cabinet picked, or, in the case of vice-presidents assuming office on the death of a president, their own first appointees unless the "holdover" Cabinet members continued in office beyond the vice-president's inauguration in his own right in which case the "holdovers" are counted as first appointees. Data are from Sobel (1971).

[h] Twelve presidents (T. Roosevelt through Nixon). See Winter (1973b, pp. 216-217) for details and list of wars. Nixon is not counted as a "war entry president"; the Vietnam conflict entry is assigned to Kennedy.

[i] Twelve presidents (T. Roosevelt through Nixon); list of agreements and definitions is found in footnote 7.

Activity (vs. Passivity): How much energy does the man invest in his presidency?

Positive Affect (vs. Negative Affect): How much satisfaction does the president feel in his political life? Is it happy or sad? Enjoyable or discouraging?

Our expectation that n Power would be positively related to both of Barber's dimensions is confirmed as is the hypothesis that n Achievement is related to both activity *and* dissatisfaction. In other words, both high n Achievement and high n Power presidents are active, but only high n Power presidents *enjoy* the activity of the presidency. Passivity is related to n Affiliation.

Concerning more specific and objectively measurable outcomes, we find that n Power is associated with assassination attempts. The two Roosevelts, Truman, and Kennedy—all of whom were the targets of would-be assassins—are high in n Power. As we noted earlier, individuals high in n Power stay "on top" by exploiting associates and attacking enemies. They are likely to arouse strong emotion in other people.

Executive turnover is another easily measured outcome. Table 2.4 shows that n Achievement is associated with more rapid turnover in the president's Cabinet. This finding appears to be a direct expression of the tendency for people high in n Achievement to prefer working with and consulting experts rather than friends and to modify their performance on the basis of feedback.

Many of the hypotheses derived from prior research involve the kind of men that the president chooses as advisors. We have taken first Cabinet appointments as the population of advisors to be studied for the reason that these appointments are most likely to reflect the president's dispositions and preferences unaffected by "reality," the demands of specific issues and groups, or the performance of advisors in office over time. Restricting the population to Cabinet members insures that the group will be roughly comparable from president to president (unlike the burgeoning number of special assistants) and that standard biographical information will be available on each advisor.

We predicted that n Affiliation would be associated with picking advisors who were similar to the president. Many possible dimensions of similarity—e.g., state of the country born in, type of education, religion—involve artifacts that are hard to remove. For example, Kennedy is the only Catholic president in the sample and he appointed one other Catholic to his first Cabinet. Does this reflect a tendency to pick dissimilar (in religion) advisors, or does it reflect adherence to an implicit "quota" of Catholics in the Cabinet and a sensitivity to the church-state issue raised in the 1960 campaign? To pick someone of the same denomination, Theodore Roosevelt would have had to confine himself to the small number of Dutch Reformed Church members, while Truman could have chosen from the far more numerous Baptists. To take another dimension, state of the country born in, Coolidge was born in Vermont and so had a number of fellow Vermonters that was much smaller than the number of New Yorkers available to

Franklin Roosevelt. For these reasons, we calculated similarity on only two indices, measures that we hoped did not reflect such artifacts: age and number of children. In each case, *n* Affiliation is negatively associated with the average discrepancy between the president and his first Cabinet (although only the first correlation approaches significance). In other words, high *n* Affiliation presidents pick Cabinet members who are relatively more similar to them than do low *n* Affiliation presidents. *N* Achievement and *n* Power are positively associated with at least discrepancy in age. Thus, it appears that the high *n* Affiliation president does, in fact, seek the security of interacting with those who are like him, while the high *n* Power (and perhaps high *n* Achievement) president seeks advisors on some other basis. In fact, the high *n* Power president may actually seek diversity among his advisors in order to enhance his own power as head of the Cabinet and final arbiter.

While none of the motives is associated with the president's having had a legal background nor is there any relationship between the president being a lawyer and the proportion of lawyers chosen in his first Cabinet (r_{pb} = -10, n.s.), we do find that high *n* Power presidents pick relatively more lawyers and high *n* Affiliation presidents pick relatively few. Further, *n* Power is associated with picking advisors with previous experience in Congress or state legislatures, while *n* Achievement is (modestly) associated with picking advisors with previous experience in the relevant department of the executive branch. These correlations seem to support the following general hypotheses outlined above: (1) high *n* Achievement presidents will pick experts as advisors—men with knowledge of the actual area of their job; (2) high *n* Power presidents will pick advisors not necessarily with expert knowledge but rather with political or "power experience" (legislative experience) or "power skills" (legal background). In terms of overall presidential performance, we would suggest that *n* Achievement presidents get good advice that is, unfortunately, politically "naive" and therefore likely not to be approved or implemented. High *n* Power presidents are probably good at getting their advice enacted by Congress and carried out by the bureaucracy but the advice itself may be less than expert.

As we hypothesized, *n* Affiliation is positively associated with scandal. High *n* Affiliation presidents are vulnerable to the self-serving behavior of others. Scandal was assessed by counting the number of pages per year devoted to a president during that president's tenure in Woodward's (1974) recent report to the House Judiciary Committee on presidential charges of misconduct and by noting whether a Cabinet member or White House staff member had resigned or been indicted for political (not personal) misconduct that occurred during a president's tenure. According to Woodward (1974), the following presidents had Cabinet and staff members leave under such circumstances: Harding (Fall, Daugherty), Truman (Connelly), Eisenhower (Adams), and Nixon (numerous forced resignations and indictments with Watergate).

Perhaps two of the most important aspects of a president's behavior are committing his country to war and initiating or adhering to agreements to limit or reduce armaments. Although the causal chain between presidential motives and the outcomes of war or arms limitation agreements is complex, it is striking to observe that, as predicted, the power motive is associated with war and lack of arms limitation agreements, while n Affiliation and n Achievement are positively associated with entering into or adhering to agreements to limit or reduce arms.[7] These findings are directly parallel to the results of Terhune's (1968a, 1968b) research on motives and interpersonal bargaining referred to in Table 2.1; that is, n Achievement was associated with rational cooperation, n Affiliation with cooperation under some circumstances, and n Power with exploitation and conflict. Overall, the results presented in Table 2.4 are impressive, even if their general applicability depends upon future research.

During the final revisions of the manuscript of this chapter, President Nixon resigned and President Ford was inaugurated. We have included motive scores from Ford's inaugural speech (the speech made immediately after taking the oath of office on August 9, 1974, which is generally considered to be an "inaugural speech" despite Ford's disclaimer) in Table 2.3. Given the findings about presidential behaviors associated with each motive, we venture to make predictions about Ford's Presidency on the basis of his motive scores. (Let us note that this paragraph was written in October 1974.) Ford's motive pattern appears to be extraordinarily high n Affiliation with low n Achievement and n Power. From this pattern, we would predict that Ford will be neither particularly strong nor particularly successful in office (Maranell scales). Yet, ironically, he will likely avoid war and assassination and conclude further peace or arms-reduction agreements. He will be seen as flexible (Maranell scale) and will surround himself with advisors similar to himself by whom he will be readily influenced. These advisors will have comparatively long tenure in office. Ford's biggest problem may lie in these advisors: first, they are likely to be friends rather than experts—that is, they are likely to be without the appropriate administrative or political experience; and, second, they may precipitate another scandal via Ford's influenceability, Watergate notwithstanding. Indeed, Ford's most noteworthy act in his first two months in office—the pardon of Nixon—clearly reflects his motive pattern: a warm and friendly act, counselled by those close to the president (high n Affiliation) and taken without full awareness of

---

[7]"Arms limitation agreements" are defined as the conclusion of, or adherence to, an agreement with one or more other major powers for the mutual limitation or reduction of one or more of the major powers' weapons systems. Whether the agreement eventually breaks down or continues is not considered. The following constitute "arms limitation agreements" by such a definition: Harding—Washington Armament Conference (1921-22); Hoover—London Naval Conference (1930); Eisenhower—Implicit cessation of atmospheric nuclear testing (1958-59); Kennedy—Nuclear Test-Ban Treaty (1963); Nixon—Seabed Treaty (1971), SALT agreements (1972), renunciation of chemical and biological warfare. It should be noted that: (1) the Second London Naval Conference (1936) accomplished, in effect, nothing; (2) until Nixon's presidency, the U.S. did not ratify the 1925 Geneva Protocol; and (3) the nuclear non-proliferation treaty was not an agreement to limit or reduce arms among *major* powers.

the political and technical judicial consequences (low *n* Achievement and *n* Power).

One can imagine a wide variety of applications of motive content analysis to the speeches and writings of political actors. Any group of speeches or writings which constitute a standardized series, whether over the political life of one actor or across several political actors, could be coded to yield comparable motive scores. State of the Union messages, the Sovereign's speech from the throne in the United Kingdom (written by the party in power), and standard speeches of other heads of state are of obvious interest. Winter (1976) coded and analyzed the announcement speeches of the major presidential candidates in the 1976 primaries. News conference transcripts and other ad hoc speeches may present more of a problem because they are often affected by specific issues and are, as a consequence, not really comparable with each other. Nevertheless, pilot research could establish whether motive levels varied with topic (war, economy, domestic turmoil, etc.); if they did, motive scores could be computed and compared by controlling for topic mentioned. A final problem is translation of non-English speeches. McClelland (1961, p. 114) argues, however, that this is no problem for the motive scoring systems. Moreover, Winter (1973b, pp. 92-93) reports support for McClelland's argument, finding a very high correlation between *n* Power scores for German stories (scored in German) and English translations of the same stories, scored in English. The only caution is that the translation be fairly literal to preserve motive imagery and that any abbreviations or other references in the original language which might not be clear to an English-speaking scorer be explained.

This chapter has reviewed some of the major applications of psychological content analysis to the speeches and writings of political actors. We have reviewed four methods—intensive clinical interpretation, value-analysis, evaluation assertion analysis, and motive scoring—and have discussed many of the more important studies of this general type which have been conducted over the last forty years. This review led us to propose several different issues or standards against which past and future research should, in our minds, be compared in order to produce the most valid, psychologically interesting inferences about important political actions from scrutiny of political actors' verbal and written content.

CHAPTER 3

Nonverbal and Paralinguistic Analysis of Political Behavior: The First McGovern-Humphrey California Primary Debate*

Robert S. Frank

Editor's Introduction

Most oral communication is accompanied by some nonverbal behavior. The speaker uses a gesture, moves his body, smiles, blinks. The present chapter is concerned with this nonverbal behavior as well as with the communication itself. In effect, Frank combines content analysis and observation in collecting his data.

The type of observation which Frank uses is field observation. In such observation the researcher goes to the subject's natural habitat and observes him

*I am indebted to Robert Meadow and Laurel Tanner for extensive assistance on earlier drafts of this chapter and to the editor for continued patience and insightful suggestions throughout the preparation of this manuscript.

performing his usual activities. Moreover, the researcher tries to intrude as little as possible into the setting. With the increased television coverage of political events, however, Frank did not have to attend the first 1972 McGovern-Humphrey California primary debate to collect his data. He used a videotape of the debate which had the added advantage of permitting him to replay the debate as many times as coding demanded.

Frank builds on a burgeoning literature in psychology which has examined how nonverbal behavior and paralinguistic verbal behavior relate to stress and states associated with stress like anxiety, fear, uncertainty, and defensiveness. For example, see Dittmann (1972), Ekman and Friesen (1975), Goldman-Eisler (1968), Kasl and Mahl (1965), Mehrabian (1972), Murray (1971), Siegman and Pope (1972a), and Wiener and Mehrabian (1968). Paralinguistic verbal behavior here refers to how the communication is spoken (e.g., fast, slow, loud, soft) and to the kinds of words that are used (e.g., number of different words used, number of repetitions, number of negatives). Interest in measures of this sort developed first in psychotherapy. Therapists wanted to determine in a systematic way how stressful certain material was to the patient. By monitoring specific nonverbal and paralinguistic indicators of stress, the therapist could see how the patient dealt with the stressful material and when changes occurred in the course of the therapy. Essentially Frank has followed this same procedure. He examines certain indices of stress, relating them to the issues discussed by McGovern and Humphrey in their first debate during the California primary in 1972. Which specific issues and types of issues are most stressful for each candidate? Although Frank does not explicitly explore how the candidates deal with stress, he provides some clues on their behavior in his discussion of the issues each found most and least stressful and in his discussion of the responses in which the candidate defended his own position or attacked his opponent's position.

Chapter 14 by Hermann is much like the present chapter in its focus. Taking high- and low-stress periods in the course of a negotiation, Hermann notes indicators of stress in the negotiators and the ways they respond to the stress. Both of these chapters are ultimately concerned with the impact of stress on their subjects' own political behavior. As a result of analyses like those performed by Frank and Hermann, the researcher can begin to say what kinds of issues are likely to be stressful for specific political leaders and how they are likely to respond to stress.

Ever since his dissertation drew him into this area of research, Frank has been interested in applying nonverbal and paralinguistic analysis to the study of political leaders. The present chapter is a sequel to his Sage Professional Paper in International Studies on linguistic analysis of political elites (see Frank, 1973). Frank, a political scientist, is currently a Research Scientist at the University City Science Center in Philadelphia.

CLUES TO THE PSYCHOLOGICAL makeup of political actors are available from the analysis of a given actor's verbal and nonverbal behavior. Although such clues have been successfully used for years in the fields of psychometrics and psychotherapy, only recently has their potential contribution become recognized in political analysis. The purpose of this chapter is to illustrate how verbal and nonverbal behavior can be utilized to study the personal characteristics of political leaders.

Before proceeding much further, however, some definitions are in order. Verbal behavior can be broken down into two dimensions. The first dimension encompasses the subject's *linguistic* behavior in which the *manifest content* of the subject's communication is recorded and analyzed. The second dimension of verbal behavior, the *paralinguistic* dimension, includes the aspects of speech in which *nonsemantic verbal* data (e.g., voiceprints, speech rate, and voice pitch) and *semantic but "noncommunicatively significant"* data (e.g., type-token ratios, frequency of self references) are recorded and analyzed. Nonverbal behavior can likewise be broken down into a number of subcategories: maintenance of physical distance in interpersonal interaction, posturing behavior, gesturing and facial affect, and so forth. All three kinds of behavior—the linguistic, the paralinguistic, and the nonverbal—provide valuable clues to psychological states.

The analysis of linguistic behavior, i.e., the manifest content of dialogue, has enjoyed tremendous popularity not only in political science but also across the social sciences. The analysis of paralinguistic and nonverbal behavior, on the other hand, has not enjoyed to date the popularity afforded to the analysis of manifest content even though such analyses offer the same advantages as an examination of manifest content. Nonverbal and paralinguistic techniques, like linguistic techniques, afford the researcher the opportunity to study political actors "at a distance" in a temporal as well as in a locational sense. Given an audio and/or video record of a political actor's behavior, the researcher can gain access to his subject whether that subject be living or deceased, available or unavailable for direct face-to-face testing, and willing or unwilling to be analyzed.

These techniques offer an additional advantage—they are nonreactive. The great majority of interview and survey techniques require that the researcher actually meet and talk to the subject, i.e., initiate a face-to-face confrontation. The intrusion of the researcher into the situation which he or she wishes to investigate often changes the situation that is to be studied. Such intrusion even for the purpose of detached analysis can generate the social scientific equivalent of the Heisenberg Effect. The subject responds not only to the questioner's interrogations but also to the investigator. Often those areas of greatest interest to the researcher are the very topics or value questions that the subject would like to retain as private knowledge. Therefore, knowing that the investigator is in some way recording any responses, the subject may attempt to "mask" his or her true feelings and opinions through lying, evading the questions, or simply refusing to respond. Through the use of paralinguistic and nonverbal techniques, however, a subject can be kept unaware that crucial aspects of his behavioral routine are being studied. Consequently, while the subject may attempt (and perhaps succeed) in "masking" the more manifest aspects of his behavior (such as the semantic content of his responses), his own paralinguistic and nonverbal behavior may not be (in some cases cannot be) as closely self-monitored.

In short, the use of paralinguistic and nonverbal techniques affords access to subjects who might otherwise be inaccessible and, in many instances, results in minimal intrusion of the researcher into the observed situation. For both of these reasons, it can be argued that the use of such techniques will provide valuable data that cannot be collected through direct and fully explained assessment techniques such as focused interviews and survey research designs.[1] The maximal payoffs for the social scientist, of course, lie in combining direct and indirect techniques, supplementing the findings from one strategy with the findings from the other. One of the objectives of this chapter is to encourage social scientists to make broader use of such indirect assessment techniques as paralinguistic and nonverbal analysis.

Research Method

PROCEDURE

This chapter applies some of the extant and readily available paralinguistic and nonverbal techniques to the psychopolitical examination of two political actors, George McGovern and Hubert Humphrey, as they appeared during their first televised debate in the 1972 California Presidential primary. To facilitate this research we videotaped the first California primary debate using ½-inch Sony machines. All responses for both candidates were coded for three types of nonverbal behavior (nods, blinks, and gross bodily movements) and two types of paralinguistic behavior (speech disturbances and "non-immediacy" frequencies). We also categorized the responses according to the nature of the issue being discussed. Our analysis involved comparing the manifest content of the responses with concurrent paralinguistic and nonverbal behaviors of the two candidates. Given that the five types of nonverbal and paralinguistic measures in this study are indicative of certain types of stress reactions, we ascertained what types of issues elicited what types of stress responses. Through this exercise we attempt to demonstrate how the utilization of such indicators can shed new insights into subjects' personality dynamics and particularly into their orientation toward specific types of political stimuli. The issues which McGovern and Humphrey were questioned about and addressed in the first of their California primary debates are listed in Table 3.1.

[1]There are a series of ethical questions posed by this research strategy. However, adequate answers to such ethical questions would require another complete paper. The reader interested in this issue should see, for example, Rogers and Skinner (1956) and Selltiz, Jahoda, Deutsch, and Cook (1959).

Table 3.1.   Description of Manifest Content of Questions and Answers during
First McGovern-Humphrey 1972 California Primary Debate

Humphrey		McGovern	
Question Number	*Issue*	*Question Number*	*Issue*
1.	How to beat Nixon	2.	How to beat Nixon
3.	Is California crucial?	4.	McGovern Vietnam record
5.	McGovern record on Vietnam	7.	Humphrey Vietnam record
		9.	Humphrey support of Vietnam policies*
6.	McGovern record on Vietnam	10.	Bombing in Vietnam
8.	McGovern voting record	12.	McGovern record on Vietnam
11.	McGovern record on aid to Israel	15.	McGovern defense budget
13.	McGovern defense budget*	16.	Submarine force proposals*
14.	Humphrey defense budget	20.	Defense budget
17.	Attacks McGovern budget cuts	22.	McGovern welfare proposals
18.	Nature of Soviet military threat	23.	Cost of welfare proposal
19.	McGovern defense budget makes the U.S. a second-class power	29.	Cost of welfare proposal
		30.	Wallace phenomenon
		35.	Bussing*
		36.	Bussing
21.	Basis of Humphrey estimate of McGovern welfare plan costs	37.	General budget proposals, soundness of McGovern programs
		39.	Proxmire endorsement*
24.	McGovern welfare plan	43.	Can you win the Humphrey supporters?
25.	McGovern welfare plan	44.	Concluding statement
26.	McGovern welfare plan		
27.	Humphrey welfare plan		
28.	McGovern welfare plan		
31.	McGovern is for "handouts"		
32.	Nature of Wallace phenomenon		
33.	Bussing		
34.	Bussing*		
38.	Proxmire opposes McGovern tax reforms*		
40.	Proxmire opposes McGovern tax reforms*		
42.	Can you win the McGovern supporters?		
45.	Concluding statement		

*Answer has less than fifty words.

PARALINGUISTIC AND NONVERBAL INDICATORS AND
    RATIONALE: A TENTATIVE THEORETICAL MODEL

All of the paralinguistic and nonverbal indicators used in this study in one way or another represent a certain degree of negative arousal or, in less formal language, "stress." At the outset it is important to note that the concept of stress as a generic term might well encompass various types of negative arousal. As Lazarus (1966, pp. 4, 11) notes: "Problems arise when we try to set the lower limits of stress. . . ." He continues by observing: "The compound dilemma in the popularization of the term 'stress' is that multiple meanings of the term exist, and a variety of other terms are used to refer to similar phenomena." In this chapter we shall conceptualize stress as a deviation away from an active-positive-strong response to a given stimulus. Figure 3.1 positions the five measures used in this study—blinks, nods, non-immediacy responses, speech disturbances, and gross bodily movements—in a three-dimensional matrix to show the types of stress responses or deviations from an active-positive-strong response which they indicate.

The reader will recognize the three dimensions in the matrix in Figure 3.1 as those that Osgood, Suci, and Tannenbaum (1957) found in their measurement of meaning. Although these meaning dimensions tap the perception of meaning in the eyes of those who fill out a semantic differential scale, we argue that there

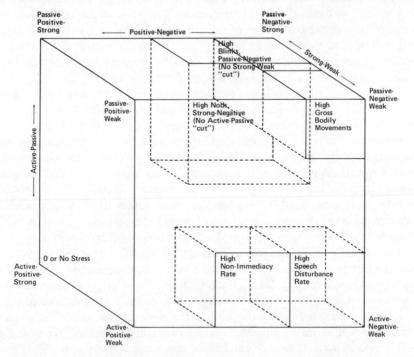

Figure 3.1. Three dimensional representation of indicator characteristics.

is a correspondence between the perception of meaning and the actual attributes of the people and objects being perceived. Carroll (1959, p. 73) makes this same point in his review of *The Measurement of Meaning:*

> If evaluation, activity, and potency are such persuasive components of adjectival characterizations they must correspond to fundamental psychological attributes of persons and to the organization of perceptual and conceptual processes. . . . Let us propose that the three principal SD [semantic differential] dimensions represent fundamental dimensions in the adjustment of the individual to the objects in his environment.

One decade later, in a review of research using the meaning dimensions to assess personality, Wiggins and Fishbein (1969) come to a similar conclusion.

The meaning dimensions represent the parameters of possible responses to stress. A lack of stress, or the absence of a stress response, is located at the origin of the matrix in Figure 3.1 (corner "0") and is characterized as an active-positive-strong response. Stress, in our formulation, is conceptualized as a movement away from "0"; the stress response can consist of one or more shifts, from active to passive, positive to negative, and/or strong to weak. If one wanted to consider stress as a unidimensional phenomenon, a diagonal from the origin to the passive-negative-weak corner of the matrix in Figure 3.1 would be most appropriate, with this latter area representing a response to the highest degree of stress. Although the positioning of our indicators in Figure 3.1 is only relational and ordinal (and should not be taken as rigid multidimensional scaling), if more precise locations for these indicators could be achieved we could use vector analysis to determine a quantifiable aggregate "stress-score."

The paralinguistic indicators, non-immediacy references and speech disturbances, are placed in the active-weak region of Figure 3.1. Both non-immediacy references and speech disturbances occur during active attempts to communicate or respond to the verbal questioning of interviewers, but both are relatively weak types of response. A non-immediacy reference is viewed as being more positive than a speech disturbance in that non-immediacy represents a psycholinguistic coping strategy, i.e., a strategy of "pushing away" linguistically the stressful object or situation. Speech disturbances, on the other hand, do not represent any conscious psycholinguistic strategy. Speech disturbances represent "verbal stumbles" with no conscious (or unconscious) coping strategy involved.

Mahl (1958) has provided incontrovertible evidence that various types of disturbances in speech during the act of verbal communication are valid indicators of personal anxiety. Mahl's findings dovetail very nicely with conventional wisdom on this subject. Under conditions of great tension, embarrassment, and so forth, it is a common phenomenon that the given speaker will be "at a loss for words" or will verbally "stumble" during oral communication. We coded the oral record of both Humphrey's and McGovern's responses using the Mahl verbal slip dictionary. The number of repetitions ("I am going to, going to try to continue. . . ."), stutters or incoherent intruding sounds ("It is our feeling the result will be b-b-bad."), word omissions ("The bombing will halt [omission] August."), sentence changes ("We're going to drive, fly to Chicago."), and sentence incompletions ("I'm worried about . . .") were all coded.

The second paralinguistic measure, the frequency of non-immediacy references, is fully described by Wiener and Mehrabian (1968) and has been used successfully on the speeches of political elites by Frank (1973). The notion of non-immediacy can be summarized as follows. Under conditions of perceived negative affect toward a given object or situation, the speaker in referring to that object or situation will tend to linguistically "distantiate" himself or herself from that which is negatively evaluated. The speaker will place himself in a "non-immediate" linguistic relationship with the given object or situation. For example, as I sit here at the typewriter, there is a cup of coffee about 18 inches away on my desk. Without in any way changing the objective relationship between myself and the cup of coffee, I can refer to the cup of coffee as either "this cup of coffee" or "that cup of coffee." The latter pronoun, "that," is an example of non-immediacy or psycholinguistic distantiation. Wiener and Mehrabian (1968) give a series of eight content categories which they argue are examples of non-immediacy. We coded for all categories cited by Wiener and Mehrabian.

The three nonverbal indicators—blinks, gross bodily movements, and nods—are also located in the matrix in Figure 3.1. Blinks are positioned all along the passive-negative areas of the cube. We have not placed a full "partition" between blinks and gross bodily movements as we did between non-immediacy references and speech disturbances because there is no "strong-weak cut" for the blink indicator. Past research has demonstrated a relationship between blink behavior and negative affect (see, e.g., Kanfer, 1960; Ponder and Kennedy, 1927; Russell and Snyder, 1963). We accept Darwin's (1965) initial formulation that blinking is passive in nature.[2]

Gross bodily movements, on the other hand, are limited to the passive-negative-weak corner of the cube. By gross bodily movement is meant a major shifting of the torso of the body (e.g., shifting or "squirming" in one's chair). We conceive the "squirming" behavior of gross bodily movements as behaviorally more "weak" than blinking behavior for the latter is not necessarily associated with any bodily "giving" in the face of stressing stimuli. Dittmann (1962) and Sainsbury (1954, 1955) have reported that gross bodily movements increase as negative affect increases. Like blinks, gross bodily movements represent passive responses to stressful situations; there is little attempt at coping with the stress.

Vertical head nodding is seen as a strong but negative response to stress. Nods are viewed as negative because nodding represents a need to communicate. That is, the speaker feels that there is something that needs to be communicated

---

[2]Darwin (1965, p. 38) notes that blinking in adults is most often a habitual and not a reflex action "as the stimulus is conveyed through the mind and not by the excitement of the peripheral nerve." We hold this general principle—that physiological responses are related to psychological and not to physiological stimuli—to be true throughout the analysis of our data.

which otherwise would not be or which would not be communicated as effectively were the communication not emphasized. Here we are equating a psychological need with the existence of some degree of stress. Nodding behavior is obviously a directed and strong response (for example, as contrasted with gross bodily movement behavior). While the demarked region in the cube for nods does not extend to the "floor" of the cube, this truncation is visually presented only so as not to confuse the reader. In fact, we are postulating that nods run the gamut of the active-passive dimension as blinks run the gamut of the strong-weak dimension. Nods can represent an active attempt to cope with the stress as well as a passive way of acknowledging the presence of the stress stimuli.

Results

INTERCORRELATIONS AMONG MEASURES

The intercorrelations among four of the paralinguistic and nonverbal indicators used to code the Humphrey and McGovern responses during the first 1972 California primary debate are found in Table 3.2. These correlations are based on the 15 McGovern answers and the 21 Humphrey answers which exceeded 50 words. Responses of less than 50 words occurred when the speaker was successfully interrupted by the other candidate, a newsman questioner, a station break, or a commercial. Such answers did not appear to be "normal" responses and, thus, were not included in the analysis. To control for differences in the length of answers for both candidates, the speech disturbance and non-immediacy scores for each answer were divided by the number of words in the answer while the number of blinks and nods in a response were divided by the number of seconds the response took. These rates were used in determining the correlations in Table 3.2.

Table 3.2 shows statistically significant correlations between the two paralinguistic measures, speech disturbance rate and non-immediacy rate, for both Humphrey and McGovern. While the correlation between the two nonverbal measures, blink rate and nod rate, was not statistically significant for Humphrey, it was for McGovern. For both candidates the negative relationships between the paralinguistic and nonverbal indicators suggest a trade-off between these two types of behavior—when one is present, the other tends to be absent (or present to a lesser degree) and vice versa.

The gross bodily movement indicator is not included in Table 3.2 because there were only 29 gross bodily movements by the candidates during this debate—4 for Humphrey and 25 for McGovern. Indicating the presence or absence of gross bodily movements along the rank-ordered answers for each of the other four indicators, we conducted runs tests (Siegel, 1956, pp. 52-58) to examine the association between gross bodily movement and these indicators. We found that gross bodily movements were directly associated with blink rates

Table 3.2.   Intercorrelations among Indicators (Spearman *rho*)

Indicator	Humphrey				McGovern			
	1	*2*	*3*	*4*	*1*	*2*	*3*	*4*
(1) Speech Disturbance Rate (.95)	—				—			
(2) Non-Immediacy Rate (.80)	.81**	—			.60**	—		
(3) Blink Rate (.95)	-.22	-.09	—		.04	-.46	—	
(4) Nod Rate (.85)	-.39	-.39	.43	—	-.09	-.51	.54*	—

$*p<.05$ $**p<.01$
Note: Numbers in parentheses following indicator are inter-coder reliabilities using the Holsti (1969, p.140) simple agreement formula.

for both McGovern and for Humphrey, with the strength of association reaching statistical significance for the Humphrey data ($p < .05$, two-tailed test). However, gross bodily movement was not associated with speech disturbances, non-immediacy references, or nod rate for either Humphrey or McGovern.

The interrelationships among these five indicators lend some support to their placement in the cube in Figure 3.1. Speech disturbances and non-immediacy references are located together at an end of the cube opposite the three nonverbal indicators. While blinks overlap in location with both nods and gross bodily movements, nods and gross bodily movements remain in separate locations.

RELATIONSHIPS WITH POLITICAL CONTENT

There are several ways of relating the paralinguistic and nonverbal indicators to the political issues in Table 3.1. These various methods differ according to how

Table 3.3.   McGovern and Humphrey Blink Rates by
Answer for Attack and Defend Responses

Humphrey		McGovern	
Answer Number	*Blink Rate*	*Answer Number*	*Blink Rate*
Attack Responses		*Attack Responses*	
5	.10	2	1.03
6	.15	7	1.05
8	.15	23	1.14
11	.07	29	.87
13	.22	30	1.14
17	.15	44	.85
19	.07		
24	.20	Mean =	1.03
25	.08		
26	.18		
28	.15		
31	.44		
Mean =	.16		
Defend Responses		*Defend Responses*	
1	.48	4	.72
3	.67	10	.78
14	.40	12	.43
18	.14	15	.48
27	.31	20	.64
32	.35	22	.66
33	.33	36	.78
42	.11	37	1.24
45	.37	43	1.22
Mean =	.35	Mean =	.76

the political content of the McGovern and Humphrey responses is classified. To start with, the Humphrey and McGovern answers were dichotomized into those responses during which the candidates *defended* their own political positions and record and those responses in which the candidates *attacked* each other's position and record. Of the five paralinguistic and nonverbal indicators in this study only blink rate differed significantly (or almost significantly) for the two candidates during attack and defend responses ($t=4.25, df=19, p < .001$ for Humphrey; $t=2.08, df=13, p=.06$ for McGovern). The data for blink rate are presented in Table 3.3.

Interestingly, as Table 3.3 shows, the direction of the differences for blink rate between attack and defend responses differs for Humphrey and McGovern. We see McGovern manifesting more anxiety when he attacked the Humphrey position and the Humphrey record. We see Humphrey manifesting more anxiety when he had to defend his own record. From the data in Table 3.3, Humphrey seemed most confident (least stressed) when he was on the attack, while McGovern seemed least confident (most stressed) when on the attack. Of course, we do not know the relative perceptions that McGovern and Humphrey had of the strengths and weaknesses of their own as opposed to their opponent's record and position. It could be argued that Humphrey felt his own record/position to be suspect, thus the higher blink rates for defense statements than for attack statements. Likewise it could be argued that McGovern was more confident of his own record/position than he was convinced of the weakness of Humphrey's record/position. Here supplemental interview data from the candidates concerning their recollections of the relative strengths and weaknesses of their positions/records vis-à-vis their opponent would be extremely valuable.

Another way of relating our five indicators to political issues is to categorize the issues according to the problems they address. Some nine problem areas were found in the questions and answers of this first California primary debate. Table 3.4 shows the means and z-scores for the paralinguistic and nonverbal indicators by problem. The z-scores indicate the deviation of the indicator for that problem from the overall mean for the indicator—a positive z-score means that the indicator was more prevalent than normal when that topic was discussed; a negative z-score means the indicator was less prevalent than usual. To achieve a rough approximation of the "most stressed problem areas" by candidate for this first debate, we decided to average the z-scores for the five indicators for each problem area. The reader should remember that such a procedure is somewhat suspect in that there is no firm evidence that such a unidimensional conceptualization of psychopolitical stress can be generated. However, we still believe that such an exercise is of some preliminary utility. These results are also presented in Table 3.4.

Working from the data in Table 3.4, a series of political conclusions are possible. At the time of the first debate, tax reform was the most stressful subject for McGovern and a very low stress subject for Humphrey. Humphrey continually challenged McGovern's various tax reform proposals throughout the first debate as being too radical, unworkable, and ill-conceived. Interestingly

Table 3.4. Means and z-Scores for Five Indicators for Humphrey and McGovern Responses by Political Problem Area

	Humphrey		McGovern	
	Mean	z-Score	Mean	z-Score
Vietnam				
Sp. dist.	.004	− .33	.018	±.00
NI	.010	− .59	.016	− .20
Nod rate	.104	− .21	.104	− .23
GBM's	.000	− .25	.002	− .39
Blink rate	.130	− .60	.928	+ .02
Mean		− .40		− .16
Domestic Politics				
Sp. dist.	.001	− .67	.004	− .78
NI	.014	− .41	.017	− .13
Nod rate	.282	+ 1.96	.193	+ .71
GBM's	.004	+ .25	.018	− .25
Blink rate	.428	+ 1.26	.920	− .01
Mean		+ .48		− .09
Military Spending				
Sp. dist.	.009	+ .22	.017	− .06
NI	.018	− .28	.017	− .13
Nod rate	.107	− .17	.084	− .45
GBM's	.000	− .25	.028	− .16
Blink rate	.211	− .09	.790	− .40
Mean		− .12		− .24

	Humphrey		McGovern	
	Mean	z-Score	Mean	z-Score
Mideast				
Sp. dist.	.000	− .78	No Responses	
NI	.018	− .28		
Nod rate	.133	+ .15		
GBM's	.000	− .25		
Blink rate	.067	− .99		
Mean		− .43		
Welfare				
Sp. dist.	.009	+ .22	.010	− .44
NI	.024	+ .04	.023	+ .27
Nod rate	.086	− .43	.137	+ .12
GBM's	.006	+ .50	.015	− .28
Blink rate	.193	− .21	.830	− .28
Mean		+ .02		− .12
Bussing				
Sp. dist.	.000	− .78	.026	+ .44
NI	.020	− .14	.039	+ 1.33
Nod rate	.229	+ 1.32	.108	− .17
GBM's	.000	− .25	.025	− .19
Blink rate	.212	− .09	.976	+ .16
Mean		+ .01		+ .31

Table 3.4. (Continued)

	Humphrey		McGovern	
	Mean	z-Score	Mean	z-Score
Soviet Union				
Sp. dist.	.033	+3.00	No Responses	
NI	.026	+ .14		
Nod rate	.125	+ .05		
GBM's	.000	− .25		
Blink rate	.146	− .50		
Mean		+ .49		
Current Election				
Sp. dist.	.008	+ .11	.013	− .27
NI	.019	− .18	.021	+ .13
Nod rate	.133	+ .15	.158	+ .34
GBM's	.004	+ .25	.061	+ .13
Blink rate	.378	+ .95	1.184	+ .78
Mean		+ .25		+ .22
Tax Reform				
Sp. dist.	.011	+ .44	.042	+1.33
NI	.023	± .00	.003	−1.07
Nod rate	.056	−2.16	.145	+ .20
GBM's	.000	− .25	.266	+1.96
Blink rate	.212	− .09	1.121	+ .60
Mean		− .41		+ .60

	Humphrey		McGovern	
	Mean	S.D.	Mean	S.D.
Totals				
Across Problems				
Sp. dist.	.007	.009	.018	.018
NI	.023	.022	.019	.015
Nod rate	.121	.082	.126	.094
GBM's	.002	.008	.046	.112
Blink rate	.226	.160	.923	.331

Note: The following abbreviations are used in this table—Sp. dist. = speech disturbance rate; NI = non-immediacy rate; GBM's = gross bodily movements; S.D. = standard deviation.

enough, when the interviewers attempted to move the line of inquiry away from the tax reform issue toward a discussion of the "Wallace phenomenon," Humphrey refused to move away from this former issue and eventually couched his answer to the Wallace question in terms highly critical of the McGovern tax reform ideas. A brief excerpt from the transcript of the first debate indicates the "enjoyment" or the lack of stress which is associated with Humphrey's continued desire to press the tax reform issue, especially as associated with welfare issues.

> *Question:* "I would like to explore further the Wallace phenomenon with you, Senator."
>
> *Humphrey:* "This is an important part of the entire debate in this country today. Do the American people want to have the welfare program, that does not put an emphasis on jobs, but puts an emphasis on a handout that costs seventy-two billion dollars. Or do they want one that costs two hundred and ten billion dollars? That's what Senator McGovern is proposing. And I submit that he has no evidence that he can finance either one. And I submit that the middle income tax payer will pay the lion share of the bill. The Senate Finance Committee studies say that even under the best of circumstances, if you took all of the corporate profits, if you closed all of the tax loopholes which Senator McGovern talks about, and by the way, I have this specific tax loophole closing program, that you'd still be fifty-one billion dollars short. Now, how are you going to do that?"

Across the five measures we also find low levels of stress for Humphrey when he deals with the Mideast issue. Given his traditional Jewish support and the fact that McGovern was calling for a general retrenchment of foreign commitments, this finding is understandable. The low level of stress associated with the Humphrey Vietnam answers is not so understandable, although, perhaps, Humphrey felt his explanation of the relative Humphrey and McGovern Vietnam positions was valid and would be accepted by the public. Humphrey's continued attacks on the McGovern voting record (as opposed to McGovern's rhetorical position), combined with the continued Humphrey slogan that neither he nor McGovern were "right from the start," seemed to keep Humphrey fairly self-confident on this issue.

Humphrey's low level of stress on the military spending issue is also unexpected. In part, this low level can be explained by Humphrey's feeling that his Jewish constituency would not want military spending to be cut if this meant a probable reduction in aid to Israel. On the other hand, if military spending answers had been combined with "the nature of the Soviet threat" responses (Soviet Union in Table 3.4), the combined score (representing a more general category of military spending) would have displayed a higher level of stress (z-score = .17). Indeed, we almost opted for combining these two issues. From reading the transcript of the debate, the nature of the Soviet threat did enter the interview in the context of military spending.

McGovern's low levels of stress during his discussions of military spending, Vietnam, and domestic politics are fairly understandable in the political context of the time and in the questioning context of this first debate. McGovern's low level of stress on the welfare issue, however, is somewhat unexpected. Perhaps McGovern's low z-score on this topic can be understood by noting that McGovern perceived this issue as contributing to his political platform if only through default. When pressed by Humphrey on the issue of welfare reform, McGovern's ultimate argument was "nothing can be worse than the system we have now."

What happens if we examine more carefully the most and least stressful problem areas for both candidates? Table 3.5 presents the mean z-scores for each indicator for those issues which appeared to be most and least stressful for McGovern and Humphrey. Most and least stressful topics were those with the most extreme aggregate z-scores from Table 3.4. Two indicators stand out as important in differentiating most and least stressful topics for Humphrey—nods and blinks. These two indicators were quite evident during discussion of stressful issues but not very evident during discussion of comfortable topics. In Figure 3.1 we note that the one characteristic which nods and blinks have in common is that both are negative. By combining the characteristics of nods and blinks in Figure 3.1, we find Humphrey focusing on passive-negative-strong responses in a stressful situation. One might conceive of using these two indicators on future occasions to ascertain when Humphrey is experiencing stress.

McGovern, in contrast to Humphrey, shows a fairly general paralinguistic and nonverbal reaction to stress. All indicators have positive z-scores for the high stress topics and negative z-scores for the low stress topics. An examination of the differences between the z-scores across the five indicators for the most and least stressful issues suggests that gross bodily movements and blinks differentiate the best between these two types of problems. A check with Figure 3.1 shows that these two nonverbal indicators denote a passive-negative response to stress. It is interesting that for both McGovern and Humphrey nonverbal behaviors which are fairly easy to observe and count are also the most relevant to understanding the stress responses of these two candidates in their first California primary debate. Such nonverbal behaviors may be difficult even for highly trained political actors to control.

Conclusion

The utilization of nonverbal, paralinguistic, and psycholinguistic indicators can contribute to the researcher's understanding of political actors. In some cases the findings obtained by using such measures corroborate what is obvious from a simple investigation of the manifest semantic content and the manifest behavior of the subjects involved. Nevertheless, in other instances the use of such techniques can highlight some readily available semantic and behavioral routines

Table 3.5. Mean z-Scores by Indicator and Candidate for Most and Least Stressful Problem Areas

Humphrey		McGovern	
Indicator	Mean z-Score	Indicator	Mean z-Score
Most Stressful Problems (Soviet Union, Domestic Politics, Current Election)		*Most Stressful Problems (Tax Reform, Bussing, Current Election)*	
Speech disturbance rate	.81	Speech disturbance rate	.50
Non-immediacy rate	−.15	Non-immediacy rate	.13
Nod rate	.72	Nod rate	.12
Gross bodily movements	.08	Gross bodily movements	.63
Blink rate	.57	Blink rate	.51
Least Stressful Problems (Vietnam, Tax Reform, Mideast)		*Least Stressful Problems (Vietnam, Military Spending)*	
Speech disturbance rate	.22	Speech disturbance rate	−.03
Non-immediacy rate	−.20	Non-immediacy rate	−.20
Nod rate	−.74	Nod rate	−.34
Gross bodily movements	−.25	Gross bodily movements	−.28
Blink rate	−.56	Blink rate	−.19

that the scholar might inadvertently overlook in the course of his or her investigation. Also, these techniques can help to unearth new and fresh dimensions of actor-behavior and orientation which would be otherwise unavailable were the researcher to concentrate solely upon an anlysis of the image that the subject is consciously trying to portray in his particular sociopolitical role. Examples of all these uses for five paralinguistic and nonverbal techniques have been provided in this study of the first Humphrey-McGovern 1972 California primary debate.

CHAPTER 4

Operational Codes and the Prediction of Leadership Behavior: Senator Frank Church at Midcareer*

Loch K. Johnson

Editor's Introduction

Whereas the previous two chapters have illustrated quantitative content analysis, the present chapter by Johnson is an example of *qualitative content analysis*. In contrast to quantitative content analysis, qualitative content analysis involves no exact counting process. The procedure entails making a thorough examination of a body of material and gaining some sense of the material based on the research questions under examination. Unlike the quantitative analyst, the qualitative

*An earlier version of this chapter was presented at the 1973 Annual Meeting of the American Political Science Association, New Orleans, September 4-8. The author would like to express his appreciation to the American Political Science Association Congressional Fellowship Program for supporting a year of participant observation in the office of Senator Church; to Senator Church and his staff for providing a stimulating environment for learning; to the Ohio University Research Committee for financing a research trip to Idaho; to Idaho political editor, Sam Day, for his insights and hospitality; to Leena Sepp Johnson for editorial assistance; to the editor of this volume for her helpful advice; and to Ole R. Holsti for encouraging this study and providing valuable suggestions along the way. Of course, any errors in this chapter are strictly the responsibility of the author.

content analyst is not adverse to using all sorts of supplementary information if it can help provide a basis for his conjectures. This sensitivity to the various contexts—semantic, political, historical, situational—in which communications are embedded is critical to the functioning of the qualitative analyst. As proponents of qualitative content analysis argue, the frequency with which something is said does not always indicate its importance to the speaker, particularly the political leader who must be acutely aware of what his audience wants to hear. One reference in such a context may be as important as many; moreover, what is not said may also prove relevant. To date, most qualitative content analysts are less systematic in collecting their data than are quantitative content analysts. The qualitative analyst rarely indicates which of his results are based on frequently appearing pieces of information and which involve some inference. Nor does he check to see whether a second person reading the same material would describe the political leader in a similar manner. Such procedures, if followed, would help in comparing outcomes of quantitative and qualitative content analysis.

In this chapter, Johnson is interested in discerning information about political leaders' beliefs. The operational code technique is suggested as one way to use content analysis in ascertaining what a political leader's beliefs are. The operational code as used by Johnson is based on George's (1969) reformulation of this construct which was developed by Leites (1951, 1953) for his now classic study of Bolshevism. George (1969, p. 197) views the operational code as "a political leader's beliefs about the nature of politics and political conflict, his views regarding the extent to which historical developments can be shaped, and his notions of correct strategy and tactics." A political leader's operational code is seen as setting the boundaries within which the leader will act. The operational code is composed of two kinds of beliefs—philosophical and instrumental beliefs about political reality. Philosophical beliefs refer to a political leader's "fundamental assumptions" about the nature of politics; instrumental beliefs represent the political leader's beliefs about the styles and strategies appropriate to acting in a political world defined by the philosophical beliefs. In applying the operational code technique, the researcher examines all the material available on a specific leader, seeking the answers to a series of ten questions—five are concerned with philosophical beliefs and five with instrumental beliefs.

Using the operational code framework outlined by George (1969), a rather large number of studies have been done on a variety of political leaders. We have classified them by type:

U.S. Senator
Frank Church (present Chapter)
J. William Fulbright (Tweraser, 1973)
Arthur Vandenberg (Anderson, 1973)

U.S. Secretary of State
Dean Acheson (McLellan, 1971)
John Foster Dulles (Holsti, 1970a)

Henry Kissinger (Walker, 1975)
Dean Rusk (Gutierrez, 1973)

Head of State
Willy Brandt (Ashby, 1969)
Lyndon Johnson (Malone, 1971)
William Lyon Mackenzie King (Gibbins, n.d.)
Ramsay MacDonald (Kavanagh, 1970)
Mao Tse-Tung (White, 1969)
Lester Pearson (Lawrence, 1975)
Pierre Trudeau (Thordarson, 1972)
Getulio Vargas (Dye, n.d.)

The present chapter is unique among this operational code research in several ways. First, Johnson suggests the dimensions which he perceives to underlie the operational code questions posed by George (1969). Such dimensions enable Johnson to compare the operational codes of several leaders. Second, he shows how the operational code can change over time and points to some of the events that promote change. Johnson is currently in the process of carrying research with the operational code one step further by examining how the operational code influences what a political leader does—for example, how he votes, the political decisions he makes, the job assignments he accepts.

In addition to illustrating qualitative content analysis, this chapter indicates how observation and interview can be used in the study of political leaders. Johnson employs two types of observation—participant observation and informant observation. As an intern on Senator Church's staff, Johnson gained firsthand knowledge about Church's operational code. In this position he was both a participant and an observer. Johnson has been lucky in the type of informant observations available to him. Among others, Church's mother and son have served as informants, providing information on the sources of the Senator's operational code. With regard to the interview, Johnson used this technique to query his informants. Moreover, Church's responses to the operational code questions in an interview format were an important input into the qualitative content analysis.

Johnson is an assistant professor of political science at Ohio University. His interest in doing the operational code of Senator Church was sparked by his work on Church's staff. Johnson continues to be a participant observer of Church's behavior, working in his 1974 re-election campaign and, most recently, on the staff of the Senate Select Committee on Intelligence Activities which Church chairs.

THIS CHAPTER EXPLORES some possibilities for explaining and predicting the behavior of political leaders. Its organization is in four parts. First, a brief time-space framework is presented for placing the "operational code" approach (see George, 1969) used in this study into perspective. Second, the operational code (or *Weltanschauung*) of Senator Frank Church (Democrat, Idaho), as recorded in a 1972 interview, is examined, concentrating on its international aspects. Third, this code is treated as a dependent variable to explore its continuities with the Senator's beliefs on foreign affairs in 1956 at the beginning of his political career. Finally, the 1972 code is viewed as an independent variable influencing Church's subsequent behavior as a political actor.

Senator Church, the "laboratory" for these investigations, was first elected to the U.S. Senate in 1956 at age 32—the youngest senator at the time and the fourth youngest in history. Since then he has climbed the seniority ladder to the penultimate rung on both the Interior Committee and the Foreign Relations Committee. He is also chairman of the Special Committee on Aging, co-chairman of the Special Committee on the Termination of the National Emergency, and chairman of the Select Committee on Intelligence Activities.

In July, 1976, Church celebrated his 52nd birthday. He is 12 years younger than the senior Democrat on Interior (Henry Jackson, the chairman, is 64), and—more significantly—more than 20 years younger than each of his two seniors on the Senate Foreign Relations Committee (John Sparkman, the chairman, is 77 and Mike Mansfield is 73). Should the Democrats retain a majority, his relative youthfulness makes his chances to accede to the chairmanship of the Senate Foreign Relations Committee (SFRC) during the next decade seem very good, at least statistically; all but two of the fourteen previous chairmen of that Committee in this century have retired before their 80th birthday. Moreover, his electoral position in Idaho appears reasonably secure; in 1974 he won with over 56 percent of the popular vote.

Church, then, is a political figure on the threshold of power in the Senate. Whether the process takes a few years or several, he seems destined to be the senior-ranking Democrat on the Senate committee for foreign affairs. Accession to the SFRC chairmanship would represent for Church the realization of an early boyhood aspiration. As a youth, he greatly admired another Idahoan from his home town: William E. Borah, Republican chairman of the Senate Foreign Relations Committee from 1924-1934. His mother recalls him hoping as a pre-teen to grow up to be like Borah; and he, also, traces his early interest in politics to the "Lion of Idaho."

For several reasons, it is important to study the beliefs and actions of individuals like Church who are moving toward leadership positions. Prolonged research access is somewhat less of a dilemma at this earlier stage; and, more importantly, such studies can provide data to help explain and predict orientations that the leader is likely to assume upon his "arrival." Furthermore, oral history, participant observation, and related methods applied during this developmental period can generate rich information about matters that may be difficult to investigate in later years.

In the case of Church, for instance, many of the still vivid impressions of his octogenarian mother regarding his childhood have been captured now, but would have been lost to researchers in later decades. It is precisely such impressions that may help to provide a key to the often puzzling genesis of a leader's operational code. While an examination of leadership behavior from lengthy historical vantage point has certain advantages (among them a greater wealth of established fact), the recording of a leader's moods and beliefs as he faces the strains and uncertainties of his early political career can produce unique developmental data on the maturation of leadership styles and perspectives. Moreover, as Barber (1972, p. 10) notes: "It is often much easier to see the basic patterns in early life histories. Later on a host of distractions—especially the image-making all politicians learn to practice—clouds the picture." For these reasons, a relatively young American political figure has been chosen for scrutiny.

Data on the operational code of an individual or group may be obtained through various methods (see George, 1969, pp. 221-222): (1) qualitative or quantitative content analysis of material written by the subject (or subjects); (2) interviews with the subject and those who know him, using the operational code construct as a basic guide for developing questions; (3) participant observation, if access is possible; and (4) case studies of the actor's responses to particular situations. This chapter is based on a qualitative content analysis of Church's public statements, open-ended and in-depth interviews, and participant observation. In the qualitative content analysis used here, Church's scrapbooks, his Idaho "newsletters," his legislative files, various newspapers and periodicals, and *The Congressional Record* were all canvassed in search of statements that directly addressed, or at least suggested "answers" to, the philosophical and instrumental questions set out in the operational code framework. (These questions are outlined in the following section.) Interviews helped to fill in gaps in the public record—and sometimes these gaps can be substantial for politicians since they are not in the habit of waxing philosophic about operational codes. In one lengthy interview in 1972, Senator Church was asked to respond to each of the "op code" questions. Other interviews ranged more widely, covering such topics as his first political success and his approach to specific issues and decisions. Follow-up questions attempted to ascertain any changes in beliefs or decision-making approaches over time and the reasons for change. His responses were contrasted with the impressions of others interviewed about his political life.[1] Participant observation allowed this researcher to note at first hand the

---

[1] Several lengthy interviews have been conducted with Senator Church—the first one in August, 1970, near the end of the author's ten months as an American Political Science Association Congressional Fellow in Church's office and the second (the operational code interview) in September, 1972. Both interviews were taped without the slightest indication of any decline in candor or spontaneity. Extensive notes based on several less formal sessions with the Senator in Idaho and in Washington supplement these taped interviews. Taped interviews were also held with five other individuals with whom candor and spontaneity seemed no problem: the Senator's mother, Mrs. Laura Church; his mother-in-law, Mrs. Jean Clark; his son, Forrest Church (a Harvard divinity student); and two political editors on Idaho newspapers. Other interviews—some 65 thus far—were not taped. Questions were asked from memory and the responses were dictated immediately following each session. This chapter draws chiefly upon the 1970 and 1972 taped interviews with Church, plus a few additional observations about the 1956 election obtained in interviews held with several Idahoans in Boise during March, 1973.

correspondence between the actor's expressed beliefs and his behavior. This technique, however, should be verified with additional checks, such as cross-referencing policy-oriented speeches with subsequent votes on the policy.[2]

This study marks the beginning of a time-series analysis on one American politician. The larger study of which this chapter is a part will include quantitative content analysis (see Holsti, 1969) and voting analysis in order to develop increased precision in the charting of Church's operational code. The analysis here is theoretical and empirical rather than normative. As Wolfenstein (1969, p. 7) correctly observes: "Moral judgments should grow out of the study of men's lives, as Plutarch and all other self-conscious biographers have recognized; but empirical analysis of men's lives should be one thing, the moral evaluation of them, another." The objective of this study is to place Senator Church under a microscope rather than on a balance or a pedestal.

Operational Codes: A Time-Space Perspective

The point of departure for this theoretical overview is the operational code framework devised by George (1969) for the systematic investigation of a "political leader's beliefs about the nature of politics and political conflict, his views regarding the extent to which historical developments can be shaped, and his notions of correct strategies and tactics . . ." (p. 197). According to George (1969, p. 200), a leader's "answers" to such philosophical and instrumental (ends-means) questions "can help the researcher and the policy planner to 'bound' the alternative ways in which the subject may perceive different types of situations and approach the task of making a rational assessment of alternative courses of action." In brief, the explanation and prediction of leadership behavior are improved by understanding the leader's political beliefs. The researcher will still be unable to predict with confidence the precise behavior of the subject in any specific circumstance, but he will have an idea of the probable range of choices acceptable to the subject in a decision situation.

In this sense, the operational code is an independent variable helping to explain and predict leadership and policy-making behavior. "We can also consider the operational code as a dependent variable," Holsti (1970a, p. 155) points out, "in which case our attention is turned to quite different questions." In the first case, we are directed toward the relationship between beliefs and subsequent actions; in the second case, toward the genesis and evolution of these beliefs. One view projects forward in time, the other backward.

Several studies of leadership behavior emphasize the explanatory value of specific time periods during the formation of a leader's personality. Wolfenstein (1969, pp. 100-101) writes that "the process of character formation begins at birth, if not before, and is largely completed by the end of adolescence." Much

---

[2]Though beyond the scope of this chapter, an analysis in progress suggests a strong correlation between Church's beliefs and subsequent voting behavior which reinforces my impressions (as participant observer) of his belief-behavior consistency.

of the work by Erikson (see, for example, 1968) points to the importance of the "identity crisis" in late adolescence for understanding the formation of adult personality traits. Temporally close to Erikson's focus, Barber (1968, 1970) stresses an identifiable formative period in early adulthood—that of the first independent political success—in which the major elements of political leadership are exhibited. As Barber (1968, p. 78) observes, personality formation is a long, developmental process, but "the *main, adaptively strategic, politically-relevant action patterns* [emphasis in original] " are evidenced most clearly when a young man emerges as a successful young adult. We are directed to that period in a leader's development "when he came out of relative smallness into relative greatness" (Barber, 1970, p. 393).

Less psychologically oriented, other studies (e.g., Hoffmann, 1967; Rosenau, 1968) have noted the significance of past and immediate historical and institutional forces on leadership development and behavior. Several authors have underscored in particular the importance of the immediate situation preceding a decision. The authors of *The American Voter* (Campbell, Converse, Miller, and Stokes, 1960), for instance, emphasized in their theoretical construct, the funnel of causality, that the point in time just before the occurrence of a political act (such as voting) can provide a rich source of data for explaining the actual behavior. While this point in time can be fruitful, others (Golembiewski, Welsh, and Crotty, 1969, p. 405) have commented on the dangers of assuming that "events preceding this point will be somehow reflected in their analysis." A truly complete critique of leadership beliefs and behavior would take into account as many of the psychological, historical, and institutional influences along the time axis as proved fruitful to the analysis, including a sensitivity to the feedback effect of actions upon subsequent beliefs. Greenstein and Lerner (1971, p. 99) capture several of the most important relationships: "Social background works on physiological raw materials to engender psychological orientations [here one might add 'and operational codes'] that mediate the specific situational stimuli that lead to political behavior." This breadth suggests the desirability of an interdisciplinary research team analyzing different "zones" along the subject's time axis, according to the skills and training of each team member.

In contrast, then, to what might be done, this study will be sharply limited. It is primarily interested in comparing Church's beliefs on foreign affairs during two time periods: 1956, the year of his first independent political success, and 1972. Figure 4.1 portrays the time dimension in Church's life, emphasizing the periods of primary interest in this study of his operational code.

The time dimension is but one axis for organizing and ordering the variables affecting the leader's operational code. The evolution of the code and its effect upon behavior actually take place in a complex and dynamic coordinate system of time and space. For instance, each leader's operational code has at least five fundamental philosophical and instrumental dimensions:

THE NATURE OF POLITICS AND POLITICAL CONFLICT

1. *Politics*

   Philosophical: Does harmony or conflict characterize the political universe?

   Instrumental: What is the best approach for selecting political goals (moralist-ideological versus pragmatic-problem solving)?

2. *Opponents and Allies*

   Philosophical: What is the fundamental character of one's opponents (zero-sum versus cooperative-bargaining)? What is the fundamental character of one's allies, i.e., is collective action vital or should one pursue goals autonomously?

   Instrumental: What is the best way to deal with opponents and allies; should one emphasize foreign affairs or domestic affairs when determining goal-selection priorities?

SHAPING HISTORICAL DEVELOPMENTS

3. *Control of History*

   Philosophical: How much control can one have over historical development?

   Instrumental: How can the risks of political action be calculated; should one pursue a high- or low-risk strategy?

4. *Predictability*

   Philosophical: Is the political future predictable?

   Instrumental: What is the best "timing" of action to advance one's interests; should one negotiate from strength, parity, or weakness?

5. *Optimism*

   Philosphical: Should one be optimistic about the prospects for achieving one's political ends?

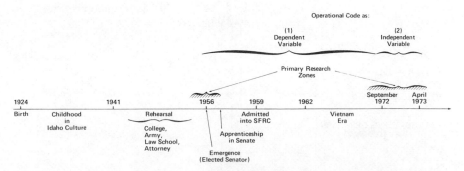

Figure 4.1.   The temporal dimension of the Church operational code.

Instrumental: What are the best means for achieving one's ends (armed intervention versus nonintervention)?

While the "answers" to these and related questions (see Anderson, 1973) will produce a picture of the leader's code, an assumption of enduring stability to these answers is unwarranted. For example, in the case of Lyndon Johnson a change may have occurred in his optimism-pessimism dimension when he discovered that his style of politics worked less well in the White House than in the

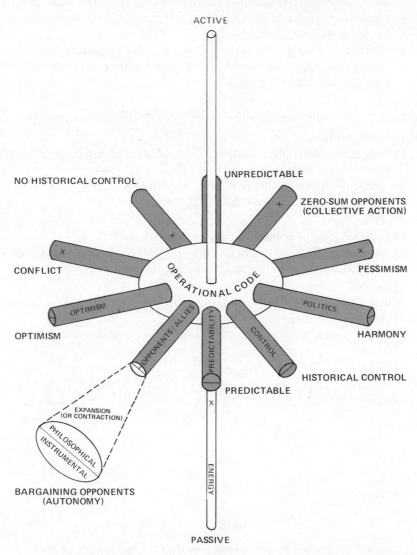

Figure 4.2. A spatial depiction of selected operational code dimensions.

Senate. Instead of static continuity, a more realistic conception of the code would include a flexible structure composed of at least the above five dimensions, each susceptible to differential states of gradual or rapid expansion or collapse as the political actor modifies his beliefs in response to the changing mix of psychological and situational pressures upon him.

In place of a set of beliefs held steadily and consistently in a unidimensional, stable amalgam of time and space, one can envision a more dynamic, multidimensional relationship. It may be that little change takes place in a leader's code, as appears to be the case with John Foster Dulles (Holsti, 1970a). For others, changes may be dramatic. While the individual patterns must be determined empirically, the working model should be designed to facilitate various reasonable possibilities. Figure 4.2 represents one way of imagining the operational code.[3] The political actor's approximate position on each of the code dimensions can be illustrated by placing an "x" at the proper location along each of the continua based on the observer's best judgment. The hypothetical subject in Figure 4.2, for example, is—among other things—highly pessimistic about the prospects for achieving his political goals.

As Barber (1972, p. 11) points out, an important question to probe in analyzing leadership behavior is: How much energy does the actor invest in his job? Is he a human cyclone like Lyndon Johnson or does he spend half the day sleeping like Calvin Coolidge? The continuum runs from highly active to highly passive. This "energy" dimension is introduced into the spatial depiction of the operational code to provide an indication of how vigorously the actor works at propagating his philosophical and instrumental beliefs. The hypothetical actor in Figure 4.2 is on the passive side.[4]

Thus, we have at least five "belief" dimensions and one "energy" dimension along which the actor can be placed. Together they help us categorize the basic political nature of the subject. It should be remembered that each of the five belief dimensions has a philosophical and an instrumental component. Moreover, each dimension may be more or less salient than another dimension at any given time, and the salience of each may vary with passing time. For instance, a subject may have virtually no interest in or beliefs regarding his opponents at one time in his career, perhaps because of their relative weakness; however, for various reasons (such as a sudden mushrooming in the political or military strength of his opponents), this aspect of the subject's code may expand rapidly as he grows more conscious of those in opposition to him. In short, the salience

[3]See Figure 4.3, also, in which each of the philosophical and instrumental dimensions discussed above is treated separately and comparatively for several American foreign policy makers.

[4]In his study of American Presidents, Barber (1972) also emphasizes the concept of positive-negative affect for understanding leadership. The idea is to discover how happy or sad an individual is in his leadership role. This happiness-sadness continuum would appear to be related to the optimism-pessimism dimension of the operational code, though Barber is less interested in a "philosophical conclusion" than he is in "a general symptom of the fit between the man and his experience, a kind of register of *felt* satisfaction [emphasis in original]" (pp. 11-12).

of the dimensions can expand and contract with conditions. The actor may move along each continuum, furthermore, as conditions change—or he may prove to be relatively set in both his fundamental beliefs and in his quantity of energy exerted. The model should be imagined as "living" and dynamic, like the mind it seeks to characterize.

Also, we feel it is more realistic—at least in the case of elected legislators—to view codes in a three-tiered fashion: a cluster of beliefs illustrating legislative orientations toward domestic *constituency* politics, a second cluster for domestic *national* politics, and a third cluster for *international* politics. In conducting research on Senator Church, it became clear that his "opponents" varied from the state to the national to the international levels as did his sense of optimism-pessimism about what he could accomplish, his sense of the severity of political conflict, and so on—including the amount of energy output he committed (active versus passive). Although pattern models like the one here can suffer from too much detail, the three-tiered perspective seems to reflect reality better than a one-tiered perspective—at least to this observer.

Finally, to order the units of analysis, the operational code may be thought of as a three-tiered configuration of space traveling through time within the mind of the *individual* actor as perceived and codified by the observer. Simultaneously, the actor (and his code) is traveling with and within a semipermeable matrix of constituency, national, and international events and personalities which may influence him (and which he may influence). It is within this extremely complex set of relationships involving time, psychological and situational forces, layers of government, and multidimensional belief systems that the operational code of a political leader takes form.

With these relationships in mind, the "international" operational code of Senator Church is singled out for inspection. Two hypotheses guide the research: (1) the 1972 code (as dependent variable) will be reflected, in basic form, in Church's beliefs during the 1956 period of "emergence," and (2) the 1972 code (as independent variable) will foreshadow Church's subsequent beliefs from October, 1972, to April, 1973.

The Church Code, 1972

The analysis of Senator Church's operational code at the "international tier" begins with a "snapshot" of his philosophical and instrumental beliefs derived from an interview with him in September, 1972.

PHILOSOPHICAL BELIEFS

The Nature of Politics
BELIEF 1. Politics is an undertaking to try and resolve the problems that face the people.

BELIEF 2. Politics is beset with conflict, disagreement, and argument.

For Church, politics is the process by which a nation or community resolves its problems. The process inevitably leads to conflict since individuals often have different problem priorities and solutions. These differences are made all the more combative for the elected politician, since he must first compete with opponents to win political office and then continue the contest periodically in order to keep the office.

BELIEF 3. There is both goodness and evil in men.

BELIEF 4. Peace and harmony can be maintained only through law and well-functioning governmental institutions.

Church places a high value on "the framework of law and government methods for living in peace together." He points to Russia, China, and the United States today and the Roman Empire in the past as examples of immense tracts of land held together by law and government. In a similar fashion, world peace can be attained only when "institutions are established that will and can enforce meaningful international law." While such institutions may be a long time in coming, Church believes that ultimately they will come; then world peace will be preserved "for a long period of time, for as long as these institutions can be maintained."

Image of the Opponent

BELIEF 5. Neither the Russians nor the Chinese are inherently evil.

BELIEF 6. Nationalities do not differ markedly one from another.

BELIEF 7. Communist nations have shown no greater tendency toward aggression than the United States.

BELIEF 8. Under certain circumstances and certain leaders, nations will be carried into adventures of aggression.

Church rejects the notion that historical events can be interpreted from the standpoint of the aggressive tendencies in one people as compared to another. Although, after two wars with the Germans, we often view them as highly militant and aggressive, Church points to new historical interpretations suggesting that World War I was actually just a tragic blunder—an unanticipated accident—and not the demonic scheme of a nation bent upon the conquest of Europe and the world. More accurately, the Senator maintains, the German Kaiser was "just a rather foolish man—prideful—a man who thought he was honor-bound to come to the rescue of his ally, the Austro-Hungarian emperor, Franz Josef." In this way, the world was "catapulted almost mindlessly into war." Only after the war began did nations determine what the purpose of the war should be. In contrast to the Kaiser, Hitler is seen by the Senator as a vengeful, aggressive man able to hypnotize the German people with his own inspired demagoguery and to inflame their sense of anger and frustration resulting from defeat in the First World War and the agony of the Depression. What these examples illustrate to Church is not that certain people tend to be more aggressive than others, but that "at certain times in history under the impact of certain circumstances and the effort of certain leaders, nations are given to undertake adventures of aggression."

The Senator finds other countries to be no more aggressive than the United States. "Our history is one of conquest," he observes. "Beginning at Plymouth Rock in 1620, and proceeding to conquer an entire continent, we drove the aboriginal people into reservations by force of arms." He regards it as a process of self-deception for critics of Israel to denounce that nation's seizure of Arab lands. On the one hand, these critics insist this is aggression and that these lands ought to be relinquished to the Arab countries; yet, on the other hand, they disregard similar events in our own history. Church doubts that the United States would have had much patience during the War with Mexico with demands for us to back up and accept our prior borders; instead we settled for half of Mexico. He reasons: "We seized a continent and we built a country upon it; and the Israelis today have seized certain territory and they're not going to relinquish that part they think is vital to their survival as a nation."

BELIEF 9. We must deal cautiously with and respect those countries with great military might, but no country should be considered a necessary enemy of the United States.

BELIEF 10. No country keeps a treaty that does not serve the interests of that country as seen by the government in power at the time.

BELIEF 11. Moral judgments must be discounted on many questions of international relations, since spheres of influence and the hegemony of large nations over their smaller neighbors have been historical facts of life.

Church is wary of the ability of the Soviet Union (and, perhaps, one day China) to destroy or inflict grievous injury upon the United States. Their power is a serious matter that must always be taken into account, just as our opponents take our power into account in their dealings with us. He rejects, nevertheless, the school of thought that says it is impossible to negotiate any kind of treaty with our opponents because they do not keep their treaties. For him, this argument misses the point: "The fact is, no country keeps a treaty that doesn't serve the interests of that country, as seen by the government in power at the time." Church recalls a string of treaties in the past that America has broken, including some 18 to 20 solemn treaty covenants the United States broke in entering ("with very little reason") the Dominican Republic in 1965.

One of the most important principles to remember about relations between nations, the Senator believes, is that "big countries have always tended to behave aggressively toward their smaller neighbors." When the Russians have done this in Eastern Europe, we in the West have called it naked aggression; yet, Church notes, the United States has insisted at the same time upon maintaining a very large hegemony in our own hemisphere. This insistence goes back to the early days of the Republic when we declared in the Monroe Doctrine that we would exercise the dominant political, economic, and military influence in the Western Hemisphere. Even before really becoming a great power, we staked out a sphere of influence for the United States that consisted of half the world. The Monroe

Doctrine was only the beginning; as we grew to power, we were no longer content with that hegemony. In Church's words:

> In the years following the Second World War we extended our sphere of influence to the middle of Europe, incorporating the whole of the Atlantic and Pacific Oceans; and not content with the Pacific Ocean—the widest moat on earth—we extended our hegemony on to the mainland of Asia itself and established permanent American military bases on the mainland of Asia.

This latter area the Senator views as China's "natural sphere of influence." He sees no chance at the present for normalizing relations with China until adjustments are made on mainland Asia "that will give to China what large nations are accustomed to demanding for themselves."

Church is sensitive to the way "opponents" of the United States perceive our actions. He notes that the Chinese did not enter the Korean War until American troops approached the Chinese borders. Reflecting upon this conflict, he points out that we viewed this war as one in which the United States sought to re-establish a boundary in the name of the preservation of world order and world peace. However, Church suggests that "from the standpoint of the Koreans, it might have looked quite different. They may have viewed the reunification of Korea as an essentially internal question that should be left to the Koreans themselves to decide."

Image of Allies

BELIEF 12. Short of attacking vital American interests, sovereign nations as powerful as the United States are free to do just about as they please.

BELIEF 13. More important than the choice of collective or individual action should be the determination of whether American vital interests truly require intervention in a given case.

BELIEF 14. The vital interests of the United States should be the safety of the American people and the survival of free government in this country.

BELIEF 15. The vital interests of the United States should not include the guaranteed protection of American corporate investments abroad.

Church is struck by the capacity and willingness of the United States to become involved in affairs overseas without the support or consent of our allies. Vietnam demonstrates to him just how far the United States is willing to go unilaterally, with only the slightest pretext of collective security. He ponders our interpretation of the SEATO Treaty; when aggression occurred in Southeast Asia, no country that was a party to the SEATO alliance was willing to intervene—except the United States. Pakistan refrained; England and France withdrew from the area; Australia and New Zealand gave nothing more than token assistance in order to keep credit in the American bank against the day they might really need American help. Thus, it turned out to be essentially a unilateral act on the part of the United States, a result of the "curious" Rusk Doctrine that we were obligated under the SEATO Treaty to act even though other partners to the same treaty did not. "Certainly this is an innovation in the law of contracts and must be an entirely unique American addition to the law of international responsibility under treaties," remarks the Senator wryly.

For Church, the Vietnam experience clearly demonstrates that the principle of collective security is secondary to individual action in American foreign policy. The important question for him is not whether collective or individual action is desirable, but "whether the interests of the U.S. in a given case require intervention." He concludes that in Southeast Asia they never did since the security of the American people was never at stake. "Why, it's preposterous," he declares, "to think a little country like that had any real relationship to the vital interests of the United States."

Within his definition of American vital interests, Church provides two reference points: the safety of the American people and the survival of democracy in the United States. He refuses to broaden the definition to include the guaranteed protection of American corporate investments abroad. This is one reason why he is chairing a SFRC *ad hoc* subcommittee to look into the role of large multinational corporations; he wants "to determine the extent that American foreign policy may have become the handmaiden of large American corporate interests."

Control of History

BELIEF 16. While some events lie beyond our mastery, a large and powerful country like the United States has a large measure of control over its own future.
BELIEF 17. Only limited goals can be accomplished by individual senators.

The possibility always exists that the United States can be "victimized by events that lie beyond our reach," comments Church. An accidental nuclear war would be an example. A *country* as large, wealthy, and powerful as ours, however, can have "a very large measure of control over its future, for better or for worse." On the other hand, the role of the *individual* in mastering events in America is limited at best, since a person "can accomplish only what lies within the reach of his office."

Given the constraints on his office as senator, Church states that his goals must be limited and modest. Because they are limited, he believes he has a "pretty good chance to achieve them." Specifically, these goals consist of initiating and passing bills of lasting benefit to Idaho, influencing national legislation insofar as he is able, and bringing such influence as he can to bear on "tempering" American foreign policy.

BELIEF 18. It is very difficult through legislation to affect foreign policy.
BELIEF 19. Programs are almost impossible to stop once they have gathered bureaucratic momentum.

In only a very few cases has the Senate been successful in affecting foreign policy, Church observes. One such case was the Cooper-Church Amendment of

1970 which used the power of the purse to prevent the expansion of American ground forces throughout Southeast Asia. For the first time in American history, the Senate voted during a war to impose spending limitations on the Commander-in-Chief, refusing to make funds available for troop deployments into countries neighboring Vietnam. Usually, though, the Senate is "obliged to accept the foreign policy as laid down by the President."

Furthermore, large and impenetrable bureaucracies grow up around the programs passed by Congress to implement the President's foreign policy. These bureaucracies soon have an inertia that is difficult to overcome. To illustrate, Church points to Senate attempts to stop foreign aid in 1971. "We just voted it down, we finally got so disgusted with it," he recalls. This vote sent a "terrible shock wave" through Washington because for 25 years the Senate and the Congress had dutifully passed the foreign aid bill. "It was not thought possible that the Senate would simply reject it," Church reflects, "and as it turned out, it wasn't possible." The big agencies just could not be terminated. In the end, the Senate passed a modified foreign aid bill, but essentially the program continued.

The most the Senate seems able to do, Church notes, is to pare down some programs that the majority is against. Even when legislative standards or conditions are written into bills, they may or may not be respected in the administration of the program—"to prove that they haven't been is very difficult." The President has too much latitude in applying these standards, laments the Senator. The President "decides what he wants to do and whatever finding the law requires, he makes." Church believes that 40 years of warfare have exalted the presidency until it is now "a new Caesardom": "It is the return of the Caesars I think we are seeing enacted here."

He sees the House of Representatives succumbing to this new Caesardom even more readily than the Senate. House members must come up for election every two years and are fearful the President may turn on them and hold them responsible for certain failures abroad, particularly if the United States is engaged in war. Members are afraid that if they cross the President, the "people will side with him and vote them out of office." The Senate has expressed more dissent against presidential power and has been more willing to challenge the President's policies because, Church explains, the six-year term for senators gives them a greater measure of protection: "Even though the public may strongly side with the President, as it usually does in the case of national emergency, senators feel they can ride that out before they have to face the people at election time."

BELIEF 20. The role of chance in human events is very large.

"Chance is a big thing," Church emphasizes. Church notes that were it not for Kennedy's defeat of Lyndon Johnson, who wanted to be President so badly, and his choice of Lyndon Johnson as running mate, Johnson never would have been President. And, perhaps, we never would have sent an expeditionary force to Southeast Asia with all of its fateful consequences.

Predictability
BELIEF 21. The future is not predictable.

Church believes that human behavior is not predictable in any precise sense, "even individual behavior, let alone collective behavior." He does think, however, that it is possible to estimate the future based upon the experience of the past and an analysis of the present: "That's about the best guideline we have to anticipating what the future may be like."

Optimism
BELIEF 22. I'm basically optimistic; we learn from our mistakes.
BELIEF 23. Our ultimate weapons are so awesome that we dare not use them.
BELIEF 24. Rational men will prevail and arms accords will be reached before a thermonuclear holocaust occurs.

The Senator places himself clearly on the optimistic side of this continuum, though he is no pollyanna. Regarding warfare with the Soviet Union or another nuclear power, he agrees that thermonuclear destruction could occur by accident, "mushrooming out of some kind of initial mistake or some momentary act of madness." Short of this, however, he can see no cause for such a war because nothing worth saving would survive. In the Senator's opinion, more probable than accidents of nuclear war or suicide is the slow movement toward agreements limiting and, ultimately, reducing nuclear weapons. At least this is more probable "as long as governments prevail on either side that are run by rational men." He thinks that, presently, both the American and the Russian leaders are rational, although both must contend with strong military influences within their governments.

INSTRUMENTAL BELIEFS

Selecting Goals
BELIEF 25. Some individuals are driven by ambition stemming from a personal sense of insecurity.
BELIEF 26. Political decisions to a very large extent are made in a highly opportunistic way.
BELIEF 27. Politicians should adopt a problem-solving approach to politics, examining issues in the light of the available facts, public opinion, and their own consciences.

In Church's opinion, politicians like Lyndon Johnson and Richard Nixon are insecure in many ways. The need for popular recognition and acclaim can lead men like Johnson and Nixon on the quest for high office. Building upon this assumption, Church suggests that many political figures attempt to find along the way the issues with which they can succeed; they tend to test public opinion at the moment, trying to weave together certain programs that have widespread appeal. "It's not so much a creative, innovative kind of thing," he says, "as it is a sort of on-going fishing expedition." He acknowledges that a person's general philosophy may lead him toward the selection of different issues than his opponent might select, but the process is pretty much the same. "Each is trying to find a common denominator that will have sufficiently large appeal to forge a majority behind his candidacy." Church would prefer a politician to take a more independent stance, keeping in touch with public opinion but also speaking out on issues as the facts and his own conscience dictate.

Goal Priorities

BELIEF 28. Foreign policy ought not to be the tail that wags the national dog.

BELIEF 29. Nations must recognize the limits of their power.

BELIEF 30. Powerful nations must learn to live with change, ferment, and revolution in the world.

The "glamour of foreign adventure" must be subordinate to the solution of domestic problems, the Senator declares, unless we wish to follow the pathway of empires in the past that have been destroyed from within. He emphatically urges keeping foreign policy in perspective, not letting it dominate.

He also believes that a great deal is going to happen in the world that the United States and other large nations will be powerless to prevent. The United States has a tendency to think it is omnipotent, Church observes; only the future will reveal whether or not we have learned from Vietnam that we are not. Foreseeing much change ahead in the world, particularly in the underdeveloped areas, he thinks we can learn to live with ferment and revolution "only if we realize there are limits in our own power to prevent revolutionary change from occurring." Our gravest mistakes in the last 20 years have come from the assumption that we do have the wealth and power to mold the world to our own liking. "We don't," the Senator states flatly, "and the sooner we learn to impose some reasonable restraint on our own tendency to intervene too much in other people's affairs, the happier land we will have and the less burden we will place upon our own people to undertake sacrifices that are not really related to their own good or the good of their country."

Control of Risks

BELIEF 31. We should not apply a double standard in world affairs, one for ourselves and another for our opponents.

BELIEF 32. War between the Soviet Union and the United States is no longer a sensible option, since it would only serve to destroy both nations.

A major theme running throughout the interview was the Senator's belief that America must avoid interfering needlessly in the affairs of other nations. The world must be permitted to make its own adjustments. For instance, rather than trying to isolate China from the rest of the world or to be implacably opposed to the Russians, the United States should help thaw out the Cold War. Church gave former President Nixon high marks for his relations with the Chinese and Soviet leaders.

Part of the problem with United States foreign policy, in Church's opinion, is its dual standard. He points to the Cuban missile crisis as an example. At the time, the United States had a tremendous lead in missile and nuclear strength. Khrushchev's gambit to place intermediary missiles in Cuba was made, Church believes, to redress this imbalance with a dramatic move; the Soviets did not have the capacity to close the missile gap quickly in any other way. Khrushchev probably also saw it as a bargaining lever to induce the United States to withdraw some of its intermediate range missiles from places like Turkey and other countries right next to the Soviet Union.

So the Russians looked at the Cuban gambit from a different perspective than the United States. We saw it as an act of aggression against our country; we were unwilling to note that we were involved in similar acts with respect to the Soviet Union. The fact that we were surrounding the Soviet Union with weapons and alliances which we regarded as purely defensive in nature led us, in the Senator's words, "to apply a double standard." To the Russians our military deployment throughout the world did not appear to be strictly defensive. They harbored the same suspicions of us as we did of them; they regarded us as the aggressors in the world. They pointed to the fact, Church notes, that we had been insisting on forward bases outside of our own country and close to the Soviet Union and had ringed the Soviet Union with missiles and bases of every kind. "To them," he observes, "this was evidence of aggression."

Only when Khrushchev realized that Kennedy was going to make it an issue of war between Russia and the United States did the Soviet leader understand he had made a grave miscalculation. The United States was not going to accept in the Caribbean what the Russians had been forced to accept in the Mediterranean. Khrushchev decided to back down rather than risk thermonuclear war at a time when the United States had the preponderant advantage.

Now that advantage has been lost. "Our own foolishness in Southeast Asia has led us to simply expend our resources so lavishly on nothing that, in the interim, the Soviet Union has caught up by assiduously applying itself to the development of large intercontinental ballistic missiles." Today the Soviets have an arsenal "fully as large and menacing as ours." Thermonuclear war is beyond the limits of the rational, the Senator observes, "unless national suicide is thought to be an acceptable objective of national policy."

Timing

BELIEF 33. Negotiations require a certain parity, not overwhelming strength.

"Do not undertake negotiations with the opponent until you enjoy a situation of strength" was a basic belief of former Secretary of State Dean Acheson (McLellan, 1971, p. 72). To Church, this principle "makes no sense at all." He admits that any nation would prefer to negotiate from a position of strength; but if the strength is preponderant, "there is no need to negotiate." If the strength is not preponderant, he reasons, then negotiations may be necessary to reach a settlement. The chance for successful negotiations depends "almost mathematically upon a certain parity on either side, a certain balance." Without this balance, the weaker side will refuse the negotiations if it can; and if it cannot refuse—if the preponderance of strength is so great on the opposing side that it cannot—then there will be no negotiations anyway. "There'll be ultimata," says Church, "and the will of the preponderant power will be imposed." The Acheson position was "a silly business," Church concludes, speculating that perhaps Acheson didn't really believe it himself; instead such a position might have been just "a formula of convenience for the time to fortify the foreign policy position that we had undertaken to establish."

The Senator's thoughts moved to an interview he had with Premier Kosygin in 1971 in the company of David Rockefeller, Charles Yost, and General Gavin. His part of the interview was to focus on the possibilities for arms limitations agreements, especially on nuclear weapons, through SALT (strategic-arms-limitations talks). Throughout the discussion, Kosygin emphasized that Russia was willing to enter into agreements to limit all nuclear arms, to reduce arms, or, ultimately, to eliminate arms, but the agreements had to proceed on the principle of parity or equality. The Soviet Union was a nation that had achieved nuclear power equal to that of the United States and, if the two countries were to have any agreements, Kosygin continued, such agreements would have to be based upon a recognition of that equality. It was clear to Church in the whole tone of the conversation with Kosygin that Russia felt able to negotiate with the United States for the first time because equality had been achieved. If the agreements reflected the principle of equality, then it would be possible for progress to be made; but Russia could not deal with the United States in any way that would give to us an advantage—any more than we could give them any advantage.

This is what makes negotiation possible in the Senator's view. Of course, one is still left with the problems of what constitutes advantage. Such a dilemma makes negotiations extremely difficult and time consuming and, perhaps, only a little progress can be made at a time. Nevertheless, Church prefers this situation to what existed during the Acheson era. In this earlier era, the fact that the United States had predominant power prevented any meaningful negotiations at all. The arms race just continued from one level to another as each state jockeyed for advantage. The only possibility of ever ending the arms race, Church believes, comes when the two sides recognize that there's nothing more to be gained for both sides to continue—other than greater dangers and costs.

Utility of Means
BELIEF 34. War is the worst means for the United States at this stage in her history.

War is not rejected out of hand by the Senator as always unnecessary or unproductive. "There are times when wars are necessary in the history of a people," he states. The war for American independence, for instance, was justified, given the circumstances of the time and the desire of the colonies to establish a government of their own. He points to other wars in American history, however, that he believes were foolish. The War of 1812 contributed little except casualties and costs, and in the end in his view accomplished nothing. He observes that the final peace treaty did not even refer to the reasons for which the war started in the first place. Other wars we have fought in the last century were largely related to the "appetite of the country for expansion, in the course of which we conquered a continent."

The wars of this century have been very costly in terms of casualties and debt accumulation. The great plans that Wilson had for a better world in the wake of the First World War never materialized. Our victory in the Second World War did destroy the fiendish Nazi regime, but, Church suggests, we did not achieve peace by war. Instead only a new contest emerged on an even larger scale with adversaries of greater potential power. Church notes that, ironically, one might have to conclude the Japanese were the principal victors of the Second World War, and after them the West Germans, and after them the Italians. The defeated countries were liberated by their defeat and have been able to achieve far higher living standards and a far greater measure of freedom than they have ever known before. The victorious nations, in contrast, have not fared as well, the Senator believes. The United States, for example, has been burdened by the "tremendous and naive attempt on our part to take over the collapsed empires of the Western world, and to subsidize them in various ways, in a futile effort to make them malleable to our own will." All of this has been terribly unsuccessful and costly, he emphasizes, and in the end led us into Vietnam and created a divided and embittered America—and a nation of young people disillusioned with their government.

He is also alarmed that the Second World War and the following wars have saddled the United States with an immense military machine which has reworked the economy to feed the needs of the machine and which, to a very large extent, has militarized the American people in their thinking. For all these reasons, the Senator concludes that "on balance these wars have done more to damage our society than to benefit it."

BELIEF 35. The United States must relax her hold on the world and not try so feverishly to control it.

"We not only can live with a great deal of ferment and change," says the Senator, "but there is no reason why we cannot allow a relationship to develop between countries that we need not dominate." Church refers to Asia as an illustration. He believes that were it not for the insistent intervention of American military power in Asia following the Second World War, a "natural equilibrium" would have developed there between Russia, China, and Japan in the North ("the triangle of power") and India and Indonesia in the South, both bulwarks of power that will resist any external penetration. "The smaller countries were really incidental," Church declares, "and would develop relationships with the larger countries as was natural to their situation, as they had done historically through the ages." The unnatural element injected into Asia was the

American presence and her insistence upon establishing alliances that, in fact, made no sense except for the presence of American power. Our alliances with Taiwan, the Philippines, and Thailand did not really forge "a circle of steel" around China at all. "It was only to the extent that the United States was willing to commit her own sons and her own money to fight wars in Asia that a circle of steel existed."

For Church, the argument that the U.S. has a moral obligation to protect the oppressed peoples of Asia is a "perversion of morals." "Protect them from what?" he asks. "What we end up giving them is Thieu and a corrupt dictatorship in South Vietnam." He asks how it is possible to justify the sacrifice of 50,000 American lives, 300,000 wounded and maimed, and $175 billion lost in a war that divided and demoralized our own people. "For what? For the day that we inevitably have to leave, when the indigenous forces once more will determine the destiny of these areas?" he asks. Church believes that our invasion of Southeast Asia with a Western army is looked upon by most Asians who live in that part of the world as "the last gasp of Western imperialism." Moreover, "the people we engulfed in the very act of protecting them are dismissed as contemptible puppets of Western power." Church hopes that America will continue to disengage from Asia. Above all, he concludes, the United States must "live with the world and not try so feverishly to control it."

The interview with Senator Church using the operational code construct reveals the broad outlines of his views on American foreign policy in late 1972. Philosophically, he believes that: (1) even though politics is conflictual, international law and peace-keeping institutions can bring harmony to the world eventually; (2) the United States must respect the spheres of influence of large nations, just as we demand they respect ours in the Western Hemisphere; (3) principles of collective security or individual action matter less than whether American vital interests (essentially the safety of the American people) in a given case require intervention; (4) we can be basically optimistic that rational men will achieve arms control; and (5) the United States has the ability to control its fate to a large degree even though precise prediction or mastery of the future is impossible.

Instrumentally, the Senator thinks that: (1) American leaders ought to be less opportunistic and more innovative in their selection of goals; (2) United States foreign affairs ought to play a subordinate role to domestic affairs; (3) the United States must realize the limits of her power and allow other nations to settle their own futures; (4) progress in negotiating with other large powers requires a parity of strength; and (5) war is the worst means for the United States to use in achieving its goals, the relaxation of her grip on the rest of the world—living with change—the best.

Diagrammatically, the Senator can be placed along the "belief" dimensions approximately as in Figure 4.3 (designated by "C" for Church). For comparative purposes, former Secretaries of State John Foster Dulles ("D") (1953-1959), Dean Acheson ("A") (1949-1952), and Dean Rusk ("R") (1961-1968) are also placed on the continua along with two former Chairmen of the Senate Foreign Relations Committee, Arthur H. Vandenberg ("V") (1946-1948) and J. William Fulbright ("F") (1959-1974). The placements, based on the author's understanding of recent operational code studies (Anderson, 1973; Gutierrez, 1973; Holsti, 1970a; McLellan, 1971; Tweraser, 1973), are rough estimates—though the "center of gravity" for each actor would appear to be generally accurate.

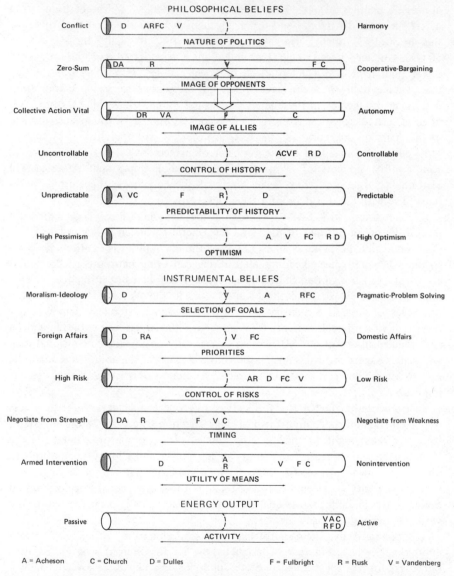

Figure 4.3. A comparison of Church and other leaders along operational code dimensions.

As illustrated in Figure 4.3, Church differs philosophically from the former Secretaries of State chiefly in (1) his stronger beliefs in the possibility of cooperation and relationships of trust with our opponents and (2) his de-emphasis of principles or maxims of collective military action. Instrumentally, Church differs from the Secretaries mainly in being (1) less internationally oriented, (2) less willing to seek situations of overwhelming strength, and (3) less interested in intervening militarily. While falling relatively close to Fulbright on each dimension, Church stands apart from Vandenberg philosophically in his image of "Opponents" and "Allies" and instrumentally in his approach to the "Selection of Goals."

No doubt differences between Church, on the one hand, and Acheson, Dulles, and Vandenberg, on the other hand, reflect in part the changing nature of the international milieu. In 1972, Church spoke in an atmosphere of rapprochement; the others expressed their beliefs during some of the most trying periods of the Cold War. As the following section illustrates, the view of the opponents and allies held by Church in the late 1950s was more like that of Vandenberg and the Secretaries (as seems to have been the case for Fulbright, too). Why Church (and Fulbright) experienced a change in some key beliefs from the 1950s to the 1960s while Rusk apparently did not is beyond the scope of this chapter. Only the single question of Church's belief modifications will be examined here.

These sketchy observations merely illustrate some of the possibilities for the comparative analysis of operational codes. Through more systematic comparisons of many leadership codes, we may be able to generate typologies of political beliefs useful for both explanation and prediction. Sophisticated typologies will need to consider more carefully than space permits here the comparative evolution of beliefs, tracing important changes and discovering their catalysts.

The 1972 Code as Dependent Variable

Holsti (1970a, p. 157) suggests that we address ourselves "not only to the effects of political beliefs on policy processes, but also to their sources and to the means by which they are sustained, modified, or discarded." Before examining Church's 1972 code as an independent variable, his 1956 beliefs regarding foreign affairs are surveyed to see which of them were "sustained, modified, or discarded" in the 1972 interview.

Church's first political success in 1956 is of special interest because of the impact such a time period may have on an individual's belief system. While personality formation is a long developmental process, Barber (1972) theorizes that the important elements of style and character are evidenced most clearly when a President emerges as a successful young adult. "Where in a man's past are the best clues to his Presidential style?" Barber (1969, p. 33) asks, and then answers: "He tends to hark back to that time when he had an analogous emergence—to his first independent political success, usually in early adulthood, when he developed a personal style that worked well for him" (p. 34).

In a similar manner, the *early beliefs* of a politician may be a useful guide to his later beliefs. Put another way, the politician's early operational code—even if fragmentary—may be useful for predicting his more mature code. This section of the chapter is designed to explore this possibility.

EMERGENCE

On February 23, 1956, Church walked into the office of a fellow attorney and proclaimed: "I'm going to reach for the moon!" The next day—four months before his 31st birthday—he announced his candidacy for the U.S. Senate. The reaction of state Democratic leaders to Church's candidacy was as chilling as the snowstorm in Boise that weekend: "He's a fine kid," said one (*Boise Journal*, 1956c), "but we can't elect him to the U.S. Senate; he's just too young and inexperienced." A week after Church entered the contest, the headlines of the nation's newspaper read: " 'I Shall Accept Nomination,' says Ike." The President's heart attack five months earlier was not going to force his retirement as Church had anticipated, and the incumbent GOP Senator, Herman Welker, would have Eisenhower's considerable coattails to grasp.

The picture began to look all the more bleak for Church as several candidates filed for the Democratic primary—including the experienced campaigner, Glenn Taylor. Taylor had been a U.S. Senator from Idaho a few years earlier and the Vice Presidential candidate for the Progressive Party in 1948. He was one of the last barn stormers in American politics, having already been in nine statewide campaigns in Idaho. Taylor was an immensely energetic campaigner. He would drive into town with his family in a speaker-equipped automobile, leap up on its roof to belt out a few rousing country-Western songs while strumming his cowboy guitar, and then fill the air with campaign rhetoric as his hat passed among the crowd. It was quite a tent show and he had a popular following.

The other Democratic candidates were soon outdistanced by Taylor and Church. The lead between these two see-sawed back and forth as the precinct results came in. Finally, Church was declared the winner by 170 votes—the closest margin of victory in Idaho history. Taylor could not believe he had been beaten. He protested the election outcome, declaring possible voting irregularities, and began going from house to house in an Idaho precinct where he had done well in the past, asking housewives how they had *really* voted. This process offended the local citizenry and he was arrested under the Green River Ordinance against house-to-house solicitation. Further enraged, Taylor decided to run against Church as a write-in candidate in the general election.

Thus, in the general election Church faced the write-in candidacy of Taylor as well as the Republican candidate Welker. In his youth, Welker had been the youngest prosecuting attorney in the nation at age twenty-one; those who knew him during these early days remember a bright, talented, warm, and gregarious person. In the 1950s, he became an outspoken critic of Communist subversion within the United States. A Senate classmate of Joe McCarthy, they became closely associated and Welker soon was referred to by many as "Little Joe from Idaho." Around 1954, Welker fell very ill; he was frequently mean and angry without cause, his daughter recalls. His behavior during the 1956 campaign was often puzzling. He was uncharacteristically slow in speech and movement; he often seemed irrational and sometimes slurred his words (and hence was accused unfairly of alcoholism). His daughter remembers that he bought a home in Idaho before he ran for re-election; she now believes he seemed to know he would not be re-elected and that, in fact, he did not have long to live. Shortly after the campaign Welker died of a brain tumor.

Despite the fact that Welker was not the man he once was and Taylor would have a difficult time winning as a write-in candidate, most experienced observers at the time in Idaho and in Washington, D.C. believed the Church campaign was finished. They reasoned that Taylor would carry his ardent supporters with him, splitting Church's vote and assuring Welker's re-election. Church's father-in-law, former Idaho Governor Chase A. Clark, predicted a different outcome: Church would be in the middle between two extremists and, therefore, would capture the most votes. This prediction proved correct. As Church recalls: "Taylor attacked me for being a candidate mortgaged to the corrupt corporate politicians and Welker charged me with being a puppet of the pinks and the punks; and the people concluded that a man might be one or the other, but he couldn't be both. So I came sailing through the middle." In the end, he had 46,315 more votes than Welker and 75,000 more than Taylor, while Ike carried the state by 60,000 votes.

That Church was able to sail through the middle of two extremists, one deathly ill and the other staging an uphill write-in campaign, suggests an element of good fortune in his win. This experience no doubt contributed to Church's beliefs regarding optimism, unpredictability, and the limited control over history. Good fortune is, however, only part of the explanation for the victory. Church's use of those rhetorical skills which he had developed and practiced as a champion school and college debater was also a vital ingredient. During the election, a reporter noted (*Boise Journal,* 1956b): "Only two shows brought out the crowds or entertained and interested the people—the old trooper, Glenn Taylor, and the sparkling young orator, Frank Church."

The Church campaign was perhaps the most personally vigorous in Idaho history. Leaving their young son in the care of grandparents, Church and his wife, Bethine, sold their home to raise money and set off in their secondhand car to visit virtually every part of the state. He was "out-Keefing Kefauver in handshaking and corner perorations," wrote one correspondent (*Washington Post,* 1957). Another noted (*Boise Journal,* 1956a) that he was "as tireless as an Adlai Stevenson and as plodding as Estes Kefauver. . . ." The new Senator-elect (Church, 1957) commented after the election: "I have no secret formula. I worked hard and went into all corners of the state." His politically astute wife worked beside him just as tirelessly in the campaign, driving the car and urging him to "shake some more hands" at the end of an exhausting day. In retrospect, Church's 1956 campaign supporters stress three main elements in his success: (1) his speaking ability; (2) his television "presence"; and (3) his efforts to shake hands with over 75,000 people throughout the state. Above all, skillful and energetic oratory again paid off for the young campaigner, as it had in his debating days.

After the election a reporter noted (*Idaho Statesman,* 1957): "The great issues of the nation and world were virtually neglected by the candidates . . . Personalities were injected into the campaign from the beginning and it was fought out on that basis." Church did provide glimpses, nevertheless, into some dimensions of his 1956 international code during a few campaign addresses.

PHILOSOPHICAL BELIEFS

Nature of Politics
EMERGENCE BELIEF 1. We live in a "world of ferment" (Church, 1956d).

Although his 1956 speeches do not elaborate on this theme, the youthful attorney was clearly mindful of the potential for conflict in the international realm. He had seen it first hand during the Second World War, and the Suez crisis reminded him daily during the 1956 campaign. Moreover, he (Church, 1956c) complained bitterly during the campaign about the political conflict in Eastern Europe where people lived "under a Communist yoke imposed upon them by bayonets."

Image of Opponents and Allies
EMERGENCE BELIEF 2. Communism must be prevented from spreading throughout the world.
EMERGENCE BELIEF 3. The Free World must stand united against Communism.

As a lieutenant serving in China, Church often expressed in his letters a respect—even an enthusiasm—for the Communists in that enormous country. He wrote to his parents on July 22, 1945 from Kumming, China:

> The Communists, as you know, have fought brilliantly against the Japs for many years. They are completely isolated, cut off from all supplies, and forced to rely entirely on their own ingenuity. In the organization of their society and in the extent of their sweeping reforms they appear to have equalled their astonishing military success.

By 1956, however, Church had accepted the Cold War and its rhetoric. For example, a speech (Church, 1956c) in September of that campaign year warned: "We must not permit the change in Russian tactics to cause us to drop our guard. Communist objectives have not changed." In October, Church (1956d) spoke of the necessity to halt "the further spread of Communism abroad" and deplored (Church, 1956e) "the Communist yoke imposed upon Hungarians and Poles by bayonets." During the campaign he (Church, 1956e) would point to his service as Idaho state chairman of the Crusade for Freedom in 1954-55: "I am grateful that I had the opportunity to support the Radio Free Europe program which has helped to keep the support of freedom alive in the satellite countries by broadcasting the truth about the Free World to these captive peoples."

In a 1970 interview, Senator Church spoke about these early statements. "I was convinced, as nearly everybody was convinced, that the Cold War policies of the United States were absolutely sound," he reflected. "Our duty, as we conceived it then, was to quarantine Communism and to protect the world from the further extension of the Communist system." Church remembered how the United States felt threatened by the Communist system because it was viewed as a mighty monolith. Any extension of Communism anywhere was seen as merely "adding another tentacle to the octopus, while the brain of the octopus was in Moscow. And, thus, the world was divided into two parts: the Red part and our part, which we liked to call the Free World." Among the most salient international beliefs held by Church during his period of emergence, then, were the containment doctrine and support for a strong, united Western Alliance.

Control of History, Predictability, Optimism
EMERGENCE BELIEF 4. "The first objective of our foreign policy should be the preservation of peace . . ." (Church, 1956e).
EMERGENCE BELIEF 5. The future is not predictable.
EMERGENCE BELIEF 6. One can be basically optimistic about improving American foreign policy, but concerning the future of mankind one cannot be a complete optimist.

As the campaign proceeded, Church spoke on several occasions about ways of changing American foreign policy to improve the quality of life here and abroad. He believed that one day a trustworthy system of enforced disarmament would be securely established among the nations of the world; he supported "every effort" to promote and maintain the peace; and he listed several instrumental beliefs for strengthening the effectiveness of U.S. foreign relations. These statements indicated both a belief in some control over the shaping of history and a sense of optimism regarding the future. Events in the future could not be predicted with confidence, however, and certain gloomy possibilities prevented a full optimism. The Suez crisis, for example, was to Church (1956a) "a burning fuse on a powder keg that could ignite a third world war."

INSTRUMENTAL BELIEFS

Selection of Goals
EMERGENCE BELIEF 7. "Our foreign policy must continue to be a bipartisan policy" (Church, 1956d).

According to Church (1956d), bipartisan policy was to be "the instrument through which we seek to make our country safe in a world of ferment." Much later in his career he (Church, 1970a) would reject blind allegiance to the ideology of bipartisanship and Presidential prerogative: "The lure of that beguiling slogan, 'politics stops at the water's edge,' led us to the erroneous conclusion that any action taken by the President abroad demanded bipartisan backing at home."

Priorities

EMERGENCE BELIEF 8. Surplus food should replace tax dollars in our foreign aid program.

EMERGENCE BELIEF 9. The United States cannot afford to subsidize the rest of the world indefinitely.

These beliefs—fundamental to Church throughout his career—are in some ways less a product of Church's own unique thinking than a reflection of Idaho political culture. In the 1956 election, Senator Welker (1956), too, complained about the foreign aid program, calling it "a 100 billion dollar spending spree, an extravagance in which the United States has been shoveling out billions of dollars each year." The other incumbent senator from Idaho, Henry C. Dworshak, had also hit continuously at foreign aid budgets. One long-time political observer in Idaho (Swisher, 1957) has commented that "Idahoans wince at the size of the federal budget and, after a long isolationist tradition, are critical of the dollar approach to foreign relations."

Control of Risks, Timing

EMERGENCE BELIEF 10. "The first principle of American foreign policy is to keep our guard" (Church, 1956b).

Throughout the campaign, Church criticized Welker for voting to cut Air Force funds and two divisions of ground troops. "I don't think in these dangerous times," said Church (1956b), "that we can afford to take such risks with the safety of our country." Although the phraseology was not used at this time by Church, he was obviously a "negotiate from strength" man at the beginning of his career.

Utility of Means

EMERGENCE BELIEF 11. Technical aid should be made available to the free people of the world.

EMERGENCE BELIEF 12. Trade expansion should replace massive foreign aid.

EMERGENCE BELIEF 13. The aspirations of colonial people for independence should be given greater recognition.

Foreign aid of the Point Four variety was, in the opinion of the youthful candidate, the best possible path to follow in international relations with poor countries: "Such aid will help them more, make them better friends of ours, and cost much less money" (Church, 1956d). This emphasis on technical aid, trade, and self-determination was all part and parcel of Church's underlying commitment to domestic priorities and nonintervention.

In summary, the young Boise lawyer spoke specifically during the 1956 campaign about the virtues of a foreign aid program based upon technical assistance, food packages, and improved trade relations. Each of these beliefs would be repeated virtually every single year henceforth in his Congressional career (each more frequently than any other beliefs)—though it was not until 1968 that he began to vote against the Foreign Aid Authorization Bill. Church (1971b) later observed that because of the technical assistance aspect of the Foreign Aid Bill, and in hopes the other features of the Bill would be "whittled down and ultimately displaced," he had "tarried too long as a supporter and indulged in too much wishful thinking." The origins of his favorable views on technical aid appear to have come from his admiration for the Truman Point Four successes. His devotion to agricultural aid probably stems from a confluence of his agricultural constituency and his recollections of the famine he witnessed in the Far East during the Second World War.

Also in 1956, Church declared that permitting independence and self-determination was the best approach for the United States to follow in the Third World, since the United States could not afford to subsidize the world anyway—a view commonly held in the fiscally conservative political culture of Idaho. He further noted that national security should be the first principle of U.S. policy. And, though the future was not predictable, he remained basically optimistic that efforts to preserve and promote peace could succeed even in a world characterized by instability and ferment.

Each of these positions remained with him, though by the 1960s he saw no need to maintain American troops in Europe and Korea at their current levels for the sake of U.S. security and he believed that long-range American security would be better served by negotiating from a basis of parity with our opponents rather than strictly from a basis of strength. However, three other major campaign positions—bipartisanship in foreign policy, a cohesive Western Alliance, and a staunch anti-Communism (maxims embraced by most American politicians at the time)—were modified substantially in the 1960s.

BELIEF MODIFICATIONS

During his first two years in the Senate, the young Idahoan applied himself to learning his new trade and, at least on foreign policy matters, was seldom heard. After this period of apprenticeship, three events in Church's life did more to refine, and sometimes reformulate, his views on foreign affairs than did any other events or experiences: (1) his admission to the Senate Foreign Relations Committee (SFRC) in 1959, (2) transformations in the Communist "bloc," and (3) the Vietnam War.

Naturally, the young Senator learned a great deal about U.S. foreign policy as a member of the SFRC, through hearings, travels abroad, and associating with senior members of the Committee and experienced staff aides. "The best post-graduate course I know of in the area of foreign relations," he observed in an interview, "is membership on the Foreign Relations Committee." The major influence of the Committee upon Church, however, seems to have been a reinforcement of his earlier beliefs regarding foreign aid, the Third World, and other international matters. Once on the Committee, Church found that he had several basic beliefs in common with certain other members. As he remarked in 1970:

> I have that kind of close connection with Stu Symington and Albert Gore and Claiborne Pell and the Chairman [Fulbright] and George Aiken and John Sherman Cooper and, to a considerable extent, Javits.[5] And this simply means that usually I can depend on them to side with me because of this commonality of attitude, and more often than not they can depend on me to side with them. But it's not done on the basis of "Well, you helped me yesterday on this particular point and I'm going to help you today in return." That's seldom the way the thing works . . . It's not that kind of *quid pro quo* at all.

Already inclined toward taking a new and critical look at U.S. foreign policy and already viewing Executive power with skepticism, the young Senator was no doubt drawn quickly into the group of SFRC activists seeking a greater role for the Senate in the making of American foreign policy. Within this group of older, more experienced senators, he acquired a new sophistication for his viewpoints; the basic form of his orientations, however, was visible prior to entry into the Committee.

As Thomson (1968) describes so well, the "fall of China," the Korean War, and the rhetoric of the McCarthy Era gave the impression in the 1950s of a Communist bloc on the march. Most American politicians reacted, in varying degrees, by viewing the Communist world as a highly dangerous threat. Only with the Sino-Soviet split and other manifestations of polycentric Communism in Eastern Europe and Asia did many American leaders re-evaluate the nature of this threat, exploring the possibilities for rapprochement. By the mid 1960s, Church was convinced that nationalism, not Communism, was the dominant political force in the world. "There is now an unraveling within the Communist world," he (Church, 1964) noted. "It isn't all one great Red dominion as it appears on the maps."

For Church, the Vietnam War was a turning point: a zero-sum view of Communism led only to catastrophic embroilments in areas far removed from American national interests. Reflecting upon his early Cold War rhetoric, Church said in 1970 that during his first years in the Senate he had never really studied questions of foreign policy: "I merely parodied these concepts." It was "only with our deep embroilment in that misbegotten war in Asia that I began to see where the excesses of this old notion had led us and what a catastrophic cause it had been."

---

[5]Four of the men listed here are no longer in the Senate. Gore (Democrat, Tennessee) was defeated in 1970; Cooper (Republican, Kentucky) retired from the Senate in 1972; Fulbright (Democrat, Arkansas) was defeated in 1974; and Symington (Democrat, Missouri) retired from the Senate in 1976.

The war in Vietnam did more than modify Church's earlier beliefs on international Communism; in a sense it was also the making of the Senator. It tempered his basic code, making it hard and strong. Because of the Vietnam experience he was no longer willing just to speak against parts of the aid program, but began to vote against the whole package. He no longer just occasionally spoke about the inability of the United States to support the Third World, but began to argue adamantly and regularly against U.S. interference in a world of revolutionary turmoil. He no longer just sporadically criticized the Executive Branch for monopolizing information, but began to compare the American Presidency to a Roman Caesardom demanding a restoration of the Congressional role in foreign affairs in order to prevent further Executive excesses like the covert escalation in Vietnam. He rejected bipartisanship in foreign policy as a misleading slogan designed to curtail legislative criticism of Presidential policy, and he began to see U.S. foreign policy in Asia as no less aggressive than the policies of our opponents.

The war also cast Church into the role of a leader in foreign affairs, as one of the original dissenters to speak against the Indochinese involvement. Since the majority of his constituents were "hawks" during the earlier stages of the Vietnam War, he had taken a courageous stand. Many who had thought of him before as merely the "boy orator" of the Senate began to view him in a new light.

This review of Church's operational code had as its primary objective an examination of the "fit" between the Senator's international beliefs in 1956 and later in 1972. The results are summarized in Table 4.1. Among the Senator's philosophical beliefs in the 1972 interview, his view of American opponents and allies represented the most significant change from 1956. The Vietnam War had made him highly skeptical of alliance politics that did not coincide directly with the vital interests of the United States; and the Vietnam War—plus the changing nature of international Communism—led him to consider favorably the possibilities for detente with our old adversaries.

Instrumental beliefs which deal with the selection of policy tactics and strategies are apt to be much more specific than philosophical beliefs, as illustrated by Church's 1972 interview responses. While antecedents for the 1972 instrumental beliefs can be seen as early as the "emergence phase" (for example, the criticism of U.S. aid policies), many of the 1972 instrumental beliefs appear to be a product of the Vietnam experience and the thawing of the Cold War. Some of the 1972 beliefs, such as the interest in multinational corporations and the stress on military parity for negotiations, have even shorter roots. Church's interest in multinational corporations grew out of a review of U.S.-Latin American policy in the late 1960s, though the interest is a basic part of the long-standing theme of nonintervention (in this case, nonintervention on behalf of U.S. private business investments). The "negotiate from parity" stand represents a sharp reversal from the "negotiate from strength" position that Church had long accepted. The modification seems related to progress in the strategic-arms-

Table 4.1.   Development of the Church International Code

International Beliefs from 1956	Emergence 1956	Apprenticeship 1956-1957	SFRC/Vietnam Era 1957-1972	September 1972
Philosophical				
World of ferment	Source	Sustained	Sustained	Sustained
Zero-sum Cold War	Source	Sustained	Modified	Modified
Free World bloc	Source	Sustained	Modified	Modified
Preservation of peace	Source	Sustained	Sustained	Sustained
Future not predictable	Source	No record	Sustained	Sustained
Basic optimism	Source	Sustained	Sustained	Sustained
Instrumental				
Bipartisanship	Source	Modified	Discarded	Discarded
Food instead of aid	Source	No record	Sustained	Sustained
U.S. funds limited	Source	No record	Sustained	Sustained
Keep up guard	Source	Sustained	Sustained	Sustained
Technical aid best	Source	Sustained	Sustained	Sustained
Trade instead of aid	Source	No record	Sustained	Sustained
Nonintervention	Source	No record	Sustained	Sustained

limitation talks (SALT) which Church attributes to the relative military equality between the United States and the Soviet Union in recent years.

Thus, ten of Church's thirteen basic international beliefs in 1956 have been sustained over time. The three beliefs modified or discarded, and the catalysts for change, are:

	Modified	Discarded
Old Outlook (1956)	Zero-sum Cold War; Free World bloc	Bipartisanship
Catalyst	Polycentrism; Vietnam War	Executive excesses in Vietnam
New Outlook (1972)	Modus vivendi with opponents; greater emphasis on national autonomy	Increased Congressional criticism of Executive

Could one have predicted much about the 1972 Church code back in 1956? The refinements and deepening convictions growing out of the Vietnam conflict, of course, could not have been anticipated, nor could the very important changes in beliefs about our allies and our opponents as a result of the thaw in the Cold War. Nevertheless, the beliefs most characteristic of the man—notably his criticism of foreign aid and foreign intervention—stood out in bold relief in his 1956 campaign and have been sustained ever since. No single time period will ever reveal the whole individual. However, the Church example suggests that the most fundamental dimensions of the operational code may develop early in the career and endure with a few (albeit sometimes important) exceptions. The exceptions for the Senator were, in most instances, the result of critical events in the international realm—especially the Vietnam War and changes in the Cold War.

The 1972 Code as Independent Variable

What is the relationship between the beliefs of the Senator in September, 1972, and his statements in the six months following? Practically all of Church's internationally oriented remarks and votes during this period fall into four categories, each growing out of his earlier beliefs: (1) opposition to further direct American involvement in Indochina, (2) continued support for Congressional efforts to reclaim lost Constitutional authority, (3) criticism of American private business interests affecting U.S. policy abroad, and (4) opposition to any

American foreign aid to North Vietnam and any U.S. unilateral aid to the rest of Indochina.

In an effort to guarantee that American involvement in Indochina would not be resumed solely by Executive order after only a temporary withdrawal, Senators Church and Case (Republican, New Jersey) introduced legislation in January, 1973, which would require Congressional approval for the re-entry of U.S. military forces into that part of the world. The bill (Church and Case, 1973, p. S1341) provided that "no U.S. Government funds may be used to finance the reinvolvement of U.S. military forces in hostilities in, over, from, or off the shores of North or South Vietnam, Laos, or Cambodia without prior, specific Congressional authorization." As the Nixon Administration continued to conduct bombing missions over Cambodia, Church helped formulate legislation specifically to deny further funding for these missions. Regarding the South Vietnamese, Church (1973c, p. S2598) concluded: "Having done all that one country can do for another, the future of South Vietnam must now be left to the Vietnamese. Whether they stand or fall is now up to them."

The proposed vigorous use of Congressional power over the purse to influence U.S. policy in Indochina was one manifestation of Church's attempts during these months to restore the Constitutional balance-of-power between Congress and the President. Another was his co-chairmanship of a new Senate Committee: the Special Committee on the Termination of the National Emergency. In January, 1973, this Committee began to study all emergency powers legislation now in force and, in particular, the question of terminating the national emergency declared by President Truman on December 16, 1950, which after more than two decades still remained in effect. In discussing this new Committee, Church (1973b, p. S1693) stressed the overriding need for Congress to recover its normal role in matters such as the power of the purse and the emergency powers: "Not only must Congress retrieve powers it gave away, it must hold them in a firmer grip."

The Senator's interest in the role of American private business in U.S. foreign policy surfaced initially in addresses during the late 1960s on U.S.-Latin American relations and emerged again with his concern about the influence which American global corporations exert on international affairs. Pointing out as he had in the past that nationalism is the dominant political force in the world, Church (1973a) observed that multinational corporations are in conflict with this nationalism. This conflict occurs, he noted, because the corporations often fail to recognize the constraints, frontiers, and traditional authority implicit in nationalism and because the corporations are frequently more powerful than their national host. Thus, the sovereignty of an individual nation becomes threatened. U.S. corporation interference in the affairs of other nations could have "a most profound impact on American foreign policy," the Senator (1973e) has stressed, referring especially to allegations concerning the role of the International Telephone and Telegraph Company (ITT) and the CIA in the 1970 Presidential elections in Chile.

Not a year in the Senator's political career has gone by without some expression of his concern about the U.S. foreign aid program; 1973 was no exception. Opposing U.S. aid to North Vietnam, Church suggested that if this Communist country needs help to rebuild "she should get it from her wartime allies, China and Russia." He (Church, 1973b; see, also, Church, 1973d, p. S4489) also opposed unilateral aid to other Indochinese nations: "After all, there are international agencies equipped to do this task. . . ." Unilateral aid, moreover, would make it much more likely for the U.S. "to become ensnared in the war again, should the fighting be resumed."

Each of these four major foreign policy positions was foreshadowed during the 1972 operational code interview—and with some depth in the case of Church's comments on the need to relax our influence in Indochina and to be alert to possible dangers that could result from U.S. corporate interests abroad. The *specific* positions on aid to North Vietnam, the Constitutional imbalance, and the damaging influence of U.S. private business in Latin America, however, were not (though the aid position was in accord with his 1956 statements on that subject). To anticipate these more specific beliefs required knowledge about the Senator's evolving beliefs during the Vietnam War era.

Church, for example, first voted against Administration foreign aid requests in 1968, as part of an effort to maintain the integrity of the dollar and to pressure the Government into reducing the U.S. role overseas. "All that Congress has left, with which to influence our course abroad, is the power of the purse," Church (1968, p. 3811) said. "If we shrink from using it, we abdicate our role, and obtain nothing in return but temporary postponement of the inevitable day when the ledger must be balanced on our international payments." Reiterating a theme that had been with him since the 1956 election, Church (1969b, p. 33671) urged in another address ". . . less reliance on external aid and more reliance on improved trade. . . ." On several occasions during the late 1960s, he (e.g., Church, 1967) recommended spending money at home instead of in Indochina: ". . . .our first duty is to put our own house in order. . . ."

The roots of Church's interest in questions regarding the Constitutional balance between Congress and the President reach back as far as his first year in the Senate, when he initially criticized excessive Executive secrecy. Again, however, it was the Vietnam War that intensified and focused his concern on this fundamental issue. As he recalled in a 1970 interview:

I didn't think we were going to go to war in Vietnam. That is, I didn't think we were going to take over the War with an American army. And Johnson was saying at the time: "We're not going to send American boys to fight wars that Asian boys should fight." He was out stumping the country and pressing the flesh and telling people what a peaceful guy he was and what a bomb thrower and saber rattler and hair trigger character Goldwater was. The whole issue [in the 1964 election] was that: responsibility—restraint in the use of power. And I was not only astonished, I was

mortified—and angered—when after the election this man began doing the
very things he led the people to believe he wouldn't do.

By 1970, the specter of a "new Caesardom" in the United States was a
frequent image in Church's speeches. He (Church, 1970b, p. 13563) warned
listeners that "the Roman Caesars did not spring full blown from the brow of
Zeus. Subtly and insidiously, they stole their powers away from an unsuspecting
Senate." Similarly, the authority of Congress was steadily declining while the
Executive gained more and more power. "It is not too much to say that the very
preservation of the Republic, itself, is the ultimate issue at stake," he stated.
"Therefore, it is the duty of Congress to redress the imbalance which has arisen
by reclaiming its authority under the Constitution."

Church first began to examine in depth the impact of U.S. private business
overseas when he became the Chairman of the SFRC Subcommittee on Western
Hemisphere Affairs in 1967. Reviewing U.S.-Latin American relations, Church
(1970a, p. 11214) declared: "What is necessary is that we first get off the back
of our neighbors. We must learn to hold ourselves at arm's length; we must come
to terms with the inevitable, letting changes take place without insisting upon
managing or manipulating them. We must begin to show some self-restraint."
Specifically, he (Church 1970c, p. 38853) urged the business community to: (1)
adopt fairer trade practices; (2) undertake joint business ventures in which Latin
Americans would share largely in both ownership and management; and (3) look
for investment opportunities which are more labor intensive to help alleviate
unemployment in South America. The next year, Church (1971b) once more
criticized the U.S. aid program to Latin America, saying it was "designed
primarily to serve private business interests at the expense of the American
people. In far too many countries, as in the case of Brazil, we poured in our aid
money for one overriding purpose, the stabilization of the economy in order to
furnish American capital with a 'favorable climate for investments.' "

Armed with this additional background information on Church's evolving
beliefs, each of the four major positions which he took in the period between
September 1972 and April 1973 is more "predictable" in the sense that each is
a continuation of beliefs that were firmly a part of the Senator's thinking. We
could not have predicted, of course, when and to what degree Church would
address himself to such questions as multinational corporations or foreign aid to
North Vietnam; but once these questions arose, his responses were entirely
consistent with beliefs he had been expressing and refining for years. Thus, for
an understanding of these four issue positions, the more inclusive examination of
Church's beliefs over time was far more useful than examining those of the 1956
period alone or the operational code interview immediately preceding the
position-taking. It should be stressed, nevertheless, that the speeches of the 1956
period did anticipate the future antipathy toward overseas intervention and
massive financial foreign aid and that the 1972 interview did reveal the broad

underlying roots of each specific action in the six months following the interview. Of course, a few months is too brief a period to permit confident judgments, but the continuation of "expected" behavior by the subject throughout this period does encourage further investigation of the operational code as a predictive device.

Conclusions

The two guiding hypotheses of this research were verified in the main, though both required modification in light of the findings. First, the 1972 code as a dependent variable *was* reflected in basic form in Church's beliefs during the period of "emergence," notably his consistent antipathy toward most forms of U.S. foreign aid and intervention. A more complete and refined understanding of his midcareer code required, however, knowledge of important subsequent events which shaped his beliefs, especially: (1) the changing nature of international Communism, (2) the Vietnam War, and (3) his Senate Foreign Relations Committee experiences. The most significant change brought about by these events was a modification of the Senator's "image of the opponents" from stark negativism to a mood of conciliation. Second, the 1972 code as an independent variable *did* foreshadow Church's subsequent beliefs from October 1972 to April 1973. Some positions, however, such as the Senator's opposition to foreign aid for North Vietnam, were best anticipated or "predicted" by an understanding of his more complete, evolving record over the years rather than reliance on a single "snapshot" interview or examination of a single period. With this more comprehensive understanding of his code, the post-1972 code responses were predictable in a broad sense. The basic conclusions can be stated simply: (1) noninterventionism, the quintessential feature of Church's 1972 international operational code, was also the keystone of his code during the "emergence" period; (2) the initial source of these noninterventionist beliefs seems to have been primarily the influence of the Idaho political culture—especially the traditional criticism of profligate Government spending; and (3) the few modifications of the Senator's code have resulted chiefly from far-reaching events in the international realm, like the Vietnam War.

Virtually all of Church's beliefs can be subsumed under the concept of nonintervention. For example, his effort to restore the role of Congress in foreign affairs is motivated in large part by a desire to prevent further U.S. interference overseas (unless the national security is at stake); his criticism of U.S. business interests abroad stems from his concern about intervention via this route; his hostility toward foreign aid comes not only from his Idaho fiscal conservatism but from a realization that aid can lead to deep military involvement. Throughout his career Church (e.g., 1969a) has emphasized that "nationalism—rather than preference of the great powers—is the engine of change in modern history," cautioning against overseas involvement except when the national security of the U.S. is under "clear and present danger." This noninterventionist stance has appeared regularly throughout his life: in his schoolboy admiration (see Church, 1965) for the career of Idaho Senator William E. Borah, a popular noninterventionist; in criticism of British imperialism as an army lieutenant (in a letter to his parents dated 2 August 1945, Kumming, China); in his 1956 campaign speeches urging global self-determination; and in annual denouncements of U.S. interference abroad since he became a member of the Senate Foreign Relations Committee in 1959. One of the Senator's favorite quotations (see Church, 1971a, p. 12668) is from John Bright, the nineteenth-century English critic of empire, on the disastrous Crimean campaign:

> I believe, if this country, 70 years ago, had adopted the principle of nonintervention in every case where her interests were not directly and obviously assailed, that she would have been saved from much of the pauperism and brutal crimes by which our Government and people have alike been disgraced. This country might have been a garden, every dwelling might have been of marble, and every person who tread its soil might have been sufficiently educated.

Yet it would be a mistake to earmark Church as an isolationist; instead, he is more accurately viewed as a selective interventionist, willing to make those international commitments necessary to enhance the safety of the American people and to preserve the American form of government. While Church does believe these goals are best served by meeting the domestic needs of the nation, he also accepts the usefulness of certain international political commitments, such as helping to maintain a strong and free Western Europe.

Not all the operational code dimensions are equally valuable for understanding the political beliefs of Senator Church. Philosophically his "image of opponents and allies" and, instrumentally, his views on "utility of means" and "priorities" are most important. These dimensions, along with "selection of goals" (refer to Figure 4.3), may prove to be particularly insightful when those interested in the operational code approach begin to contrast the belief systems of various political figures.

The precise interconnections among the code dimensions have yet to be traced; data on more individuals will be required to map out these relationships with any degree of confidence. In the Church case, an emphasis on alliance politics seemed to go hand in hand with a zero-sum perception of the opponent. Moreover, an emphasis on domestic priorities was linked to a "utility of means" based upon noninterventionism. Ties such as these need to be explored in greater detail. Furthermore, considerable work remains to be done in improving conceptual clarity, in integrating those theoretical and empirical contributions made thus far, and in relating this approach to other theories on leadership behavior.

Despite the need to refine the operational code framework, the overall consistency and durability of Church's political beliefs suggest the usefulness of this approach for helping to predict the most likely reactions of this legislator to a wide range of future international issues.

CHAPTER 5

The Leader Behavior of United States Senators: An Example of the Use of Informants*

*Ralph M. Stogdill,
Omar S. Goode, and
David R. Day*

Editor's Introduction

One set of astute political observers who have been largely ignored in political leadership research are the members of a political leader's staff. Here are individuals who observe each day what a particular political leader does and how he does it. They are sensitive to what pleases and displeases their "boss," to his beliefs, his decision-making style, and his ways of interacting with others. The present chapter by Stogdill, Goode, and Day uses U.S. senators' staff members to learn about the leader behavior of U.S. senators. The researchers were interested in finding out which of some nine leader behaviors characterized senators and in comparing the leader behavior of senators to such behavior for other types of leaders—corporation presidents, college presidents, and union

*Portions of this chapter appeared in *The Journal of Psychology,* 1963, 56, 3-8, and are reprinted with permission of The Journal Press.

presidents. To do this, members of senators' staffs were asked to fill out a questionnaire describing the leader behavior of their bosses.

The technique which Stogdill and his associates employ we have called informant observation. Informant observation involves asking persons who know a political leader well, either through personal contact or concentrated study, to answer some questions about him. This type of observation is a stock tool of news reporters who often find informants helpful in getting a story. Oral history projects on political leaders like that on John F. Kennedy at the Kennedy Library are also examples of the use of informants. The researcher interested in this technique needs to consider several issues before employing informants in this study. First, does his research focus on behaviors which can be observed? Informants can only report with confidence what they can perceive. Second, are informants more accessible and likely to be more cooperative than the political leader himself? Given the time constraints on some political leaders, informants may be a more realistic alternative than trying to see the political leader. Finally, consider the effect on the results of the research of informants who like (as opposed to dislike) the political leader and of informants who have been associated with the political leader for a short time (as opposed to a long time).

Let us examine the present chapter to see how Stogdill and his associates dealt with these queries in planning their research. Stogdill et al. were interested in studying behaviors which could be observed. Their research focused on the kinds of behaviors which a senator uses to insure that he stays in office. Assuming that senators would not take the time to fill out their questionnaire, particularly when it arrived by mail, Stogdill, Goode, and Day decided to get the information they wanted from informants. Moreover, in this case the behavior under investigation was probably more easily described by an observer than by the political leader, i.e., what is it that the senator does to gain and keep voter support. By asking the senators to select the informants, Stogdill et al. used informants who were likely to be favorably disposed toward the senators. Thus, where possible in the questionnaire they probably described the senator as having what appeared to them as "good" leader behaviors. We know little about the informants' experience in observing the senator as Stogdill et al. did not ascertain this information. One might expect, however, a more stereotyped set of responses the less experience the informant has had in observing and interacting with the senator.

In addition to illustrating a certain method, the present chapter contains information on who becomes a political leader. Stogdill, Goode, and Day suggest the kinds of behaviors involved in becoming and remaining a senator. Their research characterizes the kinds of leader behaviors important to a senator vis-à-vis his constituents. Carrying their research one step further, we can ask if persons exhibiting these leader behaviors are more likely to become candidates for the Senate and, in turn, to be elected to the Senate. Moreover, what other personal characteristics relate to these leader behaviors; for example, what characteristics relate to persuasiveness? By building on previous research on these leader behaviors in the social sciences, we can suggest sets of personal characteristics which may relate to being a U.S. senator.

Stogdill, the senior author, is a professor of management science at Ohio State University. His long-term interest in the study of leadership culminated recently in *The Handbook of Leadership* (Stogdill, 1974). Goode is a programmer in administrative systems development at Ohio State University. Day, a psychologist, teaches at Sangamon State University in Illinois.

RECENT EMPIRICAL RESEARCH on leadership has been concerned primarily with studies of small groups and such formally structured organizations as business firms, military organizations, and school systems. Comparatively less empircal research effort has been devoted to another important type of leadership in our society—that of the political leader who is elected by a large number of widely dispersed and loosely organized individuals.

Whereas much of the behavior of the executive is concerned with the structure and function of the organization that maintains and supports his leadership, the political leader must appeal directly to the people whose votes he desires. The latter can depend only to a limited degree upon his party organization. His success in gaining votes is likely to be based upon his persuasiveness and visible representation of the interests of his followers rather than upon behaviors that maintain an effectively functioning formal organization.

The research reported in this chapter was designed to determine the perceived leader behavior of outstanding political leaders. In accordance with the suppositions advanced in the preceding paragraph, we hypothesized that high-ranking political leaders, such as United States senators, will be described by informants as high in persuasiveness and representation of the interests of their followers.

THE SAMPLE

Two copies of the Leader Behavior Description Questionnaire (described later) were mailed to each senator in the United States Senate, with the request that the questionnaires be given to "two persons who know you well enough to describe you accurately as a political leader in the state that you represent." The describer was asked to identify neither himself nor the senator whom he described. No follow-up was used to increase the number of replies.

Forty-four usable questionnaires were returned. This number represents 44 descriptions, not necessarily 44 senators. In regard to political party, 15 questionnaires were checked as descriptions of Republicans, and 29 as descriptions of Democrats. Although it cannot be stated that the sample is strictly representative of the total population of U.S. senators, the number of returns is large enough for meaningful analysis.

THE QUESTIONNAIRE

The Leader Behavior Description Questionnaire (LBDQ) was developed by the Ohio State Leadership Studies Staff (see Stogdill and Coons, 1957) to describe different aspects of leader behavior. What does a leader do while acting as a leader of a group or organization? The particular version of the LBDQ used in this study was developed by the authors (Stogdill, Goode, and Day, 1962). It contained 65 items, divided among nine subscales or possible patterns of leadership behavior as follows:

1. *Representation*—speaks and acts as the representative of the group (5 items).
2. *Tolerance of Uncertainty*—is able to tolerate uncertainty and postponement without anxiety or upset (8 items).
3. *Persuasiveness*—uses persuasion and argument effectively; exhibits strong convictions (10 items).
4. *Initiation of Structure*—clearly defines own role, and lets followers know what is expected (10 items).
5. *Tolerance of Freedom of Action*—allows followers scope for initiative, decision, and action (5 items).
6. *Role Retention*—actively exercises the leadership role rather than surrendering leadership to others (7 items).
7. *Production Emphasis*—applies pressure for productive output (5 items).
8. *Consideration*—regards the comfort, well-being, status, and contributions of followers (10 items).
9. *Demand Reconciliation*—reconciles conflicting organizational demands and reduces disorder to system (5 items).

The person asked to describe the leader reacted to each item in the LBDQ by circling one of five possible responses: always, often, occasionally, seldom, never. In scoring the questionnaire, each item received a score value that ranged from five to one (or one to five for negatively stated items), as shown in the following examples.

He is a very persuasive talker:
Always (5) Often (4) Occasionally (3) Seldom (2) Never (1)
He fails to take necessary action:
Always (1) Often (2) Occasionally (3) Seldom (4) Never (5)

The score for each subscale consisted of the sum of the values received on the items in the subscale.

METHOD OF ANALYSIS

The scores on the nine subscales describing the senators' leader behavior were intercorrelated and factor analyzed, using the method of principal factors. Due to the small number of subscales, it was decided to continue the analysis until all residual entries were reduced to zero. All communalities are necessarily 1.00. The orthogonal factors were rotated by the varimax method. The matrix of intercorrelations, means, standard deviations, and reliability coefficients are shown in Table 5.1.

As hypothesized, the highest corrected mean score in Table 5.1 is obtained for Persuasiveness (42.5). However, the corrected mean for Representation (41.4) is the same as, not higher than, the means for Role Retention and Demand Reconciliation. The lowest average score (35.3) is on Tolerance of Uncertainty. The means do not differ to a statistically significant degree.

RESULTS

The rotated factor loadings are shown in Table 5.2. Inspection of this table indicates that several subscales have appreciable loadings on Factor I. Role Rentantion has a loading of .89 and Demand Reconciliation a loading of .51. Other subscales weighted on this factor are Representation (.30), Initiation of Structure (.27), and Consideration (.32). This factor describes a dimension of behavior that is characterized by actively assuming a role of leader, controlling conflicting demands, clearly defining role expectations, and being willing to represent and to consider the interests of followers. The combination of Role Retention, Demand Reconciliation, and Initiation of Structure suggests that the leadership role is under active and firm control. The factor is identified as *Control of the Leadership Position.*

On Factor II, Production Emphasis shows a loading of .97 and Initiation of Structure a loading of .58. Here, pushing for production is associated with the clarification of role expectations. The factor appears to merit the title *Facilitation of Productive Outcomes.*

Factor III shows a loading of .93 on Tolerance of Uncertainty. Also loaded on this factor are Consideration (.39) and Demand Reconciliation (.47). Tolerance of uncertainty and postponement is associated with the ability to reconcile conflicting elements for one's group and with consideration of the welfare of one's followers. The factor is identified as *Reconciling Tolerance of Uncertainty.*

Factor IV appears with loadings of .95 on Persuasiveness and .38 on Representation of the follower group. This factor may be regarded as a measure of *Follower-Oriented Persuasiveness.*

Factor V, with loadings of .97 on Tolerance of Freedom of Action and .31 on Consideration of the interests of one's followers, is essentially descriptive of *Considerate Tolerance of Follower Freedom of Action.*

Factor VI has a loading of .80 on Representation. Also loaded on this factor are Initiation of Structure (.29), Role Retention (.24), Consideration (.26), and

Table 5.1.   Intercorrelations Among Nine Subscales

Subscale	1	2	3	4	5	6	7	8	9
1. Representation	—								
2. Tolerance of Uncertainty	.30	—							
3. Persuasiveness	.63	.25	—						
4. Initiation of Structure	.63	.21	.30	—					
5. Tolerance of Freedom of Action	.27	.39	.24	.22	—				
6. Role Retention	.64	.35	.39	.59	.16	—			
7. Production Emphasis	.34	-.21	.25	.68	-.04	.32	—		
8. Consideration	.63	.62	.40	.53	.50	.62	.20	—	
9. Demand Reconciliation	.44	.64	.23	.44	.29	.72	.18	.77	—
Mean	20.7	23.2	42.5	38.8	18.3	28.8	20.6	41.1	20.7
Standard deviation	2.5	6.1	4.6	5.5	3.1	4.0	2.6	5.9	3.5
Reliability	.80	.83	.82	.72	.64	.65	.38	.85	.81
Mean (10 items*)	41.4	35.3	42.5	38.8	36.6	41.4	41.2	41.1	41.4

*Estimated mean for 10 items to correct for unequal numbers of items in the subscales.

Table 5.2. Rotated Factor Loadings

Subscale	I	II	III	IV	Factor V	VI	VII	VIII	IX	Commonality h²
Representation	.30	.19	.11	.38	.13	.80	.17	.18	.07	1.00
Tolerance of Uncertainty	.15	-.14	.93	.12	.20	.09	.14	.05	.11	1.00
Persuasiveness	.13	.11	.09	.95	.11	.21	.07	.04	.03	1.00
Initiation of Structure	.27	.58	.14	.08	.12	.29	.13	.67	.06	1.00
Tolerance of Freedom of Action	.05	-.01	.15	.09	.97	.07	.11	.04	.06	1.00
Role Retention	.89	.18	.17	.17	.03	.24	.14	.15	.13	1.00
Production Emphasis	.12	.97	-.13	.12	-.04	.09	.05	.10	.03	1.00
Consideration	.32	.13	.39	.17	.31	.26	.69	.13	.21	1.00
Demand Reconciliation	.51	.14	.47	.03	.11	.11	.29	.06	.63	1.00
Fractional Contribution of Variance	.152	.156	.148	.129	.126	.102	.074	.060	.053	1.00

Persuasiveness (.21). This factor appears to merit the title *Active Representation of Followers*.

In Factor VII, Consideration exhibits a loading of .69 and Demand Reconciliation a loading of .29. Here, consideration of the welfare of followers is associated with reconciliation of conflicting demands. This factor is identified as *Reconciling in Favor of Consideration*.

Factor VIII is a specific factor, with a loading of .67 on *Initiation of Structure*.

Factor IX, with loadings of .63 on Demand Reconciliation and .21 on Consideration, is identified as *Reconciliation of Conflicting Demands*.

DISCUSSION

As hypothesized, U.S. senators are described by informants as high in persuasiveness. We did not anticipate that Control of the Leadership Position would emerge as a strongly defined factor, but a bit of reflection suggests that this is a reasonable finding. The elected political leader cannot depend upon a formal organization structure for the maintenance of his position of leadership. He can accomplish this only through an active and continuous assumption of the leadership role.

The LBDQ has also been used to collect descriptions from informants on the leader behavior of corporation presidents (Stogdill, Goode, and Day, 1963), presidents of international labor unions (Stogdill, Goode, and Day, 1964), as well as college and university presidents (Stogdill, Goode, and Day, 1965). When the scores on the subscales for these leaders are interrelated and factor analyzed, similar factors emerge to those found in the present study with senators.[1] In other words, no factor emerges which clearly differentiates political leaders from other types of leaders. The factors appear to describe high level leaders in general.

Even though the factors do not differ across the four kinds of leaders, there are, however, some differences in emphasis. Since, in general, the factors for each kind of leader tend to be strongly dominated by a single subscale, it is possible to compare the factor loadings for these subscales to learn more about the leadership behavior of these leaders. Table 5.3 shows the factor loadings—or correlations of the variables with the factors—by factor for the dominant subscales by kind of leader. Two of the behaviors seem of about equal relevance to all four kinds of leaders. These two behaviors are emphasis on production or output (Production Emphasis subscale) and an ability to tolerate uncertainty and postponement without anxiety (Tolerance of Uncertainty subscale). Three of the behaviors are more characteristic of corporation presidents, union presidents, and college presidents than of senators. These behaviors involve acting as a representative of a group (Representation subscale), consideration of followers (Consideration subscale), and reconciliation of conflicting organizational de-

---

[1]For a more detailed discussion of these factors across the four types of leaders, see Stogdill (1974, pp. 142-155).

mands (Demand Reconciliation subscale). Persuasiveness appears to be more descriptive of senators and corporation presidents than union presidents or college presidents. Tolerance of Freedom of Action for followers is more descriptive of senators and union presidents than of corporation presidents or college presidents. Thus, Table 5.3 suggests some cross-institutional similarities and differences in leadership behavior.

In conclusion, we would like to raise some of the problems in doing research of this nature. Because the LBDQ requires that informants be knowledgeable about a leader's leadership behavior, unless the researcher is a close associate of the leader in question, he needs the leader's cooperation in designating informants. Political leaders, however, unlike business executives and educational administrators, seem reluctant to participate in behaviorally oriented research. One incident which occurred in connection with the present study illustrates some of the difficulties in gaining the cooperation of political leaders. When the LBDQ was mailed to the members of the United States Senate, a copy was brought to the attention of a Washington journalist (Dixon, 1961) who ridiculed the project in his syndicated column. The journalist stated that "every senator I interviewed admitted, on being pinned down that he either filed the questionnaire in his wastebasket or turned it over to his staff to fill out." Several items from the questionnaire were quoted and humorous answers fabricated for them, purportedly by members of the senators' staffs. It would appear that at least one senator or recipient of the questionnaire had hoped to sabotage the

Table 5.3.   Factor Loadings for Dominant Subscales by Kind of Leader

| Factor[a] | Dominant Subscale | Kind of Leader | | | |
		Senator	Corporation President	Union President	College President
I	Role Retention	.89	.93	.81	.95
II	Production Emphasis	.97	.95	.94	.91
III	Tolerance of Uncertainty	.93	.95	.94	.94
IV	Persuasiveness	.95	.90	.74	.77
V	Tolerance of Freedom of Action	.97	.89	.97	.89
VI	Representation	.80	.94	.92	.92
VII	Consideration	.69	.94	.90	.86
VIII	Initiation of Structure	.67	.71	.71	.82
IX	Demand Reconciliation	.63	.83	.76	—[b]

[a]See Table 5.2 for factor loadings of other subscales on each factor.

[b]This subscale was not administered to the college president sample.

study, even though other senators wrote the authors to express their interest in the research and their willingness to cooperate.

As the present results suggest, the LBDQ should provide a useful tool for studying political leaders. It ranks relatively low in stress value when compared to tests of personality. The purpose of the LBDQ is to provide an instrument which enables followers to describe the behavior of leaders as they see it. A leader should suffer little discomfort or embarrassment from having his behavior described by an informant, particularly if he can designate who the informant is.

Perhaps the problem lies not in the nature of the observational method being employed, but rather in the reluctance of many political leaders to submit themselves to scientific observation and evaluation. In view of the influence that political leaders exert upon the lives of men, it would appear that the scientist is under some obligation to develop effective methods for studying their behavior. But the best research techniques that can be devised will yield less than the needed amount of information unless the cooperation of the leaders themselves can be obtained. Such cooperation can only be contingent on convincing assurances that participation in research will not have any adverse effect on the leader's image, reputation, or career.

One possible method of reducing apprehension might be to include with any request for cooperation a brief abstract of reports of research in which similar methods have been used with other samples of subjects. Still more effective might be two or three letters from well-known leaders who have participated in the research. Each letter could state that the research was conducted in such a manner that neither the writer nor his associates were adversely affected by it.

Probably the most effective method of gaining information about the political leader's behavior would be for more researchers to become participant observers in the political process to act as the informants in describing what a political leader does. Barring many such opportunities, we could try to capitalize on the experiences of political interns, asking them to describe the leader behavior of the politicians with whom they worked using a tool like the LBDQ.

In the present study we have reported some initial data on the leader behavior of senators and compared these data with the leader behaviors of four other types of leaders. Future tasks involve relating the leader behaviors to measures of group performance, of follower satisfaction, of leadership stability, and of social power. Neither the items nor the factorially derived subscales of the LBDQ are of much significance standing alone. Only when the relationships from these future tasks are known do we gain insight into the effects of such leader behaviors and, in turn, their importance.

CHAPTER 6

The Q-Sort and the Study of Political Personality*

Thomas W. Milburn

Editor's Introduction

The present chapter, like the previous one, employs informant observation. Instead of members of a political leader's staff, however, in the present chapter Milburn uses academic political specialists as his informants. Here is another group of potential informants who have been underutilized by researchers interested in studying political leaders. Many political scientists, in particular, spend their professional careers as area specialists, Kremlinologists, Congress "watchers," academic advisors to political units, urban experts, and so on. They follow closely changes in political leaders and the behavior of political leaders while in office. In some cases they interact with the political leader.

Milburn's chapter suggests a technique—the Q-sort—to aid in getting information on political leaders from these experts. In the Q-sort, individuals are asked to describe either themselves or another person by sorting a series of descriptive statements into categories running from most to least characteristic. The statements describe the subject's personal characteristics. As Cronbach (1953) has observed, the Q-sort provides a way of obtaining a qualitative description of an individual in quantifiable form. In effect, the Q-sort gives the researcher a tool by which to debrief the expert.

*I am indebted to my wife, JoAnne F. Milburn, for collecting some of the judgments and analyzing some of the data included in the studies described here.

As we noted in our introduction to the previous chapter, the researcher using informant observation must consider several issues in pursuing this technique. Two of the issues mentioned there concerned the effects that (1) informants' liking or disliking of the political leader and (2) their knowledge about the political leader had on their observations. Milburn in the present chapter seeks to examine how these two variables affect the results of experts' Q-sorts. Moreover, Milburn raises some further issues for the researcher to consider. Does the informant have a preconceived notion of a political leader's personal characteristics which is likely to influence his report on a specific leader? If the informant is asked to describe a political leader in another culture, does he have any cultural biases which might affect his description? It is possible to gain some information on these potential biases by having informants describe the typical political leader or, at the least, several political leaders. By comparing the description of the specific leader with the stereotyped image of a political leader or the description of another leader, the researcher can learn something about how these biases are affecting the data.

The particular Q-sort that Milburn employs, the California Q-set, was formulated to describe an individual's personal characteristics. What is the person like? Which traits are most and least characteristic of him (her)? Recently another type of Q-sort has been developed to use in the study of political leadership (see Paige, 1966). This Q-sort, the Political Leadership Q-set, focuses on the tasks which characterize a particular political role. What must the political leader do in performing his role? One can conceive of merging the information from these two types of Q-sorts to examine the match between the personal characteristics of a political leader and the tasks that his role demands. Moreover, it would be interesting to study how the political behavior of leaders differs when personal characteristics match role demands as opposed to when there is a mismatch between personal characteristics and role demands.

Milburn is a professor of psychology and public policy at the Mershon Center, Ohio State University. He has had a long-standing interest in the discovery of ways of assessing political leaders which do not involve the leader's cooperation. When he was director of Project Michelson for the Naval Ordnance Test Station in China Lake, California, Milburn participated in and supported research aimed at finding such techniques. He is currently involved in a propositional inventory of research on leadership in the social sciences.

THE STUDY OF POLITICAL LEADERS by psychological means can prove difficult. Political leaders of interest often are unavailable or at least unwilling to serve as subjects of study while they are in power. Because students of personality have primarily focused on cooperative subjects (for example, experimental subjects in a laboratory, patients and clients, survey respondents), few techniques have been developed for doing research on the reluctant subject. The present chapter describes one such technique—the Q-sort—and illustrates its use in studying political leaders.

The Q-sort technique was first developed by Stephenson (1953). It involves making a set of judgments concerning the applicability of a series of descriptive statements to a particular subject. The statements refer to individual characteristics, for example, "is a talkative individual," "is basically anxious," "is cheerful," "is verbally fluent." The purpose of the Q-sort is to aid the researcher in discovering what attributes are most and least characteristic of a person. Accordingly, the judge is asked to sort the descriptive statements into a series of categories ranging from most to least characteristic of the subject. The statements are sorted into the categories so as to form a normal distribution—the fewest statements fall into the most and least characteristic categories.

The Q-sort technique differs from most other methods of assessing personality in several important ways. In the first place, its results are multivariate. The Q-sort examines multiple individual variables at the same time. Many psychologists feel that the ideal research strategy for producing a *science* of personality is to work with one variable at a time, establishing its validity, before working with others (e.g., see McClelland, 1961). Multivariate approaches in general are quite infrequent. The Q-sort also emphasizes the structure of the personality. In other words, what are the relations among the personality variables? Knowing the relations among personality variables provides the researcher with valuable information about a person. For example, someone who values achieving and values intellectual activity will probably try to achieve in intellectual rather than in business areas; whereas the opposite is probably true of someone who values achieving but does not value intellectual activity.

The particular Q-sort which was used in the research to be reported in this chapter is the California Q-set (CQ-set) developed by Block (1961). The CQ-set contains 100 statements which a judge is asked to sort into nine categories from most to least characteristic of a specific subject with 5, 8, 12, 16, 18, 16, 12, 8, and 5 statements falling into the nine categories. The CQ-set statements were designed to: (1) reflect no theoretical orientation, (2) suggest a continuum rather than have either-or implications, (3) express single psychological characteristics, (4) be conceptually independent from other items, and (5) be as neutral and unevaluative as possible (see Block, 1961, pp. 52-55).

To examine the usefulness of the Q-sort technique with political leaders, several U.S. political experts on the Soviet Union were asked to use the CQ-set to describe a Soviet political leader, Nikita Khrushchev. The results of the Khrushchev study raised some questions about the validity of the Q-sort as a technique for studying political leaders, particularly at a distance. These questions were explored by examining CQ-set sorts for two local level political leaders on whom much psychological data had already been collected.

Study of Khrushchev

Some nine U.S. Soviet experts consented to use the CQ-set statements to describe Khrushchev. While not one of these experts knew Khrushchev intimately, all had written articles about him, two had published scholarly biographies on him, and several had interviewed him at length. An attempt to include among the expert judges the full ideological spectrum on the Soviet Union from left to right met with little success. The Soviet experts whom we invited to participate who were clearly left- and right-wingers expressed suspicion of the project and refused to cooperate. As a result, the experts who participated varied from ideological "middle-of-the-roaders" to somewhat right of center.

Each expert sorted the 100 statements in the CQ-set by himself or herself, following some instruction in how to do a Q-sort. There was no collaboration among the experts either preceding or during their Q-sorts. By intercorrelating the experts' Q-sorts we can ascertain the extent of agreement among these individuals on Khrushchev's personality. The intercorrelations are presented in Table 6.1. The average intercorrelation among the experts is .48. An examination of Table 6.1 suggests that the major disagreements among the experts were with one person, labeled "H" in the table. This expert, a psychologist, had completed a study of Khrushchev's thought processes just prior to his participation in the present research, and may have been overly influenced by his results in sorting the CQ-items. At least, it appears his data base on Khrushchev differed from that of the other experts. Without "H's" Q-sort data, the average intercorrelation among the experts is .56.

How did the experts describe Khrushchev? If we assign each of the nine categories into which the CQ-items were sorted a number (one for least characteristic or most uncharacteristic to nine for most characteristic), a composite picture of Khrushchev can be developed. By averaging the experts' category

Table 6.1. Intercorrelations among Expert Q-Sorts of Khrushchev

Expert	A	B	C	D	E	F	G	H	I
A	—								
B	.55	—							
C	.52	.59	—						
D	.51	.62	.64	—					
E	.15	.62	.69	.70	—				
F	.63	.58	.49	.62	.53	—			
G	.59	.68	.60	.48	.58	.61	—		
H	.06	.24	.28	.35	.24	.16	.16	—	
I	.52	.49	.58	.54	.59	.44	.52	.14	—

scores for each of the 100 CQ-items, we can ascertain which items were judged as most and least characteristic of Khrushchev across the nine experts. The five items seen as most characteristic and uncharacteristic of Khrushchev as well as the eight items seen as quite characteristic and uncharacteristic of him appear in Table 6.2. The reliability of the composite for Khrushchev using the Spearman-

Table 6.2.   **CQ-Set Items Perceived by Nine Experts as Highly Characteristic and Uncharacteristic of Khrushchev**

Q-Category		CQ-Item	Average Score
Most characteristic (5 items)	91.	Is power-oriented; values power in self and others.	8.8
	18.	Initiates humor.	8.4
	52.	*Behaves* in an assertive fashion.	8.2
	71.	Has high aspiration level for self.	8.0
	98.	Is verbally fluent; can express ideas well.	7.8
Quite characteristic (8 items)	54.	Emphasizes being with others; gregarious.	7.8*
	65.	Characteristically pushes and tries to stretch limits; sees what he can get away with.	7.8
	1.	Is critical, skeptical, not easily impressed.	7.4
	4.	Is a talkative individual.	7.4
	24.	Prides self on being "objective," rational.	7.4
	57.	Is an interesting, arresting person.	7.4
	99.	Is self-dramatizing; histrionic.	7.2
	83.	Able to see to the heart of important problems.	7.0
Quite uncharacteristic (8 items)	79.	Tends to ruminate and have persistent, preoccupying thoughts.	3.2
	6.	Is fastidious.	3.0
	42.	Reluctant to commit self to any definite course of action; tends to delay or avoid action.	3.0
	45.	Has a brittle ego-defense system; has a small reserve of integration; would be disorganized and maladaptive when under stress or trauma.	3.0

Table 6.2   (Continued)

Q-Category		CQ-Item	Average Score
	9.	Is uncomfortable with uncertainty and complexities.	2.8
	78.	Feels cheated and victimized by life; self-pitying.	2.8
	100.	Does not vary roles; relates to everyone in the same way.	2.8
	19.	Seeks reassurance from others.	2.6
Most uncharacteristic (5 items)	22.	Feels a lack of personal meaning in life.	2.6
	30.	Gives up and withdraws where possible in the face of frustration and adversity.	2.0
	97.	Is emotionally bland; has flattened affect.	2.0
	14.	*Genuinely* submissive; accepts domination comfortably.	1.8
	55.	Is self-defeating.	1.8

*When the averages for items were tied where the break in the categories of the composite should have occurred, the items were randomly assigned to higher and lower categories.

Brown prophecy formula (based on average inter-judge correlation and number of judges) is .89.

The composite picture of Khrushchev in Table 6.2 represents how the nine American experts on the Soviet Union described Khrushchev's personality. At this point, the reader might ask whether the composite in Table 6.2 would differ for other Soviet political leaders? In other words, are we getting the experts' stereotyped description of the typical Russian political leader or can these experts differentiate Khrushchev from other Soviet political leaders? Two of the experts (A and B in Table 6.1) in the present study were generous enough to do Q-sorts on Lenin and Stalin as well as Khrushchev. The intercorrelations among the Q-sorts of these two experts for the three Russian political leaders are presented in Table 6.3. The results in Table 6.3 suggest that although there are some parallels between these experts' descriptions of the three Soviet political leaders, the Q-sorts do not overlap enough to be describing a single type of individual. The experts seem able to discriminate among the three political leaders.

In some sense, this study of Khrushchev raises more questions than it answers. For example, the informants or experts describing Khrushchev here were all Americans bearing the inescapable intellectual and ideological trappings of American culture. How would the Q-sorts of Khrushchev by East Europeans or Asiatics differ from the present composite? Is the lack of perfect intercorrelations among the experts' Q-sorts of Khrushchev the result of differences in how well the experts liked Khrushchev or how well they knew him? The second study to be reported in this chapter was undertaken to try to examine these issues. It focused on local political leaders for whom we already had much psychological data (e.g., MMPI scores, in-depth interviews).

Study of Local Political Leaders

The two local political leaders whom we studied we will refer to as "Smith" and "Brown." In addition to being community leaders, Smith was a physicist-inventor with many patents to his credit while Brown was director of a large organization with a budget of well over a hundred million dollars a year. Both men did a self Q-sort and completed a number of psychological tests; they also permitted themselves to be interviewed at length.

Six raters or judges were employed to describe the two local political leaders via Q-sorts. The six raters were chosen on the basis of their presumed familiarity with the social sciences and psychological tests. They represented three different levels of education (B.A., M.A., and Ph.D.) and three different disciplines within the social sciences (psychology, sociology, and social work). Along with the Q-sorts, the six raters were asked to complete a questionnaire indicating whether they had observed Smith or Brown six or more times, fewer than six times, or never, and whether the contact was work-related or social in nature. The raters were also asked to check whether they liked or disliked the two subjects. Provision was made for the indication of neutral or ambivalent feeling.

Table 6.4 presents the intercorrelations among the raters' Q-sorts, as well as the correlations of Smith's and Brown's self-sorts with the Q-sorts of the six raters, and the correlations between each rater's Q-sorts for the two political leaders. The average inter-rater correlation across the six raters for Brown is .51 and for Smith is .36. For Brown there was fairly consistent agreement among the

Table 6.3.   Intercorrelations among Two Experts' Q-Sorts
              of Khrushchev, Stalin, and Lenin

	Khrushchev	Stalin	Lenin
Expert A's Q-Sorts			
Khrushchev	—		
Stalin	.08	—	
Lenin	.12	.22	—
Expert B's Q-Sorts			
Khrushchev	—		
Stalin	.14	—	
Lenin	.20	.37	—

Table 6.4. Intercorrelations among CQ-Sorts for Brown and Smith

Rater	Intercorrelations for Brown						Intercorrelations for Smith						Rater's Intercorrelations for Brown and Smith
	_1_	_2_	_3_	_4_	_5_	_6_	_1_	_2_	_3_	_4_	_5_	_6_	
1	—						—						−.17
2	.18	—					.43	—					.27
3	.35	.48	—				.49	.31	—				.48
4	.55	.46	.67	—			.39	.43	.57	—			.43
5	.50	.30	.52	.65	—		.00	−.16	.32	.44	—		.66
6	.52	.45	.68	.69	.68	—	.22	.00	.53	.50	.65	—	.52
Brown (Self-Sort)	.49	.41	.48	.65	.62	.59							
Smith (Self-Sort)							−.05	−.22	.36	.40	.72	.55	

raters. Moreover, the raters' Q-sorts on Brown were consistently rather similar to Brown's self-sort. For Smith, however, two of the raters' Q-sorts (1 and 2) appear to have been quite different from those of at least two other raters (5 and 6) and from Smith's self-sort. These two raters, it was discovered in checking their like-dislike ratings for Smith, had indicated a dislike for Smith. On the other hand, raters 5 and 6 stated that they liked Smith. Interestingly, the highest correlation between Smith's self-sort and the raters' Q-sorts occurred with the psychologist (rater 5) who had studied Smith at length for several years and who had available the results of a battery of psychological tests on Smith. Perhaps because of their dislike for Smith and liking for Brown, the Q-sorts of raters 1 and 2 for these men show a smaller relationship. For the other raters there was a fair degree of similarity between their Q-sorts of Brown and Smith.

The composite descriptions of Brown and Smith taken from the six raters' Q-sorts appear in Tables 6.5 and 6.6. These tables also contain the results of Brown and Smith's self-sorts. For the six raters the CQ-items in Tables 6.5 and 6.6 represent those statements which, on the average, appeared as quite and most characteristic as well as quite and most uncharacteristic of Brown and Smith. The reliability of the composite is .86 for Brown and .77 for Smith. The self-sort items listed in Tables 6.5 and 6.6 are the statements which Brown and Smith perceived to be quite and most characteristic as well as quite and most uncharacteristic of themselves.

An examination of the overlap between the raters' highly characteristic and uncharacteristic items and the self-sort highly characteristic and uncharacteristic items in Tables 6.5 and 6.6 indicates the least overlap (4 items out of 13 or 30 percent) for Brown among the items characteristic of him. There is agreement on 7 of the 13 items (53 percent) seen as uncharacteristic of Brown. For Smith agreement on the items is much greater. The raters and Smith agree on 11 of the 13 items (84 percent) which are highly characteristic of him and on 9 of the 13 items (69 percent) which are highly uncharacteristic of him. If we look carefully at Brown's self-sort items and the raters' items for Brown, we note a difference in orientation in the items. Brown's items are introspective, e.g., "tends toward over-control of needs and impulses," and, thus, characteristics less likely to be observable. The raters' items on Brown, in contrast, tend to be task-oriented, e.g., "is productive; gets things done," which are reflective of their interactions with him.

How do the descriptions in Tables 6.5 and 6.6 compare with the results from the psychological tests which Brown and Smith completed? We will let the reader decide. The tests suggest that Brown is a person of much warmth and considerable focus and organization. He has much drive and is effective at dealing with leaders reporting to him who are themselves jockeying for power. Moreover, Brown tends to think not of *principles* but only of *hypotheses* of organization. Typically, he considers the multiple potential consequences of contemplated policy decisions (a fairly rare attribute). Brown is gregarious, affable, and socially skilled; he operates in a decisive way and deals effectively

Table 6.5. CQ-Set Items Perceived as Highly Characteristic and Uncharacteristic of Brown

Q-Category		CQ-Items from Composite for Six Raters		CQ-Items from Brown Self-Sort
Most characteristic (5 items)	2.	Is a genuinely dependable and responsible person.	28.	Tends to arouse liking and acceptance in people.
	24.	Prides self on being "objective," rational.	33.	Is calm, relaxed in manner.
	26.	Is productive; gets things done.	35.	Has warmth; has the capacity for close relationships; compassionate.
	29.	Is turned to for advice and reassurance.	70.	Behaves in an ethically consistent manner; is consistent with own personal standards.
	83.	Able to see to the heart of important problems.	84.	Is cheerful.
Quite characteristic (8 items)	8.	Appears to have a high degree of intellectual capacity.	3.	Has a wide range of interests.
	17.	Behaves in a sympathetic or considerate manner.	17.	Behaves in a sympathetic or considerate manner.
	51.	Genuinely values intellectual and cognitive matters.	25.	Tends toward over-control of needs and impulses; binds tensions excessively; delays gratification unnecessarily.
	52.	*Behaves* in an assertive fashion.	29.	Is turned to for advice and reassurance.
	70.	Behaves in an ethically consistent manner; is consistent with own personal standards.	54.	Emphasizes being with others; gregarious.
	71.	Has high aspiration level for self.	66.	Enjoys esthetic impressions; is esthetically reactive.
	91.	Is power oriented; values power in self or others.	83.	Able to see to the heart of important problems.
	96.	Values own independence and autonomy.	86.	Handles anxiety and conflicts by, in effect, refusing to recognize their presence; repressive or dissociative tendencies.

Table 6.5. (Continued)

Q-Category	CQ-Items from Composite for Six Raters		CQ-Items from Brown Self-Sort	
Quite uncharacteristic (8 items)	14.	*Genuinely* submissive; accepts domination comfortably.	27.	Shows condescending behavior in relations with others.
	22.	Feels a lack of personal meaning in life.	50.	Is unpredictable and changeable in behavior and attitude.
	30.	Gives up and withdraws where possible in the face of frustration and adversity.	53.	Various needs tend toward relatively direct and uncontrolled expression; unable to delay gratification.
	34.	Over-reactive to minor frustrations; irritable.	62.	Tends to be rebellious and nonconforming.
	38.	Has hostility towards others.	67.	Is self-indulgent.
	53.	Various needs tend toward relatively direct and uncontrolled expression; unable to delay gratification.	78.	Feels cheated and victimized by life; self-pitying.
	67.	Is self-indulgent.	82.	Has fluctuating moods.
	99.	Is self-dramatizing; histrionic.	94.	Expresses hostile feelings directly.
Most uncharacteristic (5 items)	37.	Is guileful and deceitful, manipulative, opportunistic.	22.	Feels a lack of personal meaning in life.
	40.	Is vulnerable to real or fancied threat, generally fearful.	36.	Is subtly negativistic; tends to undermine and obstruct or sabotage.
	45.	Has a brittle ego-defense system; has a small reserve of integration; would be disorganized and maladaptive when under stress or trauma.	37.	Is guileful and deceitful, manipulative, opportunistic.
	55.	Is self-defeating.	38.	Has hostility toward others.
	78.	Feels cheated and victimized by life; self-pitying..	40.	Is vulnerable to real or fancied threat, generally fearful.

Table 6.6. CQ-Set Items Perceived as Highly Characteristic and Uncharacteristic of Smith

Q-Category	CQ-Items from Composite for Six Raters	CQ-Items from Smith Self-Sort
Most characteristic (5 items)	8. Appears to have a high degree of intellectual capacity.	3. Has a wide range of interests.
	24. Prides self on being "objective," rational.	8. Appears to have a high degree of intellectual capacity.
	39. Thinks and associates to ideas in unusual ways; has unconventional thought processes.	39. Thinks and associates to ideas in unusual ways; has unconventional thought processes.
	51. Genuinely values intellectual and cognitive matters.	51. Genuinely values intellectual and cognitive matters.
	96. Values own independence and autonomy.	96. Values own independence and autonomy.
Quite characteristic (8 items)	2. Is a genuinely dependable and responsible person.	2. Is a genuinely dependable and responsible person.
	3. Has a wide range of interests.	26. Is productive; gets things done.
	16. Is introspective and concerned with self as an object.	48. Keeps people at a distance; avoids close interpersonal relationships.
	26. Is productive; gets things done.	62. Tends to be rebellious and nonconforming.
	48. Keeps people at a distance; avoids close interpersonal relationships.	70. Behaves in an ethically consistent manner; is consistent with own personal standards.
	70. Behaves in an ethically consistent manner; is consistent with own personal standards.	71. Has high aspiration level for self.
	71. Has high aspiration level for self.	72. Concerned with own adequacy as a person, either at conscious or unconscious levels.
	72. Concerned with own adequacy as a person, either at conscious or unconscious levels.	83. Able to see to the heart of important problems.
Quite uncharacteristic (8 items)	14. Genuinely submissive; accepts domination comfortably.	4. Is a talkative individual.

Table 6.6. (Continued)

Q-Category	CQ-Items from Composite for Six Raters	CQ-Items from Smith Self-Sort
	15. Is skilled in social techniques of imaginative play, pretending, and humor.	9. Is uncomfortable with uncertainty and complexities.
	22. Feels a lack of personal meaning in life.	15. Is skilled in social techniques of imaginative play, pretending, and humor.
	43. Is facially and/or gesturally expressive.	22. Feels a lack of personal meaning in life.
	45. Has a brittle ego-defense system; has a small reserve of integration; would be disorganized and maladaptive when under stress or trauma.	30. Gives up and withdraws where possible in the face of frustration and adversity.
	53. Various needs tend toward relatively direct and uncontrolled expression; unable to delay gratification.	53. Various needs tend toward relatively direct and uncontrolled expression; unable to delay gratification.
	92. Has social poise and presence; appears socially at ease.	97. Is emotionally bland; has flattened affect.
	94. Expresses hostile feelings directly.	99. Is self-dramatizing; histrionic.
Most uncharacteristic (5 items)	4. Is a talkative individual.	14. Genuinely submissive; accepts domination comfortably.
	36. Is subtly negativistic; tends to undermine and obstruct or sabotage.	37. Is guileful and deceitful, manipulative, opportunistic.
	37. Is guileful and deceitful, manipulative, opportunistic.	63. Judges self and others in conventional terms like "popularity," "the correct thing to do," social pressure, etc.
	78. Feels cheated and victimized by life; self-pitying.	78. Feels cheated and victimized by life; self-pitying.
	99. Is self-dramatizing; histrionic.	94. Expresses hostile feelings directly.

with conflicts. Smith appears in the tests as very bright and socially perceptive. He values initiative and original thought processes in others while possessing strong curiosity and considerable intellectual thrust as well as much independence of thought himself. Smith's thought processes are indeed unusual ones for a physicist since he has a marked preference for metaphor. His operating style is to make tentative suggestions or to express interest in projects in order to get others excited enough about them to carry them out with considerable zest.

We have noted already how the raters' liking and disliking for Smith influenced their Q-sorts of him. Can we learn in more detail how liking affected the raters' Q-sorts? One way is to examine how the Q-sort items are affected by liking item by item. To do this, we first divided the raters into those who indicated that they liked Smith ($N = 3$) and those who indicated that they disliked Smith ($N = 3$). Raters noting ambivalent or neutral feelings toward Smith were placed in the dislike group. To see where these two types of raters differed in their sorting, we averaged their scores by item. There were seven items (9, 13, 15, 23, 28, 97, and 98) on which the two types of raters differed by 2.5 or more intervals in their sorting. According to Block (1961), for typical Q-sorts a difference of 2.5 intervals is significant at the .05 level. For these seven items the mean category placement by the like-raters was closer to that of Smith's self-sort than the mean category placement of the dislike-raters. With one exception, if the like-group indicated the item was characteristic of Smith, the dislike-raters indicated that it was uncharacteristic and vice versa. Interestingly, however, these items represent only seven percent of the total CQ-items. In other words, for most items the effect of liking is less dramatic.

We hypothesized that the Q-sort might also be affected by how well the rater knows the subject he is rating. We have already noted some effect of this kind with Smith. The correlation between his self-sort and that of the psychologist who knew his test results was higher than the correlations of Smith's self-sort with the Q-sorts of the other raters. To examine the effect of contact on the Q-sorts for Smith, we assigned a score of two to raters who indicated that they had six or more contacts with the subject, a score of one to raters indicating fewer than six contacts, and a score of zero to raters with no contacts. Each rater was given a score for his social contacts with the subject, his work contacts, and his total contacts. We divided the scores for each type of contact at the median creating high contact and low contact groups of raters. An item analysis similar to that with like- and dislike-raters yielded no item with a difference of 2.5 intervals for any of the types of high and low contact raters.

In summary, our study of local political leaders indicates that liking can affect how a rater will do a Q-sort on a political leader. However, with a large number of judges and a wide range of feeling for the subject, the effects are fairly marginal. Moreover, while contact with the subject seems not to affect the Q-sort, expert knowledge about the subject does. Furthermore, as the composites suggest, the raters can come close to matching the subject's self-sort on the most extreme categories.

Conclusions

We have used a Q-sort, in particular the CQ-set of items, to describe the personal characteristics of a national political leader and two local political leaders. Our results suggest that this technique has potential promise for the study of political leaders. Other research is, of course, called for since the Q-sort technique has not been employed very often with political leaders until now. There remain many questions to answer. For example, are there characteristics in the Q-sort which are descriptive of political leaders in some roles but not in others, in some situations but not in others? How does the implicit personality theory of the Q-sort user influence his (her) sorting of the items? How does cultural bias affect Q-sorts on persons from other cultures? These questions suggest areas of interest for future research.

We have used the Q-sort to learn more about the personalities of individual political leaders. One can conceive, however, of other ways of using the Q-sort to study political leaders. If we could collect Q-sorts on a number of world leaders, we could factor analyze them, producing a typology of international leaders. Using factor scores for such leaders, we could investigate how much variance their personal characteristics account for in their political behavior and in their nation's policies. Moreover, one could compare the Q-sorts for groups of political leaders engaging in different kinds of political behavior to examine what personal characteristics appear related to the differences in their behavior.

As we noted at the beginning of this chapter, the study of political leaders by psychological means can prove difficult. We need ways to learn about the personal characteristics of political leaders who are inaccessible to us—one type, in particular, is the political leader from another country. By using informants such as area specialists and political experts and by using the Q-sort, we can gain some information about the personal characteristics of these otherwise reluctant or unavailable subjects.

PART 2

WHO BECOMES A POLITICAL LEADER?

CHAPTER 7

Politicians and Personality: A Cross-Cultural Perspective*

Gordon J. DiRenzo

Editor's Introduction

What kinds of people enter into politics? Who becomes a political leader? Do political leaders possess certain personal characteristics which differentiate them from their constituents? The next five chapters deal with these questions. Each chapter explores some facet of entry into politics and all the chapters attempt to show the complexities of the relationship between personal characteristics, role, and recruitment in the achievement of a position of political leadership.

DiRenzo in this chapter examines the dogmatism of political leaders. He is interested in how open or closed to change the belief systems of political leaders are when compared with nonpoliticians. His hypothesis is that political leaders will be more dogmatic than their constituents. DiRenzo's political leaders are members of the Chamber of Deputies of the Italian Parliament and state

*Funds for the studies reported in this chapter were provided by grants from the following sources: Italian Ministry of Education, Indiana University, Social Science Research and Training Laboratory of the University of Notre Dame, and the General University Research Fund of the University of Delaware. The author is most grateful for this research support and extends his appreciation as well to Milton Rokeach and William V. D'Antonio for their assistance in these studies. Invaluable help in the analyses of the data was rendered by Marty Smith, Anne Pottieger, and Michael Pravetz. A special word of gratitude is recorded for the editor of this volume who provided many helpful suggestions and was most patient.

legislators from Indiana and Michigan. In other words, his political leaders are elected officials who serve a legislative function. To test his hypothesis, DiRenzo compares the dogmatism scores of these elected officials to dogmatism scores of control groups composed of nonpoliticians. DiRenzo, however, is not content simply to explore this bivariate relationship but tries to ascertain from the backgrounds of the political leaders at what point the dogmatic politician enters into the political arena and what his perspective is on politics as an occupation.

The title of the present chapter contains the words "cross-cultural." And, indeed, DiRenzo's study is cross-cultural in the sense that it examines political leaders from two cultures—the United States and Italy. Although DiRenzo's intention in the beginning in using two cultures was to show that his hypotheses, if supported, held across cultural boundaries—political leaders do have distinctive personal characteristics—his study instead provides a graphic illustration of the importance of culture on who becomes a political leader. His contradictory results for the two cultures suggest the limits to generalizability inherent in research on political leaders that is focused on only one culture. What applies to political leaders in the United States may not describe political leaders elsewhere.

Two methods are used in acquiring the data for the DiRenzo study—the interview and the personality questionnaire. By employing a short, ten-item scale and by embedding it in an interview context, DiRenzo was able to get all but one of the Italian deputies he interviewed to consent to complete the scale. Moreover, he appears to have had few problems with the Indiana and Michigan state legislators. Although, as DiRenzo notes, it took much resourcefulness to schedule the interviews, once rapport was established in the interview situation, administering the personality questionnaire was relatively easy. DiRenzo's experience suggests that researchers in the area of political leadership may want to give consideration to the use of the personality questionnaire in planning their research rather than automatically assuming that the difficulties in using this method with political leaders are insurmountable. The payoff, of course, in using the personality questionnaire is that one's results become comparable to other research employing that questionnaire. Since most current research on personal characteristics measures such characteristics by means of personality questionnaires, the payoff can be great.

DiRenzo is a professor of sociology at the University of Delaware. This chapter is one of a long series of publications by this author on political psychology. Two which are noteworthy for the student of political leadership are his recent book, *Personality and Politics* (DiRenzo, 1974) and the extensive report of his research on the Italian Chamber of Deputies, *Personality, Power, and Politics* (DiRenzo, 1967c).

ONE OF THE MORE INTRIGUING hypotheses in the area of the psychology of politics is that professional politicians have a distinctive type of personality. This hypothesis derives from the thesis that certain kinds of personalities tend to be attracted and/or recruited to particular occupations in a differential rather than in a random or unsystematic fashion, and seemingly so disproportionately as to constitute modal personality types for these occupations. Inkeles (1959) describes some empirical evidence to support this position and suggests the tentative, but plausible, explanation for this situation is that there is a congruent relationship between the personality and the occupational system which is organizationally functional for the work system and psychologically gratifying for the individual.

While students of politics have described many of the roles involved in political behavior, frequently even in terms of psychological considerations, they have not done so with a concern for the total personality[1] of the political actor. If given political roles are characterized by a relative concentration of distinctive types of personality, then the modal personality[2] hypothesis has highly significant implications for political dynamics in general and the structure and function of political roles and systems in particular. As Lane (1959, p. 97) states: "The idea of a distinctive type of person, political man, is attractive in many ways: if there were such a type, it would do much to clarify the problems of leadership selection, circulation of elites, and so forth." Any meaningful concept of a distinctive political personality, however, must be related to its cultural, and perhaps even social, milieu in order to determine whether or not such a personality type indicates an accentuation relative to the normal expectancy, such as the national modal character, of a particular society.

We report in this chapter on two studies designed to explore, within a cross-cultural perspective, the hypothesis of modal types of political personality and to assess its significance for political behavior. The empirical data for our presentation·are drawn respectively from the Chamber of Deputies of the Italian Parliament and the state legislatures (both House and Senate) of Michigan and Indiana.

The two American legislatures are diversified structurally in a number of ways. Some of the principal differences between the two legislatures revolve

---

[1] The term "personality" has been used for many diverse denotations—to include or to exclude more or less of what often are referred to as the aspects, elements, and levels of personality. We define personality as the acquired, dynamic, yet relatively enduring, unique system of one's predispositions to behavior. As a systematic entity, personality necessarily has content (beliefs, ideologies, values, attitudes, motives, drives, psychodynamics, emotions, temperament, abilities, capacities, etc.) and organization or structure. Our focus in this analysis is on *personality structure,* since it is this aspect that accounts for the uniqueness that characterizes every personality, and, as such, provides a more viable means for explaining the interaction of psychological dynamics and social behavior.

[2] "Modal personality" refers to that type which is found so predominantly as to be designated the central characteristic or central tendency within a given range.

around the duration of the legislative assembly and the full-time or part-time involvement of the legislator. Such differences lend themselves to the hypothesis that a different type of "political man" (personality) could be attracted to, and recruited into, each legislative system. Indeed, it is these structural differences which in great part motivated our utilization of two state legislatures. We wanted to explore the possible ways in which differences in the American legislative system and role are related to personality.

Method

The professional politician—in fact, political man in general—has been described rather extensively as a fundamentally authoritarian personality who is motivated basically by the search for personal power. This view dates back to Spranger (1928) who contended that every personality is characterized by the dominance of one cultural value, of which he distinguished six: science, wealth, art, love, power, and religion. This arrangement yielded a classification of six basic types of men. Power became the dominant or supreme value for the "political type" of man. The most extensive writings on the concept of *homo politicus* from this personality perspective are those of Lasswell (1948, 1960) who similarly conceives of the political man as one who is distinctive by virtue of his pursuit of power and adds that the power motive derives from feelings of personal deprivation and subordination.

This general characterization of political man as a fundamentally authoritarian personality has been stated to a lesser extent by several others (see, e.g., Schumpeter, 1950; Matthews, 1954, 1960; Gottfried, 1955; Downs, 1957; Heberle, 1959; Lane, 1959; Michels, 1962). Empirical evidence for this position of authoritarianism as the distinctive mark of the politician, however, is almost totally lacking. Only five pieces of research (McConaughy, 1950; Hennessy, 1959; Harned, 1961; Milbrath and Klein, 1962; Browning and Jacob, 1964) are more or less directly relevant to this question, and—although their findings are inconsistent—none of them reports any significant associations between various kinds of political people and personality type. Other research which shows that authoritarian personalities vote no more nor less than others (Lane, 1955), that they are less likely to join political groups (Sanford, 1951), and that they are more apt to be politically apathetic (Mussen and Wyszynski, 1952; Janowitz and Marvick, 1953) has cast further doubt upon the positive relationship of authoritarianism to political activity. Perhaps one reason for this state of affairs is that actual professional politicians (or, as Lasswell says, the active elite of government or political parties) have not been studied. Another, more serious, problem concerns the theoretical bias in the concept of authoritarianism and its principal instruments of measure, such as the well-known F scale,[3] which—with the exception of McConaughy's study and the work by Browning and Jacob—have been the foci of all these earlier studies.

Authoritarianism as conceived in the classic study by Adorno and associates (1950) admittedly focused on a particular substantive or ideological content, namely Nazism. Yet, we know that there can be authoritarianism with regard to almost any ideology or belief—regardless of its specific, substantive content. Critics (see Christie and Jahoda, 1954) have alleged that the F scale was designed not to disclose the authoritarian personality as such, but rather to measure only authoritarianism of the extreme political right. These claims have been substantiated by independent research (see Barker, 1963). Not only is the F scale ideologically biased and hence content laden, but it has been shown (see Rose, 1966; DiRenzo, 1967c) that the scale is culture-bound as well.

One way of surmounting these difficulties is to focus on the phenomenon of dogmatism which Rokeach (1954, 1960) has offered as an alternative approach to that of *The Authoritarian Personality* (Adorno et al., 1950). Rokeach has made a conceptual distinction that allows for different kinds of authoritarianism by avoiding reference to the specific substantive content of authoritarian ideologies and concentrating instead on formal content (what they seem to share in common) and, even more particularly, by concentrating on the structural properties common to various authoritarian ideologies. Dogmatism is defined by Rokeach (1954, p. 195) as "a relatively closed cognitive organization of beliefs and disbeliefs about reality, organized around a central set of beliefs about absolute authority which, in turn, provides a framework for patterns of intolerance and qualified tolerance towards others." It is, thus, not so much what as how one believes that distinguishes the dogmatic (or authoritarian) personality structure.[4] Dogmatism is the personality variable studied in this chapter.

POLITICAL SAMPLES

Italian Parliament. Subjects for the Italian study constituted the male[5] membership of the Chamber of Deputies of the National Parliament for the year

---

[3]The "F" here stands for fascism. The name derives from the dominant world of authority in the social and political structures of fascist systems. The "authoritarian character" is meant to represent the personality structure which is the human basis of fascism. Hence the term "fascist" is often used synonymously for the "authoritarian personality."

[4]The term "dogmatic personality" is not used by Rokeach. It should be understood, therefore, as an innovation of the present writer.

[5]Since the smaller parties had no female representatives and the total number of women in the Chamber was 22, only a few could be expected in our sample. Accordingly, in order to derive as homogeneous a sample as possible and to reduce any bias for uncontrolled variables, our study was confined to the male membership.

1961 (Third Republican Parliament). We established a sample to include all of the members of the smaller political parties and a twenty percent selection of the larger parties, drawn by means of a table of random numbers. We managed to make direct contact with 145 deputies out of the potential sample of 193 (32 percent of 596 Chamber members). Of this number, six had to be deleted from our analysis due to their lack of response on key questions, seven accepted instruments for self-completion but failed to return them, and three openly refused to be interviewed.

The final number of subjects in the Italian study was 129, which constitutes about 22 percent of the Chamber membership. While our sample represents about one-fifth of the total membership of the Chamber, the percentage of the smaller parties represented in the sample is much greater in many cases than the percentage of the larger parties because we tried to contact all the members of these smaller parties. Overall, however, the political sample appears to be adequately representative of the membership in the Chamber of Deputies. Approximate frequency distributions have been obtained for the following factors: age, education, occupation, parliamentary experience, and regional constituencies represented. Table 7.1 contains the relevant data for the universe and sample.

American State Legislatures. Subjects for the American studies constituted the male[6] membership of both houses of the 1967 Indiana (95th General Assembly) and the 1967-68 Michigan (74th Legislature) legislatures. In Michigan, we utilized the Senate membership (excluding one female) exhaustively. This procedure made for a potential N of 37 for this subsample. In the Michigan House, five females were excluded which gave us a corrected universe of 105, from which was drawn a 50 percent random sample. The actual sample N's for the Michigan House and Senate were respectively 52 and 34 which represent 61 percent of the membership of the entire legislature.

We followed similar procedures in Indiana. The Senate membership (two females excluded) was used exhaustively, a procedure which made for a potential N of 48 for this body. The corrected universe for the House (six females excluded) was 94: 63 Republicans and 31 Democrats. The universe of House Democrats was used exhaustively, while a 50 percent random sample was taken of the Republicans. We obtained an actual sample totaling 77 for Indiana—33 Senators and 44 Representatives—which represents 54 percent of this legislative universe.

These two American samples appear to be adequately representative of the membership of both houses of each legislature in terms of party affiliation,

---

[6]Again there were relatively few women in these universes; only one or two could be expected to enter our samples. Thus, it was decided to omit females from the respective samples in order to control for whatever bias could have entered the study on the basis of sex differences.

Table 7.1.   Distribution of Italian Political Sample by Political Party

Party	Universe		Sample		
	Number	Percent	Number	Percent Universe	Percent Sample
Christian Democratic	273	45.8	31	11.3	24.0
Italian Communist	141	23.6	25	17.7	19.3
Italian Democratic	19	3.1	3[a]	15.7	2.3
Italian Liberal	18	3.0	11	61.1	8.5
Italian Social Democratic	17	2.8	8	47.0	6.2
Italian Social Movement	24	4.0	18	75.0	13.9
Italian Socialist	87	14.5	21	24.1	16.2
Miscellaneous[b]	17	2.8	12	70.5	9.1
Total	596	99.6	129	21.6	99.5

Note: This table is reproduced with permission from DiRenzo (1967c).

[a]Five defected members (Independent Monarchists) are classified as miscellaneous. Thus, this subsample actually constitutes 42 percent of the Italian Democratic Party.

[b]Includes five of the six deputies of the Italian Republican Party.

regional distribution, seniority, and other background variables such as age, education, religion, and primary occupations. Table 7.2 contains the relevant data for these samples.

A comparison of the Indiana and Michigan legislative samples on social and political background factors reveals some differences between the legislatures on certain political variables. The Michigan legislators tended to be more politically experienced and more professionally career-oriented to politics than the Indiana legislators. The following three variables revealed statistically significant differences between the two state samples (House and Senate combined): (1) previous number of legislative terms—an average of 37 percent in Michigan had served more than three terms versus an average of only 11 percent for Indiana, (2) professional role orientation—the Michigan sample had more people (68 percent) that perceived themselves as "professional" or "semi-professional" as opposed to "nonprofessional" politicians than in the Indiana sample (36 percent), and (3) political career orientation—two-thirds of the Michigan legislators indicated that their "political activity is based on a political career or political vocation," while an equal percentage of the Indiana people responded negatively to this question.

These differential patterns of professional orientation and experience, given the different legislative structures in the two states, are not wholly unexpected. The state legislator in Michigan is engaged in what amounts to a full-time

Table 7.2.   Distribution of American Political Sample
by State, House, and Party

	Universe		Sample		
	Number Used	Percent Selected	Number	Percent Universe	Percent Sample
Indiana					
House	(94)		(44)	(46.8)	(27.0)
Democrats	31a	100	19	61.3	11.6
Republicans	63a	50	25	39.7	15.3
Senate	(48)		(33)	(68.7)	(20.2)
Democrats	27b	100	16	59.3	9.8
Republicans	21b	100	17	81.0	10.4
Total	(142)		(77)	(54.2)	(47.2)
Michigan					
House	(105)		(52)	(49.5)	(31.9)
Democrats	50c	50	25	50.0	15.3
Republicans	55	50	27	49.1	16.6
Senate	(37)		(34)	(91.9)	(20.8)
Democrats	18	100	17	94.4	10.4
Republicans	19	100	17	89.5	10.4
Total	(142)		(86)	(60.6)	(52.8)
Overall Total	284		163	57.4	100.0

aExcludes three females.   bExcludes one female.   cExcludes five females.

occupation for the entirety of the calendar year, with the legislature being in session annually for an average period of nine months. The Indiana legislature, on the other hand, meets biennially for a fixed period of 60 days (special sessions excluded). Here the role of legislator and his corresponding compensation ($1,800 per annum at the time of the research) are indicative of part-time activity. Thus, politics for many Indiana legislators is, at least in the formal sense, more in the nature of an avocation.

Comparing state senators and representatives on a number of social and political background variables, we found only one statistically significant difference—on "previous elective office." Sixty-eight percent of the state representatives had no previous elective experience versus 39 percent for the state senators.

CONTROL GROUPS

In order to compare the findings for the political samples to nonpoliticians, control groups were established for both the Italian and American studies.

Italian. A simple quota sample of about 500 individuals was established for Italy. Each of 25 freshmen students at the University of Rome who were taking courses in public opinion was instructed to select 20 respondents to interview. Specific directions were given to approximate proportional distributions of the political sample in terms of sex, age, education, and professional backgrounds. The choice of individual subjects beyond these requirements was left to the student pollsters.

Some difficulty was experienced in obtaining respondents because of questions on religious affiliation and political party preference.[7] Nevertheless, well over 500 respondents were obtained. From this number was extracted a usable sample of 436 "nonpolitical" individuals who had not been elected to political office or been political candidates. All these subjects were drawn from the metropolitan area of Rome.

American. An available sample of about 1,000 individuals was similarly established for the American studies. Unlike the Italian control group, however, no attempt was made to confine the dimensions of the American sample to an approximation of those expected in the legislative samples. Hence, both males and females were included, although in a two to one ratio of male dominance, and the control sample is more heterogeneous than the legislative samples in terms of age, education, and occupational backgrounds. The American control group was drawn from the Standard Metropolitan Statistical Area of South Bend (St. Joseph County) in the state of Indiana. Subjects were selected and interviewed by a team of undergraduate students from Indiana University, South Bend. The final usable N for this control group was 922.

Since professional politicians at the parliamentary level are seldom representative of the total general population, the nonpolitical samples which were selected were not expected to be precisely matched controls for political party affiliation and such social background variables as religion, occupation, age, and education. The Italian control group, in fact, is skewed somewhat in terms of religion toward Catholicism and in terms of education toward the upper levels. Moreover, the party distributions are not comparable in all cases. The Italian control group in these and other respects may be more representative of the general Italian population than of the deputies.

Similarly, the American control group, on the whole, is probably more representative of the general population of the states of Indiana and Michigan

[7] Apparently this reticence is a rather common problem. Almond and Verba (1963) reported that 32 percent of the Italians in their studies on political culture refused to reveal voting decisions to their interviewers. This statistic contrasts to a figure of only two percent for people in the United States.

than the corresponding legislators. However, unlike the Italian study, the American control group contains a number of individuals—about seven percent—who claim to have been either elected (9), appointed (15), or a candidate (45) for political office. These persons were not deleted from the American control group because the data were collected for another study and it was no longer possible to perform subcategorical analyses on them. For these many reasons, we use the nonpolitical samples in a suggestive rather than in a probative manner for testing our hypotheses. Used in this way, they appear to be suitable controls.

MEASUREMENT OF DOGMATISM

The most widely used measure of dogmatism is the Rokeach (1960) Dogmatism Scale. The Rokeach instrument appears to be theoretically superior to other instruments as a measure of general authoritarianism. That this scale assesses general authoritarianism has been established independently by Barker (1963). Furthermore, the structure—rather than content—orientation of the Dogmatism Scale makes it a more suitable tool for cross-cultural research on authoritarianism.

Since we felt that the length of a personality inventory would be a crucial consideration with political subjects, we adopted an abbreviated version of the Dogmatism Scale, known as the D-10 Scale, for our studies. This shortened form was developed by Schulze (1962) who utilized Guttman's scalogram analysis to select those items from the Dogmatism Scale which best met the criteria of unidimensionality, item consistency, and reproducibility, and which were most representative of the single factor of dogmatism. Schulze tested the D-10 Scale for validity with two samples and found coefficients of correlation between the final 40-item version of the Dogmatism Scale (D-40) and the D-10 Scale of .76 and .73 respectively. These correlations are somewhat inflated, of course, since identical elements appear in both scales. Coefficients of correlation similar to those of the parent scale were obtained when the shortened version was associated with instruments measuring other elements in the dogmatism syndrome.

The D-10 Scale was standardized for Italian usage by the author with the assistance of Italian psychologists. Validity data on the Italian instrument were gathered by using a modification of the "Method of Known Groups" (see DiRenzo, 1967c for details). Favorable statistical results were obtained in several applications of this procedure. Directions for answering the Italian version of the D-10 Scale were basically the same as those used by Rokeach in his original work with one modification. The usual six alternative answers of the Likert form were modified to four (agree-disagree partially, agree-disagree completely) which are more standard in Italian psychological terminology and usage.

In both the Italian and American studies no "neutral attitude" response was used in order to force a selection on the abbreviated instrument. However, with the American samples, the six alternative answers were used. Given the difference in the response formats of the D-10 Scale for the Italian and American studies, the dogmatism score ranged from -20 to +20 for the Italian study and from -30 to +30 for the American studies.

PROCEDURE

One serious obstacle to this kind of research in the field has been the difficulty of inducing professional politicians to submit to the research techniques involved. The use of personality questionnaires is quickly rejected, often as inappropriate, and leads to scoffs on the part of politicians. Accordingly, we were apprehensive about submitting the personality inventory to men of political stature, not so much because it was a psychological tool but rather because of the fear and suspicion that might be aroused by its obviously projective nature which could, in turn, jeopardize the validity of the responses. After much anguished consideration, we decided to utilize various methods of data collection.

In Italy, the D-10 Scale was administered to the political sample as part of a fairly long private interview with each subject on "social and political questions." Every resourceful means was used to arrange interviews with the Italian political sample (see DiRenzo, 1967c). In addition to the D-10 Scale, our instrument included measures of political interests and activity as well as a number of questions designed to elicit attitudes regarding legislative (parliamentary) and political organizations and the motivations for participation in them. The D-10 Scale was "disguised" by positioning it well into the interview—almost at the end—after sufficient rapport had been established. Given the complexity of the response format for the personality inventory, the deputies were given a copy of these questions to hold while the interview took place. Only one deputy absolutely refused, without explanation, to respond to the D-10 Scale, even though he was extremely cooperative otherwise.

The interviewing process was initiated by a short statement of introduction designed to cover the researcher's university affiliation, the general nature of the research study, its sponsorship, the selection of subjects, and a guarantee of anonymity. The interview commenced immediately with open-ended questions about social problems and political events of a general nature. This procedure gave the respondent an opportunity at the outset to offer brief discourses about the social and the political scene. In addition to providing a smooth introduction, this method yielded an excellent fund of unsolicited background information. Questions about personal backgrounds were confined to the conclusion of the interview. The usual interviewing procedures and techniques were followed. Although the majority of our questions were precoded, the respondents were encouraged to talk at length in every case. A supportive approach was used at all times.

The nonpolitical sample in Italy was also interviewed. Their interview was brief, however, consisting of the D-10 Scale and several questions relating to social background and political activity. The only difficulties encountered with these people concerned a reluctance to respond to questions on religion and political party affiliation. The data for both the Italian political and nonpolitical samples were collected during the months of May-August, 1961.

With regard to the American studies, a similar procedure of data collection was followed in Michigan, a different procedure in Indiana. In Michigan, representatives and senators were interviewed by a team of graduate students from Michigan State University during the period from March to June, 1967. In the Indiana House and Senate data were collected by means of a mail-back questionnaire in May, 1967. Two waves were used with respective return rates of 48 and 43 percent. No particular difficulties were encountered in the collection of the data for the American political samples. Since the D-10 Scale was used in both the mail-back questionnaire and the interview schedule, the data for the two legislative bodies are comparable and the legislatures can be treated as one unit for purposes of analysis.

The American control group was interviewed in much the same way as the Italian one. These subjects were given the D-10 Scale and asked several questions about their political activity and social background. The collection of these data presented no problems.

HYPOTHESES

The specific hypotheses that constitute the focus of this analysis are: (1) that professional politicians are modally characterized by dogmatic personality structures, and (2) that professional politicians can be distinguished from nonpoliticians in terms of greater degrees of dogmatism. The tests of these hypotheses will be made by comparing dogmatism data for the political samples to those for the nonpolitical samples.

Findings

ITALIAN

Our data show that parliamentarians appear to be extensively dogmatic in personality structure. Seventy-six percent of the sample scored positively (dogmatic) and 21 percent negatively (nondogmatic) on the D-10 Scale. Within the possible range of -20 to $+20$, the mode for the political sample was +6, and the mean dogmatism score was 5.51 with a standard deviation of 6.75.

For the nonpolitical control group, we found that 74 percent of the 436 individuals scored positively and 20 percent negatively on the D-10 Scale. The remaining six percent obtained neutral scores. The mode for the entire control group was +3, and the mean dogmatism score was 3.66 with a standard deviation of 5.36.

Comparable data for the two samples are presented in Table 7.3. Proportionately speaking there is no substantial difference between the two samples ($X^2 = .03$, $df = 1$, not significant). In terms of valence, however, there is a crucial

Table 7.3. Comparison of Dogmatism Scores for Italian Political and Nonpolitical Samples

Sample	Dogmatic	Nondogmatic	Totals	Mean	S.D.	Modal Score
Political	98 (75.9%)	27 (20.9%)	125 (96.8%)[a]	5.51	6.75	+6
Nonpolitical	322 (73.8%)	86 (19.7%)	408 (93.5%)[b]	3.66	5.36	+3

[a]Four neutral scores not included here.
[b]Twenty-eight neutral scores not included here.

Table 7.4. Mean Dogmatism Score Comparisons of Italian Political and Nonpolitical Samples by Political Party

Party	Political Sample			Nonpolitical Sample			t-value	p
	N	Mean	S.D.	N	Mean	S.D.		
Christian Democratic	31	7.96	6.48	139	3.91	4.58	4.069	.001
Italian Communist	25	.92	5.49	35	2.88	5.01	1.425	n.s.
Italian Democratic	3	9.33	4.64	28	3.07	4.86	2.059	.05
Italian Liberal	11	4.00	5.29	44	4.52	5.36	.285	n.s.
Italian Republican	5	8.00	3.52	28	4.10	5.09	1.590	n.s.
Italian Social Democratic	8	9.00	3.39	37	1.41	7.30	2.804	.01
Italian Social Movement	18	9.55	3.90	60	3.91	5.58	3.949	.001
Italian Socialist	21	2.23	7.70	40	5.20	5.57	1.692	.10

Note: This table is reproduced with permission from DiRenzo (1967c).

difference. A *t*-test examining the difference between the means of the political and nonpolitical samples yielded a *t*-value of 3.24 which is statistically significant at the .01 level of confidence. This evidence supports the research hypotheses and suggests that politicians, at least Italian deputies, not only can be modally distinguished in terms of the dogmatic personality structure, but also that they are more dogmatic than nonpoliticians.

Political Parties.   Can we discover some reasons why Italian deputies are generally more dogmatic than the public at large? One variable worthy of examination is political party. Table 7.4 presents mean dogmatism scores for the political and nonpolitical samples by political party. As an inspection of Table 7.4 reveals, the political sample mean was greater than that of the nonpolitical sample for five of the parties. These parties are the Christian Democrats, the neo-Fascists (Italian Social Movement), the monarchists (Italian Democratic Party), the Republicans (Italian Republican Party), and the Social Democrats. For four of the parties the differences between the means are statistically significant. The one exception is the Italian Republican Party. For the other three parties—Communists, Socialists, and Liberals—the mean dogmatism score for the nonpolitical sample was greater than that for the political sample. None of the differences between means were significant, however, for these three parties. The results suggest that politicians representing parties of the political center and the political right tend to differ in personality structure from their nonpolitical counterparts; whereas little difference in personality is found between politicians and nonpoliticians for parties on the political left.

For both the political and the nonpolitical samples the distribution of party means was subjected to an analysis of variance. The *F*-ratio for the political sample is statistically significant ($F = 4.37$, $df = 7/114$, $p < .01$), while that for the nonpolitical sample is not significant ($F = 1.73$, $df = 7/403$). Political leaders appear to differ among themselves in personality structure along the lines of political party affiliation. Such is not the case for political followers. It is important, however, to bear in mind that "political party affiliation" for the nonpolitical sample is merely a matter of expressed preference and, thus, may not represent a strongly-held ideology.

We also measured the ideological orientation of the political sample by means of a self-rated, six-point, Likert-type scale running from "Left" to "Right." These data are presented in Table 7.5. The mean dogmatism scores for persons selecting the six scale points differed significantly ($F = 5.07$, $df = 5/118$, $p < .01$). The results show a generally consistent pattern of increasing dogmatism from the extreme political left to the extreme political right.[8] This scale was not used with the nonpolitical control group.

[8] A similar measure using five scale points, but referring to one's party rather than to personal ideology, yielded continually increasing scores from the left extreme to the right extreme (see DiRenzo, 1967c, pp. 129-133).

Table 7.5. Dogmatism and Ideological Orientation
of Italian Political Sample

	Scale Point	N^*	Mean	S.D.
"Left"	1	27	1.25	6.13
	2	27	3.70	7.12
	3	37	6.78	6.43
	4	14	9.50	4.95
	5	3	1.66	2.62
"Right"	6	16	9.62	3.99

*Five deputies had no score for ideological orientation.

Career Orientation. In addition to party and ideological orientation, we attempted, in a very general way, to measure the political career orientations of our political sample. The deputies were asked the following question: "Would you say your political activity is based on a professional vocation to politics?" Although two-thirds of our deputies were not career oriented, there was no statistically significant difference in the mean dogmatism scores between those indicating politics was a career and those indicating it was not a career. Proportionately just as many career-oriented deputies were dogmatic as nondogmatic scorers and vice versa.

Social Background. With the exception of religion, our data show no significant relationships between dogmatism and such social background variables as age, educational level, and geographic region of constituency. With regard to religious practice, Table 7.6 shows that the lowest dogmatism mean (1.73) in the political sample was found for nonbelievers, whereas respondents professing varying degrees of Catholicism had an average dogmatism score of 7.33—clearly a marked discrepancy. Again, the findings for the religious variable are not consistent between the political and nonpolitical samples. An analysis of variance on the categories of religious practice for the political sample yielded an F-ratio of 4.51 which is statistically significant ($p < .01$). On the basis of the same procedure no statistical significance was found for the nonpolitical sample ($F = 1.14$); there is, however, a pattern of response similar to that for the political sample.

In the political sample, the political left is very heavily—even characteristically—represented by nonbelievers and Catholic nonchurchgoers. Only 17 of the 59 deputies representing parties of the political left were Catholics. Nine of these said that they never went to church. Accordingly, 13 percent in the leftist parties may be considered as practicing Catholics. This finding contrasts sharply with the fact that all the members representing parties on the political right are Catholic, and only four out of these 70 individuals claimed never to go to

Table 7.6.   Mean Dogmatism Scores of Italian Political and Nonpolitical Samples by Degree of Religious Practice

Religion	Political Sample			Nonpolitical Sample				
	N	Mean	S.D.	N	Mean	S.D.	t-value	p
Catholic (1)	38	7.55	6.64	144	3.82	6.01	3.309	.001
Catholic (2)	11	9.18	3.48	95	4.18	4.90	3.258	.01
Catholic (3)	5	6.80	4.87	66	3.39	4.87	1.489	n.s.
Catholic (4)	17	8.35	6.07	64	3.75	4.81	3.264	.01
Catholic (5)	13	4.76	5.88	20	2.80	6.11	.885	n.s.
None	41	1.73	6.38	20	2.80	5.34	.637	n.s.

Note: Catholic categories indicated here refer to the intensity of religious practice—(1) attends church at least once a week, (2) nearly every week, (3) about once a month, (4) only for the major festivities, and (5) never attends church.

church. More specifically, the Christian Democrats who had one of the highest dogmatism means had 30 of 31 representatives in the political sample claim to be Catholics of the most fervent variety. For the least dogmatic Communists, 23 out of 25 deputies claimed to be nonbelievers, and many of these openly professed to be atheists. Our findings, thus, show a parallel between religious affiliation and/or practice, political ideology, and dogmatism. This association will be instrumental in our subsequent discussion concerning the nature of Italian political parties as contrasted to American ones.

AMERICAN

The American data are not consistent with the Italian findings. State legislators appear to be modally nondogmatic in personality structure. Within the possible score range of −30 to +30, 67 and 65 percent of the Michigan and Indiana samples respectively scored negatively (nondogmatic) on the D-10 Scale while 29 and 26 percent scored positively (dogmatic). This ratio of approximately two to one is in marked contrast to the one to three ratio which we found in the Italian study. The respective dogmatism means for the Michigan and Indiana legislators are −5.16 and −5.56, which are not significantly different using a t-test ($t = .30$), allowing us to combine the scores in the analysis. The combined dogmatism mean for the American political sample is −5.35, with a standard deviation of 8.31. The modal score for the state legislators is −12. These data can be inspected in Table 7.7.

For the 922 individuals in the American nonpolitical control group, our data show that 40 percent scored positively and 54 percent negatively on the D-10 Scale. The remaining five percent obtained neutral scores. The mean dogmatism score for the control group was −.958, with a standard deviation value of 8.56. These data also can be found in Table 7.7.

Proportionately there is a significant pattern of difference between the American political and nonpolitical samples ($X^2 = 8.77, df = 1, p < .01$), but one which is contrary to our research hypotheses. American politicians are *less* rather than more dogmatic than American nonpoliticians. This suspicion is confirmed when the means of the two samples are compared. A test of the difference between the mean dogmatism scores for the political and nonpolitical samples yielded a t-value of 6.06, which is statistically significant ($p < .001$). Not only does this evidence not substantiate the research hypotheses that politicians are modally characterized by dogmatic personality structures and are more dogmatic than nonpoliticians, it supports instead totally contrary theses.

Political Parties. A comparison of the D-10 Scale scores for the American political and nonpolitical samples by political party affiliation shows the same general pattern that we found for the samples not broken down by party. Both Democratic and Republican legislators were less dogmatic than their nonpolitical constituents. These data are reported in Table 7.8.

Table 7.7.   Comparison of Dogmatism Scores for American Political and Nonpolitical Samples

	Michigan		Indiana		Total Political		Nonpolitical	
	N	%	N	%	N	%	N	%
Dogmatic	25	29.1	20	25.9	45	27.6	371	40.2
Nondogmatic	58	67.4	50	64.9	108	66.3	501	54.3
Neutral	3	3.5	7	9.0	10	6.1	50	5.4
Total	86	100.0	77	100.0	163	100.0	922	100.0
Mean	−5.16		−5.56		−5.35		−.958	
S.D.	8.42		8.25		8.31		8.56	

Table 7.8.   Mean Dogmatism Score Comparisons of American Political and Nonpolitical Samples by Political Party

Party	Political Sample			Nonpolitical Sample				
	N	Mean	S.D.	N	Mean	S.D.	t-value	p
Democrats	77	−5.44	7.93	449	−.588	8.99	4.47	.001
Republicans	86	−5.20	8.64	390	−1.425	8.16	3.82	.001
Others	—	—	—	83	−.917	8.07	—	—

Our American political sample reveals no appreciable differences in the pattern of dogmatism on the basis of political party affiliation. The ratio of dogmatic to nondogmatic scorers in the political sample is one to two for both Democrats and Republicans. A t-test on the mean dogmatism scores for the two parties is not statistically significant ($t = .184$).

An analysis of the dogmatism data by political party for the control group reveals a somewhat more evenly balanced distribution of dogmatic and nondogmatic scores for members of both major American parties as well as for independents. However, no statistically significant patterns of difference were found among the mean dogmatism scores for the three political parties ($F = .996$) nor, specifically, between Democrats and Republicans ($t = 1.46$).

We also asked our American legislators to indicate their ideological orientation on the six-point, Likert-type scale used in the Italian study. No statistically significant relationship was found between dogmatism and ideological orientation for the American politicians, although the data did reveal an expected decreasing pattern of nondogmatism in moving from the extreme left to the extreme right. Comparable data for the American control sample were not collected.

Career Orientation. In the American political studies as in the Italian study, we attempted to explore the relationship of personality to political career orientation. To assess this variable, the legislators were asked whether or not they considered themselves to have and/or desired to have a professional career in politics. The results reported in Table 7.9 show that the dogmatic scorers were positively career oriented to politics in approximately a two to one ratio, while the nondogmatic scorers were about equally divided in their orientation toward a political career. Statistical analysis of the difference between dogmatism scores for those legislators indicating a positive orientation toward politics and those indicating a negative orientation toward politics yielded a t-value of 1.93 which approaches significance ($p = .06$).

Role Orientation. In the American studies we attempted to pursue a number of other questions related to our fundamental hypotheses which are concerned with the exercise of political roles. One specific question dealt with role orientation. We sought to determine whether or not the politician could be distinguished in terms of personality structure on the basis of the "style" of his political activity.

Our data show that legislators who perceived themselves as either "professional" or "semi-professional" politicians were more dogmatic in personality structure than those politicians who had a "nonprofessional" role orientation ($F = 3.48$, $df = 2/158$, $p < .05$). Only 35 percent of the dogmatic scorers considered themselves to be "nonprofessional" politicians as opposed to 54 percent of the nondogmatic scorers. See Table 7.9 for these data.

Table 7.9.   Dogmatism and Political Career and Role
Orientations of American Legislators

Orientation	Dogmatic		Nondogmatic				
	N	%	N	%	N	Mean	S.D.
Career							
Positive	23	62.2	44	47.8	67	−3.97	8.56
Negative	14	37.8	48	52.2	62	−6.73	8.19
Total	37	100.0	92	100.0	163[a]	−5.35	8.31
Role							
Professional	7	16.3	16	14.8	24[b]	−4.54	9.88
Semi-Professional	21	48.8	34	31.5	60[c]	−3.61	7.14
Nonprofessional	15	34.9	58	53.7	77[d]	−7.15	8.17
Total	43	100.0	108	100.0	163[e]	−5.35	8.31

[a]This total includes 34 legislators who gave no response or had an uncodable response for the career-orientation question.

[b]Includes one neutral response to dogmatism scale.

[c]Includes five neutral responses to dogmatism scale.

[d]Includes four neutral responses to dogmatism scale.

[e]Includes ten neutral responses and two responses to role-orientation question which were uncodable.

These particular findings are important for our hypotheses because they indicate a positive association between personality type and political man for the American sample with more refined specification of the political role variables that are involved.

Social Background.   No statistically significant relationships were found between dogmatism and the following social background variables for the American political sample: (1) previous elective office, (2) number of terms served, (3) educational level, (4) social class, and (5) religious preference.

COMPARISON OF ITALIAN AND AMERICAN FINDINGS

Unfortunately, our use of different response formats for the D-10 Scale in the Italian and American studies precludes any valid statistical analysis comparing the two sets of data. A juxtaposition of the separate findings, nonetheless, can provide some insights. These comparative data are found in Tables 7.3 and 7.7. The dogmatism findings for the Italian and American samples appear in strong contrast to one another. Moreover, despite the statistically significant differences between the political and nonpolitical samples in each study, the data for each nonpolitical sample is more consistent with the data for its respective political sample than with the data for the other study. Seen in this light, the comparison of the four sets of data suggests that there may be a strong cultural component accounting for the marked contrasts observed in our findings.

Discussion

The Italian findings support our hypotheses; the American ones do not. The American legislative data, nevertheless, do provide some support for the relationship of personality structure to political role when aspects of the political role are considered.

Perhaps, however, our findings merely reflect substantial differences in the national modal character of the two countries. Modern students of national character are convinced that societies with a long history of democracy, such as the United States, are peopled by a majority of individuals who possess a personality structure that is conducive to democracy—namely, a nonauthoritarian one, while societies which have experienced prolonged or recurrent forms of authoritarian, totalitarian, or dictatorial government, such as Italy, are inhabited by a proportionately large number of individuals with corresponding types of personality. Such an explanation may indeed be applicable to the situation at hand; but politics, of course, is not a homogeneous activity—not even for the so-called political elite.

The contradictions presented by these two sets of data seem to suggest that the relationship between personality and political role may be a function of variations in the structure and content of legislative and political party systems as well as differences in the processes of political recruitment. Underlying these specific considerations there appear to be a number of very significant sociocultural differences. We shall offer some comments on them for each set of national data, and then return to a comparative discussion.

ITALIAN

Not all the subjects in our Italian political sample manifested the political personality in the hypothesized direction. By no means are we maintaining that all professional politicians are the same type or kind—on whatever criteria of classification. We hypothesized the existence of a modal type which was confirmed for both the entire political sample as well as for several subdivisions of it. A host of sociological and psychological factors could be at work in individual cases to account for higher or lower scores on the dogmatism measure. Among such concerns, for example, are party factions (see DiRenzo, 1967c, pp. 162-168) and the status level and functions of particular political offices within the system. Lasswell (1960, p. 262) speaks to this latter question about different types of political man by suggesting:

Political types may be distinguished according to the specialized or the composite character of the functions which they perform and which they are desirous of performing. There are political agitators, administrators, theorists, and various combinations thereof. There are significant differences in the developmental history of each political type.

Perhaps a more precise delineation of the Italian parliamentarian's role orientation, as we were able to do in the American legislative studies, would reveal similar signficant differences in the political personality structure. Considerations such as these provide the basis for more precise analyses of our fundamental hypotheses about which we shall have more to say subsequently.

We offer two explanations to account for the outcome of the Italian parties which show lower dogmatism means than the corresponding nonpolitical samples. One focuses on fundamental ideology, while the other involves the process of political recruitment.

The parallel associations among political ideology, religious practice, and dogmatism which our Italian data show make for theoretical consistency. Although no religious tenet is explicit in some political ideologies, in their platforms all parties tend to be either anticlerical or quite respectful of the Church. The "pro-Church" parties—the more dogmatic ones—are found on the conservative right, while the "anti-Church" and less dogmatic parties are on the liberal left. Specifically, there is a marked correlation between membership in either the Italian Communist Party or the Italian Socialist Party and the lack of adherence to any religious ideology. This finding is consistent with the political ideology of these two socialist parties.

Politicians probably are more committed to party ideology than nonpolitical followers for whom party affiliation, at least in this study, is merely a matter of expressed preference. Moreover, Italian people—that is, the general population—are not usually ideologically oriented, except in terms of religion, in their political behavior (see Kogan, 1964, p. 5). Therefore, in the cases of the Communist and Socialist Parties, we would expect to find more atheists among the political sample and more Catholics among the nonpolitical sample, given the religious orientation of the nation. And, indeed, 92 percent of the Communist Party deputies professed no religion; whereas, in the Communist nonpolitical control group 61 percent claimed to profess Catholicism. Sixty-two percent of the Socialist Party deputies as opposed to eight percent of the Socialists in the nonpolitical control group claimed to be nonbelievers. Commitment to political ideology may account for the lower degree of dogmatism in the political samples for these two parties.

The second, and perhaps more crucial, explanation of the findings for personality structure centers on recruitment procedures. Under the election system used in Italy, the political parties are able to exercise considerable control over the candidates who are offered to the voters and, to a great extent, actually determine the results of the popular elections and those who will be recruited into the system.[9] Methods of recruitment are not consistent in the individual parties. There is some evidence that the parties of the political left—the Communist and Socialist parties—are the least democratic in the selection of candidates or the recruitment of representatives. Almost one-fourth of our political sample—and these came with but two exceptions from the two parties in question—stated that the decision to place themselves as candidates for the Chamber was not their own but that of their party.

We contend that the difference in dogmatism scores for the individual political parties may be influenced strongly by the various methods of recruitment. There is probably a selective bias operating in that party leaders choose, knowingly or unknowingly, individuals with particular kinds of personalities. Kogan (1964, p. 9), in speaking of the Italian situation particularly, states: "The party leaders are more likely to choose candidates who will be reliable followers rather than independent and individual thinkers." And we suggest that they do so because these particular kinds of personalities are functionally necessary for the party and its political system. This situation, then, raises the question of whether such political representatives are recruited (appointive) or self-recruited (elective) politicians. Our hypotheses are directed principally to the latter type, but apparently both types of political man are present in our sample. Unfortunately, a lack of sufficient data keeps us from testing this hypothesis of party versus self-recruitment. However, informal evidence—mostly volunteered by our respondents—suggests that where self-recruitment is allowed to operate politicians are more likely to be dogmatic and authoritarian personalities, but where the recruitment process is controlled a differential selection of personalities may be operating according to the needs of the system, which may or may not require dogmatic individuals. This element of differential recruitment provides another basis for the more precise specification of our research hypotheses regarding the professional politician.[10]

AMERICAN

At first glance, one might suspect—as indeed some critics have—that the Italian findings are spurious. Such a view is advanced on the grounds that the American results, with their nondogmatic modality, are more consistent with the expectations and requirements of political roles in a democratic society. Some students

[9]The method of voting in Italy is known as the *scrutinio di lista* or list vote. Although there are variants of this method which have been adopted by countries on the European continent, the basic principle is that the elector votes not for individual candidates but rather for a party list of candidates. Strictly speaking, therefore, the competition is not among individual candidates but among political parties. The electors determine how many seats each party shall receive, but it is the party organization that decides who shall occupy them. The route to political office in this system is more in the nature of an ascribed rather than an achieved social status, which is an important fact to bear in mind in reading the analysis of our data. For more details on this method of voting as it applies to Italy, see DiRenzo (1967c, pp. 243-246).

[10]More details on the dynamics of party recruitment and their relationship to dogmatism are given in DiRenzo (1967c, pp. 154-162).

of the psychology of politics (e.g., Milbrath and Klein, 1962) contend that authoritarianism is a barrier to political activity. Milbrath (1965), in particular, argues that authoritarians are not apt to succeed in politics because they lack necessary qualities; specifically, (1) they cannot tolerate ambiguity (which he suggests is important in politics) and (2) they lack the necessary psychological skills for the job. Success in politics, of course, is a more specific issue than attraction to, and entry into, political roles. Lasswell (1954, p. 222) spoke to this issue when he offered the hypothesis: "Intensely power-centered persons tend to be relegated to comparatively minor roles." He claims that such a situation is likely to be true for dogmatic personalities. Also relevant are the observations of Sanford (1951) and Levinson (1964) that authoritarians are among the most apathetic political personalities. To the contrary, Barker (1963) contends that there are as many authoritarians among political passives as there are among political actives and militants.

A number of speculations can be advanced to explain why the American data do not support the earlier Italian findings. First of all, the American state legislator role may not be conceived as a "professional" political role, which is the focus of our hypotheses. Secondly, notwithstanding the element of professionalization, there is a question of structural differences in the political hierarchy: politics at the American state level may be a substantially different ball game from the big leagues of a national parliament. Perhaps there are some very real—sociological and psychological—differences between national and state (or provincial) politics such that persons with different types of personality are attracted into politics at different levels and for different functions.

These seemingly irreconcilable sets of data, however, take on more theoretical significance when a number of more precise considerations are taken into account. We believe what the American data show is that the relationship between personality and professional political role occurs at a more refined level of specificity than was proposed in the hypotheses. This contention is based on the significant differences in dogmatism scores which were found for the American sample for the variable assessing professional orientation to the political role of legislator. Our American data, in these respects, are somewhat similar to those of Harned (1961) who, in a Connecticut study, found that people who worked for political parties were likely to be neither authoritarian nor non-authoritarian, but that authoritarianism did seem to be associated differentially with the way in which the political role was performed.

The argument of spuriousness, however, cannot be dismissed. We prefer, however, to believe that the inconsistency in our findings is not totally unexpected and that this belief can be supported by a more refined analysis of these data from a cross-cultural perspective. We will turn to such a discussion at this point.

SOCIO-CULTURAL CONTRASTS

With regard to cultural factors, one need not elaborate at great length about the differences between the political history of America and that of Italy. We have had a highly stable democracy since its inception as contrasted with a country which, during only the past thirty years, has witnessed three different forms of political rule. Specific comparisons of the contemporary political systems of America and Italy reveal a number of structural and substantive variations of democracy in these two nations. First, we have a presidential versus a parliamentary republic, concretely represented in the past 30 years by eight governments in America versus 38 in Italy. Secondly, there is a two-party system in America versus a multi-party one in Italy. Italian elections often include hundreds of different political organizations. For example, in 1948, for the election of the first parliament under the newly formed Italian Republic, over 300 different political parties were listed on electoral ballots throughout Italy. Even in more recent national elections like those held in March 1972, over 80 parties presented slates of candidates in competition for parliamentary seats.

Much more significant, perhaps, from the perspective of personality are the substantive differences between "ideological" and "methodological" parties in these two political systems. Political parties in Italy—of which there are eight major or national ones that we discussed earlier (see Table 7.4)—are ideological ones. Each party advances a different political doctrine and philosophy of life. American political parties, on the other hand—for all intents and purposes there are only two principal ones—represent no such ideological or philosophical differences. The differences between major American political parties are more methodological in nature. Each party offers primarily methodical or procedural variations on the same fundamental ideology. Differences in political ideology— however rare—in American parties are found more often within a party in the form of a specific political philosophy or methodological orientation of a faction and/or particular candidate for political office (see DiRenzo, 1968).

Our data provide some support for this distinction between the American and Italian political systems. The Italian data show that statistically significant differences in dogmatism can be found on the basis of political party affiliation for the political sample. Such is not the case for the American data. The distribution of personality types is practically identical for Republicans and Democrats in both the political and nonpolitical samples. We have found this same lack of association between dogmatism and political party affiliation/ preference rather consistently in several American studies (see, e.g., DiRenzo, 1968, 1971). We believe that this kind of result is reflective of the nonideological nature of American political parties.

Moreover, unlike the Italian study, no statistically significant patterns of association between personality type and religious preference were found in either the American political or nonpolitical samples. Whereas religious ideology is intrinsic to the political ideology of the major Italian parties, religious preference does not seem relevant to American parties, unless one wishes to consider a nonspecific theistic belief. Such a belief, however, is common to both major parties in the American political system. In sum, we believe that the differences in the substantive nature, as well as in the number, of political parties in Italy and America accounts for much of the inconsistency in the dogmatism findings in our two sets of national data.[11]

The hypothetical issues we have studied, while clarified and delineated in a more complex formulation, are not resolved. We believe our hypotheses remain tenable, but they require further specification. The dimensions of our cross-cultural analysis are meant to be suggestive rather than exhaustive.[12] The cultural elements which we have considered—as well as the more sociological and organizational factors which were raised earlier, such as the status level of the political office and full-time versus part-time activity—represent a host of considerations that need to be explored for their modifying influence on the relationship of personality to political role. Elsewhere (DiRenzo, 1974) we have suggested that further attention needs to be given to such things as: (1) different types (e.g., mayor, alderman, judge) and status levels (e.g., municipal, state, federal) of political office, (2) kinds of recruitment (e.g., elective or appointive), (3) distinctions between "leaders" and "representatives," (4) the focus of political representation in terms of whose interests are being represented,[13] (5) styles and forms of political activity,[14] (6) self-images, (7) conceptions of the political role,[15] and (8) role of party factions. Personality, we submit, may be related in significant and systematic ways to such variables and, in turn, such relationships may affect how the political actor defines a political situation.

THEORETICAL SIGNIFICANCE

The ultimate significance of the hypothesis of distinctive modal personality types will be known only when we examine the effects such types have on the quality and the functioning of political roles and systems. The fundamental question is whether the structures and processes of political organization are related in any way to the kinds of personality types which are attracted into the political system. The importance of the present findings for explaining political behavior may be noted in a consideration of the functional congruence between

[11]A more elaborate statement on the relationship of personality to methodological and ideological parties can be found in DiRenzo (1967c, pp. 119-170).

[12]For example, in this cross-cultural analysis mention at least should be made of the role of national character. Considerations of space, however, do not permit a pursuit of this concern. For a discussion of the role of national character with regard to the Italian findings, see DiRenzo (1967c, pp. 80-91).

[13]Relevant here are the following role conceptions of Wahlke et al. (1962): (1) the parliamentarian, (2) the representative, and (3) the clientelistic.

[14]For work related to this type of variable, see Matthews (1960), Barber (1965), and Hargrove (1966).

[15]One of the focal aspects in any examination of the relationship of personality to occupational structures should be a study of the conceptions of the social roles which are involved and the specific role behavior which takes place. Our data suggest that among the parliamentarian and legislative subjects there is by no means a homogeneous conception of their political role—in terms of either what it is or what it ought to be.

personality systems and political systems. In order for social systems to function as they have been structured to function, the personality systems involved have to operate in harmony with the social system. The problematic situation is that social systems may recruit personalities that, by and large, do not or cannot function effectively within them.

Our argument implies that the form of government in a particular social system is related to the kinds of personalities that are recruited into the polity or who are potential recruits for that system. Specifically, with reference to the personality characteristics in our data, it has been argued that the dogmatic and authoritarian personality is antithetical to the democratic process (see, e.g., Lane, 1962). Yet, dogmatic and authoritarian personalities can and do function within democratic structures. We do not contend that all agents of a particular system need to be either democratic or authoritarian in personality structure, as the case may be, but only that the active cooperation of a sufficient number of the appropriate type is required for a political system to function in either a democratic or an authoritarian manner. In fact, it is possible that all decision making from a functional perspective is not the result of an exclusively democratic or authoritarian process. Certain political roles need more authoritarian or dogmatic personalities, just as others may need more democratic or open-minded personalities. Similarly, authoritarian structures may be functionally dependent to some extent upon more democratic personalities. Hence both types of personality, although in varying proportions, may be required in any political system. The crucial factor is the modality of the personality structure that characterizes the system. Any political system—of whatever form—needs the functional support of a sufficient number of congruent personalities. There is some empirical evidence by Dicks (1950) on Nazism, as well as Inkeles et al. (1958) on the Soviet socio-political system, which strongly suggests that this situation does indeed obtain.

Any situation that does not maintain an effective degree of congruence between the functional requirements of the personality and political systems is apt to result in dysfunctional consequences in either or both (see Inkeles, 1959). Stability and change in political systems is, to some extent, a function of the congruity or incongruity which is shared with the respective personality systems.[16] The greater the congruity, the more stable the organization and the more minimal the social change. For example, political consensus and cleavage—exemplified in such forms as alliances, coalitions, factions, and changes in party affiliation—may be a function, at least in part, of the congruent composition of the total personality structures within any given political system (see DiRenzo, 1967b, 1967c). These theoretical questions are challenging and exciting. Substantially more cross-cultural research, however, needs to be undertaken before we can make more definitive statements and predictions on the interrelationships of personality and socio-political systems.

[16]Data on the relationship of personality to modes of socio-political change may be found in DiRenzo (1970).

CHAPTER 8

Self-Other Orientations and Political Behavior

Robert C. Ziller, William F. Stone, Robert M. Jackson, and Natalie J. Terbovic

Editor's Introduction

Ziller and his associates in this next chapter approach the question of who becomes a political leader in a different manner from DiRenzo and, indeed, from most previous research on this topic. Instead of comparing politicians with nonpoliticians, they sought out candidates for an election and asked: Are there personal characteristics associated with winning and losing an election? It is noteworthy that candidates have not been used earlier as subjects for such research. Here are persons who are interested in a political position and have passed through the recruitment process. Each candidate is attempting to influence the eligible voters to vote for him. Only some candidates, however, are successful in this influence attempt and are elected. What conditions have an impact on which candidate is successful in his influence attempt? The candidate's personal characteristics are one type of variable which can affect the electorate and how it votes. How often have we heard journalists and news analysts refer to a particular election campaign as a contest of personalities

174

rather than issues? Ziller and his colleagues suggest two personal characteristics which seem to influence who is elected, specifically which candidates for state legislative positions are elected. By examining losing candidates, as well as winners, Ziller et al. also provide information on the kinds of persons who are interested in a political position but unsuccessful in achieving one—information that is not available in a comparison of politicians with nonpoliticians.

The two personal characteristics which are examined in this chapter are self-esteem and complexity of the self concept. Self-esteem has already received some consideration as an important characteristic in the determination of political leaders. As Ziller and his colleagues note, Lasswell (1930, 1948) has proposed that people become politicians to compensate for feelings of insecurity or low self-esteem. Moreover, one of the defining characteristics of Barber's (1965) typology of freshmen state legislators was self-esteem. Biographies of Wilson (George and George, 1956), Forrestal (Rogow, 1963), and such revolutionaries as Gandhi and Lenin (Wolfenstein, 1967) lend support to the importance of self-esteem in determining who becomes a political leader. On the other hand, complexity of the self concept as defined by Ziller and his associates has been talked about very little in relation to political leaders. This personal characteristic, however, bears a resemblance to a more general personal characteristic, cognitive complexity, which has intrigued researchers studying political leadership. Two other chapters in this book, Chapter 12 by Hermann and Chapter 13 by Driver, explore the relationship between cognitive complexity and political behavior.

Like the Milburn research on the Q-sort (Chapter 6), the studies Ziller and his associates report are multivariate. Ziller et al. show that it is the combination of these two personal characteristics which affects electoral success rather than each by itself. Although most research on the personal characteristics of political leaders examines one characteristic at a time, the ultimate goal is to explore how the characteristics interact in determining who becomes a political leader. After all, most people are characterized by many rather than a single trait. It is the mix of these traits that affects what an individual does. With their research Ziller and his associates have advanced us toward this goal.

Chapter 8 is also relevant to an examination of the effects of a political leader's personal characteristics on his political behavior. These researchers study the effects of self-esteem and complexity of the self concept on behavior in a state legislature. They explore the question of whether or not characteristics relevant to success with the electorate are helpful in achieving legislative success. Although Ziller and his colleagues could not follow their successful candidates into the state legislature, they do examine the behavior of another group of freshman state legislators. Their research allows the reader some glimpse into the parallels between winning at the ballot box and being an effective legislator.

The authors of this chapter, like DiRenzo in the previous chapter, use a questionnaire to gather data on personal characteristics. Their measures are short and easily filled out, requiring only 15 minutes to complete. The questionnaires demand little of the subject's time. Ziller et al. indicate little difficulty in getting either candidates or state legislators to answer the questionnaire. Only 10 percent of these political figures declined to participate in the studies. Ziller and his associates combine their field studies on candidates and state legislators with two laboratory studies which examine intervening mechanisms relevant to explaining the field results. Their research demonstrates how studies in the laboratory can complement studies in the field and vice versa.

   Ziller's interest in examining the personal characteristics of political leaders is an outgrowth of his theoretical work on patterns of self-other orientation presented in his recent book, *The Social Self* (Ziller, 1973). He is a professor of psychology at the University of Florida. Stone, who is a professor of psychology at the University of Maine at Orono, indicates he became intrigued by the many ways politics and psychology are interrelated during his involvement in the 1968 Democratic National Convention. In his *Psychology of Politics* (Stone, 1974), he examines how research in personality and social psychology aids in explaining why people become politically active. The other two authors of this chapter, Jackson and Terbovic, were graduate students of Ziller. Currently Jackson is an associate professor of political science at Chico State University in California. Terbovic is an instructor in the Division of Women at York College of the City University of New York.

ALTHOUGH OBSERVERS PROLIFERATE examples of political events that were critically mediated by the personal characteristics of key actors, Greenstein (1968) has noted the lack of systematic research relating personality and politics. The research in this chapter was conducted to help fill this void. The studies which are reported focus on what types of persons are elected to political office. The research is based on a social psychological theory of personality which is concerned with the concept of self and the development of notions of self in relation to significant others (see Ziller, 1973).

   In examining personality and politics, a central construct of importance from this theory of the social self is the responsiveness of the political candidate to others. How sensitive is the candidate to the views of others? An individual is responsive if he will change his opinion in the direction of greater agreement with those of significant others in the environment. In other words, the responsive individual is not only aware of and sensitive to the opinions of others but also acts on the basis of this awareness.

   In what ways does responsiveness affect political recruitment and selection? The pattern of behavior viewed as crucial in American politics is the process of negotiation, accommodation, and bargaining among diverse groups under conditions of conflict. The relative power of the diverse groups is assumed to be a variable relevant to the consistency of political behavior. In an environment in which a single group or a coalition is clearly dominant, consistent political behavior congruent with the opinions of the power component of the constituency may be the basis for recruiting candidates and for political survival. Persons who practice this approach to politics we will call ideologues. The ideologue is responsive to a single dominant subgroup, that is, he responds consistently to the range of opinions supported by the dominant group in the constituency. On the other hand, where the balance of power among diverse subgroups is tenuous, a pragmatic approach to politics may be indicated. In the pragmatic approach the politician seeks an ad hoc policy decision rather than a decision in terms of his own guiding principles or those emerging from the opinions of a given segment of the constituency. The pragmatic politician is responsive to a pluralistic constituency.

SELF-ESTEEM AND RESPONSIVENESS

In the theory concerned with self-other orientations, responsiveness is associated with two components of the self concept: self-esteem and complexity of the self concept (see Ziller, 1973). Self-esteem is that component of the self system which is involved in regulating the extent to which the self system is maintained under conditions of strain such as occur during the processing of new information relative to the self. For example, neither positive nor negative evaluations evoke immediate corresponding action by the individual with high self-esteem. The response is mediated by the self concept. New information relative to the self is examined in terms of its relevance and meaning for the self system, and the social stimulus may be ignored or transformed in such a way as to maintain consistency in behavior. In this way the person with high self-esteem remains somewhat insulated from the environment and is not completely subject to environmental contingencies. Thus, high self-esteem is associated with integration of the self system and consistency of social behavior. The individual is not a victim of events nor does he feel compelled to accommodate the self to the situation.

Persons with low self-esteem, on the other hand, do not possess a well-developed conceptual buffer for evaluative stimuli. The individual with low self-esteem is field dependent; that is, he tends to passively conform to the influence of the prevailing field or context (Witkin, Dyk, Faterson, Goodenough, and Karp, 1962). Since the individual's behavior is directly linked to immediate environmental circumstances and is not mediated and integrated through the self concept, he is inclined toward inconsistency (Mossman and Ziller, 1968).

The relationship between self-esteem and political candidacy has been discussed at length by both Lasswell (1930) and Barber (1965). Lasswell (1930) described political figures as individuals suffering from marked feelings of personal inadequacy or inferiority who seek out political opportunities to compensate for these feelings. Barber (1965, p. 224) pictured two types of political candidates: (1) those who have such high self-esteem that they can manage relatively easily the threats, strains, and anxieties involved in the role of candidate; and (2) those who have such low self-esteem that they are ready to become involved in the extraordinary procedures of political candidacy in order to raise their self-esteem.

COMPLEXITY OF THE SELF AND RESPONSIVENESS

The second component of the self system which is related to responsiveness is complexity of the self. Complexity of the self is defined as the number of facets of the self perceived by the individual or the degree of differentiation of the self concept. In Lewin's (1935) terms, complexity becomes the number of parts perceived as composing the whole.

It has been proposed that the earliest stage of self-awareness involves the separation of the self from the not-self. Since this primary differentiating cognitive process concerning self identity is one of the earliest and most enduring, it may also serve as a model for subsequent differentiating cognitive processes. Of course, the bifurcation of the universe into the categories of self and not-self is but the first step in an infinite sequence. The self can be further differentiated into an unlimited number of subparts. Following the first gross categorization of self and not-self, the infant begins to discriminate among other objects, both social and material, and among his feelings and emotions. The relationship of the self to others, particularly the parents, provides information about the self. As the child strives for independence from the parents, he learns to distinguish new aspects of the self. Group affiliations add further information about the self through comparisons and contrasts with the members and with other groups. By identifying with a group, the individual establishes that he is distinguished from those who are not in the group. Thus, the self is discovered by successive approximations in an external-internal direction.

Inherent in the developmental process is the tendency to evaluate the self in comparison with others (see Festinger, 1954). In fact, Festinger's theory of social comparison is based on the assumption that a correct appraisal of one's own opinions and abilities in relation to those of others is motivated by the need for a clearly defined self concept (Ziller, 1964). Through the process of social comparison, the individual establishes a frame of social reference with the self as a point of reference. In the process, the self is distinguished from others in terms of similarities and contrasts of opinions and abilities.

Expanding the theory of social comparison, it is proposed that meaningful encounters with a wide variety of others are associated with increased self dimensionality or complexity of the self concept. In order to establish similarities and contrasts with a wide variety of others, a more highly differentiated self-social concept evolves. Each person with whom the self is compared presents one or more facets different from those of other persons. The perceiver tends to code these facets as being included in or excluded from the self definition. The inclusion of more facets within the self definition increases self complexity. Continuous confrontation with diverse others is assumed to encourage closer scrutiny of the self followed by the emergence of a more highly differentiated self concept. The result is a multifaceted self concept. In support of this theoretical position, Elton and Rose (1973) found that subjects with many work experiences earned a significantly higher mean score on complexity (as measured by the Omnibus Personality Inventory) than did those with few work experiences.

Assuming that complexity of the self concept reflects the number of dimensions along which stimuli relevant to the self are ordered (see Harvey, Hunt, and Schroder, 1961) and that the ordering and organizing of stimuli is facilitated by attending to a wide range of stimuli, it is anticipated that individuals with complex self concepts may be aware of or consider a great number of stimuli as being potentially associated with the self. In terms of interpersonal perception, the complex person has a higher probability of matching some facet of the self with a facet of the other person, since there are a larger number of possible matches. The complex individual is more inclined toward assimilation of self and others or perceiving similarities between self and others; whereas, the simplex individual is inclined toward contrasting self and others. In general, then, it is proposed that persons with more complex self concepts attend to a broader range of social stimuli, perceive more similarities between self and others, and are more responsive to others. Direct support for these hypotheses relating complexity of the self concept and responsiveness to diverse others is provided by a study by Thompson (1966). Persons with complex as opposed to simplex self concepts (complexity of the self concept was measured by enumerating the number of adjectives checked as descriptive of the self) were found to perceive strangers twenty years their senior as being more similar to themselves. Moreover, children with complex self concepts have been found to be more sociometrically popular than children with simplex self concepts (Ziller, 1973).

SELF-ESTEEM AND COMPLEXITY OF SELF MATRIX

The research reported in this chapter is based upon a classification of subjects according to their self-esteem (high-low) and the complexity of their self concepts (high-low). The four cells generated by high-low self-esteem and high-low complexity of the self describe four possible combinations or patterns of self-other orientation. Each cell indicates a different degree of responsiveness to others.

The high self-esteem, high complexity cell includes individuals with a differentiated and integrated theory of social behavior. However, while the high-high person is capable of assimilating new information concerning the self without jeopardizing the self system, there are distinct limits on his responsivity. Indeed, individuals in this category are inclined to develop personal guidance systems which are too abstract and too removed from the guidance systems of the general population. They have difficulty being responsive to the general population. Henceforth, we will refer to a person in this category as *apolitical.*

The low self-esteem, high complexity cell describes the person with a very tentative theory of social behavior, a person who is responsive to a wide range of

social stimuli. In terms of political behavior, a low-high person is quite responsive to the opinions of others in his constituency. We will refer to a person in
this category as a *pragmatist*.

The high self-esteem, low complexity quadrant includes persons with closed
theories of behavior. They are generally nonresponsive to the opinions of others.
Rokeach's (1960) concept of dogmatism may also be describing these individuals
who render absolute rather than tentative judgments. With regard to political
behavior, the *ideologue* is included in this cell.

It is more difficult to characterize succinctly persons in the low self-esteem,
low complexity cell. We will tentatively propose that these individuals are highly
responsive within a narrow range of social stimuli. This category of persons will
be referred to as *indeterminate*.

In the rest of this chapter we will present the results of four studies designed
to explore the relationship between self-other orientation, responsiveness, and
selection for a political office. Studies 1 and 2 were conducted in the field. They
examine the kind of self-other orientation found in candidates who win elections
and who are successful in their political role. Studies 3 and 4 were conducted in
the laboratory. They investigate the link between self-other orientation and
responsiveness which we have posited as important in explaining the outcomes
of the field studies.

Study 1. A Political Personality Syndrome[1]

The first study explores the patterns of self-other orientation which occur most
frequently among persons holding political positions. Moreover, the findings are
cross-validated with regard to winning an election for political office. Political
districts in the region studied (Oregon) were assumed to be pluralistic. Thus, it
was hypothesized that winning political candidates would be pragmatic or
responsive politicians (low self-esteem, high complexity of the self concept).
Changes in self-esteem were also analyzed in association with winning or losing
an election for political office.

METHOD

Subjects.   The subjects included 91 politicians who had already won the
primary election and who were candidates in the general election for the

[1]The research program from which Study 1 emanated was supported by a grant to the
senior author from the National Science Foundation. An earlier report of this study was
presented at the Western Small Groups Meetings, San Diego, California, March 27, 1968,
and appears in Ziller (1973). We are deeply indebted to the school personnel and the
political candidates who graciously cooperated in this study, to Gary Gregor, Daniel
Langmeyer, and Peter Shockett who helped in the data collection phases of the project, and
to Joseph McGrath, University of Illinois, who shared his insights with us in the early stages
of data analysis and interpretation.

legislature of the state of Oregon, 104 male elementary and high-school teachers, 150 male school principals, and 44 school superintendents. The sample of politicians represents 90 per cent of the candidates in the general election for state legislature approached by the data collectors. Public school superintendents were studied because they hold a political position not unlike that of the state legislator (Wriston, 1959) in terms of the pressures on the position for responsiveness and conflict resolution by a pluralistic community. Indeed, it may be said that a superintendent of schools is a politician without benefit of political party. The teachers and principals were selected as a convenient control group of adult males. The role of teacher was assumed to be least associated with the role of politician.

The sample of school personnel were selected from the states of Oregon, Nevada, Washington, and Idaho. The school communities included in the sample were determined in part by geographic proximity. Eighty-two per cent of the public school personnel approached agreed to complete the instruments and returned them to the research organization. The teachers selected to be in the sample were always from the same school building as one of the principals who, in turn, were usually under the supervision of one of the superintendents in the sample. Moreover, the teachers selected were those closest in age to the principal.

Procedure. The data collector traveled to the home community of the subjects and usually approached the subject personally concerning his participation in the study. This visit was preceded by a letter explaining the nature of the project in general terms. The political candidates usually completed the form while the data collector waited. School personnel returned the forms to the university office of the project director. The directions on the cover of the Self-Other Orientation Tasks for school personnel were: "The questions which follow are designed to provide an indication of the way you look at yourself in relation to significant other people. In this description of yourself and others, words are avoided. This is a social psychological instrument designed for research purposes only. Hopefully, it will tell us something about differences in the perceptions of self and others among educators in the states of Idaho, Nevada, Oregon, and Washington. This instrument has been approved by the Department of Health, Education, and Welfare, Office of Education. Please work as quickly as possible. It should require about fifteen minutes or less."

The measure of self-esteem was administered twice to a sample of 44 political candidates—once about six weeks before the general election and a second time two to four weeks after the general election. The latter sample was determined simply on the basis of proximity to the data collector and availability.

Measures. The measures of self-esteem and complexity of the self concept were derived from two instruments in the Self-Other Orientation Tasks (Ziller, 1973). The measure of self-esteem (see Ziller, Hagey, Smith, and Long, 1969) presents the subject with a horizontal array of circles and a list of significant others which includes doctor, father, a friend, a nurse, yourself, someone you know who is unsuccessful. The subject is asked to assign each person to a circle in the horizontal array. The score is the weighted position of the self. In accordance with the cultural norm, positions to the left are associated with higher scores. Significant other persons provide the social context for self evaluation and also serve to mask the intent of the item.

Previous research concerning self-esteem has not emphasized sufficiently the social nature of the self system. The failure to incorporate and weigh social factors within the self-evaluation framework may have contributed, in part at least, to the disappointing state of theory and research on self-esteem. Perhaps a more serious problem is that previous research has largely involved verbal, self-report measures of self-esteem. Such measures assume that a subject's word labels for his constructs mean what the examiner thinks they mean which may not be the case (see Kelly, 1955). To avoid this problem Kelly (1955, p. 268) suggests that if a test "can be arranged to produce a kind of protocol which can be subjected to a meaningful analysis, independent of words, we shall have made progress toward a better understanding of the client's personal constructs."

The method of communication between the subject and investigator in the measure of self-esteem used here involves the medium of a structured projective technique with limited verbal demands. The subject is asked to arrange symbols of the self and significant others. The arrangement is presumed to be an expression of his perceived relationship with others. The outcome may be referred to as a cognitive sociometric of self and other. In developing the theory and measures of self-other orientation, it was assumed that the human organism finds it expedient to order, map, or structure the multitude of social stimuli. The processes used by persons are expected to be somewhat idiosyncratic, but owing to commonality among human experiences, sensory processes, classification systems, and normative processes, the evolving abstraction systems possess sufficient similarity that a basis for a communication system exists.

The most relevant ordering process with regard to self-esteem is what DeSoto, London, and Handel (1965) refer to as "spatial paralogic" and "linear ordering." It is observed that people are prone to place elements in a linear ordering to the exclusion of other structures and that they handle linear ordering more easily than most other structures. Indeed, DeSoto, London, and Handel (1965) note that serial ordering proceeds more readily in a rightward direction than in a leftword direction. The tendency to attribute greater importance to the object placed in the extreme left position in a horizontal display has also been noted by Morgan (1944). Moreover, children in both American and Asian Indian cultures have been found to use the left-right spatial paralogic.

Research using this self-esteem measure by Ziller and his associates suggests a certain degree of validity for the scale. For example, low status others are located on the extreme right of the horizontal array a disproportionally higher percentage of the time than high status others (Ziller, Long, Ramana, and Reddy, 1968). It has also been found that sociometrically unchosen children tend to show lower self-esteem than highly chosen children (Ziller, Alexander, and Long, 1966). Moreover, neuropsychiatric patients in comparison with normal patients and depressed patients in comparison with other neuropsychiatric patients show lower self-esteem (Ziller, Megas, and DeCencio, 1964). Furthermore, neuropsychiatric patients who participated more frequently in a group discussion were found to have higher self-esteem than those who participated less frequently (Mossman and Ziller, 1968). Finally, persons with high self-esteem were more consistent in their frequency of participation across group therapy sessions than persons with low self-esteem (Mossman and Ziller, 1968).

The measure of complexity of the self concept used in this study was an adjective check list of 109 high frequency adjectives selected from the Thorndike-Lorge (1944) Word Book. The subject is asked to check each adjective which he thinks is descriptive of him. Consistent with the definition of complexity of the self concept as the number of facets of the self perceived by the individual, the measure of complexity of the self concept is the total number of words checked. The concept and measure derive from a study of accuracy of perceptual recall (Glanzer and Clark, 1963) in which it was suggested that the length of a subject's verbalizations may serve as an index of perceived complexity of the stimulus. It has been found, for example, that fewer words are required to describe a square or circle than a very irregular or unusual figure. A similar assumption is made by Zajonc (1960).

Like the self-esteem measure, research using this measure of complexity of the self concept shows some validity for the scale. For instance, it has been found that persons with high complexity of the self concept tend to be more popular (Ziller, Alexander, and Long, 1966), have a wider range of social experiences (Golding and Ziller, 1968), use wider category widths, identify with a wider range of others (Thompson, 1966), and require more time to reach a decision in an information search group decision-making situation (Smith, 1967). Moreover, Ridgeway (1965) found that persons who check a greater number of adjectives as descriptive of the self also rate themselves higher on a self-report measure of complexity of the self concept and draw more lines connecting a circle which represents the self to circles which represent other people. Finally, a Pearson correlation of .50 ($p < .05$) was found between complexity of the self concept and perception of the self as located within as opposed to outside a field of significant other people (Golding and Ziller, 1968).

Corrected split-half reliability coefficients on the present sample of subjects for self-esteem and complexity of the self concept were .90 and .92 respectively. Self-esteem was also found to be negatively correlated with complexity of the self concept ($r = -.28, p < .01$).

RESULTS

Changes in the self-esteem of political candidates were analyzed after the experience of winning or losing the general election. Candidates who were elected to office tended to gain in self-esteem (65 percent increased, 17 percent

Table 8.1.   Frequency of Four Self-Other Orientations among
              Teachers, Principals, Superintendents, and Legislators

Type of Subject	Complexity of Self	Self-Esteem High	Self-Esteem Low
Teachers	High	28	21
	Low	33	22
Principals	High	41	28
	Low	48	33
Superintendents	High	4	11
	Low	17	12
Legislators	High	9	11
	Low	19	19

decreased, and 17 percent remained unchanged); whereas, candidates who were not elected increased in self-esteem a lower percentage of the time and decreased in self-esteem a higher percentage of the time (38 percent increased, 52 percent decreased, and 10 percent remained the same). The chi-square for these data was significant ($X^2 = 6.01, df = 2, p < .05$). It is noteworthy that the candidates who were not elected yet increased in self-esteem were all nonincumbents. The publicity associated with candidacy may be reinforcing.

In analyzing the frequency of occurrence of patterns of self-esteem and complexity among teachers, principals, superintendents, and legislators, the distribution of scores of the total sample was divided at the mean and the frequencies with which the patterns occurred were tabulated (see Table 8.1). Only the political candidates who were elected to office were included in this analysis. Table 8.1 shows that the high complexity, high self-esteem (apolitical) pattern occurred with lower frequency among superintendents and legislators. In order to test the significance of this observation, the four categories of subjects were analyzed with regard to high and low self-esteem and high complexity and with regard to high and low self-esteem and low complexity. The results for high complexity were statistically significant ($X^2 = 4.12, df = 1, p < .04$) and indicate that superintendents and legislators in contrast with principals and teachers were less likely to be characterized by the high complexity, high self-esteem (apolitical) pattern. The results with regard to low self complexity were not statistically significant.

In an effort to cross-validate the previous results, the total sample of political candidates (not merely those elected as legislators) was divided according to the outcome of the general election. These data are presented in Table 8.2. Again, only the results for high complexity were statistically significant ($X^2 = 9.95, df = 1, p < .002$). Those elected to office showed the high complexity, high

Table 8.2. Frequency of Four Self-Other Orientations among
Elected and Nonelected Political Candidates

Subject's Election Outcome	Complexity of Self	Self-Esteem	
		High	*Low*
Elected	High	5 (28%)	14 (88%)
	Low	22 (69%)	14 (56%)
Nonelected	High	13 (72%)	2 (12%)
	Low	10 (31%)	11 (44%)

Note: Percentages listed indicate the proportion of persons with the particular self-other orientation elected or not elected to office.

self-esteem (apolitical) pattern less frequently, but showed the high complexity, low self-esteem (pragmatist) pattern more frequently. Of the 18 high-high (apolitical) candidates only 5 (28 percent) were elected to office; whereas 14 (88 percent) of the 16 high complexity, low self-esteem (pragmatist) candidates were elected to office.

The analysis just reported compares each of the self-other orientations with one other. It is possible, however, with the data in Table 8.2 to compare each self-other orientation with every other. In addition to the results already presented, the other significant chi-square (X^2=6.22, df=1, $p > .05$) indicates that the high-high (apolitical) candidates were also elected less frequently than the candidates who were low in complexity, high in self-esteem (the ideologues). The chi-square comparing the election and nonelection frequencies for the high complexity, low self-esteem (pragmatist) candidates with those for the low complexity, low self-esteem (indeterminate) candidates approached significance ($X^2 = 3.13$, $df = 1$, $p = .08$). Not only were the high-high (apolitical) candidates less likely to be elected than the high complexity, low self-esteem (pragmatist) candidates, the low-low (indeterminate) candidates also were less likely to be elected than the high complexity, low self-esteem (pragmatist) candidates.

Finally, let us note that only one of the 31 incumbents who were candidates for re-election lost in the election. The personality pattern of the nonelected incumbent was high self-esteem, high complexity (apolitical).

DISCUSSION

We consistently observed that the high self-esteem, high complexity of the self concept pattern of personality was associated with nonelection to a political office or nonappointment as public school superintendent. As proposed earlier, the high-high pattern appears to indicate the apolitical personality. Moreover, as we initially suggested, the high complexity, low self-esteem pattern (the pragmatic politician) appears to denote the political personality or, at least, the personality pattern associated with the highest likelihood of election to office.

The results are somewhat contradictory to those of earlier studies (e.g., Barber, 1965; Lasswell, 1930) which focused on only one aspect of the self system, self-esteem, and suggested that becoming a political candidate compensated for low self-esteem. Table 8.2, for example, shows that candidates with low self-esteem were more likely to be elected if they were high in complexity (pragmatist) and less likely to be elected if they were low in complexity (indeterminate). Moreover, candidates high in self-esteem were likely to be elected if they were low in complexity (ideologues). Of course, previous investigators have used observations or self reports as measures of self-esteem as opposed to the more indirect, limited verbal approach described here. Under conditions of self report, some persons proclaiming high self-esteem are simply describing what they half-believe themselves to be and would like to be, but they need continual confirmation (including self reports) in order to buttress their unsure self image (Maslow, Hirsh, Stein, and Honegmann, 1945).

The results are also somewhat incongruent with the theoretical frameworks of Lewin (1935) and Schroder, Driver, and Streufert (1967). The latter theorists suggest that the highest level of adaptation is achieved by persons whose life space is highly differentiated (high complexity of the self concept in terms of self-other orientation) yet highly integrated (high self-esteem here)—the apolitical personality in the present framework. The focus, however, of these earlier frameworks is individual adaptation within a social environment where the individual can select social encounters to a greater degree than a politician. The results of the present study suggest that a low self-esteem, high complexity personality pattern (pragmatist) may be more viable in the social-political environment because social responsiveness is a critical social demand. The politician is required to be other directed and aware of a multiplicity of social presses in order to deal with his pluralistic political district. The apolitical or high self-esteem, high complexity personality is less suited for a political role because he is, in Reisman's (1954) terms, inner directed. He shows little responsiveness to the diverse others in a pluralistic social unit.

We have been discussing which self-other orientations are associated with being elected to a state legislature. Another question of interest is how do these self-other orientations affect the political behavior of newly elected state legislators once they arrive in the legislature? The different roles available within a legislature may demand a variety of self-other orientation patterns. For example, legislators who are responsible for initiating, formulating, and seeking approval of new public policies—the lawmaker in Barber's (1965) terms—may be characterized by the usually apolitical high self-esteem, high complexity orientation. These legislators "are freed by virtue of exceptionally strong personal resources—particularly a deep sense of personal identity and self-acceptance—to deviate from the common path precisely because they are in possession of powerful techniques for dealing directly with accompanying strain" (Barber, 1965,

p. 224). The second study examines the political behavior of new state legislators in the state of Maine on whom there is information about self-other orientations.

Study 2. Political Personality and Legislative Success[2]

Voter attention to legislative compaigns and candidates is usually slight, barring some particularly compelling issue. How then do personality differences among candidates affect election outcomes? It seems unlikely that differences in responsiveness among candidates directly affect the voter, since so few voters have actually interacted with the candidate. Rather, it seems likely that electoral success is a two-stage process (see Stone, 1974). The first stage involves the impression a candidate makes on a relatively few people in face-to-face interaction. Those people who are favorably impressed by the candidate work for his election, raise money for his campaign, and talk with other people in the candidate's behalf. Thus, appeal to larger constituencies, which Stone (1974) has termed *remote* political leadership, depends upon effectiveness in the more intimate *face-to-face* leadership situation.

According to this line of thought, a candidate's self-other orientation will affect how he relates with others which, in turn, determines how much enthusiasm, time, and money are devoted to his campaign. Of course, the candidate's looks and ideology also affect electoral outcomes so that the correlation between personality and campaign success is necessarily inperfect. If the observed relationship between electoral success and self-other orientation does depend upon differences in impressions made in personal encounters, we would expect politicians of different orientations to be differentially evaluated by their intimates.

The impact of the hypothesized differences in interpersonal behavior related to the self-other orientations should be particularly pronounced in a state legislature, where members are in daily face-to-face interaction over a prolonged period of time. If the suggested behavioral differences among self-other types do exist, it seems likely that legislators will react to these differences among their fellows. In addition, it seems probable that differences in self-other orientation will affect a legislator's approach to his work. The present study was designed to look into these matters, using as subjects newly elected state legislators in the state of Maine.

The Maine House of Representatives numbers 151 members. In the term which began in January 1973, 46 of the 151 were in their first term of office. The plan for this study called for the measurement of self-other orientation in

[2]Study 2 reports the current status of ongoing research being conducted by William F. Stone with the assistance of Galen L. Baril. They wish to express their gratitude for the cooperation of the members of the House of Representatives of the 106th Maine Legislature.

these freshman legislators early in the session, followed by an assessment of their activity and their impact upon their fellows toward the end of the legislative session.

Based upon the theory of self-other orientation which has been presented here, we predicted that the pragmatic political type (high complexity, low self-esteem) would be more highly regarded by his colleagues than would representatives characterized by the other types. The ideologue (high self-esteem, low complexity) was expected to be more task oriented, that is, more actively involved in his legislative work. We have previously suggested that these two types might be serving different constituencies in their electoral districts. In other words, their districts are either pluralistic or homogeneous. In their legislative interaction, legislators with these two self-other orientations might also be expected to appeal to similarly defined subgroups in the legislature itself. Both the pragmatic and the ideological types were expected to be more positively evaluated by their peers than the apolitical type (high in both complexity and self-esteem). No predictions were made regarding the fourth type, the legislator who is low on both self variables.

METHOD

Self-other orientation questionnaires were administered to 42 of the 46 freshman legislators in January during the first three weeks of the legislative session. (The other four legislators declined.) The questionnaires included the six self-esteem items and the complexity measure previously described, as well as items designed to measure self-centrality and social interest (Ziller, 1973). Only the self-esteem and complexity data will be discussed here. The tests were given on a one-to-one basis by one of four graduate students who explained the tests briefly to the legislator, usually in the legislative chamber. Those legislators who agreed to complete the tests were allowed to complete them in private.

Information on the activity of these first-term legislators was obtained from legislative records. The number of bills introduced by each legislator and the number which passed were obtained from such records. In addition, the transcripts of the proceedings of the House were searched and a count was made of the number of column lines spoken by each freshman legislator. (Maine legislators do not have the privilege of amending the remarks which they make on the floor during legislative sessions.)

In early June, just before the end of the legislative session, a questionnaire was mailed to the 148 incumbent House members (three had died during the session). Responses to the questionnaire were anonymous. The respondent was asked only to indicate his political party and term of office. The names of the 46 freshman members were listed in a column on the right-hand side of the page. In the blank spaces provided, the respondent was asked to write the names of the three of these freshman legislators whom he or she felt were most likely to be successful in a subsequent legislative term. Next, the legislator was asked to check seven others on the list who also promised to be successful. On the following page, using the same procedure, respondents were asked to indicate their liking for their first-term colleagues. With one follow-up request from the investigator, 79 of the 148 members (53 percent) responded to the mailed questionnaire. There was no bias in the returns, either by party or by term of service.

RESULTS

The distributions of self-esteem and complexity scores were divided at the respective medians, with scores at the median being assigned to the "low" classification. Only 36 of the 42 first-term legislators who were tested had usable scores on both measures. Of the six subjects whose test scores were not usable, one had checked all of the adjectives on the complexity instrument and five had completed the self-esteem items in a stereotyped manner. By stereotyped manner we mean that they listed themselves and the significant others in the exact order in which they were listed on the test item. These six subjects were discarded for purposes of the analysis. The number of subjects in each personality category based on the median split is shown in Table 8.3.

Success scores were computed from the post-session questionnaire responses by the following procedure. A legislator who was among the first three mentioned (in writing) as being most likely to be successful received 8 points. Four points were awarded to a freshman whose name was among the other seven listed as having some promise of being successful. The sum of these scores across all respondents was the freshman's "success" score. Liking scores were similarly computed. Mean success and liking scores are also presented in Table 8.3.

Success scores were analyzed by means of a two-way analysis of variance with self-esteem and complexity as the independent variables. Neither main effect was significant. That is, neither self-esteem nor complexity alone accounted for variation in success scores. The predicted interaction between self-esteem and complexity was significant, however ($F = 5.19$, $df = 1/32$, $p < .05$). The interaction is shown in Figure 8.1. The highest mean success ratings were obtained by the pragmatic and ideological types, the lowest by the apolitical and indeterminate types.

Success and liking were not independent, however. The product-moment correlation between success and liking scores was .75. There is some question, therefore, whether a new legislator was seen as successful by his peers because of his personal likability or because of the amount and quality of his legislative work. Independent evidence relating to this question was provided by the activity measures from legislative records.

The legislative activity indices chosen were "lines spoken" and "bills introduced." These data are summarized in the last two columns of Table 8.3. It is apparent from inspection of these two columns that the ideologue is clearly higher on both activity measures than his colleagues of the other self-other orientations. Legislators in this ideologue category who are low in complexity

Table 8.3. Mean Success and Liking Ratings for First-Term Legislators with Four Self-Other Orientations

Type of Self-Other Orientation	Self-Esteem	Complexity of Self	N	Mean Success Score	Mean Liking Score	Mean Activity	
						Lines Spoken	Bills Introduced
Pragmatist	Low	High	9	136 (139)*	106 (70)	849 (848)	8.1 (6.7)
Ideologue	High	Low	9	123 (69)	94 (36)	1139 (602)	13.1 (6.8)
Indeterminate	Low	Low	10	68 (57)	85 (59)	688 (661)	6.3 (4.5)
Apolitical	High	High	8	55 (66)	53 (38)	551 (739)	7.6 (3.4)

*Numbers in parentheses are standard deviations.

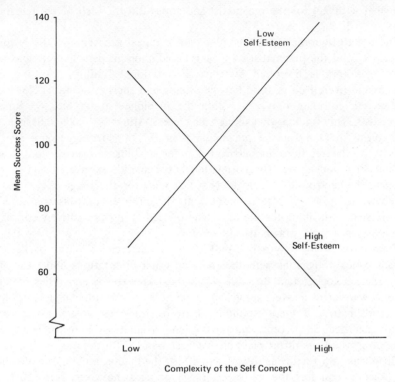

Figure 8.1. Success scores of freshman legislators as a function of self-esteem and complexity of the self concept.

and high in self-esteem sponsored significantly more bills than either the apolitical or the indeterminate types. Similar trends are apparent in the data on speaking on the House floor. Even though the differences by an analysis of variance do not reach conventional levels of significance because of between-subject variability ($F = 2.44$, $df = 1/32$, $p < .20$), the ideologue is shown to speak more than the apolitical when the two groups are compared by a t-test ($t = 1.81$, $df = 15$, $p < .09$).

The ideologue and the pragmatist, then, are seen as more promising legislators than are the apolitical and the indeterminate. Some additional observations provide hints about differences between the two successful types. We have seen that the ideologue tends to be more active than the pragmatist as measured by his sponsorship of bills and the amount of speaking he does on the floor of the legislature. Although there are no differences in the effectiveness of legislators with the four self-other orientations as measured by the percentage of bills sponsored which are passed—the percentage hovers around 35 percent for each type—because of his greater activity the absolute number of bills successfully sponsored by the ideologue is higher. His mean number of bills passed is 3.9 as compared with 2.4 for the pragmatist and about 2.6 for each of the remaining types.

The overall hypothesis that the ideologue's appeal is based upon his lawmaking activity and the pragmatist's appeal is based upon his personal relations with other legislators is bolstered by some correlational findings. For instance, whereas the overall correlation between liking and success ratings is .75, liking and success correlate only .59 within the ideologue group but .86 for the pragmatists. This finding, that liking and success ratings by one's colleagues are more highly related for the pragmatist than for the ideologue, also receives support in the relationship between number of bills sponsored and success predicted by colleagues. The correlation between bills sponsored and success ratings is higher for the ideologue ($r = .56$) than for the pragmatist ($r = .45$). Moreover, it is of interest to note that the number of bills sponsored is uncorrelated with liking for the ideologue ($r = -.12$) but is positively correlated with liking among the pragmatists ($r = +.63$).

Finally, there are only a few indications of differences in the background characteristics of persons with the four self-other orientations under examination. The ideologues tend to come from the larger towns and cities—all (100 percent) were at or above the median on an index of the urban character of the legislator's district. The corresponding figure for the pragmatist was 66 percent, for the apolitical 38 percent, and for the indeterminate 40 percent. There seem to be no marked age differences; median ages were 32 for the pragmatist, 33 for the ideologue, 35 for the apolitical, and 40 for the indeterminate. The ideologue classification contains the narrowest range of ages, however, from 26 to 41 years; whereas the other groups each contain members in their 50s and 60s. Moreover, there appear to be no departures from equivalence among persons with the four types of self-other orientations with regard to political party or sex.

DISCUSSION

In the setting of the Maine Legislature, there seem to be two distinctly different types of successful legislator. The first type corresponds to the electorally successful candidate in the Oregon legislative race. This type of legislator, high in complexity and low in self-esteem, has been termed the pragmatic politician. The second type, low on complexity and high in self-esteem, was termed the ideologue. The apolitical type delineated in the Oregon studies, high on both self-esteem and complexity, received the lowest ratings among the four types on success and liking, and was relatively inactive when compared with the ideologue and pragmatist.

While the data are not conclusive on the reasons for the differences between the two successful types, the available information supports the theory that they are responsive to differing constituencies. The pragmatist, who is thought to represent a pluralistic constituency, is more oriented toward interpersonal relationships and is a diligent practitioner of the art of compromise. He both needs and is skillful at gaining personal approval. The ideologue, on the other hand, represents a narrower constituency; he is more issue-oriented and more dogmatically attached to these issues. Both the trend toward higher liking ratings for the pragmatist and the objectively higher activity of the ideologue support these hypothetical differentiations. The two types parallel the two leadership roles which have been observed in small groups, the task role (ideologue) and the socio-emotional role (pragmatist).

The "constituencies" to whom the successful legislative types appeal is reflected in the face-to-face relationships which these freshman lawmakers establish. In the legislative setting, it seems clear that much of the lawmaker's activity is oriented toward his fellow legislators rather than to the people in his district. Moreover, it is likely that the pragmatist's behavior is oriented toward a different subgroup of legislators than is that of the ideologue. The ideologue is more apt to associate with people who are similarly concerned about issues of the day, whereas the pragmatist is more likely to react to the dominant social pressures of the moment. Further analysis of voting records may help to clarify the groups to which these two types of legislators are most strongly oriented.

An alternative to the idea of separate constituencies is the possibility that legislators in general respond positively to either of these successful types. Legislators may like the pragmatist personally and enjoy having him or her around. They may be rewarded by his compliments, and enjoy his friendliness and lack of contentiousness. It would not necessarily be self-contradictory for the legislators to admire as well the task-oriented person, the ideologue who works hard and well in support of those ends in which he strongly believes.

There do seem to be some parallels between the fourfold personality typology used to differentiate freshman legislators in the present study and that developed by Barber (1965) in his study of Connecticut freshman legislators. The criteria which Barber used to categorize his four types of legislators were: (1) activity, high or low, and (2) willingness or reluctance to serve in future legislatures. Barber's *lawmaker,* who is active and interested in further service, is described on the basis of interview data as high in self-esteem. This lawmaker type seems to correspond to the legislator we have termed the ideologue, who is high in self-esteem and low in complexity. The second active type of legislator identified by Barber, the *advertiser,* was reluctant to return for further sessions of the legislature. The advertiser was characterized as being low in self-esteem and as being concerned with favorable notice from his constituents. His activity was attributed to these motives rather than sincere interest in the issues of the day. The advertiser bears some resemblance to the pragmatic type described in the present study. Both of the other types described by Barber, the *reluctant* and the *spectator,* were characterized by inactivity, but both were also seen as being low in self-esteem. The correspondence between Barber's two inactive types and the apolitical and indeterminate types described here is less compelling than the correspondence among the active types. Nevertheless, the similarities between the legislative types identified by entirely different criteria in the two studies suggest that the findings of each have an important degree of generality.

The two field studies which we have just described related four patterns of self-other orientation to election to political office and to success in political office. In positing these relationships it was necessary to refer to the bridging concept of responsiveness. We proposed that certain patterns of self-other orientation are related to the interpersonal process of responsiveness which, in turn, is related to winning elections and to certain kinds of success in the legislature following election. Now let us seek support for the concept of responsiveness, especially how this intervening variable relates to self-esteem and complexity of the self concept. Two laboratory studies will be described. The first concerns the question of how the pragmatist accepts (or responds to) feedback from others about his behavior. The second study concerns the nature of the feedback that the pragmatist gives others in a bargaining situation. We turn to the laboratory at this point because in laboratory experiments it is possible to isolate particular behaviors for closer scrutiny, behaviors which are difficult to observe in a field setting. Moreover, through the use of laboratory manipulations we can place in bold relief those behaviors assumed to be critical for political success.

Study 3. Political Personality and
Responsiveness to Feedback[3]

The mediating variable in the foregoing studies was responsiveness. In the first two studies responsiveness was assumed to be affecting the results. Now we turn to an examination of responsiveness, exploring in this third study responsiveness to positive and negative information about their performance by persons with high or low self-esteem and high or low complexity of the self concept.

Previous research (Dittes, 1959; Jones, Hester, Farina, and Davis, 1960; Mossman and Ziller, 1968; Rosenbaum and deCharms, 1960) implies that the greater behavioral and affective consistency of persons with high self-esteem is associated with lower responsiveness to evaluation feedback. For example, Dittes (1959) found that low self-esteem subjects' liking for a group was more influenced by acceptance or rejection from the group than was high self-esteem subjects' liking for a group. Persons with high self-esteem were found to be less dependent on external circumstances with regard to liking for others. The behavior of high self-esteem individuals indicates that they have more stable internal standards on which to base their self evaluations. Persons with low self-esteem are more dependent upon others for guides to behavior; that is, they are more responsive.

Consistent with studies one and two, the second aspect of the self concept proposed to be relevant to determining an individual's responses to evaluation

[3]Study 3 represents part of Natalie J. Terbovic's unpublished master's thesis, "The Self Concept as a Mediating Factor in Determining Reactions to Positive and Negative Evaluations," University of Oregon, Eugene, Oregon, 1970.

feedback is self complexity. The most relevant finding, cited earlier (see Ziller, 1973), is that persons with complex as opposed to simplex self concepts tend to process more information before making a decision. Moreover, since complexity of the self concept is associated with perception of similarity with others, it is proposed that the complex person is more likely to accept information from others.

METHOD

Procedure.   Prior to participation in the experimental tasks subjects completed the self-esteem and complexity items described earlier as part of a set of self-other orientation tasks. A baseline rate for each subject's use of positive reinforcement in evaluating others was obtained in a "training session." Then, within the framework of a 2 x 3 repeated measures design, subjects acted as explainers in three similar but separate dyadic tasks supposedly with a different co-worker in each task. The co-worker evaluated the subject's explanation at 30-second intervals during the course of each task by sending either a green (positive) or red (negative) light signal. The ratio of positive to negative signals was pre-arranged so that every subject received ten green lights and two red during one task, two green and ten red in another, and six green and six red in another.

Subjects.   The subjects were 40 female undergraduate students from the University of Oregon. They were recruited through the student employment service and were paid two dollars each for their participation.

Apparatus.   The major equipment consisted of two electronically connected light panels. One of these panels had red and green buttons that, when pressed, lighted red and green lights on the second panel. The panels were located in separate laboratory rooms. A one-way microphone operated between the two laboratory rooms permitting the person with the light panel to communicate with the person pressing buttons.

Experimental Task.   When a subject had completed the self-other orientation tasks, she was taken by the experimenter to the room containing a light panel on which messages could be sent. The initial phase of the experiment served partially as a training session to familiarize the subject with the experimental tasks and partially to convince the subject of the authenticity of the experimental situation. The experimental tasks involved describing a drawing consisting of six rectangles to a partner who could not see the drawing and asking the partner to reproduce the drawing from the descriptions received verbally across a one-way intercom system. In the "training session" the subject was given the role of listener with the job of reproducing the drawing. The instructions read to the subject by the experimenter were as follows:

In the first part of this experiment you are being asked to follow another subject's instructions about how to reproduce a simple drawing. The other subject is in the next room and has a copy of this drawing. This other subject will describe the drawing to you over the intercom system. We are interested in the effectiveness of a very simple two-way communication network. Therefore the only way that you will be able to communicate with the other subject (your partner) is by means of the red and green lights you see there on that black panel. When you press one of the buttons, a corresponding light will flash on a panel next door. We have you in separate rooms so that there will be no opportunity for any nonverbal communication such as sounds, gestures, and facial expressions.

After 30 seconds of explanation on the part of your partner, you will hear a bell. When you hear this bell, you are to push either the red or the green button communicating to your partner your reaction to the instructions.

If you are dissatisfied in any way with the explanation being given, you may indicate this by pressing the red button. For instance, if you do not understand, are not following, or feel that the instructions are too slow or too rapid you may indicate this by pressing the red button. On the other hand, if you feel that you are satisfied and are not having any trouble understanding, then you may indicate this by pressing the green button. This will indicate that you want the other person to continue in the same manner.

Once you have responded your partner will begin to explain again. This sequence will continue until your partner has completed the explanation to your satisfaction or until a certain time limit is exceeded.

Do you have any questions? All right, I'll check next door and let the other subject know that we are ready to start.

The "subject" in the other room was actually the experimenter's assistant. The experimenter would inform the assistant that the subject was ready and return briefly to the subject to turn on the sound system so that the subject could hear the explanation. Then the subject was left alone in the room. The experimenter kept time in the room with the assistant, sounding a bell after every 30 seconds of explanation by the assistant. The explanation given by the assistant was pre-written and delivered in a manner designed to sound spontaneous. A live reading was considered preferable to a tape recording because it allowed some flexibility in acknowledging any red lights sent by the subject. If the subject sent a green light, the assistant simply read on. However, when a red light was sent, it was acknowledged by an "oh" and a repeat of the previous instruction before going on to new material.

The first phase of the experiment continued for approximately five minutes or ten 30-second intervals of explanation plus the brief period of time necessary for the subject to indicate her reactions by pressing a red or green button. A record of how many green and red lights were used by each subject was kept, providing an indicator of the subject's baseline use of positive and negative reinforcements when interacting with another. At the completion of this phase of the experiment the subject was told that she would now take over as explainer for new subjects who had not seen the drawings. The subject was taken to the room with the microphone and light panel without buttons where the experimenter read this second set of instructions:

> Now you are going to take over as explainer. You will be given a card with six rectangles drawn on it. We will ask you to describe what is on this card to another subject who cannot see the card. The other subject (your partner) will be asked to reproduce the drawing as you describe it just as you were asked to do in the first part of this experiment. Since your partner must depend on your description for all the information needed to reproduce the drawing, you should try to make your explanation very clear and include all details. Again, in order to keep this communication system as simple as possible, the other subject will be able to communicate her reaction to your instructions only by means of the green and red lights you see there before you on the black panel. Each time that 30 seconds have passed, a bell will sound. This will indicate to your partner that she may push one of the buttons.
>
> When I sound the bell be sure to look at the light panel. If the green bulb lights, it will indicate that your partner is satisfied with your explanation. If the red bulb lights, it will indicate that your partner is somehow dissatisfied with your explanation, that she feels confused, or that she is not following properly, or that you are going too quickly or too slowly. Are there any questions so far?
>
> Here is the first drawing. You will describe three of these all together to three different individuals. After each trial, you will be asked to fill out a questionnaire asking about the task, your partner, and your own view of your performance. None of the persons you work with will see any of the questionnaires you complete.
>
> If you do not complete your explanation within a certain time limit, you will be stopped. Work as quickly as your partner seems able to follow. Now, are there any questions before we begin?

During the phase of the experiment in which the subject was acting as explainer, the assistant took over the position of the partner who received the explanation and dispensed the light signals. Each of the three explanations made by the subject was accompanied by a different ratio of positive to negative lights: six green to six red (neutral condition), ten green to two red (positive condition), and two green to ten red (negative condition). The order in which these conditions were presented was counterbalanced across subjects. Each of the subject's explanations was allowed to continue for 12 time intervals of 30 seconds each. This limit was selected because it was sufficiently brief to prevent anyone from completing the task, thereby allowing everyone to receive the same number of light flashes in all trials. After each task, the subject completed an evaluation form.

In each interactional situation the subject's knowledge of his partner was restricted to the positive and negative feedback received via electronically transmitted light flashes. Holding the situation contentless except for the evaluative feedback provided control over such confounding factors as appearance and nonverbal cues, while the interactive aspects appeared to remain highly credible. Subjects did not hesitate to speak into the microphone nor did they question filling out a partner evaluation form on the basis of the restricted interaction.

The evaluation forms contained items asking about the number of positive (green) and negative (red) lights the subject recalled receiving during that particular trial. Moreover, there were items asking for appraisals (on a five-point scale ranging from strongly agree to strongly disagree) of their perceived similarity and attraction to their most recent partner, of that partner's performance, of the value of the information conveyed by that partner's signals, of their expectations as to how that partner would rate them, and of their own performance. The most recent partner was also rated on seven semantic differential items and two nonverbal measures adapted from the self-other orientation tasks—items assessing intensity of identification with the partner and relative power over the partner (Ziller, 1973).

RESULTS

The main results of this study support the proposed relationship between the political personality and responsiveness. First, subjects with high as opposed to low self-esteem were more consistent in their evaluation of their self performance across the three tasks in spite of the different ratios of positive and negative feedback. To determine this relationship subjects were divided into very high esteem and very low esteem groups on the basis of scores obtained on self-esteem items administered prior to the experimental tasks. The mean self-esteem score for all subjects was 4.00. The scores of the high self-esteem group were 5.0 and above ($N = 9$) and those of the low self-esteem group were 3.0 and below ($N = 8$).[4] The ranges of the self performance ratings across the three conditions were calculated for the subjects in the high and low self-esteem groups, and these ranges were treated as scores. With ranges from zero to eight possible, the mean range of the ratings of self performance was 1.78 for the high self-esteem group and 3.21 for the low self-esteem group. The difference between these means is significant ($t = 2.81, df = 15, p < .05$).

The second result supporting the responsiveness hypothesis concerns complexity of the self concept. In order to explore the relationship between responsiveness and complexity, subjects were divided into high and low complexity groups. The mean overall complexity score across all subjects was 38.4. High complexity was defined as a score of 49 and above ($N = 9$), and low

[4]In order to examine the purest cases of high and low self-esteem and complexity of the self, only those subjects in the upper and lower quarters of the distribution were used in the analysis.

Table 8.4.   Mean Ratings of Value of Information
by High and Low Complexity Subjects

Complexity of Self	Evaluation Condition		
	Positive	*Neutral*	*Negative*
Low	2.38	3.19	3.88
High	2.00	2.17	3.39

Note: The higher the number the less favorable the rating.

complexity as a score of 28 and below ($N = 8$). A two-way analysis of variance was calculated comparing the ratings for the high and low complexity subjects of the value of the information conveyed by their partners in each of the three experimental conditions. These ratings of the value of the information yielded a significant main effect for complexity ($F = 7.91$, $df = 1/15$, $p < .05$). Mean ratings for the high and low complexity groups by experimental condition are shown in Table 8.4. Inspection of the means in Table 8.4 shows that persons with high complexity consistently rated the information transmitted to them by their partners more favorably than low complexity persons.

The results from this study provide support for the hypothesis relating the political personality to responsiveness. The results indicate that individuals with high self-esteem reveal more stable self evaluations that permit them to be more independent of external evaluations. To some extent the person with high self-esteem is less sensitive to feedback from others or, in the present context, is less responsive to the feedback of others. On the other hand, persons with low self-esteem were found to alter self evaluations in response to different ratios of approval and disapproval from others. Moreover, individuals with high complexity of the self concept tended to assimilate both negative and positive feedback more easily than individuals with low complexity. Persons with high complexity were more responsive. Together, the results suggest that the most responsive individuals are probably characterized by low self-esteem and high complexity of the self concept or, in other words, by the pragmatic self-other orientation.

Study 4. Strategies of Reinforcement for the Political Personality[5]

In the previous study we found that persons with characteristics like the pragmatic politician were more responsive to information from others than persons with the three other self-other orientations. The study we will describe now also investigates the notion of responsiveness. Of interest is the nature of the

[5]Study 4 represents part of Robert M. Jackson's unpublished doctoral dissertation, "Personality and Political Behavior: An Empirical Analysis Using Gaming Research," University of Oregon, Eugene, Oregon, 1970.

feedback which people with the various self-other orientations use to reinforce others in the interaction process. Specifically, does the person rely predominantly on punishment or reward in reinforcing another's behavior?

Emphasis on both punishment and reward as reinforcement strategies appears in the behavior of political leaders. For example, while vice-president, Agnew was noted for his attacking style. His speeches generally focused on criticizing opponents of the Nixon administration (see *New York Times,* 1970). John Kennedy, on the other hand, is an example of a political leader who was usually rewarding in his feedback. As Hilsman (1964, p. 48) states:

> He had patience and a pragmatic willingness to settle for the possible, to see the other side of questions and to provide opponents a way out. Yet he wanted to change the world and was eager to get on with the change. Much has been said about John F. Kennedy as a man, as a friend, a statesman—and much will yet be. Still, I think his greatest, almost magical quality was the ability to inspire men to help in bringing about this change, to "get America moving again."

The question which the present study asks is whether or not reliance on such strategies is an outgrowth of a particular self-other orientation.

METHOD

Experimental Task. One type of situation which allows for constant interaction between two parties is the bargaining situation. The two bargaining parties offer and counter-offer, promise and threaten, agree and disagree, maximize and minimize their goals, lose and gain. In some sense, the bargaining process is fundamental to the political process. Legislators bargain with one another for votes; agencies within a government bargain with one another for support and resources; nations bargain with one another to determine international policy.

The experimental situation we used in this study was a bargaining situation. The participants' instructions were as follows:

> You are going to participate in a simple foreign policy exercise. As the foreign secretary for your nation, you have been asked by your premier to negotiate a treaty with the country of Utro. The main clause of this treaty would allow you to establish a military base which would permit you to keep 500 MFs (military forces, i.e., men, weapons, munitions, vehicles, etc.) in Utro. Your premier has told you that the signing of this treaty is very basic to your national security and the military level of 500 MFs is the barest minimum. Talks with Utro have been hampered by two factors: historically, relations between your country and Utro have not always been friendly; secondly, Utro does not want 500 MFs in her country. She has agreed to 50, and it will be your task to convince her that 500 MFs is necessary.

Before you is a pile of 20 chips. These chips represent your nation-state's capabilities that have been made available to you: natural resources, economic and military resources, diplomatic resources, and so forth. The negotiator for Utro also has 20 such capabilities. Your negotiations will make use of these capabilities. The session will begin with Utro's negotiator communicating to you how many MFs he is willing to have in his country. You will respond to this offer by either showing your pleasure by *giving* him *one or two* of your capabilities (which will be added to his pile) or your displeasure by *taking one or two* of his (though you won't receive it). Your sole concern is to use the instruments available to you in order to induce him to agree to the 500 MFs level. If you are successful, you will receive a bonus of 10 points (or that fraction equivalent to Utro's last offer in relation to 500 MFs) which will be added to your grade after the final curve has been established. The ultimate concern of Utro's negotiator is twofold: to have as many capabilities as possible and to have as few MFs in his country as possible.

The negotiator from Utro is a hired assistant. He has agreed to have his pay contingent upon his performance in the negotiation; in this way you are not hurting the grade of a fellow student.

You will have a fixed number of interactions to reach an agreement. I am the only one who knows what this is. In short, you do not have forever to negotiate the agreement.

Use the message forms (the white ones for ± 1 and the pink for ± 2) in front of you to communicate to Utro's negotiator your responses to his offers. The negotiation will begin with Utro knowing how many MFs you desire. In other words, both of you have total information.

Raise your hand when you are ready to begin.

Confederate's Role.   The behavior of the confederate negotiator was programmed so that each participant received identical stimuli. By using a confederate with programmed responses for one of the bargaining parties, it was possible to control the bargaining situation for research purposes. In order to facilitate bargaining under these controlled conditions, communication was greatly simplified. One bit of information was exchanged per communication. This was accomplished by asking the confederate to submit a single offer in each communication. The subject of the study then simply responded to this offer with a reward or a punishment.

The confederate's responses were designed to make him appear recalcitrant, yet willing to make some concessions for the sake of reaching some agreement. Thus, on trial 1 the confederate offered 50 MFs, on trial 5 he switched to 100 MFs, on trial 6 back to 75, on trial 7 to 100 again, on trial 8 to 135, on trial 9 to 200, and on trial 11 to 220.

Procedure.   In an effort to avoid the demand characteristics of an experimental setting and to create a degree of verisimilitude, the 61 male subjects were drawn from an introductory international relations course where the concepts of persuasion had been integrated into the course content. The students were told that they were going to participate in a role-playing exercise where they would have an opportunity to learn something about the pressures which real diplomats face by experiencing these forces themselves. Furthermore, the setting was presented in the form of a scenario. Every effort was made to clearly label the situation as political. Printed forms were used with hypothetical national seals, and the military, economic, and diplomatic resources were labeled as such.

The game began with the confederate communicating an offer to the subject. In order to induce his opponent to make the offer that he desired, the subject responded by either positively or negatively reinforcing the confederate's offer. The response was followed by another predetermined offer and the cycle continued. The self-other orientation tasks, including the items pertaining to self-esteem and complexity of the self concept, were administered in the class prior to the exercise.

Dependent Variable.   Each of the participant's 11 responses to the confederate's offers was collapsed to denote either rewarding or punishing behavior. In other words, the qualitative difference between rewarding with one or two chips or punishing by taking one or two chips was ignored. What was counted was whether the subject rewarded or punished. A person with 6 to 11 rewards for 11 trials was classified as a rewarder. A person with 0 to 5 rewards out of 11 trials was classified as a punisher.

RESULTS

The results of the analysis of the relationship between political personality and political behavior are presented in Table 8.5. The self-other orientations were determined by dividing the self-esteem and complexity scores at the median.[6]

Table 8.5.   **Relationship Between Self-Other Orientation
and Reinforcement Strategy**

Type of Self-Other Orientation	Self-Esteem	Complexity of Self	Preferred Reinforcement Strategy	
			Reward	*Punishment*
Apolitical	High	High	12	6
Pragmatist	Low	High	5	10
Ideologue	High	Low	5	14
Indeterminate	Low	Low	3	6

[6]The perceptive reader may have noted that in determining high and low scorers on the self-esteem and complexity measures, the researchers have used different procedures in these four studies. In two studies (1 and 3) the distributions were divided at the mean; in two studies (2 and 4) the distributions were divided at the median. Although these procedures may introduce slight differences in the meanings of the high and low categories in the studies, the distributions of scores for these two variables across the four studies are roughly comparable.

Kendall's *tau-c* was .311 which is statistically significant at the .0002 level of confidence. The high complexity, high self-esteem personality (apolitical self-other orientation) was the only type who used rewarding behavior predominantly. The remaining types were classified as punishers at least twice as often as they were classified as rewarders. Besides relating the four self-other orientations to preferred reinforcement strategy, each of the two components of the self-other orientations was related to behavior. Only the results for complexity were statistically significant (*tau-c* = .23, $p < .004$). Persons with high complexity in their self concepts were classified as rewarders more frequently than individuals with low complexity. The Automatic Interaction Detection technique corroborated these findings, indicating that rewarding behavior was associated with high complexity and high self-esteem, while punishing behavior was associated with low complexity.

Curiously, these results suggest that the political personality (pragmatist and ideologue) in contrast with the apolitical personality is inclined to use coercion more frequently in a persuasion situation. Our results indicate that what has often been referred to by political analysts as the "arm-twisting" technique may indeed be an important strategy for political leaders. Why this strategy is more effective than reward for the political leader remains a question for further research.

Conclusions

What appear to be two important components of the political personality were examined in the studies recounted here. Self-esteem and complexity of self concept, taken together, bear a remarkably consistent relationship to political success, at least for state legislators. Two of the four self-other orientations obtained by combining these two variables are related to both electoral success and legislative success. These two types of self-other orientation we have labeled the pragmatist (low self-esteem, high complexity) and the ideologue (high self-esteem, low complexity) orientations. The results suggest that the state legislator who is a pragmatist is alert and responsive to the desires of his constituents while running for election and, once elected, to the desires of his legislative colleagues. On the other hand, the state legislator who is an ideologue is more issue-oriented in his candidacy and, when elected, is quite active in the legislative arena.

Although these two political self-other orientations seem to lead to different kinds of political behavior, there may be reasons why both are successful. As we posited earlier, both the ideologue and the pragmatist may fulfill the task and socio-emotional roles so often found to be important for group functioning in small group research. The ideologue and the pragmatist may also appeal to different types of constituencies—the ideologue being elected by the constituency in which a single group or coalition is dominant, the pragmatist being elected in the pluralistic constituency. Moreover, both the pragmatist and the ideologue may be responsive but to different kinds of stimuli. The pragmatist listens to the people around him; the ideologue responds to the issues and problems he encounters, interpreting these stimuli so that they aid him in achieving the kind of policy that he desires. Further research on political leaders with these two types of self-other orientation is needed.

The four studies that we have described also suggest the type of self-other orientation not conducive to success as a state legislator—persons with an apolitical orientation, that is, individuals who are high in self-esteem, high in complexity. Such persons were elected less often and when elected were less successful in the legislative arena.

We have tried in the research described here to mesh findings from field studies with results from the laboratory. Whereas the field setting enables the researcher to examine his theoretical statements in the actual situation they are purported to explain, the laboratory environment allows the researcher to isolate and manipulate variables difficult to observe in the field. As the results of the four studies suggest, one research setting complements the other.

CHAPTER 9

Birth Order and Political Leadership

Louis H. Stewart

Editor's Introduction

One personal characteristic which has proven fascinating to social scientists during the last two decades is birth order. Both because it is relatively easy information to obtain on an individual and because it would appear to have an impact on social development, birth order has been widely studied (e.g., see Datta, 1967; Roe, 1953; Rosenfeld, 1966; Sampson and Hancock, 1967; Schachter, 1959; Stotland, Sherman, and Shaver, 1971; Sutton-Smith and Rosenberg, 1970). The next chapter follows in this tradition by investigating the relationship between birth order and political leadership, in particular the association between a specific ordinal position and a style of political leadership.

Continuing our examination of the question of who becomes a political leader, Louis Stewart explores a facet of the age-old "great man" versus zeitgeist controversy. At issue is whether the political leader will emerge regardless of the political setting or if the political times must be right for his emergence. For example, could a Washington have been elected president in the roaring twenties or did it take the revolutionary days of the late 1700s to secure his election? Stewart is interested in the interaction between situation and personal characteristics in the emergence of political leaders, hypothesizing that different styles of leadership and, in turn, different ordinal positions are relevant for different types of situations. Political leaders are chosen whose personal characteristics match the political demands of the times. Such a position is in line with recent reviews of studies on leadership (cf. Fiedler, 1967; Gibb, 1969; Searing, 1972; Stogdill, 1974) which suggest that neither a trait theory nor a situation-oriented theory can explain the research results. They call for more investigations of the interaction between personal characteristics and situation in the study of leadership.

Stewart uses an explanation for why birth order impacts on social behavior different from that which is generally encountered. The usual interpretation focuses on the different types of interaction which only, first-born, and later-born children have with their parents. Stewart emphasizes, however, the relations which persons from different ordinal positions have with their siblings. He speculates that the methods which an individual learns to use in dealing with his siblings will influence all his subsequent peer encounters. Moreover, observation of sibling interactions indicates that first-born children have different ways of relating to their siblings than do younger children. Stewart extrapolates from such styles of interaction to the political arena suggesting which methods seem appropriate to which national political conditions.

Birth order is an example of a biographical statistic. Although birth order would seem like a very easy piece of data to collect, it is deceptive. As Stewart notes, there are many ways of looking at ordinal position—for example, position as child (first-born child, second-born child), position as son or daughter (first-born son, second-born daughter), ratio of brothers to sisters, number of siblings, sex of siblings, density of siblings (how close in years are siblings to one another). Moreover, does one include children who die in infancy in calculating birth order? There are many questions to be answered in selecting the specific measure of birth order one will use. Researchers seeking the methodological implications of the various birth order measures should consult E. Sampson (1965), Schachter (1963), Schooler (1972), Sutton-Smith and Rosenberg (1970), and Warren (1966).

The author of this chapter, Louis Stewart, is a psychologist. He is a professor at San Francisco State University as well as a Jungian analyst. His interest in the relation between birth order and political leadership grew out of his clinical experience and his research on human development. For the curious reader, Stewart is both the first child and first son in a family of two children or, in the notation of the chapter, his birth order is M1M.

THE STUDY OF BIRTH ORDER is only just coming into its own. Deceptively simple in appearance, birth order turns out on close acquaintance to be surprisingly complex. In part this complexity arises from purely methodological considerations which we shall discuss in some detail later on. Its deeper source lies in the very nature of the variable itself. Since the present research is itself exploratory in an area in which there have been no previous investigations, let us briefly review our understanding of the variable with which we are dealing.

In the ontogeny of the individual, the assignment of birth order is a "primordial" event, so to speak. It is known to the parents before birth and is slipped over the newborn infant like an invisible envelope. Inescapably, we are received into this world not just as a child, a boy or a girl, but as a first-born, a second-born, etc., boy or girl. What significance this a priori quality has for individual development is still little known, but that birth order has been of the greatest significance to society from time immemorial we cannot doubt. The myth and ritual of all peoples as well as the laws of inheritance and of royal succession everywhere reveal its pervasive presence. We are not yet in a position to say whether this is an expression of purely social and political expedience, as some contend (Graves, 1955), or whether, as is our predilection, it has deeper roots in the recognition of an underlying psychological fitness. But regardless of the conclusion we reach, the aura of mystery which surrounds birth itself extends to encompass birth order.

It was this birth aspect of the vast reservoir of family romance found in myths and legend which first captured the attention of psychologists.[1] Rank's (1959) *Myth of the Birth of the Hero,* originally published in 1909, stands as a landmark of this early interest. Intrigued by the unusual set of circumstances that surrounded the birth of the Hero in many cultures, Rank isolated a characteristic pattern of features, among which were the Hero's virgin birth, dual parenthood, and exposure after birth. Subsequent study by other investigators have confirmed and extended Rank's basic findings (for example, Jung, 1956; Kerenyi, 1959; Slater, 1968). In one of the most systematic examinations of the Hero myth, Raglan (1956) identified some 22 elements which clustered around the three universal rites of passage: birth, initiation, and death.[2]

Our interest is limited here to the cluster of features surrounding the birth of the Hero. A re-examination of the mythological sources indicates that, in actuality, genealogical and family information about the Hero falls into two basic patterns. One of these, like the "begat" sections of the *Bible,* is clearly intended as a means for affirming the Hero's divine origins and establishing rights to the inheritance of privilege and power. The second pattern furnishes details of

---

[1] Along with Cassirer, Jung, and others, we view myth as a meaningful product of our symbol-producing psyche. Its universal features symbolize stages in man's psychological development. Its myriad variations reflect social, political, and religious aspects of the culture within which it originates.

[2] Psychologists, it would seem, are as vulnerable as anyone else to the myth of the birth of the Hero. This is manifest in the long pursuit of the will-o'-the-wisp notion that first-borns are more likely than others to scale the heights of eminence. A re-examination of the early studies (Stewart, 1961) revealed that they do not prove what they contend. Some are riddled with errors, others do not control for such factors as family size, use biased samples, and so on. There may be, however, some association between birth order and vocation. For example, it is in such hierarchical professions as the military and the church, as we might expect, that younger sons shine, whereas in the law and some intellectual pursuits, first-born and only sons are slightly more likely to attain eminence. However, all professions considered, there is little, if any, evidence to support a belief in the greater frequency of eminence in first-borns. Harris (1964) reaches similar conclusions on slightly different grounds.

the family, even to such specificity at times as the age spacing of siblings. The universal features of the Hero's birth, which fall for the most part into the first pattern, may be interpreted as symbols appropriate to the Hero's divine fate. At the human level, this corresponds to the sense of destiny evoked by the fated accident of birth, as witness the Greek myth of the Fates, the three sisters, spinning out the linen thread of our destiny from which we are suspended at birth. Underlying this myth we can detect vestiges of the ancient custom of swaddling the newborn infant in a linen band "on which his clan and family marks were embroidered and thus assigned to him his destined place in society" (Graves, 1955, p. 204).

If the universal features of the Hero myth have to do with the Hero's divine inspiration and his call to destiny, the variable details of setting and family serve mainly to define the Hero's task and his fitness to accomplish it. With this we are in a position to suggest the hypothesis that the Hero of myth and the heroic leader coalesce in a common psychological reality. That is to say, the legendary Moses and the contemporary Mahatma Gandhi, each a liberator of his oppressed people, should be identical psychological types. If we pursue this example for a moment, many obvious parallels spring to mind. *Homo Religiosus* is applicable to both; but beyond that, their lives exhibit a mysteriously successful blend of religion and politics for which Erikson (1969) has coined the apt phrase "religious actualism." It would be easy to multiply parallels and a much more thorough analysis of identical elements in the lives of Moses and Gandhi would be an illuminating study, but for the moment we shall limit ourselves to mentioning one additional element of similarity—the one most pertinent to this research—birth order. Each is a last-born and has a next older brother and an older sister.

This little excursion into mythology in search of the cultural significance of birth order has now brought us close to our thesis. It has also served to remind us of the elemental dilemma of our human existence, suspended as we are between two realms of being, the mythological vision and the everyday world. This reminder prepares us for thinking about findings we shall present later on which urgently suggest that the careers of such world renowned leaders as Lincoln, Roosevelt, and Churchill, to mention a few, would be but footnotes to the pages of history were it not for a fateful concatenation of events in which birth order and the political zeitgeist are essential elements. No mystical explanations are implied in the foregoing. To the contrary, our intent is resolutely empirical and hypothesis-building as will become evident. A critical factor in our research is the individual's sense of mission which, coupled with a complementary response from others, leads to success. In effect, we shall be considering the question which Erikson has explored so deeply in *Gandhi's Truth:* "Why certain men of genius can do no less than take upon themselves an evolutionary and existential curse shared by all, and why other men will be only too eager to ascribe to such a man a god-given greatness surpassing that of all others?" (Erikson, 1969, p. 129).

Now for a closer look at the everyday world of the family where the roots of political leadership are to be found for a Gandhi as surely as for the leader of lesser stature. Family life through its major functions of cultural transmission and the nurturance of children insures that every child is equipped with a microcosmic vision of society while at the same time being provided with a relatively sheltered arena for the testing of life's practical skills. Parents are the prime agents of all this and, as we well know from personal experience and the findings of depth psychology, their character and personality, the values they cherish, and the quality of their personal relationship carry critical significance for a child's development.

Yet, be that as it may, underlying and intermingling with these parental influences at all levels of the child's conscious and unconscious experience lies the filtering envelope of birth order. Parental influences alone are probably not sufficient to account for the impact birth order may have on development. There must also be an ongoing system of reinforcement which is built into the very structure of the family itself which we have reason to believe resides in the age differences between siblings. From this basic element of family life a whole host of consequences may be seen to flow.

First among such consequences are the purely existential priorities which are so indelibly imprinted on our memory by the ritual observance of birthdays. Far greater in importance, though, are the cumulative effects of the daily ebb and flow of family life which faces children time after time after time with the often painful awareness of just where it is they stand with their siblings in the hierarchies, for example, of size and strength, of mobility, of privilege, and of knowledge and experience which exist simply because of age differences and, in turn, by virtue of the order of their births. Need we look further? The deep-flowing currents of emotion implicit in these sibling relationships are surely what make birth order related experiences so binding and so freighted with far-reaching consequences.

Just listen to this recital by ten-year-olds of the tactics they employ to get a sibling to do what they want: "I beat him up, hit him, boss him, spook him, belt him, exclude him;" or "I get mad, shout and yell, cry, pout, sulk, ask other kids for help, threaten to tell Mom and Dad" (see Sutton-Smith and Rosenberg, 1970). So elemental and universal are these responses that no one need be told that the participants are older and younger brothers and sisters, nor need anyone be in doubt that the high power tactics are those of the older siblings. This is the litany of sibling rivalry. We may deplore, moralize, excuse, and point to other kinds of behavior, but it is impossible to deny that this is often how it is with brothers and sisters. If we now permit ourselves the vagrant thought that Mahatma Gandhi was once just such a brother among brothers and sisters, we come abruptly face to face with the near impossibility of comprehending the transformation that takes place from childhood to sainthood.

But to return to our litany of sibling rivalry, are not these the raw materials of power politics? It requires no great leap of imagination to perceive in adult political leaders the same kinds of behavior: Lyndon Johnson, a first-born son, in the Capitol cloakroom "twisting arms"; Richard Nixon, a second-born son, angry, pouting, crying on television; John Foster Dulles, a first-born son, exploiting atomic brinkmanship; or Dwight Eisenhower, a third-born son, holding Nixon at arm's length. Is this not the true state of political affairs?

With this background we are now in a position to discuss more specific hypotheses. Briefly stated, our major thesis is that birth order provides the basis for a psychological typology comprising four principle types and a number of variants. The basic types correspond to the four sibling situations: the only, first-born, middle, and last-born child. Each has an absolutely unique bit of experience. The only child never knows what it is like to have siblings; the first-born begins life as an only child and then experiences the birth of a sibling; the middle-born begins life as a last-born and then experiences the birth of a sibling; and the last-born is always last and never experiences the birth of a sibling. These types have many variations which are a function of family size, sex of siblings, and other personal and family factors. Each psychological type arises in a particular family constellation. For example, there is a first-born male type with sisters only and a first-born male type with brothers only, and so on. It is obvious that the number of possible combinations of ordinal position, sex of sibling, and family size is large but finite.

No two children in a family have quite the same experience. Each, from his own individual sibling perspective, interiorizes—to use Laing's (1972) concept—a particular 'family' experience. Birth order is one of the structural elements of such interiorized 'families.'[3] Moreover, it is an a priori position in the individual's ontogeny that places birth order at the center of the process of identity formation.

With respect now specifically to leadership, the burden of the argument is that within the family each sibling position promotes a unique view of society and provides a unique experience in dealing with power and authority. This view of society and the acquired leadership skills are normally refined in the peer play group, and then become the repertoire of adult political behavior. From this perspective, the family's role in the development of political expectations and behavior is as a microcosm of society:

> . . . .the primary group (what one might call the political system of the family) influences the expectations of the individual with regard to authority in the larger political system. Within the primary group, the individual receives training for roles that he will play within the society.

[3]Although the concept of the interiorized 'family' was developed through studies of schizophrenic families, it provides a useful way of thinking about the internalization dynamics of any family. Laing's (1972, p. 3) definition is as follows: "The family here discussed is the family of origin transformed by internalization, partitioning, and other operations, into the 'family' and mapped back onto the family and elsewhere. (Single inverted commas are used . . . to make clear that it is the internalized family that is in question.)"

This training consists in both the teaching of certain standards of behavior that can be applied to later situations and, perhaps more significantly, the playing of roles in the family and other primary groups that are similar to roles later to be played in the political or economic system (Verba, 1961, p. 31).

From our assumptions it follows, as we have said, that there should be four basic styles of leadership corresponding to the four unique sibling experiences—the only, first-born, middle, and last-born child. Moreover, we believe "successful leadership . . . rests on a latent congruence between the psychic needs of the leader and the social needs of the followers" (Rustow, 1970, p. 23) and, as a result, that there should of necessity be four major crises of the body politic which cry out for the leader of appropriate birth order. These crises, insofar as they have come clear in our research to date, are respectively: (1) the breakdown of social institutions, e.g., the 1930s Depression; (2) imperialist expansion and confrontation, e.g., World War I; (3) retrenchment and realignment of domestic and foreign commitments, e.g., the 1950s; and (4) rebellion and revolt, e.g., the Civil War.

The exercise of fitting this empirically derived matching of leadership styles and social crises to birth order hypotheses is obviously a complex one. As a starter we offer for its suggestive value the following example of the pathway our speculations have followed. Let us begin with the notion that leadership styles and social crises may be mirror images, so to speak, of childhood birth order experiences. Take, for example, the only child. If we assume that from the child's eye view of the family the parents represent past society and the children represent present society, it follows that of all the birth order positions the only child, being the sole heir of past society and the sole member of present society, would on both counts be the best able to identify with society as a totality. Thus in a crisis involving the collapse of vital social functions where the essential task of leadership is to unite all the people in a genuinely cooperative effort of regeneration, it would presumably be the only child who is most likely to succeed.

Pursuing this line of thought with the other birth-order experiences we arrive at the following for the first-born. As first heir of past society and first citizen of an expanding society all the members of which are of lower rank than himself, the first-born would be uniquely in touch with the demands of an expanding society while also inheriting responsibility for weaker members. This experience prepares him presumably for effective leadership in times of territorial expansion and confrontation.[4] The middle-born shares with the first-born the experience of an expanding society, although in other respects his situation is quite

---

[4]Much of what has been said here regarding the first-born child is applicable to first-born sons—first male heirs in a male dominated society—and, as will be seen, our results tend to bear this out. However, when we are able to accumulate larger samples of all of the critical family constellations we should be able to differentiate more clearly the specific aspects of leadership which distinguish first-born children from first-born sons.

different. For example, he finds himself in the midst of a society with higher ranking classes on one side and lower ranking classes on the other—a position which appears to maximize opportunities for diverse relationships while at the same time demanding adeptness at mediation and accommodation. This experience, it would seem, would incline the middle-born to peacemaking and leadership skills in disengagement and the realignment of power. Finally with the last-born, society has completed its growth and all classes are obviously of higher rank than the lowly last-born. Just so, we may imagine, is created the natural champion of the oppressed and the leader of choice in times of rebellion.

In concluding this section we trust that the foregoing will be accepted in the same free spirit of speculation and hypothesizing in which it is proferred. Some of it seems quite certainly provable; other aspects appear more problematic, although still worthy of consideration. In the succeeding pages, we shall demonstrate to what extent the results of our investigations of American presidents and British prime ministers support the hypotheses we have set forward. Following that we shall have another opportunity to review our position.

Methodology and Birth-Order Research

Before proceeding further, some questions of nomenclature and methodology need to be clarified. For example, there are at least three basic definitions of birth order (see Jones, 1933). One is pregnancy order. For research in which pregnancy order is appropriate data, it is often not imperative that full-term infants be born. A second definition is based upon the actual births occurring but may include still-births and deaths early in infancy. (This is the birth order frequently reported in general biographical sources.) In the third definition of birth order, which concerns the family constellation, interest centers primarily upon the children who survive birth and who live with one another for any significant portion of their early childhood. The last of these definitions is what we will use here.

Now for the complications of the family constellation, one of the best ways to come to grips with these is to make use of a traditional genealogical diagram like that in Figure 9.1. In the bottom row of this diagram we have the children in a family listed in the order of their birth from left to right. (A proper diagram would include birth dates beneath each child.) In the row just above the children are their parents. The parents are likewise represented in order of birth among their siblings. And above the parents are their parents (the grandparents of row 1). We could go on adding generations ad infinitum or, at least, until we reached the original progenitors.

The totality of this genealogical chart would constitute the most comprehensive definition of the term "family constellation." For most research purposes we would be more than delighted if it were possible to obtain data for three generations of a family, i.e., the bottom three rows of the diagram.[5] In actual fact, and certainly with respect to historical and public figures, the data we can readily obtain from general biographical sources is often limited to the bottom row.

If we examine this bottom row (our "family constellation" in practice), we note that the basic elements are ordinal position, sex of siblings, and the relative ages of siblings. The relevance of these elements to personality development is fairly easy to grasp in the extreme. For instance, it is not difficult to conceive that a first-born child who is 15 years older than his next sibling would in many ways resemble an only child. Nor is it unreasonable to postulate that the only boy among several sisters has vastly different experiences from a boy who has many brothers and no sisters. Naturally it becomes increasingly difficult to hypothesize the differential effects of less extreme age spacings and less drastic sex imbalances among siblings. The research which has been conducted in these areas will be referred to in later sections of this paper.

Although we have spent more time than may seem warranted in this discussion of relatively simple, even self-evident facts, it is precisely over such issues that much birth-order research has come to grief. These basic methodological requirements were formulated by Jones (1933) over 40 years ago, but they have been more honored in the breach than in the observance. A major reason for this

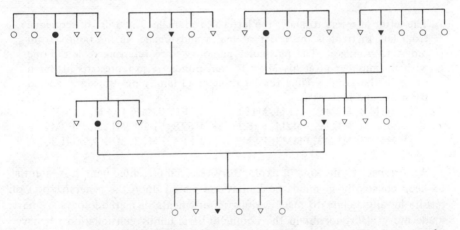

Figure 9.1.   Traditional genealogical diagram. Circles stand for females, triangles for males. The blacked in figures represent the individuals in question, i.e., grandparents and parents.

[5]We know very little yet about the effects of parents' expectations as a function of their own birth order and family constellation on the development of children. There are many suggestive examples of the apparent preference for, or rejection of, a particular child which may be related to birth order, for example, the elder and younger Pitts who were both second sons, the singular education of John Stuart Mill by his father James—both of whom were first-borns, younger son Neville Chamberlain's rejection by his first-born father, and first-born Joseph Kennedy's high hopes for his first-born, Joseph, Jr.

neglect of such elementary considerations is the complexity they introduce. As one recently disillusioned investigator (Schooler, 1972, p. 174) frankly admits, "if, in order to be fruitful, the study of birth order necessitates dealing with the complexities of such variables as sex of siblings and family density, or of collecting data on hard-to-define control groups, it loses much of its appeal." Although Schooler's re-assertion of methodological strictures is welcome, the very selective nature of the review and the apparent lack of acquaintance with a significant body of earlier literature makes the other conclusions less tenable. A much more thorough and well-informed analysis of the total body of birth order research is to be found in the recently published volume *The Sibling* (Sutton-Smith and Rosenberg, 1970). One of the significant contributions made in this work is the demonstration of consistent findings by a persistent group of investigators—Koch (1958), Lasko (1954), Levy (1937), Sears (1961), to mention a few—who were not deterred by the difficulties and complexities of the subject matter. Throughout the later sections of this paper, reference will be made to various portions of *The Sibling,* in particular the chapters on "Sex Status Effects" and "Sibling Power Effects." We have also adopted for use here the system of signs proposed by Sutton-Smith and Rosenberg for simplifying reference to family constellations. This system which applies to families of all sizes is summarized as follows (Sutton-Smith and Rosenberg, 1970, p. 17):

> The letter M refers to male; the letter F, to female. The order of sequence from left to right is the order of males and females in the family from oldest to youngest. The particular person we are referring to is the one with the number after his M or F; that number also represents his birth order in the family. Thus the 24 three-child family positions are labeled for males and females as:
>
> | | |
> | --- | --- |
> | M1MM, M1MF, M1FM, M1FF | F1FF, F1MF, F1FM, F1MM |
> | MM2M, MM2F, FM2M, FM2F | FF2F, FF2M, MF2F, MF2M |
> | MMM3, MFM3, FMM3, FFM3 | FFF3, FMF3, MFF3, MMF3 |

With respect to the kind of exploratory research presented here, it is essential to keep constantly in mind the limitations placed upon the generalization of results by any failure to meet various requirements of methodology. We have made every effort to obtain the complete basic family constellation whenever possible. This has been achieved in all but a few instances for our primary subjects, U.S. presidents and English prime ministers. It will also become obvious as the results are discussed that some of the implications of this research cannot be pursued with the data at hand. We have at times identified family constellations which appear to stimulate characteristic types of psychological development only to find ourselves unable to do more than speculate because of the limitations of the data. Because of these limitations, whenever results are presented we have tried to make clear our frame of reference, what the data are, and how complete they are so that others may be enabled to draw their own conclusions.

Sources of Biographical Data

Completely satisfactory data for this kind of research is difficult to obtain. Ellis, while preparing his *Study of British Genius* in 1900, was probably the first to encounter the frustrations imposed by incomplete, unsystematic, and ambiguous biographical facts. Not one to suffer in silence, Ellis for many years used his not inconsiderable influence to convince editors of the value of accurate facts about the origins and family life of eminent individuals. He eventually achieved limited success with the *English National Dictionary of Biography* (perhaps also indirectly with the *Dictionary of American Biography*), which began to supply with increasing regularity both birth order of children and birth order of sons. This, of course, is only a beginning and is far short of what would be desired, namely, ordinal position, sex of siblings, birth dates, indications of death in infancy and childhood for at least two generations.

Still, all is not lost. Though the frustration level remains high, there are just enough usable facts provided with a reasonable degree of accuracy to make the use of basic biographical source books worthwhile, particularly for preliminary explorations. Fortunately, these general source books can often be supplemented by individual biographies. With biographies it is a pleasure to report the situation is definitely improved and improving. There one can see clear evidence of the impact of Freud's psychological revolution. Early childhood experiences which 50 years ago were relegated to a few pages or even paragraphs now command respectable attention, and a genuine effort is made by many biographers to integrate the events of childhood with later life.

Nevertheless, the accumulation of any sizeable sample of accurate and relatively complete family constellation data on public and historical figures remains time-consuming. The present study, as may be expected, suffers to some extent from the vagaries of the biographical sources just described. This will be made clear whenever it is felt these deficiencies may seriously affect the results.

The primary sources of the biographical data used in these studies were J. N. Kane's (1959) *Facts About the Presidents* (FATP), the *Dictionary of American Biography* (DAB), the *National Dictionary of Biography* (NDB), the journal *Current Biography* (CB), and some hundred or more individual biographies. In an effort to insure accuracy in the family data, one or more individual biographies were consulted whenever possible for each of the presidents and prime ministers. This procedure was also followed with the other political leaders referred to in the research. In cases where biographies were not available and in the few instances where biographies were in disagreement, the NDB, DAB, or CB were relied upon.

As was noted earlier, the type of birth order used in these studies is the family constellation with interest centering primarily upon the children who survived birth and who lived with one another for any significant portion of their early childhood. (We have settled more or less arbitrarily on the period from birth to at least five years of age by which time many researchers suggest the nucleus of character formation has been established.) It will occasionally occur that there is some discrepancy between the birth orders reported here and those found in biographical source books which, as mentioned, often include stillbirths and deaths in infancy.

The American Presidents

The 31 elected U.S. presidents, George Washington to John F. Kennedy, form the basic sample of this study. However, in addition, biographical data were obtained on 44 defeated presidential candidates and 123 presidential hopefuls.

BIRTH-ORDER PREFERENCES

First we have tested to see whether there are any birth order preferences for presidents. In Tables 9.1 and 9.2, the birth ranks of the presidents (treating each election separately) are presented with reference to all the children in their families and with reference to the sons only. From these tables it is evident that a significant degree of clustering occurs in the birth ranks of first and third children and first and third sons. Most striking is the distribution of sons; in 68 percent of the elections, the person elected U.S. president was a first or third son. Furthermore, only once has a son of birth rank greater than three been elected; this in spite of the fact that in nearly 50 percent of the elections, the presidents have come from families of four to seven sons. This significant absence of sons of birth rank four or higher is not limited to presidents but is equally true of the 44 defeated candidates of whom all but one were first, second, or third sons. One other comparison which is not readily apparent in the data presented in Tables 9.1 and 9.2 is that between first-borns and last-borns. If we sum across all family sizes, first-borns have a sizeable edge, both with respect to children (twelve to seven) and sons (seventeen to six). However, the numbers are small; moreover, the relationship is true for certain family sizes and not for others.

BIRTH ORDER AND POLITICAL ZEITGEIST

Now let us turn to our central research question, the relationships between birth order and political zeitgeist. A chronological examination of the birth orders of the presidents suggests that the distribution of birth orders is not random with respect to time. Presidents of the same or similar birth ranks follow each other in close succession across time. For example, between 1788 and 1824 there were five presidents who were first-born sons and only one of any other birth order; whereas between 1828 and 1858 there were five presidents who were second, third, or fourth sons and only one first-born. This cyclical alternation is clearly evident in Table 9.3 where the elections have been grouped in sequences of ten.

Table 9.1. Birth Order of U.S. Presidents (Washington to Kennedy, 1789-1960)*

Number of Children in Family	Position in Family								Total
	Only Child	1st Child	2nd Child	3rd Child	4th Child	5th Child	6th Child	7th Child	
1	4								4
2		1	2						3
3		2	1	3					6
4			1	2	1				4
5		2	1						3
6		2		1					3
7				2				1	3
8		2		2	2		1		7
9				1	1	2		3	7
10		3	1						4
Total	4	12	6	11	4	2	1	4	44

*Each election is treated separately.

Table 9.2.   Birth Order of U.S. Presidents Based on Position as Son[*]

Number of Sons In Family	Position in Family						Total
	Only Child	Only Son	1st Son	2nd Son	3rd Son	4th Son	
1	4	3					7
2			6	3			9
3			5		3		8
4			3	1	4		8
5					4	1	5
6			1	1	1		3
7			2		2		4
Total	4	3	17	5	14	1	44

*Each election is treated separately.

A comparison has been made between the presidents who were first-born and only sons and those who were younger sons.

The next question to be answered is whether or not this cyclical alternation in the birth order of the presidents is correlated with meaningful variations in the political zeitgeist. A comparison of the two eras 1788-1824 and 1828-1856 suggests that this is so. In the 1788-1824 era the newly established government of the United States was primarily engaged in expanding and consolidating its boundaries and asserting its sovereignty. Here are some of the outstanding political events and issues of those days (see Langer, 1948): 1791-1794, Indian wars leading to expansion westward; 1794, Jay's treaty leading to evacuation of border posts by the English; 1795, Pinckney's treaty negotiated with Spain to establish southern boundaries and rights to navigation on the Mississippi; 1797-1799, the XYZ affair and near war with France; 1801, Marines sent to Tripoli to prevent pirating; 1802, Ohio becomes the seventeenth state; 1803, Louisiana Purchase; 1804-1806, the Lewis and Clark expedition; 1806-1807, the Chesapeake Affair with American shipping threatened by England; 1810, rise of the War Party and growing demand for war with England and conquest of Canada; 1812-1814, war with England; 1815, Jackson wins battle of New Orleans; 1817-1818, Seminole War with Jackson invading Florida and the consequent treaty with Spain and acquisition of Florida; 1819-1824, Supreme Court decisions supporting centralization of power in the Federal government; 1820, the Missouri Compromise and admission to statehood of Louisiana, Indiana, Mississippi, Illinois, and Alabama; 1823, the Monroe Doctrine.

In sharp contrast the period following the election of Andrew Jackson in 1828 was, with one notable exception (1844-1848), a time primarily devoted to

Table 9.3. Birth Order (Order as Son) of U.S. Presidents by Election Period

Birth Order as Son	Election Periods				
	1788-1824	*1828-1864*	*1868-1904*	*1908-1944*	*1948-(1960)*
Only or First-born Son	8	4	3	8	1
Younger Son	2	6	7	2	3

Table 9.4. Birth Order (Order as Son) of U.S. Presidents in Crisis and Noncrisis Elections

Birth Order as Son	Crisis Elections[a]	Noncrisis Elections[b]	Total
Only or First-born Son	8	9	17
Younger Son	1	12	13
Total	9	21	30

[a]Crisis Elections: 1812, 1844, 1860, 1864, 1896, 1916, 1940, 1944, and 1948.

[b]Noncrisis Elections: 1796, 1800, 1804, 1820, 1824, 1828, 1832, 1836, 1852, 1872, 1876, 1880, 1884, 1888, 1904, 1908, 1924, 1928, 1932, 1956, and 1960.

internal adjustments. The issues of the day were in large part monetary and political, with the dispute over slavery gaining in ascendance (see Langer, 1948): by 1829, white manhood suffrage established in all the states; 1829, the Working Man's Party organized; 1830, the Mormon Church founded; 1831, William Lloyd Garrison established the *Liberator* advocating unconditional abolition of slavery; 1830-1834, Jackson's policy of relocating Indians west of the Mississippi; 1832, the U.S. Bank controversy; 1833, General Trades Union formed; 1833, the Whig Party organized; 1838, the Underground Railroad; 1838-1839, Congress adopts gag resolutions against anti-slavery petitions; 1850, the Compromise of 1850 making California a free state but leaving other territories undecided; 1850, Clayton-Bulwer Treaty with respect to British encroachments in Latin America; 1853, the Gadsden Purchase; 1853, railroad between New York and Chicago; 1854, Kansas-Nebraska Act repealing the Missouri Compromise allowing home-steaders to decide for or against slavery; 1854, trade treaty with Japan; 1854, Ostend Manifesto warning Spain of U.S. interest in Cuba; 1854, the Know-Nothing and Republican parties appear.

The preceding brief summary of the era from 1828 to 1856 does not include President Polk's term of office from 1844-1848. This period stands out in bold relief from the preceding sixteen and the following eight years. The single overriding issue of the election of 1844 was the outcry for annexation of Texas and Oregon; "54-40 or Fight" became a popular campaign slogan of the Democratic Party. Polk, as it turned out, was the first "dark horse" candidate to be nominated by a major political party, his nomination hinging on support of an expansionist position in the annexation controversy. Immediately following his election he set out with a will to acquire, in addition to Texas, both New Mexico and California. In this he was successful although not without provoking a war with Mexico. Also during his term in office, Polk negotiated with England for the acquisition of Oregon, offered to buy Cuba from Spain, and obtained a Latin American treaty that gave the U.S. rights of passage across the Isthmus of Panama for a future railroad or canal. At the end of his four-year term, he claimed not immodestly that "the acquisition of California and New Mexico, the settlement of the Oregon boundary and the annexation of Texas, extending to the Rio Grande, are results which, combined, are of greater consequence and will add more to the strength and wealth of the nation than any which have preceded them since the adoption of the constitution" (Whitney, 1967, p. 105).

From this sketchy, although fairly representative review, it is evident that periods of expansive nationalism and aggressive confrontations, leading at times to war, occurred far more frequently, in fact almost exclusively, when the presidents in office were first-born sons (four were also first-born children), that is, John Adams (M1MM), Thomas Jefferson (FFM3FFFFM), James Madison (M1MMFMFFMMM), James Monroe (M1MMMF), and James Knox Polk (M1FFMMMFFMM); whereas, during times when attention focused more on internal affairs, the presidents were younger sons, that is, Andrew Jackson (MMM3), Martin Van Buren (MFMFFM6MM), Zachary Taylor (MMM3MFMM-

FF), William Henry Harrison (FFMFMFM7),[6] and Franklin Pierce (FMFMFMM7FM).

This apparent trend was put to a rough statistical test in Table 9.4 by comparing the proportion of first-born and only sons with the proportion of younger sons among presidents in "crisis" and "noncrisis" times as defined by the presence of war or peace. Elections considered to occur in crisis situations were those happening during the War of 1812, the War with Mexico, the Civil War, the Spanish-American War, World Wars I and II, and the Korean War. Noncrisis elections were defined as those occurring eight or more years preceding or following any one of the crisis elections. The results of a chi-square test met a .05 level of significance ($X^2 = 4.30$, $p < .05$). During six of the seven wars the president was a first-born or only son. The exception was McKinley and the Spanish-American War which has been called "Hearst's War" because of the influence which Hearst's newspapers had in arousing public opinion. McKinley (MFMFFFM7FM), it appears, was a most reluctant participant in that conflict (see Whitney, 1967).

To summarize at this point, we have found that Americans seem to prefer first and third-born sons as presidents. Fourth-born or later sons are given short shrift and second-borns are definitely slighted. In addition we have evidence for a systematic relationship between the political zeitgeist and the birth order of the presidents. Our understanding of this relationship is as yet confined to a distinction between periods of expansion and aggressiveness leading to war and other periods devoted more to internal readjustments of a political-social nature—the former having first-born and only sons as presidents, the latter having younger sons as presidents. Further on we shall identify other aspects of this correlation between zeitgeist and birth order. For the moment, however, let us consider some of the implications of these findings with respect to the political process. The critical questions are where and when such selections are made and by whom?

In attempting to answer these questions, recall us noting that a similar preference for first and third-born sons was found in the sample of defeated presidential candidates. This result suggests that the selection process takes place at the national conventions or even earlier. To learn more about the selection process, birth order data were obtained for a sample of nominees for the presidency at national conventions during the period from 1832 to 1920. This sample represents nearly all of the leading contenders in each election. Those for whom biographical data were not available fall mainly into the category of "favorite sons" who were nominated for honorary reasons. As may be seen from Table 9.5, there is apparently some selection made by the convention delegates,

---

[6]Both Zachary Taylor and William Henry Harrison died in office and were succeeded by Vice-Presidents Tyler and Fillmore. Our data do not include Tyler and Fillmore nor the other two vice-presidents, Andrew Johnson and Chester A. Arthur, who succeeded to office on the death of a president but who were not subsequently elected president themselves.

Table 9.5.   Birth Order (Order as Son) of Presidential Nominees (1832-1920)

Birth Order as Son	All Nominees		Presidential Candidates	
	N	%	N	%
Only Son	21	15	5	11
First-born	44	32	16	35
Second-born	36	26	7	15
Third-born	21	15	16	35
Fourth-born (or Higher)	17	12	2	4
Total	139	100	46	100

since the ranks of second-born and fourth-born sons are somewhat reduced and the ranks of third-born sons somewhat increased among those who are actually chosen as presidential candidates. However, the data of Table 9.5 also suggest that part of the selection process whereby fourth-born and later sons are eliminated from presidential candidacy occurs prior to the national conventions, since the 12 percent of fourth-born and later sons who appear as nominees seems to be a lower percentage than would be expected on the basis of the size of the nominees' families of which 41 percent contain four or more sons.

Let us turn now to consideration of the degree of choice left to the citizen at the ballot box. In many elections, in fact more often than not, the voter has no choice at all since both candidates are of the same birth order. For example, in a comparison of the elections from 1828 (when the public first began to have a direct impact on the elections) to 1960, we find there have been 19 elections in which the major candidates were of matched birth order in contrast to 13 in which they were mismatched. Although this difference is not very large, it may be more significant than it appears, particularly if the hypothesis is correct that the birth order of the president and the political zeitgeist vary concordantly. There would inevitably be some elections in which the president-elect is of a different birth order than the incumbent. A good example of this state of affairs is the election of 1838 when Andrew Jackson, a third-born son (MMM3) (with whose election it has appropriately been remarked the flood gates of democracy were opened) defeated John Quincy Adams, a first-born son (FM2FMM). As we have seen, Jackson's election marked the end of an unbroken succession of first-born sons covering a span of 28 years and inaugurated a period of similar length dominated by second and third-born sons. Other examples would be Polk's election in 1844 and the election of Franklin Delano Roosevelt (M1) in 1932 when the country was in the throes of the Depression.[7]

From the foregoing it is apparent that we have plunged into the truly difficult

[7]Although a test of this matching hypothesis is not statistically significant (with the elections of Jackson vs. Adams, Polk vs. Clay, and Roosevelt vs. Hoover removed, $phi = .33$); nevertheless, a clear trend is evident as noted in the following table:

question of how and where in the electoral process the correlation between political zeitgeist and the president's birth order is achieved. Sometimes that decision is made by the voter; more often than not, however, it is made somewhere else prior to election day. Some further understanding of this issue may be provided by a closer look at what actually occurs in critical election periods. Let us begin with one of the most memorable conventions in this country's history, the Republican convention of 1860. Roseboom, in his *History of Presidential Elections* (1957, p. 180), has captured a not uncommon reaction to that convention: "To the believers in the hand of Providence in American history, the Chicago nomination must afford an amazing example of its mysterious way. Midnight conferences of liquor-stimulated politicians, deals for jobs, local leaders pulling wires to save their state tickets, petty malice, and personal jealousies—a strange compound and the man of destiny emerges."

Before proceeding, let us return briefly to our historical survey of the period from 1828 to 1856 to refresh our memory as to the political climate. What is of highest interest, of course, are the signs of a continual escalation of the dispute over slavery. A signal event was the establishment by William Lloyd Garrison in 1831 of the *Liberator* with its editorial policy advocating the unconditional abolition of slavery. In short order followed the Underground Railroad of 1838, the gag rules of Congress against anti-slavery petitions, the 1850 Compromise, the Kansas-Nebraska Act of 1854, the Dred Scott decision of 1857, and in 1859 John Brown's famous raid on Harpers Ferry. This then was the political climate in which the Republican delegates convened in Chicago in 1860.

When the convention opened, Seward was the leading contender, with Lincoln a close second. Earlier in the year Seward had been far and away the favorite, but in the months just before the convention Lincoln's star had risen rapidly, largely as a consequence of his famous Cooper Union speech. In the final analysis, however, most observers agree (e.g., Roseboom, 1957; King, 1960) that the whirlwind campaign conducted at the convention by Lincoln's manager, William Winter David, must be given a fair share of the credit for toppling Seward and swinging the convention to Lincoln. For our purposes it should be noted that of all the leading nominees at the convention, Lincoln alone was an only son (FM2); Seward was a third son, with the other potential candidates likewise younger sons.

		Defeated Candidates		
		Only or First-born Son	*Younger Son*	*Total*
Elected	*Only or First-born Son*	10	3	13
Candidates	*Younger Son*	7	9	16
	Total	17	12	29

The matching of candidates may also be considered in terms of other aspects of the family constellations such as family size, ratio of brothers and sisters, and the ordinal position and sex of siblings just surrounding the subject. All these ways of matching show a considerable degree of concordance.

Another factor to be considered in Lincoln's selection by the Republican delegates is the fact that he had originally gained national fame in his debates with Douglas which Lincoln was generally conceded to have won (although he subsequently lost the Illinois Senatorial race). Moreover, Douglas who had long been actively seeking the Democratic Party nomination seemed assured of success in 1860. Such, of course, turned out to be the case, although not without some slight hitches. When the Democratic Party convened in the South, the delegates became deadlocked in the selection of a candidate and split into two factions, one of which met in Baltimore and nominated Stephen Douglas, while the other remained in the South and nominated John Cabell Breckinridge. Like Lincoln (FM2), both Douglas (FM2) and Breckinridge (M1FFF) were only sons; Douglas was of exactly the same birth order as Lincoln, both having a single older sister. Thus, in that decisive election year in which the nation anxiously faced the threat of rebellion, the slate of presidential candidates presented to the electorate made certain that, no matter what party won the elections, the presidency would be held by a man who was an only son.

From the above we might draw the conclusion that there is an increased proportion of candidates of the appropriate birth order in critical elections. Such a trend is clearly evident in the data of Table 9.6, where the percentage of first-born and only-son candidates is compared with the percentage of younger-son candidates for the five elections just preceding and including the Civil War (1852-1868) and World War I (1904-1920), and for a similar number of elections just prior to these crisis periods, namely, 1832-1852 and 1884-1900. These data suggest that the selection of a candidate of a birth order concordant with the temper of the times is statistically more probable ($X^2 = 7.43$, $p < .01$ for comparison of Civil War crisis and noncrisis periods; $X^2 = 6.30$, $p < .05$ for comparison of World War I crisis and noncrisis periods) just on the basis of the greater availability of appropriate candidates.

We draw attention to this greater frequency of potential candidates of appropriate birth order not because we believe these frequencies are indicative of underlying shifts in birth rates—for which there is no evidence and which on any grounds would be difficult to imagine considering the time spans involved as well as the wide range of ages of candidates in any election year—but rather as suggesting the need to bring consideration of the candidates' motivation into the birth order-zeitgeist equation. It could be argued that there must occur at some stage in the political process a mutual responsiveness between candidates of the appropriate birth order and some segment of the population to account for the results which we find. Hence, we would expect to encounter in critical elections candidates of the appropriate birth order in contention for some period of time before the election. Such was the case in 1860. Lincoln and Douglas, as we know, had been rivals. In 1850, they contested for the U.S. Senate in Illinois. Their widely publicized debates propelled them both to national attention. John Cabell Breckinridge had also attained national exposure in 1856 as the vice-presidential running mate of Buchanan.

Table 9.6.   Birth Order (Order as Son) of Presidential Nominees During Crisis and Noncrisis Periods

Birth Order as Son	Crisis Periods				Noncrisis Periods			
	1852-1868		1904-1920		1832-1848		1884-1900	
	N	*%*	*N*	*%*	*N*	*%*	*N*	*%*
Only or First-born Son	26	55	29	66	7	22	14	36
Younger Son	21	45	15	34	25	78	25	64

In concluding this discussion of the election of 1860, we wish to note that in the Civil War we have identified an example of a third type of political zeitgeist and leadership style. This type of political situation involves a threatened breakdown in major functions of society due either to unresolved tensions among divergent factions as in the Civil War or, as we shall see later on, through a failure to meet fundamental social needs. The correlated birth order for this political situation appears to be the only son or only child.[8]

DISCUSSION

So far we have identified three types of political zeitgeist, each implying a particular style of leadership. The first type is characterized by expansive, nationalistic, and imperialistic aims which frequently lead to military conflict; the second is more domestically oriented, preoccupied with adjustments of power among different internal factions such as business, labor, political parties; and the third involves a threatened breakdown of major functions of a society due either to unresolved tensions among divergent factions or through a failure to meet fundamental social needs. As we have seen, the leaders are in the first case first-borns, in the second case younger sons, and in the third case only sons or only children.

There is one other type of political situation which may be clearly distinguished from the three we have already identified. We are referring, of course, to revolution. It is obvious why our study has so far failed to turn up revolutionary leaders, since we have confined ourselves to governments which have been able to maintain national unity. The one situation in our data which approached revolution was the American Civil War. In our original analysis we viewed that struggle from the standpoint of the federal government. If we now turn our attention to the Confederacy we find a different type of leadership. The president chosen by the rebellious southern states was Jefferson Davis, a long-time advocate in the U.S. Senate of the rights of the individual states to resolve for themselves such domestic issues as slavery. Davis was a last-born son, the youngest of ten children (MMMFMFFFFM10). Is this a characteristic birth order for revolutionary leaders? A brief survey suggests that in many cases they were last-born children, e.g., Ho Chi Minh (FMM3), Sun Yat-sen (MMM3), Gandhi (MFMM4), and Bolivar (FFMM4). Others such as Lenin (FMM3FFM), Castro (FMM3MF), and Garibaldi (MM2MMF) were younger sons.

It is difficult to determine whether the American and French revolutions fit this pattern. One reason is that in neither of these cases did one person emerge as the single, undisputed leader. However, in America it was certainly Samuel Adams (a younger son) in the New England colonies who organized the Sons of Liberty, who inspired the initial acts of rebellion, and who was instrumental in organizing the Continental Congress. In the South-

---

[8]The election of Franklin Delano Roosevelt (M1) during the Depression in 1932 is the other example in this category. Roosevelt was the first, and through 1960 the last, only child to be elected president.

ern colonies, it was Patrick Henry (MM2FFFFFF) who first gave clear expression to the cry for liberty.[9] In France the original revolutionary impulse was eventually co-opted in a military coup led by Napoleon (MM2MFMFFM), the most famous general of the revolution. As we see, each of these leaders was a younger son.

The identification of this fourth type of political zeitgeist poses some interesting questions. With respect to birth order, the leadership type in revolution seems to be the same as in the domestically oriented political situation. Can these be the same men? At first that seems unlikely, since a major distinguishing feature of revolution is aggression and usually armed conflict; whereas a hallmark of the domestically oriented era seems to be the absence of confrontation and military engagements. But perhaps we are overlooking more important characteristics of revolutionary periods. First, it may not be true that revolution implies military engagement. Gandhi, for one, has demonstrated the possibility that a resolute, one-sided refusal to resort to arms may have revolutionary effects. Also we should note that Jefferson Davis, the pre-revolutionary leader, was merely one among many advocates of change. If we examine the lives of revolutionary leaders before their emergence as prime movers in a revolution, we note that they have engaged for many years in advocacy of the causes they support. It is primarily the nature of the government under which such revolutionary leaders live which determines the extent to which they are free to hold office and to seek change through the establishment. Thus, up until the time at which it is no longer possible for a dialogue to continue between divergent factions, there is probably no marked distinction between advocates and potential revolutionaries (cf. Gipson, 1962).

Issues like the foregoing, which we have barely touched upon, make us aware of the many perplexing questions raised by our findings. For example, while we have cleared away some of the statistical underbrush, we have still left largely untouched such basic problems as just how the selective matching of birth order and zeitgeist may occur at various levels of the electoral process, quite without any awareness on the part of the participants of the facts we have investigated here. Before pushing further into these difficult questions, let us check our findings by doing a similar investigation with the British political system. It should be evident to the reader by now that in our discussion of the American data, we recapitulated history at times. This procedure seemed desirable in order to revive acquaintance with some of the events of political history, particularly with the transitions from one period to another. Our analysis of British prime ministers will include less of a guided tour of British history. However, in view of the unique characteristics of the British mode of government, we think such an analysis illuminates the interactions among political leaders during periods of transition.

[9]George Washington (MMFM4FFMMF) probably belongs here also, although his revolutionary role was always overshadowed by his unquestioned position as commanding general of the army.

The British Prime Ministers

The choice of the British political system as a source of validating data was natural on several counts. The British prime minister is a close analogue to the U.S. president. He is the leader of his political party; he is the head of government and, like the American president, is given the responsibility for forming a cabinet. Secondly, although the British and American electoral processes differ in important details, they both require popular election of their heads of government. The prime minister is not, as is the president, elected directly by all the people. However, in a general election, he is known throughout the country and is the spokesman for his party's platform. In earlier years the choice of prime minister depended upon a number of factors. At one time the monarch had the power to actively intervene in the selection, as did the House of Lords. But, nowadays, although the monarch nominally requests the prime minister to form a government, there is no question but that the leader of a political party will ordinarily become prime minister when that party has a majority in the House of Commons. The House of Lords no longer has a say in the matter nor can a member of the House of Lords become prime minister (cf. Mathiot, 1967).

A comparison of the relative powers and responsibilities of the prime minister and the president shows that they are very similar. Historically, the office of president and the office of prime minister have gradually acquired greater and greater powers. If there is anything that students of government agree about, it is the increasing concentration of power in the hands of the U.S. president and the British prime minister (see, e.g., Berkeley, 1968).

Most students of British government also agree that the first true prime minister was Robert Walpole. As Berkeley (1968, p. 21) puts it: "Walpole virtually created the office of prime minister and made possible the evolution of the modern system of ministerial responsibility." However, following Walpole's 30-year tenure as prime minister, there was a period of some 32 years in which no further progress was made in the development of the office of prime minister, primarily because of internal party division and the fact that George III had no intention of allowing authority to pass into the hands of his ministers. According to Berkeley, not until William Pitt the Younger became prime minister in 1783 was there any further substantial development in the powers of the office. In view of this, as well as the less accurate data available in the earlier years, the principal emphasis in the present study will be the time between 1783 and 1963 or, in other words, from Prime Minister William Pitt the Younger to Prime Minister Macmillan. The earlier period from 1721 when Walpole first became prime minister to 1783 has been studied, however, and data from that period have been utilized in some instances.

RESULTS

It is evident in Tables 9.7 and 9.8 that there is no clear-cut preference for any particular birth order. First-born sons appear to have a slight edge in families of

Table 9.7.   Birth Order of British Prime Ministers (Pitt to Macmillan, 1783-1963)[a]

Number of Children in Family	Position in Family								
	Only Child	*1st Child*	*2nd Child*	*3rd Child*	*4th Child*	*5th Child*	*6th Child*	*7th Child*	Total
1	6								6
2		2	1						3
3			1	3					4
4			1	1	1				3
5		2	2		7				11
6		2	2	1	1	4			10
7		3							3
8				1				1	2
9									0
10									0
11				2					2
Total	6	9	7	8	9	4	0	1	44[b]

[a]Each ministry is treated separately.
[b]For five prime ministers, data are not available as to precise ordinal position or number of children. Of these, one was an only son, two were first-born sons, and two were younger sons.

Table 9.8.   Birth Order of British Prime Ministers Based on Position as Son[a]

Number of Sons In Family	Position in Family						
	Only Child	*Only Son*	*1st Son*	*2nd Son*	*3rd Son*	*4th Son*	Total
1	6	1					7
2			6	4			10
3			3	6	4		13
4			2	2	1	5	10
5			2		1	1	4
6			3				3
Total	6	1	16	12	6	6	47[b]

[a]Each ministry is treated separately.
[b]For two prime ministers who were first-born sons, data are not available as to the number of sons in their families.

two and more than five sons. This trend might be slightly increased by the addition of the two cases for which our data is incomplete. Just what significance attaches to this pattern is difficult to assess. However, when these data are compared with those for the American presidents, we find an impressive degree of correspondence. For example, a Spearman rank order correlation comparing the family positions of presidents and prime ministers is .77 (data are found in the last rows of Tables 9.1 and 9.7). The rank order correlation relating position as son for presidents and prime ministers is .70 (data appear in last row of Tables 9.2 and 9.8). Moreover, the range of birth order is the same in both samples; the most extreme presidents and prime ministers are seventh children and fourth sons. It is also notable that in both samples, there are appreciably more large families (five or more children) than small families (four or less children)—the percentages are about 66 percent to 33 percent for both presidents and prime ministers. Furthermore, although there are nearly twice as many first-born as last-born presidents (12/7 or 1.7) and prime ministers (9/5 or 1.8), the proportion of first-borns from large families (five or more children) to first-borns from small families (four or less children) is three to one. These findings offer some support for our contention that coping with siblings is an important element in the development of political skills.

Finally the comparisons over time presented in Table 9.9 show that like American presidents, prime ministers of the same or closely related birth orders (i.e., first-born and only sons as contrasted with younger sons) follow each other into office for certain periods of time. Naturally, due to the greater flexibility of the British political system, ministers are replaced more frequently than are U.S. presidents. Basically, though, the shifts from one prime minister to another follow the same patterns. For example, the third-born son Walpole's reign of "peace, ease, and freedom" (Bigham, 1920) led on through a succession of second-born sons to end finally with a first-born son during the stormy period of the American revolution. A similar sequence of ministers is seen during the period of the French Revolution and the subsequent wars with Napoleon and World Wars I and II.

With respect to examining the correlation between birth order of leaders and political zeitgeist for British prime ministers, periods of British history have been classified in terms of the four types of political zeitgeist previously identified using as criteria the presence or absence of war or peace for types one and two respectively, severe economic depression and threatened breakdown of important social functions for type three, and open, prolonged civil conflict for type four. The worst international crises faced by the British between 1783 and 1963 were the Napoleonic Wars (particularly 1806 to 1815) and World Wars I and II. Other less serious conflicts were the War of 1812, the Crimean War of 1854, the Indian Mutiny of 1857, the Afghan and Zulu Wars of 1874-1880, and the Boer War of 1899-1902. The more peaceful periods which were devoted extensively to internal affairs were 1784 to 1801, 1828 to 1852, 1868 to 1874, 1880 to

Table 9.9. **Birth Order (Order as Son) of British Prime Ministers by Election Period**

Birth Order as Son	Election Periods													
	1720-1759		1760-1799		1800-1839		1840-1879		1880-1919		1920-1959	
	N	%	N	%	N	%	N	%	N	%	N	%
Only or First-born Son	3	50	7	70	6	46	9	75	3	28	7	58
Younger Son	3	50	3	30	7	54	3	25	8	72	5	42

1895, 1905 to 1916, and 1945 to 1963. Type three is represented by the period 1924 to 1937 which included the long period of labor unrest culminating in the general strike of 1925 and the severe economic stress of the world-wide depression. The struggle for Indian independence led by Gandhi (MFMM4) may be considered representative of type four.

The prime ministers in the crisis periods were Liverpool (M1M),[10] Lloyd George (FM2M), Churchill (M1M), Palmerston (M1FMF), Disraeli (FM2MM), and Salisbury (MFFM4M). Among these six prime ministers there were five first-born sons of whom three were also first-born children. During the noncrisis periods we find Pitt (FMFM4M), Wellington (MMFM4MM), Melbourne (MM2MMF), Russell (MMM3), Grey (eldest of five sons, one sister), Peel (FFM3MMFFMMMF), Salisbury (MFFM4M), Gladstone (MMMFM5F), Roseberry (FFM3M), Asquith (MM2FF), Campbell-Bannerman (FMFM4), Atlee (MMFFFMM7M), Churchill (M1M), Eden (FMMM4M), and Macmillan (MMM3). Eleven of these 15 prime ministers were younger sons. Using a Fisher exact probability test, a comparison of first-born sons with younger sons in crisis and noncrisis periods is statistically significant at the .05 level, confirming the similar finding in the sample of U.S. presidents. Type three prime ministers or those leading the country through periods of severe economic depression were Baldwin (M1) and MacDonald (M1). Type four, the revolutionary leader, is represented by Gandhi (MFMM4) who is not, of course, a prime minister.

As we suggested earlier, the workings of the British political structure provide an opportunity to observe more directly the forces at work which determine shifts in political power from one birth order to another. In this regard, Lord Beaverbrook's *Politicians at War* (1926) furnishes us with an insider's account of Herbert Henry Asquith's early World War I ministry and its transformation to a coalition ministry under David Lloyd George. Asquith, as Campbell-Bannerman's first lieutenant, inherited the ministry at Campbell-Bannerman's death in 1907. In 1914, war broke out and a year later, Asquith was forced to reconstruct the ministry on a coalition basis. But this did not relieve the growing tensions over the conduct of the war, either in the Cabinet or in the House of Commons. These tensions became focused around two Cabinet members, first Winston Churchill (M1M) and then Lloyd George (FM2M). The problem that Asquith (MM2FF) found with each of these men was the same; they were aggressive, impatient, ambitious for power, and interested in pressing the war effort more vigorously. Asquith managed to thrust the young Churchill out of the Cabinet, but Lloyd George soon gained ascendancy and in 1916 became prime minister. Here is Beaverbrook's (1926, p. 23) account of how that occurred:

> People have sometimes talked and written as though his [Asquith's] downfall in December 1916 was a sudden, inexplicable catastrophe—or

[10]Liverpool was fourteen years older than his younger brother which implies that he was as much an only child as a first-born child. But this fact only increased his fitness for leadership at this time, since as a consequence of the long drawnout crisis of the Napoleonic Wars, England faced near paralysis of its civil functions.

only to be explained as the result of a secret intrigue hastily engineered by unscrupulous rivals. Nothing could be further from the truth. Ever since the spring of 1915 the Premier had been engaged in knocking the props out from under him[self] or in watching them fall without replacing them. ... Why did not Asquith simply take up Lloyd George and make him his executive arm while retaining the titular authority? In this summer, the answer to the question is a simple one. Asquith would not promote Lloyd George for the same reason that he had come to distrust Churchill, even to the point of permitting his dismissal the year before. Asquith was the *man of peace in the war*—these ministers of nervous action fretted his very soul. He did not want them about him—always bustling and hurrying and driving. This tendency of his seems to have increased as the war went on.

In this graphic description we can see portrayed at the personal level the struggle between second-born son Asquith (MM2FF) and first-born sons Churchill (M1M) and Lloyd George (FM2M) over the very issue which our hypothesis would predict, the aggressive conduct of a war. Obviously Churchill's time came later in World War II when the British government once again backed into war under the leadership of a second-born, Neville Chamberlain (FMM3FFF), only to switch almost immediately to Churchill's leadership as hostilities broke out and England itself was threatened.

Churchill's history is also illustrative of the issue we raised much earlier concerning the role the individual plays in effectuating his own destiny. Were it not for World War II, Churchill would most probably be remembered today as a politician of great promise who never quite made it.[11] More than likely political pundits would be explaining his failure as due, in part, to the difficult traits in his personality such as overbearing ambition, egocentricity, and aggressiveness. Such criticisms would not be wide of the mark. However, once Churchill's star had risen, it would be these very same traits which would stand him in good stead. Then he was praised for his indomitable will, his bulldog courage, and his fierce vengeance.

Churchill's mercurial political career actually spanned some 60 years, many of which were spent in and out of the government, switching back and forth between political parties, often at odds with the leadership. For the ten-year period just prior to World War II he was deliberately kept out of the Cabinet, isolated, often ignored, a one-man political party unto himself. Throughout this period of his splendid isolation, Churchill was viewed as a Jeremiah, thundering

[11]Two other leaders mentioned earlier in this regard were Abraham Lincoln and Franklin D. Roosevelt. Both were relative failures until their great opportunity arrived. Lincoln for the better part of his career was a relatively obscure lawyer and politician. Defeated for the U.S. Senate in 1858, he was unexpectedly elected president two years later, just as the Civil War erupted. Roosevelt as a vice-presidential candidate in 1924 suffered a disastrous defeat. Not long afterwards he contracted polio and his political career seemed over. However, only a few years later during the depths of the Depression he was elected president.

his dire prophecies of death and destruction, lamenting England's lack of preparedness. Of course, as the war clouds gathered in 1936 and 1939, his prophecies began to be heard and, almost miraculously, when war struck he became at the age of 65 the only choice to lead England through the years of her gravest crisis (cf. Taylor, 1952).

Summary and Conclusions

We have now come full circle. In two political systems we have found that the heads of state are selected in a manner which tends to maximize the probability that the leaders's birth order and the political zeitgeist will be matched in a systematic fashion. The parameters of this matching have been only roughly specified as yet, but we have identified four, more or less distinct, political situations: (1) international crisis and war, (2) peace and adjustment of internal affairs, (3) collapse of social functions and civil conflict, and (4) revolution. Corresponding to these are the four leadership styles, respectively, of the first-born, middle-born, only, and last-born son. Moreover, the relationships between these leadership styles and the political zeitgeist appear in general to meet our expectations based on an analysis of the power relationships of each sibling position. The first-born male has the greatest experience of dominance and of successful intervention in the affairs of others. The middle-born son, starting life in a position of dependence and relative weakness, gains later on an opportunity for dominance, having the most experience in mediation. The last-born son is from beginning to end in a position of dependence and relative weakness, probably harboring the greatest resentment toward all authority. Both the middle- and the last-born son, in view of their relatively weaker positions, have a greater need than the first-born son for devious and subtle tactics as well as appeals to "higher authority." The only child, dealing entirely with "higher authorities" whose favors he need never share, is most at home on center stage and least vulnerable to peer rivalry.[12]

How the relationship between birth order and zeitgeist comes about remains the most interesting and puzzling of questions. On the one hand, we must account for just where and by whom selections are made. But, on top of that, we must face the fact that, as far as we know, wherever and by whomever such choices are made the matching process goes on (or has until now) without any awareness on the part of the participants of the significance that birth order may have in the determinations. Presently, our best educated guesses as to how the matching takes place are based on observations of the British House of Commons and Cabinet, where, it seems, a proving ground is provided for the

[12]This analysis of sibling power relationships may be compared with the model suggested earlier which focused on the expectations of society derived from birth order experience. As may be seen, the two models supplement each other.

testing and training of prime ministers. In the House of Commons, the neophyte politician is subjected to the closest scrutiny by his colleagues, who give him ample opportunity to soar or to fall flat on his face (cf. Taylor, 1952). Party leaders are particularly attentive. Once such leaders are assured of their party loyalty, talented young men are drawn into closer association with their elders in party committee work or in minor government appointments, if the party is then in power. In this process, the weak, the unstable, and the incompetent are weeded out, while the chosen ones gain the opportunity to test their abilities in the more demanding situation of the Cabinet. There, as our earlier example of the Asquith Cabinet showed, the business of government is also the business of power—of who can work with whom, of who has the most direct insight into dominant trends of the country and hence the support of a major constituency, and of who can influence his colleagues to support his assault on the pinnacle of power (cf. Mathiot, 1967).

All these impressions lend support to the proposition that it is in small groups such as high-level party committees and Cabinets that, at least in Great Britain, the final matching of birth order and zeitgeist often takes place. The vehicle appears to be the competitiveness of the potential candidates and the complementary response of their colleagues in judging their likelihood of success. Such judgments most certainly are a function of the politicians' well-trained sixth sense for reading the needs, the demands, and the limitations of their constituencies. In all this, as we have said before, the individual's sense of his own fitness for the political situation at hand must play a considerable role in determining success or failure.

The American political system does not have the advantage provided by the interlocking of the British House of Commons and Cabinet, so that the training ground for American presidents occurs primarily in local level politics and the national party structure. We would surmise, though, that, just as in Great Britain, it is in small group interactions that most of the selection takes place. Exactly how is a question for further research.

Before leaving this topic, it is important to note that sometimes the matching of birth order and zeitgeist is made at the ballot box. It can occur in England in those instances where a government, no longer assured of a majority, must go to the people for support in a general election. At that point, if the opposition party leader is of a different birth order than the incumbent prime minister, the choice is up to the people. In actual fact, just as in the United States, this is true in a minority of instances. But even so, it happens, and our results suggest that in those cases matching may result from the people's decision.

This leads us most naturally into the question of how much impact a leader can actually have on history. Is it conceivable that some of the apparent matching of birth order and zeitgeist is a function of the management of affairs by a president or prime minister in pursuit of personal propensities perhaps related to birth order? This issue is answered in the affirmative (although not, of course, with any study of birth order) by Barber (1972) in his *The Presidential*

Character. In its broadest form this question has been debated by philosophers and historians for centuries. Here we pause. It is true that a host of problems—some old, some new—take on a new perspective with birth order as the vantage point. For example, to what extent does history repeat itself? Can the wrong man be elected or the right man neglected? When, if ever, can one believe what a politician says? But these questions, fascinating as they may be, carry us far beyond our present limits. Their solution, along with all the other unfinished business of this research, must await future endeavors.

If we turn our thoughts for a moment to consideration of such future endeavors we can readily distinguish three areas of research which are in dire need of further investigation. First, we obviously know very little yet about the family origins of the different leadership styles. Developmental studies of total families with particular emphasis on sibling interactions would be most helpful in providing such information. Second, as we have already noted, our knowledge of the process whereby birth order and zeitgeist are related is limited. Field studies in political settings where aspiring candidates could be followed over some period of time would prove fruitful in this regard. The British House of Commons with its interlocking structure of political parties, House membership, and Cabinet appointments appears to offer a most intriguing arena for such studies. Another potentially effective approach to the matching problem would be the study of small groups in which the variables of birth order, family constellation, and leadership task could be manipulated. Finally, there is a need for greater differentiation in our analyses of family constellations, leadership styles, and related social demands. There were a number of instances in the present research when such a differentiated analysis was called for but we were thwarted by limitations of sample size. To give just one illustration, what about the family constellation which begins sister, brother (FM2) and has many variations thereon. It is just this brother with an older sister who of all male siblings is the most susceptible to female influence (see Sutton-Smith and Rosenberg, 1970). Could we expect to find political leaders with this family constellation giving expression to women's influence? Examples immediately come to mind: the compassion of Abraham Lincoln (FM2), Woodrow Wilson's (FFFM3M) idealism, and the all-embracing democracy of Thomas Jefferson (FFM3FFFFM).[13] Following this line of thought, we were led to hypothesize a possible relationship between tenure in office of leaders from this family constellation and timing of achievements in the women's movement. A re-examination of our data with this proposition in mind did produce results suggesting that the hypothesis might be tenable; but only with further research will we know for certain.

In conclusion, the very last word belongs without question to the man whose inspiration shines everywhere throughout these studies: Alfred Adler (MM2FMFMM).

[13]Lest this be misunderstood it should be acknowledged that the qualities ascribed here to men are not necessarily "feminine." However, in a patriarchal society such as ours, it is inevitable that they should be associated with the influence of women.

CHAPTER 10

Attitudes of Regional Soviet Political Leaders: Toward Understanding the Potential for Change*

Philip D. Stewart

Editor's Introduction

If we know the attitudes of a political leader, can we discover some of the influences that determined these attitudes by looking at the political leader's biographical statistics? In Chapter 10 Philip Stewart attempts just such an exploration, using Soviet regional Party first secretaries as his subjects. Stewart suggests that there are several types of Soviet political leaders described in the literature on the Soviet Union, each type having different attitudes and

*I wish to express my appreciation to those who assisted in this research: to the editor for inspiration and encouragement; to Judy Ruth for assistance in coding the data; to William Messmer and Barbara Nelson for assistance in development of some of the ideas presented here; to Richard Hofstetter, Giacomo Sani, and Herbert Asher for conceptual and methodological guidance; to James McGregor and James Ludwig for programming and computer assistance; and to numerous graduate students for helpful comments. I am also indebted to the following facilities at Ohio State University: the Instructional and Research Computer Center for generously allocating the required computer time; and the Polimetrics Laboratory, Department of Political Science, College of Social and Behavioral Sciences, Stuart Thorson, Director. Of course, responsibility for any shortcomings belongs to the author alone.

antecedent social and political experiences. His research seeks to ascertain which of these types of leaders is most descriptive of the Soviet regional political elite.

In many respects the Stewart study parallels one done by McClosky (1967) on American regional political elites. McClosky examined the foreign policy orientations of American Democratic and Republican party leaders (delegates and alternates to the 1956 national conventions). Like Stewart, McClosky first ascertained the attitudes of the party leaders and then related them to biographical statistics on the leaders. Unlike Stewart, however, McClosky used attitude questionnaires to gain information about the attitudes of his subjects; Stewart content analyzed published articles written by Party first secretaries in determining their attitudes. Both studies introduce more complexity into the question of who becomes a political leader. Their data suggest that contradictory or nonsignificant findings regarding the relationship between personal characteristics and political roles may result from the divergent attitudes and backgrounds held by the occupants of the roles. Once the focus is more specific, say on a particular attitude, the researcher can find positive results showing the effects of personal characteristics in the selection of political leaders.

Two of the biographical statistics which Stewart uses deserve special mention. By dividing his sample on the basis of age into a younger and older group, Stewart is able to make some forecasts concerning future attitudes of Soviet political leaders. He can suggest from his data which attitudes held by older regional officials are likely to disappear and which attitudes held by younger officials are likely to become more germane across time. In effect, by choosing to look at regional Party first secretaries, Stewart is gaining information on future national Soviet leaders. Moreover, when his research is extended to include all Soviet regional Party first secretaries during the 1953-1968 time period, he will be able to compare the attitudes and background characteristics of those who go on to higher Party positions with those who do not.

The other background variable of interest concerns the time at which the Soviet regional official entered the Communist Party. The hypothesis has been advanced (e.g., see Barber, 1968, 1972; Cutler, 1971; Inglehart, 1971; Lambert, 1971; Mannheim, 1952; Nagle, 1973) that the circumstances surrounding the first successful political experience and the period of political socialization (roughly between the ages of 17 and 25) have a significant impact on consequent beliefs, attitudes, and political behavior of political leaders. Stewart's data indicate that certain of the attitudes characteristic of those officials in his sample who came into the Party during the establishment of Stalinism (1921-1939) differ from the attitudes characteristic of officials entering the Party during World War II. As Nagle (1973, p. 8) notes: "During these years (1921-1939), the drive for enforced party unity reaches its (irrational) peak, the openness of the party to a broader membership and to debate disappears behind a tightening process of membership screening, and a facade of unanimous votes and toadying to official party leadership." On the other hand, Hough (1967, p. 25) indicates that persons entering the Party during the war years found a Party "[which] was no longer engaged in warfare against the peasants or its own members. On the contrary, it was leading the country in the defense of the motherland against a foreign invader. At this time the Party de-emphasized Marxist-Leninist ideology, and even restored fairly close relations with the Orthodox Church." This type of analysis is called generational or age cohort analysis. Johnson's (Chapter 4) analysis of Senator Church's belief system also lends support to the general socialization hypothesis. His data show how the political environment of the late fifties influenced Church's views of the world.

In addition to biographical statistics, Stewart uses content analysis. Unlike the content analysis of Winter and A. Stewart (Chapter 2) in assessing presidential needs for power, achievement, and affiliation or Johnson's (Chapter 4) development of Church's operational code, the content analysis in the present chapter involves little inference on the part of the coder. More like Frank's (Chapter 3) count of the repetitions used by Humphrey and McGovern in their California Primary Debate, Stewart focuses on manifest content. What does the Party first secretary say? Of interest is how many times in his writing the regional official refers to certain attitude objects such as consumers, economic production, and Party initiatives, and whether he praises them, criticizes them, or demands changes in them. Stewart wants to learn what the concerns of the regional officials in his sample are. Moreover, Stewart has tried to avoid some of the translation problems which can plague cross-national research with content analysis by coding the original Russian documents. Such translation problems include finding translated materials, knowing how "free" the translator has been with the material, and, if words are the unit of analysis, what the word counts would be in the original when compared to the translation (cf. Brislin, Lonner, and Thorndike, 1973).

Philip Stewart is a professor of political science at Ohio State University. The research reported in this chapter is part of a larger, ongoing project, the Soviet Elite Studies Project. In pursuing his study of the Soviet Union, Stewart has spent a year at Moscow University and has participated in four recent Dartmouth Conferences between high-level political, economic, and scientific leaders from the United States and the Soviet Union.

CAN THE SOVIET UNION survive until 1984? This question, made famous as the title of the controversial essay by dissident Soviet historian Andrei Amalrik (1971), is but an extreme variation of a concern that has increasingly engaged the attention of Soviet specialists in the West in recent years. While Amalrik characterizes the Soviet polity as hopelessly stifled by an unresponsive bureaucratic Party and envisions the system ultimately succumbing under the impact of a Sino-Soviet war, most Western views are less apocalyptic. Serious academic interpretations of the nature and direction of change in Soviet politics range from a position that portrays a dynamic Stalinist totalitarianism degenerating into a kind of "oligarchic petrifaction" (Brzezinski, 1970), to an image of an essentially static, unchanging totalitarianism (Kassof, 1964), to an interpretation stressing gradual movement toward "institutional pluralism" (Hough, 1972).

An adequate understanding of the adaptive capacity of the Soviet system, of the kinds and direction of change occurring within the Soviet Union today, is of far more than academic interest to Americans. The business community, on the threshold of committing vast financial and material resources to the Soviet economy on the assumption of long-term mutual interest and benefit, needs to know whether the generation of leaders who will soon come to power will continue to perceive these relationships as beneficial and appropriate or whether a fearful, distrustful, xenophobic leadership might appear and renege on present commitments. The political leadership in the United States, and especially in the Congress, is anxious to discover to what extent the present détente, with its potential for far-reaching agreements on nuclear weapons and arms and on European security and trade, reflects a basic shift toward essentially instrumental attitudes among the Soviet leadership, wherein calculations of national self-interest and mutual benefit might increasingly replace ideologically motivated dogmatism and revolutionary messianism. Similarly, broad segments of the American public, especially the intellectual community, hopeful that détente may lead to broader areas of information exchange and to greater collaboration in the interests of solving problems common to all of mankind, are concerned whether changes now occurring in the Soviet polity will inhibit the further development of present cooperative activities.

Unfortunately, there exists no satisfactory, relatively objective knowledge upon which either scholars or interested publics can rely in choosing among competing images of Soviet political change. Instead of a commonly accepted image, dramatic and fundamental differences of interpretation have arisen among informed and thoughtful observers. Why has this occurred? Rigby (1972a) identified a major reason when he noted that it is not the basic political structures, about which we have much information, that have been altered, but rather political processes about which we know relatively little. Moreover, much of what we do know suggests that political processes reflect primarily the beliefs, orientations, values, and attitudes of the elites who fill political roles. Such abstract factors as norms, institutions, ideology, industrialization, and modernization make their impact on the political process primarily as they influence the attitudes and condition the behavior of individual political elites. Brzezinski (1970, p. 155) notes, for example, that "political change in the Soviet Union will necessarily be influenced by the emergence of a new social elite . . . but it will be even more affected by the changes in the internal character and outlook of the professional, ruling Party bureaucracy. . . ."

Yet, there have been only a few efforts to study systematically the orientations, values, and attitudes of the Soviet elite. Two pioneers (Angell, 1964; Singer, 1964) sought to compare the basic social values and foreign policy attitudes of a spectrum of Soviet and American elites. Lodge (1969) attempted to identify the participatory orientations of a number of Soviet elites as well as to classify statements on an "ideological/instrumental" continuum. None of these, however, provides adequate evidence about the *range* of orientations or attitudes expressed by the most powerful Soviet elite—the Party leadership. To fill this knowledge gap, the present study undertakes, in an exploratory and tentative manner, to examine the potential for long-term adaptation of the Soviet Party elite to challenges arising from domestic and international environments. The core assumption of this analysis is that the capacity for successful adaptation over the next ten to twenty years is dependent to a large degree on the extent to which attitudes responsive and accommodative to a broad range of "legitimate" interests in Soviet society exist today among the next generation of Soviet political leadership. This premise is consistent with views of political change in both Western (Almond and Powell, 1966, esp. Ch. 8) and Communist systems (C. Johnson, 1970, pp. 1-32).

Images of Political Change

Three distinct images of the adaptive capacity of the Soviet system have gained currency and some degree of support in the literature on Soviet politics over the past decade. Table 10.1 summarizes the behavioral and attitudinal implications of each image as well as its implied experiential antecedents. Although the development of each image is associated primarily with the work of a single scholar, as elaborated here each image also incorporates the ideas of a number of observers who share similar perspectives.

THE "BROKER POLITICIAN"

As formulated by Hough (1972) in this image the Soviet system is perceived as showing signs of moving in the direction of "institutional pluralism," or a de facto sharing of political authority, under the leadership of a Politburo that is increasingly dominated by the "frame of mind of the broker politician." The dominant ethic of the political elite becomes pragmatism at the expense of ideological dogmatism. The direction of change is toward an institutional pluralism in which change reinforces patterns of accommodation of group demands (Hough, 1972, p. 29). The remoteness of the current and future leadership from the revolution and the realities of running an industrial society have moved the Party elite increasingly away from such ideological concerns as the creation of a new "Soviet man" and toward concerns with plan fulfillment, efficiency, and economic growth.

The high adaptive potential of the Soviet political leadership arises from its increasing acceptance of the attitudes of the political broker who mediates conflicting, but legitimate interests. In this image, the Soviet elite is committed to Marxist-Leninist ideology, both as legitimating the rule of the Party elite and, perhaps most importantly, as a principal factor motivating the people to strive

Table 10.1. Attitude Antecedents, Attitudes, and Behavioral Tendencies for Three Images of Soviet Political Change

Attitude Antecedents	Attitudes	Behavioral Tendencies
"Broker Politician": Younger Post-1938 political generation Coopted into Party work Agricultural or industrial education Extensive agricultural or industrial experience	Ideology as instrumental effects Trust in the masses Industrial manpower orientation Aggressive activism to improve consumer welfare	"Institutional pluralism" Adaptive, responsive accommodation to "legitimate" interests of social forces "Creative" change toward pluralism
"Administrative Dictator": Older and younger Pre-1939 and post-1938 political generation Recruited or coopted into Party work Extensive Party experience Industrial education	Ideology as doctrine Distrust in the masses Aggressive Party activism in agriculture Symbolic affirmation of consumer welfare	"More perfect totalitarianism" Greater Party control, repression of dissent, creation of new Soviet man, and remolding of society Adaptation only to improve control
"Regime of Clerks": Older and younger Pre-1939 and post-1938 political generation Recruited into Party work Industrial or technical education Extensive Party experience	Ideology as symbolic affirmation Distrust in the masses Assertive dissatisfaction with agriculture Assertive dissatisfaction with consumer welfare	"Bureaucratic stagnation" Rigid unresponsiveness, little innovation due to "ideological petrifaction," bureaucratic stability the most-sought-after goal Minimal adaptation to social demands

actively for the attainment of the Party's goals. Rather than a set of rigid doctrines to be preserved or a set of severe constraints on creative approaches to policy, ideology plays an instrumental role in the perception of the "broker politician."

The central concern of the Soviet "broker politician" is a belief in a humanistic, responsive, yet highly productive and efficient, socialist society. This conviction finds expression in attitudes emphasizing: (1) concern for high economic productivity, (2) genuine commitment to improved consumer welfare, and (3) leadership based on a fundamental sense of trust in the masses, in their support of the Party and its goals. This trust, in turn, provides the basis for flexibility and responsiveness in managing social change and in responding to the "legitimate" interests of other elites and social groups (cf. Hough 1969; P. Stewart, 1969).

Among the multitude of factors that may form or condition political attitudes, those studied most fully in the American context include early learning experiences, the family, personality, social institutions, relevant others—especially peers, adult occupational role expectations, and the immediate political environment (cf. Sigel, 1970). A far more limited range of antecedents is susceptible to analysis in the case of Soviet political elites. Moreover, because of the lack of systematic information on elite attitudes, there is relatively little agreement on the expected impact of specific background and career variables on elite attitudes. Nevertheless, the image of the "broker politician" is generally perceived to be strongest among the younger political elites, particularly those who entered Party political work either during or since the second World War. For the most part, elites exhibiting the "broker politician" attitudes are believed to be drawn from individuals with extensive industrial or agricultural experience following a technical education. Such persons were coopted into Party work.

The prognosis for long-term adaptiveness based on the "broker politician" image is. very optimistic. As the younger generation moves up through the Party's professional staff, or apparatus, the elite should become increasingly responsive to legitimate social interests within the context of the preservation of one-party rule in a socialist society.

THE "ADMINISTRATIVE DICTATOR"

According to this widely held image, the major feature of Soviet politics is continuity, not change. Aside from relatively minor adjustments in the manner in which terror is applied, the Soviet Union remains a totalitarian dictatorship. By means of appropriate administrative controls and programs of intensified ideological indoctrination, the Soviet system is able now to function without "the large-scale and often self-defeating use of psychological terror and physical coercion as the basic means of social control" (Kassof, 1964, p. 25). Increasing utilization of advanced administrative science coupled with the dominance of the single Party make the "administered society" possible (cf. Cocks, 1970). The basic feature of Soviet political life remains the ideologically determined drive "to establish a highly organized and totally coordinated society" (Kassof, 1964, p. 25).

In this society, concern for social welfare is merely an "incidental and instrumental element" in the overall plan of control. "The ultimate form of welfare," this model posits, "is total coordination." Recognizing that real and vast changes have occurred since Stalin's death, this image "insists" that these have not affected the basic goals or orientations of the leadership. "Far from developing alternatives to totalism, Soviet society is being subjected to new and more subtle forms of it" (Kassof, 1964, p. 28).

The elite within this image is seen as jealously guarding their dictatorial prerogatives against all challenges. Elite intransigence is based upon continuing acceptance of the ideology as a body of doctrine that embodies the essential blueprint for a perfect society. This ideology emphasizes that the Party alone embodies infallible truth. Rather than serving as brokers of interests, the Party elite are perceived as utterly convinced of the need for ceaselessly strengthening inner-Party and social discipline. Only under these conditions can the Party prevent the masses from defection to bourgeois ideology.

Given the essential continuity in beliefs and attitudes of the political elite posited by this image, as well as the asserted high degree of homogeneity of outlook among Party officials, differences in age, recruitment patterns, education, and type of experience should not be related to differences in attitude. The only career-related difference observed should be a somewhat stronger commitment to their attitudes by those with more extended Party experience. Lengthy service as a Party professional should intensify commitment to the attitudes of an "administrative dictator."

Whatever adaptation occurs as a result of this image is not likely to affect the totalitarian dictatorship exercised by the Party elite. Social interests will remain illegitimate. The regime will continue to engage in combat with its people. The Soviet Union will continue its ideologically derived enmity with the non-Communist world.

THE "REGIME OF CLERKS"

One of the originators of the formerly dominant "totalitarian" model, Brzezinski (1970, p. 165), during the past decade has developed a new image which he calls "oligarchic petrifaction." The essential traits of the Soviet polity today arising out of this image include: (1) maintenance of the "essentially dogmatic character of the ideology" and (2) retention of the "dominant role of the Party." However, instead of a revolutionary, transformational policy line that seeks to create the "new Soviet man" as the basis of a perfectly integrated and totally coordinated society, the Party now: (3) places major emphasis on rote "ideological indoctrination" and (4) rejects "imposing major innovations" upon society. The next decade, in Brzezinski's view, may see a gradual, reluctant accommodation to the interests of the technologically oriented elite, while retaining the essential features of the system.

The dominant factor in the orientations of the political elite for Brzezinski (Brzezinski and Huntington, 1963, p. 139) is an overriding commitment to a dogmatic ideology that makes compromise politics anathema and leads to a tendency to "simplify issues and to reduce them to black and white categories." Referring specifically to the Brezhnev-Kosygin generation, Brzezinski (1969, pp. 7-8) argues that "to this new generation of clerks bureaucratic stability, indeed, bureaucratic dictatorship, must seem to be the only solid foundation for effective government." This regime of clerks, then, is committed to an ideology that is not so much a living doctrine as an increasingly sterile set of symbols that inhibit creative thought and adaptation. Rather than eroding, ideological petrifaction has set in.

Although Brzezinski (1970) describes the Soviet Union as the most developed of the underdeveloped countries, he does argue that the Party elite, irrespective of its distrust of the commitment of the masses, does wish to make the economy more productive. One side benefit of such interest is improvement in living standards, which is perceived as desirable.

Brzezinski and Huntington (1963) have noted the potential significance of lateral entry, or cooptation, in Soviet political work. As one approach to meeting the need for administrators with technical skills, the Party coopts into its ranks and into its professional staff persons who have already established a career in some other line—usually industrial or agricultural administration, but sometimes military or police work. Many see in this process "the danger that the Party will gradually be turned into a club for professional engineers and managers." The "danger" is seen as arising from "concomitant changes in styles and attitudes" (Brzezinski and Huntington, 1963, p. 169). In general, it is assumed by this image that those who are recruited will be more ideological, more political in their orientations, and more committed to Party dominance in all matters while the coopted officials, although "loyal and dedicated" (Brzezinski and Huntington, 1963, p. 40), are probably more instrumental, pragmatic, flexible, and accommodative (Fleron, 1969).

A combination of lengthy political or Party experience and an engineering education, Brzezinski and Huntington (1963, p. 144) argue, is likely to give Soviet political elites a "highly focused, direct, and down to earth problem-solving approach, without concern for legal niceties, and with little tendency toward compromise solutions." The technical education is perceived to develop a pragmatic orientation, but the "ideological background" of Party work is posited to arouse a "militant style" inimical to meditation and compromise.

Based on this image the major impediment to responsive adaptation by the Soviet political elite over the next several decades is the ideological petrifaction that grips the leadership. Change in the system will occur, and probably in the direction of a slight broadening of the oligarchy, but it will always be made very reluctantly. A fearful, distrustful elite will be unable, in the long run, to stop the trend toward bureaucratic ossification.

In the following sections we begin to consider to what extent each of these images is consistent with publicly articulated orientations and analytic constructs of Soviet elite attitudes. Although the relationship between attitudes and behavior is not yet clearly established (Fishbein and Ajzen, 1972, pp. 495-496), analysis of the orientations and attitudes of the Soviet Party elite will not only provide substantive illumination of this neglected area, but will create a firmer empirical basis for accepting, modifying, or rejecting present images and for creating more adequate models of change in Soviet politics.

Research Design

IDENTIFYING SOVIET ELITE ATTITUDES

In the burgeoning and multifaceted literature on Soviet elites, at least seven different kinds of information have been utilized as bases for inferring elite attitudes, beliefs, and values: (1) reified constructs such as "ideological and instrumental systems," "industrialization," and "modernization" (Brzezinski, 1966, 1970; Moore, 1954; Rostow, 1953); (2) the institutional environment including the imperatives of one-Party rule (Fainsod, 1953, 1963, 1969; Schapiro, 1971); (3) textual analysis or esoteric communication (Conquest, 1961; Linden, 1966; Rush, 1959; Tatu, 1970); (4) official policies or policy preferences of elite groups (Azrael, 1970a, 1970b; Brzezinski, 1969, 1970; Hough, 1969, 1972; Kassof, 1964; Morton and Juvelier, 1967; Schwartz and Keech, 1968; Skilling, 1966; Skilling and Griffiths, 1971; P. Stewart, 1969); (5) career associations and experiences (Armstrong, 1959, 1966; Fleron, 1969, 1970, 1973; Hough, 1969, 1972); (6) demographic factors, especially age and education (Armstrong, 1966; Blackwell, 1972; Fleron, 1973; Hough, 1969, 1972); and, in a very few instances, (7) measures of attitudes derived from content analysis of documents or from refugee interviews (Angell, 1964; Inkeles and Bauer, 1959; Lodge, 1969, 1973; Singer, 1964). As sources for the identification of elite attitudes, each approach involves, to one degree or another, the same shortcoming. Namely, lacking basic prior knowledge of the relationships between the indicator and the postulated attitude, there can be no agreed-upon rules for inferring from the indicator to the attitude. The same indicator can and does lead to quite different inferences about elite attitudes. Even where, for example, a given policy such as Brezhnev's "war on poverty" may appear to some to reflect a genuine commitment to improved consumer welfare (Hough, 1972) to another the policy is interpreted as merely a cynical "incidental and instrumental" element in a general drive for greater social control (Kassof, 1964). Moreover, even where there is relatively high agreement on the values and attitudes reflected in a given set of policies, for example, repression of intellectual dissent, or even when direct measures of the attitudes have been developed (Lodge, 1969), there exists no common basis for assessing the salience or relative importance of a given attitude or set of beliefs in the overall structure of elite attitudes. Thus, each of the authors of the above models tends to ascribe greater salience to those inferred attitudes that are most consistent with his viewpoint and to denigrate the overall importance of contradictory evidence.

How might we seek to resolve some of these problems? This paper proposes and illustrates in a tentative, exploratory spirit a three-stage approach to the study of the attitudes of Soviet political elites. The phases proposed and illustratively elaborated here are: (1) development of a comprehensive mapping of the orientations of an important subset of the Party elite—the first secretaries (i.e., leaders) of regional or provincial Party committees in the Russian republic, (2) identification of the underlying attitudinal patterns of this elite, and (3) examination of the differential salience of the identified attitude constructs for groups of regional political elites defined on the basis of selected background and career variables.

PROBLEMS IN STUDYING ATTITUDES

In all probability every student of Soviet politics would agree that, ideally, we should directly and systematically study Soviet elite attitudes. The great majority, however, doubtless would argue that such a study is simply not possible for several reasons. First, although Soviet scholars have increasingly utilized systematic survey research (Mickiewicz, 1973), neither for Soviet citizens nor, particularly, for Americans, is it possible to interview a large, probability sample of the Soviet political elite. At best, isolated, unsystematic interviews are all we may expect (Frolic, 1970; Hough, 1969). Second, although several scholars have attempted to use the writings of elites in journals and the press, the validity of such attitudinal measures has been challenged on three grounds. Since all Soviet publications are censored in a prepublication and comprehensive manner any writings, but especially those by political elites, will reflect nothing more than official policy. At best, observed differences will reflect only the range of views existing within the Politburo, with individual authors merely acting as spokesmen for their mentors (Schwartz and Keech, 1968). Some have even asserted that differing viewpoints are not those of authors, but of the editors or censors themselves. (For interesting evidence on this assertion, see P. Stewart, 1968.) A third kind of objection is sometimes raised by those who accept as genuine the diversity observed in official Soviet publications. While individual political elites are able to express in writing their own views, the constraints of their role and their perceptions of acceptable or politically useful views mean that the measured orientations and attitudes are merely those an individual wishes at the moment to be associated with his name in public. At best, analysis of publications yields only variations in perceptions by the elite of approved, or useful, public images rather than the actual, private beliefs and attitudes of the political elite. A final objection is that it is meaningless to associate background or career or any other variables with individual attitudes measured from public documents since we possess no good information as to whether even those articles signed by a first secretary are his own creations or that of some ghost-writer or subordinate.

In responding to these objections we note the frequently observed, well documented differences in viewpoint that are expressed in the Soviet press (Conquest, 1961; D. Kelly, 1972; Linden, 1966; Rush, 1959; Schwartz and Keech, 1968; Skilling and Griffiths, 1971; P. Stewart, 1968; Tatu, 1970). This record of diversity in publicly expressed viewpoints, particularly well established over the past 20 years, gives us some confidence that the writings of regional Party officials, as of others, express more than official policy. It is indeed difficult to conceive of official policy including mutually contradictory attitudes toward similar objects at the same time. Moreover, the overall effects of any role and environmental constraints as well as any censorship should be to reduce the differences in the orientations and attitudes expressed by regional Party officials. Such factors should reduce the extent to which patterned relationships occur between background, career, and contextual variables and attitudes. To the extent that differences in orientations and attitudes are found among regional Party officials and that patterned relationships are found between antecedent factors and attitudes in this study, our confidence in the use of content analysis for attitude identification and measurement will be increased.

Finally, let us observe that Soviet regional Party first secretaries, the subjects of our study, occupy a position of major political and administrative responsibility in the Soviet system (cf. Hough, 1969; P. Stewart, 1968). When they utilize their time to write, they do so in order to achieve a particular objective, to resolve a specific problem, or to influence a particular group. In such activity, a regional secretary doubtless will reflect his own perceptions of what is politically legitimate or desirable, especially since he can be held responsible for all of his actions. What these perceptions are likely to show, however, is the totality of the regional secretary's socialization, his prior experience, and his immediate environment as mediated through his personality. Fundamentally, then, we take the position that individual attitudes of Soviet political elites can be measured through content analysis of their writings in the Soviet periodical literature. Based on this premise, the present study utilizes the writings of regional Party secretaries as the data base for a mapping of elite orientations and attitudes.

THE SAMPLE USED: PROVINCIAL PARTY FIRST SECRETARIES

Since changes in the attitudes of regional Party secretaries are a central element in models of Soviet political change, they were selected as the subjects for this research. Furthermore, since direction and pattern of change are most clearly observed across an extended time frame, the sample of writings analyzed here is drawn from articles authored by regional Party secretaries over a 12-year period—1955 through 1966. The sample of writings that were selected include 75 articles authored by 39 different regional secretaries during their tenure in that post. The following are the regional Party first secretaries included in the sample and their regional assignments: Abrasimov (Smolensk), Afanasyev (Magadan), Antonov (Astrakhan), Cherkasov (Lipetsk), Chernyshev (Kaliningrad, Maritime Kray), Demichev (Moscow Oblast, Moscow City), Drygin (Vologda), Galanshin (Perm), Georgiyev (Altay), Grishin (Ryazan), Gustov (Pskov), Kalmyk (Smolensk), Kandrenkov (Kaluga), Khitrov (Voronezh), Konotop (Moscow Oblast), Konovalov (Kaliningrad), Kovalenko (Belgorod, Orenburg), Kozlov (Leningrad Oblast), Kuzyukov (Chelyabinsk), Kulakov (Stavropol Kray), Larionov (Ryazan), Leonov (Sakhalin), Morosov (Amur), Nikolayev (Sverdlovsk), Petukhov (Kirov), Popov (Leningrad City), Shcherbina (Tyumen), Shchetinin (Irkutsk), Shibayev (Saratov), Sokolov (Novgorod, Perm, Orlov), Solomentsev (Rostov), Tolstikov (Leningrad Oblast), Vasilyev (Belgorod), Vorobyev (Krasnodar), Voronov (Orenburg), Yegorychev (Moscow City), Yermin (Penza), Yeshtokhin (Kemerovo), and Zolotukhin (Tambov, Krasnodar). The regions in this sample are representative of the various types of regions found in the Soviet Union. Moreover, in terms of socialization, background, and experience variables our sample is representative of the much larger group of regional secretaries who held the position during this time period.

If it is our objective to understand the attitudes of the Soviet political elite, why limit the present study to one subset of that elite? Why not include the entire Politburo, Secretariat, and Central Committee as well as regional political elites? In what sense are regional secretaries' attitudes central to the processes of political change? While entirely agreeing that as broad a sample of elites as possible is desirable, there are several compelling reasons—theoretical and practical—for focusing on the regional elite. First, given the objective of assessing the potential of a political elite for adaptation and change, it is important to capture as much of the full spectrum of elite attitudes as possible. Second, since public documents form the basic data source for the attitude study, it is necessary to focus on the more prolific sectors of the political elite. For both these reasons, the Politburo and Secretariat are not as useful as the regional elite as a focus of study. The relatively small size of these bodies, the apparent paucity of materials authored by these officials—except for a few leading figures—and the tendencies, especially in the post-Khrushchev era, to present a united front advise against an exclusive focus on these groups. The Central Committee, on the other hand, is a conglomerate of many different kinds of elites—military, industrial, and cultural, as well as political. If we accept the arguments of Brzezinski (1966, 1970) and Hough (1972) that it is precisely the professional political elite whose views decisively influence the degree and direction of change, then we should focus more directly on the political elite. Third, and perhaps more significant for understanding political change, the regional Party secretaries constitute the major recruiting ground for new Politburo and Secretariat officials. Of the 25 men who constituted these two bodies in 1966, 16 held the post of regional Party first secretary immediately prior to appointment to the Republican or All-Union Central Party apparatus (P. Frank, 1971). Across time, moreover, the number and percentage of Politburo members with this experience has steadily increased, from 55 percent of the 1951 Politburo to 87 percent in 1971 (Rigby, 1972b, p. 16). Fourth, not only does the mean of 6.9 years spent as regional Party first secretary by the 1971 Politburo members account, on the average, for more than a third of all their previous professional Party experience, but service in this role is interpreted by some as having an especially strong impact on the attitudes and orientations of those who serve in it. Brzezinski (1969, p. 9) asserts, for example, that such experience leads the Soviet politician to acquire the skills of "initiative, direction, integration, as well as accommodation, compromise and delegation of authority." Fifth, the diversity of backgrounds and experience represented by this group, the wide variety of contexts within which they carry out their similar roles—from highly urbanized, industrialized Moscow to the frozen forests of Kamchatka—suggest that this group will reflect nearly the full range of views existing among the mature political elite as a whole. Finally, this very diversity of experience and environment provides a desirable basis for examining the differential impact of such factors on attitudes.

CONCEPTUALIZING ISSUE-ORIENTATION AND ATTITUDE

In the more than 100 years since the concept of attitude first appeared in the psychological literature, no commonly accepted definition has emerged (Greenwald, 1968). The conceptualization employed here is based primarily on the work of Fishbein and Ajzen (1972, pp. 488-510). An attitude is a predisposition to respond either positively or negatively toward or in the presence of some object. Regional secretaries, for example, may be predisposed to be critical of labor discipline on the basis of a belief, among others, that all workers tend to be lazy. As this example suggests, attitudes are influenced by beliefs and opinions about objects. The valence, or *affect,* of a particular attitude is some function of the affective value of the beliefs that make up the attitude. However, any single belief, such as that workers are lazy, may have little or no relation to an attitude, such as a feeling of sympathy for the plight of the workers. Thus, an attitude is related to the entire range of a person's beliefs or opinions about an object. Attitudes, then, while related to opinions, beliefs, and intentions to behave in particular ways, are conceptually separate from cognition and conation (Fishbein and Ajzen, 1972, p. 493).

Our approach to the identification and measurement of Soviet elite attitudes emerges from these conceptual considerations and encompasses these three elements: (1) Consistent with the premise that beliefs, or opinions, are the constituent elements of attitudes and the assumption that it is beliefs which are expressed most directly in the writings of Soviet elites, our first objective is to identify these beliefs. (2) Since attitudes reflect the totality of opinions about an object, a *comprehensive* approach to the identification of elite beliefs is more likely to yield valid indicators of attitudes. (Of course, such an approach does not assure or test the validity of our constructs.) Since we not only lack systematic knowledge about elite opinions toward specific objects but also about the classes of objects in the world of Soviet elites from which opinions are formed, our design includes identification of all significant objects of orientation as well as opinions expressed toward them. The result of this portion of the analysis is a mapping of the issue-orientations, or opinion worlds, of the regional Party elite. (3) The generally accepted approach to attitude measurement is to attempt to place each subject "along a bipolar dimension of *affect* with respect to a given object" (Fishbein and Ajzen, 1972, p. 493). This placement is normally achieved by administration of a standard attitude scale which produces a single number indexing the individual's positive or negative feelings toward an object. In the case of Soviet elites, standard attitude scales cannot be utilized. But one approach to attitude scaling that has been widely used—i.e., factor analysis—appears appropriate here as a tool for exploratory, tentative identification of attitudes from the totality of expressed elite opinions. A common factor analysis of elite opinions will organize, on the basis of correlational association, a maximum of elite opinions into a minimum number of bipolar dimensions. Each opinion will be scaled in terms of its association with the underlying attitude construct. Factor scores will locate each individual along each bipolar dimension of interrelated beliefs (Rummel, 1970).

The highly tentative nature of any attitude construct generated by factor analysis, however, needs to be emphasized. Factor analysis provides no tests of significance for identified relationships nor does it offer any effective means of controlling the reliability of input correlations. Furthermore, not only are the number and meaning of identified factors dependent upon the input variables but, more importantly, the names assigned each dimension are highly subjective, reflecting only one's best judgment. At this point the validity of these attitude constructs cannot be tested. Once more let us emphasize that this is an exploratory approach designed to provide insight rather than definitive results.

DATA GENERATION TECHNIQUE

Content analysis is the general approach most suited to the identification of opinions in public documents (cf. Holsti, 1969). The specific form utilized here we call thematic analysis. Rather than coding every aspect of every sentence in a variety of ways (cf. Holsti, 1969), we coded only statements of issue-orientation or opinion, ignoring all purely descriptive statements. This approach is based upon both our objective of mapping orientations and the consideration that although purely descriptive statements may be correlated with attitudes (McGuire, 1969, p. 155), in the case of our data—at least at this stage—the assumption seems warranted that descriptive statements are reflective primarily of role prescriptions—of the need to communicate specific information—rather than underlying attitudes.

An issue-orientation or opinion is differentiated from other statements in that it contains *both* an affective or evaluative element and a cognitive or knowledge component (McGuire, 1969, p. 155). In the thematic form of content analysis employed here, all themes containing both of these elements were coded. Of course, a given sentence may express affect toward several objects, as in the statement: "An unusually high level of ideological preparedness is displayed by our Party cadres, by factory workers and the Soviet intelligentsia in our region as a result of the creative efforts of our political education programs."

Seeking a comprehensive mapping of issue-orientations, from a sample of 25 percent of all articles to be coded we prepared a list of all cognitive objects occurring with any kind of associated affect. Virtually all expressions of affect found in this sample could be unambiguously included within one of three classes of affect: praises, criticisms, or demands. These were selected, therefore, as our coding categories for affect. Eighty-six specific cognitive objects which were subsumed under 13 distinct categories were created from the list of objects referenced. Since any of these cognitive objects could potentially be praised or criticized or a demand made with reference to it, our final coding form permitted the coding of 258 distinct orientations. In practice, however, because of the relatively small sample size, all coding was aggregated using the 13 major categories which yielded 39 issue-orientations. This aggregation was carried out only after completion of the coding, of course. The 13 major categories with some of their cognitive objects are: content of ideological work (e.g., propaganda and indoctrinational activities, exposition of ideological themes and ideas), state of ideological preparedness (e.g., among Party members, youth, general populace), industrial production (e.g., personal production initiatives, concern with production efficiency), industrial manpower (e.g., use of labor reserves, education of labor force), agricultural production (e.g., existence of mechanization and technology, physical output), agricultural manpower (e.g., use of labor reserves, education of labor force), state of social and labor discipline (e.g., organization of labor forces and populace, acceptance and understanding of responsibilities), consumer welfare (e.g., medical services, worker income, food supply in retail trade), group cooperation (e.g., industry/ agriculture, industry/schools), Party initiatives (e.g., ideological work among non-Party personnel, youth indoctrination), upper-level attention (e.g., toward upper Party levels, Ministry levels), concern for internal Party life (e.g., education of Party cadres, discipline), and Party support (e.g., for Komsomol activity and other youth initiatives, local Soviets, particular workers and brigades).

The unit of enumeration is the theme. If an individual secretary praised industrial production five times in all of his coded articles, then his final score would be "five." Our assumption is that the intensity of an opinion is best measured here in an additive manner by the frequency with which it is expressed (McGuire, 1969, p. 154). In order to make scores comparable for all individuals, i.e., to control for differences in the total number of issue-orientations expressed, all scores were converted into proportions—the frequency of each opinion as a proportion of all expressions of opinion, calculated separately for each individual.[1]

A Mapping of Elite Issue-Orientations

EXPECTATIONS

Expectations about the kinds of concerns toward which the regional Party secretary might develop and express opinions or take positions derive primarily from our knowledge of the role of regional Party officials in the Soviet political system. As is well known, all formal political power in the Soviet Union is a monopoly of the Communist Party in general and in particular of its full-time professional staff, known as "the apparatus." Moreover, the conception of the appropriate scope for politics is far broader than in most non-Communist countries. The Soviet press frequently observes that there are no questions in the life of the country to which the Party can remain oblivious—about which it can say "this is none of my affair." Thus, to some degree the Party official must be involved in providing ideological guidance, in supervising industrial and agricultural production, and in satisfying the needs of the populace for housing, education, food, and recreation. Nor can the Party official ignore questions concerning the moral and political authority of the Party, in particular the social and labor discipline of the people as reflected in their commitments to and willingness to sacrifice for the goals of the Party based upon a conscious understanding and acceptance of "socialist obligations" (Hough, 1969; P. Stewart, 1968). The role of the Soviet politician is more, then, than that of political leader. He must be both a decision maker and an executive (Brzezinski and Huntington, 1963, p. 170).

To accomplish these tasks the Party is organized into a centralized, hierarchical structure that penetrates all Soviet society through production and territorial units. The basic organ of this institution is the Primary Party Organization. Every one of the more than fourteen million members is, in principle, associated with one of the more than 330,000 primary cells at his place of work—on a farm, in a factory, in a ministry, or in a military unit. These cells are coordinated and supervised by some 4,000 *raion* or rural county Party committees and over 700 urban or city Party committees. In turn, responsible for all political functions in a region or territory—which vary in size from smaller than Rhode Island to twice the size of Alaska (Hough, 1969, p. 8)—there are approximately 139 regional Party organizations. In the Russian republic, the largest of the 15 republics in which most of the regional subdivisions are located, the

[1] As a test of coding reliability, 20 percent of the articles used in the study, chosen at random, were independently scored by a second coder. There was 91 percent agreement between the two coders. Errors appeared to be randomly distributed throughout the coding categories.

regional Party officials report directly to the Secretariat of the Central Committee in Moscow. Although each Party committee is composed of both full-time Party workers and the most important local officials from most sections of society and the economy, it is the first secretary who acts as the "head" of each Party body and who bears ultimate responsibility for the state of affairs in his area (cf. P. Stewart, 1968). The regional Party first secretary, then, is the highest political authority outside of Moscow, at least in the Russian republic. It is his job to interpret and oversee the fulfillment of general policy made in the Central Committee and Politburo.

In carrying out these responsibilities, however, the regional Party first secretary is not all powerful. While he controls many of the critical power sources—especially the right to appoint and remove many of the key officials in his region (Harasymiw, 1969)—his real power is the power to persuade (Hough, 1969; Kochetov, 1962; P. Stewart, 1968). Many of the most critical activities in the regions are also directly controlled by central ministries in Moscow. Even in agriculture where the local Party committees have long been quite directly involved, the Party officials are normally dependent upon central ministries for fertilizer, seed, and new machinery, as well as upon their own ability to persuade the peasants to labor for the common good. It is these factors which led Hough (1972) to interpret the role of the regional Party secretary as that of a "political broker" and even Brzezinski (1969, p. 9) to stress the importance of "initiative, integration, accommodation and compromise" for those in this position.

What are the general kinds of issues, then, that might reasonably be expected to elicit either positive sentiments or negative feelings from the regional Party secretaries as a group? From this review of the secretary's role we suggest four kinds of issues that are probably germane to these officials: (1) ideology, (2) leadership of the regional economy, (3) leadership of society, and (4) leadership of the Party organization as a component of a larger institution and as the structural basis of political authority.

GENERAL CHARACTERISTICS

Table 10.2 indicates the relative frequency with which regional Party first secretaries express issue positions in each of the four areas of leadership just proposed. The figures are for the sample as a whole and so represent only average salience. While no specific conclusions can be drawn about the importance of issue-orientations for individuals from this table, the coefficients of relative variation do provide some indication of the range of individual differences.

Consistent with the assertions of Hough (1969), the material and manpower aspects of production account for more than twice as many issue-orientations as any other area of leadership. The figures suggest that economic matters, overall, account for nearly half of the publicly expressed opinions of regional Party officials. Ideology appears as the least salient concern. It is the area least likely

Table 10.2.   A Mapping of the Salience of Issue-Orientations
for Regional Party First Secretaries

Issue-Orientation	N	%	C.R.V.*
Ideology	*156*	*11.9*	
Praise the content of ideological work	75	5.7	1.4
Praise the state of ideological preparedness	42	3.2	1.4
Demand improved content of ideological work	16	1.2	2.5
Demand improved state of ideological preparedness	11	.8	2.5
Criticize the content of ideological work	6	.5	4.2
Criticize the state of ideological preparedness	6	.5	2.8
Leadership of the Regional Economy	*623*	*47.2*	
Praise agricultural production	192	14.5	1.2
Praise industrial production	130	9.8	1.6
Criticize agricultural production	61	4.6	2.9
Praise agricultural manpower	54	4.1	1.8
Criticize industrial production	52	3.9	2.8
Demand improved industrial production	30	2.3	2.6
Praise industrial manpower	30	2.3	1.7
Demand improved agricultural production	26	2.0	2.3
Demand improved agricultural manpower	16	1.2	2.5
Criticize agricultural manpower	13	1.0	1.9
Demand improved industrial manpower	10	.8	3.1
Criticize industrial manpower	9	.7	3.4
Political Leadership of Society	*291*	*22.0*	
Praise the state of social and labor discipline	113	8.6	0.9
Criticize the state of social and labor discipline	55	4.2	1.6
Praise the level of consumer welfare	44	3.3	1.8
Demand improved social and labor discipline	28	2.1	2.8
Demand improved consumer welfare	13	1.0	3.5
Criticize the level of consumer welfare	11	.8	5.5
Praise the level of group cooperation	11	.8	3.5
Criticize the level of group cooperation	8	.6	4.2
Demand improved group cooperation	8	.6	7.8
Institutional Leadership	*253*	*19.1*	
Praise Party initiatives	63	4.8	1.6
Praise the degree of upper level attention	30	2.3	3.3
Demand increased upper level attention	28	2.1	2.6
Criticize insufficient upper level attention	26	2.0	2.4
Praise the state of internal Party life	25	1.9	1.6
Demand increased Party initiative	22	1.7	1.7
Praise the level of Party support	19	1.4	2.0
Criticize the state of internal Party life	15	1.1	2.4
Criticize insufficient Party initiatives	13	1.0	2.4
Demand improved internal Party life	11	.8	4.1
Demand improved Party support	1	0.0	0.0
Criticize the level of Party support	0	0.0	0.0
Total	1,323	100.2	

*C.R.V. stands for coefficient of relative variation, which is the ratio of the standard deviation to the mean frequency of each orientation.

to elicit the psychological involvement of the first secretary, accounting for only 11.9 percent of all orientations. As areas of concern to the regional officials, both political leadership of society and institutional leadership appear to be underrated by Western observers (e.g., see Hough, 1969; Linden, 1966; P. Stewart, 1968), accounting for 22 percent and 19 percent of expressed opinions, respectively.

The three types of affect—praise, criticism, and demands—when associated with cognitive objects probably suggest different modes of adjustment to the perceptually significant elements of the environment. The "praise" mode is the predominant affective orientation for regional first secretaries, with nearly 63 percent of all expressions of affect involving praise, while criticisms and demands make up 21 percent and 16 percent respectively. Brzezinski (1970, p. 153) gives one possible interpretation of "praise" when he suggests that "bureaucratic sterility in thought prompts intensified emphasis on revolutionary rhetoric and symbolism." If "praise" is seen as symbolic affirmation, reflecting a minimal degree of conscious involvement, then Brzezinski's conception of the current state of "arrested ideological development" or "ideological petrifaction" is given some support by our data showing that nearly three-fourths of the expressed issue-orientations involving ideology are "praise" or symbolic orientations.

Our general position on the adaptive function of affect as well as the overall salience of "praise" suggests an additional interpretation. This view of "praise" as affect emerges from Hough's conception of the "political broker." On the one hand, the regional official is dependent on the upper levels for his continued status and for necessary resources. Such dependence places him under constant pressure to drive the citizens in his region to ever higher levels of performance (Fainsod, 1953; Hough, 1969). Frequent expressions of praise may be designed to please one's superiors by creating an atmosphere of achievement and, thus, minimize pressures from the center. Indeed, the tone of most articles read seemed to suggest that one principle audience was the Moscow authorities, even though they were seldom mentioned by name. On the other hand, given the absence of "direct" power over many facets of local life, the regional official must rely upon persuasion to develop cooperative, harmonious relations among the frequently conflicting interests in the provinces. The "praise" orientation, both learning and reinforcement theory suggest, would be an appropriate method of adapting to this need.

Although criticisms and demands together account for less than 40 percent of all valences expressed, these two affects may well provide more meaningful indications of psychological involvement than praise. They may more fully reflect underlying attitudes than praise. Critical and demanding orientations may be indicative of perceptions of responsibility for effecting social change and economic growth or of a perceived need to improve leadership. Relative to each other, demands are seen as involving a higher level of psychological commitment than criticisms since the former implies that some kind of action be taken while the latter involves primarily an expression of dissatisfaction with a state of affairs (McGuire, 1969, pp. 151-153).

ORIENTATIONS TOWARD IDEOLOGY

Turning now to an examination of the specific issue-orientations comprising the perceptual world of the regional secretary, several features of opinions on ideology should be noted. There are two kinds of cognitive objects reflected in the measures of ideology. One, "content of ideological work," indicates concerns about doctrinal matters—the substance of ideology, its formulae, and effective articulation in books and other media. This is the aspect of ideology usually implied in descriptions of the Party elite as "ideologues." With the waning of the revolution, many observers see these concerns as increasingly relevant only to ideological specialists such as the Suslov's and Illichev's (cf. Brzezinski and Huntington, 1963, p. 41). It is significant, therefore, that we find these concerns accounting for nearly two-thirds of the expressed ideological orientations.

The second cognitive object in the ideology orientation centers on the *impact* or motivational effect of ideology. Specifically, this measure of ideology aggregates statements about the level of ideological preparedness or the state of ideological work among various groups, including workers, peasants, intelligentsia, and Party members. This conception of ideology in terms of its impact is consistent both with Hough's (1972) notion of the "broker politician" for whom ideology is a useful and necessary motivational tool and with Brzezinski's (Brzezinski and Huntington, 1963, p. 41) concept of the regional elites as "action program generalizers" who "implement the action program without extremes of either dogmatism or sheer pragmatism knowing that their power requires ideological backing." If one accepts this conception of ideology as consistent with Hough's (1972) image, then what is surprising about our finding is that this orientation accounts for only about a third of all ideological opinions.

Strongly suggestive of the symbolic role of ideology, and of possible "ideological petrifaction" (Brzezinski, 1970, p. 153), is the fact that fully three-fourths of all ideological opinions expressed were "praises," more than the average of two-thirds for all issue-orientations. At the same time, the finding that "demands" related to ideology occurred twice as frequently as "criticisms" when overall demands were less salient than criticisms indicates a relatively high level of involvement with ideology, especially with concern for its doctrinal component, among at least some groups of regional Party secretaries.

ORIENTATIONS TOWARD LEADERSHIP OF THE REGIONAL
ECONOMY

Concerns in two different areas of the economy—industry and agriculture—are found in the writings of regional secretaries and reflected in our measures. In particular the regional secretaries focus within each of these areas on: (1) the physical elements of production, especially problems of raw materials and new technology, and (2) the human component, including labor productivity, labor mobilization, and motivation.

Party officials frequently complain of their reluctant but nearly constant involvement in questions of material-technical supply, arguing that these are matters more properly within the domain of the economic and planning organizations (Hough, 1969; P. Stewart, 1968). That 78 percent of all opinions expressed about leadership of the economy related to physical production is further confirmation of the secretaries' involvement in this area. Only 22 percent of issue-orientations concerning economic matters related to those activities that the Party sees officially as one of its major concerns, i.e., the political function of selecting, training, placing, and motivating cadres and workers (Harasymiw, 1969). It is possible, however, that the high salience of the former is due more to inescapable demands from the environment than to inner attitudinal leanings. If so, we should find that mobilizational concerns are more dominant within the structure of attitudes, as analyzed in the next section, than concerns about physical production.

Three-fifths of the expressed affect toward the economy consists of positive, praising orientations. It seems reasonable to interpret this as evidence of an instrumental, motivational approach to production problems. This interpretation appears to be reinforced by the finding that Party secretaries, on the average, are almost four times as likely to criticize physical elements of either agricultural or industrial production than they are to criticize productive manpower.

ORIENTATIONS TOWARD THE POLITICAL LEADERSHIP
   OF SOCIETY

The political leadership of Soviet society, most scholars probably would agree (Fainsod, 1953, 1963; Kassof, 1964), is primarily a matter of ensuring and enforcing control. Pursuit of social welfare may be instrumental to such control, but there is little, if any, genuine commitment to a high standard of living as a goal (Kassof, 1964). Some, however, accept Hough's (1972) and Fainsod's (1969) later view that as a result of its economic successes, the Party has won greater legitimacy and genuine support from the people. One result of this support is evident in the decline in distrust of the masses as reflected in a lessening of demands for greater social and labor discipline and an increase in a commitment to consumer welfare as a "right" of a people in whose loyalty the Party is confident (*Pravda,* March 12, 1971; Hough, 1972).

Analysis of the salience of opinions alone, unfortunately, does not clarify these points of view greatly, although our examination of attitudes which follows in the next section should provide more persuasive evidence. A slightly less than average tendency to praise the level of social and labor discipline (57 percent as compared to an overall average of 62.7 percent) and, thus, possibly to indicate trust in the masses is offset by a nearly 40 percent greater than average tendency to criticize the state of social and labor discipline (28 percent versus 20 percent). At the same time, a relatively deeper involvement in problems of discipline as indicated by "demands" occurs with slightly less than average frequency (15 percent against 16 percent).

The three kinds of issues related to the social leadership role appear to reflect three different approaches to that function. Concerns with social and labor discipline may reflect a style emphasizing "moral" stimuli to appropriate behavior patterns. This mode of leadership is based upon the Leninist interpretation of the Marxist notion of "labor for the good of society" as a "moral" and psychological drive that, under the Communist society, will become as compelling as the need for food and sleep. Conscious discipline is the Leninist method of hastening the emergence of this need in socialist society. The principal task of political leadership, in this conception, is to make people more fully aware of their social responsibilities and obligations, to generate conscious social discipline. A second mode of social leadership emphasizes "material" rewards (consumer welfare) as the principal inducement to socially desirable behavior. This approach grows out of a conviction that the "heroic struggles and sacrifices" of the Soviet people in the building of a socialist society have amply demonstrated the deep commitment of the Soviet people to their Party. Trusting in the people, the task of leadership is to accommodate the legitimate but divergent interests in society. Still a third approach emphasizes the role of leadership in harmonizing the activities of the various sectors of Soviet society through facilitating group cooperation. The basis for successful cooperative activity, however, is a high degree of conscious discipline. In effect, the political leader's role is viewed as comparable to that of a symphony conductor (*Pravda,* March 8, 1963). As reflected in issue-orientations, the discipline image of leadership predominates, occurring three times as frequently as expressions of concern for consumer welfare and five times as frequently as opinions directed to group cooperation.

ORIENTATIONS TOWARD INSTITUTIONAL LEADERSHIP

Issue-orientations in the area of institutional leadership reflect the regional officials' perceptions and feelings about the Party as an institution. The "Party initiatives" variable aggregates references to the Party as responsible for initiating activities of specialists to the delivery of materials and improvement of consumer welfare. In effect, this variable reflects the degree of satisfaction or discontent with the Party's leading role. This is the aspect of institutional leadership most likely to elicit opinions, accounting for nearly 40 percent of the opinions expressed in this area. While expressions of satisfaction with the current scope of Party activities predominate, demands for expansion of Party initiatives are almost double criticisms of Party initiatives.

"Upper-level attention" represents the regional officials' response to the support and attention the region receives from both Party and government organizations at the center. Now nearly all of the literature on the Soviet political system stresses the importance of strict centralism and subordination of lower bodies to higher—particularly within the Party but also in the state hierarchy—irrespective of official descriptions of "democratic centralism." Hough (1969) was one of the first to develop a detailed image of the regional Party officials as strong defenders of the interests of their regions against the center, especially against ministries but also to some degree against Party authorities. It is highly suggestive of the validity of Hough's interpretation that, in spite of the overwhelming general tendency to "praise" and the minimal frequency of "demands" (62.7 percent to 16 percent, respectively), the orientations of regional Party secretaries toward upper-level attention are divided almost evenly among the three affects: "praise," 2.3 percent; "criticism," 2.1 percent; and "demands," 2 percent.

Complementing the Party's role as leader and initiator of action is its function of supporter of the activities and initiatives of others. This support may include verbal, policy, material, or organizational support provided by the Party to assist other organizations or social groups in achieving their objectives. The apparent overriding involvement of Party officials with their own institution and with *its* leading role is indicated by the fact that there were no criticisms of the level of Party support for other institutions and only one demand for greater Party support.

From the time of Lenin's "What is to be done?" in 1902 there have been two conflicting tendencies in internal Party life (in fact, this was the principal issue dividing the Russian social-democrats). One suggests the need for greater democracy and participation by Party members in the formation of Party policy and the selection of leadership (Hough, 1972), while the other stresses the necessity of strict, iron discipline and unity. Because of the relatively small size of our sample, opinions on both these questions are aggregated in the measure of "concern for internal Party life." Although the precise meaning is not yet clear, it is worth noting that the number of criticisms and demands for improvements in internal Party life, in contrast to the usual pattern, exceeds the number of praises of the state of Party life. Tentatively, this finding may indicate some meaningful degree of underlying restiveness and dissatisfaction with Party life, even among those leaders who appear to benefit most from that institution.

Attitudes of Regional Party First Secretaries

The results of a principal component factor analysis of the correlations among the issue-orientations of the regional Party first secretaries is presented in Table 10.3. Each of the resulting factors is considered as indicating one attitude. The factors, or attitudes, are orthogonal based on a varimax rotation of the principal

Table 10.3. Attitudes of Regional Party Secretaries

	Factor Loading	Eigen-value	% Variance Explained
Ideological Attitudes			*29.06*
1. *Ideology as Instrumental Effects*		4.34	11.73
Criticize ideological preparedness	.923		
Demand ideological preparedness	.869		
Criticize level of Party initiative	.798		
2. *Ideology as Symbolic Affirmation*		3.90	10.56
Praise level of Party initiative	.927		
Praise ideological preparedness	.914		
Praise content of ideological work	.869		
3. *Ideology as Doctrine*		2.71	7.31
Criticize content of ideological work	.899		
Demand improved content of ideological work	.851		
Praise upper level attention	.532		
Criticize upper level attention	.544		
Trust and Distrust: Leadership Style			*18.50*
4. *Distrust in Masses: Need for Discipline*		3.02	8.16
Demand concern for internal Party life	−.966		
Criticize concern for internal Party life	−.964		
Criticize state of social and labor discipline	−.829		
5. *Group Cooperation: Harmony through Discipline*		2.23	6.02
Demand improved group cooperation	.888		
Praise level of group cooperation	.861		
Criticize level of group cooperation	.578		
Demand improved social and labor discipline	.549		
6. *Trust in Masses: Possibility of Accommodation*		1.60	4.32
Praise state of social and labor discipline	.813		
Praise concern for internal Party life	.816		
Praise level of Party support	.714		
Production and Manpower Attitudes			*24.66*
7. *General Industrial Manpower Orientation*		4.69	12.69
Criticize level of group cooperation	.577		
Criticize industrial manpower	.898		
Demand improved industrial manpower	.782		
Praise industrial manpower	.665		
Criticize industrial production	.547		
8. *Aggressive Party Activism in Agricultural Sphere*		2.50	6.76
Demand improved agricultural production	.790		
Demand upper level attention	.727		
Demand Party initiatives	.693		
9. *Assertive Dissatisfaction with Agriculture*		1.93	5.21
Criticize agricultural manpower	−.753		
Demand improved agricultural production	−.686		
Criticize agricultural production	.515		
Praise industrial production	.579		
Consumer Welfare Attitudes			*9.18*
10. *Assertive Dissatisfaction with State of Consumer Affairs*		1.33	3.59
Criticize level of consumer welfare	.806		
11. *Symbolic Affirmation of Consumer Well-Being*		1.05	2.83
Praise level of consumer welfare	−.806		
Praise agricultural manpower	−.658		
Praise agricultural production	−.514		
12. *Aggressive Activism to Improve Consumer Welfare*		1.02	2.76
Demand improved consumer welfare	.847		
Total Variation in Observed Issue-Orientations Explained by 12 Attitude Dimensions			*81.94*

components solution.[2] Table 10.3 contains all factors in the analysis with an eigenvalue greater than unity; Table 10.3 also reports the issue-orientations with factor loadings of ± .5 or higher on each factor and the percentage of the total variance explained by each factor.

The reader is asked to compare the attitudes in Table 10.3 with the Soviet elite attitudes listed in Table 10.1 which are implied by the three images of Soviet political change discussed at the beginning of the chapter. For the sample as a whole, many of the attitudes posited by the three images of change are found among Soviet regional Party first secretaries. Moreover, as might be expected from the careful, thoughtful scholarship represented by these three images, our analysis provides partial support for each one. In effect, we find widely divergent conceptions of their role and their world among regional Party officials. At this point a more detailed examination of each type of attitude is in order.

IDEOLOGICAL ATTITUDES

More than 29 percent of the variation in all issue-orientations is explained by attitude dimensions whose defining characteristics are predominantly ideological concerns. Comparing this percentage with the modest proportion (11.9 percent) of all expressed opinions that were considered directly ideological, ideology appears far more significant as an underlying, organizing concern than analysis of opinions alone would suggest. Indeed, the finding that nearly a third of all issue-orientations are given directionality and coherence by ideological attitudes provides fairly striking confirmation of the widely accepted proposition about the dominant role of ideology in organizing the outlook of Soviet political elites.

When we examine the specific kinds of ideological attitudes, however, it is clear that each of the images of Soviet political elites is partially adequate but also to some degree inadequate in identifying salient ideological attitudes. The finding that an attitude conceptualizing ideology primarily as an object of symbolic affirmation accounts for more than 10 percent of all issue-orientations is relevant to Brzezinski's (1970) view of "ideological petrifaction" and, in turn, to the "regime of clerks" image. Although it is the least significant organizer of opinions, "ideology as doctrine" does not disconfirm Kassof's (1964) conception of the salience of ideology as content. This attitude lends support to the "administrative dictator" image. Similarly, that an instrumental attitude toward ideology, "ideology as instrumental effects," accounts for more variation in elite opinions than any other ideological attitude tends to justify Hough's (1972)

_____

[2]Since the use of orthogonal dimensions as descriptions of attitude structures is most appropriate only when there is reason to believe that the underlying structure is close to orthogonal, we compared our solution with an oblique rotation. We found that the highest intercorrelation of factors in the oblique solution was .2 with most factors intercorrelated in the range .02 to .08. The structure of each dimension was almost identical in the two rotations. This result gives us confidence in the appropriateness of the varimax solution.

emphasis on the "pragmatism" of political elites and the "broker politician." What is equally obvious, at the same time, is that all three ideological attitudes occur with similar degrees of salience. In other words, the Soviet elite conceptions of ideology range from an instrumentalist concern with "impact" to an unquestioned and positive acceptance of ideology to involvement with ideology as doctrine.

LEADERSHIP STYLE ATTITUDES

We find the same pattern of partial support for the three images of Soviet political elites in Table 10.3 when other types of attitudes are examined—in this case, leadership style. Both Brzezinski (1970) and Kassof (1964) hypothesize a leadership style emphasizing dictatorship and control, stressing a perceived need for continuous if not ever-increasing social and labor discipline among the masses as well as tighter discipline within the Party. Fundamentally, the political elites are seen as suspicious and distrusting of the masses, both within the Party and in society. Certainly, this attitude is not absent among the regional political elite; indeed, this attitude accounts for more variation in elite orientations than either of the other two leadership attitudes.

At the same time, irrespective of its relatively minor role in organizing orientations for the group as a whole, we cannot ignore the finding that the psychological bases for a "broker politician" leadership style also appear to exist among at least some elites. That we find an attitude of trust in the masses and Party at all is significant in light of the former predominance in Western images of Soviet politics of totalitarianism dependent upon coercive terror for survival (cf. Kassof, 1964; Friedrich and Brzezinski, 1956). Moreover, finding this attitude lends some credence to Fainsod's (1969) warning that we should not underestimate the impact on the Soviet system of its many economic, social, and political successes in the last 20 to 30 years.

Perhaps we should not be surprised that a major organizing dimension among attitudes toward the leadership function is an orientation that appears to correspond closely to the official image of the ideal Party leader—the leader who conceives his role as essentially that of an orchestra conductor (*Pravda,* March 8, 1963). Two ingredients are important to this image as portrayed in Soviet writings: (1) leadership resulting from group cooperation in the performance of Party tasks, and (2) a high level of conscious discipline among the masses. Issue-orientations indicative of both these positions define the group cooperation attitude dimension. Although the model of the "administered society" appears to imply that this official image is only a mask for a distrusting, disciplinary approach to total control, our findings indicate that these are two separate, independent kinds of attitudes toward leadership.

The identification of the trust and distrust in the masses attitudes among regional Party elites may have far-reaching significance for an examination of Soviet political change. Considerable research on trust and distrust has shown that persons exhibiting the former quality are far more flexible and capable of absorbing and adapting to new information and situations than are those displaying distrust. If we find later that trust is stronger than distrust among the emerging leadership, there may be some psychological basis for inferring a capacity for effective adaptation to social and political change among at least a portion of the Soviet political elite.

PRODUCTION AND MANPOWER ATTITUDES

The model of the "broker politician" is based upon the view that the major, if not primary, preoccupation of political leadership is physical production—planning, technology, material-technical supply. As our analysis of issue-orientations has shown, these concerns were the occasion for a large proportion of all opinions expressed. But, as we also observed, the high frequency of comment in this area may have been more the result of unavoidable environmental demands than of underlying attitudes. In another place, Hough (1969, pp. 66-69) has suggested that what probably distinguishes Party officials from their similarly trained colleagues in the industrial ministries is the preponderance of a political, generalizing approach in the former as contrasted with an essentially technical orientation to problems among the latter. Our findings lend support to this interpretation. Although 37 percent of all issue-orientations concerned the physical elements of industrial and agricultural production, these expressions constitute the defining characteristic of only one of the twelve principal attitudes identified by our method. While physical production orientations are moderately involved (factor loadings near .5) in several dimensions, the predominant elements in attitudes toward production are what the Party defines as a major political role, that is, recruiting and placing cadres and mobilizing people (cf. Harasymiw, 1969).

The one exception is the attitude, "aggressive Party activism in the agricultural sphere." Here, demands for more upper-level attention combine with demands for improved agricultural production to form a single attitude dimension. While in general, then, a political, mobilizational approach appears to characterize two of the identified attitudes toward production problems, an attitude supportive of intensive institutional and political involvement in agricultural production is also revealed. This "aggressive activism" may represent the psychological basis of what some (Bauer, Inkeles, and Kluckhohn, 1956; Fainsod, 1953, 1963) have identified as a "campaign approach" to production problems.[3] In effect, this attitude may be an extreme form of a more general, but less intense, mobilizational orientation to production problems by the political elite.

The findings on production attitudes are not inconsistent with any of the images of Soviet political change that we have reviewed. However, there are

[3]For an illustration of this approach to agriculture, see P. Stewart (1968, Ch. 6).

differences in emphasis. While the "broker politician" is seen as production oriented, emphasizing pragmatic, efficiency concerns, our findings exhibit a mobilization approach more appropriate to the "administrative dictatorship." Yet even here mobilization concerns are not as dominant as that model might suggest.

CONSUMER WELFARE ATTITUDES

Differences in attitudes toward consumer welfare are more evident in the three images than was the case with production problems. The "broker politician" is postulated as exhibiting a strong, assertive commitment to improved consumer welfare, not merely for its utilitarian value but as a basic right. In the "administrative dictatorship," welfare is only "an incidental and instrumental" element in the pursuit of more perfect social control. Brzezinski (1970) in his "regime of clerks" tends to downplay the economic achievements of the Soviet economy but he does appear to perceive some mild concern if not commitment to consumer well-being.

Again, we find evidence that all three of these attitudes exist among the regional elite. Moderate concern over consumer needs is the strongest organizing attitude dimension, but two sharply divergent attitudes on welfare are also of some importance. "Symbolic affirmation of consumer well-being" reflects a basic satisfaction both with the existing levels of welfare and with its most unreliable component—agricultural production. In sharp contrast is an attitude dimension defined almost entirely by an aggressive activism to improve consumer well-being—demands for improved welfare.

Sources of Soviet Elite Attitudes: Potential for
Adaptive Change

Our analysis of Soviet regional political elite attitudes has shown that rather than a monolithic unity of views there exists within the Party elite a broad spectrum of attitudes. This range of attitudinal diversity, while in no sense embracing those views thought of as consistent with democratic politics (cf. Almond and Verba, 1965) does extend from the instrumental, responsive, trusting attitudes of the "broker politician" to embrace the outlook of the "administrative dictator" and attitudes consistent with a "regime of clerks." In attempting to understand the present and to assess the direction of political change, each of the images of Soviet political change incorporates inferences about the background traits and kinds of experience necessary for the development of those attitudes central to the image. These hypothesized antecedent characteristics, the reader will recall, are found in Table 10.1. Observed alterations in such elite characteristics can be used as a principal means of hypothesizing the pace and direction of change in elite attitudes and behavior and, in turn, of system transformation, perfection, or degeneration. Since we have now, in a tentative way, shown that attitudes consistent with each major image are found among the Soviet regional elite, it may be useful to seek to identify and to assess the impact of these antecedent factors on elite attitudes. By establishing whether, for example, it is the younger men and those with extensive industrial experience who tend to display most strongly the attitudes of the "broker politician" as opposed to the "administrative dictator" or the "regime of clerks," we may begin to create a more adequate basis for inferences about the probable direction of system development.[4]

The antecedent variables examined here are those suggested in the literature (see Table 10.1) as most directly related to the attitudinal differences postulated by the three images of Soviet elites. The four background variables employed are age, mode of entry into the Party, political generation, and type of education. Four measures of career experience are utilized. These are rate of career development, length of industrial experience—both in economic and Party posts, length of Party experience including all Party experience prior to acquiring the post of regional Party first secretary for the first time, and agricultural experience—both directly in agriculture and in related Party positions. Consistent with the illustrative approach taken here, as well as to maximize clarity and ease of interpretation, each of the antecedent variables was dichotomized. The dividing point selected for each was the mean score for the sample on that indicator. Selected marginals for these variables in their continuous and dichotomous forms are found in the first two columns of Table 10.4. Table 10.4 also contains mean factor scores on the attitude dimensions for each subgroup created by dichotomizing the background and career experience variables.

Factor scores are used in this analysis for several reasons. First, our measures of attitudes themselves are factored dimensions. Second, since factor scores are reported as standard scores and indicate the precise degree of individual involvement in each attitude, they make possible a clear and direct interpretation of the findings, and results are comparable across all attitudes. Third, the use of standardized factor scores means that a "zero" score represents just "average" involvement with an attitude. As a result, all positive scores indicate that the background or career experience variable has a greater than average involvement with the attitude, which is precisely the objective of this analysis. Finally, the interval level of measurement which factor scores provide means that the distances between unit scores are equal and conceptually meaningful and, thus, interpretation is facilitated.

Several caveats are important at this point before we present the results of this analysis. Space does not permit presentation of findings showing the involvement of each background variable controlling for the others. Such an analysis enables a more complete understanding of the relationship between

---

[4]Another approach to this problem is to examine temporal trends in the expression of attitudes. Because of the small size of our sample, however, this approach is not appropriate here; in a later study, with a far larger sample, such will become possible.

Table 10.4. Impact of Background and Experience on Ideological, Leadership Style, Production and Manpower, and Consumer Welfare Attitudes

Antecedent Variables	Mean	N^a	Ideology Instrument	Ideology Symbolic	Ideology Doctrine	Distrust Masses	Trust Masses	Group Cooperation	Industrial Manpower	Agricultural Dissatisfaction	Agricultural Activism	Consumer Welfare Dissatisfaction	Consumer Welfare Affirmation	Consumer Welfare Activism
Background Variables														
Year of Birth														
Born post-1912	1916	19	-.028	.184	-.099	-.214	.044	-.291	.048	.301	.063	-.156	-.225	.184
Born pre-1913	1909	18	.072	-.135	.125	.216	-.208	.291	-.308	-.261	-.047	.194	.283	-.196
Mode of Entry to Party[b]														
Recruited	3.4	15	-.175	-.143	-.144	.241	.044	-.108	-.020	-.146	-.098	-.068	-.297	-.039
Coopted	15.0	12	.110	.089	.090	-.151	-.028	.067	.013	.091	.610	.042	.185	.024
Political Generation														
Joined Party pre-1939	1929	10	-.142	-.365	.265	.375	-.217	-.187	-.316	-.178	-.144	-.112	.357	-.198
Joined Party post-1938	1941	28	.060	.157	-.086	-.148	-.056	.070	.111	.083	.044	.043	-.085	.091
Education[c]														
Agricultural	—	16	-.343	.284	.153	.127	-.026	.015	-.238	.152	.216	-.393	.473	.213
Industrial	—	14	.551	-.042	-.050	-.015	-.178	.219	-.139	-.030	-.157	.473	-.393	-.003
Experience Variables														
Career Development[d]														
Slower than average	24.5	14	-.259	.248	.272	.287	.193	-.235	-.191	.286	.194	.474	.040	-.191
Faster than average	17.8	23	.162	-.155	-.170	-.179	-.120	.147	.120	-.179	-.121	-.297	-.025	.120
Industrial Experience (Yrs.)														
Lower than average	0.2	25	-.223	.005	.099	.020	.054	.137	-.246	.103	.096	-.202	.170	.078
Higher than average	8.4	12	.398	-.009	-.176	-.037	-.096	-.245	.439	-.184	-.171	.362	-.304	-.139
Party Experience[e]														
Lower than average	6.3	18	.103	.008	-.197	-.193	-.031	.117	.281	-.061	-.003	.003	-.182	-.046
Higher than average	15.8	19	-.108	-.009	.208	.203	.032	-.123	-.295	.065	.003	-.003	.192	.049
Agricultural Experience (Yrs.)														
Lower than average	0.5	27	.166	-.155	-.145	.017	-.035	-.213	-.032	.027	.080	.156	-.004	-.204
Higher than average	13.5	10	-.374	.259	.372	-.159	.079	.480	.073	-.061	-.180	-.350	.010	.460

[a]The N's for a variable may not total 39 due to missing data for that variable.
[b]Defined as years between education and first full-time Party post.
[c]Several categories are not included here because of small N's—political with N of 1, university with N of 3.
[d]Defined as years between joining Party and becoming regional Party first secretary.
[e]Defined as years in full-time Party positions.

antecedent experiences and attitudes. This type of analysis has been performed on these data and is available upon request from the author.

With respect to our ability to generalize from the findings reported here, the reader should recall the descriptive, exploratory spirit in which these results are presented. While we are persuaded that our sample is representative of the larger universe, as we examine more cases and a larger sample of writings, the relationships reported here may well be altered in significant ways.

IDEOLOGICAL ATTITUDES

The attitude, "ideology as instrumental effects," is found predominantly among those with an industrial education and those who possess considerable industrial experience. This finding is consistent with the rational-technical image of Soviet political development (Moore, 1954; Rostow, 1953) (of which the model of "institutional pluralism" is a contemporary adaptation) which suggests that industrial experience will lead to an instrumental, pragmatic orientation as contrasted with a dogmatic, ideological view of the world. But in contrast to the usual hypothesis in the literature that these tendencies will result in a *lessening* of the importance of ideology in the cognitive structure of industrialists, we find that this *most* salient of the three identified ideological attitudes is especially important to industrialist-politicians—just those whose background and experience is supposed to make ideology among the least important elements of their world view.

One kind of explanation for this phenomenon suggests itself. Ideology may be reconceptualized in a manner consistent with the industrialists' overall perspectives. Rather than developing affect toward its content or reducing ideology to the level of symbolic affirmation, the psychologically significant element of ideology becomes an overriding concern with the impact of ideological work on people. Ideology is valued pragmatically as a mechanism for motivating workers.

The conception of ideology as symbolic affirmation is found most clearly among those regional Party officials who: (1) are younger than average, (2) joined the Party after 1938, (3) completed an agricultural education, (4) rose more slowly than usual in the apparatus, and (5) acquired greater than average experience in agricultural work. Whereas industrialist-politicians tend to adopt an instrumental view of ideology, agricultural specialists approach ideology as a set of symbols to be lauded.

Why should agriculturalist-politicians display this orientation? One possible explanation is that as the revolution recedes further into the past, even politically oriented younger cadres may find it increasingly difficult to become really "involved" with the ideology. While those from an urban, probably middle-class, background transform their ideological interests in an instrumental direction in the process of industrial training and experience, the very abstractness of much of the ideology as doctrine may simply be beyond the grasp of those from a rural, peasant background who spend most of their life in agricultural work. As a result of their political interests, however, the ideology becomes learned by rote and internalized; their superiors talk and think in ideological terms and the younger agriculturalists respond similarly, conscious of the need to observe ideological form. This process is seen by some (e.g., Brzezinski and Huntington, 1963, p. 42) as reinforcing an ideological vocabulary and style. Rather than resulting in "ideological erosion," the behavioral consequences of this process in Brzezinski's (1970, p. 153) view are an "intensified emphasis on revolutionary rhetoric and symbolism." This emphasis leads, in turn, to rigidity and inflexibility in thought, and to a stifling of "intellectual innovation."

Concern for ideology as doctrine also is salient for regional Party first secretaries with higher than average agricultural experience. Yet, the fact that a concern for doctrine occurs predominantly among those who are *older* and those who joined the Party *prior* to 1938 provides some evidence of generational differences among the agriculturalist-politicians. For the younger agriculturalist-politicians ideology as symbolic affirmation is more salient. Thus, rather than doctrinal concerns becoming ever more central to the leadership as implied by the model of the "administrative dictator," these differences are precisely in the direction suggested by Brzezinski (1970) with his "regime of clerks." There is an evident trend among these regional Party officials away from doctrine and toward ideology as more rhetoric and style than substance.

LEADERSHIP STYLES

Three distinct approaches to leadership, reflecting divergent attitudes toward the masses, were identified in the previous section: (1) distrust in the masses, (2) trust in the people, and (3) cooperation based upon discipline. Information on the impact of background and experience on these attitudes is found in Table 10.4.

From Table 10.4 we note that distrust is a predominant orientation among older officials who were recruited into the Party, among those who joined the Party before 1938, among those whose career development was slower than average, and among those with higher than average Party experience. In striking contrast, the data for the trust attitude is more suggestive of which types of regional Party secretaries show little interest in trust than for which types of secretaries this attitude is salient. The attitude stressing group cooperation based upon discipline is found mainly among regional Party secretaries who are *older* than average, who received an industrial education, and who have had extensive agricultural experience.

Many Western observers, pointing to the restrictions on individual, political, and administrative initiative during the Stalin period and to the general atmosphere of tension that existed throughout most of this period, argue that a basic distrust of the masses and an emphasis on the need for vigilance and control will characterize all political officials who acquired much experience in this repressive environment. Our findings lend support to this hypothesis. Those regional officials who acquired their early political experience during the late twenties and early thirties (joined the Party pre-1939) show a distrusting orientation toward the masses.

The predominance of "cooperation through discipline" among older officials and among those with much agricultural experience, but not among their younger counterparts, suggests that the conditions associated with agricultural work in the 1930s and perhaps 1940s may have reinforced a belief in both the values of cooperation and of discipline. One reasonable interpretation is that in an area of the economy where the Party assumed major responsibility for directly supervising production, but where relatively few concrete rewards or coercive tactics could be used to increase productive activity, an emphasis on group cooperation combined with conscious discipline may well have been seen as the only effective style of leadership (cf. Fainsod, 1956). Why is this approach not found among younger agriculturalist-politicians? Khrushchev's half-hearted and Brezhnev's more extensive efforts at providing material rewards for agricultural production suggest evidence for the view that an instrumental approach, stressing material incentives over "moral" rewards, may now be perceived by younger cadres as both essential to motivate a more advanced and skilled peasantry and as appropriate in a more developed socialist economy.

While the general implication of these attitudes for conceptions of change was discussed in the previous section, we can see a clear trend away from both distrusting and cooperative disciplinary attitudes toward the masses. The younger regional officials display little interest in either of these attitudes. In effect, "regime of clerks" and "administrative dictator" images with their emphasis on distrust of the masses may well be more descriptive of the behavioral tendencies of older elites—those who are fairly rapidly leaving the scene except at the highest levels—than of the younger elites. The younger professional politicians may be still experimenting with their leadership style, some adopting the trust attitude, others using styles not identified in this study.

PRODUCTION AND MANPOWER ATTITUDES

As noted in Table 10.4, the "general industrial manpower orientation" is most pronounced in regional officials who have extensive industrial experience, belong to the post-1938 generation of Party members, and rose to prominence at an above-average rate. Regional elites with a birthdate post-1912, with an agricultural education, and with a slower than average career development exhibited the "assertive dissatisfaction with agriculture" attitude. Party first secretaries with an "aggressive Party activism in agricultural sphere" were those who were coopted into the Party, who had an agricultural education, and who were slower than average in their movement up the career ladder.

It is reflective of the dominant role of the Party in agriculture that the strongest expression of agriculture manpower orientations (agricultural activism) is found primarily among the coopted Party professional and not the agriculturalist-politician. The driving, critical, and demanding approach to

agricultural manpower problems of these later-entering, slow-rising Party professionals contrasts sharply with the "group cooperation" orientation of the older
agriculturalist-politicians.

The two attitudes concerned with agricultural production and manpower
appear to be held by different regional officials. The younger officials express
dissatisfaction with agricultural production and manpower while the coopted
officials demand changes in the agricultural sphere. The desire for change may
result, in part, from a slow promotion rate within the Party.

ATTITUDES TOWARD CONSUMER WELFARE

According to Table 10.4 differences in attitudes toward consumer welfare
appear to correspond to variations in education and to diversity of career
experiences. An attitude of assertive dissatisfaction with consumer welfare but
with an underlying emphasis upon the value of "moral" rewards is expressed
most strongly by those regional Party secretaries with an industrial education
and extensive industrial experience. Affirmation of consumer well-being and
activism on consumer welfare, on the other hand, are found in regional officials
with an agricultural education. Those regional Party secretaries actively seeking
changes in consumer welfare politics have had extensive agricultural experience,
while those affirming present consumer well-being have higher than average
Party experience. Dissatisfaction with consumer welfare appears to be the
attitude of the industrialist-politician, affirmation of consumer well-being the
attitude of the Party professional, and activism on consumer welfare the attitude
of the agriculturalist-politician. Future consumer welfare policies will be determined by which type of politician goes on to higher office. Interestingly, the
data in Table 10.4 suggest that regional officials with a faster than average career
development exhibit the activism attitude on consumer welfare.

The three consumer welfare attitudes are also espoused by different age
groups. Dissatisfaction with consumer welfare and affirmation of consumer
well-being are expressed by older officials while activism on consumer welfare is
the attitude of the younger regional officials. The strength of the consumer
welfare activism attitude among both the young and agriculturally oriented
officials lends support to Hough's (1972) contention that Brezhnev's "war on
poverty," especially its agricultural component, probably has considerable support within this segment of the Party elite. The relative youth of this supportive
group also is a potential source of confirmation of Hough's image of the
direction of political change within the Soviet Union. That conflict over the
consumer welfare issue, particularly over the question of the "right" of Soviet
citizens to a higher standard of living, does exist among the political elite itself
and probably will continue to do so in the future is indicated by the contrasting
views of the young and old officials. Support for the position that no real
improvements are needed at all, however, appears to be a thing of the past, at
least among the regional Party elite.

Conclusions

While some of the substantive conclusions presented in this chapter have been dramatic and unexpected and may even help to create a firmer empirical basis for our continuing efforts to understand Soviet political change, a more important objective will have been achieved if this research has contributed to the following ends: (1) increasing our awareness of the complexity and diversity of the Soviet political elite, a group all-too-often perceived as homogeneous in outlook; (2) enhancing our awareness that *not only* should our efforts at constructing more adequate images of the Soviet political system be based on systematic study of the attitudes of the Soviet elites, *but* (3) that it is possible to do so by using Soviet public documents. Only the reader can judge whether we have been successful in achieving these ends.

Identification of the diversity of attitudes among regional Party first secretaries and preliminary examination of the factors influencing this diversity, however, constitute only first, very tentative steps in the elaboration of more adequate images of the political culture of the Soviet Party elite and of its potential for political adaptation. Some of the most important substantive questions and methodological issues have either been entirely ignored or only briefly touched upon here. Some discussion of a few of these may suggest appropriate directions for future work on Soviet political elites.

Ultimately, the crucial factor in the successful adaptation of the Soviet polity will be whether the policy behaviors of the Party elite result in outcomes that increase support for the Party. Policies of international détente and cooperation, actions aimed at substantially improving the working and living conditions of the Soviet people, and a broadening of meaningful political participation would appear to indicate behavior appropriate to this end. Our analysis indicates that attitudes appropriate to the continuation of these policies are found among a portion of the regional elite. Yet, the crucial linkage between attitudes and behavior in the Soviet case remains undemonstrated.

Future efforts must explore to what extent differences in attitudes among the Party elite lead to differences in policy emphases and to differences in other forms of behavior. If such relationships are found, it may then become possible to identify, on the basis of similarity of attitudes or policy positions, policy coalitions among the Party elite. Even rough estimates of the extent of support for, let's say, the policy of détente versus alternative foreign policies, would enormously enhance our understanding of the probable endurance of such policies. This knowledge would, moreover, provide a more adequate basis for conceptions of the policy process and leadership succession.

One of the critical methodological issues that must be confronted in order to address the attitude-behavior linkage in the Soviet context is creation of distinct measures of the separate components of attitude—belief, affect, and behavioral intention. As recent research has indicated (see Fishbein and Ajzen, 1972, p. 516), behavior tends not to be related to the belief and affect components of attitude but to be fairly consistently related to behavioral intentions. Our own preliminary coding efforts from published materials suggest to us that such distinctions probably can be made with this type of data source.

A second important substantive issue is the extent to which the attitudinal diversity among the regional elite observed in the present research finds its reflection among the central Party leadership. Leadership recruitment policies that systematically screen out from top Party positions those with, for example, attitudes of the "broker politician" while advancing "administrative dictators" would result in far different policies and implications for long-term adaptation than if a different screening process took place. As the research reported here is carried into its next phase, our intention is to extend our sample both vertically—to include Politburo and Secretariat officials, as well as officials from major city Party organizations—and horizontally—to bring in a considerable portion of the regional Party officials. Such an approach should make it possible to address more adequately the issue of the impact of recruitment processes on policy and system change heretofore examined primarily on the basis of biographic data alone.

The durability of elite attitudes is a third, important concern for future research. By examining the writings of individual Party elites over an extended time frame, the following question can be addressed: To what extent do measured attitudes change with alterations in the environment, such as (1) a shift in central policy, (2) change in issue addressed, (3) a shift in top leadership, (4) transfer from one region to another, or (5) promotion from the region to the center? Only by intensive examination of these issues can we develop confidence in the validity of attitude measures derived from content analysis. By separating out the impact of situational factors, those elements of elite beliefs having a long-term impact can be specified. The end result should be considerably more sophisticated images of elite political culture and the potential for effective long-term adaptation.

CHAPTER 11

Effect of Career and Party Affiliation on Revolutionary Behavior among Latin American Political Elites*

William A. Welsh

Editor's Introduction

Scholars have often mused about what it is that makes a revolutionary leader. For example, note L. Stewart's (Chapter 9) discussion of the relationship between being a last-born or younger son and being a revolutionary leader. But to date there is little systematic research with which to begin to answer this question. The present chapter by Welsh describes some research which attempts

*The research design, data gathering, and preliminary data analysis phases of this project have extended intermittently over a 15-year period. Many people have contributed a great deal of time and effort to the project: the names of Kathleen Coffman Davis, Anna Elizabeth Powell, Jane Gibson Gravelle, and Michael Altimore come especially to mind. The project has been supported at various times by the Graduate College of the University of Iowa, the Office of General Research of the University of Georgia, and the Program of Graduate Training and Research in Comparative Politics at Northwestern University. Peter G. Snow and George I. Blanksten have been kind enough to use their knowledge of Latin American affairs to redirect at least the most errant and misguided of my uninformed forays into the study of Latin American elites; however, I hasten to absolve them of any responsibility for the sundry insensitivities that remain in this manuscript.

to discover what personal characteristics are related to revolutionary activity and *coups d'etat*. As the focus of his study Welsh has chosen one part of the world noted for its reliance on extralegal means of achieving political succession—Latin America. His subjects are individuals who held cabinet level or high level party positions in seven Latin American countries from 1935 to 1960.

The Welsh chapter continues our examination of who becomes a political leader. His chapter provides a contrast to the chapter by Ziller and his associates (Chapter 8). Ziller et al. were interested in the personal characteristics related to gaining political power by legal means, through election; whereas, Welsh is interested in personal characteristics related to achieving political power through extralegal procedures, namely, the *coup d'etat*. The Welsh chapter also forms a bridge to the next section of the book which is concerned with how the personal characteristics of political leaders affect political behavior. In addition to *coups d'etat*, Welsh investigates what personal characteristics are related to participation in revolutionary activities. As defined by Welsh, revolutionary activities include assassinations, joining in public protests and general strikes, and civil violence.

Welsh examines another type of behavior, not considered by the other authors in Part Two, but meaningful to an examination of who becomes a political leader. He is interested in the personal characteristics related to being thrown out of office by extralegal means. Toward what kinds of individuals are *coups d'etat* generally directed? Can we learn the kinds of characteristics related to lack of success as a political leader? The exploration of who becomes a political leader is not usually couched in terms of those who fail to become a political leader though they strive for such a position and those who are relatively unsuccessful at maintaining themselves in a leadership position. To some extent Ziller and his associates (Chapter 8) suggest some personal characteristics related to trying but not succeeding in becoming a political leader by discussing the characteristics of defeated candidates. By examining who is deposed in a *coup*, Welsh's research indicates some characteristics of individuals who succeed in becoming political leaders but are unable to sustain themselves in office. As these two chapters suggest, there may be different personal characteristics associated with attempting political leadership, becoming a political leader, and sustaining political leadership across time.

The Welsh study bears a resemblance to the previous two chapters (L. Stewart, Chapter 9; P. Stewart, Chapter 10) in that it uses biographical statistics. There are some differences, however, in the way the chapters deal with biographical data. In Chapter 9, L. Stewart focuses on only one piece of biographical information—birth order. Chapter 10 (P. Stewart), like the present chapter, examines multiple biographical variables. Although several of the variables in these two chapters are similar, such as type of education and level of party activity, the authors operationalize them differently. To date this lack of comparability between variables has been one of the failings of research using biographical statistics. Recently Quandt (1970) has urged that researchers adopt a similarly defined set of biographical variables in order to increase the comparability between studies. The variables in these last three chapters which relate to becoming a political leader are good candidates for such a set of indicators.

Welsh introduces a new type of biographical statistic which he proposes as complementary to background and career variables. This new type of biographical data we will call concurrent facts—biographical information descriptive of the political leader at the moment, unrelated to his past. Welsh places nature and extent of nonparty organizational ties in this concurrent facts category, two variables which were good predictors in his study. Other possible concurrent facts are party affiliation, age, and physical health. Given the proximity in time of such biographical variables to the behavior to be explained, concurrent facts may prove good predictors of who becomes a political leader and of political behavior.

Welsh is a professor of political science at the University of Iowa. He has written extensively about Latin American and East European elites (see, e.g., Welsh, 1969, 1970, 1971, 1973). Moreover, he has recently completed a survey of theoretical and empirical work on elites entitled *Leaders and Elites* (Welsh, 1976). Currently Welsh is working on a book on political leadership in Latin America.

THIS CHAPTER EXAMINES several social background and career attributes of Latin American political elites as predictors of their involvement in *coups d'etat* and related "revolutionary" political acts. The purpose of the study is to illuminate certain aspects of the nature of political leadership and to increase our understanding of procedures of political succession in Latin America— procedures which are sometimes viewed as aberrant, yet can be highly institutionalized phenomena. Inferentially, then, the study also is concerned with the nature of political stability and instability in Latin America.

Scholarly writing on Latin American politics[1] reflects substantial agreement on its most salient characteristics, especially on the central features of political leadership. For our purposes, five generalizations may be culled from previous studies. First, there seems to exist in Latin America a deep-seated "revolutionary commitment" to liberal democracy (Gomez, 1961). This revolutionary commitment to a democratic way of life has at least three specific manifestations. One manifestation is an ideological attachment to the symbols of democracy. Indeed,

---

[1]For convenience, this paper adopts the common practice of referring inclusively to "Latin American politics" or "political leadership in Latin America." This practice should not obscure the fact that there are important differences among the polities and the political leadership institutions in Latin America. Indeed, it is important to guard against the tendency to refer to Latin America as if the area were essentially homogeneous (see Welsh, 1970).

political leadership groups in Latin America appear to be more overtly and ideologically committed to such democratic symbols than the leaders of many political orders in which democracy as an operating system seems to be better established. However, at the same time, this Latin American commitment to liberal democracy is sufficiently revolutionary in nature that it may well have contributed to the institutionalization of extralegal, and often violent, acts as recurrent elements of political life. That is, the ideological commitment to democratic symbols and ends is not matched by a commensurate commitment to nonviolent, regularized procedures for achieving these ends. And, finally, the overt "constitutionalism" which accompanies a commitment to liberal democracy is rendered essentially meaningless by the countermanding reality of a lack of respect for political institutions established in constitutions as well as for the constitutions themselves. Thus, it is widely remarked that Latin American political leaders attach great importance to constitutional documents as programmatic statements of abstract goals, but regularly violate the constitutionally stipulated procedures through which the desired goals are supposed to be achieved (Alexander, 1965, pp. 10-17; Mecham, 1959).

A second oft-noted characteristic of Latin American politics is its chronic "instability." The concept of instability has been given a wide variety of meanings in the literature of comparative politics and by scholars of Latin America (cf. Duff and McCamant, 1968; Needler, 1968; Von Lazar, 1971, pp. 45-48). For some, instability is indicated by the presence of recurrent and intense political violence. For others, instability is most obviously manifested by the continual constitutional reworkings which have occurred in nearly all Latin American countries throughout their independent histories. And for still others, instability may be demonstrated by the absence of patterns or regularities in the processes of change which characterize politics. That is, it is sometimes remarked that there is a frustrating degree of "randomness" in Latin American political developments (C. Anderson, 1967, p. 87).

A third feature of political leadership in Latin America is the dominance of the executive branch over the other branches of government, especially the dominance of the president of the republic over other leading political actors (Alexander, 1965, pp. 18-21; Gomez, 1961; Von Lazar, 1971, pp. 30-36). At the same time, despite the almost universal agreement that the executive is politically dominant, there is considerable implicit disagreement as to the implications of that dominance. Some students of Latin American affairs (e.g., Alexander, 1965) seem to believe that the dominance of the executive branch means that the president and his cabinet are especially salient for determining political outcomes in these societies. Other writers, although agreeing that the executive is politically dominant, feel that the basic character of the political, social, and economic orders is largely determined by factors which cannot be, or are not being, manipulated by any political actors within these systems (see Hirschman, 1963). In this latter view, the executive branch dominates the corps, but the corps consists wholly of toy soldiers. The principal business of the political system is thought to be the making and unmaking of governments rather than the shaping of the social and physical environments to facilitate societal development.

A fourth, and related, generalization frequently made about political leadership in Latin America is that this leadership is highly personalistic (Silvert, 1966; Von Lazar, 1971, p. 30). This personalism has its roots in the *caudillo* system, but has been sustained and even magnified by twentieth century developments, including the impact of military and communications technology on the ability of a limited number of individuals to control large numbers of others (Friedrich and Brzezinski, 1966, pp. 23-27). Personalism in political leadership has numerous manifestations, but one of the most important for our purposes is the supposed lack of pattern or predictability that it injects into the process of leadership change. That is, patterns of leadership change in Latin America are determined essentially by factors peculiar to the personalities and backgrounds of the individuals who are in power, or who are contending for power, rather than by characteristics of the established institutions or by practices of government.

Fifth, it is broadly agreed that the varying, but almost universally important, political roles of military groups in Latin America have a central effect on the nature of politics and on the character of political leadership. Several different typologies of military involvement in Latin American politics have been offered. One of the most useful is by Germani and Silvert (1961). For our purposes, what is important is to recognize that the military has played an important role in politics in most of these countries and that a significant number of political leaders in Latin America at any given point in time are likely to be military men or to have significant military backgrounds.

Based on these generalizations drawn from the literature on Latin American politics, we can derive two basic propositions which might serve to structure this study: (1) It is important to study political leadership in Latin America because political leadership is important for an understanding of the political process as a whole and may be highly salient for the nature of societal outcomes. (2) Political leadership in Latin America reflects many of the characteristics of political life in general; namely, political leadership is (a) unstable, (b) substantially ideological in nature, (c) often violent in practice, (d) often extralegal or extraconstitutional in its succession procedures, and (e) often at least superficially unpatterned in terms of the regularity of the change process.

For the social scientist there is more than a little frustration implied by these generalizations. A very great number of unanswered questions remain before us; a few of these unanswered questions constitute the foci of this chapter. The answers tentatively offered here will be incomplete, both because it is sometimes unclear how the questions can best be asked and because the data available with which to address such questions are not wholly adequate. But some tentative first steps seem appropriate, given the importance of this area of research.

Foci of Chapter

This chapter attempts to bring us closer to explaining involvement in Latin America in *coups d'etat* and related "revolutionary" acts. We shall look at certain social background and career characteristics of individuals who have held high government and party positions in seven Latin American countries, examining these variables as predictors of extralegal political activity. We will give special attention to the contrast between military and nonmilitary backgrounds and to the nature of political party affiliation, especially contrasting ideological and nonideological parties.

There is considerable recent research suggesting that career variables are better predictors of elite attitudes and behaviors than are social background characteristics (e.g., Beck et al., 1973; Edinger and Searing, 1967). In a broad sense, the present study should contribute to the growing literature contrasting social background and career characteristics as predictors of behavior. But, more specific to Latin America, numerous studies have suggested that persons with military backgrounds and persons affiliated with ideologically oriented political parties have been disproportionately involved in *coups d'etat* and other "revolutionary" political activities (e.g., Alexander, 1964, 1965; DiTella, 1971; Horowitz, 1967). From such research we are led to infer that the likelihood of involvement in these extralegal political activities is greater on the part of persons with military backgrounds and/or persons identified with ideological political organizations. These generalizations have high face validity.

At the same time, such studies generally have not cast their explanations so as to account for variance in the dependent variable, e.g., involvement in extralegal political succession. These studies have pointed out that, for example, military men are often involved in *coups,* but the research usually has not asked whether a military background covaries significantly with this kind of behavior, i.e., whether the military/nonmilitary career distinction is a useful predictor of the likelihood of involvement in *coups.* In other words, we must ask not only if many of the persons involved in extralegal political succession are military men or from ideological parties but also whether nonmilitary individuals and persons from nonideological political organizations tend not to be involved in such behaviors. Relatedly, it is important to ascertain whether military background and affiliation with an ideological political organization have independent predictive significance or whether they may be functions of other causative factors.

This chapter, then, attempts to move toward formal, variance-based explanatory statements by examining the relative strength of a number of social background and career variables as predictors of involvement in *coups d'etat* and related "revolutionary" activities. Moreover, it seems worthwhile to examine not only extralegal accession to power but also extralegal deposition. Thus we ask whether there are regularities in the backgrounds or careers of those who have been thrown out of office through *coups* as well as whether certain social background and career variables are good predictors of involvement in *coups d'etat.* Further, it seems important to distinguish between revolutionary behavior in general and involvement in *coups d'etat* in particular. There is considerable doubt as to whether *coups d'etat* in fact constitute "revolutions" in any meaningful sense of that word. The issue has been joined frequently in literature on Latin American politics (e.g., Horowitz, 1967, pp. 150-153; Needler, 1968) and need not be explicated again here. But it does seem important to distinguish between involvement in political behaviors which are not directed immediately toward the overthrow of a given group of political authorities and attempted *coups* whose clear and expressed purpose is to unseat a group of political authorities then in power.

In this study the "revolutionary activities" variable includes essentially all extralegal involvements not directed toward the immediate overthrow of a government, e.g., leadership of or participation in general strikes, organized protests, sabotage, political assassinations, and organized street violence. It may well be argued that those who engage in these activities usually have in mind social change substantially more "revolutionary" in nature than the changes envisioned by participants in *coups.* Participation in *coups* is defined broadly to include not only those persons directly involved in the attempts to seize power but also those who accept positions in governments formed immediately as a result of *coups.* This broad definition seems necessary because it is sometimes difficult to distinguish precisely who was involved in the *coup* itself. Moreover, it is reasonable to assume that persons who are close enough to the conspirators to move immediately into positions of political importance might well show similar regularities in background or experience to those who are actually involved in the seizure of power.

The independent variables in this study include urban/rural upbringing, age, amount and type of education, occupation, foreign travel and study, nature and number of organizational affiliations, type and level of government positions, type and level of political party activities, and the nature of political party affiliation or identification. Particular attention, for reasons indicated above, is given to party affiliation and to the military/nonmilitary dimension of training and occupation.

The classification of political parties used in this analysis is three-dimensional.[2] The dimensions are ideological/pragmatic, traditional/nontraditional, and liberal/conservative. The ideological/pragmatic dimension was operationalized by coding the nature of the platform statements made by the political parties and the nature of the demands made by the parties upon their members or adherents. Political parties were coded according to the extent to which their platforms and appeals to adherents and supporters were stated in

---

[2]This political party typology was initially suggested by Anna Elizabeth Powell, a graduate assistant working on the early stages of the project. The typology was devised and initial coding of the data begun in 1965. As a result, this typology does not reflect the thoughtful suggestions presented by Ranis (1968).

expressly doctrinal, abstract, value-based prescriptions. Those parties ranking high on this dimension were considered ideological; parties which were non-doctrinal and did not make ideological demands on their adherents were coded as pragmatic. The traditional/nontraditional dimension refers to the nature of the issues which were stressed or considered most salient by these political parties. Traditional parties were ones which emphasized issues having to do with landholding, the social class structure, and the relationship between church and state. Nontraditional parties were ones which emphasized other issues that have emerged out of more contemporary political circumstances, including relations with the United States and the extent and distribution of social welfare. The liberal/conservative dimension was defined by the parties' positions on domestic, economic, and social issues. Liberal parties tended to favor a greater measure of social welfare, greater redistribution of economic wealth, and greater state involvement in the ownership and/or regulation of productive enterprises. Conservative parties favored the status quo or less involvement in these areas.

The three party dimensions were grouped together to form an eight-category typology of political organizations. For purposes of analysis, however, the party dimensions were treated both conjointly and discretely; that is, the relationship of the party variable with the dependent variables of extralegal activity was examined using the three-dimensional polychotomous classification as well as each of the three dichotomized dimensions. In other words, we asked not only how well party affiliation as an eight-category polychotomy predicted, e.g., involvement in *coups,* but also whether there was a distinction between liberals and conservatives with respect to the likelihood of their involvement in *coups.*

Some brief elaboration of the categories into which the other predictor variables were divided may be helpful. In this study, the occupation variable was dichotomized into military and nonmilitary categories. In distinguishing urban from rural origins, a population of 25,000 or more was considered to indicate an urban location. In the absence of evidence to the contrary, persons born in urban locations were assumed to have grown up there, and vice versa; however, where locale of upbringing was known to be different from place of birth, the former was used. The variables referring to level of government and party activity were eventually dichotomized into national and subnational categories. A person's "level of principal activity" was assumed to be that level of political activity at which he had spent the greatest amount of his time prior to entry into the subject population for this study, i.e., prior to assuming a cabinet-level government post or a national party position. The variable of type of government activity similarly refers to that activity at which the individual spent most of his time before entry into the national elite; it was divided into categories of executive, legislative, and judicial careers. Type of party activity was eventually dichotomized into policy-making and nonpolicy-making positions, that is, into essentially a line-staff distinction.

The variables describing the number and nature of an elite's nonparty organizational affiliations turned out to be especially important in this study. A good deal more will be said about how these variables were handled later on in the course of reporting the data analysis; however, an initial general comment is in order. There is no doubt that many organizational affiliations of Latin American elites are not reported in the sources used in this study. More than half of our subjects are not known to have had formal nonparty organizational affiliations, which seems doubtful. What may be safer to assume is that our sources identified organizational affiliations for which an elite's involvement was significant either in terms of the commitment of the person's time or identity or in terms of the behavioral relevance of the organizational membership for the individual. Thus, in this chapter, as a matter of convenience, we refer to persons who have "no" formal nonparty affiliations. The reader should translate this shorthand as meaning a person not having formal nonparty affiliations important enough to be self-reported or reported in the many secondary sources used in this study.

The parent data collection on which the analysis is based includes 46 variables describing 1,347 persons who held high political office in one of seven Latin American countries between 1935 and 1960. The countries are Argentina, Bolivia, Brazil, Ecuador, Mexico, Paraguay, and Uruguay. The political positions used as a basis for defining the population were cabinet-level positions in the executive branch of government and formal offices at the national level in political parties with parliamentary representation.[3]

Data Analysis

As might be expected with data gathered largely from secondary sources, the level of missing data for this collection is relatively high. Conservative procedures for excluding cases have been used, resulting in the ultimate inclusion in the multivariate analysis of about two-thirds of the total population for the seven countries for the period 1935-1960.[4] Furthermore, for purposes of analysis the

[3]Data for this study have been collected from a variety of sources. Lists of cabinet members and party leaders were developed from the *Political Handbook and Atlas of the World*, the *Statesman's Yearbook*, the *South American Handbook*, and U.S. Department of State lists. All standard biographic works, including international, regional, and country directories, were examined. Some biographic data were made available through the Pan American Union. Mail questionnaires were sent to both subjects and researchers in Mexico and Uruguay in an effort to improve the data collections for these two countries. Newspaper files were searched by a student research assistant in Buenos Aires to expand the Argentine data. Much of the event-related data was coded from *Facts-on-File, Keesing's Archives*, and the *New York Times Index*. Finally, some biographic data were culled from descriptive scholarly writing.

[4]In order to insure comparability among the several multivariate and bivariate analyses, cases were excluded on the following bases: (1) All cases with missing data on any of the three dependent variables were excluded. (2) All cases with missing data on more than three of the 13 independent variables were excluded. (3) Any additional deletions required were handled on a pair-wise, analysis-by-analysis basis. Even with these conservative procedures for handling missing data, some of the bivariate cross-classifications which deal with the full 25-year period of this study include less than the 896 subjects constituting the basic "sample."

25-year period covered by the study is divided into two segments, 1935-1950 ($N = 564$) and 1951-1960 ($N = 332$). This *a priori* division grew out of the general agreement in the literature on Latin American politics that the 1935-1950 period was substantially different from the later period because of the effects of the world-wide economic depression and of World War II. The use of 1950/1951 as the dividing point for the two periods was arbitrary. Since 1950/1951 coincides with government changes in a few of the countries, it might have been more appropriate to use a different cutting point for each of the seven countries. This procedure, however, would have introduced additional problems of cross-national comparability into the data. For this reason a common year was decided upon.

In addition to simple bivariate cross-classifications, the data analysis involves Multiple Classification Analysis (MCA). MCA is an analogue of multiple regression which does not make assumptions concerning either the level of measurement or the shape of the distribution of values of the independent (predictor) variables. The predictors may be nominal scales and substantially skewed; the dependent variable can be a dichotomy. Consequently, the technique seems well suited to the data at hand. MCA permits us to determine both the collective strength of the predictor variables in accounting for variance in the dependent variable and the independent contribution made by each predictor variable when controlling for the effects of the other predictors. For a detailed discussion of this technique and its use, see Andrews, Morgan, and Sonquist (1967).

Explaining Revolutionary Behavior

One category of political behavior we are interested in explaining is what we have called "revolutionary behavior." This variable includes all anti-regime or anti-government behavior other than participation in *coups d'etat* or guerrilla warfare. Revolutionary behavior includes such things as political assassinations, civil violence, and participation in general strikes and public protests. Revolutionary behavior is behavior of political opposition, but it is not immediately or directly aimed at the extralegal overthrow of any particular set of political authorities.

Revolutionary behavior, so defined, is predicted reasonably well by the 13 independent variables used in this study. Thus, the conventional notion that such behavior is unpatterned and, therefore, unpredictable does not receive support. The R^2 (the amount of variance in revolutionary behavior accounted for by the 13 independent variables) from a multivariate Multiple Classification Analysis (MCA) is -.60 for the full 25-year period and, even higher, .74 for the period 1951-1960. As the reader will discover when we discuss the bivariate analyses, party affiliation has an ambiguous and apparently changing relationship with revolutionary behavior, while there is a consistently strong positive relationship between a military background and participation in revolutionary acts.

Significantly, however, the bivariate relationships between military background and party affiliation, on the one hand, and revolutionary behavior, on the other, nearly disappear in the multivariate analysis. Indeed, in the MCA, variables having to do with the nature and extent of an individual's affiliation with nonparty organizations appear as the best predictors of an inclination toward revolutionary behavior for leaders in Latin America. The remainder of this section is devoted to elaborating and explaining these findings.

Because of our *a priori* interest in the possible significance of military background and of affiliation with ideological political parties in understanding revolutionary behavior, it seems appropriate to begin with a look at the bivariate ties between these variables and revolutionary behavior. Table 11.1 shows a significant association ($X^2 = 73.22$, $p < .001$; Cramer's $V = .29$) between a military background and participation in revolutionary acts. (Cross-tabulations for the temporal segments, 1935-1950 and 1951-1960, are not presented here; the relationship is equally significant in both time periods.) Some 26 percent of the military men in our population engaged in revolutionary activity as compared with 5 percent of the nonmilitary elites. Indeed, more than half of the "revolutionaries" under study were military men. Consequently, when we examine only the two-way relationship between a military background and revolutionary behavior, the relationship seems positive and strong.

Table 11.1 reveals a similar picture with regard to the relationship between membership in ideological political parties and revolutionary behavior ($X^2 = 23.73$, $p < .001$; Cramer's $V = .19$). The bivariate relationship is strong; 16 percent of the members of the ideological parties under study had engaged in revolutionary behavior as compared with 5 percent of the members of the pragmatic parties. Further, 74 percent of the subjects who had engaged in revolutionary behavior were members of ideological parties. The cross-tabulations for the two time segments show that the relationship between ideological party affiliation and revolutionary behavior declines in strength in the later period even though the relationship is statistically significant in both periods.

In view of these expected and, consequently, comfortable findings linking military background and ideological party affiliation with revolutionary behavior, an examination of Table 11.2 which reports the results of the MCA is particularly disquieting. In Table 11.2 we discover that party affiliation performs poorly as a predictor of revolutionary behavior explaining less than 1 percent of the variance. The military/nonmilitary distinction (occupation) performs little better, explaining, at best, a little more than 2 percent of the variance (for the 1935-1950 time period). In light of the fact that the overall proportion of explained variance in revolutionary behavior is relatively high in this analysis, the statistical insignificance of these two independent variables raises doubts about their theoretical usefulness.

The two variables which account for an overwhelming proportion of the variance in revolutionary behavior have to do with the nature and extent of an

Table 11.1. Involvement in Revolutionary Activity by Occupation (Military/Nonmilitary) and Party Affiliation (Pragmatic/Ideological Dimension): 1935-1960

	Revolutionary Activity						Total	
	No			*Yes*			*Total*	
	Frequency	Column %	Row %	Frequency	Column %	Row %	Frequency	Column %
Occupation								
Nonmilitary	708	(86	95)	35	(47	05)	743	(83)
Military	113	(14	74)	40	(53	26)	153	(17)
Total	821	(100	92)	75	(100	08)	896	(100)
Party Affiliation								
Pragmatic	356	(58	95)	18	(26	05)	374	(55)
Ideological	255	(42	84)	50	(74	16)	305	(45)
Total	611	(100	90)	68	(100	10)	679*	(100)

Note: For simplicity of interpretation the dependent variables are dichotomized in the bivariate tables. In the multivariate analysis runs the dependent variables were treated as quantitative scales, reflecting the number of times an individual was involved in that activity.

*217 of the 896 persons on whom this analysis focuses had no known political party affiliation.

Table 11.2. Strength of Predictors of Revolutionary Activity among Latin American Political Elites (Multiple Classification Analysis)

Predictor	1935-1960 (N=896) R²=.60		1935-1950 (N=564) R²=.58		1951-1960 (N=332) R²=.74	
	% of Total Variance	Rank	% of Total Variance	Rank	% of Total Variance	Rank
1. Number of Nonparty Organizational Affiliations	24.55	1	9.23	2	34.65	1
2. Nature of Nonparty Organizational Affiliations	17.51	2	22.53	1	28.55	2
3. Foreign Study (Number of Instances)	4.46	3	4.79	4.	0.49	8
4. Foreign Travel (Number of Instances)	4.10	4	2.36	7.5	2.91	4
5. Level of Party Activity	2.59	5	4.65	5	0.25	10
6. Level of Positions Held in Nonparty Organizations	2.30	6	4.86	3	1.25	5
7. Occupation (Military/Nonmilitary)	1.51	7	2.36	7.5	0.11	13
8. Level of Formal Education	1.30	8	1.86	9	0.90	6
9. Population of Birthplace (Urban/Rural Origins)	1.15	9	2.58	6	0.35	9
10. Party Affiliation	0.65	10	0.62	11	0.22	11
11. Level of Government Activity	0.11	11	0.54	12	0.18	12
12. Type of Government Career	0.07	12	0.52	13	0.53	7
13. Type of Party Career	—	13	0.86	10	3.21	3

individual's affiliation with nonparty organizations. The organizational affiliations of our subjects can be divided into four categories: "organizational marginality" (which is descriptive of persons who have no known formal nonparty organizational memberships), professional associations, intellectual/cultural/educational groups, and political agitation groups. This last category includes nonparty groups whose avowed purposes are to engage in militant political activity in an attempt to influence government policy. In our analysis, we examined both this qualitative variable—nature of nonparty organizational affiliations—and a quantitative measure of the number of formal nonparty organizational affiliations held. It must be noted that these two variables overlap operationally in that the characteristic of having no organizational affiliations is a category of both variables. While this overlap may be statistically inconvenient (the resulting multicollinearity is clear), it seems substantively necessary. The decision—especially for a political elite—not to affiliate formally with nonparty organizations would seem to constitute an important qualitative posture toward the organizational environment and cannot be excluded from the variable of "nature of nonparty organizational affiliation."

For the full 25-year period and for 1951-1960, the number of nonparty organizational affiliations is the most powerful predictor of revolutionary behavior in the MCA run. There is not an immediately obvious explanation for the importance of this variable. Table 11.3 shows the bivariate relationship between number of nonparty organizational affiliations and revolutionary behavior ($X^2 = 5.68$, $p < .10$; Cramer's $V = .08$). It appears as if persons with "few" (as opposed to none or "many") nonparty organizational memberships constitute an especially "revolutionary" subset of these Latin American elites. A comment about the initial distribution and subsequent recoding of this variable may help in interpreting Table 11.3. The initial distribution of values was tri-modal; the three categories in Table 11.3 reflect these modes. A substantial number of the subjects had no known formal nonparty organizational affiliations. A second mode was at two nonparty organizational affiliations; the third mode was much higher at seven affiliations. This finding led to a decision to trichotomize the number of affiliations into none, few (one-three), and many (four or more). The recoding of this variable thus reflects the modes of the initial distribution and was not done to maximize the explanatory significance of the variable.

We discover in Table 11.3 that elites with few nonparty organizational affiliations (one-three) are substantially more likely to engage in revolutionary behaviors than elites having either no nonparty organizational affiliations or many. To be sure, the majority of persons with records of revolutionary behavior had no nonparty organizational affiliations; however, the population under study includes more persons without nonparty organizational affiliations than occurs in either of the other two categories. The *row percentages* in Table 11.3 are critical; the probability of engaging in revolutionary behavior is distinctly higher among the group defined by row two (few nonparty organi-

Table 11.3. Involvement in Revolutionary Activity by Number and Nature of Nonparty Organizational Affiliations: 1935-1960

	No			Yes			Total	
	Frequency	Column %	Row %	Frequency	Column %	Row %	Frequency	Column %
Number of Affiliations								
None	546	(67	91)	51	(68	09)	597	(67)
Few (1-3)	83	(10	86)	13	(17	14)	96	(10)
Many (4 or more)	192	(23	95)	11	(15	05)	203	(23)
Total	821	(100	92)	75	(100	08)	896	(100)
Nature of Principal Affiliations								
None	546	(67	91)	51	(68	09)	597	(67)
Professional Associations	174	(21	94)	11	(15	06)	185	(21)
Intellectual/Cultural/Educational	88	(11	94)	6	(08	06)	94	(10)
Political Agitation	13	(01	65)	7	(09	35)	20	(02)
Total	821	(100	92)	75	(100	08)	896	(100)

Revolutionary Activity

zational affiliations) than it is for the elites defined by the other two rows in the table. [5] The relationship is especially strong for the period 1935-1950.

The second most important predictor of revolutionary behavior was nature of nonparty organizational affiliation. The bivariate relationship between nature of affiliation and revolutionary acts ($X^2 = 20.15$, $p < .001$; Cramer's $V = .15$) is also shown in Table 11.3. There are distinct differences among the types of nonparty organizational affiliations held by Latin American political elites, on the one hand, and their likelihood of being involved in revolutionary activities, on the other hand. Perhaps not surprisingly—but still importantly—we discover that members of political agitation groups are especially likely to engage in revolutionary activity. The best predictor of political protest is reflected, in effect, in the holding of membership in nonparty organizations whose aims seem particularly consistent with such protest behavior. Again, the largest single subgroup among our "revolutionaries" consists of persons who have no nonparty organizational affiliations. However, it is among those having affiliations with political agitation groups that the probability of revolutionary behavior is highest.[6] Some 35 percent of the members of political agitation groups engaged in revolutionary acts; the percentage is 9 among those with no affiliations, 6 among members of intellectual and related organizations, and 6 among members of professional associations.

At this point let us attempt a summary statement about the principal predictors of revolutionary activity. It appears as if the likelihood of revolutionary behavior can be traced to two distinct forms of "elite marginality." One manifestation of elite marginality is represented by the decision to join nonparty organizations devoted to militant political protest. The second form of elite marginality consists of a decision to join few nonparty organizations—a decision

[5]It may be worth underscoring why the row percentages rather than the column percentages reflect the critical explanatory dimensions in many of these two-way tables. Although persons with no nonparty organizational affiliations constituted the most "revolutionary" subset since most "revolutionaries" had no nonparty organizational affiliations, persons with no such affiliations also constituted a majority of the subjects under study so that their numerical preponderance in a given category of any other variable was highly likely. For this reason, our focus needs to be on the proportions of persons *within* each category of the nonparty organizational variable who engaged in revolutionary acts, i.e., on the *probability* that a person with, say, many nonparty organizational ties will also exhibit revolutionary behavior. This probability is reflected in the row percentages of the table. A similar way to look at this point is in terms of our ability to predict revolutionary behavior from number of nonparty organizational affiliations. The probability of our being accurate in predicting that a person with few nonparty organizational memberships will be revolutionary is higher than our probability of being accurate in predicting that a person with no affiliations will be revolutionary. The MCA technique proceeds in an analogous way. The association between any given category of a predictor variable and the dependent variable is based on the mean Y (dependent variable) value for cases in that X (predictor variable) category.

[6]It is worth stressing that the independent and dependent variables in question here do not overlap operationally. That is, membership in a political agitation group was not enough to cause a subject to be coded as having engaged in revolutionary activity. Revolutionary activity is a behavioral measure indicated by involvement in specific events. The relationship between membership in political agitation groups and involvement in revolutionary acts or *coups* is not tautological; some of our elite subjects who were members of such groups did not engage in revolutionary or extralegal behaviors.

which might be considered unusual for a person who occupies, or hopes to occupy, a position of societal importance. This elite marginality hypothesis is reinforced by the fact that persons who belong to a *large* number of organizations are distinctly disinclined toward revolutionary behavior; only 5 percent of the subjects with "many" nonparty organizational affiliations engaged in revolutionary behavior as compared to 14 percent of the persons with few affiliations and 9 percent of those with no affiliations.

This finding might seem uninteresting, perhaps even tautological, at first glance. Upon reflection, however, it emerges as neither trivial nor tautological. The unambiguous thrust of much of the literature on Latin American politics is that revolutionary behavior has become institutionalized and is fully, and perhaps primarily, associated with the functions of established societal institutions such as ideologically oriented political parties and the military. The data presented here do not support this conventional explanation for the occurrence of revolutionary behavior among Latin American political elites. Rather, the data suggest that the best predictors of revolutionary behavior in Latin America are similar to what one would expect to find in societies in which such behavior is not thought to be so substantially institutionalized: namely, either limited organizational links with the political "establishment" or membership in organizations expressly devoted to the concept of political agitation. To repeat, neither a military background nor membership in an ideological political party is a useful component of a multivariate model predicting revolutionary behavior among Latin American political elites. If we wish to maximize our ability to predict the likelihood of revolutionary behavior among these elites, we apparently should inquire about the nature and extent of their nonparty organizational affiliations.

Yet it remains for us to explain how the bivariate relationships between ideological party affiliation and military background, on the one hand, and revolutionary behavior, on the other hand, could have been so strong if the multivariate relationships are so meager. The answer is straightforward and no less significant than our findings concerning the importance of nonparty organizational affiliations. One of the virtues of multivariate data analysis is that spurious relationships can be identified and more systematic bases for causal statements can be provided by determining the extent to which any given variable contributes to explaining variance in a dependent variable *with the effects of other variables held constant.* When we control for other variables, the relationships of military background and ideological party affiliation with revolutionary behavior decline drastically. It must therefore be the case that these two variables simply reflect other more genuinely causative factors which operate to increase the likelihood of revolutionary behavior. An examination of the bivariate relationships between military background and ideological party affiliation, on the one hand, and some of the independent variables which emerged as more powerful predictors of revolutionary behavior in the MCA runs, on the other hand, shows this to be the case.

The prototypic, politically active military man in Latin America is a composite of several background and career factors that are positively related to revolutionary behavior. Similarly, *the prototypic member of an ideologically oriented political party in Latin America reflects most of these same characteristics.* It is because these two groups—military men and members of ideological parties—reflect a composite of revolution-related personal characteristics more faithfully than any other occupational or functional group that these two groups are disproportionately represented among revolutionaries. The relationships with revolutionary behavior, therefore, derive not from any intrinsic characteristics of the military or of ideological parties as such, but rather from the agglomeration of characteristics exhibited by a substantial proportion of their members.

Some specifics will illustrate the argument. As we have just seen, the nature and extent of nonparty organizational affiliations are the best predictors of revolutionary behavior. Table 11.4 shows that Latin American military men are underrepresented among the political elites who have substantial nonparty organizational ties in society. Many military men have no known nonparty organizational affiliations; those who do belong to organizations tend to belong to only one or two. Thus, the overall extent of organizational ties of military men is low, substantially lower than that for any of the other occupational groupings examined in this study (X^2 = 17.70, p < .001; Cramer's V = .14). The military men who do have organizational affiliations tend to be linked to professional associations, i.e., organizations of military officers (X^2 = 10.97, p < .02; Cramer's V = .11). As Table 11.5 shows, there is a positive relationship between rural or small-town origins and revolutionary behavior (X^2 = 3.18, p = .10; Cramer's V = .08); moreover, the military men tended to be from the small towns or the countryside (X^2 = 13.34, p < .001; Cramer's V = .15). Table 11.5 also shows that less-educated elites were substantially more inclined than their better-educated colleagues to engage in revolutionary behavior (X^2 = 111.82, p < .001; Cramer's V = .45) and that military men tended to be less-educated than the other political elites (X^2 = 35.47, p < .001; Cramer's V = .23). As noted in Table 11.5, experiences of study abroad and foreign travel are positively related to revolutionary behavior (X^2 = 9.63, p < .01; Cramer's V = .10 for foreign study and X^2 = 19.94, p < .001; Cramer's V = .15 for foreign travel); moreover, the military men were far more likely to have records of foreign study and foreign travel than the other occupational groups among the elites studied (X^2 = 31.83, p < .001; Cramer's V = .20 for foreign study and X^2 = 24.73, p < .001; Cramer's V = .16 for foreign travel).

Much the same is the case with the characteristics of members of ideologically oriented political parties. Returning to Table 11.4, we note that members of ideological parties are less likely to have a large number of organizational ties than members of pragmatic parties (X^2 = 16.41, p < .001; Cramer's V = .18). Not surprisingly, members of ideological political parties were disproportionately represented among the members of political agitation groups (see Table 11.4; X^2 = 16.41, p < .001; Cramer's V = .18). Furthermore, members of ideological parties were more likely to be from rural areas (X^2 = 17.20, p < .001; Cramer's V = .19) and to be less-educated (X^2 = 5.12, p < .05; Cramer's V = .11) than members of pragmatic parties (see Table 11.6). Thus, a focus on the more

Table 11.4. Number and Nature of Nonparty Organizational Affiliations by Military/Nonmilitary Occupational Distinction and Party Affiliation (Pragmatic/Ideological Dimension): 1935-1960

| | Number of Affiliations | | | | | | | | | | | | Nature of Affiliations | | | | | | | | |
| | Total | | None[a] | | | Few | | | Many | | | Professional Associations | | | Intellectual/Cultural/Educational | | | Political Agitation | | |
Occupation	Frequency	%	Frequency	Column %	Row %	Frequency	Column %	Row %	Frequency	Column %	Row %	Frequency	Column %	Row %	Frequency	Column %	Row %	Frequency	Column %	Row %
Nonmilitary	743	(83)	480	(80)	(65)	75	(78)	(10)	188	(93)	(25)	167	(90)	(22)	80	(85)	(11)	16	(80)	(02)
Military	153	(17)	117	(20)	(76)	21	(22)	(14)	15	(07)	(10)	18	(10)	(12)	14	(15)	(09)	4	(20)	(03)
Total	896	(100)	597	(100)	(67)	96	(100)	(11)	203	(100)	(23)	185	(100)	(21)	94	(100)	(10)	20	(100)	(02)
Party Affiliation																				
Pragmatic	374	(55)	221	(52)	(59)	41	(54)	(11)	112	(64)	(30)	102	(64)	(27)	47	(64)	(13)	4	(21)	(01)
Ideological	305	(45)	206	(48)	(68)	35	(46)	(11)	64	(36)	(21)	57	(36)	(19)	27	(36)	(09)	15	(79)	(05)
Total	679[b]	(100)	427	(100)	(63)	76	(100)	(11)	176	(100)	(26)	159	(100)	(23)	74	(100)	(11)	19	(100)	(03)

[a] None category is the same for both number and nature of affiliation variables.
[b] 217 of the 896 persons on whom this analysis focuses had no known political party affiliation.

Table 11.5. Rural/Urban Origins, Level of Formal Education, Foreign Study Experience, and Foreign Travel by Involvement in Revolutionary Activity and Military/Nonmilitary Occupational Distinction: 1935-1960

| | Total | | Revolutionary Activity | | | | | | Occupation | | | | | |
| | | | No | | | Yes | | | Nonmilitary | | | Military | | |
	Frequency	%	Frequency	Column %	Row %	Frequency	Column %	Row %	Frequency	Column %	Row %	Frequency	Column %	Row %
Rural/Urban Origins														
Rural	338	(65)	290	(64	86)	48	(76	14)	248	(61	73)	90	(80	27)
Urban	179	(35)	164	(36	92)	15	(24	08)	157	(39	88)	22	(20	12)
Total	517[a]	(100)	454	(100	88)	63	(100	12)	405	(100	78)	112	(100	22)
Level of Education														
Secondary or Less	56	(10)	32	(07	57)	24	(38	43)	27	(06	48)	29	(26	52)
College or More	486	(90)	446	(93	92)	40	(62	08)	404	(94	83)	82	(74	17)
Total	542[b]	(100)	478	(100	88)	64	(100	12)	431	(100	80)	111	(100	20)
Foreign Study														
No	447	(50)	423	(52	95)	24	(32	05)	403	(54	90)	44	(29	10)
Yes	449	(50)	398	(48	89)	51	(68	11)	340	(46	76)	109	(71	24)
Total	896	(100)	821	(100	92)	75	(100	08)	743	(100	83)	153	(100	17)
Foreign Travel														
No	406	(45)	391	(48	96)	15	(20	04)	364	(49	90)	42	(17	10)
Yes	490	(55)	430	(51	88)	60	(80	12)	379	(51	77)	111	(73	23)
Total	896	(100)	821	(100	92)	75	(100	08)	743	(100	83)	153	(100	17)

[a]379 of the 896 persons on whom this analysis focuses had insufficient information on place of origin to classify them.

[b]354 of the 896 persons on whom this analysis focuses had insufficient information on education to classify them.

Table 11.6. Party Affiliation (Pragmatic/Ideological Dimension) by Urban/Rural Origins and Level of Education: 1935-1960

Party Affiliation	Urban/Rural Origins									Level of Education								
	Rural			Urban			Total			Secondary or Less			College or More			Total		
	Frequency	Column %	Row %	Frequency	Column %	Row %	Frequency	Column %		Frequency	Column %	Row %	Frequency	Column %	Row %	Frequency	Column %	
Pragmatic	139	(47	59)	98	(69	41)	237	(54)		18	(36	08)	218	(54	92)	236	(52)	
Ideological	157	(53	78)	45	(31	22)	202	(46)		32	(64	15)	184	(46	85)	216	(48)	
Total	296	(100	67)	143	(100	33)	439*	(100)		50	(100	11)	402	(100	89)	452*	(100)	

*Since all three variables have missing data, the total N is less than 896.

obvious institutional identifications of these elites may tend to obscure more meaningful explanations for their patterns of behavior. It is not so much that military men or political ideologues are "revolutionary" because of their military status or ideological postures; rather, the case is that these persons tend to exhibit many of the background and career characteristics which seem to contribute to revolutionary behavior.

We should not be too quick, however, to dismiss the importance of the study of ideological political parties or of the military as political institutions in Latin America. For these two types of institutions may provide a *framework* through which the kinds of political protest behavior we have been discussing can be manifested. We may wish to entertain the possibility that the existence of such organizations is a *necessary,* but not *sufficient,* condition for the relatively widespread incidence of revolutionary activity in these societies. Such behaviors can best be explained, as this analysis seems to show, with reference to certain elements of the backgrounds and political orientations of people who join the military or affiliate with ideological parties. The institutions themselves may be important in providing vehicles for the expression of the inclinations held by these persons. It seems clear that revolutionary behavior among political elites in Latin America must be described in terms of the elites' background character- istics, early career experiences, and organizational affiliations as opposed to characteristics of the institutions with which they tend to be affiliated. At the same time, the characteristics of the institutions may be important in catalyzing this amalgam of background and career factors into concrete political protest behavior. Our data do not permit us to address systematically the possible catalytic effect of military status or ideological party affiliation. Our data do suggest that revolutionary activity is carried out by organizationally marginal individuals with limited ties to established societal institutions. These individ- uals tend to come from small towns or rural areas, to have less formal education than many of their colleagues, and to have studied and travelled abroad.

Before leaving this discussion of the predictors of revolutionary behavior among Latin American elites, we need to give some further attention to the relationship between a military background and foreign travel and foreign study. The relationship between each of these three predictor variables and revolu- tionary behavior is positive and significant. However, if we remove all military elites from the two-way cross-classifications between foreign study and revolu- tionary activity and between foreign travel and revolutionary activity, the relationships disappear. Thus, it appears as if military background *interacts* with foreign exposure in producing revolutionary activity; military men with foreign exposure seem to be a particularly revolutionary subset of the elites under study. A closer look at the data on the foreign study of the military men in our sample of elites, especially that foreign study which took place between 1935 and 1945, shows some tentative locational patterns: most studied in Germany or the United States, with Germany being more common. It is tempting to infer that exposure to the particular brand of revolutionism and militarism present in Germany during this period could have had an influence on these military elites, but there is, of course, no way of knowing from our data whether this factor was operative in their participation in revolutionary acts. This line of reasoning does suggest, however, the importance of looking more carefully at possible explanations for the apparently catalytic effect of foreign exposure on the political perspectives of military elites in Latin America.

Explaining Involvement in *Coups d'Etat*

In the previous section, we focused on what we are calling revolutionary behavior—militant protest activity designed to effect major changes in public policy but not meant to unseat particular sets of political authorities, i.e., *coups d'etat*. Since a great deal is made of the significance of the *coup d'etat* as a means of leadership succession in Latin America and because there is substantial debate about whether this behavior should be considered in the same category as other forms of political protest and/or revolution, it is appropriate to give separate attention to involvement in *coups*.

Again let us begin by entertaining our two "conventional" hypotheses, namely, that military elites are substantially more inclined than nonmilitary elites to participate in *coups* and that membership in ideologically oriented political parties is associated with participation in *coups*. Table 11.7 shows that there is a significant relationship between a military background and involvement in *coups* ($X^2 = 15.31, p < .001$; Cramer's $V = .13$). (The relationship holds more strongly for 1951-1960 than for the earlier period, but is statistically significant in both periods.) The relationship between party affiliation and involvement in *coups* is more ambiguous. Surprisingly, we discover that for the full 25-year period members of pragmatic political parties are more likely to be involved in *coups* than members of ideological parties, although the relationship is not statistically significant. An examination of Table 11.8 shows that the relationship between party affiliation and involvement in *coups* is actually quite strong for both time periods, but that the relationship is reversed between the two periods. During 1935-1950 members of pragmatic parties were far more likely than members of ideological parties to be involved in *coups* ($X^2 = 18.71$, $p < .001$; Cramer's $V = .20$), while during the years 1951-1960 members of ideological parties were substantially more likely than their pragmatic counterparts to have attempted extralegal accession ($X^2 = 7.35$, $p < .01$; Cramer's $V = .19$).

Precisely what explains this temporal reversal of the relationship between party affiliation and *coups d'etat* is not clear from these data. One possibility is that the change is associated with another dimension of the political party classification, namely, the conservative-liberal distinction. Given the respective prevailing ideological climates in the seven countries under study in the two time periods, one might hypothesize that *coups* during the late 1930s and early 1940s in Latin America were primarily the product of conservative pragmatic political

Table 11.7.   Involvement in *Coups d'Etat* by Military/Nonmilitary Occupational Distinction: 1935-1960

| | Involvement in *Coups* | | | | | | | |
| | *No* | | | *Yes* | | | *Total* | |
Occupation	Frequency	Column %	Row %	Frequency	Column %	Row %	Frequency	Column %
Nonmilitary	652	(85	88)	91	(71	12)	743	(83)
Military	115	(15	75)	38	(29	25)	153	(17)
Total	767	(100	86)	129	(100	14)	896	(100)

Table 11.8. Involvement in *Coups d'Etat* by Party Affiliation (Pragmatic/Ideological Dimension) for Periods 1935-1950 and 1951-1960

Involvement in *Coups*

Party Affiliation	1935-1950								1951-1960							
	No			*Yes*			*Total*		*No*			*Yes*			*Total*	
	Frequency	Column %	Row %	Frequency	Column %	Row %	Frequency	Column %	Frequency	Column %	Row %	Frequency	Column %	Row %	Frequency	Column %
Pragmatic	216	(55	77)	64	(82	23)	280	(59)	84	(49	91)	8	(22	09)	92	(44)
Ideological	177	(45	93)	14	(18	18)	191	(41)	89	(51	76)	28	(78	24)	117	(56)
Total	393	(100	83)	78	(100	17)	471*	(100)	173	(100	83)	36	(100	17)	209*	(100)

*216 of the 896 persons (total across two time periods) on whom this analysis focuses had no known party affiliation.

groups, whereas *coups* during the 1950s were increasingly associated with more liberal political groups. However, dichotomizing the political parties along the conservative-liberal dimension yields no relationship in either time period with involvement in *coups*. Consequently, this finding must remain unexplained with reference to the data used in this study.

The results of a Multiple Classification Analysis (MCA) to predict involvement in *coups d'etat* is equally ambiguous and somewhat discouraging. The MCA results are discouraging not only because military background and party affiliation are not the best predictors of the dependent variable, but because the amount of variance in involvement in *coups* accounted for over the 25-year period and for the period 1935-1950 is so small as to render most discussion academic. As noted in Table 11.9 for the 25-year period foreign study emerges as the most powerful predictor of involvement in *coups*. However, it accounts for only a miniscule 3.55 percent of the variance. The total variance accounted for over the full period is 17 percent.

It is, however, worth examining the MCA solution for the period 1951-1960, since here the proportion of variance accounted for (42 percent) is respectable.[7] For this time period the explanatory pattern is not unfamiliar in that the second and third strongest predictors are the two nonparty organizational affiliation variables. They perform in the same way for *coups d'etat* as they did for revolutionary behavior. Thus, involvement in *coups* like revolutionary behavior seems to be associated with a small number of nonparty organizational affiliations and with membership in political agitation groups or with an absence of nonparty organizational ties.

The best predictor (10.2 percent of the variance) of involvement in *coups* between 1951 and 1960 is level of formal education. Education performs differently in its impact on involvement in *coups* than in its effect on revolutionary behavior. *Revolutionary behavior is engaged in by less-educated elites; coups d'etat are participated in by better-educated elites.* (Although the relationship holds in this form for both time periods, it is not statistically significant for 1951-1960.) In this connection, let us note that the relationship between urban-rural origins and involvement in *coups* is much less clear than the relationship between revolutionary behavior and rural origins; numerous urban-born elites have been involved in *coups*. In effect, better-educated, urban elites are somewhat more likely to be involved in *coups d'etat* than in other forms of revolutionary behavior. This finding highlights the importance of drawing distinctions between *coups* and other revolutionary acts; it also suggests that we should examine the relationship between revolutionary behavior and involvement in *coups* for the subjects in our study.

[7]The judgment as to what proportion of variance in the dependent variable must be explained before the solution is "respectable," or "interesting," is subjective. In a multiple linear regression analysis, both the R^2 and the betas for individual predictors can be evaluated for significance through the use of F-tests. The analogous MCA procedure would be misleading here because of the patterns of interaction in the data.

Table 11.9. **Strength of Predictors of Involvment in *Coups d'Etat* among Latin American Political Elites (Multiple Classification Analysis)**

Predictor	1935-1960 (N=896) R²=.17		1935-1950 (N=564) R²=.23		1951-1960 (N=332) R²=.42	
	% of Total Variance	Rank	% of Total Variance	Rank	% of Total Variance	Rank
1. Foreign Study (Number of Instances)	3.55	1	2.39	5	1.57	11
2. Population of Birthplace (Urban/Rural Origins)	2.99	2	3.44	2	3.61	4
3. Occupation (Military/Nonmilitary)	1.80	3	2.50	4	1.61	10
4. Level of Formal Education	1.66	4	1.28	9	10.20	1
5. Nature of Nonparty Organizational Affiliations	1.61	5	2.05	6	5.07	2
6. Level of Positions Held in Nonparty Organizations	1.33	6	1.50	7.5	2.54	8
7. Number of Nonparty Organizational Affiliations	1.10	7	3.33	3	4.91	3
8. Party Affiliation	0.90	8	3.55	1	3.02	7
9. Type of Government Career	0.71	9.5	0.94	10	3.10	6
10. Foreign Travel (Number of Instances)	0.71	9.5	1.50	7.5	1.73	9
11. Level of Government Activity	0.66	11	0.12	13	3.46	5
12. Type of Party Career	0.14	12.5	0.18	12	0.81	12
13. Level of Party Activity	0.14	12.5	0.67	11	—	13

Table 11.10 shows that there is a statistically significant association between revolutionary activity and *coups d'etat* (X^2 = 8.94, $p < .01$; Cramer's V = .10). This statistic may be misleading, however, since nearly three-fourths of the persons who engaged in revolutionary activity were never involved in a *coup d'etat* and only 16 percent of the persons involved in *coups* had any previous record of revolutionary behavior. Thus, while there is statistical interdependence between the two behaviors in the population we are examining, only a relatively small proportion of the cases exhibited both behaviors. Indeed, of the 184 persons who were involved in revolutionary activity and/or *coups d'etat,* only 20 (11 percent) were involved in both.

Explaining Extralegal Deposition

In addition to asking the more conventional questions about the characteristics of individuals who have been involved in revolutionary behaviors and in *coups,* it also seemed interesting to ask whether there were regularities in the backgrounds or relevant experiences of persons thrown out of office through extralegal means. For example, do those who live by the sword, figuratively speaking, perish politically by that same means? In other words, are people who have seized power through *coups d'etat* more likely than others to be thrown out of office by the same means?

We should begin by acknowledging that the multivariate model was remarkably unsuccessful in predicting variance in extralegal deposition. The R^2 for the 25-year period was .11. Although the R^2 was highest for 1951-1960, it was only .21 for that period. Perhaps the most interesting finding from the Multiple Classification Analysis (MCA) of extralegal deposition is the fact that the urban-rural distinction was the most powerful predictor, both for the full 25-year period and for each of the constituent time periods. These MCA results are presented in Table 11.11. Elites removed from office by extralegal means tended to be from small towns and rural areas. If we remember that the persons involved in seizing power through *coups* tended to be from urban areas, the Latin American *coup d'etat* may be interpreted as a political practice whereby, among other things, urban elites remove small-town and rural elites from power. Reviewing the results for our three dependent variables, we find revolutionary behavior other than involvement in *coups* associated with rural origins, involvement in *coups* related to urban origins, and removal from office through *coups* linked with rural origins.

Interestingly, there is a change in the pattern of interaction between the urban-rural distinction and level of formal education in the 1935-1950 and 1951-1960 time periods. Between 1935 and 1950 the elites removed from office by extralegal means were inclined to be less-educated and rural; in 1951-1960 those removed were rural, but better-educated. Although it is difficult to trace such patterns of change through these data, we suspect that better-educated

Table 11.10. Involvement in *Coups d'Etat* by Involvement in Revolutionary Activities: 1935-1960

Revolutionary Activity	Involvement in *Coups*									
	No			*Yes*			*Total*		
	Frequency	Column %	Row %	Frequency	Column %	Row %	Frequency	Column %	
No	712	(93	87)	109	(84	13)	821	(92)	
Yes	55	(07	73)	20	(16	27)	75	(08)	
Total	767	(100	86)	129	(100	14)	896	(100)	

Table 11.11. Strength of Predictors of Extralegal Deposition among Latin American Political Elites (Multiple Classification Analysis)

Predictor	1935-1960 (N=896) R²=.11		1935-1950 (N=564) R²=.17		1951-1960 (N=332) R²=.21	
	% of Total Variance	Rank	% of Total Variance	Rank	% of Total Variance	Rank
1. Population of Birthplace (Urban/Rural Origins)	2.80	1	3.12	1	7.54	1
2. Foreign Study (Number of Instances)	1.85	2	2.15	2.5	1.22	6
3. Level of Formal Education	1.09	3	2.15	2.5	3.02	2
4. Number of Nonparty Organizational Affiliations	0.86	4	0.96	8.5	0.98	7
5. Party Affiliation	0.81	5	1.53	7	2.56	3
6. Foreign Travel (Number of Instances)	0.76	6	1.87	4	1.58	4.5
7. Occupation (Military/Nonmilitary)	0.71	7	1.59	5.5	1.58	4.5
8. Nature of Nonparty Organizational Affiliations	0.62	8	0.62	10	0.53	10
9. Level of Positions Held in Nonparty Organizations	0.48	9	0.96	8.5	0.53	10
10. Type of Party Career	0.33	10	1.59	5.5	0.72	8
11. Level of Party Activity	0.19	11	0.26	11	0.12	13
12. Level of Government Activity	0.10	12	0.21	12	0.53	10
13. Type of Government Career	0.01	13	0.04	13	0.21	12

elites of rural origins began to move with greater frequency into positions of political prominence in several Latin American countries after 1945. Many of these same elites were then victims of extralegal ouster by less-educated rural elites during the late 1950s. In any case, it is worth noting that the urban-rural distinction and formal education are the two strongest predictors of extralegal deposition for the period 1951-1960.

There is a strong and consistent relationship over time between coming to office through *coups* and losing office by the same means (X^2 = 46.88, $p < .001$; Cramer's V = .23). These data are found in Table 11.12. Persons who used extralegal means to obtain office were significantly more likely to lose their political positions through the same method. The relationship held for both of the time periods.

Summary and Conclusions

The data examined in this study suggest several important, but highly tentative, conclusions which bear closer examination in subsequent research on political leadership in Latin America. First, these data are not consistent with the notion that recent career experiences and political positions are better predictors of elite attitudes and behaviors than are social background characteristics. Indeed, in some respects the analysis presented here implies quite the opposite: that basic social background characteristics such as rural origins, level of formal education, and extent of study and travel in foreign countries are among the important predictors of inclinations toward revolutionary political behaviors on the part of Latin American political elites. These social background characteristics seem more useful as predictors of such behaviors than recent career experiences.

Second, and related to the first point, these data raise doubts concerning the conventionally assumed causal significance of military affiliation and identification with an ideologically oriented political party for involvement in revolutionary activity. Although bivariate links were consistently observed between these two variables and revolutionary behavior, the bivariate relationships washed out in the multivariate analysis. In effect, the apparent relationships linking a military background and ideological party affiliation with revolutionary behavior probably were due to the fact that members of these two types of institutions tended to represent a kind of prototypic amalgam of background characteristics positively related to revolutionary behavior. The important question of whether these two institutions—the military and ideological political parties—may be necessary, but not sufficient, transmission belts which catalyze, mold, and implement the inclinations of their members toward revolutionary political behavior cannot be answered with the biographic data on which this study is based. But research on this question using data on the internal func-

Table 11.12. Extralegal Deposition by Involvement in _Coups d'Etat_: 1935-1960

| | Extralegal Deposition | | | | | | | |
| | _No_ | | | _Yes_ | | | _Total_ | |
Involvement in _Coups_	Frequency	Column %	Row %	Frequency	Column %	Row %	Frequency	Column %
No	673	(89	88)	94	(67	12)	767	(86)
Yes	82	(11	64)	47	(33	36)	129	(14)
Total	755	(100	84)	141	(100	16)	896	(100)

tioning of these institutions would seem critical to an understanding of revolutionary behavior in Latin America.

Third, in some sense the research reported here suggests a basis for disenchantment with *both* social background *and* career variables as predictors of elite behavior. The most important predictors for revolutionary behavior were variables describing the nature and extent of nonparty organizational ties. To date such variables have not received adequate attention from students of elite attitudes and behaviors. We have interpreted these two variables as indicators of elite marginality. The finding that elites with few formal nonparty organizational ties or with ties primarily with political agitation groups are most likely to engage in revolutionary behavior suggests the importance of more systematic efforts to operationalize concepts of elite marginality. It is worth noting here that most of the social background factors found to be positively related to revolutionary behavior were also positively and substantially related to the organizational affiliation variables.

Fourth, the data presented in this chapter underscore the importance of maintaining a distinction between *coups d'etat* and other forms of revolutionary activity. Our ability to predict behavior other than involvement in *coups* was far greater than our capacity to predict variance in involvement in *coups*. Moreover, the overlap between these two forms of behavior was less than might have been expected; few elites were involved in both *coups* and revolutionary acts. Furthermore, the important predictors were somewhat different between the two variables. In particular, the organizational affiliation variables were less important in predicting involvement in *coups* than in accounting for other forms of revolutionary behavior.

Fifth, the differential adequacy of our multivariate model for predicting revolutionary behavior, on the one hand, and involvement in *coups d'etat,* on the other hand, has implications for future research on the antecedents of *coups* in Latin America. As Przeworski and Teune (1970) suggest when variance in individual-level behaviors cannot be accounted for by reference to within-system factors, one may want to consider possible causal factors at the system level. It is possible, of course, that individual- or group-context variables not treated in this study might increase our ability to predict involvement in *coups;* more likely, however, is the possibility that system-level variables may be affecting the incidence of *coups.* Whereas revolutionary behavior can be accounted for by within-system predictor variables, involvement in *coups* probably requires a model incorporating system-level variables.

Sixth, the findings presented here suggest the importance of giving more systematic attention to processes of elite and mass socialization in Latin America. The data provide a sufficient basis for inferring a relationship between less-educated, rural/small-town origins and what we have called "revolutionary" behavior. Some of these "revolutionary" acts are illegal or extralegal (e.g., assassination, leading general strikes) while others call for fundamental social changes, but do so through legal procedures. *Coups,* on the other hand, tend to

involve urban individuals. While it is debatable whether *coups* are institutionalized forms of political succession in Latin America—and presumably this might
vary from country to country—it is clear that *coups* are not sanctioned in any
formal, legal sense. Thus, the question of whether formal education or characteristics of the social setting (e.g., the urban/rural distinction) are accompanied
by distinct patterns of socialization must remain open. The ambiguity of the
data for answering such socialization questions underscores the importance of
systematic socialization research on subpopulations in Latin America.

There are numerous respects in which the analysis in this chapter is flawed
and must be correspondingly qualified. In the first place, the seven countries
which constitute the data base for this study were chosen on the basis of their
contrasting levels and rates of economic development not with an eye to
controlling for political system variables. It is possible that the generalizations
emerging from this study might not hold for Latin American political systems on
the whole. (At the same time, it is reasonable to ask whether "representativeness" of any given geographic area or any given population of nation-states is a
meaningful criterion to apply to the selection of cases in cross-national research.[8]) Secondly, the missing data in this study is substantial, which is
probably inevitable when research covering a considerable time period is done
largely from secondary sources. Moreover, we need to stress that the subjects on
whom data were gathered and analyzed were selected because of their political
positions not because of their political behaviors. In effect, this study does not
focus on persons who engaged in revolutionary or extralegal behaviors; it is a
study of political elites, positionally defined. It is quite possible that different
explanations for involvement in these activities might emerge if a sample of
nonelite "revolutionaries" were included.[9] Generalizations from the present
study must be limited to political elites.

Finally, and perhaps most important, this research only leads us to the edge
of asking a number of important questions, most of which will require both
systematic attitudinal data and careful analyses of societal institutions to answer.
This study has proposed linkages between certain background characteristics and
aspects of organizational involvement, on the one hand, and the propensity
toward involvement in revolutionary and/or extralegal political behavior, on the
other hand. The data have suggested that the two factors often cited in
explaining these political behaviors—a military background and ideological party

[8]It can be argued that the selection of countries for inclusion in cross-national studies, as
well as the sampling of units of observation within those countries, should be based on the
notion of "sampling" the theoretically-relevant dimensions of variables rather than sampling
populations. In this view, the "representativeness" of a sample is thought of in terms of its
representation of the range of values of a theoretically-relevant variable. This position is
advocated by Willer (1967) and seems consistent with the comparative research strategy
recommended by Przeworski and Teune (1970).

[9]It is worth emphasizing that the background and socialization variables which best
predict attitudes and behaviors may well differ between elites and mass. Especially persuasive evidence of this observation is presented by Zaninovich (1973).

affiliation—may have less independent explanatory significance than generally has been assumed. These findings, however, ring somewhat hollow as explanations because they cannot speak to the crucial *attitudinal* and *institutional channels* through which background and career influences are—or are not—translated into political behavior. Why is it, for example, that foreign study seems to have such a strong, catalytic effect on the inclination of military men to participate in *coups?* How, if at all, do political socialization processes differ between urban and rural settings? To what extent are institutions such as the military critical to the *expression* of inclinations toward revolutionary behavior? Is military recruitment enhanced by a perceived opportunity to use military institutions to work around constitutional limitations in gaining access to, and the use of, political power?

We might be inclined to guess ("infer" is the more dignified term) about some of these questions, but even "educated" guesses in the absence of attitudinal data seem likely to do more harm than good. This is especially true in an area of research in which the temptation to "explain" in the absence of systematic data has been—understandably—great in the past. Rather, it seems more appropriate to stress the importance of seeking attitudinal data on Latin American political elites so that more meaningful explanations of these important background/ career/organizational affiliation/attitude/behavior relationships can be achieved.

PART 3

PERSONAL CHARACTERISTICS AND POLITICAL BEHAVIOR

CHAPTER 12

Some Personal Characteristics Related to Foreign Aid Voting of Congressmen*

Margaret G. Hermann

Editor's Introduction

The previous section of this book dealt with the question of who becomes a political leader. The next five chapters change the focus of attention to the relationship between a political leader's personal characteristics and political behavior. In this section of the book we are interested in learning whether what a political leader is like can influence what he or his political unit does. Hermann in the present chapter provides a good summary of the controversy which has developed over whether a political leader's personal characteristics can affect political behavior. To date, however, there has been little systematic research with which to confront the parties to the controversy. The purpose of the chapters in this section of the book is to provide some systematic research bearing on the linkage between personal characteristics and political behavior as well as information on variables which enhance or reduce such a relationship.

*This chapter represents a fairly extensive revision of the author's master's thesis done at Northwestern University. The revision reflects the constructive criticism of Donald Campbell, Harold Guetzkow, Charles Hermann, and James Robinson, whose comments on earlier drafts are gratefully acknowledged.

In Chapter 12 Hermann examines how the personal characteristics of Congressmen affect their voting behavior. She is interested in the effects which political leaders' personal characteristics have on their *own* political behavior. One of the problems which has often stymied research on the relationship between personal characteristics and political behavior concerns finding accessible and appropriate indicators of political behavior. By using votes Hermann chose a generally agreed upon index of political behavior. Moreover, votes are usually accessible, particularly for political units in open societies that record votes in a form which the public can monitor. Other kinds of political behavior which, like votes, are accessible to the researcher with not too much effort where legislative records are kept are amount of participation (e.g., number of sessions attended, amount spoken, number of pieces of legislation introduced), effectiveness (e.g., ratio of pieces of legislation passed to pieces of legislation introduced), and specialization (e.g., percentage of pieces of legislation introduced which focuses on one topic, percentage of speaking time devoted to one topic). Ziller and his associates in Chapter 8 used several of these indices in examining the relationship between state legislators' self-other orientations and their legislative behavior. Recent events data sets which record who participates in an event as well as the nature of the event increase present sources of political behavior. An example of a study that examines the impact of political leaders' personal characteristics on political behavior using events data as the basis for developing indices of political behavior is found in M. Hermann (1974). Based on events data, this research examines such political behavior as changes in position, conflict behavior, diplomatic activity, commitment of resources, and concern with procedural matters. A discussion of several events data sets is available in Burgess and Lawton (1972).

In the introduction to this book we noted four types of personal characteristics—beliefs, motives, decision style, and modes of interpersonal interaction—which writings on political leaders by journalists and scholars have suggested might influence political behavior. The present chapter examines specific examples of beliefs and decision style. Beliefs refer to fundamental assumptions about the world and, in this study, about political reality. The two beliefs which Hermann relates to voting on foreign aid include a belief in the importance of caring for others (humanitarian ideology) and a belief in the importance of becoming actively involved in international relations (orientation toward international involvement). For political leaders decision style variables involve the ways in which policy-making tasks are characteristically approached and dealt with. The two decision style variables which the present chapter examines concern the complexity with which a political leader structures the nature of a decision task (cognitive complexity) and the expectation that things will work out well (optimism). Two chapters in previous sections of the book explored the relationship of specific motives and modes of interpersonal interaction to political behavior. Winter and Stewart in Chapter 2 examined how such motives (reasons for action) as the needs for power, achievement, and affiliation related to presidential political behavior. Ziller and his associates in Chapter 8 studied the relationship between four self-other orientations (modes of interpersonal interaction) and legislative behavior.

The present chapter employs content analysis in measuring the personal characteristics under study. Hermann uses quantitative content analysis, counting the frequency with which certain themes appear in the statements of Congressmen during floor debate in the U.S. House of Representatives. The source of the material for her content analysis is the *Congressional Record,* a transcript of what goes on in the U.S. Congress. During the course of the chapter Hermann raises two issues regarding the type of material which should be content analyzed to assess personal characteristics of political leaders. These concern ghostwriting and content control. Hermann deals with these problems in ways different from Winter and Stewart in Chapter 2, who use inaugural speeches as the source of their data on personal characteristics. Hermann argues that materials such as speeches which are often written for political leaders by others or are designed to convey a specific image to a certain audience may not be appropriate materials to use to learn about the personal characteristics of a political leader. The researcher will probably learn what the ghostwriter is like or the image which the political leader would like to reflect. Hermann proposes that by using spontaneous material such as occurs in the give and take of a legislative debate or press conference the researcher will probably gain a more accurate picture of a political leader's personal characteristics. The researcher knows the political leader has authored the material and the political leader has less time to plan his responses. Research that compares the results of content analyses using speeches and debate or press conference responses is needed to resolve this issue of whether there is a difference in a political leader's personal characteristics when these two types of materials are used.

Hermann, a psychologist, is a research associate at the Mershon Center, Ohio State University. Challenged during graduate school to match the personal characteristics of participants in a simulation to the personal characteristics of the major political leaders in the crisis preceding the outbreak of World War I (see C. Hermann and M. Hermann, 1967), she has continued to be fascinated with studying the personal characteristics of political leaders. Currently Hermann is involved in exploring how the personal characteristics of some 45 heads of state, in office during the decade 1959-1968, influenced the foreign policy of their nations. A pretest of this research is reported in M. Hermann (1974); the conceptual scheme which provides a rationale for expecting certain personal characteristics to affect foreign policy appears in M. Hermann (1976b).

WHAT INFLUENCE do a political leader's personal characteristics have on his political behavior? Are there personal characteristics which are related to particular policy orientations and outcomes? These questions have generated much debate. Moreover, concern over the answers is not new (e.g., see Plato's *States-man,* Machiavelli's *The Prince,* the *Analects* of Confucius, and Nizam-al-Mulk's *The Book of Government or Rules for Kings).*

Controversy over the effect of leader personality on political behavior focuses on three issues. The first criticism arises from the centuries old "great man" versus "zeitgeist" debate. Must the times be right for the man or will the man be a great leader regardless of the times? For example, would Lincoln have been as effective if he had been president in the 1920s instead of the 1860s? After carefully analyzing both sides of this debate, Searing (1972) argues that these positions form two extremes along a continuum, with most cases falling some-where between the two extremes. He urges an examination of the interrelation-ship between the situation and the man.

Research on leadership also indicates that neither position seems tenable by itself (see Gibb, 1969; Stogdill, 1974). While most leaders do appear to have certain characteristics—they are self-confident, extroverted, and exhibit interper-sonal sensitivity (or empathy), a leader in one situation is not necessarily a leader in a different situation. Moreover, leadership is often bestowed on the basis of the values and needs of a constituency, all of which can change. Students of leadership propose that it is the interaction between the characteristics of the individual and the characteristics of the situation which determines who will become a leader and the kind of behavior he will exhibit (see Fiedler, 1967; Hollander and Julian, 1970). Based on such a consideration, Paige (1972, p. 69) defines political leadership as "the interaction of personality, role, organization, task, values, and setting as expressed in the behavior of salient individuals . . ." who can have an effect on policy.

The second criticism concerns the agent or representative nature of political leadership. Political leaders merely reflect the views, beliefs, and ideologies of the constituencies they lead and, as a result, react to common situations in a similar manner. Thus, as some Kremlinologists would have us believe, all Soviet foreign policy follows from the dictates of Marxism-Leninism. In order to become a political leader an individual must have internalized the goals and norms of the elite which grants him power (see, e.g., Kolko and Kolko, 1972). His personal characteristics become subservient to these group characteristics.

Interestingly, however, even advocates of this agent position (e.g., Shils, 1954; Verba, 1969) grant that in certain situations the effects of personal characteristics on political behavior are probably enhanced rather than reduced. Moreover, they have suggested some conditions which should enhance the impact of personal characteristics on political behavior. Greenstein (1969, p. 47) has rephrased this criticism in a manner appropriate to this discussion: "Under what circumstances do different actors (placed in common situations) vary in their behavior and under what circumstances is their behavior uniform?" Pro-posals (e.g., Greenstein, 1969; M. Hermann, 1976a; Holsti, 1973; Verba, 1969) of the circumstances under which political leaders' personal characteristics will influence policy focus on three types of conditions. Personal characteristics will have more impact on policy: (1) in situations that force the political leader to define or interpret them (e.g., ambiguous situations); (2) in situations in which the political leader is likely to participate in the decision-making process (e.g., crises); and (3) in situations in which the political leader has wide decision latitude (e.g., the "honeymoon" period following a landslide election).

The third criticism focuses on the organizational constraints which limit the expression of a leader's personal characteristics in policy. In effect, the critics argue that one of the ways organizations maintain their effectiveness is by the "complete elimination of personalized relationships and of nonrational considerations (hostility, anxiety, affectual involvements, etc.)" (Merton, 1940, p. 561). This criticism may be truer of those decision makers in the lower levels of an organization. There is some evidence to suggest that the personal characteristics of decision makers at higher levels in an organization may influence policy.

Snyder and Robinson (1961, p. 158) have observed from research on organizations "that when asked if personality plays as great (or greater) a part in behavior as organizational factors such as communication, officials who are at lower echelons tend to say no, while those at high echelons tend to say yes." Roles are less likely to be well-defined the higher in an organization one climbs; the role occupant has more responsibility for delimiting and/or expanding his functions. Furthermore, there are fewer, if any, people above one to change or modify the decision. Recall Truman's famous sign on his desk saying, "The buck stops here." Moreover, studies by Palumbo (1969) and Welling (1969) indicate that the higher a person is in the organizational hierarchy the fewer the organizational and role constraints which are placed on him and, in turn, the less specific the role of the individual, the greater his power. As Stassen (1972, p. 118) notes: "Top-level executives are not under tight hierarchical constraint . . . They must be persuaded and bargained with rather than simply commanded . . . Therefore, preferences and belief-sets are likely to be important for top-level executive decision-makers. . . ."

To date the debate on these three issues remains at the level of speculation, each side drawing support from research not primarily designed to assess the impact of a political leader's personal characteristics on his political behavior. As Holsti (1973, p. 9) states ". . . .these arguments are often the initial premises that guide, rather than the considered conclusions that emerge from, systematic research." The present chapter reports the results of some research explicitly designed to examine the relationship between the personal characteristics of political decision makers and their political behavior. The topic chosen is the relationship between certain personal characteristics of Congressmen and their votes on foreign aid.

In political bodies, particularly those in democracies, the one behavior which is easily retrieved is the vote on a legislative issue. Such is the case for the U.S. House of Representatives. Moreover, analyses of voting in Congress show that votes on foreign aid can be differentiated from votes on other policy issues (e.g.,

see Clausen, 1973; MacRae, 1958; Rieselbach, 1966). Clausen (1973) has argued
that votes on foreign aid form a policy dimension indicating a Congressman's
orientation or attitude toward international involvement. The Congressman
favoring foreign aid is interested in using national resources to play an active role
in international affairs, in interacting with other nations so as to influence what
happens in international affairs. The Congressman opposing foreign aid
"counsels the husbanding of national resources and takes a skeptical view of the
gains achieved by committing these resources to affect international relations"
(Clausen, 1973, p. 43). The focus of attention of the Congressman voting against
foreign aid is his own nation—its problems, its people, its wealth. Furthermore,
there is some suspiciousness of other nations and the uses toward which the aid
will be directed. On the other hand, the Congressman voting for foreign aid
focuses his attention on the world and his nation's role in it. Only through some
cooperative efforts among nations can the world and, in turn, one's own nation
be secure and continue to develop.

What personal characteristics might relate to a policy orientation toward
international involvement and, in turn, voting on foreign aid? Since the now
classic study of the authoritarian personality by Adorno, Frenkel-Brunswik,
Levinson, and Sanford (1950) first appeared, there have been a rash of studies
relating personal characteristics to policy orientations. Three characteristics seem
important in examining an orientation toward international involvement. These
three characteristics are *optimism, cognitive complexity,* and *humanitarian
ideology.*

Optimism refers to a general expectation of good or favorable outcomes in
the future and a general satisfaction with the present. In other words, the
optimistic individual makes positive references to how things are at present and
has positive expectations for the future. Moreover, the world is perceived as a
benign place in which to live. Public opinion studies report a positive relationship between optimism and interest in international involvement (e.g., see
Guetzkow, 1955; Kosa, 1957; Scott, 1965; Smith and Rosen, 1958). For the
optimist there is little to be lost and much to be gained in giving aid to other
countries. In contrast, the pessimist expects the worst—"the world is a jungle"—
and is little satisfied with the current state of affairs. As McClosky (1967, p. 74)
notes after examining questionnaire responses of political party leaders, the
pessimist regards "the world as a hostile, dangerous, or indifferent place, popu-
lated by potential enemies and harboring innumerable threats." He found such
individuals did not favor international involvement. Based on this discussion,
Congressmen who vote for foreign aid are expected to be more optimistic than
those voting against foreign aid.

The second characteristic, cognitive complexity, concerns the way an individual structures his world. How many dimensions does the person use in
characterizing his world and how many rules does he use in integrating the
resultant information (see Schroder and Suedfeld, 1971)? The individual who
uses many dimensions and many rules is considered to be cognitively complex;

the individual who uses few dimensions and few rules is considered to be cognitively simple. Adorno et al. (1950) found that the cognitively simple individual was given to stereotyping and to an ethnocentric view of other nations. The world is composed of definite ingroups and outgroups and one must be wary of who receives aid. On the other hand, Smith and Rosen (1958) report that world-minded individuals are less likely to stereotype. As Scott (1965) found, such individuals can differentiate among nations, categorizing and relating them along not just one but a series of dimensions. These dimensions provide rationales for granting aid. In the present study, then, we expect Congressmen who vote for foreign aid to be more cognitively complex than those voting against foreign aid.

Humanitarian ideology, the third personal characteristic, is defined in the present study as a frame of reference used in assessing and reacting to one's environment which involves a genuine concern for the welfare of others—an interest in the plight of people and a desire to help them. The converse of a humanitarian ideology is the frame of reference which assesses and reacts to the environment based on a concern for the consequences to the perceiver—how much can he benefit from the situation? A positive relationship between a humanitarian ideology and an attitude favoring international involvement is easily posed. Concern for others generalizes across national boundaries. And, indeed, several studies support such a relationship (e.g., Rosenberg, 1958; Smith and Rosen, 1958; Scott, 1960). Moreover, McClosky (1967) found that political party leaders in the U.S. (both Democrats and Republicans) who favored international involvement were more likely than those against international involvement to espouse humanitarian attitudes. Building on these studies, the expectation is that Congressmen who vote for foreign aid will have a more humanitarian ideology than those voting against foreign aid.

In sum, the present research examines the relationship between Congressmen's personal characteristics and their voting behavior. Congressmen voting for foreign aid are expected to favor international involvement and to be characterized by optimism, cognitive complexity, and a humanitarian ideology. The reverse will be true for Congressmen voting against foreign aid. They will favor little international involvement and will be pessimistic, cognitively simplistic, and have an ideology focused more on concern for self than others.[1]

Before describing the research, a brief methodological discussion is necessary. A major problem in assessing the personal characteristics of political leaders at

---

[1]There is a tendency in our society to value optimism, cognitive complexity, and a humanitarian ideology while finding their opposites—pessimism, cognitive simplicity, and self-orientation—less desirable. No value connotation is assigned to them in the present study. In fact, it is possible to conceive of instances for political leaders when being pessimistic, cognitively simple, or self-oriented could lead to more rather than less desirable behavior. For example, if the leadership were too satisfied, too willing to search for alternatives or information, or too open to the plight of others, their behavior might prove dysfunctional in a crisis situation where foreign troops have been mobilized at their nation's borders. The nation could be under attack while the leaders were still planning a response.

the national level is their relative inaccessibility to the usual measurement techniques—the personality test and the interview. Because of time limitations and reactions to the possible detrimental effects on one's career of personality data (witness the Eagleton affair), political leaders are less willing to be interviewed on this subject or to take personality tests. To overcome these problems, content analysis is used in the present study to assess the personal characteristics. Content analysis has been successfully employed in the study of personality with political leaders (e.g., see Eckhardt and White, 1967; Holsti, 1962; Shneidman, 1963). Such content analyses have focused on material available in the public record so that the cooperation of the subject was not required.

Content analysis, however, is not free of problems when used with political figures. One problem is "ghostwriting" or the writing of a political leader's comments by another. If, as in the present research, the investigator wants to ascertain the personal characteristics of a specific Representative, he needs to examine material communicated by the Representative himself not that written for him by another. The debates in the House of Representatives provide such material. The House of Representatives has a five-minute rule for speaking governing its debates which limits formal speeches; as a result the debates tend to be fairly extemporaneous exchanges among the members.

A second issue in using content analysis with political leaders focuses on the spontaneity of the communication. Is the response of the political leader planned or is it a spontaneous reaction? Several studies indicate the importance of spontaneous communication in the examination of personal characteristics. For example, Osgood and Anderson (1957) have found that the more carefully and deliberately planned the message, the more remote the link between a subject's attitudes and his message content. Moreover, Garraty (1959, p. 187), discussing public figures, indicated that they "reveal very little of themselves in their letters and autobiographies, held back either by personal inhibitions or by their ideas of conventionality." Analyzing Senator J. William Fulbright's foreign policy speeches, C. Downs (1963) reports changes in focus depending on the type of audience being addressed. Because the debates in the House of Representatives provide the forum for spontaneous interaction among the members, it was hoped that use of such debates would minimize planned communication.

Method

SAMPLE SELECTION

The subjects in this study are U.S. Representatives from the 81st Congress (1949-50). The particular subjects were chosen based on their votes for and against foreign aid measures considered by this Congress and on the number of times they spoke in debates on the floor of the House of Representatives.

The 81st Congress was selected as the focus for the study because of MacRae's (1958) extensive analysis of voting patterns of the Representatives in this Congress.[2] Using Guttman's (1944) scaling technique on roll-call votes in this session of Congress, MacRae developed a foreign aid scale. A roll-call vote is a vote which necessitates a roll call of the House of Representatives with each Representative present answering "yea" or "nay." Votes of this nature may be requested by one-fifth of the members present, are automatic on votes to override a presidential veto, and can be called for as an adjunct to a quorum call (absent members are summoned). There were 275 roll-call votes in this session of the House. Sixteen of these roll-call votes are included in MacRae's foreign aid scale. Seven of the scale votes dealt with the Economic Cooperation Administration (agency which distributed funds for the Marshall Plan), three with aid for Korea, two with the Export-Import Bank Act, two with foreign aid appropriations in general, one with participation in international organizations, and one with continuation of CARE. (For more detail on these votes and the scale see MacRae, 1958, pp. 237-240, 329.) Two other roll-call votes (*Congressional Record*, 1949, p. 3829; 1950, p. 16547) concerned with aid to China and Yugoslavia were added to the MacRae scale votes for purposes of this study. These two votes are the only controversial foreign aid issues discussed by the *Congressional Quarterly Almanac* (1949, 1950) for this session which were not included in some form in MacRae's scale. Moreover, the inclusion of the Yugoslavian vote permits a fuller test of foreign aid voting as an indicator of an orientation toward international involvement since it involves a nation in the Communist or "enemy" bloc.

Each Representative's responses to these 18 roll-call votes were tabulated. A minus one indicated a negative vote, a plus one a positive vote, and a zero non-voting.[3] Vote reversals were made for those issues on which a "nay" was a vote for foreign aid. The votes of some 422 of the 435 members of the House of Representatives were tallied in this manner. Twelve of the 13 not included in the tabulation were not in this Congress during the entire session (some died, others were appointed to fill empty positions). Moreover, Rayburn, as Speaker of the House, did not vote on any of the issues. From this tabulation the ten percent of the Representatives voting consistenly for foreign aid (favoring foreign aid in all or 17 of the 18 roll-call votes) were selected as typifying the pro-foreign aid position. The ten percent of the Representatives voting consistently against foreign aid (against foreign aid in from 12 to 18 of the votes) were selected as typifying the anti-foreign aid position.

Because the effective use of content analysis demands that a rather large amount of written material be analyzed, a search was made in the *Congressional Record* (1949, 1950), which contains the transcripts of House debates, for the

[2]This study was begun prior to the appearance of analyses of voting patterns on more recent Congresses (e.g., Clausen, 1973; Rieselbach, 1966), giving the author less choice than would now be available.

[3]Pairing of votes was considered nonvoting unless the paired Representatives indicated the direction of their vote.

Table 12.1.   Background Data on Representatives in Pro-foreign Aid
and Anti-foreign Aid Samples

Representative	Region of Country*	Party
Voting For Foreign Aid		
Biemiller	Great Plains	Democrat
Davenport	Middle Atlantic	Democrat
Deane	Southern	Democrat
Madden	Lake	Democrat
Mansfield	Rocky Mountain & Pacific	Democrat
Marshall	Great Plains	Democrat
O'Sullivan	Great Plains	Democrat
Spence	Border	Democrat
Walter	Middle Atlantic	Democrat
Yates	Lake	Democrat
Voting Against Foreign Aid		
Allen	Lake	Republican
Crawford	Lake	Republican
Curtis	Great Plains	Republican
Miller	Great Plains	Republican
O'Hara	Great Plains	Republican
Rankin	Southern	Democrat
Rich	Middle Atlantic	Republican
Short	Border	Republican
Taber	Middle Atlantic	Republican
White	Rocky Mountain & Pacific	Democrat

*The following are the states included in each of the regions: Southern—Alabama, Florida, Arkansas, Georgia, Louisiana, Mississippi, North Carolina, South Carolina, Tennessee, Texas, Virginia; Rocky Mountain & Pacific—Arizona, California, Colorado, Idaho, Montana, Nevada, New Mexico, Oregon, Utah, Washington, Wyoming; Border—Kentucky, Missouri, Maryland, Oklahoma, West Virginia; Middle Atlantic—New York, New Jersey, Pennsylvania, Delaware; Lake—Michigan, Ohio, Illinois, Indiana; Great Plains—Iowa, Kansas, Minnesota, Nebraska, North Dakota, South Dakota, Wisconsin. This division is taken from MacRae (1958, p. 261).

number of times each of the Representatives in the pro- and anti-foreign aid groups had spoken during this Congressional session. The examination revealed that 13 of those anti-foreign aid and 15 of those pro-foreign aid had said 120 or more words 25 or more times during this two-year session. The rest of the sample selection process focused on these 28 Representatives.

An attempt was made in selecting the sample of Representatives in the study to control for party and region of the country represented, two background variables which other researchers (e.g., Clausen, 1973; MacRae, 1958; Matthews, 1960) suggest are related to voting behavior. By controlling for these two background variables the present test of the relationship between personal characteristics and voting behavior is less contaminated by known influences on voting. However, given the Representatives who voted predominantly for and against foreign aid identified above, it was only possible to control for region of the country represented. Table 12.1 lists the ten Representatives voting consistently for and the ten Representatives voting consistently against foreign aid who were studied.

As shown in Table 12.1, most of the Representatives in the anti-foreign aid sample were Republicans (some 80 percent) while all of the Representatives in the pro-foreign aid sample were Democrats.[4] That such a finding is not unique to this study is reflected in Farris' (1958) analysis of voting in the 79th Congress. He found 96 percent of the Democratic Representatives responding to roll-call votes in support of international involvement while 65 percent of the Republican Representatives voted against international involvement. Moreover, McClosky (1967) reports that a greater percentage of the Republican party leaders he surveyed were against international involvement while a greater percentage of the Democrats favored international involvement. One characteristic, then, which appears to differentiate Representatives voting consistently for and against foreign aid is party. These data suggest control of the party variable is difficult when examining extreme voters on foreign aid issues.

MATERIAL ANALYZED

The material that was content analyzed in this study came from the debates on the floor of the House of Representatives as recorded in the *Congressional Record* for the years 1949-1950. A search was made of the *Congressional Record* in order to pinpoint where each Representative in the pro- and anti-foreign aid sample spoke and approximately how many words he said at one time. In the course of this inventory several criteria were imposed on a Representative's communication before it was counted. One criterion grew out of the following statement by Senator Richard Neuberger (1958, p. 94).

The House of Representatives allows far greater latitude even than the Senate in tolerating distortion of the *Congressional Record*. A member of the House can speak perfunctorily for two minutes on the floor and then receive unanimous consent "to revise and extend" his remarks. He later can transform such sweeping permission into an address of 60 minute proportions, which is published in the *Congressional Record* as though spoken in its entirety on the floor.

These Neuberger called "ghost" speeches. In order to avoid this type of communication as much as possible, no statement which was followed by a request "to revise and extend" one's remarks was counted. Further, no statements of

[4]The differences in party noted for the two samples of Representatives in the study are also characteristic of the other Representatives in the 10 percent voting consistently for or against foreign aid who were not included in the study. Eighty-four percent of the Representatives in the "left-over" group voting consistently against foreign aid were Republicans; 100 percent of the Representatives in the "left-over" group voting consistently for foreign aid were Democrats.

more than 900 words were tabulated, as well as no statements introduced or referred to as speeches. The last criterion concerned statements of less than 120 words. These were not counted since they were usually either factual in nature, requests for the floor, or statements of "Yes, I agree with so and so" or "No, I do not agree with so and so," with little else.

Following this search of the *Congressional Record,* 40 was chosen as the number of coding units to be analyzed for each of the Representatives in the sample. In order to keep the size of these 40 coding units constant, each coding unit was 120 words in length. Since most of the Representatives' statements exceeded this amount, the following procedure was evolved for selecting the particular 120 words to be content analyzed. Passages were chosen which made some reference to "I" and reflected (in this writer's mind) opinions as opposed to facts. An equal number of these coding units appeared in the beginning (first or second paragraph), the end (last or last two paragraphs), and the middle (between the paragraphs comprising the beginning and end) of the Representatives' statements which exceeded 120 words. Since it was not always possible to have the 120th word be the end of a sentence, the coding units were 120 words to the nearest complete sentence.

CODING CATEGORIES FOR PERSONAL CHARACTERISTICS

The particular coding schemes used to assess optimism, cognitive complexity, and humanitarian ideology will be presented briefly. The complete coding manuals for the characteristics are available from the author. In the course of coding for each characteristic in this study, presence of the personal characteristic was noted as well as presence of its opposite—pessimism, cognitive simplicity, and self-orientation. Each of a Representative's 120-word segments were scored as indicating presence of the characteristic, presence of its opposite, or neither (a neutral category).

Optimism.   In coding for optimism each coding unit or 120-word segment was examined to ascertain whether it contained statements indicating an expectation of a good or favorable outcome in the future, satisfaction with some area of life, or lack of feelings of anxiety and/or fear of danger in the present or future. If no indication of optimism was found, the coding unit was read again to see if it contained statements suggesting pessimism or an expectation of a negative or unfavorable outcome in the future, dissatisfaction with some area of life, or feelings of anxiety and/or fear of danger in the present or future. When optimistic statements were found, the coding unit was given a score of two; when pessimistic statements were found, the coding unit received a score of zero. When neither optimistic nor pessimistic statements occurred a neutral code or score of one was assigned the coding unit. If both optimistic and pessimistic statements were present, the end of the dimension which appeared to predominate was coded. Examples of statements which would indicate optimism and pessimism are found in Table 12.2. A Representative's score on this personal characteristic was the sum of the scores for his 40 coding units.

Cognitive Complexity.   Of interest in coding for cognitive complexity were statements in the coding unit that suggested varying reasons for a particular position, a willingness to entertain the possibility that there was ambiguity in one's environment (e.g., by the use of qualifying adjectives), or flexibility in reacting to objects or ideas in the environment. When such statements were present, the coding unit was given a score of two. Cognitive simplicity was indicated if the coding unit contained statements showing the choice of a position based on classifying objects into good-bad, black-white, either-or dimensions, an unwillingness to perceive ambiguity in the environment, or a tendency to react unvaryingly to objects or ideas in the environment. Coding units with statements suggesting cognitive simplicity were scored zero. Coding units with neither type of statement were scored one. Examples of cognitive complexity and simplicity are given in Table 12.2. As with optimism, a Representative's total score on this dimension was the sum of his scores over the 40 coding units.

Humanitarian Ideology.   In assessing humanitarian ideology, each coding unit was examined for statements indicating a concern for the welfare or the plight of others as well as a desire to help them. Generally such statements were part of the discussion of legislation which the Representative favored because it aided others. If such a theme was found in a coding unit, it received a score of two. In the present study the opposite of humanitarian ideology is self-orientation or the focus on one's own self-interests or those of one's group. Help is given only if it is to one's best interests. To code for self-orientation, statements indicating a lack of concern in helping others unless it served a personal interest as well as statements noting a general disdain for the plight of others, particularly if there was nothing to be gained in return, were sought in the coding unit. If such statements were found, the coding unit received a score of zero. If neither humanitarian nor self-oriented statements were found, the coding unit was scored one. Examples of humanitarian and self-oriented statements are reported in Table 12.2. A Representative's total score on this variable was the sum of the scores on his 40 coding units.

POLICY ORIENTATION

As discussed earlier, a Congressman's vote represents the sum of many pressures on him with regard to the issue under consideration. One hypothesis in the present study is that a major influence on a Congressman's vote on foreign aid issues is his policy orientation or attitude toward international involvement. Indeed, the hypotheses relating personal characteristics to voting behavior are based on this premise. In order to assess the relationship between orientation toward international involvement and vote on foreign aid issues, each coding

Table 12.2.   Examples of Statements Indicating Presence of a Coding Category

Optimism

1. Although there may be apprehension of inflation, I think we are in a better state today than ever before and will be in an even better one.

2. I am very satisfied with my position on this particular bill before us.

Cognitive Complexity

1. This situation which has arisen was not just the result of any conniving or scheming on the part of the insurance companies. Neither was it something that the Congress anticipated. Many factors contributed to its occurrence.

2. I do not usually support his positions, however, given his reasons for this bill I think I shall go along with him at this time.

Humanitarian Ideology

1. I feel that every legislator should carry out the gentleman's thought and that is that we do have an obligation to our fellow citizens.

2. I do not have too much respect for a man or a woman who always takes the position that the rights of the people are of little consequence.

Favor International Involvement

1. Point 4 shows that this country recognizes the interrelation of economic and political developments, and the interrelation of developments abroad and at home.

2. Our country should be helping to raise the level of education all over the world.

Pessimism

1. It is my feeling that business and thus the national economy has taken a turn for the worse.

2. I believe that such an undertaking would be ruinous and extremely risky.

Cognitive Simplicity

1. I feel this should be continued indefinitely; let us not change.

2. You do not kid anybody; when the great utilities and great communications systems and railroads have their taxes added to and added to, they are going to collect it from the poor and humble people that you and I serve.

Self-Orientation

1. I am not in favor of creating a precedent whereby a large number of other people might seek to claim military service and obtain extra compensation by helping these men.

2. I have voted against things that people wanted and needed on purpose because I am more interested in keeping our country solvent.

Against International Involvement

1. These nations have contempt for our form of government. I say it is time for us to get back home and look out for the American people.

2. We want to get rid of the leftists that are in the State Department and bring the State Department to the realization that they should look after the affairs of America and not assume all the responsibilities of the nations of the world, because we just cannot do it.

unit was scored for policy orientation. Interest in one's nation becoming involved internationally was indicated in a coding unit by statements showing a regard for other nations, a desire for an active role in international affairs, or the suggestion that by interacting with other nations one's own country would influence international relations. Generally such statements implied a view of the world in which more than the United States was perceived as comprising the primary in-group to which the Representative was responsive. Coding units with statements indicating an interest in international involvement were given a score of two. Statements in the coding units which placed great emphasis on the superiority of one's own nation and the importance of national honor and sovereignty with the suggestion that there was little to be gained and much to be lost in dealing with other nations were considered to indicate a lack of interest in international involvement. Statements denoting a disinterest in international involvement generally showed a view of the world in which *only* the United States was perceived as comprising the primary in-group, all other nations tended to be seen as having aims which differed in potentially threatening ways from those of the United States. Coding units containing statements manifesting disinterest in international involvement were scored zero. Coding units with neither type of statement were scored one. Table 12.2 gives illustrations of statements indicating interest and disinterest in international involvement. A Representative's score on this policy orientation was the sum of his scores across the 40 coding units.

The original plan in coding for policy orientation was to code statements that immediately preceded and succeeded the 18 roll-call votes on which the Representatives were selected. A search of the *Congressional Record,* however, revealed that less than one-half of the Representatives in either voting group had participated in the discussions of these issues. For this reason, all coding units were analyzed for policy orientation. Although this procedure does not provide as valid a check on the 18 roll-call votes used in the sample selection process, it does afford some data on each Representative's verbalized position.

CODING PROCEDURE

In order to allow for blind analysis of the coding units, identity of the Representatives was masked in the following manner. All those pages of the *Congressional Record* which contained statements included in the content analysis were xeroxed. References to names and places which might reveal who the speaker was to a coder were inked out. Each coding unit was then cut and pasted on a 5 x 8 card and given a number from 1 to 800. The coding units were arranged in chronological order. A list matching the number of a coding unit to a Representative was kept separate from the coding units and not referred to until the coding was complete for *all* categories.

The coding process *per se* proceeded in the following manner. Each dimension was coded separately. In other words, *all* 800 coding units were analyzed for optimism-pessimism before any was coded for cognitive complexity-simplicity. In order to avoid having the first coding units receive the most amateur coding on each dimension, every analysis was begun with a different part of the coding units.

Results

RELIABILITY

Three types of reliability were determined for the data in this study. The first concerned inter-coder agreement. Could another person use the rules developed by the author and code the categories arriving at the same judgments as the author? In order to ascertain the answer to this question, a second coder[5] examined and scored 100 coding units for each dimension in the study. A different set of 100 coding units was used for each dimension; the specific 100 were selected by means of a table of random numbers. The second coder received some training, consisting of reading the coding manual and doing ten sample exercises for each dimension. The scores for the sample units were discussed and an attempt was made to answer questions which were raised by the coding manual. Percentage of agreement between the author and the second coder for each dimension is listed in column two of Table 12.3.

Inter-coder agreement for the personal characteristics is not as high as that for the policy orientation. According to Berelson (1952), content analyses for personality traits have not yielded very high reliabilities primarily because categories of this nature depend heavily on inference and are not extremely conducive to explicit definition. For example, only through diligent and persistent exercises in training coders and refining their coding categories were the early researchers (see Atkinson, 1958) studying need for achievement, need for power, and need for affiliation able to achieve agreement levels of .80 and above. Since this research is a first attempt at category definition, reliabilities may be expected to be lower than .80.

An analysis of the coding errors suggests few disagreements on the categories for the personal characteristics when a decision was made that a trait was present. Disagreement occurred over whether statements indicating the presence of a personal characteristic had been made. As columns three and four in Table 12.3 indicate, of the disagreements between the two coders a small percentage involved one coder assigning one end of a dimension to the coding unit while the other coder assigned the other end of the dimension. A greater percentage of the disagreements occurred where one coder perceived the coding unit to contain statements indicating a personal characteristic and the other coder judged the coding unit as neutral or containing no statements which could be classified

[5]Thanks are due Charles Hermann for serving as the second coder.

Table 12.3. Inter-coder, Intra-coder, and Trait Reliabilities for the Coding Dimensions

Dimension	Inter-coder Reliability			Intra-coder Reliability	Trait Reliability
	% Agreement	% Disagreement on Direction of Content	% Disagreement on Presence of Category		
International Involvement	.93	.14	.86	.98	.78
Optimism	.68	.09	.91	.92	.76
Cognitive Complexity	.70	.20	.80	.90	.80
Humanitarian Ideology	.76	.13	.87	.94	.57

among the personal characteristics. This analysis of the disagreements among the coders suggests that one way to improve the inter-coder agreement among coders in any future use of these dimensions is to count the number of statements or sentences in each coding unit indicating the presence of a category. The coder focusing on the theme as in the present study is faced with a more difficult judgment than the coder merely counting statements, particularly when only one of the several statements in the coding unit suggests the presence of a characteristic.

Because the author did the majority of the coding in the study, a second important measure of consistency in the data is intra-coder reliability. How closely does the author agree with herself from the beginning to the end of the coding? Has the coding experience affected the scores so that what was coded first differs from that coded last? To ascertain within-coder agreement, the author re-coded the first 50 coding units of each dimension after finishing all 800 coding units for that dimension. The intra-coder agreement coefficients are found in column five of Table 12.3. These percentages of agreement are high enough to suggest a minimal effect of experience on the coding.

The third type of reliability calculated on the data was trait reliability. Trait reliability refers to consistency in the characteristics across time. Of interest is whether the dimensions under study are relatively invariant across time or related to a specific topic or situation and, as a result, vary across time. Consistency across time suggests that the dimension is fairly stable and not issue or situation-specific. In order to determine the consistency of the Representatives' characteristics across the coding units, split-half reliabilities were computed for each dimension. Odd- and even-numbered coding units were compared. What was odd and what was even was determined by the chronological order (order of occurrence in the *Congressional Record*) of the Representative's statements. The consistency values, corrected for length by the Spearman-Brown formula, are reported in column six of Table 12.3. Of the dimensions in the present study, humanitarian ideology seems the most affected by topic or situation. The other three dimensions exhibit some stability across time.

VOTING BEHAVIOR AND POLICY ORIENTATION

Table 12.4 shows that there is a significant difference between Representatives voting for and against foreign aid with regard to their interest in international involvement. Representatives voting for foreign aid speak in favor of United States international involvement more than Representatives voting against foreign aid. This finding suggests a consistency between policy orientation and voting behavior on this issue. The Representatives' spontaneous discussion of the relevance of United States international involvement is consistent with their votes on foreign aid.

Table 12.4. Differences Between Voting Groups on Coded Dimensions

| Dimension | Anti-foreign Aid Voting Group | | Pro-foreign Aid Voting Group | | t | df | p |
	Mean[a]	SD[b]	Mean[a]	SD[b]			
International Involvement	35.4	4.83	42.4	4.03	3.52	18	.006
Optimism	24.7 (.69)[c]	7.32 (.18)	40.6 (1.00)	7.66 (.19)	4.75 (3.84)	18	<.001 (.002)
Cognitive Complexity	31.1 (.84)	11.19 (.26)	42.8 (1.07)	11.47 (.26)	2.31 (2.00)	18	.036 (.06)
Humanitarian Ideology	47.9 (1.30)	6.76 (.20)	55.9 (1.43)	6.67 (.16)	2.67 (1.56)	18	.016 (.14)

[a]The mean represents the average of the scores for each voting group when anti-international involvement, pessimism, cognitive simplicity, and self-orientation equal zero; a neutral code (no category considered present) equals one; and pro-international involvement, optimism, cognitive complexity, and humanitarian ideology equal two.
[b]SD stands for standard deviation.
[c]Data in parentheses are for coding units with no reference to policy orientation toward international involvement.

VOTING BEHAVIOR AND PERSONAL CHARACTERISTICS

Table 12.4 also shows the differences which were found between the two voting groups on the personal characteristics. In each case the hypotheses were supported. There are significant differences between the Representatives voting for and against foreign aid on optimism, cognitive complexity, and humanitarian ideology. Representatives voting for foreign aid were more optimistic, more cognitively complex, and more humanitarian in outlook than Representatives voting against foreign aid. The latter group were more pessimistic, more cognitively simple, and more self-oriented.

The analysis, thus far, of the personal characteristics data includes all the coding units, even those units coded as indicating interest or disinterest in international involvement. Would the results differ if references to foreign content were deleted? In other words, are the differences reported above for Representatives voting for and against foreign aid merely a reflection of attitudes specific to one content domain, namely foreign affairs, or are these personal characteristics more general traits cutting across content domains? The results for the personal characteristics when coding units scored for policy orientation toward international involvement are deleted are found in parentheses in Table 12.4. Since there was a variable number of coding units remaining for each Representative after the policy orientation units were deleted, the mean score per coding unit was used in this analysis. These data show that there is still a significant difference between the two voting groups on optimism, with the difference on cognitive complexity close to significance. Only the humanitarian ideology characteristic is affected by deleting material with a foreign content. As noted earlier in exploring trait reliability, humanitarian ideology seemed most affected by topic or situation.

RELATIONSHIP OF POLICY ORIENTATION TO PERSONAL
    CHARACTERISTICS

At the outset of this study the policy orientation toward international involvement was posited as an intervening variable between a Representative's votes on foreign aid issues and his personal characteristics. In effect, the study focused on personal characteristics known to relate to an interest or disinterest in further international involvement. A pertinent question at this point is how does orientation toward international involvement, in fact, relate to the personal characteristics under study. Table 12.5 presents the correlations between policy orientation and personal characteristics as well as the interrelationships among the personal characteristics. Correlations are presented using all of the coding units and using only those coding units which were not coded for policy orientation. These latter correlations between policy orientation and the personal characteristics do not involve the same coding units and enable one to check the relationships when content differs. In other words, such correlations

Table 12.5.   Relationships among Dimensions for All Coding Units and Coding Units with No Reference to Policy Orientation

Dimension	1	2	3	4
1. International Involvement	—			
2. Optimism	.74** (.59**)[a]	—		
3. Cognitive Complexity	.72** (.61**)	.72** (.57**)	—	
4. Humanitarian Ideology	.52* (.29)	.55* (.37)	.31 (.23)	—

*p < .05   **p < .01

[a]Correlations in parentheses are for coding units for personal characteristics with no reference to policy orientation toward international involvement.

suggest to what extent policy orientation is generally—across issue and situation—related to the personal characteristics.

Table 12.5 indicates that interest in international involvement is greater the more optimistic the Representative is and the more cognitively complex he is. These relationships hold for all coding units and those units not scored for policy orientation. Moreover, optimism and cognitive complexity are positively related. These results when combined with the findings in other sections suggest that in Congressmen optimism and cognitive complexity are related to an interest in further international involvement and, in turn, consistent voting for foreign aid. On the contrary, pessimism and cognitive simplicity are related to a disinterest in further international involvement and consistent voting against foreign aid.

From Table 12.5 we also learn that humanitarian ideology is significantly related to policy orientation, but only when the content under examination deals with foreign affairs. The relationship diminishes in magnitude and is no longer significant when such content is not included.

Discussion

The results suggest that there are differences in the personal characteristics of Representatives voting for and against foreign aid. Moreover, the direction of a Representative's vote on foreign aid appears to reflect his policy orientation on the international involvement of the United States. Given the relationships among the personal characteristics and policy orientation, one possible explanation for the findings is that optimism and cognitive complexity are among the predisposing factors leading to a Representative's development of an interest in

United States involvement internationally. This policy orientation, in turn, leads the Representative to vote for foreign aid.

Such an interpretation is tempered, however, by the present researcher's inability to control for political party. Since at least eight of the ten Representatives in each voting group were affiliated with different political parties, party is a primary rival hypothesis for explaining the results of this research. The difference in the characteristics may merely reflect the personality types of Representatives who are Democrats and Republicans. Democrats are more optimistic and cognitively complex; Republicans are more pessimistic and cognitively simple. In order to distinguish the effects of party from those of policy position, further research is needed which focuses on the personality correlates of Democratic and Republican Representatives regardless of policy orientation and/or focuses on the most extreme voters for and against foreign aid within each party.

Granting the differences in party between the two voting groups, a modification of the first interpretation is possible. Utilizing the literature cited earlier (Farris, 1958; McClosky, 1967) which indicates that political leaders with an orientation toward further international involvement tend to be Democrats while political leaders with a disinterest in further international involvement are Republicans, it may be that party choice is a result of one's policy orientations and, in turn, one's personal characteristics. In other words, the Democratic Representatives in this study may be Democrats because they favor international involvement and tend to be optimistic and cognitively complex. Regardless, however, of the explanation of the differences between the voting groups which were found, the important result of this study remains intact. A Representative's personal characteristics and policy orientation are related to his political behavior—how he votes.

Several issues were raised in the course of this research which merit further discussion. The first concerns the nature of the personal characteristics. When we speak of a characteristic or trait, we think of an enduring or stable quality of an individual, something which is fairly consistent across topics and situations. In several of the analyses of these data, an attempt was made to ascertain if the characteristics under study were affected by specific topics. These analyses included the determination of trait reliability and the examination of the data using only those coding units which were not scored for policy orientation or, in effect, deleting most of the coding units dealing with foreign policy. Two of the characteristics, optimism and cognitive complexity, appeared to be fairly consistent across time and did not seem to be affected by whether the topics under discussion were domestic or foreign. The third characteristic, humanitarian ideology, was more topic-specific. Differences on this characteristic were more pronounced when foreign policy was under consideration than when the discussion focused on topics involving domestic content. Elected political leaders may have to suggest a humanitarian outlook toward their own constituents to remain in office whether or not such is their view of the world. Requisites of the role permit less manifest differences among Representatives along the humanitarian/self-oriented ideology dimension when the issues under discussion involve their constituents. Thus, two of the personal characteristics in the present study are more trait-like in quality and could conceivably affect a wide-ranging number of other policy orientations and votes dealing with both foreign and domestic topics. One characteristic is fairly topic-specific and will probably only affect policy orientations and votes involving foreign affairs.

A second issue raised in the course of the research centers around the relationship between policy orientation and roll-call vote. As studies rapidly accumulate suggesting the many influences on a Congressman's vote, the expectation of a direct relationship between a Representative's attitude toward an issue and his vote seems less realistic. Yet, in the present study, policy orientation differed with vote, at least for those Representatives most consistently voting for and against foreign aid. This result leads to two observations. First, the Representatives voting consistently for or against an issue may be those who have the strongest ideological positions on the issue. Representatives voting sometimes for and sometimes against an issue are probably those less persuaded by an ideological position on that issue and, therefore, are more open to other pressures in the legislative arena. Second, issues dealing with foreign policy, like that of foreign aid in the present study, may be more easily influenced by ideological position since some of the other pressures such as constituency pressure are less focused for foreign than domestic issues. The fact that the policy orientation categories in the present study were the most reliable and the easiest to code suggests the possibility of checking out these hypotheses by assessing the relationship between positions on other issues—e.g., race, welfare, agriculture—and votes.

A third issue which the data raise is related to the question of whether or not the findings in the present study would change or remain consistent across Congressional sessions, particularly those where there is a change in the party of the president. Clausen's (1973) analysis of roll-call votes indicates that Congressmen from the party of the president are more supportive of legislation increasing international involvement than Congressmen in the opposing party. So, did the Democratic Representatives in the present study retain their consistent voting pattern and verbal support of international involvement in the sessions when Eisenhower assumed the presidency? Research of this nature might also help to answer the question of interpretation raised by the inability to control for party in the present study. The personal characteristics are more likely to explain belonging to a specific party if there is a change across sessions; if there is consistency, the characteristics are more likely components of policy orientation. In sum, there is a need for further investigation of the relationship between Congressional voting and policy orientation.

One issue not discussed to this point but perhaps considered already by the astute reader concerns the validity of the personal characteristic categories. Do the categories tap the dimensions supposedly under study? One way of answering this question is by asking another. Are the personal characteristics assessed by content analysis similar to such characteristics when they are measured by questionnaire, interview, or observation? For example, is cognitive complexity as indicated in a Representative's speeches similar to cognitive complexity assessed by a Representative's responses to an established questionnaire measure of this trait? As noted earlier, the main reason content analysis was used in this research was the relative inaccessibility of national political leaders for the usual techniques of personality assessment. Validity studies are, thus, difficult at best. Several projects are, however, underway to attempt to establish, if indirectly, the validity of these personal characteristic categories. In one, conferences and messages written by participants in a series of Inter-Nation Simulation runs (C. Hermann, 1969; M. Hermann, 1966) are being content analyzed for these personal characteristics. Results from the content analysis will be compared with questionnaire scores for the personal characteristics on these same participants. The second project involves measuring the characteristics in a group of leaders-in-training by a variety of techniques and relating these scores to the results of a content analysis of their public speeches and interviews. These prospective leaders are training for jobs which will be political in nature.

In conclusion, the research described in this chapter has been exploratory. The sample of Representatives was small; the inter-coder reliabilities for the personal characteristics were not high; investigations of the validities of the characteristics are only now underway. However, the study does suggest a way of examining the relationship between a Congressman's personal characteristics and his political behavior. Moreover, the findings indicate that personal characteristics and policy orientations may be important influences on a Congressman's political behavior.

CHAPTER 13

Individual Differences as Determinants of Aggression in the Inter-Nation Simulation

Michael J. Driver

Editor's Introduction

We continue in Chapter 13 to examine how the personal characteristics of political leaders affect political behavior. However, whereas the previous chapter focused on the effect of a political leader's personal characteristics on his *own* political behavior, Driver in the present chapter focuses on how political leaders' personal characteristics affect the behavior of a political unit. In other words, political behavior is treated more broadly here than in the previous chapter. Driver hypothesizes that the personal characteristics of political leaders help to

*This chapter is part of a larger research effort, see Driver (1962, 1965). The author wishes to thank all who aided in the development of this particular analysis: Harold Guetzkow for his commentary, editing, and continued inspiration; Siegfried Streufert who provided significant contributions to this report as a result of many fruitful discussions; Harold Schroder who provided a theoretical framework without which the present analyses would not have been possible; Charles and Margaret Hermann and William Caspary who acted as readers and commentators; and Linda Beard, Robert Stevens, David Ayers, and John Terhorst who aided in the assembly of the text. Finally, the author is indebted to the National Institute of Mental Health Post-Doctoral Fellowship which provided the time and environment in which the bulk of the analysis was carried out.

335

determine the nature of the policy of a political unit. In this chapter, the political unit is the national government and the policy under examination is foreign policy, specifically the act of aggression on another country. One form of aggression which Driver explores is war. The impact which a political leader's personal characteristics can have on a national decision to wage war has fascinated scholars down through the ages. The present chapter presents some evidence to support such a linkage.

Several of the personal characteristics which Driver examines are similar types of variables to those which Hermann studied in the previous chapter. Driver is interested in two beliefs and one decision style variable. The two beliefs concern whether or not the political leader favors the use of force and whether the political leader perceives people to be generally good or bad. The decision style variable which Driver studies is conceptual complexity. Driver's conceptual complexity variable is similar to Hermann's cognitive complexity variable in the previous chapter. Driver also examines one mode of interpersonal interaction—how trusting the political leader is of others.

Driver's research raises an interesting question about the interaction among the personal characteristics of the leadership of a political unit in the formation of policy. How do the personal characteristics of the president and his cabinet, for example, mesh in affecting policy? If the personal characteristics of the leaders are fairly congruent, is the resulting policy different from that when the personal characteristics are incongruent? Driver's study does not provide any answers to these questions since he only examines nations where the leaders have congruent personal characteristics. His research, however, does suggest that when dealing with the behavior of a political unit, knowledge about the mix among the personal characteristics of the leaders may provide important insights into resulting policies. We will return to this point in the introduction to Chapter 16. Druckman in Chapter 16 presents research on negotiation which attempts to come to grips with how the similarity or dissimilarity among the personal characteristics of negotiators affects the outcome of bargaining.

The present chapter introduces the second emphasis of this section of the book. This theme concerns the importance of situational variables in enhancing or reducing the relationship between political leaders' personal characteristics and political behavior. As Hermann noted in the beginning of the last chapter, there are three types of circumstances which are proposed in the literature (see Greenstein, 1969; M. Hermann, 1976a; Holsti, 1973; Verba, 1969) as enhancing the relationship between personal characteristics and political behavior. Personal characteristics are likely to affect policy: (1) in situations in which the leader has wide decision latitude; (2) in situations that force the leader to define or interpret them; and (3) in situations in which the leader is likely to participate in the policy-making process. Driver's results add yet another condition to this list—the more situation-sensitizing the leader's personal characteristics. Some personal characteristics appear to make individuals more aware or sensitive to their environment so that the nature of the situation plays an important part in their decision making. With these characteristics the individual seeks out cues in the situation to aid in decision making. To the contrary, other personal characteristics reduce an individual's attention to his environment and, in turn, reduce the impact of the situation on decision making. Such characteristics lead the individual to re-interpret the situation to fit preconceived categories and schema. Interestingly, Ziller and his associates in Chapter 8 show that individuals who are sensitive to their environment—have low self-esteem and high complexity—are likely to be elected. More research like Driver's in the present chapter and that of Ziller et al. is needed to learn which personal characteristics sensitize an individual to his environment and which cues in the environment, in turn, affect the nature of the decisions such individuals make.

Driver uses simulation to explore the relationship between political leaders' personal characteristics and political behavior. In other words, he studies the impact of personal characteristics on political behavior in an abstract, simplified model of reality. Driver uses the Inter-Nation Simulation which is a person-machine simulation of relations among nations. Simulation allows the researcher some control over the situations that the political leader experiences, which is not generally available to the researcher in the field. Moreover, simulation provides the researcher with the opportunity to study problems for which "real world" data are inaccessible and to explore hypothetical situations, examining the effects of certain input variables on outcomes. The use of simulation, however, raises the problem of validity. How generalizable are the findings from the simulation to "real world" phenomena? For example, is it appropriate to generalize from high school students, who were Driver's subjects, to heads of state and their cabinets, the objects of the present chapter? Driver has been concerned with this issue and reports that analyses of the relationships between the conceptual structures of Truman, Stalin, and Kennedy and their political behavior parallel the results presented in this chapter. Truman and Stalin acted much like the low complexity participants in the simulation while Kennedy functioned like the high complexity participants (see Driver and Lintott, 1974).

Driver, a psychologist, is a professor of business administration at the University of Southern California. He has long been interested in the effects of differences in conceptual structure on behavior. The research reported here was the first in a series of studies examining how individuals differing in conceptual structure reacted to different types of decision situations (see Schroder, Driver, and Streufert, 1967).

THE RESEARCH FOCUS of this chapter is the relationship between characteristics of policy makers and inter-nation aggression. The study uses data gathered in a series of 16 runs of the Inter-Nation Simulation in the summer of 1960. The Inter-Nation Simulation (INS) is a person-machine simulation, combining the activity of human participants with a set of machine computations. For a detailed description of the INS in general and this series of runs in particular, see Brody (1963), Driver (1962), Guetzkow (1959), and Guetzkow, Alger, Brody, Noel, and Snyder (1963).

Each run in this INS series consisted of seven simulated nations, with every nation managed by three office holders. The policy makers for each simulated nation were a head of state responsible for economic planning and overall strategy, a combined minister for foreign affairs and defense, and a representative to the international organization of the simulation. Moreover, every nation had a unique, partly programmed economy, voter reaction pattern, and military establishment. The decision makers could change these factors through varied allocations of their basic resources. Their decisions interacted with the underlying programmed parameters for the nation and the results were fed back to the decision makers, thus assuming a continuous development of the nation. Military development, wars, and defense were also partly determined by underlying parameters and partly by the decision makers. Alliances, treaties, and trading were freely arranged according to the participants' wishes. Each run of this INS series lasted four days, with the nations operating four hours a day. The subjects who assumed the roles of policy makers were high-school students, mostly juniors and seniors.

In all 16 runs of this INS series some form of inter-nation aggression occurred. Serious nuclear wars occurred in five runs. Although by no means the same as war in reality, these simulation wars represent cases of emotional strain in which participants could and did lose the fruits of many days' hard work. Moreover, a nation was generally staffed by three members of the same high school, with each nation staffed by a different school. Thus, in addition to simulation developed loyalties, school rivalry added additional significance to inter-nation war in INS. For these reasons, a deliberate attack on another nation with weapons which could destroy that nation is viewed as a form of serious aggression. In this regard, let me state at the outset that it is not the burden of the chapter to present causes of real wars, but rather to present determinants of general aggression in a situation very like the international realm in many particulars (see Caspary, 1962; Brody, 1963).

The same position is maintained with respect to acts of aggression other than war; the results in these areas may provide clues in the search for causes of international tension. Included in this category of aggressive acts are: (a) unprovoked arms increase, (b) provoked arms increase, and (c) war plans. Unprovoked arms increase is defined as an increase in nuclear force by a nation already possessing military superiority, following a decrease or nonchange in force by a militarily inferior rival; or an increase by an inferior power to a level well beyond the other nation's level, following a decrease or nonchange in arms by the superior power. Such an action usually signifies hostile intent and is considered an act of serious aggression second only to war itself. Unprovoked arms increase occurred in 7 of the 16 runs in this INS series. Provoked arms increase refers to a case where a militarily inferior nation increases nuclear force to a level near or equal to that of its rival, following a decrease in the rival's nuclear force. Such an act of increase in arms following a decrease by a rival is aggressive, but in view of the higher absolute level of the rival it is not unprovoked. Two of the runs in this series had provoked arms increases. The final category—planning war with no decision reached—is self-explanatory. It is hostile, but not seriously aggressive since no overt action is decided upon. War plans occurred in 2 of the 16 runs.

The occurrence of 7 runs with unprovoked arms increase, plus 5 war runs, means that in 12 out of 16 runs serious aggression occurred in this series of INS runs. Using the binomial test (Siegel, 1956), the probability of such high incidence of serious aggression by chance is only .038; that is, serious aggression was significantly frequent in these INS runs. Adding the 4 runs with milder aggression, it appears that in all 16 runs some form of aggression occurred. Clearly aggression in simulations, as in reality, is not only a serious problem but also a frequent one.

The remainder of this chapter will examine the relationship between four individual difference variables and aggression in these INS runs. The four individual difference variables studied are: (1) characteristic level of complexity of conceptual or cognitive structure, (2) attitude on the use of force, (3) general ideology, and (4) level of trust.

By characteristic level of complexity of conceptual structure is meant the number and linkages among the concepts which underlie information processing (see Schroder, Driver, and Streufert, 1967; Driver and Streufert, 1969). Individuals are considered to have a high level of complexity, the greater the number of dimensions they use in describing stimuli and the greater the number of rules they use in integrating the dimensions into a coherent whole. Research on this personality variable in complex social situations shows that people with low levels of complexity have a small response repetoire (Driver and Streufert, 1969; Schroder, 1971; Schroder, Driver, and Streufert, 1967). One can conceive that when put into a stressful situation in the INS, persons with low levels of complexity will have few nonaggressive options. Such persons will view the international situation as one of war or peace, and when threatened have no alternative to war. The complex individual, on the other hand, can conceive of other ways to signal aggressiveness short of war.

The second individual difference variable, attitude on the use of force, bears an obvious relation to aggression. Clearly the more a man favors force, the more likely he is to employ violence with little or no provocation.

General ideology, the third individual difference variable, is related to aggression in a more diffuse manner. A major factor in general ideology is a man's view of others. More particularly, does the individual have a positive or negative view of others—does he expect the best or worst from others? The person with the negative or more normative ideology, in contrast to the person with the positive or more humanistic ideology, is likely to magnify the intensity of a threat, inducing a subjective stress greater than conditions objectively warrant. In other words, a normative, negative ideology will lead to more aggression than a more humanistic, positive ideology.

A final individual difference variable to be related to aggression is trust. Trust, like ideology, acts as a filter in the perception of threat. A high state of trust reduces the credibility of any threat and as a result reduces the necessity for aggressiveness. A low level of trust, on the other hand, tends to increase threat credibility and, in turn, increases the incidence of aggressive behavior.

These four variables were measured as follows. Level of complexity was measured by a form of the Situational Interpretation Test (SIT) developed by Schroder and Hunt (1959). The SIT consists of a series of forced-choice items which indicate a person's preferred interpretation of criticism. Previous work (Driver, 1960; Janicki, 1964; Schroder, Streufert, and Clardy, 1961; Streufert, 1961) has indicated that criticism, a form of stress, is interpreted in different ways by persons showing behavioral characteristics of varying levels of complexity. In taking the SIT, individuals are asked to imagine their reactions to criticism in a wide range of situations. For each critical situation, the respondents indicate their preference towards each of four possible reactions. Each of these reactions is believed typical for one of four increasingly more complex levels of personality structure. Four separate scores were computed per person; one score for each of the four sets of responses corresponding to the four theoretical levels of complexity—I (low complexity) to IV (high complexity). The complexity level in which a person had his highest score was assigned as his level of complexity.

Attitude toward the use of force was measured by an item from the Tomkins' (1964) Polarity Scale. The particular item contrasted the statement "no one has the right to threaten or punish another person" with the statement "some people respond only to punishment or the threat of punishment." In responding to this item, an individual checked which statement he preferred and then for each statement noted on a six-point scale whether the statement was "extremely like my view" to "extremely unlike my view." Ratings for the pro-force statement were given positive scores (0 to 5); ratings for the anti-force statement were given negative scores (0 to 5). An individual's attitude toward the use of force was the algebraic sum of these two ratings. A minus score, then, indicated a generally anti-force view; a plus score indicated a generally pro-force view.

General ideology was measured by total score on the Tomkins' (1964) Polarity Scale. This scale consists of 25 pairs of items like that discussed under attitude on the use of force. One item in each pair always takes a more humanistic, trusting view while the other item always is more normative, hostile, and suspicious. Items cover such topics as child education, law, play, science, government, friendship, and the nature of man. In scoring for general ideology, the ratings for the paired statements were ignored; only the preference boxes were used. Scoring consisted of counting the total number of humanistic statements receiving preference checks.

One way to assess an individual's level of trust is through the F Scale (Adorno et al., 1950). Some four studies (Ashmore, 1969; Berkowitz, 1968; Deutsch, 1960; Wrightsman, 1966) have shown that high F people enter into experimental games less trusting of others than low F people. For purposes of the present analysis, individual scores on the California F Scale were cast into quartiles.

If scores on the four variables of complexity, attitude on force, general ideology, and trust had been computed for all nations in this series of INS runs, the task of analyzing the data would have been formidable. Moreover, for about half of each run only two nations possessed the nuclear capability for serious aggression. These two nations, which were the large powers (LP's), were the perpetrators of all aggression with the exception of one war. In order to reduce the data to manageable proportions and to consider groups continuously capable of nuclear aggression, the analysis of individual differences in this series of runs will focus only on the two large powers (LP's) in each run.

In each run, one LP had a generally high level of complexity among its members, while the other LP had a generally low level of complexity. In other words, the three decision makers assigned to one LP were generally of the highest level of complexity while the three decision makers assigned to the other LP were generally of the lowest level of complexity. In effect, then, in these 16 INS runs there were 16 LP's that were high and 16 LP's that were low in complexity.

With regard to the other individual difference variables, raw scores have been transformed into dichotomous categories by dividing each variable's raw score distribution at the median. This dichotomous categorization was used because the scaling of these variables is too uncertain to allow more than rough categorization. The categories are defined in the following way. F scores are the sum of the F Scale quartile scores for the three decision makers in an LP. LP's with F scores above the median F (7.5) were considered "HI" in distrust; those with scores below the median, "LO." Ideological scores are the average of the Tomkins' scale scores for the three decision makers in an LP with group scores above the median in humanism (14.6) being termed "HUM" while those below the median were called "NOR" (i.e., normative). Attitude on force scores represent the sum of the combined pro- and anti-force ratings for each of the three decision makers in an LP. Scores above the median (1.5) in a pro-force direction were considered "PRO" while those below the median were considered "ANTI." As these category definitions indicate, all the labels are relative and dependent on the samples tested; but as a basis for discovering essential relationships, these dichotomized scores seem appropriate.

A question preliminary to an examination of the relationship between these individual difference variables and aggression concerns the interrelationships among the individual difference variables themselves. A series of median tests (Siegel, 1956) were applied to all pairs of variables. Only one significant relationship emerged: complexity and F scores were inversely related with a chi square of 8.17 ($df = 1$; $p = .005$). This result confirms previous findings of a negative correlation between F and complexity (e.g., Schroder, Driver, and Streufert, 1967) and should be borne in mind while interpreting the results to follow.

The rest of this chapter will deal with how these individual difference variables relate to aggression in this series of INS runs, in particular, aggression in general, serious aggression, and particular forms of serious aggression, such as war and unprovoked arms increase. An inquiry into how general aggression is related to these individual differences will initiate the analysis.

Individual Differences and General Aggression

The central problem of this discussion is why 22 LP's in this series of INS runs exhibited aggression of some kind while only 10 LP's displayed no measured aggression. Let us first examine the factors related to nonaggression in this INS. One can scan the 10 nonaggressive cases to see what variable is significantly present in all cases. The only variable which appears to be "necessary"[1] for nonaggression is complexity. In Table 13.1, note that 9 out of 10 cases of nonaggression involve high complexity LP's. Using the binomial test (Siegel, 1956), we conclude that the number of high complexity LP's among the nonaggressive cases is significantly greater than the number expected by chance ($p = .02$). High complexity is statistically necessary for nonaggression, but it is not a "sufficient cause"[2] of nonaggression; that is, we cannot say that high complexity *per se* implies nonaggression. Nine out of 16 high complexity LP's were nonaggressive, which does not significantly depart from chance expectancy. A search among the other variables reveals that none of them could serve as sufficient causes of nonaggression. Hence, if we seek for factors which sufficiently cause nonaggression, we must look to other areas, perhaps situational phenomena.

Turning to the other side of the problem, we can ask what variable is significantly present in the 22 aggressive cases. The variable which comes closest to a necessary cause of aggression is low complexity. In Table 13.1, note that 15 out of 22 cases of aggression involved low complexity LP's. The probability of such association by chance is not quite significant ($p = .067$, binomial test). No other variable even approaches being a necessary ingredient in aggression. On the other hand, there is no shortage of statistically sufficient causes for aggression. With 15 out of 16 cases aggressive, low complexity is the most impressive factor determining aggression ($p = .001$, binomial test). In decreasing order we have

[1] In this analysis, association measures will be given semi-causal implications. For instance, any personality variable which is found to be significantly present in a given aggression state will be called a "necessary" factor for that aggression state.

[2] Any personality variable which has a significant number of its cases in a given aggression state is termed a "sufficient cause" of that aggression state; that is, the presence of that personality variable in and of itself seems to induce that aggression state. Causality is assumed since aggression is measured after personality.

Table 13.1.　General Aggression and Individual Differences in INS (N = 32 LP's)

	Distrust (F)		General Ideology		Force View		Level of Complexity	
	Hi	*Lo*	*Hum*	*Nor*	*Pro*	*Anti*	*Hi*	*Lo*
Aggression	12	10	12	10	13	9	7	15
Nonaggression	4	6	4	6	3	7	9	1
X^2	<1.00		<1.00		<1.00		7.12	
p	n.s.		n.s.		n.s.		<.005	

pro-force attitude with 13 out of 16 cases aggressive ($p = .011$, binomial test) followed by high F with 12 out of 16 cases aggressive ($p = .038$, binomial test). However, with the exception of high complexity, the other categories of each of these variables (i.e., anti-force, low F) also tend toward aggression.

In Table 13.1 note that for only one variable is there a significant difference in the incidence of aggression between the two categories of the variable. Comparing the incidence of aggression vs. nonaggression between high and low complexity LP's, we obtain a chi-square of 7.12 ($p = .005$, median test). In other words, the high complexity LP's were significantly less aggressive than the low complexity LP's. The continued prominence of conceptual structure in this analysis raises some interesting questions. Are the ideological attitude variables really as important as the conceptual structural variable? Might not attitude variables occupy a largely supplemental role?

For instance, low complexity is a statistically sufficient and nearly necessary cause of aggression. Can it be that attitudes, such as those favoring violence, merely enhance tendencies toward aggression in the low complexity individual? Might such attitudes be sufficient causes of aggression only for low complexity LP's? The answer in this case is yes. For low complexity LP's, 11 out of 12 high F cases were aggressive ($p = .006$, binomial test) while all 9 normative ideology and pro-violence cases were aggressive ($p = .002$, binomial test). On the other hand, for high complexity LP's, only 1 out of 4 high F cases was aggressive (not significant); 1 out of 7 normative ideology cases was aggressive (not significant); and 3 out of 6 pro-violence cases were aggressive (not significant).

Armed with these facts, one can conclude that conceptual structure is a key determinant in the outbreak of aggression, at least in INS. Nonaggression seems highly unlikely except in conceptually complex groups. Aggression seems to emerge in a low complexity group almost by necessity, particularly if the group members have normative, pro-force attitudes and tend to be distrustful. But how can we tell what kind of aggression to expect? Can these variables predict when aggression will be serious as opposed to minor? The discussion will now focus on the answers to these questions.

Individual Differences and Serious Aggression

Serious aggression is defined as war or unprovoked arms increase. Minor aggression includes provoked arms increase and conjectural war planning. We are interested in explaining how individual differences relate to these phenomena, particularly to serious aggression. The relevant material is presented in Table 13.2.

Because minor aggression as defined in this study was such an infrequent occurrence, almost any meaningful statement about it is impossible. An examination of the individual difference data indicates only that high complex-

Table 13.2. **Serious Aggression and Individual Differences in INS**
(*N* = 32 LP's)

	Distrust (F)		General Ideology		Force View		Level of Complexity	
	Hi	*Lo*	*Hum*	*Nor*	*Pro*	*Anti*	*Hi*	*Lo*
Serious Aggression	11	4	7	8	9	6	4	11
Minor or No Aggression	5	12	9	8	7	10	12	5
X^2	5.55		<1.00		<1.00		5.55	
p	.01		n.s.		n.s.		.01	

ity is important in predicting minor aggression as opposed to no aggression. For three high complexity LP's, one or more minor aggressions occurred; while for nine high complexity LP's, there was no aggression. For five low complexity LP's one or more minor aggressions occurred; for only one low complexity LP was there no aggression. A Fisher exact probability test (Siegel, 1956) finds this pattern significant ($p = .05$). Low complexity LP's significantly exceeded high complexity LP's in acts of minor aggression. However, this result hinges on the known difference between low and high complexity LP's in nonaggression; thus, any conclusions on minor aggression must be made with caution. For the remainder of this analysis, minor aggression will be grouped with nonaggression in an attempt to pinpoint causes of serious aggression.

As can be seen in Table 13.2, 11 out of 15 cases of serious aggression occurred in low complexity LP's. Using the binomial test, it appears that an almost necessary condition for serious aggression is low complexity in conceptual structure ($p = .059$). High F scoring (distrustful) LP's had precisely the same frequency of serious aggression as low complexity LP's, indicating that high F scores may also be a nearly necessary condition for serious aggression. Thus, when serious aggression occurs, it is likely to be found in LP's with low complexity or high F members. However, LP's with such scores need not always be seriously aggressive. Only 11 out of 16 LP's in either the high F or low complexity categories were seriously aggressive ($p = .10$, binomial test). On the other hand, low F and high complexity LP's significantly avoided serious aggression ($p = .038$, binomial test). Hence, Table 13.2 shows that high F and low complexity LP's more frequently engaged in serious aggression than low F and high complexity LP's (chi-square = 5.55, $p = .01$). While neither high F nor low complexity alone necessitate serious aggression, high F *plus* low complexity is a sufficient cause of serious aggression. Of the 12 LP's with high F scores and a low complexity conceptual structure, 10 engaged in serious aggression ($p = .014$, binomial test). Among the 11 cases of serious aggression in low complexity LP's, 10 had high F scores ($p = .006$, binomial test). Thus, high F is statistically both a necessary and sufficient cause of serious aggression among low complexity LP's in this series of INS runs. Among high complexity LP's no such relationship emerges.

To summarize this and the previous section, it appears that aggression is a very frequent outcome of low complexity in conceptual structure, particularly if F (distrust) is high and force is favored; high complexity in conceptual structure is one necessary condition for nonaggression. Furthermore, while serious aggression may require either high F or low complexity as statistically necessary conditions for its occurrence, high F plus low complexity seem to necessitate serious aggression. Given these findings, can we forecast the specific form of serious aggression which will result? Can we predict either unprovoked arms increase or war as a function of F scores, of complexity, or of other attitudes? We will now consider answers to such questions.

Unprovoked Arms Increase, War, and Individual Differences

The data relating individual difference variables and unprovoked arms increases is presented in Table 13.3. No necessary causes of unprovoked arms increase can be found in our data; although low complexity with 9 out of 12 cases (p = .07, binomial test) comes close. Similarly no single variable emerges as a sufficient cause of unprovoked arms increase. However, both high complexity and low F LP's significantly avoid unprovoked arms increase (p = .01 for high complexity LP's and p = .038 for low F LP's, binomial test). Furthermore, low complexity LP's engage in unprovoked arms increase significantly more often than high complexity LP's (chi-square = 5.21, p = .01). Again the key variable appears to be complexity with F in a secondary role.

Considering high and low complexity cases separately, it appears that high F is necessary (p = .02, binomial test) but not sufficient (p = .13, binomial test) for unprovoked arms increase among low complexity LP's but such is not the case for low F among high complexity LP's. We conclude that high F plus low complexity is important in unprovoked arms increases, and that either low F or high complexity implies the absence of this form of aggression. However, there are clearly other causes of unprovoked arms increase, possibly situational in nature, involved in a complete explanation of this kind of aggression.

With respect to war itself, the only apparently necessary condition is high F which is found in all 5 of the war cases; both low complexity and pro-force attitudes come close, being involved in 4 out of the 5 war cases, but do not reach significance (p = .18, binomial test). These data are found in Table 13.4. No sufficient causes of any sort can be found in the data. In fact, all groups significantly *avoid* war except high F, low complexity cases. Thus, although we can say that high F plus low complexity implies serious aggression, we cannot say whether this aggression will be war or unprovoked arms increase.

**Interrelationship of Conceptual Structure, Attitudes,
    and Situation in Aggression**

The conceptual complexity variable emerges as a critical individual difference in forecasting aggression in this series of INS runs. High complexity groups seem to be nonaggressive or mildly aggressive, avoiding serious aggression, particularly war. The picture for low complexity groups is nearly reversed. Low complexity in conceptual structure implies the occurrence of some kind of aggression. Serious aggression—specifically, unprovoked arms increase—occurs more often in low complexity LP's than in high complexity groups. The picture is clarified by considering attitudes among low complexity LP's. High distrust (F) and pro-violence attitudes enhance the trend towards aggression. Moreover, high F in low complexity LP's implies serious aggression as an almost necessary outcome and explains much of the unprovoked arms increase in this series of INS runs.

Table 13.3.   Unprovoked Arms Increase and Individual Differences in INS
(N = 32 LP's)

	Distrust (F)		General Ideology		Force View		Level of Complexity	
	Hi	Lo	Hum	Nor	Pro	Anti	Hi	Lo
Unprovoked Arms Increase	8	4	6	6	6	6	3	9
No Unprovoked Arms Increase	8	12	10	10	10	10	13	7
X^2	<1.00		<1.00		<1.00		5.21	
p	n.s.		n.s.		n.s.		.01	

low complexity LP's. Due to the small number of low complexity LP's with stress-diminishing attitudes (two runs), these are combined with low complexity LP's having nondistorting attitudes in this table. Table 13.5 indicates that the more stress-inductive the attitudes of low complexity LP's were, the more likely serious aggression in that run of INS ($p < .005$, Fisher exact probability test, Siegel, 1956).

In summary, our discussion has shown that much of INS aggression was due to the very low aggression thresholds of low complexity groups, especially when they had stress-inductive attitudes. Much of INS nonaggression was due to the very high aggression thresholds of high complexity groups. The few low complexity groups with stress-diminishing attitudes also seemed to avoid aggression. Moreover, at least for high complexity LP's, the inherent stress in the situation itself was important for triggering aggression.

The relevance of this study to the examination of the effects of a political leader's individual characteristics on his political behavior should be readily apparent by now. The data suggest what high-level political leaders with certain structural and attitudinal characteristics will urge on their nations. Violence-oriented, low complexity leaders may be prone to aggression regardless of the situation. In fact, this potential insensitivity of low complexity leaders to situational phenomena underlines the importance of understanding leader personality. On the contrary, high complexity leaders are likely to be more cautious, only being aggressive when provoked and undeterred.

Some caution is warranted in the direct extrapolation of this simulation research to the international arena. Others (e.g., Guetzkow, 1968; C. Hermann, 1967; Snyder, 1963) have discussed the problems in such extrapolation. The INS, however, as used in this study permitted an empirical investigation of a "real world" problem which is difficult, if not impossible, to explore in a field setting.

CHAPTER 14

Verbal Behavior of Negotiators in Periods of High and Low Stress: The 1965-66 New York City Transit Negotiations

Margaret G. Hermann

Editor's Introduction

In this chapter, Hermann changes the focus of attention from an examination of traits or more stable personal characteristics to states or more transient personal characteristics. In the previous two chapters the personal characteristics under study were considered to be fairly consistent across different kinds of situations. For example, the optimistic political leader tends to be optimistic regardless of the circumstances. (Although, as Hermann noted in Chapter 12, characteristics which one might consider fairly stable, such as humanitarian ideology in that chapter, may, in fact, prove situation- or topic-specific.) Now we are going to turn to a study of characteristics which are more situation-specific or, in other words, tend to change as the situation changes. Hermann in this chapter explores how political leaders indicate that they are experiencing stress and how they react to stress. The situation which she examines is the 1965-66 New York City transit negotiations—negotiations which culminated in one of that city's longest and costliest strikes. Hermann compares the verbal behavior of the major parties to the negotiations at less and more threatening points during the course of the bargaining to see how their reactions changed as stress increased.

Hermann uses a three-step model of stress which involves the existence of a threat to a political leader's policies, the arousal of the political leader's negative affects or feelings, and some behavior on the part of the political leader to cope with his feelings or the threat. The particular types of personal characteristics that are examined in this chapter are negative affects and coping behaviors. The presence of negative affects or feelings indicates that the individual is experiencing stress. Coping behaviors describe what the individual is doing to reduce the stress. Because a political leader's ways of dealing with stress may have important consequences for his political unit, there has been a growing interest among social scientists in delimiting what coping behaviors lead to what political unit decision processes and outcomes. Thus, we have discussions, for example, on national political leaders that include Janis' (1972) notions on "groupthink" and George's (1974) description of nine possible presidential malfunctions in coping behavior as well as many case analyses of the participants in such stressful events as the outbreak of World War I, Korean decision, Cuban missile crisis, and Watergate. Hermann's results in the present chapter lend support to the contention that a political leader's own way of coping with stress will have implications for the behavior of his political unit. How the principal parties to the transit negotiations dealt with the threats in the situation influenced both the duration and direction of the negotiations.

The research in the present chapter is similar in many respects to that of Frank in Chapter 3. Both studies involve content analysis using paralinguistic coding categories. Paralinguistic refers to the noncontent aspects of speech, i.e., the manner in which one speaks and the types of words that are used. The paralinguistic indicators of stress which Hermann and Frank use are fairly easy to code since the indicators focus on single words or, at the most, phrases. Frank goes further than Hermann by examining the nonverbal behavior (nods, blinks, gross bodily movements) of his subjects as well as their paralinguistic behavior. A nonverbal analysis of Hermann's subjects would be possible since she has films of the press conferences which she used. Such an analysis, however, has not been done to date.

The Hermann and Frank studies as well as those of Johnson in Chapter 4 and Milburn in Chapter 6 are essentially research with an N of 1. Each of these authors has examined the personal characteristics of one political leader at a time. These researchers were interested in how a specific political leader's personal characteristics changed across issues, time, judges, and with increased threat. The drawback to these N of 1 studies is that the results are not generalizable to other political leaders than the one under study. Such research, however, would seem to have important policy implications. If one knows, for example, how a particular political leader manifests and reacts to stress, such information might prove instructive to the political leader and to others who are dependent on his judgment during stressful situations. Recently M. Hermann and C. Hermann (1975) have proposed that staff members of high-level political leaders be trained to observe when their superiors are experiencing stress and if they note stress to aid their superiors in avoiding some of the less desirable coping behaviors that are known to adversely affect decision making under stress. Studies indicating how specific high-level political leaders show negative affect and how they cope with stress would facilitate the implementation of such a proposal.

We have already introduced the author of the present chapter (see Chapter 12). Hermann, a psychologist, is a research associate of the Mershon Center, Ohio State University. With her husband, Hermann has conducted several Inter-Nation Simulation studies investigating how political leaders manifest and react to stress (see C. Hermann and M. Hermann, 1967; Robinson, C. Hermann, and M. Hermann, 1969; C. Hermann, M. Hermann, and Cantor, 1974). She (M. Hermann, 1966) has also tested the model of stress which is used in the present chapter.

HOW POLITICAL LEADERS react under stress has recently become a topic of much concern to both researchers and policy makers alike. Watergate, Vietnam, the Middle East, energy shortages, and economic recession have placed American political leaders, at least, in a generally stressful environment. The present chapter is concerned with how the researcher can ascertain when a political leader is experiencing stress and how he (she) is coping with the stress. Unfortunately, it is during stress situations that political leaders are least accessible to the social scientist. Public figures, however, often leave "traces" or records of their behavior such as speeches, letters, memoranda, and films of news conferences during stress situations which are available to the researcher. By examining such records using verbal and nonverbal indicators of stress developed by social psychologists and psychotherapists during the last two decades, it may be possible to note when political leaders are experiencing stress and how they are dealing with it.

Before proceeding much further a clarification of terms is in order. A three-step model of stress is used in this chapter. Stress occurs (1) when there is a threat to a policy or program which a political leader is motivated to achieve or perpetuate, (2) his negative affect (e.g., fear, anxiety, tension, hostility) is aroused, and (3) he tries to cope with his feelings and the threat (see M. Hermann, 1966; Lazarus, 1966). In other words, to ascertain when a political leader is experiencing stress one needs three types of information—indications of whether the situation presents a threat to policies which a political leader wants to achieve or to perpetuate, indicators of negative affect, and indicators of coping behavior.

Threat is used here to indicate an impending danger to a policy or program which a political leader is motivated to achieve or perpetuate rather than a misfortune which has already been experienced. Political leaders seem particularly motivated to achieve or perpetuate policies to which they have publicly committed themselves or which they have personally worked hard to attain. In effect, their success in office, if not their continuation in office, may depend on such policies. By comparing a political leader's verbal behavior in situations in which his policies are being accepted (low threat) with situations in which his policies are being strongly criticized or support for them is eroding (high threat), the researcher may be able to learn about a political leader's behavior under stress. One type of situation which can provide both these kinds of reactions to a political leader's policies is the negotiation situation. And one type of negotiation situation which receives extensive press and television coverage, providing materials for the researcher to analyze, is a contract negotiation between local officials and a service-related union. The present chapter reports the verbal behavior of the four major participants in such a negotiation—the 1965-66 New York City transit negotiations. We examined the verbal behavior of these four participants in periods during the transit negotiations when their proposals were "under fire" and the negotiations were near collapse (high threat periods) and in periods when their proposals were accepted and the negotiations were proceeding smoothly (low threat periods).

Once there is a threat to a political leader's policies, stress occurs when the political leader experiences negative affect and begins trying to cope with either his feelings or the threat. With his policies threatened, the political leader is more likely to experience negative as opposed to positive feelings or affects. He is likely to feel distressed, uncertain, anxious, tense, hostile, angry. In the presence of such feelings the political leader can try to deal with the threat or cope with his negative affect or both. By dealing with the threat to his policies, the political leader eliminates the stimulus for the negative affect. By coping with his feelings, the political leader reduces the significance of the threat. The particular negative affects which were examined in the present study are anxiety and uncertainty; the coping behaviors which were assessed are denial and stereotyping behavior. These specific variables were selected because there already existed several, rather well-validated ways of measuring them, using traces of behavior such as speeches and press conferences.

Method

SITUATION

Every two years the contract between the Transport Workers Union (TWU) local in New York City and the New York Transit Authority (TA) must be renegotiated. The contract expires on December 31 of the second year. Such was the case December 31, 1965. In hopes of reaching an early settlement of the

1966-67 contract, the TWU presented its demands to the members of the TA on November 4, 1965. A 4-day, 32-hour work week with no loss in take-home pay and a 30 percent increase in all wage rates headed the TWU list of 76 proposals. Upon hearing the TWU's demands, the TA chairman observed that the Authority was already operating with a deficit and had no money available to cover what the union requested. Thus began two months of negotiating that included two walk-outs by the negotiating parties and a 12-day strike by the transport workers.

SUBJECTS

The four persons who played the major roles in the transit negotiations are the subjects of the present study. These men were: (1) Michael Quill, long-time president of the TWU; (2) Joseph O'Grady, chairman of the TA; (3) John Lindsay, at first mayor-elect and then mayor of New York City during the course of the negotiations; and (4) Nathan Feinsinger, chairman of the mediation panel.

THREAT PERIODS AND MATERIAL ANALYZED

Film clips of press conferences held during the transit negotiations were acquired from WCBS-TV in New York City.[1] The particular dates for which film clips were requested represented high and low threat points in the course of the negotiations. Moreover, there was some indication in *New York Times* accounts of the negotiations that at least three of the four subjects held press conferences at these times. The two disruptions in the bargaining and the strike define the high threat periods in the negotiations. The presentation of requests, the resumptions in bargaining, and the settlement define the low threat periods. In the high threat periods the negotiators' proposals were being strongly criticized and all parties were using tactics which emphasized conflict; in the low threat periods, on the other hand, the negotiators' policies were generally being accepted and there was a sense of mutual problem solving among the parties. The particular press conferences that were requested took place immediately after a bargaining session in order to capture the subjects' moods as a result of the negotiations.

WCBS-TV's news procedures placed some restrictions on the filmed press conferences which were available on the specified dates. (1) The network made decisions about which news conferences to photograph when several occurred simultaneously. (2) Any part or whole of a press conference that was incorporated into a network news show was not accessible for reproduction. (3) News

[1] The author wishes to express her appreciation to Joseph Klapper and Norman Kramer of WCBS for kindly making available the duplicate copies of filmed press conferences used in this study. Costs for the duplication of the films were defrayed by Contract N60530-12284 from the Naval Ordnance Test Station, China Lake, California. Thanks are extended to Thomas Milburn for his aid in acquiring these funds. Support for the write-up of this research was provided by the Advanced Research Projects Agency, Human Resources Research Office on Office of Naval Research Contract N00014-75-C-0053.

conferences held during the strike were recorded on videotape which requires special equipment in its use not available to the author. Consequently, there were no filmed press conferences for the subjects on some of the days which were selected as high and low threat periods. Table 14.1 shows the dates of the press conferences which were examined, by subject and threat condition.

Because of the nature of the measures used in the study, literal transcriptions were made of the press conferences. Every word and part of a word was transcribed as spoken. In other words, no attempt was made to "clean up" the texts of the interviews. In order to have a number of observations of the subjects' behavior at each point in time, a response to a reporter's question was used as the coding unit.[2] Table 14.1 indicates the number of such coding units available for each subject. The average number of words in these coding units and their average length in seconds also are noted in Table 14.1.

A much larger sample of behavior was available for Quill than for the other three subjects. This discrepancy is not peculiar to the present study. Other indices of news coverage of the transit negotiations (e.g., newspaper stories, newspaper pictures) show a disproportionate amount of time spent on Quill. Quill seems to have been more willing to discuss the transit negotiations with the press than any of the other men. Moreover, because he was considered a "colorful character," reporters often sought him out hoping for a story (see Whittemore, 1968).

NEGATIVE AFFECT

The transcripts of the news conferences were analyzed using indirect verbal measures of negative affect–specifically, verbal measures of uncertainty and anxiety. Several terms in the previous statement warrant definition. By "indirect" is meant a measure which does not involve the subject's cooperation. "Verbal measures" refer to indices using the content of a communication as well as to indices which focus on how a communication is spoken or written and the kinds of words which are used. The general hypothesis, based on the model of stress outlined earlier, was that both uncertainty and anxiety would increase as threat increased. In other words, as the negotiations became more threatening, the participants would become less sure of a positive outcome and more tense. Seven indirect verbal measures of negative affect were employed altogether– three which other research has suggested assess uncertainty and four which other research has found to indicate anxiety. The rationale for choosing the specific measures and a description of each index follow.

Uncertainty.   The three measures of uncertainty which were used were the articulation rate, the ah ratio, and the use of qualifiers. Research on these

---

[2]Another way to gain a number of observations of the subjects' behavior is to use coding units of 100 words. Examining psychotherapy transcripts, Krause (1961) found both types of units to be highly intercorrelated. Because of the naturalness of the response to a reporter's question, it seemed the preferable unit for the present research.

Table 14.1.   Description of Press Conferences Examined by Subject and Threat Condition

Subject	Threat Condition	Dates*	Press Conferences		
			Number of Coding Units	Avg. Number of Words per Coding Unit	Avg. Length of Coding Unit in Seconds
Feinsinger (Chairman of Mediation Panel)	Low	Dec. 12; Dec. 22	17	93.71	36.05
	High	Dec. 30 morning; Dec. 30 evening	15	52.60	19.00
Lindsay (Mayor)	Low	Nov. 18; Dec. 12	21	70.24	20.10
	High	Dec. 30 morning; Dec. 30 evening	23	58.74	18.43
O'Grady (Chairman of Transit Authority)	Low	Nov. 4; Dec. 22; Dec. 9 evening	14	34.86	12.14
	High	Dec. 30	6	41.00	14.00
Quill (President of Union)	Low	Nov. 4; Dec. 12; Dec. 9 evening; Dec. 22	75	29.71	14.16
	High	Dec. 7; Dec. 30; Dec. 9 morning	117	19.76	9.21

*The following events were occurring on the dates mentioned: Nov. 4—presentation of contract proposals; Nov. 18—Lindsay asked to submit names for mediation panel; Dec. 7—TWU indicated would strike early, TA said would need to raise subway fare to meet demands; Dec. 9 morning—TWU noted little progress and said early strike still on despite court injunction; Dec. 9 evening—TWU noted some progress and called off early strike; Dec. 12—first meeting of mediation panel; Dec. 22—mediation panel reported negotiations going smoothly; Dec. 30—TWU broke off negotiations, TA staged sit-in in meeting room.

indicators suggests that an individual's speech becomes more cautious and hesitant as situations increase in uncertainty. The individual appears to be verbally guarded in his reaction to the situation, to be trying to "cover all bases" while figuring out what is going on, and to be searching for feedback from his environment before proceeding too far with a response. These interpretations of the indicators will become clearer with their definitions.

The *articulation rate* is the number of words in a particular response relative to speaking time. By speaking time is meant the time a person takes to respond minus any pauses. In several recent studies Siegman and Pope (1965, 1966, 1972b) have reported a relationship between articulation rate and uncertainty. These investigators found in their research that when interviewers' questions were not well-defined or were high in informational uncertainty (e.g., "Tell me about yourself"), subjects had a lower articulation rate. Moreover, in their 1966 study Siegman and Pope observed that articulation rate decreased in respondents' TAT stories as the TAT cards increased in ambiguity. Goldman-Eisler (1961) has shown that this relationship can be reversed. Articulation rate can be increased as uncertainty decreases with practice on a complex task. Her subjects were asked to describe and indicate the meaning of a series of *New Yorker* cartoons. This research by Goldman-Eisler and Siegman and Pope indicates that subjects use fewer words as uncertainty increases. The subjects appear to become more cautious and verbally guarded with increases in uncertainty.

The *ah ratio* is the number of "ah's" (also "uh's" or "er's") in a particular response relative to the total number of words in the response. The ah has also been called the filled pause (see Maclay and Osgood, 1959), since by using an ah a speaker can hesitate without appearing actually to pause. In addition to the articulation rate, Siegman and Pope (1965, 1966, 1972b) employed the ah ratio in their research. Where the articulation rate decreased with uncertainty, the ah ratio increased. The ah ratio was larger for questions which were not well-defined as well as for more ambiguous TAT cards. Kasl and Mahl (1965) have found that when subjects are asked questions by an unseen interviewer their use of ah's increases over that in a face-to-face interview. Ah's provide speakers with some time in which to consider the next part of their response; ah's also allow speakers time to seek feedback from the environment on what they are saying. As uncertainty increases, such searching behavior becomes more rewarding to the speaker and, in turn, the use of ah's increases. In the present study intercoder agreement on the number of ah's per response across the four subjects was .99.[3]

The use of *qualifiers* refers to the number of words in a response which indicate doubt or ambivalence relative to the total number of words in a

---

[3]The coefficient of agreement used here is the product moment correlation. In determining intercoder agreement, all the coding units were scored twice. One coder was the author; the second was a student unfamiliar with the measures and the aims of the study. Both times the material was coded, the subjects' responses were inter-mixed. Moreover, there were no references to the subject or the press conference on the coding units. The author wishes to thank Ted Cook for serving as the second coder.

response. These words usually qualify what has been said and, thus, the name qualifier. The following words are all qualifiers: "maybe," "possibly," "seems," "guess," "more or less." Comparing suicide notes with ordinary letters to friends and relatives, Osgood and Walker (1959) found more qualifiers in the suicide notes than in the ordinary letters. One characteristic of the suicide situation is its uncertainty—the suicide may or may not be successful, the person committing suicide may not want to succeed. These ambivalences are reflected in the qualifiers in the suicide notes. In some sense, a person qualifies what he says to indicate a lack of certainty. Thus, as uncertainty increases, the use of qualifiers also increases. Intercoder agreement on the use of qualifiers was .84 in the present study.

Anxiety.   Four measures of anxiety were used in examining the participants' behavior during the transit negotiations. These four were the type-token ratio, the rate of sentence changes, the rate of repetitions, and speech rate. Research using these measures suggests that speech becomes more redundant and flustered but faster as anxiety increases. When experiencing high anxiety, the speaker appears to want to terminate his presence in the anxiety-arousing situation as soon as he can. But in the process of speeding up, he loses some control over both the content and presentation of his material—his speech becoming redundant and flustered.

The *type-token ratio* is the number of different words in a particular response relative to the number of words used. For example, in the statement "I can't give the answer because the answer is top secret," there are nine *different* words. The words "the" and "answer" appear twice in the statement but are only counted once since the index focuses on the number of different words. An inverse relationship has been found between the type-token ratio and anxiety. For students who rated themselves significantly less frightened or anxious after giving their last talk in a speech course than after their first talk, Lerea (1956) reported an increase in type-token ratio across time. Moses (1959) had students write and talk about their most pleasant and unpleasant experiences. In both their writing and speaking the type-token ratio was higher for the pleasant than the unpleasant topic. The type-token ratio is, in effect, a measure of redundancy. As the number of different words in a statement decreases, that is, the speaker becomes more redundant, the type-token ratio decreases. The research by Lerea and Moses shows that, when anxious, speakers use fewer different words than when not anxious. In other words, when anxious a speaker becomes more redundant. Intercoder agreement on this measure in the present study was .98.

The *sentence change* rate is the number of times a speaker corrects the form or content of a particular answer relative to total number of words in the answer. For example, the following statement contains two sentence changes in it: "That was—will be two years ago in—next fall." Sentence change has been used by Mahl (1956) as one part of an index of non-ah speech disturbances. In the course of his studies of verbal expressions of patients, therapists, under-graduates, and faculty members, sentence change has consistently made up about 25 percent of all speech disruptions (see Kasl and Mahl, 1965). Only ah's occur more frequently. Maclay and Osgood (1959) have called a similar measure the "false start." More sentence changes seem to accompany heightened anxiety. In the Lerea (1956) study described previously, sentence changes occurred more often during the more frightening or anxiety-arousing speech. Kasl and Mahl (1965) have reported that sentence changes increased when students were placed in interviews designed to be anxiety-arousing as opposed to "neutral." This measure and the next, rate of repetitions, suggest that speech becomes more flustered or disrupted as anxiety increases. In other words, with increases in anxiety, speech becomes less fluent and controlled. The intercoder agreement on sentence changes was .71.

The rate of *repetitions* is the number of times a speaker repeats one or more words in answering a particular question relative to the total number of words in the answer. For example, there are two repetitions in the following statement: "They—they get along fairly well—fairly well I would say." Along with sentence changes, repetitions have also been used as a part of Mahl's (1956) non-ah ratio. Repetitions account for about 19 percent of the occurrences of Mahl's eight indices; it is third in frequency after ah's and sentence changes.[4] In the Lerea (1956) and Kasl and Mahl (1965) studies, repetitions gave the same results as those reported for sentence changes. Repetitions increased as anxiety increased. Intercoder agreement on this measure in the present study was .88.

The last measure of anxiety which we used was the *speech rate*. Speech rate is the number of words spoken per second of response time.[5] One of the first studies to examine the relationship between speech rate and affect was done by Lasswell (1935). Equating slow speech rate with rising unconscious tension in the psychoanalytic sense and fast speech rate with a decrease in this tension, Lasswell found that his subject's rate of speaking was slower when skin conductivity increased and faster when skin conductivity decreased. In 1949, Ruesch and Prestwood analyzed patients' speech behavior in therapy and reported that speech was either faster or slower when patients stated they were anxious or angry than when they indicated they were relaxed. The changes appeared to be stable for each patient across therapy sessions, although across patients the direction of change differed. More recent research has found a faster speech rate

[4]Mahl's other five speech disruption measures were not used in the present research because of their infrequency. No stutters, omissions, sentence incompletions, tongue-slips, or incoherent sounds were found in the coding units. For this reason repetitions and sentence changes were kept separate rather than combined into the non-ah ratio. Such a ratio would not be equivalent to that used in previous studies.

[5]Speech rate may sound similar to the reader to articulation rate mentioned earlier under the uncertainty measures. The difference between the two measures is that pauses in speaking are included in speech rate but excluded from articulation rate. In other words, articulation rate indicates how many words the speaker said while he was actually talking (saying words), whereas speech rate indicates the number of words spoken from the beginning of a statement to its end regardless of pauses.

associated with anxiety-arousing situations. By counting the number of words spoken in 30 second intervals, Kanfer (1958, 1959) showed that subjects talked more about anxiety-arousing than neutral topics and in the period immediately following a warning of shock. In the latter case the increase was more noticeable, the more warning periods the subject had experienced. Sauer and Marcuse (1957) have reported that subjects who are aware that what they are saying is being recorded talk at a faster rate than subjects who are unaware of the recording. Moreover, Siegman and Pope (1972b) found that patients had faster speech rates on high anxiety as opposed to low anxiety days. In some sense, speech rate is both a reflection of an aroused state and a way of coping with that state of arousal. By speeding up, the speaker can "leave the field" faster or, at least, move on to another less anxiety-arousing question, topic, or situation.

There is some evidence to indicate that the uncertainty and anxiety measures are distinct. The research of Siegman and Pope (1972b) on both uncertainty and anxiety shows that articulation rate and ah ratio differentiate subjects' responses to well-defined and ambiguous interviewer questions while speech rate and non-ah speech disturbances such as sentence changes and repetitions differentiate between subjects' responses to anxiety-arousing and neutral questions. Moreover, articulation rate and ah ratio do not differentiate between anxiety-arousing and neutral questions and speech rate and non-ah disturbances do not differentiate between well-defined and ambiguous questions.

COPING BEHAVIOR

Once in a threatening situation, his negative affect aroused, how does the political leader react? How does he deal with the threat and his emotional state? One way for the participants in the transit negotiations to reduce their uncertainty and anxiety was to narrow their focus of attention to the group which they perceived to be the opponent or the party whose position needed to be changed for the negotiations to proceed smoothly. In this way they could simplify the situation into one of "we" versus "they." Other parties were perceived as part of the "we" or "they" depending on their support. Then, by attributing inflexibility to the opponent, a negotiator could justify becoming more rigid in his own position; any problems in the negotiations could be blamed on the opponent and his unwillingness to compromise. The "we" could deny any fault in what happened. Such coping behavior allows the participants to save face with their constituencies if the negotiations fail (see Druckman, Chapter 16). To assess whether these behaviors were present in the transit negotiations, we used three indices of stereotyping and denial. Allness terms and self and other references were used to measure stereotyping; negatives were used to indicate denial.

By *allness term* is meant a word which permits no exception such as "always," "never," "completely," "forever." Osgood and Walker (1959) have proposed that allness terms indicate stereotyping. By permitting no exceptions allness terms suggest placement of an object, person, or idea at the extreme something is either-or; there is no middle ground, no chance for ambiguity. Comparing suicide notes to ordinary letters, Osgood and Walker (1959) found that the suicide notes contained more allness terms. The intercoder agreement on allness terms in the present study was .72. To control for differences in response length between threat periods and participants, the proportion of allness terms to total number of words in each response was used in the analysis.

The second stereotyping measure involved counting *self* and *other references*. In other words, we counted the number of times one of the participants used "I," "me," "my," "mine," "myself," or mentioned one of the groups involved in the negotiations (TWU, TA, mediation panel, or mayor) in answering a question. It is possible to generate a number of different measures from these totals. In addition to self references, information is available on the number of times the four major negotiating groups are mentioned. Furthermore, one can determine the number of times each subject refers to other than his own negotiating group. Self and other references were included in this study less on past successful research than to explore the focus of attention of each of the subjects and the change, if any, during stress. The hypothesis was that self references and references to one's opponents would increase as threat and negative affect increased. In other words, as a way of coping with stress each subject's center of attention becomes more clearly defined as himself and his opponent. His focus of attention narrows to himself and what he perceives to be the threat agent. For the president of the union, Quill, the opponents should be the mayor and the TA; for the chairman of the TA, O'Grady, the union; for the mayor, Lindsay, the union; and for the chairman of the mediation panel, Feinsinger, both the TWU and the TA. Intercoder agreement for these measures in the present study was .99 for self references, .91 for references to the union, .86 for references to the TA, .94 for references to the mediation panel, and .86 for mentions of the mayor. To control for differences in response length, self and other references were converted into proportions (divided by total words in a response) before being included in the analysis.

Negatives were used to assess denial. The number of times "no," "not," "nothing," "neither," "nor," and "never" occurred in a response was tallied. Weintraub and Aronson (1963) have proposed negatives as an index of denial. Noting that impulsive patients are known to retract or deny their behavior after its expression, Weintraub and Aronson (1964) compared statements from this group with those from a control group of armed forces personnel. Both groups of subjects were asked to talk uninterruptedly for ten minutes about anything they wished. As expected, the impulsive patients used more negatives than the control group. The intercoder agreement for negatives in the present study was .97. Like allness terms and self and other references, for purposes of analysis number of negatives in a response was converted to a proportion to control for differences in length of response.

Results

Results will be presented for each subject separately before any generalizations are made across subjects.

PRESIDENT OF UNION

Table 14.2 shows the verbal reactions of the president of the union, Michael Quill, to increases in stress. Five of the measures differ significantly from the low to the high threat conditions. Quill used fewer ah's ($t = 5.14$, $p < .01$), fewer qualifiers ($t = 3.67$, $p < .01$), and more different words ($t = 3.39$, $p < .01$) at high as opposed to low threat points in the negotiations. Moreover, he made more references to the mayor ($t = 3.69$, $p < .01$) and, in effect, to all the other negotiating groups ($t = 2.95$, $p < .01$) when threat was high. The difference between self references in the two conditions is close to being significant ($t = 1.84$, $p = .07$)—Quill tended to mention himself more as threat increased. The results for the ah ratio, qualifiers, and type-token ratio are opposite to what was predicted. Quill seems to have been less hesitant, less redundant, and more sure of what he was going to say in the high threat rather than the low threat situations.

Judging from the means for Quill in Table 14.2, sentence changes and repetitions are not salient measures of his verbal behavior. They were used infrequently in his press conference responses. Similarly, Quill made few references to the mediation panel or the TA, even though the latter was on paper the union's opponent in the negotiations. In both high and low threat conditions, he mentioned the mayor more than either the mediation panel ($t = 2.18$, $p < .05$ for low threat; $t = 7.17$, $p < .01$ for high threat) or TA ($t = 1.86$, $p = .07$ for low threat; $t = 6.87$, $p < .01$ for high threat).

Table 14.3 presents the intercorrelations among the measures for Quill. The correlations for the two threat conditions are listed separately in Table 14.3. Brackets are placed around correlations which are significantly different when threat is low and high. An examination of Table 14.3 indicates that there is a tendency for the relationships among the measures to be smaller when threat is high. For example, 17 of the correlations are significant for the low threat condition while only 9 are significant for the high threat condition. Furthermore, of the 11 significant changes in relationship from one condition to the other, 9 show a reduction in the correlation as threat increases.

Over two-thirds of those relationships which changed as threat changed involve self or other references. For instance, self references are associated with more words per second and more negatives under low threat but not under high threat. In high threat conditions there is a small inverse relationship between these pairs of measures. Similarly, Quill associated qualifiers with references to his union in low threat periods; but there is a small inverse relationship between these indices in high threat periods. In examining Quill's references to his opponents, we note that when threat is high statements about the mayor are

Table 14.2. Mean Verbal Reactions of Four Major Participants in Negotiations During Low and High Threat Conditions

Measure	Quill		Lindsay		Feinsinger		O'Grady	
	Low Threat	High Threat	Low Threat	High Threat	Low Threat	High Threat	Low Threat	High Threat
Articulation Rate	2.50 (.74)*	2.57 (.81)	3.10 (.65)	3.20 (.50)	3.17 (1.19)	3.29 (.72)	2.99 (1.66)	3.04 (.85)
Ah Ratio	0.05 (.07)	0.02 (.03)	0.08 (.06)	0.06 (.05)	0.008 (.01)	0.01 (.02)	0.05 (.05)	0.03 (.06)
Qualifiers	0.04 (.06)	0.02 (.03)	0.03 (.04)	0.04 (.06)	0.06 (.06)	0.04 (.04)	0.05 (.07)	0.07 (.05)
Type-Token Ratio	0.83 (.14)	0.89 (.11)	0.70 (.16)	0.70 (.16)	0.73 (.18)	0.75 (.17)	0.82 (.19)	0.76 (.18)
Sentence Changes	0.003 (.01)	0.006 (.02)	0.01 (.01)	0.01 (.02)	0.008 (.01)	0.009 (.01)	0.008 (.02)	0.00 (.00)
Repetitions	0.007 (.02)	0.006 (.02)	0.02 (.03)	0.03 (.04)	0.008 (.01)	0.02 (.04)	0.005 (.01)	0.003 (.008)
Speech Rate	2.29 (.76)	2.33 (.83)	2.92 (.72)	2.85 (.53)	2.83 (1.17)	3.03 (.85)	2.88 (1.67)	3.00 (.84)
Negatives	0.03 (.05)	0.04 (.08)	0.03 (.11)	0.05 (.09)	0.01 (.02)	0.04 (.05)	0.06 (.10)	0.02 (.03)
Allness Terms	0.01 (.03)	0.01 (.03)	0.01 (.01)	0.02 (.03)	0.01 (.02)	0.01 (.02)	0.009 (.02)	0.03 (.05)
Self References	0.03 (.06)	0.06 (.11)	0.08 (.07)	0.08 (.06)	0.03 (.05)	0.05 (.06)	0.04 (.06)	0.05 (.07)
TWU References	0.05 (.06)	0.04 (.05)	0.001 (.004)	0.002 (.008)	0.005 (.01)	0.02 (.03)	0.02 (.07)	0.02 (.02)
TA References	0.003 (.02)	0.001 (.01)	0.001 (.006)	0.004 (.01)	0.007 (.01)	0.02 (.04)	0.04 (.05)	0.04 (.05)
Mayor References	0.01 (.03)	0.03 (.05)	0.02 (.02)	0.00 (.00)	0.009 (.02)	0.004 (.01)	0.007 (.003)	0.00 (.00)
Mediation Panel References	0.002 (.01)	0.004 (.003)	0.003 (.02)	0.01 (.02)	0.05 (.05)	0.03 (.05)	0.004 (.01)	0.02 (.03)
Other References	0.02 (.04)	0.04 (.05)	0.005 (.02)	0.02 (.03)	0.02 (.03)	0.04 (.05)	0.03 (.07)	0.03 (.03)

*Number in parenthesis is standard deviation.

Table 14.3. Correlations for Quill Among Measures by Threat Condition (Decimals Omitted)

Measure	Threat Condition	1	2	3	4	5	6	7	8	9	10	11	12	13	14	15
Uncertainty																
1. Articulation Rate	Low	—														
	High															
2. Ah Ratio	Low	-31**	—													
	High	-17														
3. Qualifiers	Low	10	-01	—												
	High	11	13													
Anxiety																
4. Type-Token Ratio	Low	-10	-03	06	—											
	High	-12	-06	-02												
5. Sentence Changes	Low	02	10	03	-37**	—										
	High	-10	08	04	-06											
6. Repetitions	Low	-06	-05	-03	-31**	37**	—									
	High	04	01	10	-22*	29**										
7. Speech Rate	Low	90**	-34**	06	02	-01	-09	—								
	High	91**	-23*	09	07	-09	03									
Denial																
8. Negatives	Low	03	-16	05	01	01	51**	00	—							
	High	-07	-05	-13	10	-04	-01	00								
Stereotyping																
9. Allness Terms	Low	22	-23*	03	12	-09	17	21	31**	—						
	High	03	-09	-06	09	05	04	08	-06							
10. Self References	Low	28*	-09	14	13	-12	-10	21	26*	15	—					
	High	-07	-10	04	14	09	06	-03	-10	09						
11. TA References	Low	-14	18	-04	-07	-06	-03	-10	-06	-08	-10	—				
	High	-02	-06	-06	-29**	-02	00	-07	09	-04	-03					
12. Mayor References	Low	12	-05	-15	13	-06	-10	08	-12	16	00	24*	—			
	High	12	27**	02	-08	-02	-13	11	-07	-12	-11	-04				
13. TWU References	Low	-10	04	29*	05	-06	06	-09	03	-01	-28*	05	-02	—		
	High	07	-11	-09	-18	11	-04	02	-06	-03	-25*	-05	-10			
14. Mediation Panel References	Low	-10	01	-11	07	-06	-01	-09	-08	-04	00	-04	-01	-04	—	
	High	-03	-06	-06	-08	01	-04	-09	-03	-04	-04	09	-07	-04		
15. Other References	Low	00	03	-16	10	-09	-10	00	-14	08	-04	58**	87**	-01	28*	—
	High	11	25**	00	-14	-02	-13	08	-05	-13	-12	17	98**	-11	03	

*p < .05 **p < .01

related to more ah hesitations and fewer allness terms. The relationships are opposite in sign during low threat. Although references to the mayor were accompanied by mentions of the TA in low threat conditions, this relationship almost disappears when threat is high. Since references to the TA, mayor, and mediation panel were summed to make up the "other" reference measure, correlations between each type of reference and this category indicate the nature of the others in Quill's statements. Not surprisingly, both the TA and mayor— the union's opponents—were salient others when threat was low. However, with an increase in threat the TA became less prominent while the mayor became more prominent.

Six of the relationships are consistent across threat conditions. Among the highest correlations in Table 14.3 are those between the articulation rate and speech rate. Because articulation rate includes only speaking time while speech rate includes both speaking time and pauses during speaking, the two measures become more alike the fewer pauses the subject makes in talking. Sentence changes and repetitions also show a similar pattern of occurrence regardless of degree of threat. Furthermore, repetitions are inversely related to the type-token ratio across the two conditions. This relationship may be somewhat artifactual since fewer different words are available if there are repetitions. Two other consistently inverse relationships are those between the ah ratio and speech rate and between self references and references to the TWU. Quill tended to talk slower the more ah's he used. Moreover, he tended to choose between self references and mentions of the union in responding to reporters' questions. The uniformly high correlations between the mayor and other references have already been mentioned.

The indices in the present study are supposed to measure two types of negative affect—uncertainty and anxiety—and two kinds of coping behavior— stereotyping and denial. It is possible, using a variant of the Campbell-Fiske (1959) multitrait-multimethod matrix which has been described by Collins (1963), to explore whether the suggested division among the measures fits Quill's data. The following question is asked of the data: Are the indices which are presumed to be measuring the same characteristic more highly correlated than those measuring different characteristics?[6] In Table 14.3 the measures which are supposed to be assessing similar negative affects and coping behaviors are marked off by triangles. By comparing the correlations for each measure within the triangle with its correlations outside the triangle, we can learn whether the measures assessing the same characteristic are more highly corre- lated among themselves or with measures of different characteristics. From the self and other reference measures only Quill's mentions of himself and his

[6]This question is concerned with discriminant validity. Convergent validity is also important. In assessing convergent validity one asks if the correlations among the measures of the same characteristic exceed chance. To have convergent validity the correlations in the triangles should exceed chance.

opponents (the TA and mayor) are included in this analysis because the hypothesis on stereotyping behavior chiefly concerned them.

As evidenced in the anxiety and uncertainty triangles in Table 14.3, qualifiers and speech rate do not seem to fit for Quill into the clusters to which they were assigned. In fact, for Quill speech rate acts more like an uncertainty measure than an anxiety measure. The uncertainty measures become more cohesive when speech rate is added and qualifiers are deleted. Moreover, if speech rate is deleted from the anxiety measures, these measures form a more cohesive group. The stereotyping behaviors, on the other hand, are almost as highly correlated with the anxiety, uncertainty, and denial measures as they are among themselves. Nor are the intercorrelations among the stereotyping measures very substantial on the whole.

MAYOR

Table 14.2 also indicates Mayor Lindsay's verbal reactions to stress. Two of the measures were significantly different in the low and high threat conditions. Three of the measures are close to being significant $(.10 > p > .05)$. Lindsay used more allness terms $(t = 2.10, p < .05)$ and fewer ah's $(t = 1.71, p = .10)$ as threat increased. Moreover, although making references to his role in low threat periods, he made *no* mention of the mayor when threat was high $(t = 3.43, p < .01)$. Both references to the mediation panel $(t = 1.81, p = .08)$ and to all others $(t = 1.85, p = .08)$ increased with stress. Interestingly, when threat was low mentions of the mayor were significantly greater than references to any of the other groups $(t = 3.04, p < .01$ for TWU-mayor comparison; $t = 2.88, p < .01$ for TA-mayor; $t = 2.35, p < .05$ for mediation panel-mayor); whereas, under high threat the mediation panel was referred to significantly more often than the TWU $(t = 2.20, p < .05)$ and mayor $(t = 2.80, p < .01)$ and close to significantly more often than the TA $(t = 1.75, p = .09)$. As stress increased Lindsay seemed to see his role diminishing in importance and that of the mediation panel becoming more important. At the same time Lindsay was becoming less hesitant and more dogmatic in what he was saying. Given that the TWU and TA are the two parties Lindsay was trying to bring to a settlement, it is interesting to note the few references he made to them in either condition.

Table 14.4 shows the correlations among the measures for Lindsay for both threat conditions. Brackets are placed around correlations which differ significantly under low and high threat. In contrast to Quill, the relationships for Lindsay are not smaller in the high threat condition. In fact, there are more significant correlations when threat is high (13) than when it is low (11). Among the significant changes in correlation between conditions, about as many decrease with an increase in threat as vice versa.

Five of the relationships are consistently significant across conditions. Again verbal and articulation rates are highly related, suggesting few unfilled pauses in Lindsay's responses. References to the TWU and TA are almost identical for Lindsay—when one was mentioned the other was also. As might be expected, the

Table 14.4. Correlations for Lindsay Among Measures by Threat Condition (Decimals Omitted)

Measure	Threat Condition	1	2	3	4	5	6	7	8	9	10	11	12	13	14	15
Uncertainty																
1. Articulation Rate	Low	—														
	High															
2. Ah Ratio	Low	-33	—													
	High	-18														
3. Qualifiers	Low	14	-26	—												
	High	-22	-32													
Anxiety																
4. Type-Token Ratio	Low	-06	-43*	35	—											
	High	-21	-32	50*												
5. Sentence Changes	Low	49*	-04	-04	-04	—										
	High	-27	55**	-20	-02											
6. Repetitions	Low	28	30	14	-06	10	—									
	High	29	-11	-29	-40	02										
7. Speech Rate	Low	97**	-50*	22	01	48*	26	—								
	High	77**	-32	03	-23	-30	46*									
Denial																
1. Negatives	Low	-42	-33	-16	41	-19	-25	-32	—							
	High	-32	-23	59**	46*	-01	-04	-12								
Stereotyping																
9. Allness Terms	Low	-23	39	-33	-44*	16	-04	-24	-14	—						
	High	-12	-17	08	23	-31	-02	05	13							
10. Self References	Low	37	-18	-06	29	00	27	39	-28	-25	—					
	High	29	-51*	38	37	-40	-35	22	20	-23						
11. TWU References	Low	-32	11	-14	-02	18	-02	-31	00	24	-19	—				
	High	-07	07	-11	00	45*	-14	-07	-05	00	-22					
12. TA References	Low	-32	11	-14	-02	18	-02	-31	00	24	-19	1.0**	—			
	High	-04	07	-10	00	45*	-15	-05	-04	00	-21	.99**				
13. Mayor References	Low	45*	-07	-11	-29	25	12	40	-16	-09	-06	-16	-16	—		
	High	—a														
14. Mediation Panel References	Low	-20	11	-19	-14	-10	-19	-24	-03	32	-16	33	33	-22	—	
	High	08	15	-16	-30	03	-21	-12	-27	-25	16	-13	-13			
15. Other References	Low	-31	13	-20	-11	02	-14	-33	-02	35	-21	76**	76**	-24	87**	—
	High	02	16	-20	-23	36	-27	-13	-23	-19	-05	66**	66**	—	66**	

*p < .05   **p < .01
aBecause Lindsay made no references to his own mayoral role during high threat situations, no correlations were possible for high threat for this measure.

groups included in the other reference measure show consistently significant part-whole correlations with this measure. The TWU, TA, and mediation panel are equally related to the other reference index under high threat; the mediation panel is slightly more related to this index under low threat.

Although the results of the *t*-tests suggest that Lindsay was more confident sounding in high threat periods, the significant relationships among the measures in these same periods belie a certain insecurity. For instance, as ah's increased so did sentence changes; as more different words were used, qualifiers and negatives increased. In fact, Lindsay tended to use qualifiers and negatives together as threat increased. Furthermore, the faster Lindsay spoke the more he repeated his ideas. And sentence changes were associated with references to the TWU and TA. There seems to have been an attempt to separate the self from this sense of insecurity—as ah's increased self referents decreased. This picture can be contrasted with that when threat was low. The significant relationships under low threat show that more different words were accompanied by more allness terms and fewer ah's. Moreover, a faster verbal rate carried with it fewer ah's and more mentions of the mayoral role. The low threat correlations suggest more confidence.

Some five of the pairs of correlations for Lindsay in Table 14.4 illustrate the model of stress proposed at the beginning of the chapter. The model of stress states that as threat increases, an individual's negative affect is aroused and he tries to cope with the threat and his negative feelings. The specific correlations in Table 14.4 are those between qualifiers and negatives, the ah ratio and self references, repetitions and self references, and sentence changes and references to the TA and TWU. In the high threat situations, when Lindsay became uncertain (increased qualifiers, increased ah's), he tried to cope with this uncertainty by denial (increased negatives) and withdrawing himself from the situation (decreased self references). Qualifiers and negatives did not appear together in Lindsay's responses when threat was low; moreover, the ah ratio and self references show a small inverse relationship under low threat. Similarly, in high threat situations, as Lindsay became anxious (increased repetitions, increased sentence changes), he dealt with his anxiety and the threatening situation by withdrawing himself from the negotiations (decreased self references) and focusing attention on the two main parties to the negotiations—the TWU and TA (increased references to the TWU and TA). Self references and repetitions co-occured in low threat situations and the correlations between sentence changes and references to the TWU and TA are minimal under low threat.

The triangles in Table 14.4 indicate those measures that supposedly assess similar characteristics and should be highly intercorrelated. Since the TWU is Lindsay's opponent, references to the TWU are included with self references in the stereotyping behavior measures. A comparison of the correlations inside and outside these triangles shows that many of the cross-trait correlations exceed the within-trait correlations. Lindsay's speech rate, like Quill's, appears more similar to the uncertainty measures than the anxiety measures, particularly when threat is low.

CHAIRMAN OF THE MEDIATION PANEL

The verbal reactions of the chairman of the mediation panel, Nathan Feinsinger, when threat is low and high are found in Table 14.2. Only one of the measures is significantly different in the two conditions. As threat increased, Feinsinger increased his use of negatives ($t = 2.32, p < .05$).

Several within condition comparisons among the self and other references for Feinsinger are noteworthy. When threat was low, Feinsinger made significantly more references to his mediation panel than to the other parties in the negotiations (TWU-mediation panel $t = 4.20$, $p < .01$; TA-mediation panel $t = 4.07$, $p < .01$; mayor-mediation panel $t = 3.72$, $p < .01$). However, under high threat the mediation panel was only referred to significantly more often than the mayor (mayor-mediation panel $t = 2.18$, $p < .05$). Interestingly, as references to the mediation panel became less prominent with stress, self references were becoming more prominent. In the low threat condition self references did not differ significantly from references to the other groups. When threat was high, though, self references significantly exceeded mentions of the TWU ($t = 2.07$, $p < .05$), TA ($t = 2.01, p = .05$), and mayor ($t = 3.20, p < .01$).

Table 14.5 presents the intercorrelations among the measures for Feinsinger for both the high and low threat periods. Like Lindsay, but unlike Quill, there are more significant relationships for high threat than low threat periods (14 as opposed to 9). Among the seven significant differences between correlations in the two conditions, about as many decrease as increase with changes in threat. Brackets are placed around correlations in Table 14.5 which differ significantly under low and high threat.

Examining Table 14.5, one notices that once again speech and articulation rates are highly correlated. Two other relationships are consistently significant across conditions. References to the TWU are related to the ah ratio. Feinsinger's mentions of the union are accompanied by speech hesitations. This correlation is even more striking the higher the threat. The other consistently significant relationship is the part-whole correlation between references to the TA and others. Under low threat, references to the TWU and the mayor are also highly correlated with other references. All three play a large part in making up the "other" references score in low threat periods. On the other hand, in high threat periods only mentions of the TA are significantly related to other references. The relationship with mayor references almost disappears. (The difference between the mayor-other references correlations in high and low threat is almost significant—p of .07.) Perhaps one contributor to the change in pattern among the part-whole correlations as threat increases was Feinsinger's growing ability to discriminate between the TWU and the TA. References to these two groups are highly and positively related under low threat. But the relationship is small and inverse in high threat periods.

Table 14.5. Correlations for Feinsinger Among Measures by Threat Condition (Decimals Omitted)

Measure	Threat Condition	1	2	3	4	5	6	7	8	9	10	11	12	13	14	15
Uncertainty																
1. Articulation Rate	Low	—														
	High															
2. Ah Ratio	Low	−17	—													
	High	−55*														
3. Qualifiers	Low	13	−25	—												
	High	−16	07													
Anxiety																
4. Type-Token Ratio	Low	−05	−18	20*	—											
	High	30	04	60*												
5. Sentence Changes	Low	−09	06	−17	−06	—										
	High	−63*	52*	−08	−05											
6. Repetitions	Low	−37	−08	19	−12	−09	—									
	High	−13	−21	−44	−46	−16										
7. Speech Rate	Low	95**	−27	21	03	−22	−32	—								
	High	84**	−51*	03	41	−60*	00									
Denial																
8. Negatives	Low	−38	−33	17	−26	−12	57*	−31	—							
	High	−08	01	54*	30	−05	−39	−29								
Stereotyping																
9. Allness Terms	Low	−13	30	−08	19	17	−26	−28	−14	—						
	High	−19	63*	04	08	−02	−21	−10	08							
10. Self References	Low	−12	−15	46	−06	−05	−24	−04	40	−04	—					
	High	13	−15	35	35	−18	−43	−17	83**	−16						
11. TWU References	Low	−35	49*	−22	−29	27	19	−34	−07	−18	−14	—				
	High	−42	85**	−07	13	34	−20	−31	09	75**	−07					
12. TA References	Low	−28	45	−21	−29	32	19	−30	−08	−16	−19	92**	—			
	High	22	−06	−10	−01	−09	−15	22	01	30	−15	−15				
13. Mayor References	Low	11	19	−20	−05	−24	−01	09	09	15	00	−16	−19	—		
	High	−14	−13	12	−26	−03	−18	−08	−21	−12	−25	−22	−14			
14. Mediation Panel References	Low	40	05	69**	02	−17	−04	45	−26	00	19	−20	−25	26	—	
	High	−10	−33	−19	−28	−19	40	04	−40	−31	−20	−26	−20	08		
15. Other References	Low	−19	55*	−33	−31	07	15	−22	−06	−06	−16	72**	70**	52*	−01	—
	High	−10	45	−03	03	13	−30	00	03	72**	−23	49	77**	−08	−34	

*p < .05   **p < .01

Further examination of significant correlations in Table 14.5 suggests that there was a change in Feinsinger's perception of his role in the negotiations as stress increased. In the low stress periods Feinsinger apparently perceived the role of the mediation panel to be that of questioner; however, as the negotiations grew more serious and tenuous this role perception changed to that of legitimator and, more particularly, negator. We noted earlier that the mediation panel was Feinsinger's most frequent referent when threat was low, and the self was when threat was high. Given these facts, we observe in Table 14.5 that references to the mediation panel are significantly correlated with the use of qualifiers under low threat but not under high threat. Similarly, self references are significantly correlated with the use of negatives in high threat periods but to a lesser degree in low threat periods.

Other significant relationships among the measures in the high threat periods indicate that Feinsinger may have reacted to heightened tension by becoming more dogmatic. For example, increased ah's are related to increased use of allness terms and increased qualifiers are related to increased use of negatives. Increased sentence changes are accompanied by more deliberate speech (fewer words per second). Redundancy in speech (lower type-token ratio) is associated with the use of fewer qualifiers. Furthermore, references to the TWU which are accompanied by an increase in ah's are also related to an increase in allness terms.

The triangles in Table 14.5 indicate those measures that are supposed to assess similar characteristics and should be highly intercorrelated. Since the TWU and TA can be considered to be Feinsinger's opponents, references to the TWU and the TA are included with self references in the stereotyping behavior measures. For Feinsinger, the within-trait measures are not as highly correlated as previous research would suggest. Many cross-trait correlations are higher than within-trait correlations. The only slight indication of a match is among the anxiety measures in the high threat condition.

CHAIRMAN OF THE TRANSIT AUTHORITY

The least amount of material was available for the chairman of the Transit Authority, Joseph O'Grady. Since it is hard to draw any firm conclusions from six responses—the total available for the high threat condition—the results for O'Grady are presented even more tentatively than those for the other three subjects. Table 14.2 contains O'Grady's verbal reactions to stress. None of the differences are significant.

Table 14.6 presents the intercorrelations among the measures for O'Grady for both high and low threat periods. Although a correlation of .81 is needed for a high threat relationship to be significantly different from zero, six reach this magnitude or better. Four more correlations in the high threat periods fall between .74 and .81 $(.10 > p > .05)$. Some 12 of the low threat correlations are significant. There is less stability in O'Grady's relationships across periods than is the case for any of the other three subjects. Eighteen of the correlations

Table 14.6.   Correlations for O'Grady Among Measures by Threat Condition (Decimals Omitted)

Measure	Threat Condition	1	2	3	4	5	6	7	8	9	10	11	12	13	14	15
Uncertainty																
1. Articulation Rate	Low	—														
	High															
2. Ah Ratio	Low	01	—													
	High	-26														
3. Qualifiers	Low	-31	-38	—												
	High	-05	02													
Anxiety																
4. Type-Token Ratio	Low	-09	-71**	39	—											
	High	22	21	70												
5. Sentence Changes	Low	-07	64*	-30	-33	—										
	High	—a														
6. Repetitions	Low	-08	71**	-29	-41	93**	—									
	High	20	-23	-32	-77											
7. Speech Rate	Low	99**	-05	-29	-06	-12	-13	—								
	High	99**	-24	-01	32		07									
Denial																
8. Negatives	Low	11	-37	-15	43	-27	-27	13	—							
	High	-46	-39	21	-46		39	-52								
Stereotyping																
9. Allness Terms	Low	-03	66**	-24	-26	89**	85*	-07	-12	—						
	High	53	-37	75	65		-21	56	07							
10. Self References	Low	40	-38	15	25	-06	-11	43	06	-04	—					
	High	-65	67	57	31		-32	-62	24	-04						
11. TWU References	Low	-27	-17	78**	22	01	-01	-25	-16	08	-20	—				
	High	-60	-30	40	-10		-10	-60	88*	19	42					
12. TA References	Low	09	39	-25	-57*	-04	-06	07	-26	-10	-33	-22	—			
	High	87*	-41	-22	-14		43	83*	-06	42	-68	-29				
13. Mayor References	Low	13	-05	-17	-44	03	-12	10	-12	-13	-06	-06	34	—		
	High	—b														
14. Mediation Panel References	Low	-02	29	-17	-33	19	12	00	-18	02	-02	-11	40	-08	—	
	High	-26	99**	03	21		-23	-24	-39	-37	67	-31	-41			
15. Other References	Low	-27	-11	74**	14	05	00	-25	-20	08	-21**	98**	-13	-04	-09	—
	High	-67	75	30	14		-29	-64	24	-22	94**	41	-60		74	

*p < .05   **p < .01

[a] Because O'Grady made no sentence changes during the high threat condition, no correlations were calculated for high threat.

[b] Because O'Grady made no references to the mayor during the high threat condition, no correlations were calculated for high threat.

between measures differ significantly from one another in the high and low threat periods. Brackets are placed around the correlations in Table 14.6 which differ significantly in the two conditions. In 13 of these comparisons it is the high threat relationship which has become elevated. Furthermore, there is only one consistently significant relationship across conditions—that between the articulation rate and the speech rate.

Eleven of the 18 changes in correlation from low to high threat periods involve self and other references. As threat increased, self references became associated with verbal hesitations and deliberate, cautious speech. The opposite was the case under low threat. Similarly, under high threat, references to the TA were related to speaking faster, though there was little relationship between these measures under low threat. Heightened uncertainty and tension are expressed in different ways depending on whether O'Grady is mentioning himself or his reference group. There was also increased hesitancy in his speech with references to the mediation panel as threat increased. O'Grady seems most sure in his references to the TWU. As pressures mounted, negatives became associated with mentions of the TWU. O'Grady may have been using negatives to indicate the TWU's lack of cooperation in the negotiations—an attempt on his part to save face with his constituency, the citizens of New York. The differences among the self and other reference intercorrelations are noteworthy too. In his high threat responses, O'Grady's self references were quite likely to co-occur with references to others, specifically the mediation panel. Under low threat the relationship between self and other references is reversed. Perhaps this reversal is because the other party most likely to be mentioned in the low threat periods was the TWU, his opponent.

The significant changes in correlation from the low to high threat periods also suggest a change in O'Grady's coping behavior between high and low threat situations. Any negative feeling which O'Grady experienced in the low threat periods was accompanied by the use of allness terms or stereotyping. Allness terms in the low threat periods are associated with more ah's, more sentence changes, and more repetitions. However, in high threat periods negatives and self references are associated with indicators of uncertainty and anxiety. These changes may indicate a switch on O'Grady's part from the typical rhetoric of the adamant management negotiator laying out his position to the involvement of O'Grady, the person, in the negotiations and his attempt to save face as the bargaining became more intense.

The triangles in Table 14.6 indicate those measures which previous research suggests should assess similar characteristics and, thus, should be highly inter-correlated. Since the TWU is O'Grady's opponent, references to the TWU are included with self references in the stereotyping measures. In O'Grady's case, there is more cohesiveness among the measures of anxiety than among the measures for either of the other characteristics.

COMPARISONS ACROSS SUBJECTS

Using Table 14.2 the reader can compare the subjects' mean reactions on each of the measures during low and high threat. Although it has become increasingly evident throughout the presentation of these results, such an examination shows most clearly the idiosyncratic nature of the subjects' verbal behavior. The differences between the low and high threat reactions among the subjects are in the same direction for only one measure, the articulation rate. Self references, other references, and allness terms either stay the same or increase as threat increases. For the other measures one or two subjects decrease while the others increase across the threat conditions.

We note in comparing the subjects that in low threat periods Lindsay, the mayor, used more ah's and repetitions as well as talked faster than the other subjects; Feinsinger, the chairman of the mediation panel, used more qualifiers; O'Grady, the president of the Transit Authority, used more negatives; and Quill, the president of the union, engaged in more deliberate speech. There is little difference among the men for sentence changes, allness terms, and type-token ratio under low threat. Although Lindsay still used the most ah's and repetitions when threat was high, he also used the most negatives. O'Grady responded with the most allness terms and qualifiers under high threat. Feinsinger talked the fastest under high threat while Quill used the most different words and the most deliberate speech.

As stress increases, there are some interesting changes in the measures among the subjects. One such shift can be observed for allness terms, qualifiers, and negatives. Feinsinger and Quill increased their usage of negatives in the high threat periods of the negotiations while decreasing the qualifiers in their speech. O'Grady, on the other hand, became more contradictory (increased both qualifiers and allness terms) while using fewer negatives. Lindsay tried all three tactics, all three types of words increasing in his responses with increased threat. Most noteworthy here are the opposite reactions of Quill and O'Grady, the chief negotiators for the TA and TWU. Willing to qualify what he had to say when negotiations were going smoothly (to entertain some uncertainty), Quill became more negative when problems arose. Reversing Quill's behavior, O'Grady was more likely to qualify his statements (perceive some uncertainty) in the high threat periods. These two would be a difficult pair to bring together on an issue. A further examination of Table 14.2 shows that the two persons who were attempting to play the mediator role in the negotiations, Feinsinger and Lindsay, became more repetitious and negative as threat increased.

With regard to the participants' references to themselves and to the major parties to the negotiations, we note that, with only one exception (Lindsay's lack of references to his mayoral role under high threat), the subjects' most frequent references were to themselves and to the reference groups to which they belonged. The question can be raised: Besides one's self and one's own group which of the other parties were foremost in the participants' discussions of the negotiations? For Feinsinger, the mayor was the most predominant other referent in the low threat periods, both the TWU and TA in high threat periods. As the TWU and TA became more frequent referents with increased threat, mentions of the mayor grew less frequent. For Lindsay, the predominant other referent was the mediation panel regardless of condition; for O'Grady it was the TWU under low threat and both the TWU and the mediation panel under high threat; for Quill it was the mayor in both conditions.

Quite appropriately the TWU and TA gained Feinsinger's attention as threat increases. The prominence of the TWU and mediation panel in O'Grady's responses also seems appropriate. What is hard to explain is Quill's regard for the mayor and the mayor's regard for the medition panel. Why wasn't Quill's attention directed toward the TA and the mediation panel and Lindsay's attention toward the TA and TWU? Some of the answer to this question is suggested by a chronology of events. Because Lindsay was involved in setting up a city administration (he took office the night the strike began), he did not want to spend his time at a bargaining table. He, therefore, made the mediation panel, which he had been instrumental in appointing, his representatives to the negotiations. The mediation panel kept Lindsay informed about the negotiations and reported his ideas to the negotiators. However, since the TA's deficit prevented them from making the TWU an adequate offer without city or state aid, Lindsay finally had to join in the bargaining. Accounts of previous transit negotiations, particularly those during the preceding 12-year Wagner administration, indicate that Quill had been used to last minute compromises with the mayor in which he reduced some of his demands but also got a good package for his men (see Whittemore, 1968, pp. 265ff.). Thus, Quill's focus on the mayor was almost a habit. Moreover, Quill knew that the TA could not make an acceptable offer without outside aid. This discussion raises some doubts about the appropriateness of the TA and mediation panel's other references. Quill's focus on the mayor may have been a more realistic behavior than that of either the TA or mediation panel. As it was, the parties were talking past one another.

Discussion

If the results are taken as a whole, what kind of picture is presented of the major participants in the 1965-66 New York City transit negotiations? What different behaviors, if any, might have avoided the strike? In attempting to answer these questions we speak to the usefulness of the verbal measures employed in the present study. In other words, we inquire if the information gained from analyzing the subjects' verbal reactions added anything to what could be gotten from a chronology of events.

We have observed that Quill, the president of the union, presented a more self-assured picture in the high threat periods than in the low. His speech included fewer ah's, more different words, and fewer qualifiers. Moreover, although not significant, he increased his use of negatives. In effect, Quill's position became hardened with stress. By doing this, however, he limited his area of compromise, making a settlement more difficult. Interestingly, contrary to his general firm position, Quill's high threat references to the mayor were associated with increased ah's and fewer allness terms. As pressures mounted, Quill showed less certainty and some openness toward the one person he thought could help to bring about a settlement. This message was not communicated adequately, though, because of the hard line "smoke screen."

The verbal behavior of Quill's opponent, Joseph O'Grady (chairman of the Transit Authority), indicates a more anxious and uncertain individual as threat increased. References to himself, the Transit Authority, and the mediation panel were associated with increased tenseness. Furthermore, when threat was high, his use of qualifiers was almost twice that for any of the other subjects. Unlike Quill, however, O'Grady's uncertainty was not extended to the party that he was trying to influence. As threat increased, references to the union were accompanied by an increased use of negatives. Thus, what may have been a general ambivalence over position became a hard line toward the union. As noted earlier, although O'Grady's focus on the union and the mediation panel seems appropriate to the situation, it is curious that he did not increase his appeals to the mayor as threat increased. O'Grady continued to announce that the Transit Authority was an independent agent when, indeed, it was highly dependent on others. O'Grady's behavior lends support to the "face-saving" coping behavior hypothesis advanced at the beginning of this study.

Both Lindsay, the mayor, and Feinsinger, the chairman of the mediation panel, were outside parties to the real negotiations, but were given the role of mediator. While Lindsay put off accepting the role as long as he could, Feinsinger had to immediately shoulder the responsibility for bringing the Transit Authority and union together upon his election as chairman of the mediation panel. There is some indication that Feinsinger became more involved himself as threat increased. With this increased involvement came a change in role—from that of questioner to that of negator. Feinsinger's use of negatives quadrupled as pressures mounted. Along with this change in function, Feinsinger began to differentiate between the union and Transit Authority. In his high threat responses, references to the union are accompanied by increased speech hesitations and allness terms. Under high threat Feinsinger apparently decided that the union was the group to be dealt with and responded to Quill's hard line in kind. Had Feinsinger's perception of his role not changed or had he reacted to both the union and Transit Authority in the same manner when threat was high, one wonders if the negotiations would have been stalemated for so long.

Because he was faced with the pressing task of selecting and setting up a city administration, Mayor Lindsay elected to let the mediation panel represent his interests in the transit negotiations. Whenever asked about the negotiations, particularly in the high threat periods, he would place less emphasis on his role and more emphasis on that of the mediation panel. At the same time, he presented a confident front—things were going to work out all right and there would be no strike. His speech patterns, however, show that he was less secure about the outcome than he wanted to appear. Like the question about Fein-singer's behavior, what would have happened if Lindsay had joined actively in the bargaining earlier is one of the interesting if's of the situation.

Even though the verbal measures have been able to add information to what was already available, they are not problem free. Whenever records or traces of behavior are used, there are certain problems to be confronted. First, there are the limitations on what is accessible. For instance, in the present study, the network's film library reflected decisions made during the transit negotiations about which press conferences to film and which not to film. Thus, one must often deal with less than would be desirable for well-controlled research. Because Quill was interviewed most during the course of the negotiations, his results are probably more representative of his behavior than those for O'Grady who infrequently approached the press and vice versa. Similarly, the results for Feinsinger and Lindsay should be considered less representative. Moreover, the lack of availability of material for some of the selected periods during the negotiations permits a rival explanation for the results of the subjects. Whereas enough material was available on Quill to have low and high threat press conferences interspersed across time,[7] the low threat periods for the other subjects occurred early in the negotiations and the high threat periods were late in the negotiations. Therefore, the results for Feinsinger, Lindsay, and O'Grady may only indicate the effects of practice in the news conference situation. For example, ah's may have decreased and speech rate increased because a subject was getting used to talking to the press. Since some of the changes, however, are not easily attributed to familiarization with the news conference routine (e.g., increases in allness terms, qualifiers, or references to the union), the stress hypothesis remains credible. Moreover, because measures such as ah's and repetitions which one might expect to decrease with practice do not for all subjects (in fact, they increase for several subjects), the stress hypothesis remains credible. Furthermore, since Quill shows some of the same reactions as Fein-singer, Lindsay, and O'Grady, the stress hypothesis remains credible.

A second issue is that of content control. These men were speaking to the press. They knew that their statements might be printed or broadcast over radio and TV. It would be natural for them to want to manipulate the content of what they said to present a certain image. Content control, however, would seem to be a less important issue the more spontaneous one's materials are. Certainly content control is less salient in the give and take of a press conference than it would be in a prepared speech or statement. (The couple of prepared statements which were read in the news conferences in the present study were deleted from

---

[7]This interspersing of low and high threat periods over time for Quill helps to reduce the plausibility of a rival explanation for his results. Since Quill had a heart attack on January 4, it is conceivable that his health was deteriorating throughout the latter part of the negotiations in which he took part. Therefore, his verbal reactions may have been more a response to his physical well-being than the situation. However, with high threat press conferences occurring early and late in the negotiations, we have some control over this rival hypothesis.

the data analysis.) Mahl (1959) has argued that it is much more difficult to control such things as ah's and repetitions than themes and ideas. Ah's and repetitions are side effects of what one is saying and are less likely to be noticed when they occur. Moreover, even though allness terms and self references, for example, are more content-oriented than ah's and repetitions, it seems unlikely that material at the word level can be manipulated in unprepared speech such as occurs in a press conference.

A third issue with regard to the verbal measures is the idiosyncratic nature of the subjects' responses. In this respect the present study is like that of Krause (1961). He intercorrelated several of the anxiety measures included in the present research and reports idiosyncratic relationships among the measures across subjects. In both this study and the Krause study, indices which are reputed to be assessing similar traits between subjects do not seem to be within subjects. With physiological measures of fear, Ax (1960) has found that subjects tend to favor one mode of response over another. Such may also be the case with the present verbal measures of negative affect and coping behavior. Until there is further intra-subject research, the researcher is probably safer to refer to these verbal measures by their manifest content (e.g., the ah is a filled pause, the type-token ratio denotes redundancy) rather than as differential indicators of uncertainty, anxiety, denial, and stereotyping behavior when studying the behavior of only one subject.

In summary, the ten verbal measures in the present study have helped to shed some light on the behavior of the participants in the 1965-66 New York City transit negotiations. Although these indices are not problem free, their problems do not seem insurmountable. With more research like the present, they may prove valuable additions to the "toolbox" of the investigator interested in examining the behavior of political leaders in stress.

CHAPTER 15

An Experiment in Simulated Historical Decision Making*

*Wayman J. Crow and
Robert C. Noel*

Editor's Introduction

One of the recurrent themes in this book centers around the interaction of
personal characteristics and situation in determining who becomes a political
leader and such a leader's political behavior. Thus, L. Stewart (Chapter 9) notes
that political leaders with different birth orders are chosen in crisis as opposed to
noncrisis situations; Driver (Chapter 13) finds decision makers high in
complexity more atune to situational requirements than decision makers low in
complexity; and, in the last chapter, Hermann (Chapter 14) deliberately sets out
to find indicators of personal stress in what appear to be high and low threat
periods in a negotiation. The present chapter by Crow and Noel focuses on this

*This chapter represents a revision of an earlier paper entitled "The Valid Use of Simulation
Results" published by the Western Behavioral Sciences Institute, 1965. The research was
supported by the RAYTHEON Corporation under Contract #DA-49-146-XZ-110. We wish
to express our gratitude to the Commander of the Naval Training Center, San Diego, and his
staff, particularly Dale Lovell and Chief Coslett, for their help in assigning participants to
this study. Moreover, we wish to thank Elizabeth Lynn of San Diego State College for
statistical advice and David Newman of the Computer Center of the University of California,
San Diego, for programming the data analysis.

theme, exploring in a much more systematic way the relative effects of personal characteristics and situation on decision making. In effect, Crow and Noel examine two types of situational variables—the structure of the decision-making setting which they call the organizational context and the substantive nature of the problem which they label the situational variable.

This chapter joins a growing group of papers concerned with examining the interface among the various components of the policy-making process such as the personal characteristics of the policy maker, the nature of the policy-making unit, bureaucratic variables, characteristics of the situation, and cultural variables (e.g., see East, Salmore, and Hermann, 1977; M. Hermann, 1974, 1976a; Holsti, 1970b). These writers suggest that it is only in exploring how these types of variables interact in determining policy that we will be able to understand or explain the policy process. The proponents of this viewpoint do not expect the personal characteristics of the political leader to generally relate on a one-to-one basis with policy outcomes but hypothesize the conditions under which personal characteristics will have an effect. Thus, for example, personal characteristics have been hypothesized to have a greater effect in closed than in open societies, in ambiguous as opposed to unambiguous situations, and when decisions are made by small *ad hoc* groups as opposed to bureaucratic agencies. Although most of the effort in this direction is as yet at the hypothesis generation stage, like the present chapter there are several research projects underway to systematically explore such hypotheses (see M. Hermann, 1974; C. Hermann et al., 1973).

The organizational context variable which Crow and Noel examine takes into account both types of political behavior which we have been considering in this section of the book—both the political behavior of the individual political leader and the political behavior of a political unit. Moreover, the research in this chapter indicates how these two types of behavior can differ. What the individual political leader decides on his own often differs from the decision made in consultation with staff, in inter-agency meetings, or within-agency committees. The Crow and Noel research indicates the importance of this distinction between own and political unit behavior. Moreover, their study suggests that the examination of how the personal characteristics of political leaders affect political unit behavior is probably a more complex task than exploring the same hypothesis for the individual leader's own political behavior. Studying the interaction of personal characteristics with bureaucratic and situational variables, for example, may be more important in the case of the political unit than for the political leader himself. In other words, the link between leader personal characteristics and leader political behavior is more direct than the link between leader personal characteristics and political unit behavior.

The political behavior which Crow and Noel explore is the choice of an escalatory or de-escalatory military response in a crisis-like situation. Their results add to the composite picture begun by Driver (Chapter 13) of the type of decision maker who will participate in a decision to escalate in a stressful environment. In the present chapter, Crow and Noel examine the effects of militarism, risk-taking preference, and nationalism on choice of an escalatory response; Driver explored the effects of complexity, pro-force view, general ideology, and distrust on the decision to escalate. It is interesting to view the results of the Driver research and the Crow and Noel study in light of L. Stewart's (Chapter 9) findings that first and only sons generally are heads of state during periods of national stress and Winter and A. Stewart's (Chapter 2) findings that presidents high in need for power tend to have a more aggressive foreign policy. All of these results begin to suggest the portrait of the aggressive political leader, particularly the Western aggressive political leader.

Like Chapter 13 (Driver), the present chapter involves simulation. Persons who are not political decision makers in actuality assume the roles of political decision makers. They operate in staged political units whose structural characteristics are thought to resemble in certain critical ways actual political units. The simulated environment in the Crow and Noel research, however, is not as complex as that used by Driver since it involves only one nation and does not include feedback to the participants on their decisions. In the simulation which Driver used, feedback to decision makers was based on the application of a theory of international relations to their decisions. Both exercises are open to problems of validity. We have discussed this validity question in our introduction to the Driver chapter. Crow and Noel, however, add a twist to the validity discussion by using for their simulated environment an actual historical situation. By comparing the participants' responses with the historical outcome, Crow and Noel have some estimate of the validity of their exercise.

Crow, a psychologist, is director of the Western Behavioral Sciences Institute in LaJolla, California; Noel is an associate professor of political science at the University of California at Santa Barbara. Representing different disciplines, Crow and Noel became interested in the research in this chapter in an attempt to bridge the gap they perceived between these disciplines. Both authors have had a long-standing commitment to simulation research, having participated in some of the early research with simulation in international relations (see Crow, 1963, 1966; Guetzkow, Alger, Brody, Noel, and Snyder, 1963; Raser and Crow, 1968).

THE PRESENT STUDY attempts to extend simulation-gaming methodology in two major respects: First, a decision-making context typical of complex simulations is linked to the rigorous experimental-design techniques typical of two-person game studies. Second, the study is interdisciplinary in a much broader way than has been customary. Research topics, variables, and techniques are adapted from psychology, sociology, political science, and history. These are combined into an experimental design paradigm with sufficient replications to permit the use of advanced statistical techniques. Most importantly, the study allows assessment of the relative impact of representative variables from different disciplines and of their interactions. Such interaction among personality characteristics, social structure, and historical situations has been neglected in the approaches of single disciplines. For those who believe as the authors do that much more research effort should be interdisciplinary in nature, the present approach is intended to be a step forward.

Specifically, the study addresses five fundamental questions:

1. Do different decisions result from participants who are different in their individual characteristics?
2. Do different decisions result from different organizational contexts?
3. Do different decisions result from different information about the situation?
4. Do personality, organizational context, and situational factors interact in determining decision outcomes?
5. Do simulation decisions match decision outcomes from historical situations?

Overview of Experimental Procedure

In this study, a simulated environment is created through a scenario entitled "The Algonian Exercise." The scenario was designed to simulate events leading up to the outbreak of conflict in a fictitious international situation which roughly paralleled an historical case of international conflict (the decision facing Mexico at the time Texas declared its independence in 1836). In essence, the problem posed involved the risk of escalation. The participants were confronted with a dilemma in which low levels of military response might be inadequate to control an insurrection in a remote part of their national territory and higher levels were likely to provoke direct intervention by a neighboring power with the possibility of general war.

The study was carried out as follows. A questionnaire was administered to a pool of 1,124 potential subjects to determine their locations on three attitudinal dimensions—militarism, nationalism, and risk-taking preference. Those whose responses clustered near either extreme on a dimension were selected to participate in the study, providing two groups markedly different in terms of each attitudinal dimension. Each exercise consisted of a four-hour session and involved sixteen participants in groups of four. There were 24 such exercises conducted, with a total of 384 subjects participating in the simulated environment. After a brief introduction to the exercise, participants spent the first hour reading the exercise scenario which acquainted them with the history of their "nation," Algo, and with the factors involved in an insurrection in the Province of East Algo. After a 30-minute question-answer and discussion period, participants were divided into groups of four. Each group was assigned to a separate room which contained an individual desk for each participant in the group. Every few minutes, each participant received one of a sequence of seven "daily" scenario supplements, a "Summary of the Significant Events of the Day," in which the situation was developed further. These summaries provided a detailed account of the past week's events, the deepening crisis in East Algo, and the reactions of neighboring Utro, the other "nation" involved.

After the last of the "daily" events summaries, the experimenter announced that each participant was now to consider himself the Chief of State of Algo. As such, it would be his responsibility to decide how Algo would respond to the crisis. The entire situation was then briefly reviewed; the options available to Algo were set forth in an "Advisors' Analysis" paper which was the final information given to the participants. This Advisors' Analysis narrowed the choices which the participants had by, for example, ruling out bargaining, the issuance of threats, imposing diplomatic and/or economic sanctions as being infeasible in the present situation. Instead, the analysis focused on military alternatives; action could be taken at any one of eleven levels of intensity ranging from withdrawal and loss of the province to Utro to the declaration of general war against Utro. The eleven options were mutually exclusive; only one could be chosen.

Participants, functioning individually, were given 15 minutes in which to decide which response level Algo would make. Subsequently, they were assembled around a conference table and asked to consider themselves as members of a group of four top-level leaders of Algo, all equal in authority and responsibility. As such, they were to discuss the crisis and the situation confronting Algo and in 20 minutes to reach a consensus regarding Algo's response.

The participants' final task was to complete an "Educational Questionnaire," the purpose of which was to maintain the fiction that the study was designed to investigate the educational value of the exercise as well as to see whether any participants had recognized the historical analogue.

Method

SUBJECTS

The subjects in this study were 384 young males selected from a subject pool of 1,124 enlisted personnel at the United States Naval Training Center, San Diego, California. All of these personnel had been selected by the Navy to enter service schools after their basic training; they were thus presumably of average or above average intelligence. A battery of personality and attitude measures was administered to the subject pool prior to the experiment. Three different individual characteristics were used to identify three subsets of subjects to participate in the experiment: (1) those whose scores on an *aggressive militarism vs. nonbelligerence* scale were equal to or greater than one standard deviation above and below the mean ($N = 176$); (2) those whose scores on a *risk-taking preference* scale were equal to or greater than one standard deviation above and below the mean ($N = 112$); and (3) those whose scores on an *authoritarian nationalism vs. equalitarian internationalism* scale were equal to or greater than one standard deviation above and below the mean ($N = 96$).

DESIGN

The study was structured as a three-way analysis of variance design. The principal dependent variable was the level of military response decided upon by the participants (scaled from 1 to 11). Decisions were made under two experimental conditions that were defined by our "organizational context" variable to involve *individual vs. group decision making*. Individual decisions were made and recorded first. The consensus reached by each group of participants after discussion was considered a group decision. The four-person groups were homogeneous with respect to individual characteristics.

Three parallel experiments were conducted with different personality and situation variables. Subjects were assigned to one of the experiments with the intent of approximating a balanced design on these two types of variables. In Experiment I, aggressive militarism was varied (high vs. low) against the situational variable, *level of provocation* (high vs. low). Level of provocation refers to the nature and extent of infiltration from Utro, the potentially threatening neighbor. In Experiment II, risk-taking preference was varied (high vs. low) against a different situational variable—an "objective" estimate of the *probability of winning/losing a war* (high vs. low) with the neighboring country if such a war were to occur as a result of the subjects' decision. Experiment III varied authoritarian nationalism (high vs. low) against yet another situational variable, the potential *enemy's intentions* (expansionist vs. nonexpansionist) with regard to the subject-nation's territories.

In sum, each experiment had a personality variable, a situation variable, and involved making decisions at the individual and group levels.

THE SIMULATED ENVIRONMENT

The scenario for this study described a fictitious world of six nations, complete with map, geography, history, and a description of the economic, political, and cultural characteristics of each nation. Two nations, Algo and Utro, were the focus of attention. Together with Omne and Ingo, they were located in one hemisphere; Alland and Utland, the other two nations in this world, were located in another hemisphere.

In the scenario, the situation was presented nationalistically from the point of view of Algo—the participants' nation. Algo was an economically underdeveloped country, predominantly agricultural. Its possessions included a main continent, two sets of islands, East Algo, and the East Algonian Peninsula. East Algo was separated from Algo by water and islands. Utro bordered East Algo, the Winding River forming the boundary between them. Utro had a balanced economy. Moderately well industrialized, she had modern agriculture and stock raising on large ranges. Alland and Utland were two large world powers located 3,000 miles to the west of Algo and Utro. Algo was formerly a colonial possession of Alland but won independence in a war fought a few years ago. Utro won its war of independence against Utland several decades ago. Omne and Ingo were the two remaining vestiges of Utland's colonial power in the world. Omne was politically independent, but depended on Utland economically. Ingo was still a colonial territory.

As this simulation begins, an insurrection is under way in East Algo. The agitators, largely of former Utronian stock, are stirring up the population to demand independence from Algo or union with Utro. At the time of the insurrection, the population in East Algo was predominantly Utronian in origin. Before Algo's independence, a treaty had been negotiated between Utro and Alland allowing immigration of the expansionist Utronians into East Algo; this treaty was re-negotiated after Algo's independence and was observed until the situation demanded that further immigration be restricted. Because of political instability within Algo, a few Utronians—illegal entrants, land-grabbers, and speculators—were exploiting the situation, justifying their subversive activities on the basis of the regrettable lack of internal order and security in East Algo. Since there were only a handful of Algonian troops in East Algo, the self-proclaimed leaders of the insurrection had been able to drive them out and declare East Algo an independent nation.

The Utronians reacted to this situation by clamoring (spurred on by agitators) for Utronian intervention "to help their Utronian brothers." Since for many years expansionists within Utro had trained their sights on the rich territory of East Algo, there was much talk within Utro that this territory "rightfully" belonged to Utro anyway. Thus, there was a strong possibility that Utro would intervene. No assistance to either side in this struggle could be expected from any foreign power.

Through the series of scenario supplements, the situation unfolded. Five battalions of Algonian soldiers, ordered into East Algo to suppress the rebellion, were initially victorious and succeeded in dispersing the rebel units. Men and supplies, however, continued to filter across the Winding River from Utro. Although the Utronian government insisted that it would maintain its traditional policy of nonintervention in the affairs of other nations, the tone of its notes to Algo became stiffer, demanding that the majority in East Algo should be granted their "legitimate aspirations" for national independence. Algo demanded that Utro stop infiltrating their men and supplies into East Algo. Utro denied any official responsibility; she then placed her forces along her side of the border on alert status. A meeting of the Algonian Cabinet and the Defense Council ruled out dealing with the situation through negotiation, threat, or economic sanctions, concluding that the situation demanded some sort of military action. The

Chiefs of the Armed Forces in Algo were directed to prepare an analysis of possible actions.

It is at this point that the participants took over control of the "government." Eleven possible levels of military action were outlined, including the advantages and disadvantages of each. The levels of action ranged from disengagement with the insurgents and withdrawal of the five battalions to assuming defensive positions at the neck of the East Algonian Peninsula to an outright declaration of war on Utro. The participants had to choose which level of response should be made to the situation.

"LEVEL OF RESPONSE": THE DEPENDENT VARIABLE

The dependent variable in this study was the decision which the subjects made concerning Algo's level of military response to the insurrection in East Algo. We chose this dependent variable with two criteria in mind—the first stemming from an applied research interest, the second from a basic research interest.

This study was conducted as part of a project aimed at constructing a computer simulation of international conflict processes. An escalation submodel was under consideration which was based on a cost-effectiveness algorithm. There was interest in generating behavioral data which might indicate a possible need to change this submodel to reflect the influence of other kinds of variables on the escalation decision process. The present study thus attempted to focus on a decision with escalatory implications. Although the experimental design was static (it did not involve iterative, stimulus-response sequences), it did focus the subjects' attention on the implications of possible counter-response by the other party to the conflict.

The second criterion for choosing "level of response" as the dependent variable grew out of our basic research interest in decision-making behavior in international relations and foreign policy. We sought to examine experimentally the notion that substantive outcomes are a function of three "variable clusters": the "internal setting" of the decision (organizational context), the "external setting" of the decision (situation), and the individual characteristics of the decision makers (cf. Snyder, Bruck, and Sapin, 1962).

Response data were acquired in all three experiments in the following manner. The sequential scenario supplements structured the situation such that all nonmilitary response options were ruled out (except for Level 1, "disengagement with insurgents," which might be considered nonmilitary). The "Advisors' Analysis" sheets that were distributed prior to when the participants made their decisions explored further the implications of the situation and possible outcomes. Eleven mutually exclusive responses were described by a short paragraph in the Advisors' Analysis sheets. Moreover, their advantages and disadvantages, potential gains and/or losses, and the risks involved in choosing each were outlined. It was our intention to provide materials from which a "reasonable" argument could be advanced for selecting any one of the available responses. In this way the responses which the participants selected would depend upon their own evaluations of the total situation. These are the eleven levels of response:

Level 1: Disengagement with insurgents.

Level 2: Hold and defend present position.

Level 3: Counter-rebel action.

Level 4: Level 3 *plus* destruction of infiltration and supply lines *on our* [Algo] *side* of Winding River border.

Level 5: Heavy counter-rebel action *plus* destruction of infiltration and supply lines *on our* [Algo] *side* plus defensive precautions.

Level 6: Level 5 *plus* destruction of infiltration and supply lines *on Utro side* of border.

Level 7: Level 6 *plus* commando raids into Utro territory.

Level 8: Level 7 *plus* destruction of principal supply lines in Utronian mountains and naval blockade.

Level 9: Level 8 *plus limited* preventive action against Utronian Regular Forces in Winding River Basin and subsequent withdrawal of our forces.

Level 10: Level 8 *plus unlimited* preventive action against Utronian forces in Winding River Basin and continued presence of our forces there.

Level 11: Level 8 *plus* declaration of war, occupation of Winding River Basin, establishment of military control there and of offensive and/or defensive positions in mountains separating the Basin from southeastern Utro.

These eleven response levels were scaled according to the following procedures. Prior to the experiment, 23 subjects were put through the same orientation to the exercise that was used for the actual experiments. However, instead of making individual judgments on Algo's response to the situation described in the scenario and its supplements, they were given the following instructions:

We want to know how *restrained* or *forceful* you believe *each* of the 11 response levels is. Level 1, disengagement with insurgents, is the *most restrained* response. Level 11, declaration of war, etc., is the *most forceful* response. We want you to indicate where each of the other levels falls between these two points. We have placed Level 1 at 0 on the scale below and Level 11 at 100. Read the description of each of the other response levels (2 through 10) given in the "Advisors' Analysis." Decide where each one falls on the scale below. Select any number between 0 and 100 for each level and write it in the space by each level. It is important that you consider each judgment in relation to all of the others. You may want to re-read all of them before making your judgment.

Table 15.1.   Results of Scaling Procedure for "Level of Response"

Response Level	Mean	Variance	Range
1	0.0	0.0	0
2	10.7	67.5	38
3	20.0	78.2	45
4	27.8	109.0	43
5	39.5	114.3	41
6	51.1	104.9	40
7	58.5	117.5	41
8	68.7	65.7	25
9	77.4	50.5	28
10	88.5	73.5	33
11	100.0	0.0	0

The resulting data are summarized in Table 15.1. The data in Table 15.1 indicated to our satisfaction that there was sufficient discrimination among the points on our "level of response" scale to use it and to assume an increase in level of military involvement with each scale position from 1 to 11.

INDIVIDUAL CHARACTERISTICS

Fundamental psychological research has documented the influence of such personality variables as attitudes, opinions, values, and social experience on a variety of behaviors. Unfortunately, however, the behavior studied has rarely been decision making. Pioneering efforts in this direction, such as Freud's (1962) study of Moses or Lasswell's (1930) investigation of the relation between personality and political behavior, were almost the sole essays in this field until the more recent case studies of prominent decision makers by George and George (1956), Gottfried (1961), and Rogow (1963).

The most intensive investigation of decision making has been stimulated by game theory. Nevertheless, in their review of the voluminous game theory research, Rapaport and Orcutt (1962) cite only one study in which the effect of player attributes upon decision outcomes was investigated. Driver (1962) studied the relation of "concrete" versus "abstract" thinking to decision making in the Inter-Nation Simulation and the Hermanns (1967) used a battery of personality tests to match the personalities of student participants and world leaders in a simulation of the outbreak of World War I. Important as these studies are, they are only early steps toward a deeper understanding of the impact of personality attributes on decision making.

The individual characteristics selected for examination in this study are related to previous, but scant objective research to be discussed below. Because the first two attributes are closely related—*aggressive militarism vs. nonbelligerence* and *authoritarian nationalism vs. equalitarian internationalism*—they are considered together first in the section that follows. The third attribute—*risk-taking preference*—is dealt with separately.

Aggressive Militarism and Authoritarian Nationalism. One of the most important contemporary features of the international scene is the rise of intense nationalism and the pursuit of national goals through military and para-military conflict. It is likely that many of the leaders of these new nationalisms possessed or have adopted personal values and attitudes congruent with the international stance of their nations. Their values can be contrasted with those of the leaders who advocate international cooperation and the resolution of conflict by non-military means. Both sets of values are often deeply rooted in cultural traditions or firmly entrenched in the modern ideology of nations and, thus, are a part of the environment which shapes the personality and character of contemporary leaders. Decision makers oriented toward one extreme or the other on these variables will probably respond quite differently to the same decision occasion.

The relation of ideological orientation to personality has been established by the classic work of Adorno et al. (1950) on the authoritarian personality. Levinson (1957) extracted from research on authoritarianism those elements which were most pertinent to foreign policy orientation and devised a measure of nationalism. Using a similar scale, Lutzker (1960) found that "nationalists" made significantly fewer cooperative choices in the Prisoner's Dilemma game than did "internationalists." Also in a game-theory setting, Deutsch (1960) found that "authoritarian" subjects were suspicious and untrustworthy while "nonauthoritarian" subjects were trusting and trustworthy. Using 24 personality scales related to bargaining behavior as a source for items, including those used by Lutzker and Deutsch, Shure and Meeker (1965) developed a personality questionnaire pertinent to decision making. After a factor analysis, the questionnaire yielded six independent factors or scales, two of which were utilized in the present study.

The first of the two scales used, aggressive militarism vs. nonbelligerence, distinguished between those participants who would place reliance on the use of force, threats, and power in international diplomacy and those participants who would avoid belligerent means; between those who would use armed strength and those who would rely on trust and understanding as a foundation for negotiations; and between those who would use armed strength and those for whom resort to threats and violence would be seen as a failure of diplomacy. Here are some sample items from this scale:

If an undemocratic nation threatens to attack us, we should encourage a revolution in that nation.

Threats are never a good way to get other countries to do what we want them to do.

Our government should support revolutionary movements in undemocratic countries.

Subjects were asked to indicate their agreement and disagreement with these items on a seven-point scale from "disagree very much" (1) to "agree very much" (7). Items supporting nonbelligerence were given a negative score; items favoring militarism a positive score. The test results for this scale with our subject pool were: mean -32.34, standard deviation 11.83. Subjects with scores equal to or greater than one standard deviation above and below the mean were selected to participate in the experiment.

The second of the Shure and Meeker (1965) scales used in the present study, authoritarian nationalism vs. equalitarian internationalism, identifies persons who are ethnocentric, who glorify and idealize America, and who are hostile to outsiders. Others are seen as inferior, envious, and threatening. Moreover, there is an emphasis on national honor and sovereignty and a belief in a policy of military strength and preparedness. Persons high on this factor have an autocratic orientation to child rearing, conceive of family in hierarchical terms, and over-idealize parents, seeing them as strong authorities requiring obedience and respect. Such persons emphasize work over leisure, are punitive, fear moral contamination, are submissive to powerful authority, have an exaggerated fear of weakness, exercise a hard line, and are impatient with negotiations with other nations. There is little capacity for, indeed an avoidance of, self-awareness; there is denial of personal aggression to family members. Some sample items from this scale are:

While we should give military aid to countries which are prepared to fight our enemies, we ought to cut down on foreign economic help, or else the other countries will just play us for a sucker.

The greater the danger of war, the less use there is in working for world disarmament.

The first principle of our foreign policy should be to join forces with any country, even if it is not very democratic, just as long as it is strongly anti-Communistic.

As with the previous scale, subjects were asked to indicate their agreement and disagreement with these items on a seven-point scale from "disagree very much" (1) to "agree very much" (7). The test results for this factor with our subject pool were: mean 97.57, standard deviation 15.95. Subjects with scores equal to or greater than one standard deviation above and below the mean were selected to participate in the experiment.

Risk-Taking Preference. In a semi-erratic world where events are only partially accessible to foresight, decision making necessarily involves risks. It is the weighing of alternatives according to their probability of potential gain or potential loss that culminates in a decision. At this point the personal characteristics of decision makers might be influential, should such characteristics predispose the decision makers to take high risks or, conversely, to be very cautious.

Kogan and Wallach (1964) have argued that consistently risky or consistently conservative behavior is irrational, because it does not represent a response to situational elements that call for flexibility in risk taking. They further have pointed out that the decision-making behavior of subjects high in motivational disturbance is characterized by highly generalized "risky" or "conservative" choices. Underlining the possible implications for students of international behavior, they (Kogan and Wallach, 1964, p. 214) suggest:

> The published literature on national and military affairs has emphasized the presence of irrational elements in decision making and the possible impact of such elements on international conflict. Nowhere in this literature has any specific attempt been found, however, to isolate and describe in detail the forms of irrationality that possess particular implications for the decision making involved in matters of human survival. Nor is there evidence of attempts to delineate and document systematically the varying personality dispositions that can exacerbate or dampen tendencies toward irrationality in times of international tension and stress.

Based on Kogan and Wallach's (1964) work with risk-taking, preference for high risks versus preference for low risks was chosen as the third individual difference variable in this study.

Risk-taking preferences were measured with an instrument developed by Kogan and Wallach and used in previous studies where its reliability and validity have been established (e.g., Kogan and Wallach, 1964; Wallach and Kogan, 1965; Wallach et al., 1962, 1964). Subjects are presented with 12 hypothetical "real life" situations in which the central person must choose between alternative actions and goals. One alternative is more desirable or attractive than the other, but the desirable alternative is less likely to be attainable. The subject indicates the minimum odds (1 in 10, 3 in 10, 5 in 10, 7 in 10, 9 in 10, would not choose no matter what probability is) he would demand before recommending the more desirable alternative. The situations involve such things as: an electrical engineer with a choice between his present job at a modest salary or a new job offering more money but less security; a man with a heart ailment who must choose between restrictive changes in his way of life or a dangerous surgical operation. The complete instrument may be found in Kogan and Wallach (1964). The test results for risk taking with our subject pool were: mean 69.12, standard deviation 15.14. Subjects with scores equal to or greater than one standard deviation above and below the mean were selected to participate in the experiment.

ORGANIZATIONAL CONTEXT

National decisions are not only made by individuals with different personal characteristics, they are made in socially defined organizational contexts which prescribe divisions of labor, authority, roles, and relations. Do decision makers make different decisions when they function in different organizational contexts? If organizational context affects decision outcome, then it is important to know how.

One feature of the organizational structure in which national decisions are made which has attracted the attention of political scientists and practitioners alike is the widespread use of the committee system. Committees have often been criticized by such scholars for their tendency to inhibit innovation, boldness, and creativity, with the result that any decision is a consensus or compromise based on the lowest common denominator of agreement. As Kissinger (1962, p. 356) has pointed out, " . . . the system stresses avoidance of risk rather than boldness of conception." (See also Acheson, 1960; Neustadt, 1960; and Whyte, 1956.) Recently, however, a series of social psychological studies has shown that as a result of group discussion individual members will often shift and accept greater risks. Evidence (Wallach and Kogan, 1965, p. 1) has been adduced to support the following proposition:

> If members of a group engage in a discussion and reach a consensus regarding the degree of risk to accept in the decisions which they make, their conclusion is to pursue a course of action more risky than that represented by the average of the prior decisions of each individual considered separately.

This "risky shift" has been found in studies involving monetary gain and loss, intellectual failure, and physical pain as well as hypothetical risks. Wallach and Kogan (1965) have suggested that diffusion of responsibility through interpersonal discussion accounts for the risky shift—each individual can feel less than proportionally to blame for the possible failure of a risky decision. It is exactly this diffusion of responsibility that political scientists have seen as producing conservatism in committees.

These conflicting explanations, coupled with our prior selection of high vs. low risk preference as an individual difference variable, persuaded us to select *individual judgment vs. group consensus* as the organizational context variable for the present study. The organizational context variable was operationalized in the following manner. After reading the Participants' Manual, attending a discussion period, receiving further information through summaries and an Advisors' Analysis, each participant decided privately on the appropriate military response for Algo without knowing that a group discussion would follow. When the individual judgments had been made, the four participants seated together in a room were assembled at a conference table and were read the following instructions which paraphrase the Wallach and Kogan (1965) procedures.

> You are now a group of four top decision makers in Algo. Each of you is equal in authority. We want you to discuss the situation in East Algo. As the top decision-making group in Algo you must arrive at a unanimous decision on what response Algo should take. This means that you must agree to a consensus. A consensus is different from a majority vote. A consensus is a combination between what you personally see as the best thing to do and what you think the group can agree to unanimously. You have twenty minutes to arrive at consensus. We will tape record the discussion so that we can study the discussion later.

In this manner, individual judgments and group consensus scores were obtained for the dependent variable—level of military response. This procedure was used for each of the three experiments.

SITUATIONAL VARIABLES

National decisions are not only made by individuals of differing personal characteristics and by personnel who function in differing organizational contexts, but decisions must be made for situations which differ substantively. It seems obvious that in grossly different situations decision makers will make different decisions. It also seems obvious that selected elements of one situation could vary widely without affecting the decision outcome, while slight changes in other elements in that same situation could be crucial to the decision. Our research design anticipated that individuals with different personal characteristics will attend to different features of their environments, possibly distorting them in different ways. Unfortunately, we had little theory or evidence to suggest which elements of a situation national decision makers will attend to, which they will neglect, and what sorts of perceptual distortion will be involved. In addition to problems of attention and perceptual distortion, there is the problem of how information about a situation is interpreted and what conclusions are drawn. Even when there is agreement about the "facts" of the situation, there is often disagreement as to what they "mean" and what should be "done" about them.

Which elements of a situation most affect the conclusion that will be drawn? This question was examined in the present study. The Algonian scenario was presented to all participants in an identical fashion except for one important element which was changed in each experiment to see if it would affect participants' decisions. The three situational elements which varied across the three experiments were: (a) the level of the opponent's provocation, (b) the probability of winning should a war occur, and (c) the motive (aggressive intent) of the opponent.

Level of Provocation. The demonstration of force to influence an opponent is a practice of long standing; its history has been reviewed by Vagts (1956). Milburn (1964) and Schelling (1960) have emphasized the significance of force deployments as "communications" and "tacit bargaining" for modern contexts. One of the novel features of the present international scene is the attempt to advance national goals by indirect military means. In the nuclear age, when direct confrontation between the major powers entails such high risks, there has been a growth in actions variously labelled "wars of national liberation" or "counter-insurgency" involving "volunteers" and "advisors." Such signal actions or provocations can be expected to compel the attention of decision makers. Clearly, level of provocation may be an important situational variable which is open to different interpretations and from which differing conclusions can be drawn.

Level of provocation was incorporated in the Algonian scenario in Experiment I as part of the summary of the day's events for the 4th and 6th days. Half of the participants in this experiment received the low provocation condition and half the high. The two conditions were presented as follows:

> *Low Provocation: Fourth Day*—Our Intelligence Agency reports it has positive evidence that Utronian nationals are responding to the rebels' call for help. Individual armed volunteers are entering East Algo in small numbers to join the insurrectionists. These are not members of the Utronian Armed Forces.
>
> *Sixth Day*—Our National Intelligence Agency reports that the flow of individual armed volunteers in small numbers into East Algo continues. These are not members of the Utronian Armed Forces.

> *High Provocation: Fourth Day*—Our Intelligence Agency reports that it has positive evidence that Utronian nationals are responding to the rebels' call for help. Organized units of "volunteers," believed to be of company size or larger, are entering East Algo fully armed, equipped, and supplied. These are regular units of the Utronian Armed Forces disguised as "volunteers." It is estimated that, at the present rate of entry, this aid could increase the rebels' chances of success within two or three weeks.
>
> *Sixth Day*—(Last item presented.) Our National Intelligence Agency reports that the flow of organized and armed units of Utronian "volunteers" continues to enter East Algo. These are units of company size or larger and are regular forces disguised as "volunteers."

Probability of Winning War.   The importance of the concept, "probability that an event will occur," for theories of strategy is well known. The same considerations apply for "probability" as an element in the situations confronting decision makers. "Probability" elements of a situation are usually defined for a decision maker by the intelligence estimates and capability analyses of his staff. An analogous procedure was followed in Experiment II through the use of an

"Advisors' Analysis" which analyzed the developing crisis in East Algo and included a statement that the chances that the opponent, Utro, would intervene directly with its armed forces were 50/50. It also included a statement as to the probability that Algo would win a war with Utro should such a war occur. This latter "objective" probability differed for each group of participants depending on whether they were in the high or low probability condition. The following statements were included in the Advisors' Analysis to indicate these two conditions.

High Probability: Our present military superiority and strategic advantages give us a 75 percent chance of winning if we act with strength and decisiveness, before they can mobilize their longer range potential for military superiority. If our action is indecisive and weak, our chance of winning drops as low as 65 percent. It must be remembered that this means that *we stand a 25 percent to 35 percent chance of losing.*

Low Probability: Our present military superiority and strategic advantages give us a 35 percent chance of winning if we act with strength and decisiveness, before they can mobilize their longer range potential for military superiority. If our action is indecisive and weak, our chance of winning drops as low as 25 percent. It must be remembered that this means that *we stand a 65 percent to 75 percent chance of losing.*

Opponent Intentions. The desire to unite a separated people, the need for more living room, the lust for empire, and the need for raw materials have been advanced as reasons for impelling nations to conflict. The estimate of an opponent's intentions, particularly his willingness to engage in hostilities to accomplish expansionistic objectives, is an important consideration in national decision making. In Experiment III of the present study the intention of the opponent, Utro, to acquire the territory of East Algo was varied by means of changing the information in the scenario and in the supplementary materials. For the nonexpansionism condition, Utro's territorial ambitions were minimized. This nonexpansionism was reinforced in the "Advisors' Analysis" by the statement that 75 percent of the Utronian government and people were *opposed* to acquiring East Algo if it meant war. In the high condition, expansionism and aggressiveness were emphasized with 75 percent of the government and people *favoring* the acquisition of East Algo, even if it meant war.

Results

The results of each of the three experiments were evaluated by analysis of variance. The design was a straightforward 2 by 2 by 2 arrangement. In order to compare individual decisions and group consensus decisions in the analysis of variance, the mean of the individual decisions of the four participants in each decision group was used instead of the individual scores.

EXPERIMENT I

Data from Experiment I are presented in Table 15.2. The only variable which significantly affected response level was the individual characteristic, militarism vs. nonbelligerence ($F = 5.38$, $df = 1/40$, $p < .05$). As can be seen in Table 15.2, participants high in militarism selected higher levels of military response than those low in militarism (high in nonbelligerence). The organizational variable affected the group consensus level but not the overall magnitude of the response. In a significantly greater *number* of groups ($p < .05$, Sign Test), participants shifted to a lower as opposed to a higher level of military response after group discussion.

EXPERIMENT II

Data from Experiment II are presented in Table 15.3. There were significant main effects for both the individual characteristic ($F = 9.27$, $df = 1/24$, $p < .01$) and the organizational context variable ($F = 15.89$, $df = 1/24$, $p < .01$). Moreover, there was a significant interaction between the organizational and situational variables ($F = 4.29$, $df = 1/24$, $p < .05$). Mean response levels in Table 15.3 show that those participants preferring high risk chose higher levels of military response as compared to those preferring low risk. However, group consensus levels were consistently lower than the means for the individual decisions. With regard to the interaction between the organizational context and situational variables, the difference between consensus and individual decisions was greater for participants in the high probability condition than in the low probability condition. A shift to lower levels of military response occurred in the consensus decisions under both situational conditions, but for the low probability situation the difference was not significant.

Table 15.2.   Mean Response Level in Experiment I as a Function of Militarism, Level of Provocation, and Type of Organizational Context (Subjects = 176; Groups = 44)

Militarism/ Nonbelligerence Score	Level of Provocation	Individual Decisions	Group Consensus
High	High	6.22 (N=44)	6.07 (N=11)
	Low	5.44 (N=44)	5.77 (N=11)
Low	High	4.82 (N=44)	4.61 (N=11)
	Low	4.84 (N=44)	4.48 (N=11)

Table 15.3.   Mean Response Level in Experiment II as a Function of
Risk-Taking Preference, Probability of Winning War, and
Type of Organizational Context
(Subjects = 112; Groups = 28)

Risk-Taking Preference	Probability of Winning War	Individual Decisions	Group Consensus
High	High	6.80 (*N*=28)	4.98 (*N*=7)
	Low	5.68 (*N*=28)	5.25 (*N*=7)
Low	High	5.24 (*N*=28)	4.12 (*N*=7)
	Low	4.17 (*N*=28)	3.67 (*N*=7)

EXPERIMENT III

The data for Experiment III are found in Table 15.4. In this experiment both the individual characteristic ($F = 4.50$, $df = 1/20$, $p < .05$) and the situational variable ($F = 11.08$, $df = 1/20$, $p < .01$) had significant main effects. Moreover, like Experiment II there was a significant interaction between the situational variable and organizational context ($F = 5.56$, $df = 1/20$, $p < .05$). Table 15.4 shows that highly nationalistic individuals and those in the "opponent expansionism" situation both chose higher levels of military response than did those in the low conditions. The interaction between the situational and organizational variables was different from that in Experiment II. Whereas in Experiment II there was a downward shift in the level of military response, in the present experiment the interaction was such that in the high situational condition response levels shifted *upward* after group discussion while in the low situational condition response levels went *down*.

Table 15.4.   Mean Response Level in Experiment III as a Function of
Nationalism, Opponent's Intentions, and Type of
Organizational Context
(Subjects = 96; Groups = 24)

Nationalism/ Internationalism Score	Opponent's Intentions (Expansionism)	Individual Decisions	Group Consensus
High	High	7.43 (*N*=24)	9.18 (*N*=6)
	Low	5.53 (*N*=24)	5.51 (*N*=6)
Low	High	6.11 (*N*=24)	6.56 (*N*=6)
	Low	4.97 (*N*=24)	4.27 (*N*=6)

Discussion

RELEVANCE OF INDIVIDUAL CHARACTERISTICS
TO DECISION OUTCOME

In all three experiments, there were main effects for the individual characteristics. Decision makers' idiosyncratic traits influenced decision outcomes. Individuals who scored high on "militarism vs. nonbelligerence," high in terms of risk-taking preference, and high on "authoritarian nationalism vs. equalitarian internationalism" chose significantly higher levels of military response than did those whose scores were low on these three psychological dimensions.

RELEVANCE OF ORGANIZATIONAL CONTEXT TO
DECISION OUTCOME

In all of the experiments, organizational context affected the decision outcome in some way. In Experiments I and II group consensus resulted in lower levels of military response than were selected in individual decision making. In Experiment III the effect of group discussion depended upon the situation. Participants confronting a highly expansionistic opponent shifted to a higher level of military response as a result of group discussion, while those confronting a nonexpansionistic opponent moved to a lower response level in their consensual decision. The results from Experiment III suggest the impact which situational variables can have in determining whether a group of decision makers escalates or de-escalates their military response. One consequence of group discussion apparently is to enhance certain situational cues—something which is less likely to happen when one makes a decision for himself. While we recognize that our "organizational context" variable was only a rough approximation of the formal organizational contexts encountered in governmental decision making, these results tend, interestingly, to correspond more closely to findings concerning the effects of committee behavior on decision outcome reported by political scientists than to results of research on small groups reported by social psychologists.

RELEVANCE OF SITUATIONAL VARIABLES TO
DECISION OUTCOME

In both Experiments I and II, there were no significant main effects for the situational variables, although in the second study the situational and organizational variables interacted. Only in Experiment III did the situational variable have an effect on decision outcome. It is rather surprising that the difference between "infiltration by armed individuals" and "infiltration by company-sized organized units of regular forces disguised as volunteers" (Experiment I) did not affect the participants' decisions. It is even more surprising that the difference between a 75 percent chance of winning any eventual war and a 75 percent chance of losing such a war (Experiment II) did not importantly affect the military response levels chosen by the participants. Of the situational variables examined, only the motives of the opponent made a pronounced difference to the participants; when the opponent nation was presented as expansionistic with respect to the territory of East Algo, the participants chose a higher level of military response than when the opponent was viewed as nonexpansionistic. The strong main effect of the "opponent's motives" variable (Experiment III) suggests the central role which "attributions of another's intent" may play in the definition of a situation; "objective" events acquire different meanings depending upon the attribution of intent. Perhaps the relative unimportance of the situational variables in contrast to the individual characteristics is due to our particular participants' lack of experience in decision making.

NOTE ON EXTERNAL VALIDITY

As mentioned earlier the scenario used in the present study was structured as a rough parallel to an historical case of international conflict. While the names were changed (in part, perhaps, to protect the authors' historical innocence), the situation was meant to confront the participants with a conflict decision problem analogous to that confronting the Mexican Government (Algo) in its conflict with the United States (Utro) regarding Texas (East Algo). In spite of the many historical dissimilarities reflected in the scenario and accompanying map—many of which were intentional masks—the situation is easily recognized by persons who are even moderately familiar with that period of American/Mexican history. Nonetheless, of the 384 subjects in the three experiments, only one correctly identified the historical situation in the post-experimental questionnaire (a fact which may be disconcerting to high-school history teachers but was most reassuring to a group of experimenters!).

It may be interesting to note whether the decisions taken in the experiment conformed to the decision outcome in the actual historical case. Response levels 4 or 5 were judged by the experimenters to have been the approximate level of response taken by Mexico; we rated Mexican action at "the Alamo" as approximately similar to "heavy counter-rebel action" (level 5). Table 15.5 presents the distribution of responses over the eleven response levels for the 384 individuals and 96 groups in the three experiments. Levels 4 and 5 were chosen by 45 percent of the individuals and 57 percent of the groups.

If one considers each individual and each group as a separate replication of the simulated historical situation (which means ignoring the differences resulting from the selection of the individuals and variations in the situational conditions), then the correspondence is remarkably high. While there was wide variation in the level of response chosen, almost half of the individuals and more than half of the groups chose the level the authors judged to represent the historical decision. To be sure there were almost as many "misses" as "hits," but the agreement is remarkably high when compared to the degree of conformity to prediction usually obtained in behavioral science research. For example, to obtain correct predictions in 45 percent and 57 percent of the cases in psychological testing,

Table 15.5.   Distribution of Individual and Group
Responses for Each Experiment

Response Level	Experiment I		Experiment II		Experiment III	
	Individual	Group	Individual	Group	Individual	Group
1	0	0	0	0	0	0
2	8	1	2	0	4	0
3	5	1	3	1	4	1
4	9	1	3	0	0	1
5	74	24	53	21	33	8
6	12	2	8	3	5	1
7	10	3	7	1	4	1
8	25	4	12	0	18	2
9	3	2	5	0	5	2
10	11	1	5	0	6	3
11	19	5	14	2	17	5
Total	176	44	112	28	96	24

the validity coefficients would have to be .67 and .75 respectively. A psychological test is considered excellent if its validity is between .45 and .55.

In evaluating these results, the reader needs to know that a somewhat similar situation in Vietnam occupied contemporaneous newspaper headlines during the course of the experiments. Data-gathering was already under way as the Vietnam conflict was escalating (Winter, 1964-65) and the question of crossing some form of international boundary was much discussed in the media. When participants were asked in the post-experiment questionnaire if the exercise reminded them of some situation, past or present, Vietnam was by far the most frequent response (118 out of the 243 who were reminded of anything at all). While we do not have data on the response levels of these particular individuals (31 percent of the total number of subjects), it is possible that a "Vietnam effect" rather than a "scenario effect" accounted for some of the clustering near level 5 and, thus, added a spurious element to any inferences one might wish to make about external validity by comparing response modalities to the decision taken in the intended historical analogue.

As a further caution, we note that neither of the authors is a historian and our rendering of the scenario could be in serious error. The whole approach, however, does raise the intriguing speculation that history could become, in part, a laboratory discipline. Validation of simulations of international processes by congruence with historical situations has had strong appeal for political scientists despite difficulties in implementation. It is a different question to ask, "Can history repeat itself in the laboratory?" After all, validation is a two-way street—when a laboratory result conflicts with an historical interpretation, which is right? At our present state-of-the-art we had best avoid any challenges, but a future can be foreseen when such an issue might be taken seriously, perhaps even by historians.

Conclusion

Learning about the interrelations among different classes of variables is important because each type of variable reflects a different orientation toward the explanation of complex events such as those encountered in international conflict. These differences are implied in such parochial notions as: "the great man theory," "bureaucratic inertia (or momentum)," and "events taking control." In spite of many advances in our understanding of such phenomena in recent years, the relative importance of individual, organizational, and situational factors is still a matter of dispute; disciplinary and philosophic predispositions are very much in evidence. It is our belief that complexity is the essence of the problem. We like to think that the present study, its limitations notwithstanding, has produced evidence to show how individual, organizational, and situational variables can affect decision making. Furthermore, we hope that the study has demonstrated that, through a combination of simulated environments and modern experimental methodologies, some of the complexity of international relations and foreign policy can be addressed with rigor and without undue sacrifice of external validity for internal validity.

Specialization by behavioral science disciplines is justified by the progress it provides in understanding limited content areas. For more complex phenomena, an interdisciplinary approach has often been advocated and the interactions found in the present study provide some empirical support for this position. Progress in understanding complex social behavior can be speeded if we each stop holding all other behavioral science disciplines constant except our own.

CHAPTER 16

The Person, Role, and Situation in International Negotiations*

Daniel Druckman

Editor's Introduction

How do the personal characteristics of the negotiators involved in international negotiations affect their reaching an agreement? Is it possible to separate the impact of person, role, and situation variables on international negotiations? These are the topics of the present chapter by Druckman. The primary subjects of the chapter are negotiators. The political behavior of interest is negotiating behavior—in particular, the process and outcome of negotiations between nations. As in the Driver (Chapter 13) and Crow and Noel (Chapter 15) chapters, the emphasis here is on the behavior of the political unit. Unlike most other

*I am deeply grateful to the editor for her excellent comments and suggestions on an earlier draft. I would also like to extend my appreciation to the Academy for Educational Development, New York and, in particular, to Edward W. Barrett (Director of the Academy's Communications Institute) for support (provided by the Schweppe Research and Education Fund) of an earlier project that formed the basis for this chapter. These various efforts have benefitted considerably from Ed Barrett's continuous encouragement and enthusiasm.

previous chapters, however, the present one does not report the results of a particular piece of research but reviews the experimental research literature on negotiation since 1965 in an effort to suggest its implications for international negotiations.

Two of the kinds of person variables which Druckman describes as having an effect on international negotiations merit some introduction since they have important implications for future research on political leadership. The first type Druckman calls "cultural differences among negotiators." In effect, he argues that the experimental literature suggests that there are cross-national differences in negotiating style. There are preferred ways of behaving in negotiations which differ across nations and can come into conflict when negotiators from such nations must bargain together. The fact that Druckman has found studies which show cultural differences raises a problem for researchers interested in examining the effects of the personal characteristics of cross-national political leaders on national political behavior. Are there personal characteristics specific to certain cultures or parts of the world? For example, is there support for the oft-made claim that the personal characteristics of the Eastern or Oriental man differ from those of Western man? The research question becomes one of separating culturally derived personal characteristics from individually derived personal characteristics. As it becomes feasible to study the personal characteristics of national political leaders (and given the procedures discussed in this book, such studies should seem more feasible), research aimed at separating these phenomena is possible. Using our example of Eastern versus Western man, data on the personal characteristics of Eastern and Western heads of state would enable us to compare these two types of leaders to see if they differed on certain hypothesized characteristics and to note the range in the data for the characteristics for each type of leader.

The second type of person variable of interest Druckman describes as the "problem of coordination." As Druckman notes, negotiation depends on "negotiators coordinating their intentions and concession-making functions." Each negotiator mutually influences the other in the course of deliberations as each tries to ascertain the other's continually shifting goals, strategies, and willingness to concede. In effect, coordination depends on the dyadic interaction of the negotiators—on the match between the characteristics of the representatives of both sides to the conflict. Since few policy decisions are made by one person, the problem of coordination is probably relevant to most kinds of political behavior. The more general research question is how do the characteristics of policy makers interact to affect the resultant policies. For example, what differences are there in the policies of a dogmatic head of state and a dogmatic foreign minister as opposed to a nondogmatic head of state and a nondogmatic foreign minister, between a conservative mayor and a liberal city council president and vice versa? Driver (Chapter 13) and Crow and Noel (Chapter 15) attempted to control for such coordination effects by examining homogeneous groups of decision makers—those with similar traits. Their results, however, do suggest the policies characteristic of similar or compatible policy makers. Recently Hermann and Kogan (1976) have explored the effects on cooperation of dyads that were homogeneous and heterogeneous on eight personal characteristics. Across a series of interactions, the different types of dyads—both high on the trait, both low on the trait, mixed (high and low) on the trait—had distinctive effects on the level of cooperation. More research of this nature on political leaders is needed.

As with most chapters in this section of the book, the present chapter examines the effects of personal characteristics in concert with situational variables. Personal characteristics and situational variables often interact in determining political behavior. Druckman adds to these two kinds of variables information on role. Throughout the chapter, Druckman presents examples of how person, role, and situational variables affect one another in determining the outcomes of international negotiations.

The particular aspect of role which Druckman examines is representation. A negotiator is a representative of someone or some party, in this case a national government. The concept of representation is generally germane to the study of political leadership. Many political leaders, particularly elected officials, are representatives. An elected official supposedly represents the wishes of his constituents. Moreover, like the negotiator, this same official must respond to another party—the demands of the specific political unit to which he was elected. Druckman and others refer to the conflict between these two types of demands as the boundary role conflict. Druckman indicates some of the variables which influence how responsive a negotiator is to his own party and to his opponent. These same variables may be important to understanding the responsiveness of an elected political leader to his constituents and the political unit of which he is a part.

The research which Druckman reviews uses most of the techniques described in this book—e.g., observation, content analysis, simulation. The research, however, was conducted primarily in a laboratory setting, not with actual negotiators in a "real" negotiation. Druckman is concerned about his extrapolation from the laboratory to the field setting. In an attempt to show the relative similarity of findings in the laboratory and actual experience at the negotiating table, Druckman intertwines anecdotal evidence from actual international negotiations and negotiators with the results from the laboratory. While more field research on international negotiation in ongoing negotiations is desirable, Druckman's chapter is suggestive of the avenues of interest for such future explorations. Moreover, as Driver (Chapter 13) noted in discussing the validity of simulation, the laboratory experiment at times permits one to investigate a phenomenon which is difficult to study—because of access, political climate, national security—in a field setting.

Druckman is a psychologist and Senior Research Analyst at Mathematica, Inc., in Bethesda, Maryland. He has done much research on negotiation as the references to his chapter attest. Moreover, he is currently completing an edited book on negotiation entitled *Negotiations: A Social-Psychological Perspective*. The present chapter builds on his (Druckman, 1973) Sage Professional Paper in International Studies concerned with human factors in international negotiations.

INTERNATIONAL NEGOTIATIONS have excited the curiosity of scholars at least since Thucydides wrote about the "Corinthian Warning" in *The Peloponnesian Wars* (see the Jowett Translation, 1963). Through the years, this curiosity has served as a goad to action—for example, when scholars become statesmen (e.g., Kissinger, 1957) or when their analyses are used as prescriptions by policy makers (e.g., Chayes, 1972; Schelling, 1960)—and as a goad to the development of a scientific discipline evidenced by a growing empirical literature on negotiations which is brought up to date in various reviews and attempted integrations (e.g., Druckman, 1973). Moving in either of these directions, scholars have contributed to the harnessing of scattered informal observations in the form of decision rules for policy or propositions derived from empirical evidence. It is to these visible intellectual products that this essay is addressed.

In their search for a guiding conceptualization, social psychologists have attempted to clarify the relative influence of the person, role, and situation on behavior in a number of settings. These attempts at clarification have been largely at the empirical level where complexity is revealed by the emergence of an interactive model summarized by the general observation that "under certain conditions, particular 'person' variables influence behavior when they are not moderated by role demands." Progress at the theoretical level lags far behind as Terhune (1970) attests in his attempt at integration. This lag is due in part to the lack of a paradigm to guide analytical development. Moreover, agreement on definitions is not universal, often precipitating a philosophical debate over such issues as whether the situation is objective, existing external to the individual, or is subjective, existing only insofar as it is defined by the individual. In any event, this chapter will not contribute directly to the advancement of theory, paradigm construction, or to clarification of definition. Rather, while waiting for break-throughs to occur, this essay borrows from the progress that has been made to date in attempting to extend the conceptualization to the arena of international negotiations. Furthermore, this essay benefits from a previous review of the bargaining and negotiation literature concerned with international negotiation by Sawyer and Guetzkow (1965). They present in their review the framework for a general model of negotiation.

By interspersing material on international diplomacy with results of laboratory studies, Sawyer and Guetzkow (1965) convey a sense of the broad range of causal influences which can operate on the process and outcome of international negotiations. Their interplay between laboratory and field data serves to extend the restricted focus of experimentation while sharpening the expanded focus of traditional treatments. The two major kinds of variables which Sawyer and Guetzkow consider to have an impact on international negotiation are *background factors* and *conditions*. Background factors refer to characteristics of the negotiators and their positions or roles vis à vis their own governments and the other negotiators who are involved. Conditions are variables concerned with the setting or environment in which the negotiations are being conducted. These two components of the Sawyer-Guetzkow model parallel the person, role, and situation variables to be discussed here.

The following are some of the situation, role, and person variables highlighted in this essay. Among the person factors of interest are cognitive and ideological differences, cultural or national differences, and attitudes, strategies, and attributions of the other's intentions. Among the situation variables which will be considered are prenegotiation experience, agenda formation, open versus secret negotiations, and stresses and tensions caused by such factors as time pressures and the consequences of the outcome. The third concept, role, is considered in terms of its representational aspects. While the referent for representation in international negotiations is not always clear (e.g., all citizens, the State Department, the President), the fact of representation is. As a representative, the negotiator is constrained by instructions regarding the positions he can take, by diplomatic guidelines for his behavior, by accountability for the outcome of the deliberations, and so on.

In this essay, person, situation, and representational role variables are treated as factors which facilitate or impede *agreement* in bilateral or multilateral negotiations. Like other treatments of international negotiations, *agreement* is considered in terms of both process and outcome (e.g., Iklé's 1964) conception that the outcome emerges out of a process of continuous assessment by negotiators of their threefold choice—reach agreement, abandon negotiations, or continue bargaining). However, unlike other treatments which have relied on events and documented quotes (e.g., Iklé, 1964), personal experience (e.g., Lall, 1966), or case studies (e.g., Walton and McKersie, 1965), this effort uses experimental data as the primary, though not the exclusive, information base from which propositions and insights are drawn.[1]

---

[1]While reliance on experimental findings adds analytical rigor to the study of international negotiations, it also raises the issues of extrapolation and relevance. The issue of extrapolation will not be resolved in this paper. Rather, we *assert* that the generality of laboratory findings to nonlaboratory settings can be treated as an empirical issue, resolvable through exhaustive comparisons of parallel data sets. Moreover, we *assume* that general social psychological processes, observed repeatedly, are relevant to international negotiations. Some progress has been made in assessing the generality of laboratory findings on negotiation (see, e.g., Bonham, 1971; Guetzkow, 1968), and some support can be found for the assumption of "relevance" in the literature on international negotiations (see, e.g., Jervis, 1972; Kelman, 1965, p. 591). In general, it is claimed that the more similar the settings which are being compared, the more likely an observed correspondence in process between the settings. This principle of *proximal similarity* suggests that the studies selected for review should be those which provide information concerning a process relevant to the phenomenon of international negotiations *per se*. Such a principle guided our reading of the literature as reflected in this essay. This strategy represents a compromise between drawing exclusively upon the more general experimental literature on negotiation and limiting

The format for this essay is similar in some respects to that employed by Sawyer and Guetzkow (1965). In scope this treatment is more modest, emphasizing only the background factors and conditions components of their model. In style this treatment is more rigorous, relying more on experimental evidence and, in general, imposing an independent-intervening-dependent variable model on the phenomenon. In addition, the review serves to update the Sawyer-Guetzkow effort by focusing primarily on developments since their chapter appeared. Following each section, a summary set of propositions is suggested, based on an attempted integration of the preceding material. Plausible interactions among the three types of variables are suggested in a concluding section, and the central factors within each of these categories which have been shown to facilitate or hinder obtaining agreements are presented. The sections are arranged in a roughly temporal order in terms of influences on the negotiation process.

Person Factors Influencing Negotiation

As noted earlier, person factors consist of all those characteristics, experiences, attitudes, and problems that negotiators bring to the situation that may influence the course of negotiations. These factors exist prior to the negotiations, affecting the initial positions taken and the course of developments in the negotiations, although their influence may be moderated somewhat by role obligations and situational variables. Among the factors considered here are those cognitive, ideological, and cultural differences between parties which lead the parties to take different positions on the issues being negotiated as well as those cognitive, cultural, attitudinal, and affective differences between the negotiators that create amity or enmity among the parties. Thus, as conceived in this chapter, person factors serve as "inputs" to the initial positions taken and to the affect that lingers on through the course of the deliberations. These factors often impede the process of negotiating an agreement, as numerous experiments conducted at the interpersonal level have demonstrated. Several investigators have constructed techniques designed to assuage the negative impact of cognitive (Hammond and Brehmer, 1973), ideological (A. Rapoport, 1964), and attitudinal (Burton, 1969; Doob, 1970) differences on negotiations. Both the experimental evidence and some of the proposed "therapeutic" techniques are reviewed in this section.

selection to simulation studies and studies conducted *in situ*. The strategy is based on the contention that much of the general literature is only partially relevant to international negotiations and on the *fact* that there have been very few simulation or field studies of international negotiations completed to date. This position is not as extreme as that taken recently by Bobrow (1972, p. 55) who argued: "We should move more rapidly toward treating phenomena that cross national lines as instances of phenomena that occur in several types of social units. Accordingly, alliances become coalitions; negotiations between nations become bargaining; foreign policy choices become decision-making." While not disagreeing entirely with this position, we argue that the *differences* between settings may be as interesting as the *similarities*.

CHARACTERISTICS OF THE NEGOTIATOR

In his book on "Diplomacy," Nicolson (1939, p. 126) characterized the "ideal" diplomat: "These, then, are the qualities of my ideal diplomatist. Truth, accuracy, calm, patience, good temper, modesty and loyalty. They are also the qualities of an ideal diplomacy." This list is an improvement over the one proposed by Ottaviano Maggi some 400 years earlier which ranged from being a "genius" to being "of excellent family, rich, and endowed with a fine physical presence." Yet the difference is one of exaggeration rather than form. Francis Bacon (1890, p. 331) differentiated more precisely when he advised: "Use also such persons as affect the business wherein they are employed, for that quickeneth much; and such as are fit for the matter, as bold men for expostulation, fair-spoken men for persuasion, crafty men for inquiry and observation, forward and absurd men for business that doth not well bear out itself." These early "person-oriented" treatments have their modern-day counterparts in Gladstone (1962) who analyzes international orientations in terms of the Freudian developmental stages or Scott (1965) who searches for correlations between personal attitudes and preferences for national postures. But just how important are personal characteristics as factors which influence the process and outcome of negotiations? What does the empirical evidence suggest?

From one standpoint, Boulding (1966, p. 66) claims that since there are few decision makers in the international system, the personality characteristics of these role-occupants are important. He argues that:

> The international system is much more like a duopoly or oligopoly in economics, where we have the interaction of a few sellers. In this case the personalities of the decision makers may be important. We cannot assume that individual differences cancel out in the mass, and even though in organizations the behavior of a role occupant such as a president or prime minister is determined in considerable measure by the role which he occupies and the information system which surrounds him, different decision makers in the same role will make different decisions and it cannot be assumed that the structure of the organization determines the decisions that are made in it.

However, for other reasons, it can be argued that a decision maker's personality is not important: (a) the range of variation in personality among top level decision makers is restricted due to a recruitment process that limits selection from among a small population of persons with similar backgrounds and experiences (see Modelski's (1970) data on foreign ministers); (b) there develops over time a sub-culture shared by opposite number diplomats which serves to provide a normative framework for behavior (see Bartos, 1967; Turk and Lefcowitz, 1962); (c) role demands and accountability pressures submerge the expression of idiosyncratic factors; (d) experimental evidence from studies in which subjects were neither trained negotiators nor drawn from as homogeneous a population as professional negotiators suggests few clear relationships between personality and bargaining behavior (e.g., see Bartos, 1967; Terhune, 1970); and (e) personality variables are less likely to affect behavior in situations that are highly complex (e.g., Walton and McKersie, 1965), threatening (e.g., Terhune, 1968a), or in which normative or mediative mechanisms suggest a resolution of the conflict (e.g., Joseph and Willis, 1963). Since these are the conditions under which "real world" negotiations often occur, negotiators' characteristics are likely to have a negligible effect in such situations.

Yet, the operation of these moderating factors notwithstanding, there is evidence which suggests that personality variables may affect negotiations in a more subtle manner than can be gleaned from many of the experimental investigations. By focusing exclusively on outcomes, these investigations have overlooked the process through which such outcomes are reached.[2] When the process is examined, dramatic relationships between personality variables and behavior sometimes emerge. Personality variables have been found to affect the process of interaction in gaming situations during the early phases of interaction before the structural aspects of the situation overwhelm these effects (Pilisuk et al., 1965; Terhune, 1968a), and then again during the later phases of interaction in very long games (Bixenstine and Blundell, 1966). Moreover, personality variables can affect reactions to a specific sequence of moves, for example, cooperating on a trial after having cooperated (competed) while the opponent competed (cooperated) (Gahagan et al., 1967; Tedeschi et al., 1969). Such reaction propensities impact on different aspects of the interaction process; for example, when an immediate retaliation to a hostile act and the future course of conflict are differentially affected by Machiavellian attitudes and tolerance for ambiguity (Teger, 1970) or when "internationalists" respond to shifts in an opponent's strategy while "isolationists" do not (McClintock et al., 1965). Furthermore, opponents with different matchings on personality traits produce different trends in cooperation or competition through time—for example, a curvilinear trend results when the contestants are both "low" in cognitive complexity, dogmatism, or tendency to be conciliative while a linear trend characterizes the "low-high" and "high-high" pairings for the same traits (Hermann and Kogan, 1976).

Even more interesting, perhaps, is the finding which suggests that these effects are most likely to occur under conditions similar to those under which

---

[2]By *outcome* we are referring to indices which reflect the state of affairs at the point of termination, including the number of issues resolved, the type of resolution attained, the total amount of concession made by each of the parties, the relative amount of concession made by the parties, the satisfaction of each party with respect to each agreement, and so on. The negligible effects obtained in most of these studies on *outcome* indices have led experimentalists toward a preference for situational interpretations of conflict behavior (see Terhune, 1970), and have reinforced a preference among international relations scholars for system-theoretic perspectives (see Jervis, 1972). A closer look at the literature or more detailed data analyses on process, however, might serve to moderate the intensity with which these preferences are held. By *process* we are referring to indices which reflect such events as the exchange of bids or offers as well as the use of influence tactics and other forms of communication or debate through time from the inception of negotiation to its termination in deadlock or agreement.

"real world" negotiations occur, namely, when the situation permits a range of strategic options leading to the same outcome and when communication is permitted (Terhune, 1968a). Under such conditions negotiators with different definitions of the situation are likely to choose different options. For example, negotiators who have different "philosophies of human nature" (see Wrightsman, 1966) are likely to interpret an opponent's concessions differently—e.g., as a trick or as a sign of "weakness"—leading each to behave differently—e.g., to tighten up his own concessions or yield in an attempt to reach an agreement. Similarly, negotiators with different definitions of the purpose of the negotiations (e.g., to "win" or to "compromise") are likely to react differently to opponent concessions. Moreover, these "definition of the situation" variables may correlate with such personality variables as Machiavellianism (e.g., Geis, 1964) or dogmatism (e.g., Druckman, 1967), which also have been shown to affect bargaining behavior. On the other hand, the situation itself may suggest a particular negotiating strategy or provoke competitiveness (cooperativeness) by features inherent in its structure. Under these circumstances, the effects of prenegotiation attitudes are likely to be precluded (some of the specific conditions are discussed in Druckman, 1971, pp. 534-535).

Further support for person-process relationships comes from research conducted *in situ.* Similar to the laboratory findings, these observations suggest that the effects of personality characteristics may be stronger during certain phases or junctures in the negotiation process. Based on her observations of collective bargaining sessions, Douglas (1957) notes that bargainers rely primarily on their personal resources during the second phase of the bargaining process which she calls "reconnoitering the range." In her words, "the properties of organizational action have become too limited to meet the demands of the bargaining situation, which now calls on negotiators to put at the disposal of their respective parties their individual capacities to assay the rapid conversations going on in the environment and to improvise adaptive behaviors on the spot" (Douglas, 1957, p. 77). It is during this stage of negotiations, when bargainers are released from those role obligations that constrain their behavior during the first and third phases, that the critical adjustments are made toward an agreement. For this reason, it is important to "know the man" with whom you are negotiating. Informal meetings that take place "around" the negotiations can provide this opportunity (see Iklé, 1964, Chapter 9). While the negotiator's "official" behavior often betrays one's expectation formed on the basis of informal conversation (e.g., Westerners are often surprised by the contrast between Soviet officials' behavior at the conference table and their personal affability in informal meetings), some insight into "the man" may be of considerable aid for understanding his behavior during Douglas' second phase.

The evidence discussed in this section suggests the first set of summary propositions:

1. Background and experiential differences between international negotiators are minimized by the similar selective recruiting procedures administered

by different governments.

    a. Differences within this "pool" of selected negotiators are further moderated by a shared "negotiator subculture."

2. The *more* complex, the *more* tense, and the *clearer* the definition of roles in a negotiation situation, the *less* likely will person variables be able to affect negotiation behavior; to the extent that international negotiations occur under these conditions, person variables are likely to have a negligible effect on the course of events in this arena.

3. A limited range of characteristics and moderating conditions notwithstanding, person variables can affect certain subtle processes under certain negotiation situations.

    a. Different negotiators are likely to respond differently to a previous sequence of "moves" (as the way they react to a previous contingent response by the other or to a shift in the other's strategy) and to demonstrate different trends in "softness" or "toughness" over long periods of time.

    b. The *more* a negotiation situation permits a variety of definitions of purpose, opponent's intentions, and so on, the *more* likely are person variables to affect negotiation behavior.

    c. In situations which permit a variety of "definitions," those person variables which affect perceptions of the specific situation, or are related to well-defined aspects of the situation, are most likely to affect negotiation behavior.

4. A cyclical pattern of reliance by negotiators on "personal resources" as opposed to "official postures" causes person variables to be more important during certain junctures of the negotiation process. (Knowing this pattern may prevent a negotiator from confusing "official" behavior with the personal motivations of his opposite number.)

    a. The negotiator is more likely to rely on his own resources during the middle phase of the deliberations.

    b. Person variables are also likely to be important very early in the deliberations, before the structural aspects of the interaction become the major determinant of behavior; such is especially likely to be the case if the negotiator is not constrained at the outset by "official" instructions.

COGNITIVE AND IDEOLOGICAL DIFFERENCES

Cognitive differences between parties or, more broadly, differences in ideological orientation between negotiating parties have been shown to affect the course of negotiations. Hammond and his collaborators (e.g., Hammond, 1965; Hammond et al., 1966) have pursued a large-scale research program designed to examine the effects of cognitive differences on conflict resolution behavior in negotiation situations. Along these lines, L. Rapoport (1969) developed a procedure for assessing the cognitive structure of subjects before they participated in a laboratory experiment. Cognitive structure was defined as the way a person utilized cues in predicting a particular social event. A sample of respondents was asked to predict the amount of racial strife that they thought would be associated with different patterns of, for example, education, housing, and job discrimination. From their responses, it was possible to select pairs whose judgments were highly similar, pairs whose judgments were highly dissimilar, and pairs whose judgments were unrelated. A comparison between these three groups of respondents indicated that significantly more conflict was produced in the "cognitively different" pairs than in the "cognitively similar" pairs with the "neither similar nor dissimilar" pairs falling in between. Moreover, pre-experimental cognitive differences were found to impede learning and compromise.

The difficulty in resolving cognitive structure differences is attested to by results obtained in numerous experiments conducted by the Hammond group. Taken together, the results of some 25 experiments conducted with different types of groups and materials lead to the conclusion that "overt differences in judgment—the visible product of policies—do not converge; overt cognitive differences are not reduced" (Hammond and Brehmer, 1973, p. 386). Overt differences between subjects are differences between them in their initial prediction of an event (e.g., the level of democracy in a nation). Differences invariably occur as a result of discrepant training or experience in the utilization of cues (e.g., elections, state control) to predict social events. After the original judgments are made, respondents discuss their differences in order to arrive at a "joint judgment" which is a mutually agreed-upon prediction of the event. Following the negotiation and joint decision, each subject makes a private judgment, not reported to his opposite number, of the best prediction of the event. (This procedure is repeated for a large number of trials, each trial consisting of a prediction based on specified levels for each of the cues.) In contrast to the overt differences between subjects, these private differences do converge through time (Hammond and Brehmer, 1973, p. 386). In fact, the experiments make apparent that covert conflict is affected by one set of factors while overt conflict is affected by another. "For although covert policy-differences decrease markedly, inconsistency occurs in an amount sufficient to keep the overt judgments of the participants apart, and they continue to experience conflict" (Hammond and Brehmer, 1973, p. 386). However, as convergences occur through time at the covert level, overt differences between the negotiators are likely to become smaller.

In order to moderate the effects of cognitive differences, the investigators devised an elaborate computerized aid for facilitating the learning of another's cognitive structure. Through the use of quantitative/pictorial displays, subjects are able to discern precisely where their agreements and disagreements occur. While some evidence has been obtained demonstrating the effectiveness of this technique (see Hammond and Brehmer, 1973), the use of such techniques in international relations is questionable. The difficulty lies in getting decision makers from different nations to submit to these elaborate procedures and to admit that the only thing preventing them from reaching their joint goal is a "pure" cognitive difference.

Related to the findings obtained in the cognitive conflict experiments, but perhaps more relevant to international relations, are the results of a series of experiments which examined ideological differences and the effects of arousing such differences on attempts to resolve a conflict of interest. In repeated studies of simulated political decision-making conferences, Druckman and Zechmeister (1970; see also Zechmeister and Druckman, 1973) examined how making ideological differences salient affected attempts to resolve a conflict of interest over the funding of urban programs. When such differences were aroused, the decision makers had more difficulty in achieving a resolution and perceived larger differences between their respective conflict of interest positions than when the ideological differences remained implicit. Moreover, the studies showed this effect to be stronger in general for male negotiators and significant only for those female negotiators who identified strongly with the ideological orientations that were aroused.

In spite of the findings reported above, A. Rapoport (1964) recommended debate between the great powers at the level of principles. He argued that by focusing on specific narrowly defined issues which are bargainable (see Fisher, 1964), the negotiators may only be achieving minor adjustments which serve to preserve the system in which hostility and broader ideological divergences are maintained. He suggested a technique for conducting such a debate, called "bilateral exploration of the Region of Validity." It consists of three stages: (1) restating accurately the other person's·position, (2) exploring areas of agreement in the opponent's stand, and (3) inducing assumptions of similarity. In order for this procedure to be effective, explicit role reversing by both contestants is necessary. However, the empirical evidence on the effectiveness of role reversal is not terribly encouraging (e.g., see Hammond et al., 1966; Druckman, 1968b). The evidence indicates that very specific conditions have to be met in order for role reversal to be effective (see Druckman, 1971). Among other factors, the negotiators must be skillful role reversers (D. Johnson, 1967; Muney and Deutsch, 1968); their positions should not be incompatible (i.e., both could be true at the same time—D. Johnson, 1967); they should not be highly precommitted to their initial positions (Blake and Mouton, 1962); their negotiating orientation should be individualistic rather than competitive (Johnson and Dustin, 1970); and the issue should be one which has been the subject of considerable public discussion (Muney and Deutsch, 1968).

Thus, like cognitive differences, conflicts caused by ideological differences have been shown to be very difficult to resolve through compromise. Moreover, it is conjectured that negotiators with opposing ideologies become further polarized through time or repeated interactions, intensifying the conflict over issues derived from their contrasting ideologies (see Druckman and Zechmeister, 1973). In order to prevent such an escalating spiral, countervailing mediational mechanisms built into the negotiating situation might be invoked. For example, shared interests that cut across the ideological divisions might be emphasized both in informal discussions and in the formal deliberations. In addition, an intermediary might reveal schisms that exist within each of the contending parties on ideology or on the interests that derive from these more general positions. This tactic could serve to provide each negotiator with a more realistic and less stereotyped image of the other (i.e., as a party that is not committed to a single ideology). Perhaps this is a more effective strategy for reducing the intensity of conflicts that derive from ideological differences than direct confrontation between the contesting parties on the contrasting ideologies *per se*.

A second set of propositions is suggested by the evidence reviewed in this section:

5. Cognitive differences impede attempts by negotiators to attain an agreement; the larger the differences in cognitive structure between negotiators, the more difficult it is to achieve a resolution.
   a. Cognitive differences are more difficult to resolve at the overt or public level than at the covert or private level; overt differences are reduced more slowly than covert differences.
   b. As convergences occur through time in covert cognitive differences, the overt differences become smaller.
6. Conflicts of interest between opposing negotiators are more difficult to resolve when underlying differences in ideology are made explicit.
7. Negotiations that are *not* intended to focus specifically on the resolution of cognitive or ideological differences are facilitated to the extent that the application of techniques designed to reduce the salience of these differences is effective.
   a. A role-reversing procedure designed to facilitate debate and resolution of ideological differences is generally ineffective.
      1. Such a procedure, however, is *more* effective, the *more* competent the negotiators are as role reversers, the *more* compatible the opposing positions, the *less* competitive the negotiating orientation, the *more* the issue(s) has received public attention, and the *less* precommitted the negotiators are to their initial positions.
   b. A more effective strategy for reducing the impact of ideological differences on conflict intensity involves invoking certain mediational mechanisms built into the structure of the negotiation situation (e.g., managing the issues, emphasizing cross-cutting interests) that serve to make one's opposite number appear less of an ideologue, committed to a single ideological system.

CULTURAL DIFFERENCES

Writing in 1939, Nicolson remarked, ". . . there exist certain standards of negotiation which might be regarded as permanent and universal. Apart from these standards, which should be common to all diplomacy, there are marked differences in the theory and practice of the several Great Powers. These differences are caused by variations in national character, tradition and requirements. One can thus distinguish types, or species, of diplomacy and it is important that these distinctions should be recognized" (pp. 127-128). He went on to characterize the differences in diplomatic theory and practice that existed between Great Britain, Germany, France, and Italy. However, such descriptions do not distinguish differences due to culture from other sources of difference between negotiators such as ideology or motivation.[3] One attempt to separate cultural differences *per se* from other influences was made recently by Danielian (1967). He designed a procedure intended to sufficiently sensitize members of contrasting cultures so that they could distinguish the differences between them that were due to culturally derived underlying presuppositions common to most "personalities" within the culture from the differences that were due to individually derived stylistic features. In his example of an application of the technique, an individual trainee for overseas service was confronted with a "staged" contrasting-culture adherent whose "script" consisted of making explicit and challenging the underlying assumptions that characterized the rhetoric of the "naive" trainee. (Unfortunately, Danielian does not provide data on the effectiveness of the technique.)

With respect to international negotiations, the Danielian technique could be used for sensitizing diplomats to the various definitions of the word "compromise" employed by different cultures. Several writers have pointed out that "compromise" has an adverse connotation for a number of major cultures outside the North American continent, including the Soviet Union. For example, Triandis and Davis (1965) observed that Greeks involved in heterocultural discussions with Americans considered settling for a solution "in between" two positions to be a definite defeat. Initial demands were considered as "truths," making compromise impossible. Similarly, Summers et al. (1968) found that Arab subjects involved in heterocultural negotiations with Americans were less willing to compromise than their American counterparts. The proportion of the distance compromised by the Americans was significantly greater (they compromised about half the difference between the contending positions) than that compromised by their Arab counterparts.

Certain types of cultural differences would seem to have more of an impact on the negotiation process than others. One, in particular, is differences in preferences for committee functioning. For example, Gyr (1951) found national differences between Chinese, American, Near Eastern, and South American informants on uncertainty about motives of other committee members, on desire to cooperate in reaching a group goal, on recognition of the superiority of the leader, and on trustfulness. Moreover, differences in styles of diplomacy as described by Nicolson (1939), Iklé (1964, Chapter 12), and others (see Sawyer

[3]Often these sources are confounded in interpretation as several experiments on heterocultural negotiations illustrate (e.g., Nayar et al., 1968; Summers et al., 1968). In these studies, such other dimensions of difference between cultural representatives as ideology, involvement, and information possessed by the parties about the contended issues could have accounted for the findings.

and Guetzkow, 1965, pp. 501-503 for a review of sources) would seem to have a substantial effect on progress. Such is especially the case when incompatible goals and contrasting styles are intertwined as in Communist Chinese-American confrontations. Peking's adversary style—designed to serve its goal of total victory—consists of a tough, offensive posture, a rejection of the rhythm of bargaining and reciprocal concession making (including viewing their opponent's concessions as a trick or a sign of weakness), moves calculated to induce tension, and an unwillingness to consider smaller issues in a stepwise progression toward a resolution of larger issues (see K. Young, 1968, esp. Chapter 15). The contrasting American style of convergent bargaining (i.e., exchanging concessions) reflects a concern for tactics, emphasizing technical remedies and small gains on the way toward agreement on the larger issues (see Kissinger, 1966). These irreconcilable approaches, which are institutionalized by the foreign policy apparatus in each of the nations, have been largely responsible for prolonged deadlock in the protracted ambassadorial talks between these governments. More broadly, adversary negotiating and convergent bargaining are probably the two major negotiating styles that characterize nations in the international system. There may be emerging gradually, however, a third style which Kissinger (1966) has called revolutionary-inspired integrative negotiation where the parties cooperate toward achieving "new" solutions to "old" problems.

Some evidence on differences in negotiating styles is provided at the micro-level of dyadic bargaining by recent experiments on the effects of culture on competitiveness.[4] Among the findings of relevance to international negotiations are: (a) children from a more socialistic, Kibbutz community were more cooperative in general than their city-living (more capitalistic-oriented) counterparts, but the Kibbutzniks were more competitive when they represented a group than when they represented themselves—in contrast to the city children who responded the same in both conditions (Shapira, 1970); (b) Mexican village children were more cooperative than both their U.S. counterparts and urban children in the two cultures (Madsen and Shapira, 1970); (c) the presence of an audience when compared to a condition in which negotiations were conducted in private had the effect of increasing cooperativeness among Argentinian children while it had the effect of increasing competitiveness among American children (Druckman et al., 1976); (d) children from India were more competitive throughout the course of bargaining—making more total offers, making more extreme offers, and rejecting more of their opponent's offers—than similar age cohorts from Argentina who were, in turn, more competitive than U.S. children; moreover, the three cultures demonstrated different patterns of play across repeated bargaining "games" (Druckman et al., 1976); and (e) a marked difference was found between Japanese and American subjects in their use of relative-

[4]In contrast to the studies of heterocultural negotiations, reviewed previously, these studies are less problematic with respect to confounding factors. Simple games were used as tasks to investigate differences in competitiveness *per se*. Since there was no debate over issues, ideologies or values were not involved. For this reason, however, the implications of the obtained results for international negotiations are even more indirect.

gain and gain-maximizing strategies in bargaining (Mushakoji, 1972). The differential use of strategies or differences in competitiveness between representatives of different cultures may lead to asymmetrical outcomes as one negotiator attempts to exploit the other who is not prepared to retaliate.

While the above findings suggest behavioral differences between cultures, there is also evidence for similarity. McClintock and Nuttin (1969) found considerable similarity in patterns of competitive behavior between Belgian and American children. The only difference between these two types of subjects was in the onset of a competitive (i.e., relative-gain) orientation. The Flemish children took longer to manifest the competitive orientation. By the sixth grade, however, the children in both cultures were equally competitive. Brehmer et al. (1970) reported considerable similarity among subjects in five countries (Czechoslovakia, Greece, Japan, Sweden, and the U.S.) in their attempts to resolve a cognitive conflict. The pattern of conflict reduction behavior and other behaviors studied by the cognitive conflict paradigm (see Hammond, 1965) were *independent* of cultural factors.

Such observed similarities as those obtained in the above two studies indicate that nationals from these cultures are better able to coordinate at the negotiation table. However, the relevance of these findings is limited due to the focus of these studies on cultural differences in *intra-cultural* bargaining behavior. Perhaps more directly relevant to the international arena are studies of heterocultural negotiations. Unfortunately, with few exceptions (e.g., Nayar et al., 1968; Summers et al., 1968), experimental studies completed to date on this topic have either only simulated international conferences with subjects of the same nationality (e.g., Bonham, 1971) or have used subjects of the same culture who reported different "views of the world" (e.g., Davis and Triandis, 1965; Zechmeister and Druckman, 1973). And, as indicated earlier (see footnote 3), the results obtained by Nayar et al. (1968) and Summers et al. (1968) are merely suggestive due to a confounding of other dimensions of difference between contestants with cultural differences *per se*.

Taken together with other observations, the experimental findings suggest that, in general, cultural differences are likely to impede progress in negotiations. Yet in spite of the delays apparently caused by these differences, the everyday affairs of state seem to proceed. Cultural differences may be more important as the principal source for conflict in the international system. As Glenn and his collaborators (1970) point out, differences between cultures in broad orientations are probably irreconcilable through negotiation. These investigators characterize the United States, for example, as a case oriented (practical, inductive, issue oriented), abstractive (disciplined, systematic, deliberate) culture while the Soviet Union is depicted as a universal oriented (principled, deductive, uncomprising, generalized), abstractive culture. The Middle East conflict can be explained in terms of the implantation of an abstractive culture into a primarily associative (i.e., react to the environment immediately and intuitively) culture. Since these orientations have survived through centuries of change and realignment, it is unlikely that such a source of conflict will be eliminated in the near future. However, the authors contend that there is gradual progress toward the emergence of a pan culture largely through international participation in such specialized agencies as commercial and investment interchanges and information and educational exchanges. Participation by diverse cultures in these institutions instills an awareness of the counter-culture's orientation.

The following propositions are suggested by the literature reviewed in this section:

8. Techniques that enable negotiators to separate their cultural differences from other types of difference are important for strategic reasons.
   a. Negotiating strategy depends in part on whether a negotiating team considers itself to be confronted by a "tough culture," a "tough opposite number," or a "tough strategy" employed by the other side.
   b. While negotiators can be replaced and strategies can be countered, cultural differences are less likely to be altered in the short run; and, even over the long run, as nations continue to negotiate, cultural convergences are unlikely to occur as a result of the resolutions achieved.
9. Cultural differences between nations cause opposite number negotiators to differ on such dimensions as preferences for committee functioning (e.g., recognition of a leader), motives (e.g., rivalistic vs. joint maximization), style (e.g., cooperativeness vs. competitiveness), definitions of the situation (e.g., negotiation as compromise or as contest), and their responsiveness to aspects of the situation (e.g., the presence of an audience).
10. Negotiations between nations with irreconcilable cultural differences in style or motives are generally protracted, frequently resulting in deadlock or asymmetrical outcomes as one negotiator attempts to exploit his opposite number who is not prepared to retaliate.
11. Differences between nations on cultural presuppositions or linguistic structure are less likely to impede negotiations when opposing negotiators have received training in the concepts of the contrasting culture.

THE PROBLEM OF COORDINATION

The evidence reviewed in the previous sections highlights the effects on negotiation of *differences* between the negotiators. Differences between opposite number negotiators in cognitive structure, ideology, and more general cultural characteristics have all been shown to interfere with the negotiation process as it proceeds toward an acceptable agreement. However, there is evidence which suggests that there may be *fewer* dimensions of difference between the persons appointed as national representatives in negotiations than between other contrasting culture-adherents. For instance, Modelski's (1970) large-scale survey of foreign ministers documents the observation made by others (e.g., Bartos, 1967;

Rusk, 1955) that there is considerable background similarity among foreign ministers from different nations. This similarity is due in part to similar recruitment procedures used by different nations and is perpetuated by the emergence of a cohesive subculture of top-level negotiators. One consequence of this development is that opposite-number negotiators have a better understanding of each other's intentions and a more realistic, less stereotyped appraisal of the other culture. This effect is strengthened by frequent formal and informal contacts among opposite-number role cohorts as Druckman's (1968a) Inter-Nation Simulation data indicate. In that study the "foreign minister," the role with the most equal-status contacts, was the least ethnocentric of four roles in the simulation with regard to perceptions of members of one's own nation, its allies, and its enemies. As a result of his heightened sensitivity and low ethnocentrism, a nation's chief negotiator (e.g., the foreign minister) is likely to be responsive to the needs and concerns of the other nation. Mutual responsiveness among opposite-number negotiators should facilitate coordination although the evidence to be reviewed in this section suggests that the coordination problem is severe even among highly similar contestants (e.g., college students from the same university).

From the standpoint of a particular negotiator the strategies employed by other parties influence his own posture in a cycle of reciprocal influences. As each negotiator reacts to his opposite number, they establish a pattern which may project them on a course toward agreement or toward deadlock. Which outcome is most likely depends on their ability to coordinate their intentions and concession-making functions. The coordination problem has received considerable attention by a number of experimentalists (e.g., Kelley et al., 1967) who consider this to be the central aspect of negotiation between parties who have equal power. In this section, coordination is considered as a problem of the negotiators rather than as a problem resulting from their role or a condition of negotiations. Negotiators begin to assess the other's intentions, strategies, and interests long before the negotiations get underway and continue this assessment throughout the course of the deliberations. The coordination problem is discussed in this section from the standpoint of both prenegotiation and contemporaneous influences.

That coordination is rarely achieved is not surprising when one considers the components of (or prerequisites for) success. Shared goals, accurate perception of the others' utilities for various outcomes as these occur through time, and an agreed-upon exchange rate for concessions are only some of the conditions that must be met in order for parties to synchronize their moves toward an agreement. The difficulty in learning another's position has been documented in experiments by Blake and Mouton (1962) and by Hammond et al. (1966). In spite of lengthy pre-debate learning sessions and subjective judgments of insights into the other's position, subjects typically demonstrate very little actual understanding of the other's positions (Blake and Mouton, 1962). In controlled laboratory studies of interpersonal conflict, subjects are rarely able to achieve a high degree of accuracy when attempting to predict the other's policy judgments, even when they observe each other's judgments over a large number of trials (Hammond et al., 1966). Some of the factors which may be responsible for these learning difficulties were separated recently in an experiment on policy making by Summers et al. (1970). Their general findings indicated that policies which are *inconsistent* with the "learner's" own beliefs and expectations are more difficult to learn. Moreover, information provided in the form of *self report* by the other is considerably less beneficial to the learner than information that is provided by an objective, mathematical model of that individual's judgment policy. The latter result suggests some of the difficulty involved in self report, including inaccuracies and ambiguities inherent in language. A third factor related to learning the other's positions is *complexity*. Subjects in a bilateral-monopoly bargaining study were able to more accurately predict their opponent's concessions when the concession-rate schedule that the opponent employed was less complicated (i.e., they were constant as opposed to accel-erated concessions) (Druckman, Zechmeister, and Solomon, 1972). These diffi-culties are likely to be even further enhanced in international negotiations where policies are more complex than those used in laboratory studies and where access to the others' positions in order to employ quasi-therapeutic techniques (e.g., presenting mathematical models) is highly unlikely.

While both strategic theorists and empirical research have demonstrated the value of complete and accurate information for successful coordination (see Sawyer and Guetzkow, 1965, pp. 496-497 for a review of sources), there is some reason to believe that under certain conditions complete information may actually be a hindrance. For example, veridical perception of the other's inten-tions may reveal antagonistic motives which, if disguised, would not interfere with coordination. In a non-zero-sum situation, both sides may agree on the best solution irrespective of their feelings toward one another. The process of attaining this result can then be treated as a strategic problem which demands a task orientation that is interfered with by feelings of anger. Another advantage of incomplete information is that real position incompatibilities that may exist do not surface. Johnson (1967) presented experimental evidence which indi-cated that for highly adequate learners, greater understanding of the opponent's position increased competition when the contestants' positions were incom-patible, but decreased competition when their positions were compatible.

Incomplete information is just one of the uncertainties that burdens negoti-ators in international negotiations. The dynamics of the process as captured by Iklé (1964) in his chapter on "Shifting Evaluations" reveal that evaluations made by negotiators with regard to the threefold choice (to reach agreement, to abandon negotiations, to continue bargaining) are in constant flux as a result of uncertain criteria for assessing gains and losses, uncertain goals due to changing evaluations of the opponent's motives, and changes in events. All these factors mitigate against setting "realistic" goals that project the parties on a course toward acceptable terms. Iklé's treatment points up the intertwining of goals and process and the shaping of goals by developments monitored through time. What appears to be realistic at one point in time may be "way off the mark" at another. Agreement depends in large part on the ability of the contestants to *coordinate* in spite of the uncertainties. And, agreement often comes about because changing evaluations lead to changing expectations of the opponent's willingness to compromise which in turn softens (or hardens) a negotiator's position, producing a self-fulfilling prophecy (see Druckman, Zechmeister, and Solomon, 1972). On the other hand, this cycle can lead to undesirable consequences as when the West permitted Soviet interference in Czechoslovakia in 1948 enabling the Sovietization of this country. In this case, the Soviets could have been halted before they entered Czechoslovakia by American and British military strength; however, changed evaluations had already caused Washington to regard the Soviet coup as the expected and tolerable outcome. (Of course from the Soviet standpoint, this takeover was a desirable outcome. The Soviets were extraordinarily effective through these extended negotiations in altering Western expectations with regard to their concern for Eastern European territories.)

From another standpoint, however, there is evidence which suggests that evaluations may not shift dramatically through time. Based on limited information, negotiators are prone to attribute intentions to their opposite number. Once the intent of the opponent is established, his negotiation behavior may be interpreted in light of these intentions. For example, attributing competitive intentions to the other may lead one to interpret cooperative moves as temporary and tactical. Also, attributing competitive intentions to an opponent may serve to support one's own competitive posture and its concomitant hostility. Attributions have been shown to relate systematically to the behavior of the person making them. Wilson (1969) presented evidence which indicated that a subject's game strategy is consistent with his attributions of motives to an opponent. When the subject created a competitive situation, he saw his opponent as having untrustworthy motives. When the subject's strategy was based on cooperation, his opponent's motives were viewed more favorably. Changes in an opponent's intentions or strategy may go unnoticed as a result of this attribution process; i.e., one's own behavior and his attribution of the other's behavior are mutually supportive, the one strengthening the other through time.

Another source for inflexibility and insensitivity to changes in an opponent's goals and concession-making function is the intensive unilateral strategy preparation that each team usually engages in prior to the deliberations. Experimental results reported by Druckman (1968b) indicate that this type of prenegotiation experience strengthens within-team cohesiveness, enhances a negotiator's commitment to a position, reinforces a win-lose orientation to the bargaining process, and prolongs the negotiations as each side is less willing to yield to the other. When teams did not prepare strategies but instead engaged in informal discussion of the issues on a unilateral or bilateral basis, negotiations were facilitated. Under these conditions, negotiators were less committed to their initial positions and adopted more of a problem-solving (rather than win-lose) approach to the bargaining process than in the strategy-formation condition. The reduced committedness presumably enabled them to be more flexible and willing to yield in the negotiations while the problem-solving orientation made coordination easier as each bargainer used the other's concession rate as information that would aid *both* in achieving a mutually desirable outcome. Moreover, informal prenegotiation communication with a focus on the issues had a positive effect (as compared to strategy preparation or no preparation) irrespective of the structural arrangement of the groups (unilateral or bilateral) before negotiation (see also Bass, 1966).[5]

For all the reasons discussed above, the problem of coordination can be regarded as severe. Attempts have been made to prescribe solutions from formal models as well as to derive solutions from empirical evidence. No attempt will be made here to review, extend, or comment on these efforts. Rather, the reader is referred to a recent article by Pruitt (1971), who suggests various alternative approaches to the coordination of concession exchanges with examples drawn from international and government-industrial contract negotiations. Both direct and indirect approaches are offered, including:

> a. make a small concession and wait for a counter-concession, b. overtly propose an exchange of concessions, c. tacitly communicate a readiness to concede if the opponent concedes, d. propose an informal conference, e. transmit a conciliatory message via an intermediary, and f. propose that a mediator be called in and reveal information about own priorities to him (Pruitt, 1971, p. 233).

Other direct approaches are proposed by Osgood (1962) and by Siegel and Fouraker (1960) who base their recommendations on the most effective concession-rate strategies for eliciting reciprocation. Interestingly, each proposes a "most effective" strategy which partially contradicts the other's proposed strategy. Among the indirect approaches that have received attention are tacit communication (see Jervis, 1972; Schelling, 1960) and the use of intermediaries (see O. Young, 1972).

The literature on coordination of negotiating strategies discussed in this section suggests the following set of propositions:

12. The more mutually responsive the opposite number negotiators, the easier it is for them to coordinate their intentions and concession-making functions.

[5]However, *well-structured bilateral discussion* may indeed facilitate coordination. In particular, coordination is facilitated when negotiators have agreed on an exchange rate for concessions before the formal deliberations begin. The computation of such a rate depends on the ability of negotiators to define issues in terms of a metric. Once conceived in this manner they can determine how far each is willing to go (used to predict *amount* of movement expected) and the value and cost of a concession of a given size to each party (used to determine the *rate* of movement). When these calculations cannot be made, concession exchange is likely to occur intuitively, aided occasionally by tactical interventions performed by an intermediary. This is often the case in international negotiations where the complexity of the issues mitigates against the computation of stable utilities and disutilities.

13. The more accurately opposite number negotiators perceive each other's utilities for various outcomes, the easier it is for them to coordinate their concession-making strategies.
    a. Despite subjective contentions to the contrary, accurate learning of another's positions and values rarely occurs.
    b. The more consistent with a negotiator's own beliefs, the more precise and unambiguous the presentation, and the less complex the other's policy, the easier it is to accurately learn his positions.
14. Accurate learning of another's positions is more likely to facilitate negotiations the more compatible the opposing positions and the less competitive the intent of the opposing negotiator.
15. The more sensitive the negotiators are to *changes* that occur in the other's intentions and expectations, the easier it is for them to coordinate toward reaching an agreement.
    a. Attributions of intentions to an opponent, made early in the negotiations and based on limited information, hinder sensitivity to changes in intentions or goals that occur through time.
       1. Attributions of another's intent, which may be inaccurate, covary with one's own behavior in negotiations; for example, negotiators who adopt competitive (cooperative) strategies are likely to attribute competitive (cooperative) intentions to an opponent.
       2. Attributions of another's intent and one's own behavior are mutually supportive, the one strengthening the other through time and making one less sensitive to changes that occur in the other's intentions.
    b. The more negotiators engage in unilateral strategy formation prior to negotiations, the less flexible they are to changes in the other's ·intentions or expectations.

Influence of Role as Representative on Negotiation

Negotiators are also occupants of roles which prescribe their options and obligate them to the "home office" for the consequences of their performance. Negotiators are official representatives of policies formulated by their governments through a complex process which involves interdepartmental bargaining within a bureaucratic framework that is affected by the influence of special interest groups, public opinion, and the personal power of certain government officials (see Chayes, 1972). The policy which emanates from a coalescence of these forces presumably reflects the interests of the nation. The negotiator, among others, is responsible for its execution as an agent or delegate of the head of state who, in democratic countries, is himself a political representative. As an agent, the negotiator's posture may range all the way from that of messenger or emissary commissioned to "deliver the position" to free agent with considerable latitude in his attempts to achieve a negotiated agreement. This "decision latitude" or degree of freedom which a negotiator has varies somewhat with the status of the negotiator and the nature of the negotiations (see Iklé, 1964, pp. 123-128).

Consideration of the effects of role behavior on international negotiations shifts our focus from the inter*personal* to the inter*party* level of analysis, from the isolated dyadic bargaining process to intergroup negotiations. The negotiator as representative can be characterized as a mediator between the demands of his "home office" and the demands of his opposite number. His bargaining reputation (see Iklé, 1964, Chapter 6) depends largely on his ability to balance these two pressures in attaining an agreement which is acceptable to the party he represents. This "dual responsiveness" has been referred to as a "boundary role conflict" (e.g., Walton and McKersie, 1965). Boundary role conflict is considered in this section after a discussion of its components, that is, role obligations to one's own party and responsiveness to the other party. One mechanism for resolving these competing pressures, third-party intervention, is also discussed briefly in this section.

ROLE OBLIGATIONS: RESPONSIVENESS TO OWN PARTY

As an agent, the negotiator is responsible for representing his nation's policy in negotiations. This responsibility has implications for the progress of the deliberations. In particular, progress is likely to be impeded as a result of the negotiator's "sense" of being obligated and by the internal policy-making process within which he is ensconced. Both these factors intrude insofar as the negotiator is both an interpreter *of* policy and a messenger *for* policy (see Iklé, 1964, pp. 123-128).

The behavioral consequences of role obligations for dyadic behavior in negotiations has been documented by a number of recent experiments whose results can be summarized as follows:[6]

1. Opposite number negotiators who are representatives are more competitive during the process of negotiating than nonrepresentatives. They make more extreme offers and reject more of their opponent's offers throughout the bargaining. For these reasons it takes them longer to reach an agreement than opposite number negotiators who are not agents for a position or team (see Druckman, Solomon, and Zechmeister, 1972). Related to the behavioral results are findings which demonstrate differences in perceptions of the purpose of

[6]In several of the experiments summarized here, conducted with different age groups and in different settings, responsiveness to role obligations has been found for males but not for females. However, since most diplomats at present are male, these results would seem to have implications for international negotiations and, thus, are reported above. Moreover, these findings are based on experiments conducted with American subjects. Unless otherwise indicated, the findings summarized in this section are not based on cross-cultural data. The extent to which they are *limited* to the U.S. is an empirical question to be resolved by cross-cultural research. Promising starts along these lines are the studies by Shapira (1970) and by Druckman et al. (1976), cited earlier, which obtained cultural differences in response to role obligations.

negotiation. Representatives view the confrontation as more of a "win-lose" contest while nonrepresentatives view it more in terms of a problem to be solved through compromise (Benton and Druckman, 1974).

2. Negotiators who are representatives are more *equally* competitive, miligating against agreements that result from one bargainer submitting to the other. Asymmetrical compromise occurs more often among nonrepresentatives.

3. For representatives competitiveness increases through the course of bargaining, but each representative is more accepting of the other's competitive offers until they reach a mutually acceptable agreement or deadlock. When deadlock is discouraged, pairs of representatives in contrast to nonrepresentatives prefer a compromise solution that serves to minimize the maximum concessions of either delegate (see Hermann and Kogan, 1968; Lamm and Kogan, 1970). This process is similar in some respects to a reciprocity that each accords to the other. Such compromise is facilitated when a salient outcome is possible (Benton and Druckman, 1973).

4. The effects of role obligations on male negotiators are so strong that they occur in the presence of an audience of constituents as well as when there is no audience present and under both a competitive and a cooperative set (see Druckman et al., 1972; Shapira, 1970; Zechmeister and Druckman, 1973). Presumably, the enhanced sensitivity of males to such role requirements emanates from a cultural norm which serves to provide them with more experience in the role of "advocate." Indeed, Shapira's (1970) data suggest that differential frequency of experience as an advocate is responsible for the observed differences in behavior. In that experiment (Shapira, 1970, p. 107), sex differences were obtained in a sample where socialization experiences for boys and girls differed whereas no such differences were found in a sample where socialization experiences for boys and girls were essentially alike. Moreover, other data suggest that greater involvement in the representational role for males than for females may be another source of the observed differences in responsiveness (Zechmeister and Druckman, 1973, p. 86).

One way of characterizing the behavioral effects of role obligations is that such responsiveness legitimizes a pattern of behavior which prevents negotiators from responding spontaneously to their opposite number. These effects are likely to be most pronounced under the following conditions: (1) when a negotiator has little latitude in determining either his position or his posture (see Zechmeister and Druckman, 1973); (2) when a negotiator is held highly accountable for his performance (see Gruder and Rosen, 1971); (3) when a negotiator has sole responsibility for the outcome (see Druckman, Solomon, and Zechmeister, 1972); (4) when a negotiator is obligated to a "team" that is present during the negotiations (see Lamm and Kogan, 1970); and (5) when a negotiator is appointed rather than elected (see Boyd, 1972). Taken together, these conditions determine the extent to which a negotiator's behavior is constrained by his obligations and, indeed, can be considered the *components* of representation. The more latitude a negotiator has in constructing the positions that he represents, the more dispersed the responsibility for the outcome (e.g., see Druckman,

1967, and Lamm and Kogan, 1970, for examples of shared responsibilities for the outcome among several representatives), and the more abstract the constituency (e.g., cultures, ideologies),[7] the less the impact of representational role obligations on behavior. Instead of responding to demands from his own constituents, the "uncommitted" representative is free to respond to the demands of his opposite number. In fact, under certain conditions a negotiator may be "obligated" to be responsive to the demands of his opponent(s). Some of these conditions are discussed in the next section.

The research evidence just reviewed suggests that the negotiator in his role as representative is constrained by external pressures which affect his posture in the deliberations. The impression one gets from these findings is that the negotiator is a passive recipient of instructions for the next phase of deliberations. However, this characterization may be misleading. In most instances the negotiator is very much a part of the process of intraparty maneuvering for negotiating positions that proceeds concurrently with the interparty deliberations. Typically he is at the cross-roads between the intra- and interparty bargaining that occurs simultaneously. In fact his role of agent often blends into that of mediator between the contending parties (see Evan and MacDougall, 1967). As such, he seeks to achieve an internal consensus on the position that he is to defend at any particular time (see Walton and McKersie, 1965). Some negotiators take an active role in insuring that *all* responsible parties perceive veridically the existence of a consensus on both positions and posture.[8] Without a consensus within the negotiator's own party, his concessions are very difficult to interpret. For example, does the negotiator's party expect him to concede a particular point; from what initial position is he conceding? Under these conditions, negotiators are likely to be reluctant to offer concessions, especially when they are highly accountable to their "office." The results of a recent experiment document this interpretation.

Gruder and Rosen (1971) created conditions of high and low accountability of negotiators to their constituents by manipulating the expectation that their performance would be evaluated by their teammates following the bargaining. In addition, communications from constituents suggesting different types of postures (e.g., exploitative, fair) were manipulated. Highly accountable subjects as compared to the less accountable subjects conceded very slowly irrespective of the type of communication received from their constituents. During the negotiation process the accountable subjects desired more open communication

[7]Assessment of the effects of different types of constituencies on role behavior is a line of research that would seem to have direct implications for international negotiations. For example, are the behavioral implications of representing a large bureaucratic organization different than representing an abstract ideology or a team that is present during negotiations? To date, however, this issue has not been explored systematically.

[8]This maneuvering is especially characteristic of negotiators who feel strongly about their position or who are generally assertive and energetic. However, as research by Blake and Mouton (1962, p. 222) suggests, such differences between representatives are moderated by selection procedures which insure that appointed (or elected) negotiators are assertive, dominant, tactically competent, and strong believers in the positions that they must defend.

with their constituents in an attempt to learn *specifically* what agreement the constituents would consider satisfactory. Until the negotiators received this clarification they were unwilling to offer concessions to their opponent. Moreover, the authors (Gruder and Rosen, 1971, p. 316) suggest that the negotiator in the high accountability condition desired to "plan any bargaining strategy jointly with his constituent, and thereby share the responsibility for any risks which the subjects might take in bargaining."

Continuous collaboration between the negotiator and his own party is important in order to prevent an incorrect attribution by the negotiator of his constituency's expectations. Incorrect attributions may lead a negotiator to perform in a manner that is inconsistent with his constituency's expectations in spite of intentions to the contrary. Realizing this, the accountable negotiator is likely to go to considerable lengths to insure that his perception of his constituency's expectations is veridical. For example, he may frequently call for a recess in order to confer with team members or he may devise an elaborate signaling system for communicating with them during the deliberations. And, as data presented by Klimoski (1972) suggests, this maneuvering and the concomitant slower progression to agreement is further enhanced when the accountable negotiator is highly attracted to the team he represents.

The empirical results reviewed above can be summarized by the following set of propositions:

16. The more responsive opposite number negotiators are to their representational role obligations, the more competitive they are throughout the course of the deliberations.
    a. Competitiveness increases throughout the course of bargaining for opposite number representatives who are *both* responsive to their role obligations.
    b. Opposite number representatives who are both responsive to their role obligations are more equally competitive than those opponents who are not responsive to their role obligations or who are not under such pressures.
    c. Responsive opposite number representatives are more likely to attain agreements that are achieved by symmetrical compromises.
    d. Negotiations are longer and deadlocks are more frequent for responsive (as compared to nonresponsive) opposite number representatives.
17. Male negotiators are more responsive to their role obligations (or to their own party) than female representatives, and, as a result, are more likely to demonstrate the negotiating style just described.
18. A negotiator's responsiveness to his role obligations depends upon the following role characteristics: amount of decision latitude, degree of accountability, amount of responsibility for the outcome, type of constituents, and amount of surveillance by teammates.
    a. The less latitude a negotiator has in defining his party's positions, the more responsive he is to his role obligations.

b. The more accountable the negotiator is for the outcome, the more
    responsive he is to his role obligations.
    1. The more accountable the negotiator is for the outcome, the
        slower his concession making and the longer the negotiations.
        1a. Negotiations are delayed even further when the accountable
            negotiator is highly attracted to his team (or constituents).
c. The more the responsibility falls on the negotiator alone, the more
    responsive he is to his role obligations.
d. The more concrete (or less abstract) the negotiator's constituents,
    the more responsive he is to his role obligations.
e. The more "public" the negotiation process, the more responsive the
    negotiator is to his role obligations.

ROLE OBLIGATIONS: RESPONSIVENESS TO OTHER PARTY

As an agent, the negotiator is also responsible for achieving an agreement with
his opposite number(s). This responsibility has implications for the progress of
the deliberations. In particular, progress is likely to be facilitated to the extent
that both negotiators take into account each other's desires for an acceptable
agreement. Taking into account both the demands of their own party and the
preferences of the other party should aid them in evaluating their threefold
choice during the process of negotiating—reach agreement, abandon negotiations, or continue negotiations (Iklé, 1964, Chapter 5).

The behavioral implications of being responsive to one's opposite number are
in direct opposition to the findings summarized above on the effects of being
obligated to one's own team. High "internal" obligations on the part of both
negotiators mitigate against mutual responsiveness. "Without responsiveness each
party will tend to insist that he gain just as much as the other in every
agreement ... that an equal trade of concessions be found at once, in the
present negotiation" (Pruitt, 1962, pp. 16-17). Such a pattern of behavior was
found to be characteristic of negotiators who were under strong pressure to
represent their group (e.g., Hermann and Kogan, 1968; Lamm and Kogan, 1970;
Druckman, Solomon, and Zechmeister, 1972). In contrast, mutual responsiveness is likely to lead one party to bow to the other "in cases where the other has
much to be gained or lost, knowing that he is building up credit such that the
other will do the same for him" (Pruitt, 1962, p. 16). This behavior is similar to
that observed when nonrepresentatives bargain—one concedes to the other in
order to achieve an agreement. Other implications of responsiveness to one's
opposite number that are suggested by Pruitt (1962) include a negotiator's
increased willingness to make costly concessions to the other side, decreased
firmness in adhering to his own proposals when these have been rejected by the
other side, increased attempts to discover how advantageous each alternative is
to the other side so as to compute his utility for the alternative, and increased
favorableness toward any alternative the more advantageous that alternative
seems to the other side. For these reasons, among others, "negotiations are likely

to proceed more rapidly and with less conflict the more responsive are the negotiators to one another" (Pruitt, 1962, p. 16).

While these hypotheses have not been explored directly, there is some evidence which is suggestive. Several experiments have demonstrated different bargaining processes when pairs of friends (or opponents who have similar beliefs) negotiated as opposed to nonfriends (or dissimilar opponents). Morgan and Sawyer (1967) found that access to information about the other's expectations or intentions facilitated resolution in different ways for friends and nonfriends. Friends accepted inequality when one thought that the other might prefer it; for them, information served to introduce such well-intentioned misunderstanding and increased equal outcomes. Nonfriends were less willing to accept anything but equality whether or not they had information; however, information which enabled them to know what to expect let them come to an agreement in about 1/5 of the time. Presumably pairs of friends used the information to increase their responsiveness to the other's demands while nonfriends used the information to enhance coordination based on equal concessions without necessarily taking account of the other's "desires." In other experiments, investigators found higher levels of cooperation and higher expectations of cooperation among opponents who saw themselves as being highly similar as compared to pairs who were dissimilar or who were neither similar nor dissimilar (Kaufman, 1967; Krauss, 1966). The high level of cooperation rendered by similar opponents is perhaps based on *trust* that it will be reciprocated. Disappointments lead to a deterioration of the mutual responsiveness. The negotiator who is responsive to an opponent who does not reciprocate risks being exploited. Kaufman (1967) observed that when a highly similar opponent failed to cooperate, subjects retaliated significantly more vigorously by decreasing their own cooperative choices.

Friendships, background similarities, shared subcultures, and frequent informal conferences are some of the factors which are likely to promote responsiveness by enabling negotiators to arrive at a common definition of the situation with respect to each other's intentions and by enhancing a willingness on the part of both to be influenced by these intentions. Several developments in the international system suggest that there may be a progressive trend in the direction of increasing the familiarity and camaraderie among opposite number negotiators. Most impressive perhaps are the results of Modelski's (1970) large-scale survey which documents the observation made by others (e.g., Bartos, 1967; Rusk, 1955) that there is a developmental trend toward the emergence of a cohesive world elite among foreign ministers resembling a "close-knit" society with a normative structure. This phenomenon is facilitated by similarities in the backgrounds of foreign ministers from different nations (Modelski, 1970) and by the nature of the screening for recruitment into the role and the selective survival of those who are recruited (see Singer and Ray, 1966). One consequence of this development (and, indeed, the development of cohesive subcultures with respect to other diplomatic roles) is that it may lead to similarity in perception among opposite number role cohorts and differences in perceptions between different role cohorts.[9] Druckman (1968a) found very strong differences in the expression of ethnocentric biases among four different decision-making roles in the Inter-Nation Simulation. "Foreign ministers" were the least ethnocentric while persons with the lowest status role ("head of party out of power") were the most ethnocentric in their perceptions of members of their own nation, its allies, and its enemies. The low ethnocentrism among "foreign ministers" was interpreted to result from more frequent equal status contacts among them in both formal and informal conferences. The implication of these findings is the hypothesis that ethnocentrism covaries with responsiveness between opposing negotiators—the lower the ethnocentrism, the higher such responsiveness.

Another development in the international system is likely to increase the level of responsiveness between representatives of different nations. Nations are beginning to recognize that as they become increasingly interdependent, power politics is less effective as an influence tactic (e.g., the U.S. opening up trade and diplomatic relations with Red China). One consequence of this recognition is the emergence of specialized international agencies such as commercial and investment interchanges and informational and educational exchanges in which more than two cultures participate (see Glenn et al., 1970). Related to this recognition is the requirement within nations that agencies involved in the foreign policy formation process become more responsive to the "desires" of other nations (see Pruitt, 1962). These institutionalized mechanisms may pave the way for cultural convergence on a grand scale.

The discussion in this section leads to the following propositions:

19. Increased responsiveness to the positions and needs of the other party covaries with decreased responsiveness to the obligations imposed by one's own party.

20. The more mutually responsive opposite number negotiators are, the quicker the negotiations.

21. The more mutually responsive opposite number negotiators are, the more probable are asymmetrical outcomes (i.e., one concedes more than the other).

   a. Asymmetrical outcomes are especially likely to occur if the opposing negotiators are differentially responsive (i.e., one negotiator is more responsive to his opponent than his opponent is to him).

---

[9] Another consequence of this development is that, unlike the negotiation behavior of college students, the behavior of professional negotiators is highly predictable because such negotiators share a subculture that serves to limit the influence of their idiosyncratic motives (see, e.g., Bartos, 1967). Presumably, responsiveness is enhanced when the effects of *differences* between negotiators are moderated. However, a shared subculture does not preclude the effects of differences between negotiators; rather, it limits these effects to certain variables such as the experiential variables of self-esteem—based on prior success or failure in similar negotiations—and cognitive complexity—based on expertise in the area being negotiated.

22. The more mutual trust between opposite number negotiators, the more mutual responsiveness.
    a. Friendships, background similarities, shared subcultures, and frequent informal conferences between opposite number negotiators promote responsiveness by increasing their trust of one another.
23. The more similar the perceptions and evaluations of opposing negotiators, the more mutual responsiveness the negotiators will exhibit.
    a. Friendships, background similarities, and so on between opposite number negotiators promote responsiveness by enhancing similarities between them in perceptions and evaluations.
24. The less ethnocentric the opposing negotiators, the more mutual responsiveness the negotiators will show.
    a. Friendships, background similarities, and so on between opposite number negotiators promote mutual responsiveness by reducing ethnocentric attitudes.
    b. Mutual responsiveness is promoted by the emergence of international exchange agencies in which the nations of the opposing negotiators participate; participation in such agencies reduces ethnocentric attitudes.

BOUNDARY ROLE CONFLICT

The two conflicting aspects of a representative's role obligations were highlighted in the previous two sections: the expectations of a negotiator's own party that emerge out of an internal consensus on the positions he is to take and the expectations of the opponent that must be taken into account if an agreement is to be reached. Since these expectations conflict, the negotiator is placed in a boundary role position (Walton and McKersie, 1965, pp. 283ff.) where he must mediate the differences in order to insure that the agreement produced is acceptable to both parties. In international negotiations, the situation is further complicated by the existence of diverse constituencies which include the negotiating team, administrative personnel, public opinion, and allies. Moreover, many negotiations between nations are conducted by "lower-echelon" personnel who are stationed at the embassy of the country with which the nation is dealing (see S. Perry, 1957). As a result of their location, such negotiators may be able to appraise more accurately the positions taken by the negotiators of the opposing nation than the positions of their own nation, thus facilitating responsiveness to an opponent's desires while enhancing the conflict between their own and their "superior's" expectations.[10] How the negotiator

---

[10]From a psychological standpoint, this complexity may be represented as a juxtaposition of images that the negotiator has of the interface between the opposite number representatives, of the ingroup-outgroup relationship, and of the relationship between the various factions within his own party and his own posture (see S. Perry, 1957).

deals with his boundary role dilemma may in large part determine the process and outcome of the interparty deliberations.

One aspect of the boundary role dilemma focuses on the relationship between the negotiator's perceptions of his own party's expectations for his behavior and his perceptions of his opponent's orientation in the negotiations. The results of a recent experiment by Frey and Adams (1972) suggest that both these perceptions are important influences on negotiating behavior. They found that bargaining behavior was best predicted from an interaction between the negotiator's perceptions of ingroup and outgroup orientations along two dimensions: the constituent's trust or distrust in him and the cooperative vs. exploitative perception of his opponent. A representative who knew that he was not trusted was particularly unwilling to make concessions when his opponent was seen as being conciliatory and particularly willing to make concessions when he was seen as being exploitative. The most intolerable position for the representative was when he was both distrusted by his constituent and viewed his opposite number as being exploitative. In this condition the representative was overwhelmed by the toughness of his opponent, yielding to the opponent's desires while resenting the distrust of his own party. He could not prove himself to his constituent in this condition, causing considerable frustration. A conciliatory opponent "helped" him to resolve the internal conflict by enabling him to "prove" himself to his untrusting constituent. A second study suggests that the boundary role conflict can be reduced by relaxing constituency pressures. Benton and Druckman (1974) found that agreement between opposing representatives was facilitated when the conflicting pressures experienced by the negotiators were reduced by making constituency expectations more compatible with opponent expectations. Taken together, the results of the two studies suggest that both internal and external factors can be manipulated in order to assuage (or exacerbate) the pressures experienced by representatives in their boundary role position. These two sets of factors are likely to facilitate or hinder the negotiating process depending upon whether they are complementary or conflicting forces on the representatives.

In the situations created in the experimental studies just reviewed, the representatives did not have an opportunity to influence the perceptions of either their constituents or their opponent. Rather, they were "passive" recipients of experimental manipulations designed to influence *their* perceptions and behavior. In international negotiations which take place over long periods of time, the negotiating representatives have opportunities to employ a variety of tactics in attempting to influence the perceptions and expectations of both their principals and their opponents. With respect to his own party, a negotiator can attempt to achieve an internal consensus by resolving factional disputes over positions or he can attempt to manipulate the perception of his performance and his outcome. The skillful negotiator-tactician should be able to prevent internal expectations from becoming firm until after the opponent's position is apparent and to persuade his constituents to revise their expectations after they have been developed. Moreover, when necessary, he should be able to represent his actual level of achievement in such a manner as to minimize the dissatisfaction experienced by his teammates. In order to achieve this end, he may engage in tacit bargaining as a way of explaining to his opponent that his behavior is not to be taken seriously (see Walton and McKersie, 1965, pp. 311ff., for a discussion of these tactics as they are used in labor negotiations). Tacit bargaining and misrepresenting one's performance to his own party are tactics which are likely to be most effective when the negotiation process takes place in secrecy (see Turk and Lefcowitz, 1962).

With respect to his opponents the negotiator can attempt to manipulate their perceptions of the amount of concessions that would be tolerable for him to offer. Schelling (1960, p. 34) describes the tactic of linking one's position to a general principle as one way of communicating to an opponent an intention to remain adamant since capitulation would discredit the principle. The tactical process consists, first, of explicitly stating the principle and, second, of indicating unambiguously to one's opponent how it is related to his bargaining position. Presentation of scientific evidence or discussion of developments in one's own country may serve as another type of "commitment device." A related strategy is to magnify one's own concessions while talking to an opponent in order to convince him that agreement depends on his concessions alone. However, as Iklé (1964, p. 138) points out "... even the Russians sometimes have to steer between the Scylla of failing to magnify concessions while talking to the opponent and the Charybdis of appearing to concede too much while explaining a new position to domestic critics or allies." In general, the tactical problem for the representative in his boundary role is to convince his own party that his performance is in keeping with their expectations and that they can trust him to convince the opponent that further concessions would forfeit an irretrievable commitment to a position and would thus be intolerable. But, this maneuvering must not sidetrack the purpose of the deliberations—to achieve an agreement.

As a negotiator the representative is expected to make concessions toward achieving an agreement. As a representative the negotiator must be cautious in offering concessions and demand reciprocation for concessions made. As a tactician the negotiator-representative does not want to convey the impression that because he made some concessions further concessions are forthcoming or that he has conceded to the "superior" position of his opposite number. In this tactician role, the negotiator is an impression-manager who may be aided by certain tactical interventions performed by an intermediary. Experimental results reported by Podell and Knapp (1969) demonstrate that it is *safer* to offer concessions through an intermediary. Direct offers raise the expectations of an opponent for further concessions significantly higher than when the same offers are initiated by an intermediary. Moreover, proposals initiated by a third party who is viewed as impartial are more likely to be seen as unbiased. [11] However, as Burton (1969, p. 155) argues, "the longer mediation continues the less, and not the more, is the mediator likely to be accepted as disinterested and unprejudiced." With respect to the representative's own side an intermediary can "help a negotiator making a concession to avoid a loss of face through such devices as creating the impression that the player is conceding to the pressures of public opinion rather than to the superior position of the other players" (O. Young, 1972, p. 58). If effectively employed, this tactic is also likely to relieve those negotiators who have a strong need to save face of their sense of personal inadequacy inherent in making concessions to an opponent (see Johnson and Tullar, 1972).

The following propositions serve to summarize the discussion in this section:

25. The more compatible (conflicting) the expectations of the negotiator's own party and those of his opposite number, the quicker and easier (slower and harder) the negotiations.

26. The more a negotiator perceives that he is distrusted by his own party, the less (more) likely he will be to concede to an opponent whom he considers to be conciliatory (exploitative).

27. The more effective (or convincing) a negotiator is in conveying the impression that his performance coincides with his own party's expectations while conveying the impression to his opposite number that he cannot concede beyond a clearly defined point, the easier the negotiations.

    a. A negotiator will be more effective in conveying impressions of firmness to his own party which are in keeping with their expectations if the negotiations are secret.

    b. A negotiator will be more effective in conveying impressions of firmness to his opposite number if he can present unambiguous evidence indicating that he is unable to offer any more concessions.

---

[11] Impartiality depends on a number of factors including the extent to which the intermediary is adequately informed and his incentives for accepting the role. A third party that is given a limited amount of information concerning the dispute is not likely to have the proper context for evaluating the relative defensibility of the initial positions or of the concessions that were made by either party (see Johnson and Pruitt, 1972). A third party that is employed by only one of the parties is likely to arouse suspicions of collusion by the other parties. More interesting, perhaps, is the case of the third party that takes account of the interests of an external group which has a stake in the outcome but is not a party to the deliberations. To the extent that the third party is considered an agent for this group, it is likely to have an interest in the content of the agreement or the speed with which an agreement is produced. Third-party responsiveness to one group's interests pits it against the other parties, subverting the role of impartial intermediary. Under these conditions the third party should be regarded as another party to the negotiations capable of influencing its progress in a direction that conflicts with the interests of the other principals (see O. Young, 1972). In addition, the third party functions as a representative subject to the role obligations and boundary role conflicts just reviewed.

28. A negotiator's attempts at impression-management can be facilitated by an intermediary who will be more effective the more impartial he is viewed to be.

    a. Concessions are easier to make through an impartial intermediary than directly by the negotiator.

        1. Concessions made through an intermediary are *less* likely to be interpreted by a negotiator's own party as vulnerability to an opponent's superior position than are direct concessions.

        2. Concessions made through an intermediary are *less* likely to raise the opponent's expectations for further concessions than are direct concessions.

Influence of Situation on Negotiation

The third major influence on negotiation presented in this essay is the situation or, in other words, the conditions under which the process transpires. Considered in an approximate temporal order, person factors are antecedent, existing prior to the onset of negotiations; role is both antecedent insofar as the negotiator brings his obligations with him and concurrent insofar as intraparty negotiations occur simultaneously with interparty deliberations; and situation is concurrent, characterized by conditions which are specific to a particular negotiation setting. Since characteristics of the situation may be easier to manipulate than characteristics brought to the situation (e.g., cultural factors, role obligations), information on the situation may be more useful to those social engineers who are responsible for creating the conditions which are conducive to attaining an agreement than information on person or role variables.

A decade of experimental investigations on the effects of situational variables on negotiation is leading to the gradual accumulation of evidence relevant to policy making. Investigations have been designed to provide information germane to answering the following questions. What is the effect upon outcomes or process of increasing the number of parties in negotiation, of redefining the scope of the issues to be negotiated, of increasing the size of the audience present during negotiations, of communicating a threat to an opponent, of taking a firm stand at first followed by a loosening up, of altering the seating arrangements? Some of this evidence is reviewed in the present section in an attempt to depict the influence on negotiations of such conditions as prenegotiation experience and agenda formation, public versus private deliberations, and the stresses and tensions surrounding negotiations. These are some of the contemporaneous factors which are hypothesized to impinge upon a negotiation as it proceeds through time.

PRENEGOTIATION EXPERIENCE AND AGENDA FORMATION

The negotiation process emerges from a set of preconditions and preparations that are likely to influence its course. In order for negotiations to occur at all, the contending parties must agree on the most general objective, the necessity to convene in order to resolve their differences. Moreover, they must agree on the general normative framework within which the deliberations will be conducted. The former is referred to by Lall (1966) as the "irreducible minimum objective" while the latter is referred to by Iklé (1964) as the "rules of accommodation." These preliminary agreements set the stage for both the formal preparations made by each party and the formation of an agenda which defines the issues and the order in which they will be discussed. In this section the research on preconditions, preparations (including caucusing and learning about the other side's positions), and agenda formation are discussed.

In modern-day international politics, most nations interact within the framework of a tradition of negotiations. Considered from this perspective, negotiators from different nations can be characterized as being ensconced in a network which prescribes codes of behavior and norms learned in the process of professionalization. More visible perhaps is the corps of trained professionals within each nation prepared to "act" when the preconditions for a specific series of deliberations are met.[12] In fact, it has been argued that the negotiation process is largely predictable from knowledge about the system within which these "professionals" operate (see Bartos, 1967; Singer and Ray, 1966). This predictability is related in part to an acceptance by the contending parties of certain "rules of accommodation" (see Iklé, 1964, Chapter 7).

The realization by contending parties that it is in their best interest to conclude a satisfactory agreement leads them to accept certain rules of conduct. Adherence to such rules is reflected in an accommodating style which is likely to facilitate the negotiations and to insure a stable relationship between the parties over the long run. One of the more interesting rules is to "negotiate in good faith," including the "canon" that negotiators should not have hidden motives for their actions and should not seek to exploit their opponent or to violate an agreement (see Iklé, 1964, pp. 111-114). In certain instances, in order to insure that neither exploitation nor disloyalty will occur, negotiators may initial "protective contracts." These prenegotiation agreements are likely to be entered into when the conditions are most conducive to both exploitation and disloyalty as in negotiations between enemies and in nonself-executing agreements when violations are possible (e.g., SALT). In a series of experiments, Thibaut and his colleagues (Thibaut, 1968; Thibaut and Faucheux, 1965) made evident some of

---

[12] Among the preconditions for negotiation listed by Lall (1966, p. 82ff.) are: "(a) when there is a more or less spontaneous and shared realization by a number of countries that a particular situation should be the subject of negotiations; (b) when a relatively powerful or large State suggests negotiations to a relatively small or less powerful State; (c) when there is a tradition of friendship and common discussion among two or more States. . . ."

the conditions that lead negotiators to enter into "protective contracts." They found that when the contending parties have equal power to threaten the relationship and when the mutual threat is perceived by both as being potentially destructive—e.g., when one party is in a better position to be exploitative (a powerful nation demanding a high price for armaments from a weaker ally) while the other is in a better position to be disloyal (the weaker nation threatening to leave the alliance)—protective contracts will be signed.

Preparations for negotiation begin soon after the parties have completed their procedural negotiations and have agreed to negotiate in "good faith." The first concern is the development of an agenda which defines the issues to be negotiated and the order in which they will be discussed. The extent to which the agenda is a constraint depends on how closely it is adhered to. Moreover, the choice of the issues to be discussed may be a critical determinant of both the process and outcome of negotiations. Once the parties have defined the issues, they must seek internal clarification of positions as well as "intelligence" reports on the other party's postures on the various issues. The results of several studies indicate systematic relationships between the way in which preparations are made and the process of negotiating.

It is not the literal outline of steps specified by an agenda that defines its importance. Agendas and conference titles usually assume greater importance at the time when they are being hammered out than as a guide for the deliberations. For example, after prolonged and strenuous meetings at the beginning of the nuclear test-ban conference in 1958, East and West finally agreed on a *rotating* agenda with the topics proposed by each side considered in alternating two-day periods. However, as the conference proceeded, "even this arrangement was quietly abandoned, and each side brought up proposals or discussed issues raised by the opponent as it pleased" (Iklé, 1964, p. 96). Recognizing the tentativeness of an agenda, optional agendas with disclaimers attached (i.e., statements making it explicit that there is no penalty for deviating from the agenda) are sometimes proposed as was the case at the Eighteen Nation Disarmament Conference. Other examples can be drawn from multilateral international negotiations to illustrate that negotiators rarely adhere strictly to the preliminary plan. Rather, an agenda is critical from the standpoint of defining issues and setting the "tone" for deliberation. As Iklé (1964, p. 99) points out, "agreeing to put a topic on the agenda signifies consent that the topic is a subject of negotiation."

The manner in which issues are defined at the outset may have important ramifications for the course of negotiations. For example, smaller issues are likely to be easier to resolve than larger issues. Fisher (1964) recommended translating differences between parties on matters of principle which are not bargainable to issues on which compromise is possible and indeed sought for the sake of expediency. There is experimental evidence which supports Fisher's thesis. Deutsch et al. (1971) found that as issue size increased, bargainers had more difficulty in reaching a mutually beneficial solution. They defined "size of conflict" in terms of the expected difference in the value of the outcomes that a bargainer will receive if he "wins" compared with the value that he will receive if the other "wins" the conflict. On the basis of their results, the authors concluded that "issue control" may be as crucial as "arms control" to the peace of the world. " 'Issue control' would . . . be directed toward narrowing and limiting the scope of the conflict, to making issues as specific and focused on the here-and-now as possible" (Deutsch et al., 1971, p. 266; see also Druckman and Zechmeister, 1970).

A related issue concerns the order in which issues are discussed. Conceivably, the resolution of "smaller" issues at the beginning of negotiations could serve to enable the parties to confront the larger issues that are responsible for repeated conflicts between the nations. An illustration of this process is the resolution of "smaller" issues (e.g., agreeing on a "baseline" number) leading to the final settlement on the retirement of submarine-launched ballistic missiles at the 1972 SALT talks (see Newhouse, 1973, pp. 254-255). The order of the issues for discussion may be important for another reason. Several studies have shown that differences between parties on the relative importance of the issues under consideration hinders negotiations. Most notable are Bonham's (1971) results from a simulation of the 1955 U.S.-Soviet disarmament negotiations. He found that differences between the two parties in issue emphasis (reduction in arms vs. inspections) resulted in greater negative affect and hostility, fewer concessions, less reciprocation in concession making, and fewer major agreements than when issue emphasis was not manipulated. Other studies have shown that the *greater* the difference between parties in the priority-ordering of issues, the more difficult it is to achieve a resolution of the conflict (e.g., Druckman, 1970; Summers, 1968). The results of Bonham's study also suggest that differences in issue emphasis lead to misunderstandings and hostilities that interfere with a focus on the substantive issues *per se*. Such misunderstanding due to differences in issue-priorities was evident in the early stages of the SALT negotiations. The U.S. was eager to discuss a list of qualitative issues concerning multiple warheads (MIRVs) on missiles while Russia desired to focus on the Forward Based Systems (FBS) deployed by the U.S. in various locations around the world. Each side refused to discuss the other's "major issue." [13] The jockeying for issues continued for several stages of phase I of the SALT talks, creating antagonisms and sidetracking the proceedings from focusing on the one substantive issue that the contestants could agree on: ABM deployment (see Newhouse, 1973, pp. 173-176).

Taken together with other findings, the evidence just reviewed suggests that substantive decisions made in prenegotiation procedural conferences are likely to

[13]The Soviets were very sensitive to any suggestion made by the U.S. to limit research and development on new systems; they preferred to focus on the smaller quantitative issues. The Americans, on the other hand, were surprised that the Soviets even brought up the FBS issue since they claimed that this was not a subject for bilateral talks (a NATO agreement) and that these systems concern tactics, not strategy which is presumably what SALT was about.

have significant effects on the negotiation process and outcome. However, the effects of these meetings may not be *limited* to such decisions. Among the other functions which the bilateral structure of such conferences serves are: (a) providing a framework within which each party can obtain information about the other's intentions, (b) accomplishing preliminary activities that would take time during the early phases of the formal deliberations, and (c) diverting parties from engaging in unilateral strategy preparations. Information obtained about the other's intentions and goals can be used to facilitate coordination between parties if the parties have time to integrate the information before the deliberations begin. A "period for reflection" between the procedural conference and the formal deliberations may be helpful (see Conrath, 1970). But even if the parties do not have time to integrate the information received, the preliminary interaction may permit them to resolve their internal structuring problems and to attain diminished negative affect so that they are ready to move to a discussion of substantive issues early in the formal negotiations. Evidence presented by McGrath and Julian (1963) suggests that the earlier these problems are resolved, the more effective the negotiations. (Further opportunities for resolving structuring and affect problems are provided by informal meetings held during the procedural conference. Parties may also use these informal meetings to corroborate impressions about intentions received during the procedural conference.) Finally, as noted earlier, a negotiator who has experienced frequent preliminary bilateral meetings is likely to enter negotiations with a more cooperative, problem-solving orientation than one who has engaged in extensive unilateral strategy planning (see Druckman, 1968b). Presumably the bilateral meetings serve to divert attention away from strategy planning sessions.

The developments reviewed in this section are summarized by the following propositions:

29. Parties are more likely to enter into "protective contracts" which are designed to preserve a common interest in maintaining negotiations when they have equal power to threaten the relationship.
    a. The more likely both parties are to perceive a mutual threat as potentially destructive, the more likely they are to enter into a protective contract.
30. The more limited the scope of the issues to be discussed in the negotiations, the more likely are resolutions to be attained.
    a. The more resolutions attained on "smaller" issues, the more likely the parties will be to negotiate their differences on the "larger" issues which have served to sustain long-term hostilities.
    b. The *earlier* the resolution of "smaller" issues, the more likely the parties will be to broach their differences on the "larger" issues.
31. The more agreement between parties on the priority-order for discussion of the issues, the quicker agreements will be attained.

    a. The more agreement there is on the priority-order for discussion, the more reciprocation in concession making.

32. The more agreement between parties on the relative importance of the issues to be discussed, the quicker agreements will be attained.

    a. The more disagreement there is on the relative importance of the issues, the more hostility that will be aroused to interfere with a focus on the substantive issues *per se*.

33. Frequent bilateral conferences prior to negotiations facilitate coordination during the negotiations—the more such encounters, the easier the coordination.

    a. Negotiations are facilitated the longer the time period parties have to reflect on their bilateral experiences prior to negotiations.

    b. The more time spent prior to negotiations reflecting on bilateral experiences, the less time spent preparing strategies unilaterally.

        1. The less time spent preparing strategies unilaterally, the easier the negotiations are.

    c. Negotiations are facilitated further to the extent that parties are able to resolve internal structuring problems in preliminary bilateral conferences.

OPEN VERSUS SECRET DIPLOMACY

Secrecy is a matter of degree. All international negotiations take place under conditions that are partly secret and partly open. Negotiations that are too secretive arouse the suspicions of citizens who are concerned about the democratic control of foreign policy while negotiations that are too open are subject to a myriad of outside pressures which interfere with the process of reaching an agreement. Examples of specific cases[14] where domestic pressures have intruded upon the course of deliberations (see Iklé, 1964, pp. 131-136) remind us of the delicate balance that exists between "too open" and "too closed."[15]

In advocating secrecy, some analysts have distinguished between policy and outcome on the one hand and process on the other (see, e.g., Nicolson, 1939, Chapter 4), claiming that while the former should be public, the details involved in hammering out an agreement should be private. For example, Morgenthau (1960, p. 553) asserts: "Disclosure of the results of diplomatic negotiation is required by the principles of democracy, for without it there can be no

[14]In the American-Japanese peace treaty negotiations, the private interests of the American fishing industry influenced the course and outcome of the negotiations. Tariff negotiations and commercial agreements are characteristic arenas for the influence of private domestic interests. Occasionally, private interests from different nations align to affect the outcome of negotiations as when "munitions makers" banded together to influence disarmament conferences before and after World War I.

[15]In partially secret negotiations, the news media has wider latitude for creating impressions. The news media might "overstate the case" by conveying the impression that a critical situation exists, arousing public concern as in the Berlin negotiations of 1962.

democratic control of foreign policy. Yet ... it takes only common sense derived from daily experience to realize that it is impossible to negotiate in public on anything in which parties other than the negotiators are interested." Two types of influences are likely to intrude on open negotiations—pressure groups and third parties who are not involved directly in the conferences, and personnel present during the deliberations, including advisors, experts, and more neutral onlookers. The former type of influence has been discussed by international relations scholars while social psychologists have conducted experiments designed to assess the impact of audiences on negotiations.

Iklé (1964, p. 134) points out two major functions of secrecy: "First, it keeps domestic groups ignorant of the process of negotiation, thereby preventing them from exerting pressures during successive phases of bargaining. Second, it leaves third parties in the dark and thus reduces their influence." The availability of information on the progress of the deliberations permits public opinion to coalesce in support of a position which may be contrary to the actions taken. Widespread agreement puts pressure on the executive branch to shift policy during the course of the deliberations. To the extent that policy makers within the executive are responsive to these sectors of opinion, policy shifts may occur at any time and interfere with progress (see Gamson, 1968, for a discussion of alternative perspectives on "responsiveness" to public opinion). More often, perhaps, factions of *different* opinion develop, each placing a different interpretation on concessions offered by their negotiating team. To the extent that the policy-making apparatus is responsive to these cross-pressures, negotiators are reluctant to concede at all, resulting in a slowdown of the proceedings.

The second type of pressure discussed by Iklé is the influence of third parties in open negotiations. Third parties that have a vested interest in the outcome are likely to operate in favor of one of the parties, causing the other to withhold concessions (see footnote 11). Furthermore, a third party might be tempted to exploit the differences that exist between the principals, forcing them to emphasize their common interests against the encroachment of the "outsider" rather than to resolve the "real" differences at issue. (For further discussion of the influence of third parties, see O. Young, 1972, and Iklé, 1964, pp. 134-136.)

In addition to the more distal influence of publics and third parties, the presence of spectators is another (more proximal) source of influence on the course of the deliberations. Research evidence indicates that with an audience present negotiators tend to remain firm in their positions, attempting to place the burden for concession making on their opponents (see Druckman, Solomon, and Zechmeister, 1972). This is especially the case if the predominant motive of the negotiators is rivalistic (McClintock and Nuttin, 1969). The result can be a deadlocked negotiation. Another consequence of the presence of an audience during negotiations is that it may serve to encourage face-saving behavior. Decisions that are motivated by face-saving considerations can conflict with decisions that are necessary to achieve satisfactory agreements. In several experiments, negotiators have been shown to forego considerable rewards (or to respond irrationally) in order to save face before an audience (e.g., constituents or other members of the negotiating team), especially if that audience is in the role of evaluator (see B. Brown, 1968, 1970). A third consequence of "performing before an audience" is to delay the deliberations. It has been found that the negotiation process is impeded when negotiators are highly accountable for their performance to constituents or teammates. Under this condition, negotiators are reluctant to make concessions, impeding progress toward a settlement (Gruder and Rosen, 1971). Slower progression toward an agreement is especially likely to occur when the accountable negotiators are highly attracted to the team they represent (see Klimoski, 1972).

For all of these reasons, secret negotiations are likely to be more effective in producing an acceptable agreement. Even when negotiators are highly accountable for their performance, secrecy permits them to rationalize concessions as having been necessary in order to produce the agreement achieved. The skillful negotiator-tactician can make the result appear as less of a "sellout" than when the process is monitored. Acts of accommodation, necessary to achieve an agreement, can be made effectively in secrecy insofar as: (1) secrecy permits the representative to convey to the other party that his accommodative acts have the support of his own party; (2) secrecy reduces the likelihood of a negotiator's acts appearing as a "sellout" to his party; and (3) secrecy enables the negotiator to translate the results of the negotiations to his own party in terms which are in accord with their values. Thus, the same compromise arrived at in secrecy does not look nearly so bad as when arrived at openly (see Turk and Lefcowitz, 1962).

The discussion in this section can be summarized by the following propositions:

34. The more open the negotiations, the more likely are factions of differing public opinion concerning policy to develop.
    a. The more responsive the policy-making apparatus is to these cross-pressures of public opinion, the more reluctant are negotiators to offer concessions.
35. The presence of an audience of onlookers enhances a negotiator's tendency to remain firm in his position, placing the burden for concession-making on his opponent.
36. When an audience is in the role of evaluator, negotiators are more likely to be motivated by face-saving considerations.
37. When an audience is in the role of evaluator, negotiations are delayed, since negotiators are cautious to insure that there is an internal consensus before offering a concession.
    a. Negotiations are delayed further when the negotiators are accountable to the evaluator-audience for their performance.
    b. Negotiations are delayed even further when the accountable negotiators are attracted to the audience.

38. Secrecy facilitates achieving agreements.

    a.   Under secrecy, negotiators are less likely to be subjected to divergent interpretations of their performance and to delay negotiations in the service of insuring an internal consensus on positions taken and postures assumed.

STRESSES AND TENSIONS

The amount of stress or tension experienced by negotiators can be considered as an intervening variable, *influenced* by situation and person factors and *influencing* the prospects for obtaining an agreement. Many of the factors discussed previously can be seen to influence the level of stress experienced by negotiators. For example, different negotiators may have different thresholds for perceiving the same situation as stressful; different negotiators may represent nations which vary in the degree of agreement among various sectors of the population on the positions taken by the representative (e.g., the more factionalization, the more stress); and the presence of spectators to whom the negotiator is accountable is likely to be more stressful than when negotiations are conducted in private. While acknowledging the importance of these factors, the discussion in this section focuses on the effects of other *conditions* not considered previously, including time pressure, the consequence of nonagreement, and systemic forces. Changes in these situational variables also lead to changes in the stresses and tensions experienced in negotiations.

With regard to time pressure, the results of several experiments suggest that this variable, defined in terms of deadlines and/or costs for negotiating time, may either facilitate or hinder the attainment of an agreement. Pruitt and Drews (1969) found that acute time pressure produced more rapid concessions than did mild time pressure in an experimental buyer-seller bargaining situation. On the other hand, Bass (1966), using a simulation of collective bargaining, found that deadlines and costs for negotiating time hindered resolution (i.e., more deadlocks) more than deadlines without costs for negotiation time and more than no deadlines. One variable which may affect the direction of the relationship between time pressure and negotiation behavior is the perceived consequence of not agreeing. Johnson and Pruitt (1972) found that the anticipation of binding arbitration from a third party in case of deadlock produced more rapid concessions than when nonbinding mediation was anticipated. This effect was enhanced when the negotiator had information that led him to suspect that the binding decision might be biased against his position. Mitigating against this effect, however, are the perceived consequences of agreeing. On certain issues, such as disarmament, nations may believe that an agreement would be detrimental to their security interests, forcing them to evaluate the two types of consequences one against another (e.g., Jensen, 1963).

Another variable that may influence the behavioral effects of time pressure is an opponent's concession rate. A firm bargaining strategy employed by an opponent produces rapid concessions under high time pressure; the same strategy, however, evokes resistance and less yielding when parties are not under such pressure (Komorita and Barnes, 1969). More complicated perhaps is the relationship obtained by Bartos (1967) between concession-rate strategies and agreement under high time pressure. When unanimous agreement was required in a five-man bargaining team, the moderately firm bargainer elicited more concessions than either an extremely "tough" or a "soft" bargainer. This curvilinear relationship between strategies and agreement under high time pressure is formally equivalent to the curvilinear relationship between level of tension and agreement obtained by Jensen (1963) in his study of Soviet-American post-war disarmament negotiations. Agreements fell off during periods of both high and low tension. Taken together, these two studies suggest that a moderately firm bargaining strategy combined with moderate time pressure is most conducive to agreement. Conversely, either tough or soft strategies combined with either very high or very low time pressures are most detrimental to agreement.

Factors external to the negotiations also may cause stress that affects the course of the deliberations. Specific events that occur concomitantly with the negotiations (e.g., an oil embargo) and the general state of the international system at the time when negotiations are taking place (e.g., friendly vs. hostile interaction among nations) are likely to be reflected in the "tone" of the relationship between the parties. Similarly, the process and outcome of the negotiations may affect the level of tension in the international system in a cycle of reciprocal effects. The following hypotheses suggest the impact of system tension on the negotiation process: a high level of tension in the international system is likely to lead to *overreaction* by one nation to another nation's provocations, causing a breakdown in the negotiations; a low level of system tension leads to *underreaction* by one nation to another's provocations, facilitating negotiations or leading parties to seek mediational mechanisms for resolving their differences (see Druckman, 1973; Pruitt, 1969).

These hypotheses on system tension were tested recently by Hopmann and Walcott (1973) in a simulation of arms control negotiations. They compared the effects of three conditions on negotiation behavior: a malign condition (i.e., a news report announcing an increase in tensions), a benign condition (i.e., an announcement of an agreement between the parties on nondisarmament matters), and a control condition in which no news bulletin was issued. The results indicated that the malign environment contributed to a deterioration in negotiations resulting in tougher bargaining strategies, more negative affect, and more disagreements. These effects were especially strong in competitive bargaining between opposing nations. Increased tension did not affect bargaining between allies as much. However, an improvement in the international environment, as operationalized in the "benign" condition, did not result in a significant improvement in negotiations over the control condition. These results support the hypothesis that a high level of system tension leads to a deterioration in negotiations, but fail to support the hypothesis that a low level of system tension facilitates negotiations. One implication of these results is that agreement in arms control negotiations is likely in the absence of a significant improvement in the international environment but that it is more difficult to attain in the face of a deterioration in external conditions. The experimental paradigm used by these investigators might be extended to examine the feedback effects of a deterioration in negotiations on system tension and the spiral of effects going in both directions through time or repeated interactions.

When the conditions of negotiation cause stress that threatens the chances of concluding agreements, third-party intervention may be useful. Pruitt and Johnson (1970) found that mediation was effective in relieving the sense of personal inadequacy that might be anticipated as a result of making concessions when there is high time pressure and little movement from the other (see also Komorita and Barnes, 1969). Presumably these conditions are likely to produce conflict about whether or not to make concessions in order to achieve an agreement. With respect to stress caused by systemic processes, the conflict resolution workshops (Burton, 1969; Doob, 1970) may prove useful. Access to the appropriate decision makers and proper timing can make a workshop experience effective in preventing an incipient international crisis from occurring.

A final set of propositions is suggested by the discussion in this section on the effects of stresses and tensions on negotiation:

39. The more severe the time pressures are in a negotiation situation, the quicker (slower) the progress toward an agreement.
    a. Under high time pressure the more negative the perceived consequences of not agreeing are, the quicker the progress toward an agreement.
    b. Under high time pressure the more negative the perceived consequences of agreeing are, the slower the progress toward an agreement.
    c. The simultaneous existence of negative consequences for not agreeing and negative consequences for agreeing enhances the stress experienced by the negotiators.
40. Under high time pressure the firmer the concession-making strategy of one party, the more concessions elicited from the other party.
    a. Under moderate time pressure, a moderately firm bargaining strategy is most conducive to agreement.
41. The higher the level of tension in the international system, the more difficult it is to attain negotiated agreements.
    a. High levels of system tension are likely to lead to a deterioration in negotiations which are highly competitive, e.g., those between opposing nations.

Conclusions

The "visible intellectual products" to which this essay is addressed take the form of summary propositions derived from a blending of hard evidence and broad interpretation. These propositions underscore the importance of social-psychological factors to the understanding of international negotiations by highlighting processes which have been observed to impair or facilitate the obtaining of agreements in such negotiations. As stated, the propositions are neither prescriptive nor causal. Rather, they are descriptive statements which must be regarded as only a first step on the way to a more encompassing social-psychological theory of international negotiations. This first step is largely heuristic. It tells us where to look—which variable or cluster of variables accounts for what in negotiation behavior? It also tells us what might be done—what mechanisms can be invoked to facilitate the process of negotiating? Some general conclusions can be drawn with respect to each of the three factors considered in this essay, i.e., person factors, role obligations, and certain aspects of the situation. These are summarized in Table 16.1.

The summary of "effects on negotiation" presented in Table 16.1 suggests that each of the specific variables examined in this chapter affects some aspect of negotiation. However, the effects can be contradictory. While one set of variables is facilitating an agreement, another set is impeding progress toward an agreement. For example, the process of concession exchange is facilitated by the ability of negotiators to coordinate their strategies while the rate of concession-making is slowed by responsiveness to role obligations; matchings on certain attitudinal dispositions may facilitate coordination in trends of cooperating through time while cognitive or cultural differences interfere with progress, producing deadlocks or asymmetrical outcomes; substantive issues are discussed earlier if negotiators can resolve their structuring problems in preliminary bilateral conferences while open deliberations may impede progress by increasing the incidence of dysfunctional face-saving behaviors.

Similarly, the "intervention strategies" presented in Table 16.1 suggest that strategies tend to be variable-specific. For example, whereas *tactical* interventions seem appropriate for helping negotiators to resolve their boundary role conflicts and for transmitting concessions under stress, *workshop* interventions are more appropriate for reducing the negative effects of cognitive (e.g., through role-reversal procedures) and cultural (e.g., through concept training) differences and for reducing the level of stress experienced by negotiators. A third type of intervention, *technological aids,* is most likely to facilitate coordination. Moreover, if the particular persons doing the negotiating are the problem, the most efficacious strategy would be to "try a new team."

More generally, the strategy of blending hard evidence with broad interpretation which has been used in this essay has implications for the systematic development of a theory of international negotiations. The analytical rigor of an experimental approach contributes precision while descriptions of the phenomenon *in situ* contribute richness. The broad outlines of this strategy for building context-relevant theory are developed elsewhere (e.g., Druckman, 1968a, 1971). Here, two general recommendations are made for the *next step* in a program designed for the generation of refined theoretical propositions on the effects of the person, role, and situation on international negotiations.

Table 16.1. Summary of Salient Effects, Possible Interactions, and Intervention Strategies for Person, Role, and Situational Variables

General Type of Variable	Focus	Specific Variables	Effects on Negotiations	Possible Interactions Among Types of Variables	Intervention Strategies
Person	Negotiator	"Characteristics"	Trends in cooperation or competition through time; reaction to previous contingent responses or shifts in strategy; interpretation of other's concessions; strongest effects during middle phase and very early in the deliberations	Differential importance of role/person during different phases; audience presence, expanded range of options enhance effects of person	Change negotiators
		Cognitive and ideological differences	Deadlocks; escalating spiral of conflict intensity	Effects of ideological differences may be confused with effects of representing an ideological constituency	Role reversal; invoking mechanisms built into structure of negotiating situation
		Cultural differences	Protracted negotiations; asymmetrical outcomes; differences in cooperativeness or competitiveness	Effects of formal cultural representation may be confounded with effects of cultural differences between representatives; are responsive to different aspects of negotiating situation	Training in concepts of other culture

Table 16.1. (Continued)

General Type of Variable	Focus	Specific Variables	Effects on Negotiations	Possible Interactions Among Types of Variables	Intervention Strategies
		Attributions and coordination of strategies	Coordination facilitates concession exchange; attributions hinder sensitivity to changes; preplanned strategies protract negotiations, enhance inflexibility in evaluation of alternatives	Conditions (agenda, informal conferences, intermediary intervention) can facilitate or hinder coordination	Intermediary to transmit concessions and information; informal conferences; computation of exchange rates; technological aids
Role	Representation	Responsiveness to own party	Delays; deadlocks; slower concession making; increased competitiveness through phases; symmetrical compromise more likely	Responsiveness moderates the impact of idiosyncratic influences; are cultural differences in responsiveness to role obligations; audience presence enhances responsiveness to role obligations	
		Responsiveness to other party	Facilitates agreements; quicker progression toward agreement; asymmetrical compromising more likely	Attitudinal, cognitive, and cultural similarity facilitates mutual responsiveness; mutual responsiveness facilitates coordination	
		Boundary role conflict	Delays caused by consultation with own party; slow progression of concessions; increased frequency of tacit bargaining	Secrecy facilitates resolution of boundary role dilemma; more assertive negotiators take a more active role in resolving this conflict	Tactical interventions by intermediary who transmits concessions and manages impressions

Table 16.1. (Continued)

Situation				
Conditions of negotiation	Prenegotiation experience and agenda formation	Preliminary agreements can serve to sustain the relationship between parties; agreement on agenda issues hastens negotiated agreements by producing reciprocation in concession making, fewer misunderstandings, positive affect; informal bilateral conferences facilitate reciprocation in concessions, speed up discussion of substantive issues	Preliminary bilateral conferences and agreement on agenda issues can facilitate coordination	
	Open vs. secret negotiations	Secrecy facilitates agreement; openness leads to delays, face-saving behavior, competitiveness, deadlocks	Audience presence prolongs delays when negotiators are accountable to the onlookers	Engineering the situation to convert open negotiations into secret negotiations
	Stresses and tensions	High levels of tension lead to unsatisfactory outcomes and a deteriorated relationship among parties; time pressures lead to faster (slower) concessions depending on consequences of agreeing	High levels of stress moderate the effects of person and role variables	Third parties can facilitate concession making under high stress; conflict resolution workshops might mitigate against effects of stress caused by systematic factors

INTERACTIONS AMONG FACTORS

The few studies that have examined interrelationships among person, role, and situational factors are more suggestive than conclusive (see, e.g., Druckman, 1967; Holsti, 1970b; Terhune, 1968a). In general, these findings suggest that a negotiator's behavior is a complex function of his response to the external situation, to his role obligations, and to his internal state. At different times and under certain conditions or settings, the negotiator may be relatively impervious to the situation, his role, or the unique qualities of his personality. Programmatic research along these lines could specify more precisely the pattern of interaction among these classes of variables.

As presented in Table 16.1, interactions can occur between the various combinations of person-role, situation-role, and person-situation variables as well as in the three-way interaction among person, role, and situation. For example, following Douglas' (1957, p. 77) lead, the relative effects of person and role can be observed during the *process* of negotiating, with negotiators responding predominantly to their role obligations during the first and third phases while during the second phase negotiators must "put at the disposal of their respective parties their individual capacities to assay the rapid conversations going on in the environment and to improvise adaptive behaviors on the spot." Similarly, with respect to situation-role interactions, negotiators may be more responsive to the presence of an audience at certain junctures than to their role obligations. Or, as the results of several studies suggest, some negotiators may be more responsive to role obligations (e.g., males) than to situational pressures, while others (e.g., females) respond more to environmental pressures than to their role obligations (e.g., Druckman, Solomon, and Zechmeister, 1972). With regard to person-situation interactions, the situation may serve as a moderating or enhancing influence on the expression of idiosyncratic variables. Extrapolating from the results of a number of gaming studies (see Druckman, 1971), it may be conjectured that the effects of person factors are *enhanced* in the early phases of interaction, in situations which provide for a variety of strategies leading to the same outcome, under conditions that heighten the intensity of a conflict, and in the presence of an audience of onlookers. On the other hand, the impact of person variables is *moderated* in situations that are well-defined or where there are a limited number of options for a course of action.

More complex, perhaps, is the possible three-way interaction among person, role, and situation. For example, consider the hypothesis that intense boundary role conflicts are more likely to be resolved by highly skillful or experienced negotiators under conditions which permit strategic communications to their constituents and tacit bargaining with their opposite numbers. One such condition is secrecy; another is frequent informal conferences during the formal deliberations. How different negotiators under varying degrees of responsiveness to their role obligations (or accountability for the outcome) and under varied conditions (e.g., secrecy vs. openness) attempt to resolve their boundary role dilemma is a research issue worth pursuing. More generally, each of the interactions just described is worthy of further exploration in an attempt to separate the relative impact of these sources of variation on negotiation behavior. This analytical approach, however, must be complemented by an inferential strategy for determining the *relevance* of information to the arena of concern.

CONTEXT-RELEVANT KNOWLEDGE

As noted earlier (see footnote 1), the more similar a model of a particular "reality" is to the "reality" itself, the more likely will processes observed within that model be relevant to the "reality" being modeled. According to this principle of proximal similarity, the inferential base for complex simulations of international negotiations is likely to be stronger than for less complex abstract experiments (e.g., the Prisoner's Dilemma game or bilateral monopoly bargaining tasks). Following this reasoning, it can be argued that the findings obtained by Bonham (1971) on the effects of the relative importance of the issues to be negotiated and by Hopmann and Walcott (1973) on the effects of external stress have more relevance for international negotiations than findings reported from matrix-game experiments or simulations of collective bargaining. Both of these studies used simulations of arms control negotiations modeled on real world events. Results obtained in other experiments reviewed in this essay achieve their relevance more indirectly by examining a *process* presumed to be important in international negotiation. A more systematic appraisal of the relevance of laboratory findings depends upon the development of a technology for assessing similarity between diverse contexts (see Sells, 1966, for a promising start along these lines). The principle of proximal similarity can be used to underwrite the development of such a technology.

In concluding, we recommend the development of a general methodology which combines the strengths of experimentation with the strengths of model construction. Such a development would entail rigorous exploration of inter-relationships within a context-relevant framework. One strategy for achieving this methodology is to bring the technology of experimental social psychology into closer contact with the literature on international relations.[16] For example, hypotheses and variables can be drawn from case studies of real negotiations while manipulations of these variables can be performed within a constructed model of the phenomenon. This general approach is spelled out more elaborately by Ackoff and Emery (1972, see pp. 230-235) in their discussion of building a theory of large-scale social conflicts. These authors recommend a methodology in which theory and experimentation are intertwined as an investigator moves between drawing variables from observations of the "real" phenomenon and

[16]From one standpoint it might be argued that social-psychological investigations focus on negotiation as *conference*, whereas the international relations literature construes negotiation in terms of a broader *confrontation* perspective. The juxtaposition of these two levels of analysis places the study of international negotiations at that interdisciplinary juncture where international relations merges with the social psychology of debate and bargaining.

constructing artificial models of that reality. Once constructed, the model is then decomposed into simpler experiments, the results of which can be used to modify the model in an attempt to bring the construction closer to the reality being captured. One type of product that would evolve from this approach is a more sophisticated model of the interplay among factors affecting agreement in international negotiations.

CHAPTER 17

Conclusion: Directions for Future Research

Margaret G. Hermann

IF THE AUTHORS of the chapters in this book have been at all effective in presenting their research, the reader at this point has many constructive criticisms to offer that would improve the studies, has seen several hidden relationships which the researchers missed, and has some follow-up studies already designed in his (her) mind. The purpose of this last chapter is to aid the reader in summarizing what the authors have said about the three issues raised at the beginning of the book. (Recall that these issues concerned how to assess or measure the personal characteristics of political leaders, who becomes a political leader, and how a political leader's personal characteristics affect his political behavior and the behavior of his political unit.) Based on our summarization of the research in this book, we will suggest directions which future studies on the personal characteristics of political leaders might profitably take.

Assessment

The first issue that we addressed concerned how the researcher could assess the personal characteristics of political leaders. Six techniques—questionnaire, interview, observation, content analysis, biographical statistics, and simulation—were

posited as alternative ways of measuring political leaders' personal characteristics. The reader has now perused at least two studies illustrating the use of
each of these techniques. Table 17.1 shows which chapters illustrate which
techniques. This table also contains other information indicating how these
techniques were used in each study. The information includes the nature of the
source of the data on personal characteristics (self, judge, or behavior), whether
or not the cooperation of the political leaders was required to use the technique
(obtrusive vs. unobtrusive), whether the source of the data was available in the
public domain or required special access (public vs. private), and the degree of
inference required in using the technique to assess a political leader's personal
characteristics (little, some, or much inference). Elaboration of each of these
categories follows.

As Table 17.1 shows, the personal characteristics which were examined in this
book had three origins. Some were based on self reports which political leaders
made about themselves; some were the results of judges' or informants' observations on the political leaders; others were inferred from political leaders'
behavior. Only one of the studies combined information from all three sources.
Johnson (Chapter 4) in ascertaining Senator Church's operational code interviewed Church (self as source) asking him the operational code questions;
Johnson also interviewed other people associated with Church (judges as source)
and content analyzed Church's speeches and remarks (behavior as source).
Church's operational code represents a synthesis of these various perspectives on
him. All the other chapters assessed personal characteristics using only one
source of information for each characteristic. Even where two sources are listed
in Table 17.1, the authors did not use both sources to assess each personal
characteristic which they were studying but rather used one source for information on one characteristic and the other source for information on a second
characteristic. Given the single source emphasis in these studies, one can wonder
if what political leaders report would be reflected in their behavior and noticed
by close associates and observers. If there is a convergence among these various
sources of information can we be more confident in our assessment of the
political leaders' personal characteristics? To date researchers studying political
leaders have not confronted this issue. Where multiple sources of information are
available—e.g., the political leaders can be interviewed, close associates will
consent to fill out a questionnaire, and speeches are accessible—future investigators are urged to compare and contrast the data which these three perspectives
provide to check what the effect of source is on assessment of personal
characteristics.

The second category in Table 17.1 concerns whether or not the cooperation
of the political leaders was required to learn about their personal characteristics.
We call the need for cooperation "obtrusive" because the researcher must
obtrude or intrude into the political leader's environment long enough to ask the
political leader questions or to observe his behavior. In the unobtrusive study the
researcher has no actual contact with the political leader. The investigator who

Table 17.1. Summary of Techniques Used by Authors in Book

Chapter and Author	Measurement Technique					
	Questionnaire	Interview	Observation	Content Analysis	Biographical Statistics	Simulation
2. Winter & A. Stewart				Behavior, Unobtrusive, Public, Some Inference		
3. Frank		Behavior, Unobtrusive, Public, Some Inference	Behavior, Unobtrusive, Public, Some Inference	Behavior, Unobtrusive, Public, Some Inference		
4. Johnson		Self & Judge, Obtrusive, Private, Little Inference	Behavior, Unobtrusive, Private, Little Inference	Behavior, Unobtrusive, Public, Some Inference		
5. Stogdill, Goode, & Day	Judge, Obtrusive, Private, Little Inference		Judge, Obtrusive, Private, Little Inference			
6. Milburn	Judge, Unobtrusive, Public, Some Inference		Judge, Unobtrusive, Public, Some Inference			
7. DiRenzo	Self, Obtrusive, Private, Little Inference	Self, Obtrusive, Private, Little Inference				
8. Ziller, Stone, Jackson, & Terbovic	Self, Obtrusive, Private, Little Inference					
9. L. Stewart					Self & Behavior, Unobtrusive, Public, Little Inference	
10. P. Stewart				Behavior, Unobtrusive, Public, Some Inference	Self & Behavior, Unobtrusive, Public, Little Inference	
11. Welsh					Self & Behavior, Unobtrusive, Public, Little Inference	
12. Hermann				Behavior, Unobtrusive, Public, Some Inference		
13. Driver*						Unobtrusive, Much Inference
14. Hermann		Behavior, Unobtrusive, Public, Some Inference		Behavior, Unobtrusive, Public, Some Inference		
15. Crow & Noel*						Unobtrusive, Much Inference

Note: Chapter 16 by Druckman is not included in this table because it reviews many studies rather than reporting the results of a single piece of research.
*The nature and source of data categories are not applicable to these simulation studies since the personal characteristics of simulation participants who were not actual political leaders were assessed.

intrudes into the political leader's environment needs to have several concerns. First, what is the nature of the situation—are there things which have just happened to the political leader which might have an impact on his responses? Second, how many times is the political leader interrupted or forced to attend to other events while interacting with the researcher; in other words, how distracted is he from the researcher's concerns? Third, is the political leader essentially cooperative and interested in the research or does he indicate problems with the questions and general suspiciousness about the project? Fourth, does the political leader seek reassurance that he has responded as the researcher wanted him to respond or indicate in some other way that he hopes the researcher has received the information he wanted to hear? Noting the answers to these questions can provide the researcher with some check on how the obtrusive research setting may have affected his data.

The person who uses material gained in an unobtrusive manner also has some issues to consider. Such a researcher needs to learn what policies exist concerning the material which he has used. Is there any bias which influences what material is kept? Moreover, are there any changes made in the material as a consequence of the recording process? For example, if verbatim speech is being recorded, are repetitions, use of ah's, and sentence changes deleted to clean up the transcript or are they left in when they occur? In short, when using either obtrusive or unobtrusive means of assessing the personal characteristics of political leaders, researchers need to consider how their research setting may be influencing their data. For a more extensive discussion of the possible effects, see Webb, Campbell, Schwartz, and Sechrest (1966).

Somewhat related to the obtrusive-unobtrusive issue is the notion of whether the material which is used to assess personal characteristics is from public or private sources. By public material we mean material which is in the public record and available to anyone in the public-at-large. Private material refers to material which is not available to the public-at-large. Private material is usually acquired from a political leader or his close associates and friends. Such materials are not part of the public record. An example of the difference between public and private materials is found in Nixon's speech in public situations and on the Watergate tapes. As Table 17.1 indicates, both types of material are used in the chapters in this book. With political leaders there are two important issues to consider in using public materials—ghostwriting and content control. Has someone else written the material for the political leader? What image is the political leader trying to maintain, i.e., does the audience or topic necessitate a certain rhetoric from the political leader? We have already raised these issues in the introduction to Chapter 12. Ghostwriting is not an issue with private materials as we have defined them. Content control may, however, be a problem with private materials if the researcher is present in their acquisition, although probably not nearly to the extent of public materials. If one is limited to public materials, use of the most spontaneous material available and the collection of materials across topics and audiences may help to control for the political leader's attempts at image maintenance. A far better strategy, though, when private materials also are accessible, would be to use both public and private materials, comparing the results from each type of material to see what the effects of content control are and which personal characteristics are particularly affected. The differential impact of public and private materials on the assessment of political leaders' personal characteristics is an area in need of much careful thought and research.

The last category in Table 17.1 indicates the amount of inference which appears inherent in our authors' assessment of their subjects' personal characteristics. There would seem to be less inference involved in moving from a political leader's own responses to a description of his personal characteristics than in moving from a simulation of heads of state to a statement about actual heads of state. In effect, what this category indicates is the remoteness of the data source from the political leader and his responses. The ratings in Table 17.1 are tentative in nature. They are dependent on the answers to the questions that we have raised concerning the convergence of self, judge, and behavior assessments of personal characteristics, the effects of obtrusive and unobtrusive measurement, and the biases in public information.

In sum, this book has illustrated how the six techniques in Table 17.1 can be used to assess the personal characteristics of political leaders. But these techniques are not problem free when applied to political leaders. We have raised four areas of concern which future researchers should consider in designing their studies.

Types of Political Leaders and Personal Characteristics Studied

Before discussing the two other topics which this book has addressed, let us summarize who the political leaders were on whom our authors' gathered information and which personal characteristics were examined. Table 17.2 indicates the types of political leaders who were the subjects of the research reported in this book. Table 17.2 presents several possible ways of classifying political leaders. For instance, there are political leaders at local, state or regional, and national levels in most governments. Such political leaders generally fulfill legislative and/or executive functions. They can be elected to office or achieve office through appointment, assassination, revolution, *coup d'etat,* intraparty maneuvering, and resignation. Moreover, political leaders have a specific role such as representative, premier, mayor, party chairman.

Table 17.2 indicates that the majority of the chapters (12 out of 15 or 80 percent) in this book focus on political leaders at the national level. Two of the chapters examine local political leaders and three study state or regional political leaders. In effect, Table 17.2 suggests that the results of the studies in this book are more descriptive of political leaders at the national level of government than at either the local or state/regional levels. There are probably

Table 17.2. Types of Political Leaders Studied by Chapter

			Type of Political Leader			
	Local		State or Regional		National	
Chapter and Author	Legislative	Executive	Legislative	Executive	Legislative	Executive
2. Winter & A. Stewart						Presidents (U.S., E)[a]
3. Frank					Senators (U.S., E)	
4. Johnson					Senator (U.S., E)	
5. Stogdill, Goode, & Day					Senators (U.S., E)	
6. Milburn		Committee Heads (U.S., A)				Head of State (U.S.S.R., A)
7. DiRenzo			State Legislators (U.S., E)		Deputies (Italy, E)	
8. Ziller, Stone, Jackson, & Terbovic			State Representatives (U.S., E)			
9. L. Stewart						Heads of State (U.S., England, E)
10. P. Stewart				Regional Party First Secretaries (U.S.S.R., A)		
11. Welsh						Cabinet (Latin America, A)
12. Hermann					Representatives (U.S., E)	
13. Driver						Heads of State, Cabinet[b]
14. Hermann		Mayor, Agency Heads (U.S., E & A)				
15. Crow & Noel						Heads of State, Cabinet[b]
16. Druckman						Diplomats[b]

[a]The material in parentheses indicates the country(ies) of the political leaders and whether they were elected (E) to office or achieved (A) office in a way other than by election.

[b]Represents simulated or experimental decision makers rather than actual political leaders.

several reasons for this emphasis on national political leaders. First, it may reflect the fascination of the general public and the mass media with national political leaders. In this era of Watergate, Vietnam, and personal diplomacy, national political leaders are continuously in the limelight. Second, traces or records of the behavior of national political leaders may actually be more accessible (in public libraries, in TV and newspaper morgues, in magazines) than similar records of the behavior of state/regional and local leaders. The reader interested in other research on the personal characteristics of political leaders at the regional and local level should see Barber (1965), Black (1972), Browning and Jacob (1964), Chamberlin (1972), Hedlund (1973), Kotter and Lawrence (1974), and Prewitt (1970).

Examining the other ways of classifying political leaders denoted in Table 17.2, we find 60 percent (9) of the chapters focus on political leaders with executive functions while 40 percent (6) of the chapters study political leaders with legislative functions. Some 60 percent (9) of the chapters are concerned with elected political leaders; roughly one quarter (4) of the chapters deal with political leaders who achieved office by other than an election. In all, 10 different political roles are examined. The roles receiving the most attention are head of state (5 chapters or 33 percent of the chapters), cabinet-level officials (3 chapters or 20 percent of the chapters), and senators (3 chapters or 20 percent of the chapters). One-third (5) of the chapters studied other than American political leaders.

Table 17.2 suggests the diversity in the subjects who have been the focus of attention in this book. With the exception of the DiRenzo and L. Stewart chapters (Chapters 7 and 9), however, the authors made no attempt to contrast the different types of political leaders. In the introduction to this book we suggested that one reason why researchers studying who becomes a political leader had found such contradictory results was that political leaders were not a homogeneous group. As we have shown in Table 17.2, there are many types of political leaders. It is not difficult to think of personal characteristics which might distinguish elected from appointed officials. Are there differences in personal characteristics between political leaders who have spent their political careers at the local level of government versus at the national level of government? In effect, we need a mapping of the political leader domain. What are the possible ways of classifying political leaders? For which types of political leaders are there differences in personal characteristics? What reasons might explain these differences? DiRenzo and L. Stewart have begun this endeavor by examining legislators and heads of state from different nations. But theirs is only a beginning to the research which is required.

Before leaving this topic let us re-examine our definition of political leader in light of the subjects actually studied in this book. We defined a political leader as an individual who has the authority to commit the resources and to select the goals of a political unit and, in turn, to affect its policy (see Chapter 1). This definition is easier to apply, at least in the United States, to the executive than to the legislative branches of government. In the executive branch there is an organizational hierarchy so that one individual does have the authority to commit resources and to select goals for a political unit. The definition is not as easily applied to the legislative branch of government. With each legislator having the right to vote, each has some authority to commit the resources and to select the goals of the political unit. Moreover, legislators are elected by constituencies who grant authority by the election process to commit their resources (e.g., taxes) and to select their goals or priorities (e.g., by legislation). Each legislator is, in effect, a political leader.

Another way to define political leader is to put less emphasis than the present book does on who has the authority or who has the position to commit resources and to select goals for a political unit and to focus, instead, on who assumes such authority. Who mobilizes the votes, whose advice is sought after and listened to, and whose bills and amendments generally receive support are questions one might raise in selecting legislative political leaders to study based on this definition. Who actually makes the policy decisions and who takes charge of implementing decisions are questions which could be asked in selecting executive political leaders. This definition is concerned with successful and effective influence. Whose influence attempts are accepted by or have an impact on the political unit? The chances are high that individuals who are both successful and effective in their influence attempts will continue to act as leaders or will be sought as leaders by the members of a political unit. Several authors who have used a definition much like this one in discussing political leaders are Edinger (1972), Katz (1973), and Verba (1961). The drawback to using this influence definition is that the researcher must ascertain who is exercising influence in a political unit before knowing who the political leaders are whom he will study. However, the knowledge that one is studying political leaders who have had an impact on the policy of their political unit may make the initial investigation worth the effort.

Table 17.3 presents a summary of the personal characteristics which were examined in the chapters in this book. The columns in this table are the types of personal characteristics which were suggested in the introductory chapter (see Chapter 1) as important to the study of political leaders. Scholars and journalists propose that these types of personal characteristics have an effect on political behavior. At first glance Table 17.3 appears to present a myriad of personal characteristics with little or no overlap among the characteristics across studies. But if one looks closer, at least for beliefs, there is some overlap. Crow and Noel's militarisim variable is like Driver's attitude on the use of force; Hermann's orientation toward international involvement variable is the inverse of Crow and Noel's nationalism variable. Hermann's humanitarian ideology variable is made specific in P. Stewart's consumer welfare attitudes, as is Driver's general ideology variable in P. Stewart's trust-distrust in the masses attitudes. In the decision style category, Hermann's cognitive complexity variable and the Driver conceptual complexity variable are similar.

Table 17.3.   Types of Personal Characteristics Examined by Chapter

Chapter and Author	Types of Personal Characteristics					
	Beliefs	Motives	Decision Style	Modes of Inter-personal Interaction	Stress Responses	Training or Expertise
2. Winter & A. Stewart		Need Achievement, Need Affiliation, Need Power				
3. Frank					Paralinguistic & Nonverbal Indicators of Stress	
4. Johnson	Operational Code					
5. Stogdill, Goode, & Day			Demand Reconciliation, Tolerance of Uncertainty, Tolerance of Freedom of Action, Initiation of Structure	Role Retention, Production Emphasis, Persuasiveness, Representation, Consideration		
7. DiRenzo			Dogmatism			
8. Ziller, Stone, Jackson, & Terbovic				Self-Other Orientations		
9. L. Stewart				Birth Order[a]		
10. P. Stewart	Ideological Attitudes, Trust-Distrust in Masses, Production & Manpower Attitudes, Consumer Welfare Attitudes, Age[a], Political Generation[a]					Nature of Education,[b] Nature of Experience[b]
11. Welsh	Party Affiliation,[a] Nature of Birthplace[a]			Nonparty Organizational Affiliations[a] (Number, Nature, Level of Position Held)		Nature of Experience,[b] Level of Education
12. Hermann	Humanitarian Ideology, Orientation toward International Involvement		Optimism, Cognitive Complexity			
13. Driver	Attitude on Use of Force, General Ideology		Conceptual Complexity	Level of Trust		
14. Hermann					Verbal Indicators of Negative Affect, Denial, & Stereotyping Behavior	
15. Crow & Noel	Militarism, Nationalism		Risk-Taking Preference			

Note: The Milburn (Chapter 6) and Druckman (Chapter 16) chapters are not included in this table since these chapters did not focus on specific personal characteristics.
[a]These variables are considered by the authors to be linked to certain beliefs and modes of interpersonal interaction.
[b]Because of space limitations several variables have been listed here under one heading. Separate experience and education variables include party, military, agricultural, and industrial experience and education as well as foreign study and foreign travel.

An insight which came to this writer as she assigned the personal characteristics to the categories in Table 17.3 appears in footnote "a" of the table. The authors who used biographical statistics assumed that these variables reflected certain beliefs and modes of interpersonal interaction. For example, "older people are more conservative than younger people" is one such proposition. The present authors use such variables as age, party affiliation, birth order, and nonparty organizational affiliations as indicators of certain beliefs and ways of interacting with others. In Chapter 9 L. Stewart is quite detailed in spelling out the kinds of modes of interpersonal interaction which he expects first-born and later-born children to adopt that can affect their selection as a political leader. In Chapter 10 P. Stewart discusses how the particular political generation which Soviet regional Party first secretaries represent can influence their attitudes. Those secretaries entering the party before 1939 in contrast to after 1938 found different environments and preoccupations within the party hierarchy which probably had an impact on their views of political reality. Can we move beyond these hypothesized relationships and show how these biographical statistics link to the other characteristics they are supposed to indicate? P. Stewart's (Chapter 10) examination of the relationship between biographical data and attitudes of Soviet regional Party first secretaries is a step in this direction. Here is an avenue in need of further research.

A perusal of Table 17.3 suggests that the personal characteristics which were studied are at different levels. In other words, some are more basic to an individual's functioning and, thus, probably are manifested earlier in an individual's development. Others result from the interaction of these early characteristics and experience. For example, consumer welfare attitudes and attitude on the use of force are probably not characteristics one possesses early in development but most likely arise in the late teens or early twenties as political ideas become more salient to the individual. Hermann's data in Chapter 12 suggests that an orientation toward international involvement is found in individuals who are generally optimistic and have a high level of cognitive complexity. What level of personal characteristic a researcher should study with political leaders has generated some controversy. Scholars working in the psychoanalytic tradition have argued for the importance of characteristics developed early in childhood (e.g., see George and George, 1964; Rogow, 1963; Wolfenstein, 1967); while others see personal characteristics like political attitudes and beliefs as more germane to what political leaders are about and, thus, more relevant to the study of political leaders (e.g., see M. Hermann, 1974; Holsti, 1973). By examining the interrelationship among personal characteristics across levels, much as Hermann did in Chapter 12, we can learn what "basic" personal characteristics result in specific political characteristics, eliminating the need for debate and enhancing our knowledge about which characteristics have payoff in the study of political leaders.

The emphasis in the previous two paragraphs on examining the linkages among personal characteristics leads naturally to a plea that research on the personal characteristics of political leaders move now beyond the single trait approach. An individual is a mix of characteristics—some are consistent over time and situation, while others change; some are basic to the individual while others develop in response to new situations and information. Although all chapters in this book studied more than one characteristic, most of the authors examined each characteristic by itself, not in conjunction with the others. As Milburn argues in Chapter 6, one learns little about the interaction of these characteristics by assuming such a univariate approach. There are several notable exceptions, however, among the chapters. Ziller and his associates in Chapter 8 examine how self-esteem and complexity of the self interact to form four self-other orientations. It is the self-other orientations which Ziller et al. study in their political leader sample. In Chapter 13 Driver shows how stress-diminishing and stress-enhancing attitudes affected the aggressive responses of political leaders low and high in conceptual complexity. In both of these studies, several personal characteristics interacted in affecting what a political leader did. The mix of characteristics was necessary for the result.

Who Becomes a Political Leader?

In the introduction to this volume (see Chapter 1) we indicated that there were three strains of research on the topic of who becomes a political leader. Research has focused on comparing the personal characteristics of political leaders to those of their constituents, on describing the personal characteristics of specific groups of political leaders, and on exploring the relationship between personal characteristics, political role, and the recruitment process. In Part Two of the book, the reader encountered examples of each of these strains of research. DiRenzo (Chapter 7) and Ziller et al. (Chapter 8) were interested in differentiating political leaders from nonpoliticians—in showing how political leaders differed from their constituents on dogmatism and self-other orientation. In Chapter 10, P. Stewart described the personal characteristics of one group of political leaders—regional Party first secretaries in the Soviet Union. The primary emphasis, however, in the research reported in Part Two of the book was exploring the interrelationship between personal characteristics and the recruitment process.

Several recruitment issues were studied. What kinds of individuals gain office through extralegal means? What kinds of individuals initiate their own political participation versus what kinds are recruited or coopted into a political role? Does a change in the informal requirements of a political role influence who is recruited? Do different types of "selectors" in the recruitment process choose political leaders with different personal characteristics? Let us see how the authors addressed these issues.

In Chapter 11 Welsh examined the issue of who tries to gain office by extralegal means, i.e., participates in a *coup d'etat.* He found that in Latin

America individuals with only a few nonparty organizational affiliations, who were better educated, and from urban backgrounds tended to achieve political roles through such extralegal means. Contrast the Welsh study to those by DiRenzo (Chapter 7), Ziller et al. (Chapter 8), and L. Stewart (Chapter 9). These three chapters focused on gaining office by election or legal means. These authors asked what kinds of persons are selected by an electorate for state and national offices. Dogmatism, self-other orientation, and birth order were the personal characteristics under study. These researchers found such elected officials were first- and third-born sons, and either pragmatists (low self-esteem, high complexity of self) or ideologues (high self-esteem, low complexity of self). The results for dogmatism were intertwined with another recruitment issue which we will consider next.

DiRenzo found differences in the dogmatism of his samples of political leaders who were elected in the United States and Italy. There appeared to be a cultural bias affecting who was selected. The Italian political leaders tended to be dogmatic while the American political leaders were nondogmatic. Moreover, the people forming the electorate differed along the same lines as the political leaders. The Italian constituents were predominantly dogmatic; the American constituents were predominantly nondogmatic. In effect, the political leaders merely exhibited more of the characteristic which was found among their constituents. The differing characteristics of the electorate were reflected in the political leaders who were chosen.

What about the kinds of individuals who are self-selected in the recruitment process versus those who are recruited or coopted? By self-selection we mean an individual's seeking out a political role. Recruitment and cooptation are processes by which persons are sought by others to take political roles. Three chapters considered this general recruitment issue. By examining participants in *coups d' etat,* Welsh in Chapter 11 studied the extreme in self-selection. Here are individuals who take over political roles without participating in the usual selection process. In effect, they bypass the whole recruitment process. Such individuals in Latin America, as we have already noted, are characterized by more than a high-school education, an urban upbringing, and few nonparty organizational affiliations. One of the biographical statistics which P. Stewart examined in Chapter 10 focused on whether a Soviet regional Party first secretary was recruited or coopted into Party work. Different attitudes on the use of ideology, trust in the masses, and consumer welfare were found between recruited and coopted officials. Moreover, DiRenzo in Chapter 7 suggests that his results for Italian parties are indicative of whether the candidate was self-selected or coopted. Self-selected legislators were more dogmatic.

A final recruitment issue centers on the informal requirements of a political role and political leaders' perceptions of these role requirements. In Chapter 9, L. Stewart proposes that as the times move from peace to war, different kinds of behavior are demanded of occupants in head-of-state positions, and persons are selected whose personal characteristics match the new role requirements. Thus, later-born sons with their early sibling experience in coalition formation and consensus making become president or prime minister in times of peace, and first-born sons who early dominate sibling relationships assume these political roles in times of crisis and war. DiRenzo in Chapter 7 examines political leaders' perceptions of the roles which they hold. He reports that state legislators who perceived their role as a profession as opposed to an avocation were more dogmatic. One might interpret DiRenzo's finding as indicating how personal characteristics can impact on the perception of opportunity which an individual sees in a political role.

This discussion of the interrelation between personal characteristics of political leaders and recruitment is merely illustrative of the research directions which are possible in the study of who becomes a political leader. That we need more research is readily apparent; we also need more thoughtful consideration of what personal characteristics might affect the recruitment issues we have discussed and what the nature of the impact might be. The authors in Part Two of this volume along with Barber (1965), Browning and Jacob (1964), Prewitt and Stone (1973), and Seligman (1971) have laid the cornerstone for such a conceptualization, but its construction has just begun.

Before leaving the question of who becomes a political leader, there is one more area of concern for future researchers which merits some discussion. There are two recruitment processes which demand the attention of the researcher. The first is recruitment into a specific political unit. For example, how does someone become a state legislator, a local councilman, a party regular, a political appointee? The second recruitment process is that which occurs within a particular political unit in selecting its leadership. For instance, how does someone become Senate majority leader, city council president, head of a party, chairman of an inter-agency committee? Although the first recruitment process has received more attention than the second, students of political leadership should be interested in the second. The effects of personal characteristics on both recruitment processes were examined in the chapters concerned on both becomes a political leader. In fact, Ziller et al. (Chapter 8) and Welsh (Chapter 11) studied both these processes in the same research. Ziller and his colleagues looked at who was elected to the state legislature and then how successful freshman state legislators with such characteristics were in influencing legislation. In addition to who comes to power via a *coup d'etat,* Welsh also examined the leaders who were deposed by a *coup.* What kinds of people can become political leaders but cannot sustain their influence? Probably the greatest potential payoff for learning how personal characteristics affect the second recruitment process is found in P. Stewart's (Chapter 10) research. Stewart has information on the attitudes and biographical characteristics of Soviet Party first secretaries. By noting who goes on to become members of the Soviet Politburo, Stewart can begin to describe the characteristics relevant to political advance-

ment in the Soviet Union. In effect, all three chapters suggest ways of systematically studying the relevance of personal characteristics in this second
recruitment process.

It is interesting to speculate on how the personal characteristics relevant to
one recruitment process affect the other. Ziller and his colleagues found that
pragmatic and ideologic self-other orientations enhanced a candidate's chances
of being elected a state legislator and of being successful in the state legislature's
influence process. Being sensitive to one's environment (the pragmatist) or
having a sense of mission (the ideologue) were useful characteristics in both
recruitment processes. Can we think of characteristics which might help one get
elected but hinder advancement or lead to slow advancement into positions of
influence in a political unit? Matthews (1959) in describing the folkways of the
U.S. Senate indicates two such characteristics—ambition and liberal ideology.
Matthews noted that Senators with these characteristics were less likely to
conform to the folkways of the Senate and, in turn, were legislatively less
effective in influencing other Senators. Ambition in this case was for an office
outside of the political unit—the presidency. Ambition for an office within the
Senate might have led to different behavior. As it was, the Senators in Matthews'
study who were ambitious for a higher office needed to be heard and seen by the
public-at-large. As a consequence of this need, they spoke a lot on the floor of
the Senate, were absent from the Senate frequently, and did not specialize—all
behaviors counter to the norms of the Senate. With regard to liberal ideology,
liberal Senators were generally elected with the notion that they would change
things. But they were usually unable to enact change on their own. Thus, liberal
Senators either postponed achievement of their objectives and conformed to the
norms until they could gain enough prestige (or lose an election) to "change
things" or they tried to initiate changes immediately and were dubbed non-
conformists, often losing their legislative effectiveness in the process.

This discussion leads naturally to the next topic—how the personal characteristics of political leaders affect their own political behavior and the behavior
of the political body or unit in which they participate. In some sense the
recruitment process within a political unit for leadership roles involves the
examination of how personal characteristics affect behavior. As we have already
noted, one might argue that an individual becomes a political leader when he or
she has been able to have an impact on the behavior or policy of a political unit.
When individuals influence the behavior or policy of a political unit, their
personal characteristics are one set of variables which may help to explain the
nature of that behavior or policy.

Personal Characteristics and Political Behavior

The chapters in Part Three of the book, plus Chapter 2 by Winter and A.
Stewart, dealt with the effects of political leaders' personal characteristics on

political behavior. Let us see how these chapters explored the three questions that we raised in the introductory chapter (Chapter 1) concerning the relationship between personal characteristics and political behavior—namely, whose political behavior is one interested in predicting; what personal characteristics affect political behavior; and are there role, situational, and/or organizational factors which enhance the relationship between personal characteristics and political behavior.

The predominant emphasis of the chapters in Part Three was on collective political behavior. In other words, the authors were interested in explaining the political behavior of the political unit in which their subjects participated. Five of the six chapters focused on collective political behavior. Only Hermann in Chapter 12 examined her subjects' own political behavior. In effect, the authors found collective political behavior a more interesting outcome to explain. Such an emphasis may be justified since it is the behavior of the political unit which has the greatest impact on the lives of those being governed. If a political leader's personal characteristics can account for some of the variance in collective political behavior, we have information of value for that political system. However, the authors may have dismissed too lightly studying the relationship between a political leader's personal characteristics and what he or she does. Political leaders do not operate in a vacuum; for example, party pressures, constituency demands, role requirements, and previous commitments may reduce the effect of personal characteristics in a particular situation. Note in Hermann's data on U.S. Representatives (Chapter 12) how a role norm on what political leaders can criticize domestically affected the verbalized humanitarianism of the Representatives. Moreover, learning how political leaders' personal characteristics influence their own behavior may suggest how such characteristics might affect collective political behavior. In the long run, research on both types of political behavior seems worthwhile.

The question of what personal characteristics affect political behavior is the primary emphasis of the chapters in Part Three. This question has two parts. What are the political behaviors which the researcher wants to explain, and which personal characteristics seem relevant to such behaviors? With the exception of Hermann in Chapter 14, the political behavior which the authors of these chapters wanted to explain was foreign policy, specifically the choice of a conflictful or cooperative national foreign policy. Winter and A. Stewart (Chapter 2) examined entry into war and agreements on arms limitations; Hermann in Chapter 12 studied votes for and against foreign aid; Driver (Chapter 13) looked at aggressive responses ranging from war to provoked arms increases; Crow and Noel (Chapter 15) were interested in military escalatory responses to a crisis situation; and Druckman (Chapter 16) examined international negotiations. From these studies we can begin to form pictures of the national political leaders who influence their nations toward aggressive and conciliatory relations with other nations. The aggressive leader is high in need for power, low in conceptual complexity, distrustful of others, militaristic, nationalistic, and prefers high risk responses. In contrast, the conciliatory leader is high in need for achievement and affiliation, high in conceptual complexity, optimistic, non-belligerent, internationalistic, and prefers low risk responses. One caveat is necessary here before these results are automatically generalized to all national political leaders—the subjects in these studies were American political leaders (e.g., U.S. Presidents, U.S. Representatives, U.S. simulation participants). At present, then, these are portraits of American aggressive and conciliatory political leaders.

Granting this caveat, let us speculate about the processes which underly the personal characteristic-foreign policy relationships for the aggressive and conciliatory leaders. In some sense such processes appear to parallel those for the ideologue and pragmatist from the Ziller et al. (Chapter 8) research. The conciliatory leader, like the pragmatic leader, is sensitive or responsive to his environment, in this case the international system. He is atune to what is going on in international relations. He is interested in having his nation interact with other nations, in working out peaceful solutions to problems jointly plaguing his own and other nations. On the other hand, the aggressive leader, like the ideologue, is responsive to an idea. He is mission-oriented. His mission is the maintenance of his national identity. Such a leader urges his nation to be suspicious of the motives of the leaders of other nations and to limit interaction with other nations. If interaction is necessary, it should be on his nation's terms. In another place the writer (M. Hermann, 1974) has explored the general foreign policy behavior of two types of political leaders, defined by a series of characteristics similar to those in the conciliatory and aggressive composites, and found that conciliatory leaders were generally more cooperative in their foreign policy while the aggressive leaders were more willing to change on their own the nature of their relationship with another nation.

In the introductory chapter we noted four types of personal characteristics—beliefs, motives, decision style, and modes of interpersonal interaction—which scholars and journalists have suggested have an impact on political behavior. Interestingly, our portraits of the aggressive and conciliatory American political leader lend support to this contention. Representatives of all four types of characteristics appear in the portraits. The nationalism-internationalism and militarism-nonbelligerence variables represent beliefs; the needs for achievement, affiliation, and power represent motives; optimism, risk-taking preference, and level of conceptual complexity represent decision style; and distrust in others represents a mode of interpersonal interaction.

We posed several responses earlier (Chapter 1) to the question of whether there were role, situational, and/or organizational variables which enhanced the relationship between personal characteristics and political behavior, in particular, collective political behavior. A rationale was presented for studying high-level political leaders. Such leaders have less well-defined roles and few people, if any, above them with authority to change or modify their decisions. Their personal characteristics have a greater opportunity to influence the behavior of a political unit. Turning to the chapters in Part Three we note that all five chapters concerned with the effect of personal characteristics on collective political behavior focused on high-level political decision makers. Presidents, a mayor, chief negotiators, and cabinet officers were among the subjects. Using high-level political leaders as subjects, these researchers generally found relationships between personal characteristics and collective political behavior.

We also argued in the introductory material that even with high-level political leaders as subjects, there are probably circumstances which enhance personal characteristic-collective political behavior relationships. One situation which appeared to have this effect in the research reported in Part Three was the stressful or high threat situation. Hermann in Chapter 14 focused on how the personal characteristics and reactions of the chief participants in the New York City transit negotiations changed as stress increased; Driver in Chapter 13 found that certain situational constraints were necessary for political leaders with high conceptual complexity to go to war. Since so many types of variables can impinge on the decision process of a political unit, examination of the interaction among leaders' personal characteristics, situation, role, and organizational variables seems an important area of concern for future research. Although Crow and Noel (Chapter 15) and Druckman (Chapter 16) go about studying such interactions in different ways, their investigations of how personal, situational, and role variables influence escalatory responses and international negotiations are prototypes for such future research.

In Summary

This book in many respects is like a toddler's first step. It is a prelude to many more steps, including some false ones. We have presented ways of assessing the personal characteristics of political leaders, indicated issues important to the examination of who becomes a political leader, and started the exploration of how political leaders' personal characteristics affect their own political behavior and the behavior of their political units. But the research contained in these chapters marks only a beginning to the study of the personal characteristics of political leaders. Much work remains. We have tried to point out directions which such future studies should take. We hope we have piqued the reader's curiosity enough for him (her) to join in these next endeavors.

References

Abelson, R. P. Psychological Implication. In R. P. Abelson, E. Aronson, W. J. McGuire, T. M. Newcomb, M. J. Rosenberg, and P. H. Tannenbaum (Eds.), *Theories of Cognitive Consistency: A Sourcebook.* Chicago: Rand McNally, 1968(a).

―――. Simulation of Social Behavior. In G. Lindzey and E. Aronson (Eds.), *The Handbook of Social Psychology.* Rev. ed., Vol. 2. Reading, Mass.: Addison-Wesley, 1968(b). Pp. 274-356.

―――. The Ideology Machine. Paper presented at annual meeting of American Political Science Association, Chicago, September, 1971.

―――. The Structure of Belief Systems. In K. Colby and R. Schank (Eds.), *Computer Simulation of Thought and Language.* San Francisco: Freeman, 1973.

――― and Carroll, J. D. Computer Simulation of Individual Belief Systems. *American Behavioral Scientist,* 1965, 8, 24-30.

Acheson, D. G. The President and the Secretary of State. In D. K. Price (Ed.), *The Secretary of State.* Englewood Cliffs, N.J.: Prentice-Hall, 1960. Pp. 27-50.

Ackoff, R. L., and Emery, F. E. *On Purposeful Systems.* Chicago: Aldine-Atherton, 1972.

Adorno, T. W., Frenkel-Brunswik, E., Levinson, D. J., and Sanford, R. N. *The Authoritarian Personality.* New York: Harper, 1950.

Alexander, R. J. The Emergence of Modern Political Parties in Latin America. In J. Maier and R. W. Weatherhead (Eds.), *The Politics of Change in Latin America.* New York: Praeger, 1964. Pp. 101-125.

―――. *Latin American Politics and Government.* New York: Harper and Row, 1965.

Allport, G. W. Attitudes. In C. Murchison (Ed.), *Handbook of Social Psychology.* Worcester, Mass.: Clark University Press, 1935. Pp. 798-884.

———. *Personality: A Psychological Interpretation.* New York: Holt, 1937.

Almond, G., and Powell, G. B., Jr. *Comparative Politics: A Developmental Approach.* Boston: Little, Brown, 1966.

Almond, G., and Verba, S. *The Civic Culture.* Princeton: Princeton University Press, 1963. (Paperback: Little, Brown, 1965.)

Amalrik, A. *Will the Soviet Union Survive until 1984?* New York: Praeger, 1971.

Anderson, C. W. *Politics and Economic Change in Latin America.* Princeton: Van Nostrand, 1967.

Anderson, J. E., Jr. The "Operational Code" Approach: The George Construct and Senator Arthur H. Vandenberg's Operational Code Belief System. Paper presented at annual meeting of American Political Science Association, New Orleans, September, 1973.

Andrews, F., Morgan, J., and Sonquist, S. *Multiple Classification Analysis: A Report on a Computer Program for Multiple Regression Using Categorical Predictors.* Ann Arbor: Institute for Social Research, 1967.

Angell, R. C. Social Values of Soviet and American Elites: Content Analysis of Elite Media. *Journal of Conflict Resolution,* 1964, 8, 330-385.

Ansbacher, H. L., and Ansbacher, R. R. (Eds.) *The Individual Psychology of Alfred Adler.* New York: Harper and Row, 1956.

Armstrong, J. A. *The Soviet Bureaucratic Elite.* New York: Praeger, 1959.

———. Party Bifurcation and Elite Interests. *Soviet Studies,* 1966, 17, 417-430.

Ashby, N. Schumacher and Brandt: The Divergent "Operational Codes" of Two German Socialist Leaders. Unpublished Manuscript, Stanford University, 1969.

Ashmore, R. D. Personality-Attitude Variables and Characteristics of the Protagonist as Determinants of Trust in the Prisoner's Dilemma. Unpublished Manuscript, University of California, Los Angeles, 1969.

Atkinson, J. W. (Ed.) *Motives in Fantasy, Action, and Society: A Method of Assessment and Study.* Princeton: Van Nostrand, 1958.

Atkinson, J. W., and Feather, N. T. *A Theory of Achievement Motivation.* New York: Wiley, 1966.

Ax, A. F. Psychophysiology of Fear and Anger. *Psychiatric Research Reports,* 1960, 12, 167-175.

Azrael, J. R. The Managers. In R. B. Farrell (Ed.), *Political Leadership in Eastern Europe and the Soviet Union.* Chicago: Aldine, 1970(a).

———. Varieties of De-Stalinization. In C. Johnson (Ed.), *Change in Communist Systems.* Stanford: Stanford University Press, 1970(b).

Bacon, F. *The Essays of Francis Bacon.* Oxford: Clarendon Press, 1890.

Barber, J. D. *The Lawmakers.* New Haven: Yale University Press, 1965.

———. *Power in Committees: An Experiment in the Government Process.* Chicago: Rand McNally, 1966.

———. Classifying and Predicting Presidential Styles: Two "Weak" Presidents. *Journal of Social Issues,* 1968, 24, 51-80.

———. Analyzing Presidents: From Passive-Positive Taft to Active-Negative Nixon. *The Washington Monthly,* 1969, 9, 33-54.

———. Adult Identity and Presidential Style: The Rhetorical Emphasis. In D. A. Rustow (Ed.), *Philosophers and Kings: Studies in Leadership.* New York: Braziller, 1970. Pp. 367-397.

———. *The Presidential Character: Predicting Performance in the White House.* Englewood Cliffs, N.J.: Prentice-Hall, 1972.

Barker, E. N. Authoritarianism of the Political Right, Center, and Left. *Journal of Social Issues,* 1963, 19, 63-74.

Bartos, O. J. How Predictable Are Negotiations? *Journal of Conflict Resolution,* 1967, 11, 481-496.

Bass, B. M. Effects on the Subsequent Performance of Negotiators of Studying Issues or Planning Strategies Alone or in Groups. *Psychological Monographs,* 1966, Whole No. 614.

Bauer, R. A., Inkeles, A., and Kluckhohn, C. *How the Soviet System Works.* Cambridge: Harvard University Press, 1956.

Beaverbrook, Lord. *Politicians and the War.* Garden City, N.Y.: Doubleday, 1926.

Beck, C., Fleron, F. J., Jr., Lodge, M., Waller, D. J., Welsh, W. A., and Zaninovich, M. G. *Comparative Communist Political Leadership.* New York: McKay, 1973.

Benton, A. A., and Druckman, D. Salient Solutions and the Bargaining Behavior of Representatives and Nonrepresentatives. *International Journal of Group Tensions,* 1973, 3, 28-39.

——— and Druckman, D. Constituent's Bargaining Orientation and Intergroup Negotiations. *Journal of Applied Social Psychology,* 1974, 4, 141-150.

Berelson, B. *Content Analysis in Communication Research.* Glencoe, Ill.: Free Press, 1952.

Berkeley, H. *The Power of the Prime Minister.* London: Allen and Unwin, 1968.

Berkowitz, N. Alternative Measures of Authoritarianism, Response Sets, and Prediction in a Two-Person Game. *Journal of Social Psychology,* 1968, 74, 233-242.

Bigham, C. *The Prime Ministers of Britain 1721-1921.* London: Murray, 1920.

Bixenstine, V. E., and Blundell, H. Control of Choice Exerted by Structural Factors in Two-Person, Non-Zero-Sum Games. *Journal of Conflict Resolution,* 1966, 10, 478-487.

Black, G. S. A Theory of Political Ambition: Career Choices and the Role of Structural Incentives. *American Political Science Review,* 1972, 66, 144-159.

Blackwell, R. E., Jr. Career Development in the Soviet Obkom Elite: A Conservative Trend. *Soviet Studies,* 1972, 24, 25-40.

Blake, R. R., and Mouton, J. S. The Intergroup Dynamics of Win-Lose Conflict and Problem-Solving Collaboration in Union-Management Relations. In M. Sherif (Ed.), *Intergroup Relations and Leadership.* New York: Wiley, 1962. Pp. 94-140.

Block, J. *The Q-sort Method in Personality Assessment and Psychiatric Research.* Springfield, Ill.: Charles C. Thomas, 1961.

Bobrow, D. B. Transfer of Meaning across National Boundaries. In R. L. Merritt (Ed.), *Communication in International Politics.* Urbana: University of Illinois Press, 1972.

Boise Journal, 2 March, 1956(a).

———, 17 August, 1956(b).

———, 21 September, 1956(c).

Bonham, G. M. Simulating International Disarmament Negotiations. *Journal of Conflict Resolution,* 1971, 15, 299-315.

Boulding, K. *The Impact of the Social Sciences.* New Brunswick, N.J.: Rutgers University Press, 1966.

Bowen, D. D. Reported Patterns of Needs for Achievement, Affiliation and Power in Studies of Thematic Apperception. Unpublished Paper, University of Pittsburgh, 1972.

Boyatzis, R. Affiliation Motivation. In D. C. McClelland and R. S. Steele (Eds.), *Human Motivation: A Book of Readings.* Morristown, N.J.: General Learning Press, 1973. Pp. 252-276.

Boyd, N. K. Negotiation Behavior by Elected and Appointed Representatives Serving as Group Leaders or Spokesmen under Different Cooperative Group Expectations. Unpublished Doctoral Dissertation, University of Maryland, 1972.

Brehmer, B., Azuma, H., Hammond, K. R., Kostran, L., and Varonas, D. A Cross-National Comparison of Cognitive Conflict. *Journal of Cross-Cultural Psychology,* 1970, 1, 5-20.

Brislin, R. W., Lonner, W. J., and Thorndike, R. M. *Cross-Cultural Research Methods.* New York: Wiley, 1973.

Brody, R. A. Some Systemic Effects of the Spread of Nuclear Weapons Technology: A Study through Simulation of a Multi-Nuclear Future. *Journal of Conflict Resolution,* 1963, 7, 663-753.

Brown, B. R. The Effects of Need to Maintain Face on Interpersonal Bargaining. *Journal of Experimental Social Psychology,* 1968, 4, 107-122.

———. Face-Saving Following Experimentally Induced Embarrassment. *Journal of Experimental Social Psychology,* 1970, 6, 255-271.

Brown, R. W. *Social Psychology.* New York: Free Press, 1965.

Browning, R. P. Hypotheses About Political Recruitment: A Partially Data-Based Computer Simulation. In W. D. Coplin (Ed.), *Simulation in the Study of Politics.* Chicago: Markham, 1968.

——— and Jacob, H. Power Motivation and the Political Personality. *Public Opinion Quarterly,* 1964, 28, 75-90.

Brzezinski, Z. The Soviet Political System: Transformation or Degeneration. *Problems of Communism,* 1966, 15, 1-15.

———. (Ed.) *Dilemmas of Change in Soviet Politics.* New York: Columbia University Press, 1969.

———. *Between Two Ages: America's Role in the Technetronic Era.* New York: Viking, 1970.

——— and Huntington, S. *Political Power: USA/USSR.* New York: Viking, 1963.

Burgess, P. M., and Lawton, R. W. Indicators of International Behavior: An Assessment of Events Data Research. *Sage Professional Papers in International Studies,* 1972, 1, No. 02-010.

Burton, J. W. *Conflict and Communication.* New York: Free Press, 1969.

Byars, R. S. Small-Group Theory and Shifting Styles of Political Leadership. *Comparative Political Studies,* 1973, 5, 443-469.

Campbell, A., Converse, P. E., Miller, W. E., and Stokes, D. E. *The American Voter.* New York: Wiley, 1960.

Campbell, D. T., and Fiske, D. M. Convergent and Discriminant Validation by the Multitrait-Multimethod Matrix. *Psychological Bulletin,* 1959, 56, 81-105.

Cantril, H. *The Pattern of Human Concerns.* New Brunswick, N.J.: Rutgers University Press, 1965.

Carroll, J. B. Review of *The Measurement of Meaning. Language,* 1959, 35, 58-77.

Chamberlin, H. B. Transition and Consolidation in Urban China: A Study of Leaders and Organizations in Three Cities, 1949-53. In R. A. Scalapino (Ed.), *Elites in the People's Republic of China.* Seattle: University of Washington Press, 1972. Pp. 245-301.

Chayes, A. An Inquiry into the Workings on Arms Control Agreements. *Harvard Law Review,* 1972, 85, 904-969.

Cherryholmes, C. H., and Shapiro, M. J. *Representatives and Roll Calls: A Computer Simulation of Voting in the Eighty-Eighth Congress.* Indianapolis: Bobbs-Merrill, 1969.

Christie, R., and Geis, F. L. *Studies in Machiavellianism.* New York: Academic Press, 1970.

——— and Jahoda, M. (Eds.) *Studies in the Scope and Method of "The Authoritarian Personality."* New York: Harper, 1954.

Church, F. *Idaho Statesman,* 4 August, 1956(a).

———. *Idaho Statesman,* 8 September, 1956(b).

———. *Idaho Statesman,* 30 September, 1956(c).

———. *Idaho Statesman,* 11 October, 1956(d).

———. *Idaho Statesman,* 27 October, 1956(e).

———. *Washington Post,* 20 February, 1957.

———. *Lewiston* (Idaho) *Morning Tribune,* 20 December, 1964.

———. Borah the Statesman. *Idaho Yesterdays,* 1965, 9 (Summer), 2-9.

———. *Constituent Newsletter,* October, 1967.

———. The Torment in the Land. *Congressional Record,* 1968, 114 (21 February), 3803-3813.

———. *Salt Lake City Tribune,* 7 February, 1969(a).

———. U.S. Aid to Latin America. *Congressional Record,* 1969(b), 115 (11 November), 33669-33672.

———. Toward a New Policy for Latin America. *Congressional Record,* 1970(a), 116 (10 April), 11211-11217.

———. Of Presidents and Caesars. *Congressional Record,* 1970(b), 116 (30 April), 13563-13566.

———. U.S. Policy in the Caribbean. *Congressional Record,* 1970(c), 116 (25 November), 38851-38854.

———. Let Us Come Out Together. *Congressional Record,* 1971(a), 117 (29 April), 12667-12668.

———. *Washington Post,* 7 November, 1971(b).

———. The Multinational Corporation—A Perception of America. *Congressional Record,* 1973(a), 119 (18 January), S989-S991.

———. Impoundment and Executive Emergency Powers. *Congressional Record,* 1973(b), 119 (31 January), S1690-S1693.

———. Let Us Have No Illusions about Peace. *Congressional Record,* 1973(c), 119 (15 February), S2597-S2598.

———. On Aid to North Vietnam. *Congressional Record,* 1973(d), 119 (13 March), S4488-S4489.

———. *Washington Post,* 30 March, 1973(e).

———. *Constituent Newsletter,* April, 1973(f).

——— and Case, C. P. *Congressional Record,* 1973, 119 (26 January), S1340-S1343.

Clapp, C. L. *The Congressman: His Work as He Sees It.* Garden City, N.Y.: Anchor Books, 1964.

Clausen, A. R. *How Congressmen Decide: A Policy Focus.* New York: St. Martin's Press, 1973.

Cocks, P. The Rationalization of Party Control. In C. Johnson (Ed.), *Change in Communist Systems.* Stanford: Stanford University Press, 1970. Pp. 154-190.

Collins, B. E. An Experimental Study of Satisfaction, Productivity, Turnover, and Comparison Levels. Unpublished Doctoral Dissertation, Northwestern University, 1963.

Congressional Quarterly Almanac. Vols. 5 and 6. Washington, D.C.: Congressional Quarterly News Features, 1949, 1950.

Congressional Record. Washington, D.C.: U.S. Government Printing Office, 1949-1950.

Conquest, R. *Power and Policy in the USSR.* New York: St. Martin's Press, 1961.

Conrath, D. W. Experience as a Factor in Experimental Gaming Behavior. *Journal of Conflict Resolution,* 1970, 14, 195-202.

Cortés, J. B., and Gatti, F. M. *Delinquency and Crime: A Biopsychosocial Approach.* New York: Seminar Press, 1972.

Cronbach, L. J. Correlations between Persons as a Research Tool. In O. H. Mowrer (Ed.), *Psychotherapy Theory and Research.* New York: Ronald Press, 1953. Pp. 376-388.

Crow. W. J. A Study of Strategic Doctrines Using the Inter-Nation Simulation. *Journal of Conflict Resolution*, 1963, 7, 580-589.

———. Simulation: The Construction and Use of Functioning Models in International Relations. In K. R. Hammond (Ed.), *The Psychology of Egon Brunswik*. New York: Holt, Rinehart, and Winston, 1966.

Cutler, N. Generational Analysis in Political Analysis. Paper presented at annual meeting of American Political Science Association, Chicago, September, 1971.

Danielian, J. Live Simulation of Affect-Laden Cultural Cognitions. *Journal of Conflict Resolution*, 1967, 11, 312-324.

Darwin, C. *The Expression of the Emotions in Man and Animals*. Chicago: University of Chicago Press, 1965.

Datta, L. Birth Order and Early Scientific Attainment. *Perceptual and Motor Skills*, 1967, 24, 157-158.

Davis, E. E., and Triandis, H. C. *An Exploratory Study of Inter-Cultural Negotiations*. University of Illinois Group Effectiveness Research Laboratory Technical Report 26, ARPA Contract NR 177-472, Nonr-1834 (36), 1965.

DeRivera, J. H. *The Psychological Dimension of Foreign Policy*. Columbus, Ohio: Merrill, 1968.

DeSoto, C. B., London, M., and Handel, S. Social Reasoning and Spatial Paralogic. *Journal of Personality and Social Psychology*, 1965, 2, 513-521.

Deutsch, M. Trust, Trustworthiness and the F Scale. *Journal of Abnormal and Social Psychology*, 1960, 61, 138-140.

———, Canavan, D., and Rubin, J. The Effects of Size of Conflict and Sex of Experimenter upon Interpersonal Bargaining. *Journal of Experimental Social Psychology*, 1971, 7, 258-267.

Dexter, L. A. *Elite and Specialized Interviewing*. Evanston, Ill.: Northwestern University Press, 1970.

Dicks, H. V. Personality Traits and National Socialist Ideology. *Human Relations*, 1950, 3, 111-153.

DiRenzo, G. J. Personality Structures and Political Consensus-Cleavage. *Research Reports in the Social Sciences*, 1967(a), 1, 13-27.

———. Professional Politicians and Personality Structures. *American Journal of Sociology*, 1967(b), 73, 217-225.

———. *Personality, Power, and Politics*. South Bend, Ind.: University of Notre Dame Press, 1967(c).

———. Dogmatism and Presidential Preferences in the 1964 Elections. *Psychological Reports*, 1968, 22, 1197-1202.

———. Personality Typologies of Students and Modes of Social Change. Paper presented at the Eighth World Congress of Sociology, International Sociological Association, Varna, Bulgaria, 1970.

———. Dogmatism and Presidential Preferences: A 1968 Replication. *Psychological Reports*, 1971, 29, 109-110.

———. *Personality and Politics*. New York: Doubleday, 1974.

DiTella, T. S. Populism and Reform in Latin America. In J. D. Martz (Ed.), *The Dynamics of Change in Latin American Politics.* 2nd edition. Englewood Cliffs, N.J.: Prentice-Hall, 1971. Pp. 246-360.

Dittes, J. E. Attractiveness of Group as Function of Self-Esteem and Acceptance by Group. *Journal of Abnormal and Social Psychology*, 1959, 59, 77-82.

Dittmann, A. T. The Relationship Between Body Movements and Moods in Interviews. *Journal of Consulting Psychology*, 1962, 26, 480.

———. *Interpersonal Messages of Emotion.* New York: Springer, 1972.

Dixon, G. "Scientific" Study of Political Leaders: Research Bureau of Ohio State University Gets "Sharp" Answers from Quiz of Senators. *Columbus Dispatch*, 25 August, 1961.

Donley, R. E. Psychological Motives and the American Presidency. Unpublished A. B. Thesis, Wesleyan University, 1968.

——— and Winter, D. G. Measuring the Motives of Public Officials at a Distance: An Exploratory Study of American Presidents. *Behavioral Science*, 1970, 15, 227-236.

Doob, L. W. *Resolving Conflict in Africa: The Fermeda Workshop.* New Haven: Yale University Press, 1970.

Douglas, A. The Peaceful Settlement of Industrial and Intergroup Disputes. *Journal of Conflict Resolution*, 1957, 1, 69-81.

Downs, A. *An Economic Theory of Democracy.* New York: Harper, 1957.

Downs, C. W. A Thematic Analysis of Speeches on Foreign Policy of Senator J. W. Fulbright. Unpublished Doctoral Dissertation, Michigan State University, 1963.

Driver, M. J. The Relationship Between Abstractness of Conceptual Functioning and Group Performance in a Complex Decision-Making Environment. Unpublished Master's Thesis, Princeton University, 1960.

———. *Conceptual Structure and Group Processes in an Inter-Nation Simulation. Part One: The Perception of Simulated Nations.* Research Bulletin RB62-15, Educational Testing Service, Princeton, N.J., 1962.

———. *A Structural Analysis of Aggression, Stress, and Personality in an Inter-Nation Simulation.* Institute Paper No. 97, Institute for Research in the Behavioral, Economic, and Management Sciences, Purdue University, 1965.

——— and Lintott, J. T. *Managerial Decision Diagnostics.* Graduate School of Business Administration, University of Southern California, 1974.

——— and Streufert, S. Integrative Complexity: An Approach to Individuals and Groups as Information-Processing Systems. *Administrative Science Quarterly*, 1969, 14, 272-285.

Druckman, D. Dogmatism, Prenegotiation Experience, and Simulated Group Representation as Determinants of Dyadic Behavior in a Bargaining Situation. *Journal of Personality and Social Psychology*, 1967, 6, 279-290.

———. Ethnocentrism in the Inter-Nation Simulation. *Journal of Conflict Resolution*, 1968(a), 12, 45-68.

———. Prenegotiation Experience and Dyadic Conflict Resolution in a Bargaining Situation. *Journal of Experimental Social Psychology,* 1968(b), 4, 367-383.

———. Position Change in Cognitive Conflict as a Function of the Cue-Criterion Relationship and the Initial Conflict. *Psychonomic Science,* 1970, 20, 91-93.

———. The Influence of the Situation in Inter-Party Conflict. *Journal of Conflict Resolution,* 1971, 15, 523-554.

———. Human Factors in International Negotiations: A Survey of Research on Social-Psychological Aspects of International Conflict. *Sage Professional Papers in International Studies,* 1973, 2, No. 02-020.

———, Benton, A., Ali, F., and Bagur, S. Cultural Differences in Bargaining Behavior: India, Argentina, and the United States. *Journal of Conflict Resolution,* 1976, 20, in press.

———, Solomon, D., and Zechmeister, K. Effects of Representational Role Obligations on the Process of Children's Distribution of Resources. *Sociometry,* 1972, 35, 387-410.

——— and Zechmeister, K. Conflict of Interest and Value Dissensus. *Human Relations,* 1970, 23, 431-438.

——— and Zechmeister, K. Conflict of Interest and Value Dissensus: Propositions in the Sociology of Conflict. *Human Relations,* 1973, 26, 449-466.

———, Zechmeister, K., and Solomon, D. Determinants of Bargaining Behavior in a Bilateral Monopoly Situation: Opponent's Concession Rate and Relative Defensibility. *Behavioral Science,* 1972, 17, 514-531.

Duff, E. A., and McCamant, J. F. Measuring Social and Political Requirements for System Stability in Latin America. *American Political Science Review,* 1968, 62 (December), 1125-1143.

Dutton, J. M., and Starbuck, W. H. *Computer Simulation of Human Behavior.* New York: Wiley, 1971.

Dye, D. R. A Developmental Approach to the Political Style of Getulio Vargas. Unpublished Manuscript, Stanford University, no date (n.d.).

East, M. A., Salmore, S. A., and Hermann, C. F. (Eds.) *Why Nations Act.* Beverly Hills: Sage Publications, forthcoming 1977.

Eckhardt, W. War Propaganda, Welfare Values, and Political Ideology. *Journal of Conflict Resolution,* 1965, 9, 345-358.

——— and White, R. K. A Test of the Mirror-Image Hypothesis: Kennedy and Khrushchev. *Journal of Conflict Resolution,* 1967, 11, 325-332.

Edinger, L. J. Political Science and Political Biography. In G. D. Paige (Ed.), *Political Leadership.* New York: Free Press, 1972. Pp. 213-239.

——— and Searing, D. D. Social Background in Elite Analysis: A Methodological Inquiry. *American Political Science Review,* 1967, 61 (June), 428-445.

Ekman, P., and Friesen, W. V. *Unmasking the Face.* Englewood Cliffs, N.J.: Prentice-Hall, 1975.

Ellis, H. *A Study of British Genius.* New York: Houghton Mifflin, 1926.

Elton, C. F., and Rose, H. A. Relationship between Variety of Work Experiences and Personality. *Journal of Applied Psychology,* 1973, 58, 134-136.

Erikson, E. H. *Childhood and Society.* New York: Norton, 1950.

———. *Insight and Responsibility.* New York: Norton, 1964.

———. *Gandhi's Truth.* New York: Norton, 1969.

Evan, W. M., and MacDougall, J. A. Interorganizational Conflict: A Labor-Management Bargaining Experiment. *Journal of Conflict Resolution,* 1967, 11, 398-413.

Fainsod, M. *How Russia Is Ruled.* Cambridge: Harvard University Press, 1953. (2nd ed., 1963)

———. *Smolensk Under Soviet Rule.* New York: Random House, 1956.

———. Roads to the Future. In Z. Brzezinski (Ed.), *Dilemmas of Change in Soviet Politics.* New York: Columbia University Press, 1969. Pp. 128-134.

Farris, C. D. A Method of Determining Ideological Groups in the Congress. *Journal of Politics,* 1958, 20, 308-338.

Festinger, L. A Theory of Social Comparison Processes. *Human Relations,* 1954, 7, 117-140.

Fiedler, F. E. *A Theory of Leadership Effectiveness.* New York: McGraw-Hill, 1967.

Finlay, D. J., Holsti, O. R., and Fagen, R. R. *Enemies in Politics.* Chicago: Rand McNally, 1967.

Fishbein, M., and Ajzen, I. Attitudes and Opinions. In P. Mussen and M. Rosenzweig (Eds.), *Annual Review of Psychology.* Vol. 23. Palo Alto: Annual Reviews Inc., 1972. Pp. 487-544.

Fisher, R. Fractionating Conflict. In R. Fisher (Ed.), *International Conflict and Behavioral Science: The Craigville Papers.* New York: Basic Books, 1964. Pp. 91-109.

Fleron, F. J., Jr. Cooptation as a Mechanism of Adaptation to Change: The Soviet Political Leadership System. *Polity,* 1969, 2, 177-201.

———. Representation of Career Types in the Soviet Political Leadership. In R. B. Farrell (Ed.), *Political Leadership in Eastern Europe and the Soviet Union.* Chicago: Aldine, 1970. Pp. 108-139.

———. System Attributes and Career Attributes: The Soviet Political Leadership System, 1952 to 1965. In C. Beck et al., *Comparative Communist Political Leadership.* New York: McKay, 1973. Pp. 43-85.

Frank, J. D. *Sanity and Survival.* New York: Random House, 1968.

Frank, P. The CPSU Obkom First Secretary: A Profile. *British Journal of Political Science,* 1971, 1, 173-190.

Frank, R. S. Linguistic Analysis of Political Elites: A Theory of Verbal Kinesics. *Sage Professional Papers in International Studies,* 1973, 2, 02-022.

Freud, S. *Outline of Psychoanalysis.* New York: Norton, 1949.

———. *Moses and Monotheism.* New York: Vintage Books, 1962.

Freud, S., and Bullitt, W. C. *Thomas Woodrow Wilson: A Psychological Study.* Boston: Houghton Mifflin, 1967.

Frey, F. W. *The Turkish Political Elite.* Cambridge, Mass.: MIT Press, 1965.

Frey, R. L., and Adams, J. S. The Negotiator's Dilemma: Simultaneous Ingroup and Outgroup Conflict. *Journal of Experimental Social Psychology,* 1972, 8, 331-346.

Friedrich, C. J., and Brzezinski, Z. *Totalitarian Dictatorship and Autocracy.* Cambridge: Harvard University Press, 1956. (2nd ed., Praeger, 1966)

Frolic, M. Soviet Elite: Comparisons and Analysis. *Canadian Slavic Papers,* 1970, 12, 440-463.

Gahagan, J., Horai, J., Berger, S., and Tedeschi, J. Status and Authoritarianism in the Prisoner's Dilemma Game. Paper presented at meeting of Southeastern Psychological Association, Atlanta, 1967.

Galbraith, J. K. *Ambassador's Journal.* Boston: Houghton Mifflin, 1969.

Gamson, W. A. *Power and Discontent.* Homewood, Illinois: Dorsey Press, 1968.

Garraty, J. A. The Application of Content Analysis to Biography and History. In I. deS. Pool (Ed.), *Trends in Content Analysis.* Urbana: University of Illinois Press, 1959. Pp. 171-188.

Geis, F. Machiavellianism and the Manipulation of One's Fellow Man. Paper presented at annual meeting of American Psychological Association, Los Angeles, 1964.

George, A. L. *Propaganda Analysis.* Evanston, Ill.: Row Peterson, 1959(a).

———. Quantitative and Qualitative Approaches to Content Analysis. In I. deS. Pool (Ed.), *Trends in Content Analysis.* Urbana: University of Illinois Press, 1959(b). Pp. 7-32.

———. The "Operational Code": A Neglected Approach to the Study of Political Leaders and Decision Making. *International Studies Quarterly,* 1969, 13, 190-222.

———. Adaptation to Stress in Political Decision Making: The Individual, Small Group, and Organizational Contexts. In G. V. Coelho, D. A. Hamburg, and J. E. Adams (Eds.), *Coping and Adaptation.* New York: Basic Books, 1974. Pp. 176-245.

——— and George, J. *Woodrow Wilson and Colonel House: A Personality Study.* New York: John Day, 1956. (Paperback: Dover, 1964)

Germani, G., and Silvert, K. H. Politics, Social Structure, and Military Intervention in Latin America. *European Journal of Sociology,* 1961, 2, 62-81.

Gibb, C. A. Leadership. In G. Lindzey and E. Aronson (Eds.), *The Handbook of Social Psychology.* Vol. 4, 2nd Ed. Reading, Mass.: Addison-Wesley, 1969. Pp. 205-282.

Gibbins, R. The Political Leadership of William Lyon Mackenzie King. Unpublished Manuscript, Stanford University, not dated (n.d.).

Gipson, L. H. *The Coming of the Revolution.* New York: Harper and Row, 1962.

Gladstone, A. I. Relationship Orientation and Processes Leading Toward War. *Background,* 1962, 6, 13-25.

Glanzer, M., and Clark, W. H. Accuracy of Perceptual Recall: An Analysis of Organization. *Journal of Verbal Learning and Verbal Behavior,* 1963, 1, 289-299.

Glenn, E. S., Johnson, R. H., Kimmel, P. R., and Wedge, B. A Cognitive Interaction Model to Analyze Culture Conflict in International Relations. *Journal of Conflict Resolution,* 1970, 14, 35-48.

Golding, L. H., and Ziller, R. C. Social-Psychological Implications of Discreditable Stigmata. Unpublished Manuscript, University of Oregon, 1968.

Goldman-Eisler, F. The Significance of Changes in the Rate of Articulation. *Language and Speech,* 1961, 4, 171-174.

———. *Psycholinguistics: Experiments in Spontaneous Speech.* New York: Academic Press, 1968.

Golembiewski, R. T., Welsh, W. A., and Crotty, W. J. *A Methodological Primer for Political Scientists.* Chicago: Rand McNally, 1969.

Gomez, R. A. Latin American Executives: Essence and Variation. *Journal of Inter-American Studies,* 1961, 3, 81-96.

Gorer, G. *The American People.* New York: Norton, 1948.

Gottfried, A. The Use of Socio-Psychological Categories in a Study of Political Personality. *Western Political Quarterly,* 1955, 8, 234-247.

———. *Boss Cermak of Chicago.* Seattle: University of Washington Press, 1961.

Graves, R. *The Greek Myth, Volume I.* Baltimore: Penguin Books, 1955.

Greenstein, F. I. Personality and Politics. *Journal of Social Issues,* 1968, 24, 1-172.

———. *Personality and Politics.* Chicago: Markham, 1969.

——— and Lerner, M. (Eds.). *A Source Book for the Study of Personality and Politics.* Chicago: Markham, 1971.

Greenwald, A. G. On Defining Attitude and Attitude Theory. In A. G. Greenwald et al., *Psychological Foundations of Attitudes.* New York: Academic Press, 1968. Pp. 361-388.

Gruder, C. L., and Rosen, N. A. Effects of Intragroup Relations on Intergroup Bargaining. *International Journal of Group Tensions,* 1971, 1, 301-317.

Guetzkow, H. *Multiple Loyalties: Theoretical Approach to a Problem in International Organization.* Princeton, N.J.: Center for Research on World Political Institutions, 1955.

———. A Use of Simulation in the Study of Inter-Nation Relations. *Behavioral Science,* 1959, 4, 183-191.

———. Some Correspondences Between Simulations and "Realities" in International Relations. In M. Kaplan (Ed.), *New Approaches to International Relations.* New York: St. Martin's Press, 1968. Pp. 202-269.

———, Alger, C. F., Brody, R. A., Noel, R. C., and Snyder, R. C. *Simulation in International Relations: Developments for Research and Teaching.* Englewood Cliffs, N.J.: Prentice-Hall, 1963.

Guterman, S. S. *The Machiavellians.* Lincoln: University of Nebraska Press, 1970.

Gutierrez, G. G. Dean Rusk and Southeast Asia: An Operational Code Analysis. Paper presented at annual meeting of American Political Science Association, New Orleans, September, 1973.

Guttman, L. A Basis for Scaling Qualitative Data. *American Sociological Review,* 1944, 9, 139-150.

Gyr, J. An Analysis of Committee Member Behavior in Four Cultures. *Human Relations,* 1951, 4, 193-202.

Hammarskjold, D. *Markings.* New York: Knopf, 1964.

Hammond, K. R. New Directions in Research on Conflict Resolution. *Journal of Social Issues,* 1965, 11, 44-66.

——— and Brehmer, B. Quasi-Rationality and Distrust: Implications for International Conflict. In L. Rapoport and D. A. Summers (Eds.), *Human Judgment and Social Interaction.* New York: Holt, Rinehart and Winston, 1973. Pp. 338-391.

———, Todd, F. J., Wilkins, M., and Mitchell, T. O. Cognitive Conflict Between Persons: Application of the "Lens-Model" Paradigm. *Journal of Experimental Social Psychology,* 1966, 2, 343-360.

———, Wilkins, M., and Todd, F. J. A Research Paradigm for the Study of Interpersonal Learning. *Psychological Bulletin,* 1966, 65, 221-232.

Harasymiw, B. *Nomenklatura:* The Soviet Communist Party's Leadership Recruitment System. *Canadian Journal of Political Science,* 1969, 2, 493-512.

Hargrove, E. C. *Presidential Leadership: Personality and Political Style.* New York: Macmillan, 1966.

Harned, L. Authoritarian Attitudes and Party Activity. *Public Opinion Quarterly,* 1961, 25, 393-399.

Harris, I. D. *The Promised Seed.* Glencoe, Ill.: Free Press of Glencoe, 1964.

Harvey, O. J., Hunt, D. E., and Schroder, H. M. *Conceptual Systems and Personality Organization.* New York: Wiley, 1961.

Heberle, R. Changing Social Stratification of the South. *Social Forces,* 1959, 38, 42-50.

Hedlund, R. D. Psychological Predispositions: Political Representatives and the Public. *American Journal of Political Science,* 1973, 17, 489-505.

Hennessy, B. Politicals and Apoliticals: Some Measurements of Personality Traits. *Midwest Journal of Political Science,* 1959, 3, 336-355.

Hermann, C. F. Validation Problems in Games and Simulations with Special Reference to Models of International Politics. *Behavioral Science,* 1967, 12, 216-231.

———. *Crises in Foreign Policy: A Simulation Analysis.* Indianapolis: Bobbs-Merrill, 1969.

———, East, M. A., Hermann, M. G., Salmore, B. G., and Salmore, S. A. CREON: A Foreign Events Data Set. *Sage Professional Papers in International Studies,* 1973, 2, 02-024.

——— and Hermann, M. G. An Attempt to Simulate the Outbreak of World War I. *American Political Science Review,* 1967, 61, 400-416.

———, Hermann, M. G., and Cantor, R. A. Counterattack or Delay: Characteristics Influencing Decision Makers' Responses to the Simulation of an Unidentified Attack. *Journal of Conflict Resolution,* 1974, 18, 75-106.

Hermann, M. G. Testing a Model of Psychological Stress. *Journal of Personality,* 1966, 34, 381-396.

———. Leader Personality and Foreign Policy Behavior. In J. N. Rosenau (Ed.), *Comparing Foreign Policies: Theories, Findings, and Methods.* New York: Sage-Halsted, 1974. Pp. 201-234.

———. Circumstances Under Which Leader Personality Will Affect Foreign Policy: Some Propositions. In J. N. Rosenau (Ed.), *In Search of Global Patterns.* New York: Free Press, forthcoming 1976(a).

———. Effect of Personal Characteristics of Leaders on Foreign Policy. In M. A. East, S. A. Salmore, and C. F. Hermann (Eds.), *Why Nations Act.* Beverly Hills, Calif.: Sage Publications, forthcoming 1976(b).

——— and Hermann, C. F. Maintaining the Quality of Decision Making in Foreign Policy Crises: A Proposal. In A. L. George, *Towards More Soundly Based Foreign Policy: Making Better Use of Information.* Report to Commission on the Organization of the Government for the Conduct of Foreign Policy, March, 1975.

——— and Kogan, N. Negotiations in Leader and Delegate Groups. *Journal of Conflict Resolution,* 1968, 12, 332-344.

——— and Kogan, N. Personality and Negotiating Behavior. In D. Druckman (Ed.), *Negotiations: A Social-Psychological Perspective.* New York: Sage-Halsted, forthcoming 1976.

Hilsman, R. *To Move a Nation.* Garden City, New York: Doubleday, 1964.

Hirschman, A. O. *Journeys Toward Progress.* New York: Twentieth Century Fund, 1963.

Hoffmann, S. Heroic Leadership: The Case of Modern France. In L. J. Edinger (Ed.), *Political Leadership in Industrialized Societies.* New York: Wiley, 1967. Pp. 155-181.

Hofstadter, R. *The Paranoid Style in American Politics and Other Essays.* New York: Knopf, 1965.

Hollander, E. P., and Julian, J. W. Studies in Leader Legitimacy, Influence, and Innovation. *Advances in Experimental Social Psychology,* 1970, 5, 33-69.

Holsti, O. R. The Belief System and National Images: A Case Study. *Journal of Conflict Resolution,* 1962, 6, 244-252.

———. Cognitive Dynamics and Images of the Enemy. In D. J. Finlay, O. R. Holsti, and R. R. Fagen (Eds.), *Enemies in Politics.* Chicago: Rand McNally, 1967. Pp. 25-96.

———. *Content Analysis for the Social Sciences and the Humanities.* Reading, Mass.: Addison-Wesley, 1969.

———. The "Operational Code" Approach to the Study of Political Leaders: John Foster Dulles' Philosophical and Instrumental Beliefs. *Canadian Journal of Political Science,* 1970(a), 3, 123-155.

———. Individual Differences in "Definition of the Situation." *Journal of Conflict Resolution,* 1970(b), 14, 303-310.

———. Foreign Policy Decision-Makers Viewed Psychologically: A Sketchy Survey of "Cognitive Process" Approaches. Paper presented at Conference on the

Successes and Failures of Scientific International Relations Research, Ojai, Calif., June 25-28, 1973.

Hopmann, P. T., and Walcott, C. The Bargaining Process in Arms Control Negotiations: An Experimental Analysis. Harold Scott Quigley Center of International Affairs, University of Minnesota, 1973.

Horowitz, I. L. The Military Elites. In S. M. Lipset and A. Solari (Eds.), *Elites in Latin America.* New York: Oxford University Press, 1967. Pp. 146-189.

Hough, J. The Soviet Elite II: In Whose Hands the Future. *Problems of Communism,* 1967, 16, 18-25.

―――. *The Soviet Prefects.* Cambridge: Harvard University Press, 1969.

―――. The Soviet System: Petrifaction or Pluralism? *Problems of Communism,* 1972, 21, 25-45.

Hunt, W., Crane, W., and Wahlke, J. Interviewing Political Elites in Cross-Cultural Comparative Research. *American Journal of Sociology,* 1964, 70, 59-68.

Idaho Statesman, 1957.

Iklé, F. C. *How Nations Negotiate.* New York: Harper, 1964.

Inglehart, R. The Silent Revolution in Europe: Intergenerational Change in Post-Industrial Society. *American Political Science Review,* 1971, 65, 991-1017.

Inkeles, A. Personality and Social Structure. In R. K. Merton et al. (Eds.), *Sociology Today.* Glencoe: Free Press, 1959. Pp. 249-276.

――― and Bauer, R. A. *The Soviet Citizen.* Cambridge: Harvard University Press, 1959.

―――, Hanfmann, E., and Beier, H. Modal Personality and Adjustment to the Soviet Socio-Political System. *Human Relations,* 1958, 9, 3-22.

Janicki, W. P. Effect of Disposition on Resolution of Incongruity. *Journal of Abnormal and Social Psychology,* 1964, 69, 579-584.

Janis, I. L. *Victims of Groupthink.* Boston: Houghton Mifflin, 1972.

Janowitz, M., and Marvick, D. Authoritarianism and Political Behavior. *Public Opinion Quarterly,* 1953, 17, 185-201.

Jensen, L. Soviet-American Bargaining Behavior in the Post-War Disarmament Negotiations. *Journal of Conflict Resolution,* 1963, 7, 522-541.

Jervis, R. Hypotheses on Misperception. In J. N. Rosenau (Ed.), *International Politics and Foreign Policy.* Rev. ed. New York: Free Press, 1969. Pp. 239-254.

―――. *The Logic of Images in International Relations.* Princeton, N.J.: Princeton University Press, 1972.

Johnson, C. *Change in Communist Systems.* Stanford: Stanford University Press, 1970.

Johnson, D. F., and Pruitt, D. G. Pre-intervention Effects of Mediation vs. Arbitration. *Journal of Applied Psychology,* 1972, 56, 1-10.

――― and Tullar, W. L. Style of Third Party Intervention, Face-Saving and

Bargaining Behavior. *Journal of Experimental Social Psychology*, 1972, 4, 319-330.

Johnson, D. W. The Use of Role-Reversal in Intergroup Competition. *Journal of Personality and Social Psychology*, 1967, 7, 135-142.

——— and Dustin, R. The Initiation of Cooperation Through Role Reversal. *Journal of Social Psychology*, 1970, 82, 193-203.

Jones, E. E., Hester, S. L., Farina, A., and Davis, K. E. Reactions to Unfavorable Evaluations as a Function of Evaluator's Perceived Adjustment. *Journal of Abnormal and Social Psychology*, 1960, 60, 105-112.

Jones, H. E. Order of Birth in Relation to the Development of the Child. In C. Murchison (Ed.), *A Handbook of Child Psychology*. Worcester, Mass.: Clark University Press, 1933. Pp. 204-241.

Joseph, M. L., and Willis, R. H. An Experimental Analog to Two-Party Bargaining. *Behavioral Science*, 1963, 8, 117-127.

Jung, C. G. *Symbols of Transformation*. Translated by R. F. C. Hull. New York: Pantheon Books, 1956.

Kaltenbach, J. E., and McClelland, D. C. Achievement and Social Status in Three Small Communities. In D. C. McClelland, A. L. Baldwin, U. Bronfenbrenner, and F. L. Strodtbeck (Eds.), *Talent and Society*. Princeton, N.J.: Van Nostrand, 1958. Pp. 112-134.

Kane, J. N. *Facts about the Presidents*. New York: Wilson, 1959.

Kanfer, F. H. Supplementary Report: Stability of a Verbal Rate Change in Experimental Anxiety. *Journal of Experimental Psychology*, 1958, 56, 182.

———. Verbal Rate, Content and Adjustment Ratings in Experimentally Structured Interviews. *Journal of Abnormal and Social Psychology*, 1959, 58, 305-311.

———. Verbal Rate, Eyeblink, and Content in Experimentally Structured Interviews. *Journal of Abnormal and Social Psychology*, 1960, 61, 341-347.

Kasl, S. V., and Mahl, G. F. The Relationship of Disturbances and Hesitations in Spontaneous Speech to Anxiety. *Journal of Personality and Social Psychology*, 1965, 1, 425-433.

Kassof, A. The Administered Society: Totalitarianism without Terror. *World Politics*, 1964, 16, 558-575.

Katz, D. Patterns of Leadership. In J. N. Knutson (Ed.), *Handbook of Political Psychology*. San Francisco: Jossey-Bass, 1973. Pp. 203-233.

Kaufman, H. Similarity and Cooperation Received as Determinants of Cooperation Rendered. *Psychonomic Science*, 1967, 9, 73-74.

Kavanagh, D. A. The "Operational Code" of Ramsey MacDonald. Unpublished Manuscript, Stanford University, 1970.

Kelley, H. H., Beckman, L. L., and Fisher, C. S. Negotiating the Division of a Reward under Incomplete Information. *Journal of Experimental Social Psychology*, 1967, 3, 361-398.

Kelly, D. R. Interest Groups in the USSR: The Impact of Political Sensitivity on Group Influence. *Journal of Politics*, 1972, 34, 860-888.

Kelly, G. A. *The Psychology of Personal Constructs.* New York: Norton, 1955.

Kelman, H. Social-Psychological Approaches to the Study of International Relations: The Question of Relevance. In H. C. Kelman (Ed.), *International Behavior: A Social-Psychological Analysis.* New York: Holt, Rinehart, and Winston, 1965. Pp. 565-607.

Kerenyi, C. *The Heroes of the Greeks.* New York: Grove Press, 1959.

King, N. L. *Lincoln's Manager David Davis.* Cambridge: Harvard University Press, 1960.

Kissinger, H. A. *Nuclear Weapons and Foreign Policy.* New York: Harper, 1957.

———. *The Necessity for Choice: Prospects of American Foreign Policy.* New York: Doubleday, 1962.

———. Domestic Structure and Foreign Policy. *Daedalus,* 1966, 95, 503-529.

Klimoski, R. J. The Effects of Intragroup Forces on Intergroup Conflict Resolution. *Organizational Behavior and Human Performance,* 1972, 8, 363-383.

Knepprath, H. E. The Nationally Broadcast Speeches of Eisenhower and Stevenson during the 1956 Presidential Campaign. Unpublished Doctoral Dissertation, University of Wisconsin, 1962.

Koch, H. L. Some Emotional Attitudes of the Young Child in Relation to Characteristics of His Sibling. *Child Development,* 1958, 27, 293-426.

Kochetov, V. *Secretar' Obkoma.* Moscow: *Molodaya Gvardiva,* 1962.

Kogan, N. *The Government of Italy.* New York: T. Y. Crowell, 1964.

Kogan, N., and Wallach, M. A. *Risk Taking.* New York: Holt, Rinehart and Winston, 1964.

Kolko, J., and Kolko, G. *The Limits of Power: The World and United States Foreign Policy, 1945-1954.* New York: Harper and Row, 1972.

Komorita, S. S., and Barnes, M. Effects of Pressures to Reach Agreement in Bargaining. *Journal of Personality and Social Psychology,* 1969, 13, 245-252.

Kosa, J. The Rank Order of Peoples: A Study in National Stereotypes. *Journal of Social Psychology,* 1957, 46, 311-320.

Kotter, J. P., and Lawrence, P. R. *Mayors in Action.* New York: Wiley, 1974.

Krause, M. S. Anxiety in Verbal Behavior: An Intercorrelational Study. *Journal of Consulting Psychology,* 1961, 25, 272.

Krauss, R. M. Structural and Attitudinal Factors in Interpersonal Bargaining. *Journal of Experimental Social Psychology,* 1966, 2, 42-55.

Laing, R. L. *The Politics of the Family.* New York: Vintage Books, 1972.

Lall, A. *Modern International Negotiation: Principles and Practice.* New York: Columbia University Press, 1966.

Lambert, T. A. Generational Factors in Political-Cultural Consciousness. Paper presented at annual meeting of American Political Science Association, Chicago, 1971.

Lamm, H., and Kogan, N. Risk Taking in the Context of Intergroup Negotiation. *Journal of Experimental Social Psychology,* 1970, 6, 351-363.

Lane, R. E. Political Personality and Electoral Choice. *American Political Science Review,* 1955, 49, 173-190.

———. *Political Life*. Glencoe, Ill.: Free Press, 1959.

———. Notes on a Theory of Democratic Personality. In R. E. Lane (Ed.), *Political Ideology*. Glencoe, Ill.: Free Press, 1962. Pp. 400-412.

Langer, W. C. *The Mind of Adolf Hitler*. New York: Basic Books, 1972.

Langer, W. L. *An Encyclopedia of World History*. Boston: Houghton Mifflin, 1948.

Lasko, J. K. Parent Behavior towards First and Second Children. *Genetic Psychological Monographs*, 1954, 49, 96-137.

Lasswell, H. D. *Psychopathology and Politics*. Chicago: University of Chicago Press, 1930. (Paperback: Viking Press, 1960.)

———. Verbal References and Physiological Changes during the Psychoanalytic Interview: A Preliminary Communication. *Psychoanalytic Review*, 1935, 22, 10-24.

———. *Power and Personality*. New York: Norton, 1948. (Paperback: Viking Press, 1962.)

———. The Selective Effect of Personality on Political Participation. In R. Christie and M. Jahoda (Eds.), *Studies in the Scope and Method of "The Authoritarian Personality."* Glencoe, Ill.: Free Press, 1954. Pp. 197-225.

——— and Lerner, D. *World Revolutionary Elites: Studies in Coercive Ideological Movements*. Cambridge, Mass.: MIT Press, 1965.

Lawrence, D. The Operational Code of Lester Pearson. Unpublished Doctoral Dissertation, University of British Columbia, 1975.

Lazarus, R. S. *Psychological Stress and the Coping Process*. New York: McGraw-Hill, 1966.

Leites, N. *The Operational Code of the Politburo*. New York: McGraw-Hill, 1951.

———. *A Study of Bolshevism*. Glencoe, Ill.: Free Press, 1953.

Lerea, L. A Preliminary Study of the Verbal Behavior of Speech Fright. *Speech Monographs*, 1956, 23, 229-233.

LeVine, R. *Dreams and Deeds: Achievement Motivation in Nigeria*. Chicago: University of Chicago Press, 1966.

Levinson, D. J. Authoritarian Personality and Foreign Policy. *Journal of Conflict Resolution*, 1957, 1, 37-47.

———. Role, Personality, and Social Structure in the Organizational Setting. *Journal of Abnormal and Social Psychology*, 1959, 58, 170-180.

———. Idea Systems in the Individual and in Society. In G. K. Zollschan and W. Hirsch (Eds.), *Explorations in Social Change*. Boston: Houghton Mifflin, 1964. Pp. 297-318.

Levy, D. M. Sibling Rivalry. *American Orthopsychiatric Association Research Monograph*, No. 2, 1937.

Lewin, K. *A Dynamic Theory of Personality*. New York: McGraw, 1935.

Linden, C. *Khrushchev and the Soviet Leadership*. Baltimore: Johns Hopkins, 1966.

Lodge, M. *Soviet Elite Attitudes Since Stalin*. Columbus: Charles Merrill, 1969.

———. Attitudinal Cleavages within the Soviet Political Leadership. In C. Beck et al., *Comparative Communist Political Leadership*. New York: McKay, 1973. Pp. 202-225.

Lutzker, D. R. Internationalism as a Predictor of Cooperative Behavior. *Journal of Conflict Resolution*, 1960, 4, 426-430.

McClelland, D. C. *The Achieving Society*. Princeton, N.J.: Van Nostrand, 1961.

———. *Power: The Inner Experience*. New York: Irvington, 1975.

——— and Watson, R. I., Jr. Power Motivation and Risk-Taking Behavior. *Journal of Personality*, 1973, 41, 121-139.

——— and Winter, D. G. *Motivating Economic Achievement*. New York: Free Press, 1969.

McClintock, C. G., Gallo, P., and Harrison, A. A. Some Effects of Variations in Other Strategy upon Game Behavior. *Journal of Personality and Social Psychology*, 1965, 1, 319-325.

——— and Nuttin, J. M., Jr. Development of Competitive Game Behavior in Children Across Two Cultures. *Journal of Experimental Social Psychology*, 1969, 5, 203-218.

McClosky, H. Personality and Attitude Correlates of Foreign Policy Orientation. In J. N. Rosenau (Ed.), *Domestic Sources of Foreign Policy*. New York: Free Press, 1967. Pp. 51-109.

McConaughy, J. B. Certain Personality Factors of State Legislators in South Carolina. *American Political Science Review*, 1950, 44, 897-903.

McDiarmid, J. Presidential Inaugural Addresses: A Study of Verbal Symbols. *Public Opinion Quarterly*, 1937, 1, 3, 79-82.

McGrath, J. E., and Julian, J. W. Interaction Process and Task Outcome in Experimentally-Created Negotiation Groups. *Journal of Psychological Studies*, 1963, 14, 117-138.

McGuire, W. J. The Nature of Attitudes and Attitude Change. In G. Lindzey and E. Aronson (Eds.), *The Handbook of Social Psychology*. Vol. 3, 2nd Ed. Reading, Mass.: Addison-Wesley, 1969. Pp. 136-314.

McLellan, D. S. The "Operational Code" Approach to the Study of Political Leaders: Dean Acheson's Philosophical and Instrumental Beliefs. *Canadian Journal of Political Science*, 1971, 4, 52-75.

Mackelprang, A. J. Missing Data in Factor Analysis and Multiple Regression. *Midwest Journal of Political Science*, 1970, 14, 493-505.

Maclay, H., and Osgood, C. E. Hesitation Phenomena in Spontaneous English Speech. *Word*, 1959, 15, 19-44.

MacRae, D., Jr. *Dimensions of Congressional Voting: A Statistical Study of the House of Representatives in the Eighty-First Congress*. Berkeley: University of California Press, 1958.

Madsen, M. C., and Shapira, A. Cooperative and Competitive Behavior of Urban Afro-American, Anglo-American, Mexican-American, and Mexican Village Children. *Developmental Psychology*, 1970, 3, 16-20.

Mahl, G. F. Disturbances and Silences in the Patient's Speech in Psychotherapy. *Journal of Abnormal and Social Psychology*, 1956, 53, 1-15.

―――. Measuring the Patient's Anxiety During Interviews from "Expressive" Aspects of His Speech. *Transactions of the New York Academy of Science,* Series II, 1958, 21, 249-257.

―――. Exploring Emotional States by Content Analysis. In I. Pool (Ed.), *Trends in Content Analysis.* Urbana: University of Illinois Press, 1959. Pp. 89-130.

Malone, C. S. The Operational Code of Lyndon Baines Johnson. Unpublished Manuscript, Stanford University, 1971.

Manley, J. F. Wilbur D. Mills: A Study in Congressional Influence. *American Political Science Review,* 1969, 63, 442-464.

Mannheim, K. The Problem of Generations. In P. Kecskemeti (Ed.), *Essays on the Sociology of Knowledge.* New York: Oxford University Press, 1952. Pp. 276-322.

Maranell, G. M. The Evaluation of Presidents: An Extension of the Schlesinger Poll. *Journal of American History,* 1970, 57, 104-113.

Maslow, A. H., Hirsh, E., Stein, M., and Honegmann, I. A Clinically Derived Test for Measuring Psychological Security-Insecurity. *Journal of Genetic Psychology,* 1945, 33, 24-41.

Mathiot, A. *The British Political System.* Palo Alto: Stanford University Press, 1967.

Matthews, D. R. *Social Backgrounds of Political Decision-Makers.* New York: Doubleday, 1954.

―――. The Folkways of the United States Senate: Conformity to Group Norms and Legislative Effectiveness. *American Political Science Review,* 1959, 53, 1064-1089.

―――. *U.S. Senators and Their World.* Chapel Hill, N.C.: University of North Carolina Press, 1960.

Mazlish, B. *In Search of Nixon: A Psychohistorical Inquiry.* Baltimore, Md.: Penguin, 1973.

Mecham, J. L. Latin American Constitutions: Nominal and Real. *Journal of Politics,* 1959, 21, 258-275.

Mehrabian, A. *Nonverbal Communication.* Chicago: Aldine-Atherton, 1972.

Merton, R. K. Bureaucratic Structure and Personality. *Social Forces,* 1940, 18, 560-568.

―――, Broom, L., and Cottrell, L. S. (Eds.), *Sociology Today.* New York: Basic Books, 1959.

Michels, R. *Political Parties.* New York: Collier Books, 1962.

Mickiewicz, E. Policy Applications of Public Opinion Research in the Soviet Union. *Public Opinion Quarterly,* 1973, 36, 566-578.

Milbrath, L. W. *Political Participation.* Chicago: Rand McNally, 1965.

―――　and Klein, W. W. Personality Correlates of Political Participation. *Acta Sociologica,* 1962, 6, 53-66.

Milburn, T. W. *Studies in Deterrence.* I. *Design for the Study of Deterrent Processes.* China Lake, Calif.: Behavioral Sciences Group, April, 1964.

Mischel, W., and Gilligan, C. Delay of Gratification, Motivation for the Prohibited Gratification, and Response to Temptation. *Journal of Abnormal and Social Psychology,* 1964, 69, 411-417.

Modelski, G. The World's Foreign Ministers: A Political Elite. *Journal of Conflict Resolution,* 1970, 14, 135-175.

Moore, B., Jr. *Terror and Progress USSR.* Cambridge: Harvard University Press, 1954.

Morgan, J. J. B. Effects of Non-Rational Factors in Inductive Reasoning. *Journal of Experimental Psychology,* 1944, 34, 159-168.

Morgan, W. R., and Sawyer, J. Bargaining, Expectations, and the Preference for Equality over Equity. *Journal of Personality and Social Psychology,* 1967, 6, 139-149.

Morgenthau, H. J. *Politics among Nations: The Struggle for Power and Peace.* New York: Knopf, 1960.

Morton, H., and Juvelier, P. *Soviet Policy-Making.* New York: Praeger, 1967.

Moses, E. R., Jr. A Study of Word Diversification. *Speech Monographs,* 1959, 26, 308-312.

Mossman, B., and Ziller, R. C. Self-Esteem and Consistency of Social Behavior. *Journal of Abnormal Psychology,* 1968, 73, 363-367.

Muney, B. F., and Deutsch, M. The Effects of Role-Reversal during the Discussion of Opposing Viewpoints. *Journal of Conflict Resolution,* 1968, 12, 345-356.

Murray, D. C. Talk, Silence, and Anxiety. *Psychological Bulletin,* 1971, 75, 244-260.

Murray, H. A. *Explorations in Personality.* New York: Oxford University Press, 1938.

Mushakoji, K. The Strategies of Negotiation: An American-Japanese Comparison. In J. A. Laponce and P. Smoker (Eds.), *Experimentation and Simulation in Political Science.* Toronto: University of Toronto Press, 1972. Pp. 109-131.

Mussen, P. H., and Wyszynski, A. B. Personality and Political Participation. *Human Relations,* 1952, 5, 65-82.

Nagle, J. D. The Soviet Political Elite, 1917-1971: Application of a Generational Model of Social Change. Paper presented at annual meeting of American Political Science Association, New Orleans, September, 1973.

Nayar, E. S. K., Touzard, H., and Summers, D. A. Training, Tasks, and Mediator Orientation in Heterocultural Negotiations. *Human Relations,* 1968, 21, 283-294.

Needler, M. C. *Political Development in Latin America: Instability, Violence, and Evolutionary Change.* New York: Random House, 1968.

Neuberger, R. L. The Congressional Record is *Not* a Record. *New York Times Magazine,* 20 April, 1958, pp. 74, 94-95.

Neustadt, R. E. *Presidential Power.* New York: Wiley, 1960.

Newhouse, J. *Cold Dawn: The Story of SALT.* New York: Holt, Rinehart and Winston, 1973.

New York Times, 12 July, 1970, p. 18 (Agnew Affirms "Partisan" Role but Bars Presidential Ambition).

Nicolson, H. *Diplomacy.* London: Thornton Butterworth Ltd., 1939.

Oppenheim, A. N. *Questionnaire Design and Attitude Measurement.* New York: Basic Books, 1966.

Osgood, C. E. The Representational Model and Relevant Research Methods. In I. deS. Pool (Ed.), *Trends in Content Analysis.* Urbana: University of Illinois Press, 1959. Pp. 33-88.

———. *An Alternative to War or Surrender.* Urbana: University of Illinois Press, 1962.

——— and Anderson, L. Certain Relations Among Experienced Contingencies, Associative Structure, and Contingencies in Encoded Messages. *American Journal of Psychology,* 1957, 70, 411-420.

———, Suci, G. J., and Tannenbaum, P. H. *The Measurement of Meaning.* Urbana: University of Illinois Press, 1957.

——— and Walker, E. Motivation and Language Behavior: A Content Analysis of Suicide Notes. *Journal of Abnormal and Social Psychology,* 1959, 59, 58-67.

Paige, G. D. *A Q-sort for Political Leadership Roles.* Unpublished Manuscript, Princeton University, 1966.

———. *Political Leadership.* New York: Free Press, 1972.

Palumbo, D. J. Power and Role Specificity in Organization Theory. *Public Administration Review,* 1969, 29, 237-248.

Perry, S. E. Notes on the Role of the National: A Social-Psychological Concept for the Study of International Relations. *Journal of Conflict Resolution,* 1957, 1, 346-363.

Pilisuk, M., Potter, P., Rapoport, A., and Winter, J. A. War Hawks and Peace Doves: Alternative Resolutions of Experimental Conflicts. *Journal of Conflict Resolution,* 1965, 9, 491-508.

Podell, J. E., and Knapp, W. M. The Effect of Mediation and the Perceived Firmness of the Opponent. *Journal of Conflict Resolution,* 1969, 4, 511-520.

Ponder, E., and Kennedy, W. P. On the Act of Blinking. *Quarterly Journal of Experimental Physiology,* 1927, 18, 89-110.

Pool, I. deS. (Ed.) *Trends in Content Analysis.* Urbana, Ill.: University of Illinois Press, 1959.

——— and Kessler, A. The Kaiser, the Tsar, and the Computer. *American Behavioral Scientist,* 1965, 8, 31-38.

Prewitt, K. *The Recruitment of Political Leaders.* Indianapolis: Bobbs-Merrill, 1970.

——— and Stone, A. *The Ruling Elites: Elite Theory, Power, and American Democracy.* New York: Harper and Row, 1973.

Prothro, J. W. Verbal Shifts in the American Presidency: A Content Analysis. *American Political Science Review,* 1956, 50, 726-739.

Pruitt, D. G. An Analysis of Responsiveness Between Nations. *Journal of Conflict Resolution,* 1962, 6, 5-18.

—––. Stability and Sudden Change in Interpersonal and International Affairs. *Journal of Conflict Resolution*, 1969, 13, 18-38.

—––. Indirect Communication and the Search for Agreement in Negotiation. *Journal of Applied Social Psychology*, 1971, 1, 205-239.

—–– and Drews, J. L. The Effects of Time Pressure, Time Elapsed, and the Opponent's Concession Rate on Behavior in Negotiation. *Journal of Experimental Social Psychology*, 1969, 5, 43-60.

—–– and Johnson, D. F. Mediation as an Aid to Face Saving in Negotiation. *Journal of Personality and Social Psychology*, 1970, 14, 239-246.

Przeworski, A., and Teune, H. *The Logic of Comparative Social Inquiry*. New York: Wiley, 1970.

Quandt, W. B. The Comparative Study of Political Elites. *Sage Professional Papers in Comparative Politics*, 1970, 1, No. 01-004.

Raglan, Lord. *The Hero*. New York: Vintage Books, 1956.

Ranis, P. A Two-Dimensional Typology of Latin American Political Parties. *Journal of Politics*, 1968, 30, 798-832.

Rank, O. *The Myth of the Birth of the Hero*. New York: Vintage Books, 1959.

Rapoport, A. *Strategy and Conscience*. New York: Harper and Row, 1964.

—–– and Orcutt, C. Experimental Games: A Review. *Behavioral Science*, 1962, 7, 1-38.

Rapoport, L. Cognitive Conflict as a Function of Socially-Induced Cognitive Differences. *Journal of Conflict Resolution*, 1969, 13, 143-148.

Raser, J. R., and Crow, W. J. A Simulation Study of Deterrence Theories. In L. Kriesberg (Ed.), *Social Processes in International Relations, A Reader*. New York: Wiley, 1968.

Ridgeway, S. Relationships among Three Measures of Self Concept. Unpublished Master's Thesis, University of Maryland, 1965.

Rieselbach, L. N. *Roots of Isolationism*. Indianapolis: Bobbs-Merrill, 1966.

Riesman, D. *Individualism Reconsidered*. Glencoe, Ill.: Free Press, 1954.

Rigby, T. H. "Totalitarianism" and Change in Communist Systems. *Comparative Politics*, 1972(a), 4, 3, 433-453.

—––. The Soviet Politburo: A Comparative Profile 1951-1971. *Soviet Studies*, 1972(b), 24, 3-23.

Robinson, J. A. Participant Observation, Political Internships, and Research. *Political Science Annual*, 1969, 2, 71-103.

—––, Hermann, C. F., and Hermann, M. G. Search under Crisis in Political Gaming and Simulation. In D. G. Pruitt and R. C. Snyder (Eds.), *Theory and Research on the Causes of War*. Englewood Cliffs, N.J.: Prentice-Hall, 1969. Pp. 80-94.

Robinson, J. P., and Shaver, P. *Measures of Social Psychological Attitudes*. Ann Arbor, Mich.: Survey Research Center, 1969.

Robinson, T. W. Lin Piao as an Elite Type. In R. A. Scalapino (Ed.), *Elites in the People's Republic of China*. Seattle: University of Washington Press, 1972. Pp. 149-195.

Roe, A. A Psychological Study of Eminent Psychologists and Anthropologists and a Comparison with Biological and Physical Scientists. *Psychological Monographs*, 1953, 67, Whole No. 352.

Rogers, C., and Skinner, B. F. Some Issues Concerning the Control of Human Behavior: A Symposium. *Science*, 1956, 124, 1057-1066.

Rogow, A. A. *James Forrestal: A Study of Personality, Politics and Policy.* New York: Macmillan, 1963.

Rokeach, M. The Nature and Meaning of Dogmatism. *Psychological Review*, 1954, 61, 194-204.

–––. *The Open and Closed Mind.* New York: Basic Books, 1960.

Rose, A. M. Prejudice, Anomie, and the Authoritarian Personality. *Sociology and Social Research*, 1966, 50, 141-147.

Roseboom, E. H. *A History of Presidential Elections.* New York: Macmillan, 1957.

Rosenau, J. N. Private Preferences and Political Responsibilities: The Relative Potency of Individual and Role Variables in the Behavior of U.S. Senators. In J. D. Singer (Ed.), *Quantitative International Politics.* New York: Free Press, 1968. Pp. 17-50.

Rosenbaum, M. E., and deCharms, R. Direct vs. Vicarious Reduction of Hostility. *Journal of Abnormal and Social Psychology*, 1960, 60, 105-112.

Rosenberg, M. Misanthropy and Attitudes toward International Affairs. *Journal of Conflict Resolution*, 1958, 1, 340-345.

Rosenfeld, H. M. Relationships of Ordinal Position to Affiliation and Achievement Motives: Direction and Generality. *Journal of Personality*, 1966, 34, 467-480.

Rostow, W. W. *The Dynamics of Soviet Society.* Boston: MIT Press, 1953.

Ruesch, J., and Prestwood, A. R. Anxiety–Its Initiation, Communication and Interpersonal Management. *Archives of Neurology and Psychiatry*, 1949, 62, 527-550.

Rummel, R. J. *Applied Factor Analysis.* Evanston: Northwestern University Press, 1970.

Rush, M. Esoteric Communication in Soviet Politics. *World Politics*, 1959, 11, 614-620.

Rusk, D. Parliamentary Diplomacy–Debate Versus Negotiation. *World Affairs Interpreter*, 1955, 26, 121-138.

Russell, P. O., and Snyder, W. U. Counsellor Anxiety in Relation to Amount of Clinical Experience and Quality of Affect Demonstrated by Clients. *Journal of Consulting Psychology*, 1963, 27, 358-363.

Rustow, D. A. The Study of Elites: Who's Who, When and How. *World Politics*, 1966, 18, 690-717.

–––. (Ed.) *Philosophers and Kings: Studies in Leadership.* New York: Braziller, 1970.

Rutherford, B. M. Psychopathology, Decision-Making, and Political Involvement. *Journal of Conflict Resolution*, 1966, 10, 387-407.

Rycroft, C. Causes and Meanings. In C. Rycroft (Ed.), *Psychoanalysis Observed.* London: Constable, 1966.

Sainsbury, P. A Method of Recording Spontaneous Movement by Time-Sampling Motion Pictures. *Journal of Mental Science,* 1954, 100, 742-748.

———. Gestural Movement during Psychiatric Interview. *Psychosomatic Medicine,* 1955, 17, 458-469.

Sampson, E. E. The Study of Ordinal Position: Antecedents and Outcomes. *Progress in Experimental Personality Research,* 1965, 2, 175-228.

——— and Hancock, F. R. An Examination of the Relationship between Ordinal Position, Personality and Conformity: An Extension, Replication and Partial Verification. *Journal of Personality and Social Psychology,* 1967, 5, 398-407.

Sanford, F. H. Public Orientations to Roosevelt. *Public Opinion Quarterly,* 1951, 15, 189-216.

Sartori, G. Parliamentarians in Italy. *International Social Science Journal,* 1961, 13, 583-599.

Sauer, R. E., and Marcuse, F. L. Overt and Covert Recording. *Journal of Projective Techniques,* 1957, 21, 391-395.

Sawyer, J., and Guetzkow, H. Bargaining and Negotiation in International Relations. In H. C. Kelman (Ed.), *International Behavior: A Social-Psychological Analysis.* New York: Holt, Rinehart and Winston, 1965. Pp. 464-520.

Scalapino, R. A. (Ed.) *Elites in the People's Republic of China.* Seattle: University of Washington Press, 1972.

Schachter, S. *The Psychology of Affiliation.* Stanford: Stanford University Press, 1959.

———. Birth Order, Eminence, and Higher Education. *American Sociological Review,* 1963, 28, 757-768.

Schapiro, L. *The Communist Party of the Soviet Union.* New York: Random House, 1960. (2nd Ed., Vintage, 1971)

Schelling, T. C. *The Strategy of Conflict.* New York: Oxford University Press, 1960.

Schlesinger, A. M. Our Presidents: A Rating by Seventy-Five Historians. *New York Times Magazine,* 29 July, 1962, 12-14.

Schlesinger, J. A. *Ambition in Politics: Political Careers in the United States.* Chicago: Rand McNally, 1966.

Schooler, C. Birth Order Effects: Not Here, Not Now. *Psychological Bulletin,* 1972, 78, 161-175.

Schroder, H. M. Conceptual Complexity and Personality Organization. In H. M. Schroder and P. Suedfeld (Eds.), *Personality Theory and Information Processing.* New York: Ronald Press, 1971. Pp. 240-273.

———, Driver, M. J., and Streufert, S. *Human Information Processing.* New York: Holt, Rinehart and Winston, 1967.

——— and Hunt, D. E. The Role of Three Processes in Determining Responses to Interpersonal Disagreement. Joint Progress Report: Office of Naval Research,

Contract Nonr-171-055 and U.S. Public Health Service, Project No. M-955, 1959.

———, Streufert, S., and Clardy, M. A. Dispositional Effects upon Conflict Resolution. Unpublished Manuscript, Princeton University, 1961.

——— and Suedfeld, P. *Personality Theory and Information Processing.* New York: Ronald Press, 1971.

Schulze, R. A Shortened Version of the Rokeach Dogmatism Scale. *Journal of Psychological Studies,* 1962, 13, 93-97.

Schumpeter, J. A. *Capitalism, Socialism, and Democracy.* New York: Harper, 1950.

Schwartz, J. J., and Keech, W. Group Influence and the Policy Process in the Soviet Union. *American Political Science Review,* 1968, 62, 840-851.

Scott, W. A. International Ideology and Interpersonal Ideology. *Public Opinion Quarterly,* 1960, 24, 419-435.

———. Psychological and Social Correlates of International Images. In H. C. Kelman (Ed.), *International Behavior: A Social-Psychological Analysis.* New York: Holt, Rinehart and Winston, 1965. Pp. 70-103.

Searing, D. D. The Comparative Study of Elite Socialization. *Comparative Political Studies,* 1969, 1, 471-500.

———. Models and Images of Man and Society in Leadership Theory. In G. D. Paige (Ed.), *Political Leadership.* New York: Free Press, 1972. Pp. 19-44.

Sears, P. S. Doll Play Aggression in Normal Young Children. Influence of Sex, Age, Sibling Status, Father's Absence. *Psychological Monographs,* 1951, 65, Whole No. 323.

Seligman, L. G. *Recruiting Political Elites.* New York: General Learning Press, 1971.

Sells, S. B. A Model for the Social System for the Multi-Man Duration Space Ship. *Aerospace Medicine,* 1966, 37, 1130-1135.

Selltiz, C., Jahoda, M., Deutsch, M., and Cook, S. W. *Research Methods in Social Relations.* New York: Holt, Rinehart and Winston, 1959.

Shapira, A. Competition, Cooperation and Conformity among City and Kibbutz Children in Israel. Unpublished Doctoral Dissertation, University of California at Los Angeles, 1970.

Shapiro, M. J., and Bonham, G. M. Cognitive Processes and Foreign Policy Decision-Making. *International Studies Quarterly,* 1973, 17, 147-174.

Shils, E. A. Authoritarianism: "Right" and "Left." In R. Christie and M. Jahoda (Eds.), *Studies in the Scope and Method of "The Authoritarian Personality."* Glencoe, Ill.: Free Press, 1954. Pp. 24-49.

Shneidman, E. S. Psycho-Logic: A Personality Approach to Patterns of Thinking. In J. Kagan and G. S. Lesser (Eds.), *Contemporary Issues in Thematic Apperceptive Methods.* Springfield, Ill.: Charles C. Thomas, 1961. Pp. 153-190.

———. The Logic of Politics. In L. Arons and M. A. May (Eds.), *Television and Human Behavior.* New York: Appleton-Century-Crofts, 1963. Pp. 177-199.

Shure, G. H., and Meeker, R. J. *A Personality/Attitude Schedule for Use in Experimental Bargaining Studies.* Technical Memorandum TM-2543, System Development Corporation, Santa Monica, Calif., 1965.

Siegel, S. *Nonparametric Statistics for the Behavioral Sciences.* New York: McGraw-Hill, 1956.

――― and Fouraker, L. E. *Bargaining and Group Decision Making: Experiments in Bilateral Monopoly.* New York: McGraw-Hill, 1960.

Siegman, A. W., and Pope, B. Effects of Question Specificity and Anxiety Producing Messages on Verbal Fluency in the Initial Interview. *Journal of Personality and Social Psychology,* 1965, 2, 522-530.

――― and Pope, B. Ambiguity and Verbal Fluency in the TAT. *Journal of Consulting Psychology,* 1966, 30, 239-245.

――― and Pope, B. (Eds.). *Studies in Dyadic Communication.* New York: Pergamon Press, 1972(a).

――― and Pope, B. The Effects of Ambiguity and Anxiety on Interviewee Verbal Behavior. In A. W. Siegman and B. Pope (Eds.), *Studies in Dyadic Communication.* New York: Pergamon Press, 1972(b). Pp. 29-68.

Sigel, R. S. *Learning about Politics.* New York: Random House, 1970.

Silvert, K. H. Leadership Formation and Modernization in Latin America. *Journal of International Affairs,* 1966, 20, 318-332.

Singer J. D. Soviet and American Foreign Policy Attitudes: Content Analysis of Elite Articulations. *Journal of Conflict Resolution,* 1964, 8, 424-485.

――― and Ray, P. Decision-Making in Conflict: From Inter-Personal to Inter-National Relations. *Menninger Clinic Bulletin,* 1966, 30, 300-312.

Skilling, H. G. Interest Groups in Communist Politics. *World Politics,* 1966, 18, 435-451.

――― and Griffiths, F. (Eds.) *Interest Groups in Soviet Politics.* Princeton: Princeton University Press, 1971.

Slater, P. E. *The Glory of Hera.* Boston: Beacon Press, 1968.

Smith, H. P., and Rosen, E. W. Some Psychological Correlates of World–Mindedness and Authoritarianism. *Journal of Personality,* 1958, 26, 170-183.

Smith, M. D. Complexity of the Self Concept and Decision-Making in Homogeneous Groups. Unpublished Master's Thesis, University of Oregon, 1967.

Smith, M. S., Stone, P. J., and Glenn, E. N. A Content Analysis of Twenty Presidential Nomination Speeches. In P. J. Stone, D. C. Dunphy, M. S. Smith, and D. M. Ogilvie (Eds.), *The General Inquirer: A Computer Approach to Content Analysis.* Cambridge, Mass.: M.I.T. Press, 1966.

Smoker, P. International Relations Simulations. In H. Guetzkow, P. Kotler, and R. L. Schulz (Eds.), *Simulation in Social and Administrative Science.* Englewood Cliffs, N.J.: Prentice-Hall, 1972. Pp. 296-339.

Sniderman, P. M., and Citrin, J. Psychological Sources of Political Belief: Self-Esteem and Isolationist Attitudes. *American Political Science Review,* 1971, 65, 401-417.

Snyder, R. C. Some Perspectives on the Use of Experimental Techniques in the Study of International Relations. In H. Guetzkow, C. F. Alger, R. A. Brody,

R. C. Noel, and R. C. Snyder, *Simulation in International Relations: Developments for Research and Teaching.* Englewood Cliffs, N.J.: Prentice-Hall, 1963. Pp. 1-23.

———, Bruck, H. W., and Sapin, B. (Eds.) *Foreign Policy Decision Making.* New York: Free Press of Glencoe, 1962.

——— and Robinson, J. A. *National and International Decision-Making.* New York: Institute for International Order, 1961.

Sobel, R. (Ed.) *Biographical Directory of the United States Executive Branch, 1774-1971.* Westport, Conn.: Greenwood, 1971.

Spranger, E. *Types of Men.* Halle, Germany: Max Niemeyer Verlag, 1928.

Stassen, G. H. Individual Preference Versus Role-Constraint in Policy-Making: Senatorial Response to Secretaries Acheson and Dulles. *World Politics,* 1972, 25, 96-119.

Stephenson, W. *The Study of Behavior.* Chicago: University of Chicago Press, 1953.

Stewart, L. H. Birth Order and Political Genius. Paper presented at annual meeting of the California State Psychological Association, 1961.

Stewart, M. D. Importance in Content Analysis: A Validity Problem. *Journalism Quarterly,* 1943, 20, 286-293.

Stewart, P. D. *Political Power in the Soviet Union.* Indianapolis: Bobbs-Merrill, 1968.

———. Soviet Interest Groups and the Policy Process: The Repeal of Production Education. *World Politics,* 1969, 22, 29-50.

Stogdill, R. M. *Handbook of Leadership Research.* New York: Free Press, 1974.

——— and Coons, A. E. (Eds.) *Leader Behavior: Its Description and Measurement.* Ohio State University, Bureau of Business Research, Monograph No. 88, 1957.

———, Goode, O. S., and Day, D. R. New Leader Behavior Description Subscales. *Journal of Psychology,* 1962, 54, 259-269.

———, Goode, O. S., and Day, D. R. The Leader Behavior of Corporation Presidents. *Personnel Psychology,* 1963, 16, 127-132.

———, Goode, O. S., and Day, D. R. The Leader Behavior of Presidents of Labor Unions. *Personnel Psychology,* 1964, 17, 49-57.

———, Goode, O. S., and Day, D. R. The Leader Behavior of University Presidents. Ohio State University, Bureau of Business Research, Unpublished Report, 1965.

Stone, P. J., Dunphy, D. C., Smith, M. S., and Ogilvie, D. M. (Eds.) *The General Inquirer: A Computer Approach to Content Analysis.* Cambridge, Mass.: M.I.T. Press, 1966.

Stone, W. F. *The Psychology of Politics.* New York: Free Press, 1974.

Stotland, E., Sherman, S. E., and Shaver, K. G. *Empathy and Birth Order: Some Experimental Explorations.* Lincoln, Nebr.: University of Nebraska Press, 1971.

Streufert, S. Attitude Generalization as an Effect of Majority-Minority Interaction in Triad Communication. Unpublished Manuscript, Princeton University, 1961.

Summers, D. A. Conflict, Compromise, and Belief Change in a Decision-Making Task. *Journal of Conflict Resolution,* 1968, 12, 215-221.

———, Stewart, T. R., and Oncken, G. R. Interpersonal Conflict in Heterocultural Dyads. *International Journal of Psychology,* 1968, 3, 191-196.

———, Taliaferro, J. D., and Fletcher, D. J. Judgment Policy and Interpersonal Learning. *Behavioral Science,* 1970, 15, 514-521.

Sutton-Smith, B., and Rosenberg, B. G. *The Sibling.* New York: Holt, Rinehart and Winston, 1970.

Swisher, P. *Lewiston* (Idaho) *Morning Tribune,* 26 September, 1957.

Tatu, M. *Power in the Kremlin.* New York: Viking, 1970.

Taylor, R. L. *Winston Churchill.* Garden City, N.Y.: Doubleday, 1952.

Tedeschi, J. T., Heister, D. S., and Gahagan, J. P. Trust and the Prisoner's Dilemma Game. *Journal of Social Psychology,* 1969, 79, 43-50.

Teger, A. I. The Effect of Early Cooperation on the Escalation of Conflict. *Journal of Experimental Social Psychology,* 1970, 6, 187-204.

Terhune, K. W. Motives, Situation, and Interpersonal Conflict within Prisoner's Dilemma. *Journal of Personality and Social Psychology Monograph Supplement,* 1968(a), 8, No. 3, Part 2.

———. Studies of Motives, Cooperation and Conflict within Laboratory Microcosms. *Buffalo Studies,* 1968(b), 4, 1, 29-58.

———. The Effects of Personality in Cooperation and Conflict. In P. G. Swingle (Ed.), *The Structure of Conflict.* New York: Academic Press, 1970. Pp. 193-234.

Thibaut, J. The Development of Contractual Norms in Bargaining: Replication and Variation. *Journal of Conflict Resolution,* 1968, 12, 102-112.

——— and Faucheux, C. The Development of Contractual Norms in a Bargaining Situation under Two Types of Stress. *Journal of Experimental Social Psychology,* 1965, 1, 89-102.

Thompson, E. H. Complexity of the Self Concept: Contrast and Assimilation Effects in the Perception and Acceptance of Strangers. Unpublished Doctoral Dissertation, University of Delaware, 1966.

Thomson, J. C., Jr. How Could Vietnam Happen? An Autopsy. *The Atlantic,* 1968, 221 (April), 47-53.

Thordarson, B. *Trudeau and Foreign Policy: A Study in Decision-Making.* Toronto, Canada: Oxford University Press, 1972.

Thorndike, E. L., and Lorge, I. *Teacher's Word Book of 30,000 Words.* New York: Bureau of Publications, Teachers College, Columbia University, 1944.

Thucydides. *The Peloponnesian Wars* (Jowett Translation). New York: Twayne Publishers, 1963.

Tomkins, S. *Polarity Scale.* New York: Springer, 1964.

Triandis, H. C., and Davis, E. E. Some Methodological Problems Concerning

Research on Negotiation between Monolinguals. Technical Report No. 28, Group Effectiveness Research Laboratory, University of Illinois, 1965.

Tucker, R. C. The Dictator and Totalitarianism. *World Politics,* 1965, 17, 55-83.

Turk, H., and Lefcowitz, M. J. Towards a Theory of Representation Between Groups. *Social Forces,* 1962, 40, 337-341.

Tweraser, K. Senator Fulbright's Operational Code as Warrant for His Foreign Policy Advocacy, 1943-1967: Toward Increasing the Explanatory Power of Decisional Premises. Paper presented at annual meeting of American Political Science Association, New Orleans, September, 1973.

Vagts, A. *Defense and Diplomacy.* New York: King's Crown Press, 1956.

Verba, S. *Small Groups and Political Behavior: A Study of Leadership.* Princeton: Princeton University Press, 1961.

———. Assumptions of Rationality and Non-Rationality in Models of the International System. In J. N. Rosenau (Ed.), *International Politics and Foreign Policy.* Rev. ed. New York: Free Press, 1969. Pp. 217-231.

Von Lazar, A. *Latin American Politics: A Primer.* Boston: Allyn and Bacon, 1971.

Wahlke, J. C., Eulau, H., Buchanan, W., and Ferguson, L. C. *The Legislative System.* New York: Wiley, 1962.

Walker, S. G. Cognitive Maps and International Realities: Henry A. Kissinger's Operational Code. Paper presented at annual meeting of American Political Science Association, San Francisco, September, 1975.

Wallach, M. A., and Kogan, N. The Roles of Information, Discussion, and Consensus in Group Risk Taking. *Journal of Experimental Social Psychology,* 1965, 1, 1-19.

———, Kogan, N., and Bem, D. J. Group Influence on Individual Risk Taking. *Journal of Abnormal and Social Psychology,* 1962, 65, 75-86.

———, Kogan, N., and Bem, D. J. Diffusion of Responsibility and Level of Risk Taking in Groups. *Journal of Abnormal and Social Psychology,* 1964, 68, 263-274.

Walton, R. E., and McKersie, R. B. *A Behavioral Theory of Labor Negotiation: An Analysis of a Social Interaction System.* New York: McGraw-Hill, 1965.

Warren, J. R. Birth Order and Social Behavior. *Psychological Bulletin,* 1966, 65, 38-49.

Washington Post, 21 July, 1957.

Webb, E. J., Campbell, D. T., Schwartz, R. D., and Sechrest, L. *Unobtrusive Measures: Nonreactive Research in the Social Sciences.* Chicago: Rand McNally, 1966.

Weintraub, W., and Aronson, H. The Application of Verbal Behavior Analysis to the Study of Psychological Defense Mechanisms: Methodology and Preliminary Report. *Journal of Nervous and Mental Disease,* 1963, 134, 169-181.

——— and Aronson, H. The Application of Verbal Behavior Analysis to the Study of Psychological Defense Mechanisms: Speech Pattern Associated with

Impulsive Behavior. *Journal of Nervous and Mental Disease*, 1964, 139, 75-82.

Welker, H. *Idaho Statesman*, 4 August, 1956.

Welling, J. F. Role and Norm Deviation. Unpublished Master's Thesis, University of Minnesota, 1969.

Welsh, W. A. Toward a Multiple-Strategy Approach to Comparative Research on Communist Political Elites: Empirical and Quantitative Problems. In F. J. Fleron, Jr. (Ed.), *Communist Studies and the Social Sciences: Essays on Methodology and Empirical Theory*. Chicago: Rand McNally, 1969. Pp. 318-356.

———. Methodological Problems in the Study of Political Leadership in Latin America. *Latin American Research Review*, 1970, 5 (Fall), 3-33.

———. Toward Effective Typology Construction in the Study of Latin American Political Leadership. *Comparative Politics*, 1971, 3, 2, 271-280.

———. Introduction: The Comparative Study of Political Leadership in Communist Systems. In C. Beck, F. J. Fleron, Jr., M. Lodge; D. J. Waller, W. A. Welsh, and M. G. Zaninovich, *Comparative Communist Political Leadership*. New York: McKay, 1973. Pp. 1-42.

———. *Leaders and Elites*. New York: Praeger, forthcoming 1976.

White, G. A Comparison of the "Operational Codes" of Mao Tse-Tung and Liu Shao-Chi. Unpublished Manuscript, Stanford University, 1969.

White, H. B. Comments. *American Political Science Review*, 1956, 50, 740-750.

White, R. K. "Black Boy": A Value-Analysis. *Journal of Abnormal and Social Psychology*, 1947, 42, 440-461.

———. Hitler, Roosevelt and the Nature of War Propaganda. *Journal of Abnormal and Social Psychology*, 1949, 44, 157-174.

———. *Value-Analysis*. Ann Arbor, Mich.: Society for the Psychological Study of Social Issues, 1951.

Whitney, D. C. *The American Presidents*. Garden City, N.Y.: Doubleday, 1967.

Whittemore, L. H. *The Man Who Ran the Subways: The Story of Mike Quill*. New York: Holt, Rinehart and Winston, 1968.

Whyte, W. H., Jr. *The Organization Man*. Garden City, N.Y.: Doubleday, 1956.

Wiener, M., and Mehrabian, A. *Language Within Language: Immediacy, A Channel in Verbal Communication*. New York: Appleton-Century-Crofts, 1968.

Wiggins, N., and Fishbein M. Dimensions of Semantic Space: A Problem of Individual Differences. In J. G. Snider and C. E. Osgood (Eds.), *Semantic Differential Technique: A Sourcebook*. Chicago: Aldine Atherton, 1969. Pp. 183-193.

Willer, D. W. Conditional Universals and Scope Sampling. In D. W. Willer, *Scientific Sociology*. Englewood Cliffs: Prentice-Hall, 1967. Pp. 97-115.

Wilson, W. Cooperation and the Cooperativeness of the Other Player. *Journal of Conflict Resolution*, 1969, 13, 110-117.

Winter, D. G. Human Motives and the No-Growth Society. Unpublished Paper, Wesleyan University, 1972.

———. The Need for Power: 1970. In D. C. McClelland and R. S. Steele (Eds.), *Human Motivation: A Book of Readings.* Morristown, N.J.: General Learning Press, 1973(a). Pp. 279-286.

———. *The Power Motive.* New York: Free Press, 1973(b).

———. What Makes the Candidate Run? *Psychology Today,* 1976(a), 9, in press.

——— and Stewart, A. J. Power Motivation. In H. London and J. Exner (Eds.), *Dimensions of Personality.* New York: Wiley, forthcoming 1976(b).

Witkin, H. A., Dyke, R. B., Faterson, H. F., Goodenough, D. R., and Karp, S. A. *Psychological Differentiation.* New York: Wiley, 1962.

Wolfenstein, E. V. *The Revolutionary Personality.* Princeton: Princeton University Press, 1967. (Paperback: Princeton University Press, 1971)

———. *Personality and Politics.* Belmont, California: Dickenson, 1969.

Woodward, C. V. (Ed.) *Responses of the Presidents to Charges of Misconduct.* New York: Dell, 1974.

Wrightsman, L. S. Personality and Attitudinal Correlates of Trusting and Trustworthy Behaviors in a Two-Person Game. *Journal of Personality and Social Psychology,* 1966, 4, 328-332.

Wriston, H. M. *Academic Procession: Reflections of a College President.* New York: Columbia University Press, 1959.

Young, K. T. *Negotiating with the Chinese Communists: The United States Experience, 1953-1967.* New York: McGraw-Hill, 1968.

Young, O. R. Intermediaries: Additional Thoughts on Third Parties. *Journal of Conflict Resolution,* 1972, 16, 51-66.

Zajonc, R. B. The Process of Cognitive Tuning in Communication. *Journal of Abnormal and Social Psychology,* 1960, 61, 159-167.

Zaninovich, M. G. Elites and Citizenry in Yugoslav Society: A Study of Value Differentiation. In C. Beck, F. J. Fleron, Jr., M. Lodge, D. J. Waller, W. A. Welsh, and M. G. Zaninovich, *Comparative Communist Political Leadership.* New York: McKay, 1973. Pp. 226-297.

Zechmeister, K., and Druckman, D. Determinants of Resolving a Conflict of Interest: A Simulation of Political Decision-Making. *Journal of Conflict Resolution,* 1973, 17, 63-88.

Ziller, R. C. Individuation and Socialization. *Human Relations,* 1964, 17, 341-360.

———. *The Social Self.* New York: Pergamon Press, 1973.

———, Alexander, M. and Long, B. H. Self-Social Constructs and Social Desirability. Unpublished Manuscript, University of Oregon, 1966.

———, Hagey, J., Smith, M. D., and Long, B. H. Self-Esteem: A Self-Social Construct. *Journal of Consulting and Clinical Psychology,* 1969, 33, 84-95.

———, Long, B. H., Ramana, K. V., and Reddy, V. E. Self-Other Orientations of Indian and American Adolescents. *Journal of Personality,* 1968, 36, 315-330.

———, Megas, J., and DeCencio, D. Self-Social Constructs of Normals and Acute Neuropsychiatric Patients. *Journal of Consulting Psychology,* 1964, 28, 50-63.

Index

506